Engineering Ethics:
Concepts and Cases

Engineering Ethics:
Concepts and Cases

Charles E. Harris
Texas A&M University

Michael S. Pritchard
Western Michigan University

Michael J. Rabins
Texas A&M University

W

Wadsworth Publishing Company

I(T)P™ An International Thomson Publishing Company

Belmont • Albany • Bonn • Boston • Cincinnati • Detroit
London • Madrid • Melbourne • Mexico City • New York • Paris • San Francisco
Singapore • Tokyo • Toronto • Washington

Philosophy Editor: Tammy Goldfeld
Editorial Assistant: Kelly Zavislak
Production Services Coordinator: Gary Mcdonald
Production: Ruth Cottrell
Print Buyer: Diana Spence
Permissions Editor: Robert Kauser
Designer: Ruth Cottrell
Copy Editor: Rene Lynch
Cover: William Reuter Design
Compositor: Ruth Cottrell Books
Printer: Malloy Lithoghraphing, Inc.

For more information, contact Wadsworth Publishing Company.

Wadsworth Publishing Company
10 Davis Drive
Belmont, California 94002
USA

International Thomson Editores
Campos Eliseos 385, Piso 7
Col. Polanco
11560 México D.F. México

International Thomson Publishing Europe
Berkshire House 168-173
High Holborn
London, WC1V 7AA
England

International Thomson Publishing GmbH
Königswinterer Strasse 418
53227 Bonn
Germany

Thomas Nelson Australia
102 Dodds Street
South Melbourne 3205
Victoria, Australia

International Thomson Publishing Asia
221 Henderson Road
#05-10 Henderson Building
Singapore 0315

Nelson Canada
1120 Birchmount Road
Scarborough, Ontario
Canada M1K 5G4

International Thomson Publishing - Japan
Hirakawacho Kyowa Building, 3F
2-2-1 Hirakawacho
Chiyoda-ku, Tokyo 102
Japan

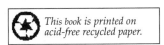

Library of Congress Cataloging-in-Publication Data

Harris, Charles E.
    Engineering ethics: concepts and cases / Charles E. Harris,
Michael S. Pritchard, Michael J. Rabins.
        p.   cm.
    Includes biographical references and index.
    ISBN: 0-534-23964-1
    1. Engineering ethics. 2. Engineering ethics--case studies.
    I Pritchard, Michael S. II. Rabins, Michael J. (Michael Jerome),
    1932–   . III. Title
    TA157.H357 1994
    174'.962--dc20   94-22112

To
  Charles E. Harris, PE retired
  R. William Eddy, the family engineer, retired
  Herman Rabins

And to our families who put us on the right road and our engineering
  students who illuminated the way

Contents

A Case Study Guide

This book contains more than 70 case studies at the ends of chapters. Below is a list of major topics the cases address, with suggested cases listed under each heading. Many cases appear under several headings, giving some indication of their complexity. The topic headings below are meant to be suggestive rather than exhaustive. No doubt each heading can be divided into various subtopics, and other major topics could be identified.

Preface

Because of the limited number of engineering ethics texts available, our book may not need special justification. Nevertheless, we believe that the following features will make it especially useful for both students and instructors.

- Cases at the ends of the chapters, as well as illustrative cases in the body of the text

- A conceptual apparatus for analyzing the cases into their component parts

- Techniques for resolving the problems presented by the cases, after they have been analyzed

- Professional engineering codes used as a starting point for considering issues in engineering ethics

- Responsible engineering professionalism as a guiding ideal in engineering ethics

- Discussions of substantive issues that are treated minimally or not at all by other textbooks

Let us consider each of these features in more detail.

The Importance of Cases

Engineers, like most professionals, are interested in real-world problems—in the specific, the concrete, and the practical. Theory is important insofar as it is useful in problem solving, but the way to get the attention of engineering students is to focus on cases.

We begin each chapter with a case, and short illustrative cases appear in every chapter. Cases that enable students to apply the concepts developed in the chapter appear at the end of each chapter. Some of the cases are what one of the authors calls the "media splash" cases that hit the front pages of the newspapers, but most are more mundane—the types that engineers are most likely to encounter in their own careers.

We have analyzed some of the cases, and we have included a few student analyses and some analyses by outside sources. We leave most of the cases for the readers to analyze.

An Analytical Frame of Mind

Exposing students to cases has another value: It convinces them that they need some conceptual tools to deal with the issues presented by the cases. The first things students need to do is to understand what is going on in a case. What are the known facts and what factual questions remain unanswered? Are there some future events whose outcome is important in a moral evaluation? Are there terms (e.g., "safe" or "clean") whose definitions are crucial to the solution?

This book helps engineering students carry their natural analytical talents into a new area: moral deliberation. It shows them the importance of being analytical. It stresses the fact that many apparent moral disagreements are really disagreements over the facts or over the definitions of crucial terms, and that the locus of moral disagreement can be discovered only by analysis.

Ethical Problem Solving

Engineering ethics is a branch of applied ethics, so it is a problem-solving discipline. Engineers are professional problem solvers, but they are usually not trained in ethical problem solving. A textbook in engineering ethics should build on the problem-solving orientation of engineers and provide techniques that will help them to come to intellectual closure about moral problems.

In this book we give a number of techniques and tests for resolving moral problems. We believe that most moral problems are either line-drawing problems or conflict problems. We provide methods for resolving both types. At the same time, we emphasize that no technique can make ethical problem solving easy or painless. The techniques show students that there can be method and structure in moral deliberation, but that there are no algorithms.

The Codes

We take engineering codes seriously. Professional codes represent the consensus of a professional community about the standards that should govern their conduct. This does not mean that the codes are complete or above criticism, or that there can be no questions as to how the codes apply in particular situations. Far from it! But the codes should be the starting point for discussion of most issues in engineering ethics.

We attempt to meet a need for a code-oriented text (not a code-dominated text!) by discussing what the codes say about a topic and —when appropriate—suggesting where the codes may be inconsistent, unclear, or in need of modification. This provides a way for students to engage themselves realistically and productively with the engineering community as a whole.

The Responsible Engineer

One of the functions of a course in engineering ethics is to help students assume intelligently the mantle of professional responsibility. The best way to do this is to help them see that their actions as engineers will affect the lives and well-being of others. The best way to do this is to focus on cases. This is another reason for the case orientation of the book.

In addition, however, we have written a whole chapter on professional responsibility. What does it mean to be a responsible engineer? Is it simply to avoid malpractice, or is there a more positive component? What are some of the impediments to professional responsibility, and how can they be overcome? We attempt to help students understand professional responsibility intellectually. Exposure to case studies helps them feel it on a more visceral level.

Other Features

We consider some topics that are not treated—or are treated minimally—in other texts. One of these is the environment. Engineers have more impact on the environment that any other professionals, yet no existing text does justice to this. Another topic is the engineer/manager relationship, so important in many engineering ethics cases. In addition, we believe that this book has fuller discussions of risk and safety, honesty in research and testing, and the proper functions of state regulatory boards and professional engineering societies than other textbooks.

Outline of the Book

Some of the topics discussed are:

• The Challenger case, role morality, personal and professional ethics, and professional ethics as preventive ethics

• Two models of professionalism, objections to codes of ethics, and why professionals should support their codes of ethics

• Responsible engineering and impediments to professional responsibility

• Factual beliefs, conceptual beliefs, and moral beliefs

• Techniques for resolving conflict problems and line-drawing problems and the standpoints of agents and judges

• Utilitarianism and the ethics of respect for persons as sources of tests for moral problem solving

• Reliability in professional services, ways of misusing the truth, proprietary information, confidentiality, expert testimony, failure to inform the public, and conflicts of interest

- Identifying risk, uncertainties and value judgments in estimating risk, acceptable risk, and lay versus expert approaches to risk

- Employee disobedience, engineer/manager relationships, organizational loyalty, responsible engineering dissent, and enhancing employee freedom in the workplace

- Management attitudes toward environmental issues, criteria for a "clean" environment, and environmental responsibility where human health is not an issue

- State boards of registration, licensure, the "industry exemption," and engineering societies

Use of the Text

This text is suitable for a full sixteen-week semester course in engineering ethics. In our courses we are able to cover all of the chapters as well as devote five or six sessions to videotapes and/or outside speakers. For shorter courses in the quarter system, we recommend using seven or eight of the chapters, leaving out some of the last five.

Acknowledgments

Our students in our engineering ethics class have been a continual source of encouragement. They tell us that the subject of engineering ethics is important and that a course in it is long overdue. Their responses have helped us to know when the ideas we have been developing are plausible and clearly presented and when they need further work. Our students should not, however, be held responsible for anything in this book.

We also want to thank the readers of our manuscript: Michael Davis, Illinois Institute of Technology; P. Aarne Vesilind, Duke University; Donald Gotterbarn, East Tennessee State University; L. S. Fletcher, Texas A&M University; and Kevin Passino, Jimmy Smith, Penny Vann, and Dave Dorchester—all associated with the Murdough Center for Engineering Professionalism and Ethics—have encouraged us since we first entered the field of engineering ethics. W. Gale Cutler and James A. Jaksa were early sources of encouragement, and of cases in engineering ethics. Rachelle Hollander at the National Science Foundation was responsible for funding some of our early work and bringing the three of us together. She deserves a special word of thanks. Engineering faculty on several campuses have been encouraging and supportive, as have Ken King and Tammy Goldfeld at Wadsworth. Several secretaries have offered invaluable assistance. The index was prepared by Joan Rabins. Finally, our families have put up with fathers and spouses who have been spending too much time in front of the computer.

Chapter 1

Introduction

On the night of January 27, 1986, Roger Boisjoly, engineer with Morton Thiokol, faced a crisis. The Space Center was counting down for a launch the next morning. In a teleconference with the Space Center, however, his superior, Robert Lund, had conveyed the recommendation of the engineers against launching. This recommendation was based on worries of the engineers about the ability of the O-rings to seal at low temperatures.

Roger Boisjoly knew the problems with the O-rings all too well. The O-rings are part of the sealing mechanism between the segments of the booster rockets. If they lose too much of their resiliency, they can fail to seal altogether. The result would be the escape of hot gasses, ignition of the fuel in the storage tanks, and a fatal explosion.

The technical evidence was incomplete but ominous: there appeared to be a correlation between temperature and resiliency. Although there was some leaking around the seal even at relatively high temperatures, the worst leakage was at 53 degrees. With a predicted ambient temperature of 26 degrees at launch, the O-rings were estimated to be at 29 degrees. This was much lower than the launch temperatures of any previous flight.

Now the teleconference with the Space Center had been temporarily suspended. NASA had questioned Morton Thiokol's no-launch recommendation, and Morton Thiokol had requested the suspension in order to allow the engineers and management at Morton Thiokol to reassess their recommendation. The Space Center would not fly without approval from Morton Thiokol, and Morton Thiokol management would not give this recommendation without approval from their engineers.

Jerald Mason, senior vice-president at Morton Thiokol, knew that NASA badly needed a successful flight. He also knew that Morton Thiokol needed a new contract with NASA, and a recommendation against launch was probably not perceived as enhancing the prospects of obtaining that contract. Finally, Mason was aware that the engineering data were inconclusive. The engineers could not give any firm figures as to the precise temperature at which it would be unsafe to fly. They were relying on the apparent correlation between temperature and resiliency and their tendency to be conservative on serious safety O-ring issues.

The teleconference with the Space Center would resume shortly and a decision had to be made. Jerald Mason turned to Robert Lund and said, "Take off your engineering hat and put on your management hat."[1] The earlier no-launch recommendation was reversed.

Boisjoly was deeply upset by this reversal of the engineers' recommendation. As a human being, he no doubt felt concern for the well-being of the astronauts. He did not want to be a part of something that could lead to death and destruction.

More than this was involved, however. Roger Boisjoly was not only a concerned citizen. *He was an engineer*. It was his *professional* engineering judgment that the O-rings were not trustworthy. He also had a *professional* obligation to protect the health and safety of the public, and he evidently believed that this obligation extended to the astronauts. Now his *professional* judgment was being overridden.

Contrary to the instructions of Gerald Mason to Robert Lund, Roger Boisjoly did not believe it appropriate to take off his engineering hat. His engineering hat was a source of pride, and it also carried with it certain obligations. He believed that *as an engineer* he had an obligation to render his best technical judgment and to protect the safety of the public, including the astronauts. Therefore he made one last attempt to protest the decision to reverse the no-launch recommendation, pointing out the low-temperature problems to Thiokol management. He frantically attempted to persuade management to stick to the original no-launch recommendation, but his protests were disregarded. Thiokol managers reversed the original no-launch decision.

The next day, just 73 seconds into the launch, the Challenger exploded, taking the lives of the six astronauts and schoolteacher Christa McAuliffe. In addition to the tragic loss of human life, the disaster destroyed millions of dollars worth of equipment and severely tarnished NASA's reputation. Boisjoly had failed to prevent the disaster, but he had exercised his professional responsibilities as he understood them.

1.1   Introduction

This dramatic story, now one of the most famous cases in engineering ethics, illustrates both the importance of engineering knowledge to the lives and well-being of the public and the consequent responsibilities that engineers bear. Roger Boisjoly's knowledge was important because it could have saved the lives of the astronauts and prevented the loss of millions of dollars worth of equipment and a national embarrassment. Because of this, Boisjoly had a responsibility that he appeared to clearly recognize, the responsibility to use his knowledge in a way that protects and benefits the public, including the astronauts.

This book focuses on the ethical context and professional issues that arise in the practice of engineering and on the response of the engineering community to these issues. Although most engineers will never face situations involving the high drama associated with the Challenger disaster, all will encounter situations requiring ethical reflection and decision making. Consider the following examples:

• Tom is designing a new chemical plant. One of his responsibilities is to specify the valves to be used in a certain portion of the plant. Before he makes his final decision, a salesman for one of the firms that manufactures valves invites Tom to a golf game at the local country club. Should Tom accept the offer?

• Mary discovers that her plant is discharging into the river a substance that is not regulated by the government. She decides to do some reading about the substance and finds that some of the studies suggest that it is a carcinogen. As an engineer, she believes she has an obligation to protect the public, but she also wants to be a loyal employee. The substance will probably be very expensive to remove and her boss says, "Forget about it until the government makes us do something. Then all the other plants will have to spend money too, and we will not be at a competitive disadvantage." What should Mary do?

• Jim's company has an in-house tool and die department that would like to bid on a contract that has been submitted to outside vendors. The department manager of the in-house tool and die department asks Jim for the quotes from the other vendors, so he can underbid them. "After all," the department manager argues, "we are both on the same team. It's better to keep the money inside if we can. You don't have to tell the outsiders what you have done." What should Jim do?[2]

Issues such as these arise in the professional experience of most engineers. We believe this book will help students and professional engineers handle such issues more effectively. Engineers can profit from a study of professional ethics and such study should be a part of their professional education. A study of professional ethics will, in fact, make engineers better professionals.

The major emphasis of this book is on professional ethics, not simply personal ethics. The two cannot of course be totally separated. In one respect it is appropriate to say that personal ethics is a foundation for professional ethics: one's desire to be an ethical engineer is part of one's desire to be an ethical person. Nevertheless, there are important differences, as the ensuing discussion will demonstrate.

The most obvious difference is that professional ethics has to do with the ethical standards adopted by a professional community. When a person becomes a professional, she joins a community of other professionals. This community has standards. One of the most obvious places to look for these is in the codes of ethics of professional societies. Engineering societies, for example, have adopted codes of ethics for their members. Several are included in the appendices of this book. The basic principles of these codes are very similar to one another, suggesting a high degree of consensus among these societies concerning the professional responsibilities of engineers.

We shall cite the ethical codes of many professional societies in this book, but we shall most often use the ethical code of the National Society of Professional Engineers (NSPE). In several respects the NSPE is unlike the societies representing the major branches of engineering, such as the American Society of Civil Engineers (ASCE), the American Society of Mechanical Engineers (ASME), the Institute of Electrical and Electronics Engineers (IEEE), and the American Institute of Chemical Engineers (AIChE). While these societies are concerned primarily with the pursuit and dissemination of technical knowledge in their respective areas of engineering, the NPSE is primarily concerned with nontechnical matters involving the engineering profession. It is concerned rather with issues such as licensing, professional development, avoiding conflicts of interest, encouraging engineers not to encroach on the practice of other engineers, and other issues in the area of professional practice. From a historical standpoint, it has also been oriented toward the concerns of civil engineers, especially those in private practice.

There are, however, several reasons for using the NSPE code. The NSPE is a professional society that all engineers are invited to join, regardless of their engineering specialty, if they are registered professional engineers. Civil engineers, mechanical engineers, chemical engineers, electrical engineers—as well as other types of engineers—are members of the NSPE. The NSPE code is also the code used by the NSPE Board of Ethical Review, to which we shall occasionally refer. Finally, it is the code which is often cited in some of the best-known contemporary texts in professional ethics.[3]

While we take the NSPE code and other engineering codes very seriously, we do not find them above criticism. Engineering codes have undergone considerable evolution in the past and no doubt will continue to evolve in the future. One of the marks of a living and vital moral community is that it grows and changes as a result of changed circumstances and intelligent self-criticism. We make some suggestions for code modifications ourselves. Therefore, we take the codes seriously as formal expressions of the ethical norms of the professional engineering community, but we do not adhere to them slavishly, nor do we think they are always adequate or complete.

We do not know how many engineers are members of engineering societies, although we surmise that many practicing engineers are not members of any professional society. This raises the question of whether the provisions of the codes apply beyond the official membership of the professional society it represents. Still, the codes reflect ideas that are inculcated into the minds of engineering students in their professional training and later confirmed by the practice of many (we hope most) practicing engineers. The codes simply state these ideas formally.

1.2　　**Professional Ethics: Standards for a Professional Community**

In this first chapter, we begin with some general remarks about the nature of professional ethics. Then we consider some more specific objectives in studying engineering ethics.

Professional Ethics As Role Morality

All of us occupy many roles. We are students, professors, children, parents, members of clubs and organizations of various types, employees, members of religious and professional communities, and citizens of countries. Many of these roles carry with them special obligations and prerogatives, which we can refer to as *role morality*. Parents, for example, have obligations to their children that they would not have if they were not the children's parents. They must provide food, clothes, and shelter and take care of them when they are sick. They must also keep them out of danger, give them emotional support and comfort, and provide for their education. Parents also have certain prerogatives with regard to their children, which they would not have if they were not parents. They have a considerable say in their children's education. They can even educate their children at home if they do not like public or private education. Parents can also deeply influence the religious and political views of their chidren.

Sometimes the obligations may conflict. On the one hand, a parent whose child has committed a crime may feel an obligation as a parent to protect the child from prosecution. As a law-abiding citizen, on the other hand, the same parent may feel obligated to cooperate with the law in prosecuting his or her own child. Employees whose company is polluting the waters in the community may experience a conflict between their obligations to the company and their obligations as citizens of the community. Persons whose religious views commit them to pacifism may feel a conflict between their roles as religious believers and their roles as citizens to defend their country.

It is also possible to separate professionals as ordinary people or as occupants of other roles from their roles as professionals. In their professional roles, lawyers may have an obligation to defend clients whom they believe to be guilty. In a recent case in Austin, Texas, a lawyer defended a client against the charge of rape by arguing that because the victim asked her attacker to use a condom, she consented to sexual intercourse. The victim argued in response that she repeatedly begged him not to hurt her. "I knew there wasn't much I could do to prevent what was going to happen. I thought maybe I could protect myself from dying from AIDS."[4] The case was complicated by the fact that the rapist had consumed twenty-five beers before the attack and had an IQ of 71. But in any case, the lawyer defending the rapist may have subordinated personal convictions to professional obligations to give the client the best possible defense before the law.

In another case in legal ethics, two lawyers defended their decision not to tell a grieving father where his daughter was buried. Their client had told them where he had buried the bodies of his victims, but they argued that this information had been conveyed to them confidentially and that, as lawyers, they could not break this confidentiality. In their defense of themselves, they emphasized that as individual human beings they deeply sympathized with the father, but as lawyers they felt compelled to protect lawyer-client confidentiality.[5]

Similar conflicts between personal morality and professional morality arise in medicine. A physician may believe that medical confidentiality compels her to refrain from telling a woman that her future husband has a serious disease that can be transmitted through sexual intercourse and that he could have contracted only from someone else. In her role as an individual human being rather than a physician, she may believe she should tell the patient about the danger.

Like lawyers and physicians, Roger Boisjoly is a member of a professional community with rules and standards governing the conduct of its members. Engineers are probably less likely than lawyers and physicians to experience a conflict between their professional ethics and their personal moral convictions, but sometimes engineers have personal convictions that go beyond the requirements of their profession, for example, in environmental concerns. It is more likely, however, that engineering codes raise two other sorts of questions for engineers.

Issues in Engineering Ethics

The first question is, *What should the codes say?* We have pointed out that the engineering community already has ethical standards, but they are subject to change. This is true in other professions as well. Some believe that the standards governing legal and medical confidentiality should be modified, especially in the defense of guilty clients and professional confidentiality. Similarly, some engineers believe engineering codes should include stronger statements regarding the engineer's obligations to the environment. At present, only the codes of the Institute of Electrical and Electronics Engineers (IEEE) and the American Society of Civil Engineers (ASCE) mention the environment.

Environmental issues raise difficult and important questions. Should engineers impose on themselves responsibilities for the environment that go beyond the law? Should professional engineering ethics protect the right of engineers to refuse to participate in projects (such as designing dams that flood farmlands or tame wild rivers) to which they object? After all, medical ethics protects the right of physicians not to participate in medical procedures (such as abortions) to which they object. Should engineers have professional obligations to protect virgin forests or endangered species?

The second question is, *What direction do the codes give in particular circumstances?* How are the standards to be applied? Consider the following examples:

1. Section 4.a of the NSPE code requires engineers to avoid "conflicts of interest," but the code does not define conflicts of interest or give directions as to how potential conflicts of interest should be handled. Suppose Scott, a design engineer, owns a small company that manufactures a device for shutting off the fuel supply to boilers when the pressure gets too high. Scott believes that his product

is superior to anything else on the market. Should he avoid specifying his valve in his designs, even though he believes it is the best available? How can he handle this situation to avoid a conflict of interest?

2. Section 10.a of the NSPE code requires engineers to "recognize the proprietary interests of others." Suppose Betty, a chemical engineer, recognizes that some of the ideas she developed for her former employer provide the basis for a solution to a problem faced by her new employer. The two companies are not competitors, and the applications of the ideas are so different that very few people would even recognize them as having a common origin. Is it ethical for her to employ her own ideas in this new and creative way?

3. The first canon of the NSPE code requires engineers to "hold paramount the safety, health and welfare of the public in the performance of their professional duties." John, a chemical engineer, notices that workers in his section of the plant are complaining of noxious fumes from hot metals. "They give me headaches every day," one worker complains. Are workers part of the "public" for whom John has a professional responsibility? Does he have an obligation as an engineer to try to remedy the problem?

4. The first canon of the NSPE code requires engineers to "hold paramount the safety, health and welfare of the public in the performance of their professional duties." The fourth canon of the same code directs engineers to "act in professional matters for each employer or client as faithful agents or trustees." Betty knows that the code gives priority to protecting the public, but this knowledge is not sufficient to resolve her problem. Her company manufactures a product that appears to have a slightly greater likelihood of harming users than similar products of the competition. Her employer does not want to change the design, and she wonders whether in this case her obligation to protect the public outweighs her obligation to be a loyal and obedient employee.

This book will contain many other cases in which the codes do not give sufficient direction. No code, in fact, could supply an algorithm with an automatic solution to all ethical problems. We need some further techniques of moral reasoning, which this book will attempt to supply.

1.3   Engineering Ethics As Preventive Ethics

The cases discussed in the last section are a part of what we call preventive ethics. Here we develop this concept.

The Importance of Thinking Ahead

In his or her professional capacity, an engineer can be faced with significant ethical choices. Some would argue that moral character is already well in place by the time this happens to a young engineer. If we have not learned the difference between right and wrong long ago, a skeptic might say, it is really too late. But engineer Samuel Florman answers:

> Skeptics—both within academe and without—argue that moral character is formed in the home, the church, and the community, and cannot be modified in a college classroom or professional symposium. I cannot agree with the skeptics on this count. Most evil acts are committed not by villains but rather by decent human beings—in desperation, momentary weakness, or an inability to discern what is morally right amid the discordant claims of circumstances. The determination to be good may be molded at an early age, but we grapple all our lives with the definition of what is good, or at least acceptable.[6]

At the very least, responsible engineering requires familiarity with the kinds of circumstances in engineering practice that call for ethical sensitivity and reflection. It also requires opportunities to gain a clearer understanding of the concepts and principles that are essential to ethical reflection in engineering.

Until quite recently, engineering education has not emphasized the importance of including ethics as a part of the engineering curriculum. However, now the Accreditation Board for Engineering and Technology (ABET) requires accredited engineering programs in the United States to make serious efforts to foster in their students "an understanding of the ethical characteristics of the engineering profession and practice."[7]

As many professional engineers can testify, they often learn ethical lessons only after something has been overlooked or has gone wrong. By requiring engineering programs to introduce students to ethical concerns, ABET is taking the position that students need to begin to think about ethical issues in engineering before things go wrong. In essence, ABET is advocating a kind of preventive ethics, which is much like preventive medicine in that one does not wait until something is obviously amiss before taking appropriate action. Preventive medicine advocates good health habits to minimize the need for more serious medical intervention later. Similarly, preventive ethics anticipates possible consequences of actions to avoid more serious problems later.

A Calvin and Hobbes comic strip nicely illustrates the importance of thinking ahead.[8] As they are cascading down a treacherous hill in Calvin's wagon, they discuss their circumstance:

Calvin: Ever notice how decisions make chain reactions?

Hobbes: How so?

Calvin: Well, each decision we make determines the range of choices we'll face next. Take this fork in the road, for instance. Which way should we go? Arbitrarily I choose left. Now, as a direct result of that decision, we're faced with another choice: Should we jump this ledge or ride along the side of it? If we hadn't turned left at the fork, this new choice would never have come up.

Hobbes: I note with some dismay, you've chosen to jump the ledge.

Calvin: Right. And *that* decision will give us *new* choices.

Hobbes: Like, should we bail out or die in the landing?

Calvin: Exactly. Our first decision created a chain reaction of decisions. Let's jump.

After crash landing in a shallow pond, Calvin philosophizes: "See? If you don't make each decision carefully, you never know where you'll end up. That's an important lesson we should learn sometime." Hobbes replies, "I wish we could talk about these things without the visual aids." Hobbes might prefer that they talk through a case study or two before venturing with Calvin into engineering practice. The classroom can provide engineering students with opportunities to absorb Calvin's lesson "without the visual aids."

What should a classroom concerned with preventive ethics aim to accomplish? Preventive ethics has two dimensions. First, engineers must think ahead to anticipate possible consequences of their actions as professionals, especially those that may have an important ethical dimension. Second, engineers must think effectively about those consequences and decide what is ethically and professionally right. Let us look at some of the aspects of ethics education that are important in achieving this.

Education in Preventive Ethics

After a two-year study of ethics programs in higher education sponsored by the Hastings Center, an interdisciplinary group of educators agreed on five main objectives.[9] These are an excellent summary of training in preventive ethics. Engineering was one of the areas explicitly considered by the team of educators gathered together by the Hastings Center, and this makes their conclusions all the more relevant. Taking our cue from the Hastings study, we can isolate the following elements involved in training in preventive ethics.[10]

1. *Stimulating the Moral Imagination.* The first teaching objective identified by the Hastings Center study is stimulating the moral imagination of students. Like most professional ethics programs, there is a heavy emphasis on cases. Cases such as the Hyatt Regency disaster; films such as *The China Syndrome, Class Action,* and *Silkwood;* and novels such as Nevil Shute's *No Highway* and Kurt Vonnegut's *Player Piano* effectively stimulate the moral imagination.

For engineers—as for anyone else—imagination is necessary in anticipating the consequences of actions as professionals and in coming up with solutions to ethical problems encountered in professional life. In order to minimize the chances of being taken by surprise, engineers must imagine possible alternatives and their likely consequences. One of the managers interviewed in Barbara Toffler's *Tough Choices* explains how he tries to deal with difficult situations:

> I first play out the scenario of what would happen if I did it one way and what would happen if I did it the other way. What would be the followup? What would be the next move? What would be the response back and what would be the consequences? That's the only way you can tell if you're going to make the right move or not because I think something that instinctively may feel right or wrong, if you analyze it, may not pan out that way.[11]

2. *Recognizing Ethical Issues.* It is not difficult to recognize that suppressing data raises ethical questions, even if deciding what to do about it is difficult.

However, the ethical dimensions of situations are not always so apparent. Consider this illustration.[12] At a meeting of engineering educators and professional philosophers, an engineer briefly described a housing project. The property adjacent to the housing development was a large, heavily treed, hilly area. The engineer then asked his audience what size drainage pipe should be recommended for the sewer system. Crude estimates were made by engineers and philosophers alike, with little consensus and much amusement. Finally someone asked the question that no doubt was on the minds of many: What did this problem have to do with ethics?

The engineer replied by asking the audience to consider what the surrounding environment might be like shortly after the completion of the housing project. Perhaps a shopping mall would replace the heavily treed, higher adjacent area—resulting in a much greater rainwater run-off problem. Should an engineer recommend a pipe size that takes into consideration such future contingencies? What if the housing developer wants to get by with minimal costs and shows no concern for who might have to bear the expense of replacing the inadequate draining system in the near future? Who should bear the expense, and to what extent, if at all, should an engineer be concerned about such questions when making recommendations?

However these background questions are answered, they make clear that the question of what should be recommended is not just a technical one. In addition, although an engineering code of ethics might address issues like this in a very general way, it will not necessarily guide engineers to a consensus.

3. *Developing Analytical Skills.*   In one sense engineering students obviously have well-developed analytical skills. However, they must use the technical, analytical skills essential to good engineering practice with some caution in analyzing moral issues. Sometimes their analytical skills may even impede moral analysis, which requires clear thinking about concepts such as utility, justice, rights, duties, and respect for persons. These concepts are not necessarily amenable to quantitative analysis.

Suppose David Weber, a highway safety engineer, has to assign priorities to projects in a county with diverse traffic patterns.[13] He considers two intersections that need safety improvements. One is an urban intersection that handles about 2,400 cars per day. The other is a rural intersection that handles about 600 cars per day. The annual number of fatal accidents at each intersection is virtually identical (approximately two), but the number of property damage and minor injury accidents at the urban intersection is substantially greater. There is just enough money left in this year's budget to improve one of the intersections. The result of the improvement at either intersection will be to cut the number of annual fatalities roughly in half. There will be a greater reduction in property damage and minor injury accidents if the improvement is made at the urban intersection. Which improvement should be given greater priority by David Weber?

Versions of this case have been presented to engineering students for more than ten years. The overwhelming initial response is always that the urban intersection should take priority. Why? As the numbers clearly reveal, more people will be served there. Invariably someone will say, "It's the greatest good for the greatest number."

If students are asked if anyone favors the rural intersection, one or two may volunteer that, in fact, the rural intersection is more dangerous. Individual drivers are at higher risk of having a serious or fatal accident. This, too, can readily be demonstrated mathematically.

So, what do the numbers settle in this case? By themselves, nothing. From the standpoint of maximizing the overall good, the numbers seem to favor the urban intersection. But the utilitarian assumption that we should promote the greatest good for the greatest number is not based on numerical analysis. It requires philosophical support. Considerations of fairness or respect for individual rights, on the other hand, strengthen the case for the rural intersection. Again, while numerical analysis can be joined with considerations of fairness or individual rights, all require philosophical support. However the numbers in this case are used, we need to ask what ethical assumptions we are making about their relevance. The temptation to take comfort in numbers may be there, but ethical analysis reveals the assumptions that underlie giving in to this temptation.

4. *Eliciting a Sense of Responsibility.* Preventive ethics can be practiced most effectively by people who have a sense of themselves as moral agents. Even though we have given the codes a central place in our conception of professional ethics, we have also pointed out that they cannot be relied upon uncritically. The codes may need modification in certain areas, and how to apply them to particular moral problems is not always evident. Practice in preventive ethics is thus not indoctrination but practice in independent thought.

5. *Tolerating Disagreement and Ambiguity.* Discussions of problems like David Weber's are often frustrating to engineering students. Sorting out the nuances of ethical concepts reveals a certain amount of vagueness, ambiguity, and, above all, disagreement. Lack of consensus on such cases may be disturbing for those accustomed to technical solutions to problems. Some may want to turn to a code of ethics to bring matters to an authoritative resolution, but we have already pointed out that the codes do not provide ready-made solutions to all moral problems. No code of ethics is self-interpreting. Its principles and rules are stated in general terms and need to be applied thoughtfully to particular circumstances, and some parts of a code might potentially conflict with one another. For example, protecting public safety and being faithful to one's employer may, on the face of it, pull an engineer in opposite directions. We have already pointed out how even the fact that the codes give priority to protecting the public may not resolve all of these conflicts. Only careful reflection and discerning judgment can adequately resolve such potential conflicts. Even then engineers might find themselves reasonably disagreeing to some extent among themselves.

The willingness to persevere in our reflections even to the point of such disagreement is itself a mark of responsibility. However, it is also a mark of responsibility to continue to search for possible points of agreement and further clarity when confronted with difficult and challenging problems.

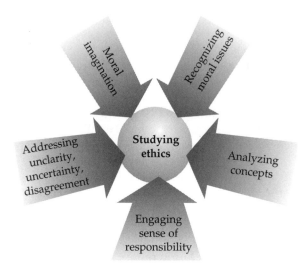

Figure 1.1 Aims in Studying Ethics

Figure 1.1 summarizes the five aims in studying ethics. As you can see in this figure, studying ethics aims at stimulating our moral imagination; helping us recognize moral issues; helping us analyze key ethical concepts; engaging our sense of responsibility; and helping us address unclarity, uncertainty, and disagreement about moral issues.

1.4   Cases, Cases, Cases!

Throughout the chapter we have referred frequently to cases in engineering ethics. Their importance cannot be overemphasized. It is by studying cases that a person can most easily develop the abilities necessary to engage in preventive ethics. Cases stimulate the moral imagination by challenging us to anticipate the possible alternatives in resolving them and the consequences of those alternatives. Through cases we learn to recognize the presence of ethical problems and to develop the analytical skills necessary in resolving them. A study of cases is the most effective way to see that the codes cannot provide ready-made answers to all moral questions that professional engineering practice generates and that the individual must become a responsible moral agent. Finally, the study of cases convinces us that there may be some unresolvable uncertainties in moral analysis and that in some situations rational and responsible professionals may disagree about what is right.

Cases appear throughout the text. Each chapter is introduced with a case, which is usually referred to in the chapter. In many chapters we present our own attempt to resolve the moral problem. We often use brief cases to illustrate various points in our argument, and we present a series of cases at the end of chapters for further discussion and analysis. Chapters 4, 5, and 6 are also devoted to methods for analyzing and resolving the moral issues presented in cases.

Cases are of several types. Some are imaginary and others are real. Some focus on highly publicized events, such as the Challenger disaster or the Ford Pinto gas tank controversy. Others concern more ordinary events and issues in the professional experience of engineers. Many of the imaginary or hypothetical ones are based on one or more actual cases. Some cases are simplified to focus better on a particular issue, while others are more complex and multifaceted. Every case furthers the study and understanding of professional engineering ethics. Two final points are important with regard to their use.

First, the use of cases is especially appropriate in a text in professional ethics. A medical school dean known to one of the authors once said, "Physicians are tied to the post of use." By this he presumably meant that physicians do not have the luxury of thinking indefinitely about moral problems. They must make decisions about what treatment to administer or what advice to give. Physicians feel tethered or constrained by the necessity of making these decisions that vitally affect the lives of others.

Engineers, like other professionals, are also tied to the post of use. They must make decisions about designs that will affect the lives and financial well-being of many people, give professional advice to managers and clients, make decisions about purchases, decide whether to protest decisions by managers and others that affect the well-being of the public, and take other actions that have important consequences for themselves and others. Engineers, like other professionals, are case-oriented. In the study of cases they see that professional ethics is not simply a gloss on professional education but is intimately related to what it means to be a professional.

Second, the study of cases is especially valuable for engineers who aspire to management positions. Cases have long been at the center of management education. Many if not most of the issues faced by managers have ethical dimensions. Some of the methods for resolving ethical problems discussed in Chapters 4 through 6—especially finding a "creative middle way"—have much in common with the methods employed by managers. Managers must make decisions within constraints, and they usually try to satisfy as many of these constraints as possible. The kind of creative problem solving necessary to make such decisions is very similar to the brainstorming necessary to satisfactorily resolve many ethical problems.

The use of preventive ethics is also a worthwhile tool for managers. If they can avoid serious ethical problems before they appear, managers can avoid many difficult and painful decisions that might otherwise arise. Some large health-care firms now employ medical ethicists on the corporate level to assist in establishing corporate policy regarding health care. Presumably the thinking of corporate executives is that if corporate policy is ethically sound, it will avoid liability lawsuits and public-relations problems that often result from unethical actions. (If these are the sole motives of such executives, we may have questions about them from an ethical standpoint.) Nevertheless, we cannot deny the importance of ethics in sound health-care management. The importance of ethics in sound engineering management is equally obvious.

1.5   Chapter Summary

Engineering ethics is a type of professional ethics and as such must be distinguished from personal ethics and from the ethical obligations one may have as an occupant of other social roles. Engineering ethics is concerned with the question of what the standards in engineering ethics should be and how to apply these standards to particular situations. One of the values of studying engineering ethics is that it can help promote responsible engineering practice.

Part of responsible engineering practice is the exercise of preventive ethics: the practice of sound ethical decision making to avoid more serious problems later. Practice in preventive ethics involves stimulating the moral imagination, developing the ability to recognize ethical issues when they arise, developing analytical skills in dealing with ethical problems, eliciting in engineers a sense of responsibility for their actions, and helping engineers to tolerate and also to resist disagreement and ambiguity.

The use of cases is an essential aspect of developing felicity in the practice of preventive professional ethics because professionals must always make decisions. Additionally, the study of cases in professional ethics is valuable practice for engineers who aspire to management, for many ethical problems are also management problems, and sound ethics usually makes for sound management.

Case Analyses

Case 1.1   The Forklifter[14]

Engineering student Bryan Springer has a high-paying summer job as a forklift operator, which enables him to attend college without having to take out any student loans. He is now staring at a 50-gallon drum filled with used machine coolant, wondering what he should do.

Just moments ago, Bryan's supervisor, Max Morrison, told him to dump half of the used coolant down the drain. Bryan knew the coolant was toxic, and he mentioned this to Max. But Max was not swayed.

Max: The toxins settle at the bottom of the drum. If you pour out half and dilute it with tap water while you're pouring it, there's no problem.

Bryan: I don't think that's going to work. Besides, isn't it against the law?

Max: Look, kid, I don't have time for chit-chat about a bunch of silly laws. If I spent my time worrying about every little regulation that comes along, I'd never get anything done—and neither will you. Common sense is my rule. I just told you—toxins settle at the bottom, and most of them will stay there. We've been doing this for years, and nothing's happened.

Bryan: You mean no one's *said* anything about it? That doesn't mean the environment isn't being harmed.

Max: You aren't one of those "environmentalists," are you? You college guys spend too much of your time in the ivory tower. It's time to get real—and get on with the job. You know, you're very lucky to have a good-paying job like this, kid. In three months you'll be back in your cozy college. Meanwhile, how many other college kids do you think there are out there wondering if they'll be able to afford to go back—kids who'd give their eye teeth to be where you are right now?

Max then left, fully expecting Bryan to dump the used coolant. As Bryan stares at the drum, he ponders his options. What options do you think he has? What do you think he should do?

Analysis

Bryan is in a difficult situation. He believes that complying with Max's order is both illegal and wrong, yet he has little if any power in the company and is in danger of losing a valuable job if he disobeys. Furthermore, he must make an immediate decision. He might decide that he just does not want to do something that he considers wrong and that he has already earned as much as most students earn in a summer. If need be, he can take out a student loan. He might also believe that his example of refusing to dump the coolant can have an effect on company policy.

On the other hand, he might decide to dump the coolant down the drain. He might try to convince himself that one more dumping will not make that much difference, and

it will give him a little more time to make a decision. He might also believe that staying on will have more effect on company policy than merely quitting or being summarily fired. This is a factual issue, having to do with the likely consequences of various courses of action.

Bryan also must be aware of what laws he may be violating if he decides to follow Max's orders. He must be prepared personally to deal with the consequences of those laws (fine and/or imprisonment) if he is indicted for the felony of toxic waste dumping under the terms of the U.S. Resource Conservation and Recovery Act (RCRA). Equally important, he must be conscious of what he personally would be doing to the environment.

As a budding engineer, Bryan should be aware of the first fundamental canon in the NSPE Code of Ethics: "Hold paramount the safety, health and welfare of the public in the performance of their professional duties." Maybe driving a forklift is not yet one of his professional duties, but it is a means for him to become a professional engineer. Also, the company he is working for is ostensibly involved in engineering-related work. It is machine coolant he was asked to dump, and the strictures of the NSPE Code of Ethics apply equally to companies and to individuals. But a company can violate one of the code items only through the actions of its employees. So, in aiming its code of ethics at individuals, the NSPE is clearly also enjoining companies to follow those same guidelines. There is not and cannot be a separate code for individuals and companies to follow.

It looks as though, if Bryan wants to convince Max to stop dumping toxins, he will need to gather information on the toxicity of the specific chemicals he is dumping and the medical evidence available about the effects of that toxic waste on the public. This is most effective if put in numerical terms such as the probability of whatever serious consequence is possible per unit level of exposure (for example, probability of the number of serious illnesses per 100,000 people exposed to one part per million in their drinking water). Next he will need to gather information on current applicable laws, and particularly what fines and penalties are at risk. Finally, he will need to present the cost of alternatives available to Max's company other than just outright dumping. That is a lot of work, but if Bryan is really disturbed about the situation and still wants to keep his summer job, he may have no other alternative to spending some significant research time in the local library.

Suppose Bryan discovers that Max's theory about how to reduce the toxic effect has no validity at all. He also confirms his suspicion that repeated dumping of the toxins into the drain is not only illegal but a considerable source of environmental pollution and a potential health hazard. If Bryan wants to persuade Max that they should not dump the toxins, he will have to proceed with great tact and diplomacy. He will likely have to convince Max that seriously considering alternatives to dumping may be in Max's and the company's best interests. He must somehow convince Max to be his ally in trying to sell the cost of the alternatives to dumping to Max's superiors in the company.

What if Bryan concludes that Max will never take his advice seriously? If the company is large enough to have an "ethics hotline" or an ombudsman or an officer in charge of corporate responsibility, he should certainly make use of the opportunities these resources afford. If not, he should consider laying his case before Max's superior or the personnel officer.

If this is done in a way that is both sincere and nonconfrontational and if Bryan manages to find a receptive person, he may have a good chance of both protecting the environ-ment and protecting his job. If this fails, he will have to face an unpleasant choice. Bryan could take his case outside the company. Some argue that this course of action makes sense only after one has resigned from the company, in other words after there is no longer anything personal (job and income) at stake. This may be a moot point since once he goes public, it is highly likely that Bryan will no longer be employed by his company.

Nevertheless, Bryan may console himself with the thought that he has done what he thinks is right rather than keeping his job at the cost of his conscience—and perhaps at the cost of the surrounding environment. And he may take some satisfaction from the thought that he is preparing himself for professional life by determining that lines may have to be drawn even in the face of serious opposition and at the risk of personal sacrifice.

Case 1.2   USAWAY[15]

John Budinski, quality control engineer at Clarke Engineering, has a problem. Clarke contracted with USAWAY to supply a product subject to the requirement that *all* parts are made in the United States. Although the original design clearly specifies that all parts must satisfy this requirement, one of Clarke's suppliers failed to note that one of the components has two special bolts that are made only in another country. There is not time to design a new bolt if the terms of the contract are to be met. USAWAY is a major customer, and John fears that not meeting the deadline can result in unfortunate consequences for Clarke.

John realizes that the chances of USAWAY discovering the problem on its own are slim. The bolts in question are not visible on the surface of the product.

Furthermore, it is highly unlikely that those who work on repairs will notice that the bolts are foreign made. In any case, Clarke is under contract to do any needed repairs. Meanwhile, it can work on a bolt design so that it will be ready with U.S. bolts when, and if, replacements are needed.

What possible courses of action are available to John Budinski? What do you think he should do?

Case 1.3 Whose Property?[16]

I

Derek Evans used to work for a small computer firm that specializes in developing software for management tasks. Derek was a primary contributor in designing an innovative software system for customer services. This software system is essentially the "lifeblood" of the firm. The small computer firm never asked Derek to sign an agreement that software designed during his employment there becomes the property of the company. However, his new employer did.

Derek is now working for a much larger computer firm. His job is in the customer service area, and he spends most of his time on the telephone talking with customers having systems problems. This requires him to cross-reference large amounts of information. It now occurs to him that by making a few minor alterations in the innovative software system he helped design at the small computer firm, cross-referencing can be greatly simplified.

On Friday Derek decides he will come in early next Monday morning to make the adaptation. However, on Saturday evening he attends a party with two of his old friends, you and Horace Jones. Not having seen each other for some time, you talk about what you have been doing recently. Derek mentions his plan to adapt the software system on Monday. Horace asks, "Isn't that unethical? That system is really the property of your previous employer." "But," Derek replies, "I'm just trying to make my work more efficient. I'm not selling the system to anyone, or anything like that. It's just for my use—and, after all, I did help design it. Besides, it's not exactly the same system—I've made a few changes."

This leads to a discussion among the three of you. What is your contribution?

II

Derek installs the software on Monday morning. Soon everyone is impressed with his efficiency; they ask about the "secret" of his success. Derek begins to realize that the software system might well have company-wide adaptability. This does not go unnoticed by his superiors either, so he is offered an opportunity to introduce the system in other parts of the company.

Now Derek recalls the conversation at the party, and he begins to wonder if Horace was right after all. He suggests that his previous employer be contacted and that the more extended use of the software system be negotiated with the small firm. His superiors firmly resist this suggestion. They insist that the software system is now the property of the larger firm. Derek balks at the idea of going ahead without talking with the smaller firm. If Derek does not want the new job, his superiors reply, someone else can be invited to do it; in any case, the adaptation will be made.

What should Derek do now?

III

Does Horace have any responsibility to alert the smaller firm about Derek's plans? Do you?

What if Horace is friends with people who work at the smaller firm? What if you are?

Case 1.4   The Thesis[17]

I

Nelson Nice is on the engineering faculty at State University. Three years ago he headed a research project that involved an undergraduate student assistant. At first Jason Smart was enthusiastic about the project, and he certainly felt honored that Professor Nice selected him as his undergraduate assistant. However, as time passed Jason grew impatient with the laboratory work and write-ups. Nelson Nice found that he had to do more and more of the work himself. Eventually Jason Smart left the project—before the work was completed.

One year later Jason, then a graduate student at another university, wrote to Nelson Nice and asked him if he would send him a copy of the final report of the work they had done together. Jason explained that he had matured considerably since his undergraduate days and was now working in a related area. "Now," he said, "I think I'm ready for more serious work. It would help me a lot if I could see how things finally worked out in the project."

Should Nelson Nice send the report to Jason Smart?

II

Nelson Nice was not anxious to share the report with anyone. Disappointed with the results of the research, Nelson had turned his attention elsewhere. As far as he was concerned, the project was dead. He also had to admit that he was still unhappy with Jason's performance. Nevertheless, he was impressed with Jason's acknowledgment of his earlier immaturity and his apparent desire to do serious work. So Nelson sent the report, pointing out to Jason that, although the research was now complete, it had not turned out as he had hoped, and that he had no plans to do further work in the area. He wished Jason well in his graduate work and hoped that this report might be of some help in giving him new ideas.

Several years later Nelson Nice discovered that Jason Smart used the report as his master's thesis—adding only a couple of introductory paragraphs, a concluding section, and an updated bibliography. No reference to Nelson Nice appeared anywhere in the thesis!

What, if anything, should Nelson Nice now do about this? Is there anything he could have done earlier that might have prevented this from happening? What might he do in the future to decrease the chances of this sort of thing happening again?

Case 1.5   Recommendation for a Friend[18]

I

Mike Hubbard sat in his study composing a work of fiction on his word processor. His efforts were not supposed to be fiction—he was actually writing a letter of recommendation for a friend from college days, engineer Tom Fellows.

Roommates at State University, both had majored in mechanical engineering. Mike was a superior student and continued on to get a Ph.D. Tom struggled with his studies, received a lot of help from Mike, spent much time on extracurricular activities, and frequently borrowed money from Mike because of irresponsible spending habits. Tom went to work in industry as soon as he got his bachelor's degree. Mike and Tom remained lifelong friends and kept in reasonably close touch over the years.

After graduate school Mike went to work for XYZ in its research laboratory. Now, ten years later, he was manager of mechanical engineering research. Tom held a series of jobs at which he had not been particularly successful and, three years ago, with Mike's help, landed a job in XYZ's computer-aided design department.

Two weeks earlier Tom informed Mike that he lost his XYZ job in a departmental budget reduction effort. At Tom's request, Mike went to Tom's supervisor to ask if his job could be salvaged. "Tom is a great guy and not a bad engineer," his supervisor replied, "but he doesn't concentrate on getting work out; he's more interested in the golf league, office gossip, the stock market, and a lot of other things. Also, he's turned in some very high expense accounts for trips and, although I can't prove it, I think he's padding some of them—maybe all of them. Given all this, I think he's one of the obvious choices for my reduction-in-force."

Mike discussed these comments frankly with Tom, at which point Tom asked if Mike would prepare a general letter of recommendation to help him find another job. "You know I won't get much of a recommendation from my supervisor," said Tom, "and, Mike, you've known me for years and know my abilities. If you help me get another job I'll really buckle down and show you how good an engineer I can be!"

So Mike sat at his word processor trying to put together a reasonably positive letter of recommendation for his friend. The letter contained a series of positive statements about Tom's ability and enthusiasm, was addressed "To Whom It May Concern," and given to Tom. Tom's weaknesses were not included. Although he did not state it explic-

itly, Mike implied that Tom had worked directly for him.

Several weeks had passed when Mike received a telephone call from the director of engineering of a small company that purchased components from XYZ. The director had interviewed Tom, was given Mike's letter, and was calling to discuss Tom's ability in regard to a specific project management assignment. Mike was as enthusiastic as possible because he felt the assignment would probably be one in which Tom would work well if he applied himself.

A few days later Tom telephoned Mike to tell him that he had the job. Mike offered Tom serious advice about giving his all to this new job, and Tom assured Mike he had learned the "error of my ways."

Identify and discuss the ethical issues Mike Hubbard faced. How do you think he should have handled Tom's request to write a letter of recommendation for him? Assuming Tom works out well at his new job, do you think Mike acted appropriately?

II

A couple of months passed, during which Mike Hubbard and Tom Fellows played golf a couple of times and Tom told him that he had "everything under control" and that the job was working out well. Mike breathed a sigh of relief and felt he had really done the right thing in writing the letter of recommendation.

Mike's peace of mind was soon rudely shattered. One day he received a call asking him to come to the office of Pat Berry, Mike's boss and XYZ's director of research. When Mike entered Pat Berry's office, he found XYZ's director of human resources, Pete Gettings, also present.

"Mike, we've got a serious situation to discuss with you," Pat opened immediately. "A couple of days ago I got a telephone call from a long-time acquaintance of mine. He's vice-president of engineering at the company Tom Fellows has joined. He said that recommending our 'dead wood' was not a very desirable way to treat a customer and wondered if they should continue to do business with us. He told me that Fellows had made an absolute mess of the management of a project assigned to him and had probably cost them a major government contract. When I questioned Pete about why we recommended Fellows, he had no record of making any recommendation at all. So I called my friend back. He said the individual in question had a letter of recommendation from you, Mike, which you further backed up in a telephone conversation with their director of engineering. What do you know about all of this?"

How should Mike answer Pat Berry's question? What action, if any, should Pat Berry take against Mike?

Case 1.6   Hitting the Glass Ceiling[19]

Brenda Jones, a chemistry laboratory technician at XYZ, returned to her laboratory frustrated and angry after her meeting with her department manager, Mike Richards. She had asked for the meeting in order to discuss a job posting for a process chemist in one of XYZ's factories. She regarded this job as a real opportunity to match her skills and abilities with her responsibilities.

Brenda had been a brilliant college student, excelling in chemistry and chemical engineering. However, when she sought employment the state of the economy made it very difficult for her to find an appropriate position. She took the only job related to her field that she could find—a chemistry laboratory technician in the research laboratories at XYZ. It soon

became obvious to XYZ's research management that Brenda was capable of handling a much more demanding position. After a short time she was promoted to a chemist's position in XYZ's technical service organization. She regarded becoming a process chemist as a good next step in her career.

What frustrated and angered Brenda at her meeting with Mike was his flat refusal to place her name in application for the process chemist position. "Brenda," he said, "you would find the atmosphere in a factory too demanding for you as a woman. That's a very high-pressure job. What would you do if your kids got sick again? The factory has got to run and they wouldn't wait for you while you stayed home to play nursemaid!"

This was not the first time Mike had indicated doubts about what she could handle. Shortly after her transfer into the technical service department, Mike told Brenda that, as the only woman in the department, she would not be invited to the department's annual off-site planning and recreational meeting. "You'd be the only woman there and I think you'd be very uncomfortable," he said, adding that "besides, the language in the discussions sometimes gets a little rough and we wouldn't want to subject you to that. OK?" Although too stunned to do anything but nod her assent, Brenda was very upset at Mike's attitude, which she considered to be quite unprofessional.

Even more upsetting to Brenda was Mike's first performance appraisal of her work. During her first year in the department, Brenda had to take several consecutive days off when one of her children became seriously ill. She had done her best not to let her work assignments fall behind and had worked many extra hours after her child's health was restored. However, during her annual appraisal, Mike had criticized her severely because of her "poor attendance record."

When she first considered whether to

transfer into the technical service department, Brenda was warned by some of her co-workers that Mike Richards did not particularly like to have women working for him. But she decided to adopt a wait-and-see attitude. She was now convinced that her co-workers were right, but she was also faced with the question of what to do. She could take a grievance to XYZ's human resource manager. But he was also male and had a reputation for giving women who complained to him a hard time. She might ask for a lateral transfer to another department in the research laboratories. She might try to stick it out and make the best of a frustrating situation, while keeping her eyes open for opportunities with another company. Or perhaps she could confide in someone she trusts and ask for advice.

What advice might such a person give Brenda? What ethical issues does this case raise?

Case 1.7 A Promotion[20]

On the face of it, Darnell, Inc. has a strong commitment to affirmative action. Five years ago less than 1 percent of its professional and managerial staff were women. Now 8 percent are women. However, few of the women are in senior positions. Partly this is because most of the women have less seniority than the vast majority of men. But it is also because, until recently, there has been widespread skepticism at Darnell that women are well suited for the responsibilities that attach to the more senior positions. This may now be changing. Catherine Morris is one of the leading candidates for promotion to chief engineer in quality control at Darnell.

Although they work in different areas of Darnell, Judy Hanson and Catherine Morris have gotten to know one another rather well

in the few months Judy has been with Darnell. Judy likes Catherine very much, but she has serious doubts that Catherine is the right person for the promotion. She does not think that Catherine has strong leadership qualities or the kinds of organizational skills that will be needed. Furthermore, she is worried that if Catherine fails at the job, this will only reinforce the prevailing skepticism at Darnell about women's ability to handle senior position responsibilities. Rather than being a mark of women's progress at Darnell, it will be, Judy fears, a setback—one which will take its toll on other women at Darnell.

Questions for Analysis

a. What, if anything, should Judy do?

b. Suppose Judy overhears several male engineers talking about Catherine's possible promotion. They remark that she will never be able to handle the job. This will show once and for all how foolish, and potentially harmful, affirmative action in the workplace is. What should Judy do?

c. Suppose it is Tom Evans, not Judy, who overhears the conversation in b. What should he do?

d. Suppose Tom and Judy overhear the conversation together. What should they do?

Case 1.8 Golfing[21]

I

Paul Ledbetter is employed at Bluestone Ltd. as a manufacturing engineer. He regularly meets with vendors who offer to supply Bluestone with needed services and parts. Paul discovers that one of the vendors, Duncan Mackey, like Paul, is an avid golfer. They begin comparing notes about their favorite golf courses. Paul says he's always wanted to play at the Cherry Orchard

Country Club; but since it is a private club, he's never had the opportunity. Duncan says he's been a member there for several years and that he's sure he can arrange a guest visit for Paul. Should Paul accept the invitation?

II

Paul accepts the invitation. He, Duncan, and two other members have a very competitive, but friendly, eighteen-hole match. Paul is teamed up with one of the other members, Harvey. Although Paul does not normally bet money in matches, Duncan and the others persuade him to play for $3 a hole ("just to keep things interesting"), along with the losers buying drinks for the winners. Paul and his partner win five holes to their opponents' two, thus winning $9 each. While they are having drinks, Duncan says, "I think it's only fair that Bob and I get a rematch. What do you say, Paul? You can be Harvey's guest on Guest Day next month." Should Paul accept the invitation?

III

Paul accepts the invitation. The match is closer this time, but Paul and Harvey win $3 each. Soon Duncan and Harvey nominate Paul for membership at Cherry Orchard. The membership committee approves, and Paul is invited to join the country club. Paul accepts, thus beginning a long golfing relationship with Duncan.

Gradually Paul overcomes his resistance to betting on the golf course, and the stakes eventually grow somewhat larger. Although Duncan occasionally beats Paul, the upper hand is clearly Paul's. In the subsequent years Paul does not keep close track of his overall winnings, but he realizes that, all told, he has won several hundred dollars

from Duncan. Meanwhile, Duncan is still one of the vendors with whom Paul interacts. Does this pose any ethical problems?

IV

Bluestone's vice-president of manufacturing calls a special meeting for engineers in her division who deal with vendors. She announces: "I've been told by the president that we have to make some cutbacks in the vending area. We're going to be in real trouble if we don't get more cost effective. So, I want each of you to do a review—your targeted cutback is 20 percent. If your unit deals with ten vendors now, cut it back to eight, and so on. Give me your recommendations—with a brief rationale—by the first of next week."

Paul next discusses the problem with the two other engineers in his unit who deal with vendors. They have to recommend the elimination of two vendors. Should Paul bring up his golfing relationship with Duncan?

V

Paul mentions his golfing relationship with Duncan. He raises the question of whether this compromises his objectivity. The other engineers reassure him, pointing out that they, too, have formed friendships with some of the vendors and that each of them will just have to do the best they can at objectively assessing the situation. As the discussion continues, it becomes more and more worrisome to Paul that, if he were to be objective about it, he would have to recommend Duncan's elimination. Should he tell the others that this is what he is thinking, or should he let them take the initiative? (This way, either they would recommend two others for elimination—thus sparing Duncan—or perhaps both would recommend Duncan and it would not be necessary for Paul to recommend against his friend.)

VI

Paul lets the other two engineers take the initiative. They both recommend that Duncan be eliminated. Paul says nothing in opposition to their recommendation. The group decides to think about it overnight and make its final recommendation the next day.

Paul and Duncan are scheduled for a golf match later that same afternoon. Since Paul and Duncan are good friends, Paul decides he should tell Duncan about the bad news he is likely to receive soon. Duncan is understandably upset. He points out that he has done his best for Bluestone all these years, and he has always been pleased with what he thought was a good working relationship—especially with Paul. Finally, he asks Paul what he said to the other engineers. What should Paul say? Discuss.

VII

Paul tells Duncan that he did not oppose the recommendations of the other two engineers. He reminds Duncan that he had to try to be objective about this: "We all talked about how hard it is to deal with this since friendships are involved. But we agreed that our basic obligation has to be to do what is best for Bluestone. Friendship should not be allowed to overturn good business. So, hard as it was, when I tried to be objective about it, I couldn't really disagree with their recommendations."

As Paul painfully explains his position, Duncan's face reddens. Finally Duncan furiously explodes, "I don't believe this! What kind of friend are you, anyway? Didn't I get

you into Cherry Orchard? And how good a golfer do you think you are, anyway? How do you think you've won all that money from me over the years? You don't really think you're *that* much better at golf than I am, do you?"

Discuss the ethical issues that you now think this case raises. Would you like to reconsider any of your earlier answers?

Notes

1. Rogers Commission, "Report to the President by the Presidential Commisssion on the Space Shuttle Challenger Accident" (Washington, D.C., June 6, 1986), pp. 772–773.
2. Michael S. Pritchard, *Teaching Engineering Ethics: A Case Study Approach,* National Science Foundation, Grant No. DIR-8820837, pp. 199–200.
3. The NSPE code is the only full code reprinted in Deborah Johnson's *Ethical Issues in Engineering* (Englewood Cliffs, N.J.: Prentice Hall, 1991). See pp. 98–104. It is also reprinted, along with other codes, in Mike W. Martin and Roland Schinsinger, *Ethics in Engineering* (New York: McGraw-Hill, 1989), pp. 352–358.
4. See *The Dallas Morning News* (May 14, 1993), p. 1.
5. Reported in several sources, including *The New York Times,* June 20, 1974.
6. Samuel Florman, "Moral Blueprints," *Harper's* (October 1978), p. 31.
7. Accreditation Board for Engineering and Technology, *Fifty-Third Annual Report*, 1985, p. 98.
8. This installment appeared in newspapers on April 4, 1990.
9. These goals are discussed in detail in Daniel Callahan, "Goals in the Teaching of Ethics," in Daniel Callahan and Sissela Bok, *Ethics Teaching in Higher Education* (New York: Plenum, 1980), pp. 61–74.
10. For a good discussion of this, see Robert Baum, *Ethics in Engineering* (Hastings-on-the-Hudson, N.Y.: The Hastings Center, 1980). Baum was an original member of the Hastings Center team of educators. His monograph is one of many prepared for use in the different disciplines.
11. Barbara Toffler, *Tough Choices: Managers Talk Ethics* (New York: Wiley, 1986), p. 288.

12. This case was presented by engineer J. Kent Roberts (University of Missouri—Rolla) at the Illinois Institute of Technology's 1980 Summer Workshop on Engineering Ethics.

13. This case was developed by civil engineer James Taylor (University of Notre Dame).

14. From NSF Grant No. DIR-8820837, in Michael S. Pritchard, ed., *Teaching Engineering Ethics: A Case Study Approach*, June 1992. The case and accompanying commentaries are on pp. 162–171.

15. Ibid., case and commentaries on pp. 431–444.

16. Ibid., case and commentaries on pp. 336–346.

17. Ibid., case and commentaries on pp. 402–410.

18. This is an adaptation of W. Gale Cutler's fictitious case, "Tom Asks for a Letter of Reference," *Research.Technology Management* (November/December 1990), pp. 47–48.

19. This is an adaptation of W. Gale Cutler's fictional case, "Brenda Hits the Ceiling," *Research.Technology Management* (January/February, 1989), pp. 51–52.

20. Pritchard, *Teaching Engineering Ethics*, case and commentaries on pp. 325–335.

21. Ibid., case and commentaries on pp. 172–189.

Chapter 2

Professionalism and Codes of Ethics

The tragic 1981 Kansas City Hyatt Regency walkway collapse received extensive coverage in *The New York Times* some four years after its occurrence. Here is how a November 16, 1985, article begins:

> KANSAS CITY Mo., Nov. 15—A state judge today found the structural engineers for the Hyatt Regency Hotel guilty of "gross negligence" in the 1981 collapse of two suspended walkways in the hotel lobby that killed 114 people.
>
> Many of those killed were dancing on the 32-ton walkways July 17, 1981, when an arrangement of rods and box beams suspending them from the ceiling failed. Others of the dead and the 200 injured were crushed under the structures.
>
> Judge James B. Deutsch, an administrative law judge for Missouri's Administrative Hearing Commission, in a 442-page ruling, found the structural engineers guilty of gross negligence, misconduct and unprofessional conduct.[1]

One day before the judge's decision, the American Society of Civil Engineers (ASCE) announced a policy of holding structural engineers responsible for all aspects of structural safety in their building designs. This policy resulted from the deliberations of an ASCE committee named in 1983 to address questions raised by the disaster.

Judge Deutsch found the project manager guilty of "a conscious indifference to his professional duties as the Hyatt project engineer who was primarily responsible for the preparation of design drawings and review of shop drawings for that project." He also concluded that the chief engineer's failure to closely monitor the project manager's work betrayed "a conscious indifference to his professional duties as engineer of record." Responsibility for the collapse, it was decided, lay in the engineering design for the suspended walkways. Expert testimony claimed that even the original box beam design fell short of minimum safety standards. Substantially less safe, however, was the design that actually was used. As one of the worst structural engineering tragedies in the history of the United States, the walkway disaster is a grim reminder of how dependent we all are on competent, responsible engineering practice.

2.1   Introduction

Judge Deutsch's language in the Hyatt-Regency case is noteworthy. Two structural engineers were charged with unprofessional conduct. Each was found guilty of "a conscious indifference to his *professional* duties. . . ." (Emphasis added.) This suggests that some duties to avoid or prevent harms are special. Although anyone could be said to have a duty or responsibility to avoid causing harms by driving a car carelessly, some people have duties to avoid or prevent harms because they are professionals. Is there a special set of responsibilities that engineers have because of their professional roles? This chapter will explore this question by considering, first, what it means to be a professional and, second, what professional engineering societies and their codes of ethics have to say about the responsibilities of engineers.

The strong role played by ASCE in the follow-up to the walkway disaster suggests comparisons with the American Medical Association (AMA) and the American Bar Association (ABA). The AMA and ABA are umbrella organizations that states rely on in regulating professional practice. Physicians and attorneys must be licensed by the state to practice, and AMA and ABA standards are used in establishing licensing criteria.

In contrast, however, only certain areas of engineering practice require licensing. Judge Deutsch recommended that the state of Missouri's Board of Architects, Engineers and Land Surveyors discipline the negligent engineers. The board could censure the engineers, or it could suspend or revoke their licenses. However, this is possible only because engineers are required to be licensed if they do the kind of work in question. Most engineering practice does not require licensing, and only about 20 percent of those who engage in engineering practice are licensed, professional engineers.

In engineering there is nothing comparable to the AMA or ABA. Instead there is a proliferation of more or less autonomous professional engineering societies. Major professional engineering societies such as ASCE, the Institute of Electrical and Electronic Engineers (IEEE), and the American Society of Mechanical Engineers (ASME) each have their own codes of ethics. But none has power or influence comparable to the AMA or ABA. In addition, there are more than eighty other specialized societies with their own codes. Efforts in recent years to establish national organizations embracing the entire engineering profession have been only moderately successful.

To better understand the aims of these efforts, it is important to discuss what a profession is and why professional status might be desirable. We turn first to the topic of professionalism in general. Then we examine the claim that there is a "social contract" that stipulates mutual obligations between the professions and the larger society. Next we consider some criticisms of professionalism, especially from the standpoint of contemporary sociology and economics. We conclude our general discussion of the professions with a brief consideration of possible alternatives to the present relationship between the professions and society. Finally we turn to a detailed discussion of engineering codes of ethics.

2.2   The Professions

The early meaning of the term "profession" and its cognates referred to a free act of commitment to a way of life. The *Oxford Shorter Dictionary* says that the earliest meaning of the adjective "professed" referred to the activity of a person who had taken the monastic vows of a religious order. We might think of a person who made a public promise to enter a distinct way of life with allegiance to high moral ideals. One "professed" to be a certain type of person and to occupy a special social role, which carried with it stringent moral requirements. By the late seventeenth century, the word had been secularized to refer to anyone who professed to be duly qualified.

Thus "profession" originally meant, according to the *Oxford Shorter Dictionary*, the act or fact of "professing." It has come to mean: "The occupation which one professes to be skilled in and to follow. . . . A vocation in which professed knowledge of some branch of learning is used in its application to the affairs of others, or in the practice of an art based upon it."

This brief historical account, however, is not sufficient for our purposes; we need to discuss the *characteristics* of professionalism in more detail. In particular, we need an account of the characteristics of professionalism that will enable us to distinguish a profession from a "mere" occupation. There is no universally accepted account. It is unwise to claim that the characteristics we will discuss constitute a true definition, i.e., a statement of the necessary and sufficient conditions for having the status of a profession. Rather, we will consider a set of characteristics that at least usually hold true of professions. A given profession might not have one of these (so the characteristic would not be necessary), or an occupation might have a characteristic without being a profession (so the characteristic is not sufficient). Nevertheless, the following five characteristics will be useful in distinguishing professions from nonprofessional occupations.

First, entrance into a profession requires an extensive period of training, and this training must be of an intellectual character. Many occupations require extensive apprenticeship and training, and they often require practical skills, but the training required of professionals focuses as much on intellectual content as practical skills. Professionals' knowledge and skills are grounded in a body of theory, described by the sociologist Ernest Greenwood as "a system of abstract propositions that describes in general terms the classes of phenomena comprising the profession's focus of interest."[2]

The acquisition of this theoretical base necessitates formal education, usually in an academic institution. Today most professionals have at least a bachelor's degree from a college or university, and many professions require more advanced degrees, often conferred by a professional school. Thus the professions are usually closely allied in our society with universities, especially the larger and more prestigious ones.

Second, professionals' knowledge and skills are vital to the well-being of the larger society. A society that has a sophisticated scientific and technological base is especially dependent on its professional elite. We rely on the knowledge possessed by physicians to protect us from disease and restore us to health. The lawyer has knowledge vital to our welfare if we have been sued or accused of a crime, or if our business has been forced into bankruptcy, or if we want to get a divorce or buy a house. Likewise, we are dependent on the knowledge and research of scientists and engineers for our safety in an airplane, for many of the technological advances upon which our material civilization rests, and for national defense. The accountant's knowledge is also important for our business success or when we have to file our tax return.[3]

Third, professions usually have a monopoly or near monopoly on the provision of professional services. According to Greenwood, this control is achieved in two ways. One way is that the profession convinces the community that only those who have graduated from a professional school should be allowed to hold the professional title. The profession usually also gains considerable control over professional schools by establishing accreditation standards that regulate the quality, curriculum content, and number of such schools. In the second way of achieving control, a profession often attempts to persuade the community that there should be a licensing system for those who want to enter the profession. Those who practice without a license are subject to legal penalties.

Fourth, professionals have an unusual degree of autonomy in the workplace. Professionals in private practice have considerable freedom in choosing their clients or patients, and most professionals exercise a large degree of individual judgment and creativity in carrying out their professional responsibilities. A physician must determine the most appropriate type of medical treatment and a lawyer must decide the most successful type of defense of her client. This is one of the most satisfying aspects of professional work. The justification for this unusual degree of autonomy is that only the professional has sufficient knowledge to determine the proper professional service. The possession of specialized knowledge is thus a powerful defense of professional autonomy.

Fifth, a professional claims to be regulated by ethical standards, usually embodied in a code of ethics. The degree of control that professions possess over the services vital to the well-being of the rest of the community provides an obvious temptation for abuse. Therefore most professions attempt to limit these abuses by regulating themselves for the public benefit. Professional codes are ordinarily promulgated by professional societies, and there is occasionally some attempt to punish members who fail to abide by the provisions of the code.

Holding these five characteristics in mind, it is easy to see that occupations form a continuum, extending from those that are unquestionably professions to those that are unquestionably not. The occupations that hold a clear title to professional status include medicine, law, veterinary medicine, architecture, accounting (at least certified public accountants), and dentistry. Some occupational groups might be considered borderline. For example, engineers are considered full professionals by many people, but others believe they are deficient in professional autonomy. Furthermore, engineers do not hold a monopoly on the provision of professional services. Finally, most probably consider counseling psychologists with a Ph.D. to be true professionals, although those with lesser academic credentials might be considered deficient with respect to the first characteristic.

2.3   The Business Model and the Social-Contract Model

There are at least two models of the professions, both of which are suggested by the characteristics of professions we have just considered. One model, the *business model*, emphasizes the ways in which professionals use their professional status for their own economic advantage. The other, the *social-contract model*, emphasizes the service orientation to which professionals are supposedly committed. Which model is most appropriate to engineering? Are engineers primarily businesspersons or guardians of a public trust? Before answering this question, let us look more closely at these two models.

The Business Model

Most engineers are employees of large organizations. These so-called "employed professionals" usually have a strong sense of loyalty to their employers, and some of them may think of themselves primarily as employees. In this way they may identify with the business model. As employees, they are also interested in increasing their own salaries and making themselves as essential to their employers as possible. They want to ensure that entrance into their profession is limited by stringent educational requirements and that their skills are vital to their employers. In these ways also, engineers may seem to be following the business model.

Some engineers are either self-employed or work in small professional firms—some civil engineers, for example. It is even more obvious that these engineers are engaged in a business enterprise, so that the business model is more appropriate. Many students of the professions believe that even when professionals appeal to the ideals of professionalism, they do so for their own economic interests. Taking suggestions from sociologist Magali Larson, we can see three ways in which professionals—presumably including engineers—can appeal to the concept of professionalism to enhance their economic position.[4] First, they often appeal to their supposed service orientation, maintaining that professionals have a special responsibility for service to all humanity, regardless of social class. This can mask the economic interests of engineers and other professionals. Second, professionals insist that their work is of unusual importance to society, which can serve to justify high prices for professional services. Third, professionals insist that they are capable of regulating themselves in the public interest,[5] an argument used to ask for relative freedom from government control.

Critics of the professions point out that many of the activities of professional societies seem to promote the economic self-interest of professionals, although their various activities often have more altruistic motivations. Professional societies often promote professional licensure and aggressively attack the "unauthorized practice" of the professional skills associated with their profession. While this is done in the name of protecting the public, it can also give the profession control of the market for a particular service. Professional societies have also traditionally opposed competitive pricing and the advertising of professional services, on the grounds that it protects the quality of professional services. Another reason for their opposition, however, might be that it keeps up the price of professional services. Professional societies perform other functions that promote the economic self-interest of professionals. They arbitrate disputes among professionals, thus perpetuating the belief that professionals are self-regulating and warding off encroachment by external regulatory agencies. They also promulgate codes of ethics, again promoting the belief that professions are self-regulating.

The business model captures some truth about the professions, including engineering. It gives an explanation of many things such professionals do and say, whether they are employees of large organizations or work in professional firms. Nevertheless, the business model does not contain the whole truth.

The Social-Contract Model

The second model takes the affirmations of the professions to a public-service orientation much more seriously than does the business model. In this model, professionals are not simply businesspersons who use the trappings of professionalism to promote their economic self-interest. Rather, they are guardians of a public trust. One way to express this idea is in terms of the concept of a social contract.

The idea of a social contract has a long history in political philosophy. The English philosophers Thomas Hobbes (1588–1679) and John Locke (1632–1704) and the French philosopher Jean-Jacques Rousseau (1712–1778) were the classical advocates of the social contract. The basic idea of a social contract is that there are implicit, unstated agreements among the members of society that explain and justify social institutions. As applied to the professions, the concept implies an understanding between the professions and the rest of society that explains and justifies the existence of the professions. The social contract embodies a set of mutual expectations. If either party to the contract fails to abide by its terms, it has "breached" the social-contract and thereby warrants moral criticism.

One source for the terms of this contractual arrangement is the codes promulgated by the professions themselves. Professional codes present a picture of what professionals understand to be an implicit agreement between themselves and the larger society. The social contract model, then, is an account of the self-understanding of the professions, as presented in their codes of ethics.

The social contract between the professions and society contains at least four provisions. On the one hand, the professions agree (1) to devote themselves to the service of society and (2) to regulate themselves in the provision of those services. On the other hand, society agrees (3) to give professionals a place of honor and adequate or above-average livelihood and (4) to allow them an unusual degree of autonomy in the performance of their professional duties. We can find suggestions of these provisions of the social contract in the NSPE code.

SERVICE

The service provision includes several elements: (1) promoting the well-being of the general public as this relates to the profession's area of expertise, (2) ensuring the competence (and continued competence) of professionals in their area of expertise, and (3) ensuring that professionals are devoted to the public welfare even when it conflicts with self-interest, particularly economic self-interest. This latter provision may sometimes imply the obligation to engage in *pro bono* work, providing free professional services to the poor and public-service organizations.

The first of the "fundamental canons" of the code of the NSPE says that engineers shall "hold paramount the safety, health and welfare of the public in the performance of their professional duties." The second "rule of practice" under this canon stipulates that "engineers shall perform services only in the areas of their competence." Under the section "Professional Obligations," the second rule states that "engineers shall at all times strive to serve the public interest." The eleventh rule under this same section requires that "engineers shall cooperate in extending the effectiveness of the profession by interchanging information and experience with other engineers and students, and will endeavor to provide opportunity for the professional development and advancement of engineers under their supervision." This includes encouraging employees to continue their education, attend meetings of professional societies, and become registered. It also includes assigning them to tasks that utilize their professional abilities.

SELF-REGULATION

Professionals must be able to create and enforce high standards of professional competence and ethical conduct for themselves. The NSPE code requires, in the first rule under "Professional Obligations," that "engineers shall be guided in all their professional relations by the highest standards of integrity." A provision under the second rule in this section is that "if a client or employer insists on . . . unprofessional conduct" an engineer should "notify the proper authorities and withdraw from further service on the project." The third rule states that "engineers shall avoid all conduct or practice which is likely to discredit the profession or deceive the public."

AUTONOMY

The other side of the contract between professions and the public is that, in exchange for competent service and self-regulation, professions are to receive public honor and recognition and to enjoy an unusual degree of autonomy in the conduct of their professional work. Autonomy includes freedom to choose whom to serve and to conduct professional services in accordance with professional standards and with a minimum of interference from nonprofessional sources. The primary statements about autonomy are in the codes of law and medicine, perhaps because lawyers and physicians are more likely to be self-employed. Concern for the independence of professional judgment, however, is expressed in section II.1.a of the NSPE code, where there is a statement that if engineers find their "professional judgment overruled under circumstances where the safety, health, property or welfare of the public are endangered, they shall notify their employer or client and such other authority as may be appropriate."

SOCIAL STATUS

Even the social-contract model maintains the right to financial rewards. According to section III.6, "engineers shall uphold the principle of appropriate and adequate compensation for those engaged in engineering work." Section III.6.b instructs "engineers, when employing other engineers" to "offer a salary according to professional qualifications."

The Emergence of the Social-Contract Model

If we were to evaluate these two models of professionalism for their conformity to the facts of professional life, we would probably have to say that both models have validity. Professionals are to some extent businesspersons: they must survive in the marketplace. Even the social-contract model recognizes the legitimacy of expecting financial rewards for professional services. Professionals also have obligations to public service that may transcend the business model and that may correspond more adequately with aspects of the social-contract model. Nevertheless, the stress on the obligations to the public—the hallmark of the social-contract model—seems to be assuming increasing importance in engineering codes, at least in the United States.

The earliest American codes typically held: "The engineer should consider the protection of a client's or employer's interests his first professional obligation, and therefore should avoid every act contrary to this duty."[6] The only stated responsibility to the public was that an engineer "should endeavor to assist the public to a fair and correct general understanding of engineering matters, to extend the general knowledge of engineering, and to discourage the appearance of untrue, unfair, or exaggerated statements on engineering subjects in the press or elsewhere. . . ."[7]

Sometime prior to 1926 the American Association of Engineers (AAE) advanced a four-part "Compilation of Specific Principles of Good Professional Conduct for Engineers." The first principle states: "The engineer should regard his duty to the public welfare as paramount to all other obligations."[8] However, AAE was short-lived, and emphasis on the primacy of the engineer's obligation to the public was not to reappear until later. Not until mid-century was greater responsibility to the public acknowledged in the major codes. In 1947 the Engineers' Council for Professional Development (ECPD) endorsed the idea that engineers have not only duties of fidelity to their employers and clients but also duties to the public. The ECPD code specified that engineers "will have due regard for the safety and health of the public." In 1974 the ECPD code was revised to say that "engineers shall hold paramount the safety, health and welfare of the public in the performance of their professional duties."[9]

If our analysis is correct, the engineering codes thus provide evidence that engineers think of themselves as professionals. They not only are attempting to sell their services in the marketplace—whether to employers or clients—but also have obligations to the safety, health, and welfare of the public. But some have argued that the codes themselves are outdated and perhaps should even be discarded. Let us consider some of these arguments.

2.4   Objections: The Very Idea of a Code of Ethics

Although professions characteristically have codes of ethics, there is no consensus about what functions such codes should have. Heinz Luegenbiehl suggests that a code of ethics is necessary for an emerging profession to gain initial recognition.[10] However, he adds, engineering codes have now outlived their usefulness. These codes are currently understood as a "set of ethical rules that are to govern engineers in their professional lives."[11] But, he argues, there are three reasons for not being satisfied with this understanding: (1) practicing engineers seldom consult engineering codes of ethics; (2) basic principles in the codes conflict with each other, and the codes provide no guidance for resolving these conflicts; and (3) codes are meant to be coercive, but this conflicts with the autonomy usually attributed to moral agents.[12] We discuss each of these problems in turn.

1. It certainly does seem to be true that practicing engineers seldom consult engineering codes of ethics. A relatively small percentage of practicing engineers are members of the professional engineering societies that have adopted these codes. But even members of these societies seldom consult their codes of ethics and many are not familiar with their contents. Still, engineers act in accordance with the principles and rules found in engineering codes of ethics and they would agree with these principles and rules if asked about them. The codes might thus be understood as making explicit the principles and standards that experienced, responsible engineers accept in practice.

Experienced engineers might not need to consult an ethical code in deciding what to do. But, as Luegenbiehl himself points out, inexperienced engineers might find a code useful in pointing out areas of ethical concern with which they will have to deal. All engineers, however, could call on the code for support in resisting the requests of others to do what it would be unethical for an engineer to do.

2. There are circumstances in which the principles or rules of an engineering code seem to conflict with each other, for example, concern for public safety and loyalty to an employer. A code of ethics cannot be expected to provide an algorithm to resolve such conflicts. Sometimes the resolution will be straightforward (e.g., if an employer presses for something that clearly violates important safety requirements). However, as already noted, codes are best understood as providing the kinds of ethical considerations to bear in mind rather than recipes for

decision making. Codes of ethics provide an ethical framework within which decisions should be made rather than specific solutions to problems.

3. It is not an inherent feature of a code of ethics that it must be coercive. A code can identify principles and rules of conduct without stipulating penalties for failure to comply. If a professional organization, or a court of law, does impose penalties for violations, this does not in itself change a code of ethics into something else (a quasi-legal code). All that follows is that the professional organization, or court of law, takes the ethical behavior of professionals so seriously that it will punish what it takes to be breaches of ethics. Whether taking such punitive measures is ethically justifiable is another matter, but this need not affect the status of the code as a code of ethics.

Some might object that it is already coercive for a professional organization to stipulate for its members what will or will not be regarded as ethical. However, if a code's provisions can be supported with good reasons, why should a profession not include an affirmation of those provisions as a part of what it professes? Further, this does not preclude individual members from autonomously accepting those provisions and jointly committing themselves to their support. The real question is whether the provisions of a particular code are reasonable expectations for practitioners in the profession. For example, is it really problematic to expect engineers to commit themselves to safety, honesty, and objectivity in their work? What would we say of an engineer who *rejected* such values?

Despite his dissatisfaction with current engineering codes of ethics, Luegenbiehl agrees that engineering students should be introduced to ethics. He advocates assisting them in becoming morally autonomous engineers. This requires respecting the basis of their own ethical beliefs, a basis that presumably comes from something other than the acceptance of a professional code of ethics. Since engineering students are not familiar with the contexts within which engineers must make ethical decisions, he believes they should be provided with *guides* (rather than *codes*). For example, a guide could define "conflict of interest" in an engineering context and provide examples of possible kinds of conflicts of interest and their likely consequences for individuals, the profession, and society.

Familiar ethical principles (such as honesty, fairness, and not causing harm), says Luegenbiehl, have their foundations outside of professional codes and therefore do not belong in them: "The profession is justified only in aiding engineers to apply their moral foundation to a specifically engineering context."[13] However, this restriction seems arbitrary and unhelpful. If, for example, honesty, fairness, and not causing harm do have specific applications in engineering practice, how are engineering students to be guided unless it is *assumed* that they accept honesty, fairness, and not causing harm as important ethical values? But if they do accept them, what objection can there be to affirming this in a code of ethics? And if they do not accept them, are they really suitable candidates for the profession? Furthermore, if these values are not affirmed in a profession's code (or set of guides), how is guidance to be provided? Again, what seems most important is that the ethical values affirmed in a code of ethics be supportable. Support, however, can come from more than one source—for example, the engineering students' own moral foundations and the profession's (and society's) understanding of what it should be about.

2.5   Functions and Contents: Down to Particulars

What functions might a code of ethics serve? Stephen Unger suggests several.[14] First, it can serve as a collective recognition by members of a profession of its responsibilities. Second, it can help create an environment in which ethical behavior is the norm. Third, it can serve as a guide or reminder in specific situations (although it should not be confused with a cookbook). Fourth, the process of developing and modifying a code of ethics can be valuable for a profession. Fifth, a code can serve as an educational tool, providing a focal point for discussion in classes and professional meetings. Finally, a code can indicate to others that the profession is seriously concerned with responsible, professional conduct.

Of course, how welcome all of this is depends on the code's contents. Unger urges the inclusion of positive ideals, not just the avoidance of wrongdoing. He also emphasizes that a code must be acceptable to people with diverse political, social, and religious views. Since reasonable people can disagree to some extent about important ethical matters, we cannot expect consensus to include everything that individual professionals regard as ethically significant in their professional lives. A code that respects political, social, and religious diversity will either leave some matters unmentioned or it will provide space for some individual differences in professional standards and ideals. An acceptable code will restrict ethical requirements to what we might call "the highest common denominator"—those standards and ideals that all can embrace, despite their differences. These, then, will not address all professional standards and ideals that an individual professional finds important.

In some instances there may be disagreement among professionals about what, specifically, a code should include. In the absence of agreement, the code may remain permissive even though individual professionals might still regard certain code-permitted behavior unprofessional and continue to urge code reform. In other instances a professional may restrict what he or she is prepared to undertake professionally because of personal or social ideals that he or she agrees it would be inappropriate to impose on the entire profession. For example, Unger himself says that he tries to avoid all engineering work that involves military projects. However, rather than seek to impose his opposition to such projects on the engineering profession, he simply insists that engineers should be accorded the right to resist conscientiously certain kinds of engineering work.

Samuel Florman questions this right of refusal to refrain from performing engineering services to which one ethically objects.[15] He compares the right to engineering services to the right to legal counsel. However, as Unger points out, the right to legal counsel is itself restricted and even where it applies does not automatically confer an obligation on any particular attorney. This is a matter for government and volunteer agencies to determine. The obligation falls directly on the legal profession, not necessarily on individual attorneys. A similar observation can be made about rights to medical care.

One difference between law and engineering is that even those believed guilty of the worst crimes are entitled to legal representation. The courts may appoint an attorney to defend such persons even if none would otherwise be willing to do so. What if no engineers were willing to provide certain kinds of services (e.g., to build gas chambers for extermination camps)? As Unger points out, even Florman agrees that it would be inappropriate to force some engineers to do this sort of work. However, given the diversity of values among engineers, it is unlikely that conscientious refusal will result in the unavailability of services except in cases of highly questionable projects. We should emphasize, however, that we are talking here about *conscientious* refusal, not mere dislike or disinterest.

If an engineering code of ethics should restrict itself to principles, rules, and ideals about which reasonable people can obtain consensus, what might we expect to be included? Unger suggests framing a code around basic principles of honesty, trustworthiness, respect for human life and welfare, fair play, openness, and competence.[16] Unger sees science and technology as a special case of cooperation—cooperation among those with expertise and with those to whom services are provided. In an engineering context, the principles he mentions are essential to science and technology's need for stability over time. They are necessary for fair treatment; for being able to count on one another; for working together to increase knowledge, understanding, and expertise; for providing needed services; and for not causing unnecessary harm to one another or to those for whom services are provided.

It is important to notice that the principles to which Unger appeals have their foundations outside the codes of ethics in which they are incorporated. Although a code of ethics may endorse and adapt such principles for its own purposes, it does not create, invent, or legitimate them. They already exist in common morality. A code simply spells out their relevance to the professional practice in question.

The preamble to the National Society of Professional Engineers Code of Ethics seems to support this independent foundation for the ethical principles and standards of engineering practice:

> Engineering is an important and learned profession. The members of the profession recognize that their work has a direct and vital impact on the quality of life for all people. *Accordingly*, the services provided by engineers require honesty, impartiality, fairness and equity, and must be dedicated to the protection of the public health, safety, and welfare. In the practice of their profession, engineers must perform under a standard of professional behavior which requires adherence to the highest principles of ethical conduct on behalf of the public, clients, employers and the profession. [Emphasis added.]

Thus, NSPE's code attempts to articulate principles and standards for all engineers, not just those who are formal members of NSPE. In this respect, NSPE is not attempting to impose its ethical values on engineers. It is acknowledging and articulating principles and standards already implicit in responsible engineering practice and presenting them in a comprehensive, coherent fashion. Further, NSPE hopes to gain explicit commitment to these principles and standards from members of NSPE, as well as from other practicing engineers who may be exposed to the NSPE code. Whether everything in the NSPE code (or in other engineering codes) is defensible in these terms needs careful attention.

2.6   Why Support a Code of Ethics?

Why should practicing engineers comply with engineering codes of ethics? We explore several possible answers, using NSPE's code as representative.

First, the most fundamental reason for complying with the code is stated in NSPE's preamble. Given the nature of engineering practice and its importance to society, certain responsibilities follow: those articulated in the code. Acknowledging this does not require being a member of NSPE but simply understanding one's role as a practicing engineer and the responsibilities to which this gives rise. The NSPE code is a product of the careful reflection of experienced engineers who want to articulate in a coherent and comprehensive manner the basic ethical responsibilities of practicing engineers. In short, it might be argued, the NSPE code is simply the best current statement of the responsibilities of engineers.

This first reason gains strength if a code's provisions are the result of the sort of deliberative process used by the ethics committee of the American Association of Engineers (AAE) in the early 1920s. As described by Carl Taeusch, a group of experienced, thoughtful leaders of the profession examined representative ethical problems engineers face. They derived from their discussions a set of principles and standards that seemed most relevant to their resolution.[17] This reason gains even further strength when we consider the more recent work of NSPE's Board of Ethical Review (BER). This board carefully examines and comments on ethical problems in terms of NSPE's code, thus providing guidance in interpreting and applying the code to engineering practice.[18] This inductive approach may not be the final word, but it does seem to deserve the respect of engineers seeking ethical guidance.

This first reason does not say that the NSPE code should be supported because it is an *adopted code*, as distinct from simply being a reliable statement of the responsibilities of engineers. As a second reason for complying with the code, it might be argued that engineers should support it because it is the code of their professional society. This is part of what they agreed to do as a condition of membership in NSPE. Now, for those who are members of NSPE, this is a reason for compliance. This is an instance of keeping one's word, keeping one's promise, or sticking to one's commitments. Unfortunately, this reason applies only to a small percentage of practicing engineers. As we have noted, most practicing engineers are not members of NSPE or any other professional engineering society.

The third reason is the implicit "contract" between the engineering profession and society. This was part of our discussion of professionalism. In return for benefits received (respectable salary, prestige, and the privilege of self-regulation), engineers understand that they owe honesty, trustworthiness, and a good service to society. We cannot easily dismiss the reciprocal relation between engineering practice and society. Whether this is best understood in quasi-contractual terms or more simply in terms of a mutual exchange of benefits is perhaps unclear.

Still, this relationship may be more between society and the engineering profession as a whole, rather than between society and any particular engineers, so a reason that can be applied more directly to particular engineers is desirable. Michael Davis presents such a reason.[19] Davis sees engineering codes of ethics as essential to advising engineers how to conduct themselves as *professionals*, to judging engineers' conduct, and to understanding engineering as a profession. A code of ethics, he suggests, is best seen as a *convention between professionals* (as distinct from expressing some agreement with society). A profession can be understood, in part, as a group of persons who want to cooperate in serving the same ideal of public service better than they could if they did not cooperate. A code of ethics is therefore part of the solution to a coordination problem. It can help engineers if they support each other by committing themselves to a code of ethics; they can help one another resist unwelcome pressures it would be more difficult to resist alone.

Davis's view explains why engineers should want to organize to form professional societies with codes of ethics. It gives those already in such societies reason to continue to support them and their codes, and to work at recruiting others to join their societies. And it gives engineers who are not members of such societies reason to join.

The advantage a code of ethics gives engineers is that ethics need no longer be just a matter of personal conscience for them. Conscience standing alone might tell us something quite different than conscience joined with others by way of the codes. With the conventions established by the codes, an engineer can appeal to a code (and its supporters) by saying, "As an engineer, I cannot do this." A code serves as a guide to what engineers may reasonably expect of one another, to what they can expect other engineers to help them do or refuse to do. In short, there is strength in numbers, at least when those numbers are morally joined.

Davis sees this convention as a "quasi-contract" or "contract in law" among engineers (in contrast to an agreement between engineers and society). Although there is no actual promise or agreement, engineers choose to become engineers and they accept the benefits that come with calling themselves engineers. These benefits depend on the support of others who also wish to call themselves engineers. Only by banding together do the full benefits come. Supporting the code is a way of doing one's fair share in supporting the engineering profession.

Davis sums up his view with four reasons for supporting an engineering code of ethics:[20]

1. It will help protect engineers and those they care about from being injured by other engineers (*self-regulation*).

2. It will help create a working environment that makes it easier for an engineer to resist the pressure to do wrong (*objecting as an engineer*).

3. It will help make engineering a practice about which they need not feel justified embarrassment, shame, or guilt (*respectability of profession*).

4. It is an obligation of *fairness* to do one's part, assuming that others do theirs.

2.7   Codes: Uses and Limitations

A glance at the National Society for Professional Engineers' (NSPE) Code of Ethics lends some support to Stephen Unger's view that a good code of engineering ethics can pivot around a small number of basic organizing principles. The code emphasizes protection of the health, safety, and welfare of the public; competence; objectivity; truthfulness; and serving as faithful agents of their employers and clients.[21] There is nothing surprising in this list (although the emphasis on protection of the public is a fairly recent addition). However, as the full body of the code reveals, the special functions of engineers in their professional life require elaborations of these basic principles in the context of engineering practice. Furthermore, even these further elaborations are no substitute for individual judgment or decision. As we have said, the NSPE code is not like a recipe in a cookbook. At best, it provides a basic framework, with general guidelines, for engineers to bear in mind when engaged in their work; and it is not self-interpreting.

This is why NSPE's Board of Ethical Review (BER) periodically presents cases with commentaries on how the code might be used to deal with them. This is an invaluable service to the engineering profession, providing paradigm examples of acceptable and unacceptable conduct according to the code. The code, in turn, expresses and confirms the shared ethical beliefs and commitments of members of NSPE. Thus, the BER serves the important function of further articulating for engineers, their employers and clients, and the public the basic ethical standards engineers should observe.

Unlike the media, the BER commentaries concentrate more on the everyday ethical concerns of engineers than on disaster stories such as the Challenger accident, Chernobyl, Bhopal, and the Kansas City Hyatt-Regency walkway collapse. Although the BER case studies are based on actual situations, few are newsworthy enough to attract the attention of the media. Their importance for most engineers and engineering students lies precisely in their ordinariness. These are problems that *any* engineer might have to deal with. Thus, they come closer to meeting ABET concerns than the less frequent, more spectacular incidents portrayed in the media. The BER discussions are useful in helping engineers and students see how NSPE's Code of Ethics should be interpreted in a variety of situations. But an exclusive focus on BER cases has several shortcomings.

First, since the case studies are designed to aid understanding of the NSPE Code of Ethics, they are essentially code driven. Analyses by the BER are quasi-legalistic in tone, mirroring the specific provisions of the code, with little analytical discussion of the underlying ethical principles or concepts. But, as we have seen, codes themselves need to be evaluated.[22] They may include some provisions that themselves are ethically problematic. A history of engineering codes reveals important changes over the years—ranging from eliminating provisions on certain forms of advertising services to adding provisions about fundamental obligations to protect public health and safety. Also, there may be other areas of ethical concern that the code either does not address or addresses only vaguely.

Second, BER commentaries almost always are consensus reports. There are very few minority dissenting opinions. Of course, it is important that students be aware of the extent to which consensus (and shared commitment) on ethical issues in engineering exists. However, more complex ethical issues do not necessarily command consensus, and students need to see examples of reasoned disagreement as well as agreement.[23]

Third, critics frequently complain that engineering codes of ethics, including NSPE's, tend to view the engineer as an independent consultant, rather than as a corporate employee who is expected to fit within a complex organizational setting. Engineers in a large corporate context typically lack the degree of autonomy that independent, consulting engineers have. They lack this both because they may not be primary decision makers themselves and because they may work in relatively isolated units that provide them with little access to the wider implications of their work. Furthermore, the expectations of engineering codes of ethics and those of managers of the units within which engineers work may not always match. These differences can result in serious ethical concerns that engineering codes do not clearly address. For example, a fundamental canon of the NSPE code is that engineers shall "hold paramount the safety, health, and welfare of the public in the performance of their professional duties." Another fundamental canon is that engineers shall "act in professional matters for each employer or client as faithful agents or trustees." The code is not specific about how to handle the conflicts that may arise between these two canons. Whistleblowing is a major area of ethical concern among engineers, yet the code offers no real guidance. It may be that codification of such matters is either unattainable or undesirable. Still, it is important for students to reflect on circumstances in which whistleblowing may be at issue.

Fourth, BER cases are limited in scope. Most of the published opinions deal with issues such as advertising professional services, engineering fees, conflicts of interest, and government employment. Relatively few deal with such concerns as negligence or incompetence.[24]

Finally, BER cases seldom require a consideration of the likely implications of initial decisions for subsequent decision making. However, decisions that seem to resolve matters for the moment do have consequences that often set the stage for even greater ethical problems later. As we noted in Chapter 1, one of the managers interviewed in Barbara Toffler's *Tough Choices* emphasizes the importance of imaginatively exploring different alternatives. This is useful advice for any engineer. Codes of ethics can remind us of the sorts of ethical concerns we need to be ready to deal with, but they cannot tell us which ones are likely to come up next—and they cannot replace the need for careful and imaginative thinking.

2.8   Chapter Summary

In this chapter we discussed professionalism as it applies to engineering. Both the business and social-contract models seem to apply to engineering. Engineers, whether self-employed or employees, must market their services and survive economically. At the same time, engineering codes of ethics have increasingly recognized an obligation to public safety, health, and welfare.

As in other professions, codes of ethics play an important role in efforts to have engineering's professional status fully defined and accepted. We have examined reasons for even those engineers who are not members of professional societies to take these codes seriously. At the very least, engineering codes of ethics reflect the efforts of experienced, thoughtful engineers to articulate the kinds of ethical principles and standards that responsible engineers should accept. Beyond this, the codes have the potential to support engineers who want to resist pressures to do less than what is ethically required. In any case, codes of ethics are an invaluable resource in thinking through the ethical problems facing engineers.

Case Analyses

Case 2.1 An Employment Opportunity[25]

Part I: A Dilemma

Gerald Wahr was not prepared for such a sudden turn of events. He was scheduled to complete his degree in chemical engineering in June. He planned to return to help his parents run the family farm right after graduation. However, in early May his father became seriously ill, and it was evident he would have an extended, expensive stay in the hospital. Gerald's mother and his older brother could continue to operate the farm as long as they could manage the bills. But without an additional source of income, the family would soon begin defaulting on the farm's mortgage payments. The best hope for saving the farm would be for Gerald to find employment as an engineer.

Since Gerald had expected to return to the farm, he had already missed many opportunities for job interviews. He would have to work quickly. After an intensive search, only one solid opportunity surfaced. Pro-Growth Pesticides, Inc. would be on campus next week to interview candidates for a supervisory job requiring a degree in chemical engineering.

Gerald certainly is academically well qualified for the job. However, there is a hitch. The Wahr farm uses strictly organic methods; Gerald's family has always opposed the use of pesticides. In fact, Gerald's father is noted in the area for his outspoken views about this and Gerald admires this in his father. As a young child he often proudly announced that he wanted to grow up to be just like his father. Harold Wahr, however, had different ideas about this. A high school dropout, Harold advised young Gerald to further his education. "Without a college degree," he told Gerald, "you'll be as ineffective as I am. You have to fight fire with fire. If you really want to show those pesticide folks a thing or two, you've got to be able to talk their language." So, Gerald decided he would go to college and study chemical engineering.

Gerald's studies have done nothing to shake his conviction that organic farming is best. Quite the contrary. He is now more convinced than ever that the pesticide industry is not only harming the environment generally, but farm products in particular. Despite this, should he go for the interview with Pro-Growth?

Gerald Wahr's situation poses a number of ethical problems. First, there is the problem of his own *integrity*. Can he accept a job with a company whose primary business is to market products he adamantly opposes? Would this compromise his principles, and therefore himself? Or in difficult circumstances such as his, could he compromise his position without compromising his integrity?[26]

Second, Gerald has responsibilities to his family. Clearly his parents and brother depend on him for support, if not survival. That they share his opposition to pesticides further complicates things. Even if Gerald can work out the problem of preserving his own integrity, his family may not find his resolution acceptable. He needs to convince not only himself but his family that taking a job with a pesticide firm is all right. What if his father, for example, rejects the thought of compromise? ("We don't *want* your money if that's where it's coming from!")

So far we have mentioned only what might be called problems of *personal ethics*. They are personal in the sense that they focus on Gerald's concerns about personal integrity and on personal relationships with others. In contrast, Gerald might focus primarily on matters that are more broadly matters of *social ethics*—e.g., social, political, and legal issues concerning the environment. No doubt in Gerald's case personal and social ethics strongly overlap, since his personal concerns about the use of pesticides also relate to social, political, and legal issues. Nevertheless, the personal and social aspects of his concerns can be roughly distinguished.

There is another complicating ethical dimension: *professional ethics*. Although Gerald is not yet a professional engineer, he is now seriously contemplating becoming one. How does this alter the picture? What is a profession, and what does becoming a professional engineer entail? These are questions Gerald should seriously consider before he decides to go for an interview.

Part II. Conversations with Friends

At first Gerald rejects the idea of going for the interview. He thinks of it as a matter of integrity. How can he work for a company that researches, produces, and markets the very products he and his family have so long opposed? However, his friends counsel him otherwise. Here are some of their arguments. How might Gerald respond to them?

Ellen: Look, if you don't go for the job, someone else will. The job won't go away just because you stay away. So, the work's going to be done anyway. Your refusing the job won't change a thing.

Bob: Right! Furthermore, you need to look at this from a utilitarian point of view—the greatest good for the greatest number.[27] If you don't go for the job, someone else who really believes in pesticides will—and that's going to make things even worse! If you take the job and aren't gung ho, that might just slow things down a little.

Don: Besides, you might be able to introduce a few reforms from the inside. That won't kill the pesticide industry, but it might make it a little bit better—certainly better than if some zealous pesticide nut takes the job.

Ellen: So, it's pretty clear what to do. All things considered, you *ought* to go for the job. It's your only real chance to save the farm; and if someone else gets the job, Pro-Growth will cause even more harm. You can't be a purist about these things. It's not a perfect world, you know.

Each of these urgings may initially seem somewhat attractive to Gerald Wahr. But he should look at them with some care. Ellen's first comment is especially troubling if taken alone. Although undoubtedly not intended to include such instances, it could be construed to endorse virtually *any* unethical act (e.g., theft, murder) as long as one is assured that someone else will do it anyway. For example, suppose Gerald knew that if he did not steal a valuable laptop computer sitting in an unlocked office, two thieves would make their way into the office and steal it. Does this really give Gerald a reason to steal the computer? At the very least, Gerald needs some assurance that what he is contemplating is not clearly unethical (or illegal). But this is precisely the question he is trying to resolve in deciding whether he should work for a pesticide company.

Bob's appeal to the greater good may impress Gerald, but there are two features of this appeal that might give him pause. First, if Gerald really wants to serve the greater good, he needs to ask whether he might do more good doing something else (e.g., holding out until an opportunity to fight the pesticide industry comes along). After all, there are probably many other kinds of job (perhaps less well paying) of which he could say, "If I take that job, I'll do less harm (or more good) than the person who will get it if I don't." Why should Gerald accept such an argument about *this* job—especially if this might damage his credibility as an opponent of pesticides? Unless he is very careful, Gerald is in danger of rationalizing the acceptance of a job that will address his short-run economic needs, but possibly at the expense of his long-run aims and his own integrity.

The second reason Gerald should worry about Bob's seeming utilitarian appeal also applies to Don's comment. Is it professionally responsible to accept a job with the intent of disappointing the expectations of one's employer and fellow workers? This is what Bob is recommending. Don's reasoning is more subtle; he suggests working for reforms. But Gerald must ask how he might go about this. Can he be up front about his aims and expect the respect and support of his employer and fellow workers? Or will this risk alienating them, perhaps resulting in the loss of his job? Is it professionally acceptable for him to be secretive about his real attitude about the pesticide industry?

Ellen's final observation is certainly worth noting. This is not a perfect world, and purist approaches to professional work are likely to result in disappointment if one's standards are exceptionally high. At the same time, Gerald needs to be concerned about whether compromising his standards may come at the cost of compromising himself. The fact that one can have unrealistically high standards does not mean that one can have no standards at all. *Where* to draw the line should be Gerald's problem, not *whether* a line should be drawn at all.[28] Once he accepts the job, Gerald's professional responsibilities (at least as seen by his employer and fellow workers) may require him to draw the line even farther from his original ideals than he anticipated. He must give these matters very careful thought before taking that first step.

Part III. The Interview

Gerald Wahr decides to go for the interview. He is quite uncomfortable during the interview, but it seems to be going rather well. However, the interviewer then asks: "There are a lot of people who disapprove of the use of pesticides in farming. Of course, Pro-Growth disagrees. What are your thoughts about the use of pesticides?" How should Gerald answer this question?

Part IV. Selecting Employment

Gerald Wahr's situation may seem extreme. However, it does raise important questions about job choices. To what extent should we be concerned about whether there is a good match between our basic ethical commitments and job selection? What kinds of engineering-related jobs, if any, would you decline because of ethical concerns?

Case 2.2   Participation in Professional and Technical Societies—Ethical Duty of Employer and Employee[29]

Facts

Engineer A has been employed by an organization for more than 20 years. During his early years of employment he was encouraged by his superiors to join and participate in the activities of both a technical society and a professional society. Within those societies, Engineer A held several board and committee positions, of which entry into the key positions was approved by his

superiors. He presently holds a committee position.

Engineer A's immediate superior, Engineer B, opposes Engineer A's participation in activities of his professional society on any other than annual leave basis, although existing organization rules encourage the use of excused leave for such purposes. It is Engineer B's view that such participation does not result in "benefits for the employer"; he feels that such participation does not constitute "employee training." Engineer B has refused to permit written communications from Engineer A asking for administrative leave to attend professional society meetings to go through Engineer B to higher level personnel.

When summoned by the chief executive officer (CEO) on another matter, Engineer A took the opportunity to ask his opinion of attendance and participation in technical and professional society meetings by his engineers. The CEO reaffirmed the organization policy.

When Engineer A prepared a travel request to go through his superior, Engineer B, to the CEO, Engineer B refused to forward the travel request and told Engineer A that he did not appreciate Engineer A's going over his head to discuss attendance and participation in technical and professional societies with his superior.

Questions

1. Was it ethical for Engineer A to discuss attendance and participation in technical and professional societies with the CEO without first notifying his superior?

2. Was it ethical for Engineer B to hinder Engineer A's efforts to obtain excused leave in order to attend technical and professional society meetings?

References

Code of Ethics—Section I.4.—"Engineers, in the fulfillment of their professional duties, shall

. . . act in professional matters for each employer or client as faithful agents or trustees."

Section III.1.f.—"Engineers shall avoid any act tending to promote their own interest at the expense of the dignity and integrity of the profession."

Section III.11.a.—"Engineers shall encourage engineering employees' efforts to improve their education."

Section III.11.b.—"Engineers shall encourage engineering employees to attend and present papers at professional and technical society meetings."

Discussion

The two questions posed are best addressed by reference to four code sections. Section I.4. requires engineers to act professionally and faithfully in dealing with their employer. Section III.1.f. cautions engineers to avoid any act tending to promote their own interests at the expense of the profession. Sections III.11.a. and b. admonish engineers to encourage their engineer employees to improve their knowledge through education and in particular through attendance and participation in professional and technical society meetings. With that background we will proceed to evaluate the actions of Engineers A and B.

It is possible for this Board to review the actions of Engineer A and to conclude that as a factual matter he was disloyal and promoting his own self-interests by going beyond his immediate superior to obtain permission to attend and participate in professional and technical society activities. However, if we were to do so, we would be ignoring the basic underlying philosophy of engineering—professionalism. The essence of professionalism is the unique service a practitioner renders to a client by virtue of having developed special capabilities. In line with that view we believe an employer of engineers has an obligation to treat engineers as pro-

fessional individuals. It is incumbent on the employer of any employed professional engineer to create an environment conducive to the continued development of professional capabilities. Of course it is the professional obligation of the practitioner to expend some time and effort to continuous expansion of his or her knowledge and capabilities. Such expansion of knowledge may be gained in a variety of ways. We believe one of those ways is by participating in the activities of a professional society. In particular, participation in the committee work of a professional society allows the practicing engineer the opportunity to gain a greater understanding of the new trends and advances in his profession, permits him to interact and exchange views and insights with other engineers, and provides the engineer with a better perspective as to the role of the engineer in society.

We are of the view that a fundamental issue was at stake when Engineer A discussed attendance and participation in technical and professional societies with the CEO. What was at stake was Engineer A's professional integrity and his obligation to expand his knowledge and capabilities.

In addition, we note that it was the general policy of the employer to encourage Engineer A's participation in the activities of technical and professional societies. It was only Engineer A's immediate supervisor, Engineer B, who hindered his efforts to participate. In view of those factors, we are of the view that Engineer A acted professionally and faithfully in his dealings with his employer.

Although it may have been more appropriate for Engineer A to first meet with his supervisor, Engineer B, to inform him of his intention to seek the CEO's permission to attend and participate in the technical and professional organizations' activities, we are not convinced that his failure to do so tended to promote his own self-interest at the expense of the dignity and integrity of the profession. Although his action might be characterized as a deception, given the intransigence of his supervisor, Engineer B, in not permitting him to communicate with his superior on the matter of participation in professional and technical society activities, one can better understand his decision to pursue this route. We find that Engineer A's failure to inform Engineer B of his intention to seek the CEO's permission to attend and participate in technical and professional society activities did not promote his own interest at the expense of the profession.

As for Engineer B, we are of the opinion that his opposition is neither in accord with the code nor supported by experience. Sections III.11.a. and b. admonish engineers to encourage their employees to participate in a variety of activities in order to foster their professional growth and development. As Section III.11.b. plainly states, among these activities are professional and technical society meetings. Engineer B was of the view that Engineer A's participation in technical and professional societies did not constitute "employee training" and did not result in "benefits to the employer." Aside from the question of whether this was in fact an accurate assessment of Engineer A's society activities, there is the issue of whether standards such as "employee training" or "benefits to the employer" are the only yardsticks by which professional and technical society activities and continuing engineering education programs should be measured. We think not but leave that question for another day. It suffices to say that in the instant case, contrary to Engineer B's view, Engineer A's participation in professional and technical society meetings was of the type intended by Sections III.11.a. and b. of the Code.

We note, however, that our decision today must not be construed to mean that an engineer should as a matter of course be granted excused leave from his employment without due regard to the needs and requirements of his employer. We believe that Section I.4. mandates that an engineer must be sensitive to the needs and requirements of his employer. When an employer chooses to limit his employees' participation in technical and professional society activity because those employees' services are critical to the operation of his organization, Section I.4. requires the employee to accede to his employer's decision. Although an engineer has an obligation to further his professional growth and development, it should never be pursued in a manner that would be adverse to the interest of his employer.

Conclusion

Q1. It was ethical for Engineer A to discuss attendance and participation in technical and professional societies with the CEO without first notifying his superior.

Q2. It was unethical for Engineer B to hinder Engineer A's efforts to obtain excused leave in order to attend technical and professional society meetings.

Board of Ethical Review
Ernest C. James, P.E.
Lawrence E. Jones, P.E.
Robert H. Perrine, P.E.
James L. Polk, P.E.
J. Kent Roberts, P.E.
Alfred H. Samborn, P.E.
F. Wendell Beard, P.E., chairman

Note: This opinion is based on data submitted to the Board of Ethical Review and does not necessarily represent all of the pertinent facts when applied to a specific case. This opinion is for educational purposes only and should not be construed as expressing any opinion on the ethics of specific individuals. This opinion may be reprinted without further permission, provided that this statement is included before or after the text of the case.

Case 2.3   Signing and Sealing Plans Not Prepared by Engineer[30]

Facts

Engineer A is the Chief Engineer in a large engineering firm and affixes his seal to some of the plans prepared by registered engineers working under his general direction who do not affix their seals to the plans. At times Engineer A also seals plans prepared by non-registered, graduate engineers working under his general supervision.

Because of the size of the organization and the large number of projects being designed at any one time, Engineer A finds it impossible to give a detailed review or check of the design. He believes he is ethically and legally correct in not doing so because of his confidence in the ability of those he has hired and who are working under his general direction and supervision.

By general direction and supervision, Engineer A means that he is involved in helping to establish the concept, the design requirements, and review elements of the design or project status as the design progresses. Engineer A is consulted about technical questions and he provides answers and direction in these matters.

Question

Is it ethical for Engineer A to seal plans that have not been prepared by him, or which he has not checked and reviewed in detail?

References

Code of Ethics—Section II.2.a.—"Engineers shall undertake assignments only when qualified by education or experience in the specific technical fields involved."

Section II.2.b.—"Engineers shall not affix their signatures to any plans or documents deal-ing with subject matter in which they lack competence, nor to any plan or document not prepared under their direction and control."

Section II.2.c.—"Engineers may accept assignments and assume responsibility for coordination of an entire project and sign and seal the engineering documents for the entire project, provided that each technical segment is signed and sealed only by the qualified engineers who prepared the segment."

Case 2.4   Gifts for Engineers[31]

Facts

Engineers A, B, and C are principals or employees of a consulting engineering firm which does an extensive amount of design work for private developers. The engineers are involved in recommending to the developers a list of contractors and suppliers to be considered for selection on a bidding list for construction of the projects. Usually, the contractors and suppliers recommended by the engineers for the selected bidding list obtain most of the contracts from the developers. Over a period of years the officers of the contractors or suppliers developed a close business and personal relationship with the engineers of the firm.

From time to time, at holidays or on birthdays of the engineers with whom they dealt, the contractors and suppliers would give Engineers A, B, and C personal gifts of substantial value, such as home furnishings, recreational equipment, gardening equipment, etc.

Question

Was it ethical for Engineers A, B, and C to accept gifts from the contractors and suppliers?

References

Code of Ethics—Section II.4.c.—"Engineers shall not solicit or accept financial or other valuable consideration, directly or indirectly, from contractors, their agents, or other parties in connection with work for employers or clients for which they are responsible."

Section II.5.b.—"Engineers shall not offer, give, solicit, or receive, either directly or indirectly, any political contribution in an amount intended to influence the award of a contract by public authority, or which may be reasonably construed by the public of having the effect or intent to influence the award of a contract. They shall not pay a commission, percentage, or brokerage fee in order to secure work except to a bona fide employee or bona fide established commercial or marketing agencies retained by them."

Section III.5.b.—"Engineers shall not accept commissions or allowances, directly or indirectly, from contractors or other parties dealing with clients or employers of the Engineer in connection with work for which the Engineer is responsible."

Case 2.5   Engineer's Dispute with Client over Design[32]

Facts

Client hires Engineer A to design a particular project. Engineer A develops what he believes to be the best design and meets with the client to discuss the design. After discussing the design plans and specifications, the client and Engineer A are involved in a dispute concerning the ultimate success of the project. The client believes Engineer A's design is too large and complex and seeks a simpler solution to the project. Engineer A believes a simpler solution will not achieve the result and could endanger the public. The client demands that Engineer A deliver over to him the drawings so that he can present them to Engineer B to assist Engineer B in completing the project to his liking. The client is willing to pay for the drawings, plans, specifications, and preparation but will not pay until Engineer A delivers the drawings. Engineer A refuses to deliver the drawings.

Question

Would it be ethical for Engineer A to deliver over the plans and specifications to the client?

References

Code of Ethics—Section II.1.a.—"Engineers shall at all times recognize that their primary obligation is to protect the safety, health, property, and welfare of the public. If their professional judgment is overruled under circumstances where the safety, health, property, or welfare of the public are endangered, they shall notify their employer or client and such other authority as may be appropriate."

Section II.1.e.—"Engineers having knowledge of any alleged violation of this Code shall cooperate with the proper authorities in furnishing such information or assistance as may be required."

Section III.1.b.—"Engineers shall advise their clients or employers when they believe a project will not be successful."

Case 2.6   Joint Authorship of Paper[33]

Facts

Engineer A and Engineer B are faculty members at a major university. As part of the requirement for obtaining tenure at the university, both Engineer A and Engineer B are required to author articles for publication in scholarly and technical journals. During Engineer A's years as a graduate student he had developed a paper which was never published and which forms the basis of what he thinks would be an excellent article for publication in a journal. Engineer A discusses his idea with Engineer B and they agree to collaborate in developing the article. Engineer A, the principal author, rewrites the article, bringing it up to date. Engineer B's contributions are minimal. Engineer A agrees to include Engineer B's name as coauthor of the article as a favor to enhance Engineer B's chances of obtaining tenure. The article is ultimately accepted and published in a refereed journal.

Questions

1. Was it ethical for Engineer A to use a paper he developed at an earlier time as the basis for an updated article?

2. Was it ethical for Engineer B to accept credit for development of the article?

3. Was it ethical for Engineer A to include Engineer B as coauthor of the article?

References

Code of Ethics—Section III.1.—"Engineers shall be guided in all their professional relations by the highest standards of integrity."

Section III.3.c.—"Consistent with the foregoing, Engineers may prepare articles for the lay or technical press, but such articles shall not imply credit to the author for work performed by others."

Case 2.7 Engineer Serving on Private Hospital Board and Performing Services[34]

Facts

A county hospital board owns a hospital facility and contracts with a private health care provider to manage, administer, and generally operate a hospital facility. Engineer

A, a principal in a local engineering firm, serves on the board of directors of the private health care provider. Certain engineering and surveying work will need to be performed at the hospital facility. Engineer A seeks and receives a contract from the private health care provider to perform the engineering and surveying work at the hospital. The decision to select Engineer A's firm was made by the private health care provider's board of directors and Engineer A participated in the decision.

Question

Was it ethical for Engineer A to seek a contract with the private health-care provider to perform the engineering and surveying services at the hospital?

References

Code of Ethics—Section II.4.d.—"Engineers in public service as members, advisors, or employees of a governmental body or department shall not participate in decisions with respect to professional services solicited or provided by them or their organizations in private or public engineering practice."

Section II.4.e.—"Engineers shall not solicit or accept a professional contract from a governmental body on which a principal or officer of their organization serves as a member."

Case 2.8 Objectivity of Engineer Retained As Expert[35]

Facts

Engineer A is a forensic engineer. He is hired as a consultant by Attorney Z to provide an engineering and safety analysis report and courtroom testimony in support of a plaintiff in a personal injury case. Following Engineer A's review and analysis, Engineer A determines that he cannot provide an engineering and safety analysis report favorable to the plaintiff because the results of the report would have to suggest that the plaintiff and not the defendant was at fault in the case. Engineer A's services are terminated and his fee is paid in full. Thereafter, Attorney X, representing the defendant in the case, learns of the circumstances relating to Engineer A's unwillingness to provide a report in support of Attorney Z's case and seeks to retain Engineer A to provide an independent and separate engineering and safety analysis report. Engineer A agrees to provide the report.

Question

Was it ethical for Engineer A to agree to provide a separate engineering and safety analysis report?

References:

Codes of Ethics—Section II.1.c.—"Engineers shall not reveal facts, data, or information obtained in a professional capacity without the prior consent of the client or employer except as authorized or required by law or this Code."

Section II.3.a.—"Engineers shall be objective and truthful in professional reports, statements, or testimony. They shall include all relevant and pertinent information in such reports, statements, or testimony."

Section II.4.b.—"Engineers shall not accept compensation, financial or otherwise, from more than one party for services on the same project, unless the circumstances are fully disclosed to, and agreed to by all interested parties."

Section III.4.b.—"Engineers shall not, without the consent of all interested parties, participate in or represent an adversary interest in connection with a specific project or proceeding in which the engineer has gained particular specialized knowledge on behalf of a former client or employer."

Case 2.9   Engineer's Duty to Report Data Relating to Research[36]

Facts

Engineer A is performing graduate research at a major university. As part of the requirement for Engineer A to complete his graduate research and obtain his advanced degree, Engineer A is required to develop a research report. In line with developing the report, Engineer A compiles a vast amount of data pertaining to the subject of his report. The vast majority of the data strongly supports Engineer A's conclusion as well as prior conclusions developed by others. However, a few aspects of the data are at variance and not fully consistent with the conclusions contained in Engineer A's report. Convinced of the soundness of his report and concerned that inclusion of the ambiguous data will detract from and distort the essential thrust of the report, Engineer A decides to omit references to the ambiguous data in the report.

Question

Was it unethical for Engineer A to fail to include reference to the unsubstantiative data in his report?

References

Code of Ethics—Section II.3.a.—"Engineers shall be objective and truthful in professional reports, statements, or testimony. They shall include all relevant and pertinent information in such reports, statements, or testimony."

Section III.3.a.—"Engineers shall avoid the use of statements containing a material misrepresentation of fact or omitting a material fact necessary to keep statements from being misleading; statements intended or likely to create an unjustified expectation; statements containing prediction of future success; statements containing an opinion as to the quality of the engineers' services; or statements intended or likely to attract clients by the use of showmanship, puffery, or self-laudation, including the use of slogans, jingles, or sensational language of format."

Section III.11.—"Engineers shall cooperate in extending the effectiveness of the profession by interchanging information and experience with other engineers and students, and will endeavor to provide opportunity for the professional development and advancement of engineers under their supervision."

Case 2.10 Engineer Misstating Professional Achievements on Resume[37]

Facts

Engineer A is seeking employment with Employer Y. As an employee for Employer X, Engineer A was a staff engineer along with five other staff engineers of equal rank. This team of six was responsible for the design of certain products. While working for Employer X, Engineer A along with five other engineers in his team participated in and was credited with the design of a series of patented products.

Engineer A submits his resume to Employer Y and on it implies that he personally was responsible for the design of products that were actually designed through a joint effort of the members of the team.

Question

Was it ethical for Engineer A to imply on his resume that he was personally responsible for the design of the products which were actually designed through the joint efforts of the members of the design team?

References

Code of Ethics—Section II.5.a.—"Engineers shall not falsify or permit misrepresentation of their, or their associates', academic or professional qualifications. They shall not misrepresent or exaggerate their degree of responsibility in or for the subject matter or prior assignments. Brochures or other presentations incident to the solicitation of employment shall not misrepresent pertinent facts concerning employers, employees, associates, joint venturers or past accomplishments with the intent and purpose of enhancing their qualifications and their work."

Section III.10.a.—"Engineers shall, whenever possible, name the person or persons who may be individually responsible for designs, inventions, writings, or other accomplishments."

[Compare this case with Case 1.3, "Whose Property?" in Chapter 1. What do you think these code provisions would suggest about that case? What do you think is the underlying ethical basis for these provisions in the code?]

Case 2.11 Disclosure of Previous Work by Consultant[38]

Facts

Engineer A agrees to provide consulting services to RMF, Inc., in connection with the development of a new product for manufacture. He develops a preliminary report, which is approved, then develops the design for the product. Engineer A and RMF, Inc., do not negotiate any terms in their agreement relating to the actual ownership of the design of the product. Neither takes any steps to seek patent protection. When the design reaches the production stage, RMF, Inc., terminates the services of Engineer A in accordance with their agreement. Thereafter, Engineer A agrees to provide consulting services to SYS, Inc., a competitor of RMF, Inc. As a part of those services, he divulges specific information unique to the product designed for RMF, Inc.

Question

Was it ethical for Engineer A to divulge specific information to SYS, Inc., unique to the product designed earlier by him for RMF, Inc.?

References

Code of Ethics—Section II.1.c.—"Engineers shall not reveal facts, data or information obtained in a professional capacity without the prior consent of the client or employer except as authorized or required by law or this Code."

Section III.4.—"Engineers shall not disclose confidential information concerning the business affairs or technical processes of any present or former client or employer without his consent."

Section III.10.c.—"Engineers, before undertaking work for others, in connection with which the Engineer may make improvements, plans, designs, inventions, or other records which may justify copyrights or patents, should enter into a positive agreement regarding ownership."

Case 2.12   Signing of Drawings by Engineer in Industry[39]

Facts

Engineer A is employed by a computer manufacturing company. She was responsible for the design of certain computer equipment several years ago. She signed off on the drawings for the equipment at that time. Although Engineer A's design was properly prepared, the equipment manufacturing process was faulty and, as a result, the equipment became too costly and suffered mechanical breakdown. The manufacturing division made a number of recommended modifications to her design that it believed would help reduce costs in the manufacturing process. Engineer A's analysis of the manufacturing division's recommendations revealed that they would reduce the reliability of the product and greatly increase the downstream costs to the company through warranty claims. Engineer A's supervisor, who is not an engineer, asks Engineer A to sign off on the changes for the new computer equipment. There is nothing to suggest that the equipment would pose a danger to the public health and safety. Engineer A raises her concerns to her supervisor but nevertheless agrees to sign off on the changes without further protest.

Question

Did Engineer A fulfill her ethical obligation by signing off on the changes without further action?

References

Code of Ethics—Section II.1.—"Engineers shall hold paramount the safety, health and welfare of the public in the performance of their professional duties."

Section II.1.a.—"Engineers shall at all times recognize that their primary obligation is to protect the safety, health, property and welfare of the public. If their professional judgment is overruled under circumstances where the safety, health, property or welfare of the public are endangered, they shall notify their employer or client and such other authority as may be appropriate."

Section II.1.b.—"Engineers shall approve only those engineering documents which are safe for public health, property and welfare in conformity with accepted standards."

Section II.2.b.—"Engineers shall not affix their signatures to any plans or documents dealing with subject matter in which they lack competence, nor to any plan or document not prepared under their direction and control."

Section II.4.—"Engineers shall act in professional matters for each employer or client as faithful agents or trustees."

Section III.2.b.—"Engineers shall not complete, sign, or seal plans and/or specifications that are not of a design safe to the public health and welfare and in conformity with accepted engineering standards. If the client or employer insists on such unprofessional conduct, they shall notify the proper authorities and withdraw from further service on the project."

NOTES

1. Article by William Robbins, special to *The New York Times* (November 16, 1985).

2. Ernest Greenwood, "Attributes of a Profession," *Social Work* (July 1957), pp. 44–45.

3. It should be noted that there is no suggestion that only the professions serve vital needs of society. Many occupations do, and they may require special expertise. The emphasis here in regard to the professions, however, is on the critical role of knowledge and expertise that is grounded in the formal educational background of professionals.

4. Magali Sarfatti Larson, *The Rise of Professionalism* (Berkeley: University of California Press, 1977), pp. 8, 66, 105. Cited in John Kultgen, *Ethics and Professionalism* (Philadelphia: University of Pennsylvania Press, 1988), p. 100.

5. This summary is taken from Kultgen, *Ethics and Professionalism*, pp. 114–115.

6. This was a principle in the 1912 code of the American Institute of Electrical Engineers, the first American code, and one that served as the model for most of the other engineering societies. For a brief summary of the history of engineering codes, see Robert Baum, *Ethics and the Engineering Curriculum*, pp. 7–10.

7. Baum, *Ethics and the Engineering Curriculum*, p. 8. Current codes have a similar provision. Given the rather low level of scientific and technological literacy prevalent today, fulfilling this responsibility presents engineers with a creative and important challenge. Mike Martin and Roland Schinzinger, *Ethics in Engineering* (New York: McGraw-Hill, 1989), suggest that engineering practice is a form of social experimentation. Those most affected by this experimentation, the general public, are likely to be the least knowledgeable about scientific and technological matters. Informed consent, as a matter of patients' rights, is now standardly recognized in medical practice. The public, it seems, is far from being in a comparable position in regard to the technology on which they depend so much.

8. Cited in Carl F. Taeusch, *Professional and Business Ethics* (New York: Henry Holt & Co., 1926), p. 102. However, according to Michael Davis and Heinz Luegenbiehl, the 1920 version of the AAE code has no such provision. (See Appendix C of their *Engineering Codes of Ethics: Analysis and Applications*, Center for the Study of Ethics in the Professions, Illinois Institute of Technology, 1986.) What accounts for this difference is not clear. Nor is it clear why no other engineering societies adopted the AAE provision at that time. AAE itself soon dissolved.

9. This provision has been adopted by all the major engineering societies with the exception of IEEE, which holds instead that engineers' responsibilities to employers and clients are limited by their responsibilities to protect public safety, health, and welfare. The function of ECPD has now been taken over by ABET, whose Code of Ethics retains the 1974 ECPD provision.

10. Heinz Luegenbiehl, "Codes of Ethics and the Moral Education of Engineers," in Deborah Johnson, ed., *Ethical Issues in Engineering* (Englewood Cliffs, N.J.: Prentice Hall, 1991), pp. 137–138.

11. Luegenbiehl, "Codes of Ethics," p. 137.

12. This is the major contention of John Ladd's "The Quest for a Code of Professional Ethics: An Intellectual and Moral Confusion," in Johnson, *Ethical Issues in Engineering*, pp. 130–136.

13. Luegenbiehl, "Codes of Ethics," p. 151.

14. Stephen H. Unger, "Codes of Engineering Ethics," in Johnson, *Ethical Issues in Engineering*, p. 105.

15. Unger discusses Florman's view on p. 110 in Johnson. Florman's view is developed in Samuel Florman, "Moral Blueprints," *Harper's*, 257 (October 1978), 30–33.

16. Unger, "Codes of Engineering Ethics," p. 107.

17. Carl F. Taeusch, *Professional and Business Ethics*.

18. Strengths and weaknesses of BER commentaries will be discussed in some detail below.

19. Michael Davis, "Thinking Like an Engineer: The Place of a Code of Ethics in the Practice of a Profession," *Philosophy and Public Affairs*, 20, no. 2 (Spring 1991), 150–167.

20. Davis, "Thinking Like an Engineer" pp. 166–167.

21. A copy of the NSPE code can be found right after this introduction.

22. See, for example, John Kultgen, "Evaluating Codes of Professional Ethics," in Wade L. Robison, Michael S. Pritchard, and Joseph Ellin, eds., *Profits and Professions* (Clifton, N.J.: Humana Press, 1983), pp. 225–264.

23. For good examples of constructive departures from BER consensus opinions, see Paula Wells, Hardy Jones, and Michael Davis, *Conflicts of Interest in Engineering* (Chicago: Center for the Study of Ethics in the Professions, Illinois Institute of Technology, 1986). Unfortunately, none of the case studies they present deal with engineers working in large organizations.

24. For a discussion of these limitations, see Donald Baker, "Social Mechanisms for Controlling Engineers' Performance," in Albert Flores, ed., *Designing for Safety: Engineering Ethics in Organizational Contexts* (Troy, N.Y.: Rensselaer Polytechnic Institute, 1982), especially p. 96.

25. Pritchard, *Teaching Engineering Ethics*. Case and commentaries on pp. 244–263.

26. For an insightful discussion of under what kinds of circumstances one can compromise without thereby compromising one's integrity, see Martin Benjamin, *Splitting the Difference: Compromise in Ethics and Politics* (Lawrence: University Press of Kansas, 1990).

27. See Chapter 6 for a discussion of utilitarian thinking.

28. For a discussion of line-drawing techniques, see Chapter 5.

29. This is BER Case No. 82-7 in National Society of Professional Engineers, *Opinions of the Board of Ethical Review*, Vol. VI (Alexandria, Va.: National Society of Professional Engineers, 1989), pp. 27–29.

30. National Society of Professional Engineers, BER Case No. 86-2. The BER discussion is on pp. 76–77.

31. This is BER Case No. 81-4 in NSPE's *Opinions of the Board of Ethical Review*, Vol. VI (Alexandria, Va.: National Society of Professional Engineers, 1989). The BER discussion of this case is on pp. 7–8.

32. This is BER Case No. 84-4 in NSPE's *Opinions of the Board of Ethical Review*, Vol. VI (Alexandria, Va.: National Society of Professional Engineers, 1989). The BER discussion of this case is on pp. 51–52.

33. This is BER Case No. 85-1 in NSPE's *Opinions of the Board of Ethical Review*, Vol. VI (Alexandra, Va.: National Society of Professional Engineers, 1989). The BER discussion is on pp. 57–58.

34. This is BER Case No. 85-2 in NSPE's *Opinions of the Board of Ethical Review*, Vol. VI (Alexandria, Va.: National Society of Professional Engineers, 1989). The BER discussion of this case is on pp. 59–61.

35. This is BER Case No. 85-4 in NSPE's *Opinions of the Board of Ethical Review*, Vol. VI (Alexandria, Va.: National Society of Professional Engineers, 1989). The BER discussion is on pp. 64–66.

36. This is BER Case No. 85-5 in NSPE's *Opinions of the Board of Ethical Review*, Vol. VI (Alexandra, Va.: National Society of Professional Engineers, 1989). The BER discussion of this case is on pp. 67–69.

37. This is BER Case No. 86-6 in NSPE's *Opinions of the Board of Ethical Review*, Vol. VI (Alexandra, Va.: National Society of Professional Engineers, 1989). The BER discussion of this case is on pp. 85–87.

38. This is BER Case No. 87-2 in NSPE's *Opinions of the Board of Ethical Review*, Vol. VI (Alexandria, Va.: National Society of Professional Engineers, 1989). The BER discussion of this case is on pp. 90–91.

39. This is BER Case No. 88-5 in NSPE's *Opinions of the Board of Ethical Review*, Vol. VI (Alexandria, Va.: National Society for Professional Engineers, 1989). The BER discussion is on pp. 111–113.

Chapter 3

On Becoming a Responsible Engineer

C arl Lawrence was alarmed by Kevin Rourke's urgent early-afternoon message: "All supervisors immediately check for open caustic valves. Supply tank is empty. Pump still running—either an open valve or a leak. Emergency order of caustic supply on the way." Only in the first year of his work as a supervisor of one of Emerson Chemical's acid and caustic distribution systems, Carl had never had to deal with anything like this before. He knew he should move quickly to see if his unit was the source of the problem.

Much to his dismay, Carl found that the problem had originated in his unit. One of his lead operators discovered that a seldom-used caustic valve was open. Although the valve was immediately closed, Carl knew the clean-up remedy would be costly. Minimally, several hundred gallons of caustic would have to be replaced, and as many as thirty drums of hydrochloric acid might need to be used to reduce the pH level of effluent rushing out of the plant toward the local publicly owned wastewater treatment works. Beyond this, Carl knew that eventually he would need to determine who was responsible for the accident.[1] But, for now, he knew his primary responsibility was to help get the problem under control.

3.1 Introduction

Although it is fictional, this is an instructive case. First, it makes clear that what engineers do matters a great deal. Accidents like this are costly, both to our environment (and perhaps public health) and to those who have to pay for the clean-up. No doubt Carl Lawrence's engineering responsibilities include much more than preventing and responding to accidents. But this is an important part of his job.

This chapter explores different ways in which an engineer might regard his or her responsibilities. Some engineers are independent consultants or members of consulting firms. Consulting engineers provide services to clients. However, most engineers are corporate employees. Whether they work for clients or corporate employers, however, engineers have basic job responsibilities. Canon 4 of NSPE's Code of Ethics emphasizes this by insisting that "engineers shall act in professional matters for each employer or client as faithful agents or trustees." We will discuss this in some detail in Chapter 9, "Engineers As Employees." In this chapter we concentrate on some broader issues of responsibility, especially those concerning possible harms and benefits to society that are associated with engineering practice. We also discuss a variety of impediments to acting responsibly.

We begin with a conception of responsibility that relies heavily on minimal legal standards. Then we consider conceptions that require more than meeting minimal legal standards. Next we explore the idea that engineers might accept responsibilities that go "above and beyond the call of duty." We show that which of these conceptions engineers embrace as their own can have very important consequences for others. Finally, we explore several impediments to responsibility, especially a variety of obstacles that stand in the way of taking fully into consideration all the factors relevant to responsible engineering practice.

3.2   Standards of Responsibility: Malpractice or Reasonable Care?

Although legal and moral responsibility are distinct, they are related to each other. Responsibility is attributed to *persons* in both law and morality. However, in law, corporations and institutions can simply be given legal standing as persons, whereas in morality it is highly debatable whether corporations and institutions can be persons.[2] These two areas aside, notions of legal and moral responsibility have much in common.

Martin Curd and Larry May explore some of these common elements in the context of the moral responsibilities of engineers for harms that might occur.[3] They draw three basic legal distinctions: *intentional, negligent*, and *reckless* causing of harm. Intentionally caused harm is done knowingly and deliberately. Negligently caused harm is not knowingly done, but it is done without "due care." The agent, we say, "should have known better." Recklessly caused harm is not done intentionally (in that harming is not one of its aims), but it is done in conscious awareness that harm is likely to result.

These three distinctions in law are also found in morality. In fact, it is plausible to say that the legal distinctions rest on their parallel distinctions in morality. We attach the legal importance we do to each because of their parallel moral importance.

Relying on these basic distinctions, Curd and May discuss two models of professional responsibility. The first, the malpractice model, holds simply that professionals have a duty to conform to the standard operating procedures of their profession. They are morally (and, most likely, legally) responsible for harms caused by their failure to fulfill this duty. Although Curd and May believe this model works well in many instances, they do not believe it is always adequate. Their concern is that standard operating procedures are typically minimalist, stipulating only minimally acceptable standards.

Curd and May favor a second position, a reasonable care model. This model adds an important qualification to the malpractice model. In some instances there may be "a standard of reasonableness as seen by a normal, prudent nonprofessional" that is more demanding than the more minimalist professional standard. In such instances, Curd and May hold, the more demanding standard should be upheld.

Curd and May apply the reasonable care standard to the Flight 191 American Airlines DC-10 crash in Chicago in 1979 that claimed the lives of 274 people. Although all the design features of the DC-10 satisfied FAA regulations at the time of the crash, Curd and May identify three causal factors that they believe raise further questions of responsibility. First, it was known that, due to improper procedures in servicing, DC-10s were in danger of suffering cracks in the pylons linking engines to wings. In the 1979 crash the left engine broke off from the left wing just before liftoff. Second, when the engine broke off it also severed hydraulic control and power lines that were located in more vulnerable positions than those in the Tristar and the 747, two DC-10 competitors. This caused severe imbalance, resulting in the plane rolling to the left. The warning system was damaged and therefore did not alert the crew. Unlike the Tristar, the DC-10 lacked a back-up warning system (an optional feature of the 747). Third, unlike the Tristar and 747, the DC-10 did not have a system to lock the slats and prevent slat retraction if the hydraulic system failed.

Since the DC-10 lacked safety features that the Tristar and 747 had, it might be argued that the DC-10 had a design flaw. But working against this idea, the Tristar and the 747 exceeded FAA regulations in this regard, so the malpractice model of responsibility was not violated.

However, the reasonable care model asks further questions. Was there reason to believe that there would be a servicing problem? Proper procedures required maintenance crews to disassemble the pylon from the engine during servicing. Failure to do this could contribute to cracking in flanges of the pylons. Curd and May maintain that it was reasonably foreseeable that maintenance crews would take shortcuts.[4]

> It has been estimated that it would have taken an extra 200 man-hours per engine to service them in the manner recommended by McDonnell Douglas. More importantly, McDonnell Douglas knew that maintenance crews were using the less time-consuming and more hazardous procedure. Continental Airlines and American Airlines were both using forklift trucks to remove the entire engine and pylon assembly as a unit. In December 1978, and again in February 1979 (several months prior to the Chicago crash), cracked flanges were discovered in planes belonging to Continental that had been serviced in this way.

Curd and May conclude that when it was apparent to McDonnell Douglas engineers that there was a serious risk of cracked flanges, they should have done something to reduce accident risks.

But why not simply attribute responsibility to those who oversee and carry out the servicing of the DC-10s? Had they done their work properly, the disaster very likely would not have occurred. The problem, one might say, was in servicing rather than design. Curd and May agree that the maintenance staff was at fault. But their view is that this does not relieve McDonnell Douglas from all blame. As the Tristar and 747 illustrate, design improvements were feasible at the time, even if, by the malpractice model, they were not required. In contrast, by the reasonable standard model, with the knowledge that others were likely to be negligent, efforts should have been made to redesign either the engine mounts or the maintenance procedure.

Whether we should agree with Curd and May's assessment of the DC-10 case is difficult to determine. We all know that hindsight is wonderful. McDonnell Douglas claimed that, on the basis of what they knew before the crash, the combination of factors leading to the crash was extremely unlikely (one in a billion). Curd and May disagree. They point out that a hazardous design defect in the cargo hatch door resulted in an even worse DC-10 crash five years earlier in Paris, France. This, they maintain, should have put McDonnell Douglas engineers on alert.[5]

The FAA, like most governmental regulatory agencies, sets only *minimal* standards of safety. We believe that reasonable risk is not the same as minimally acceptable risk, especially in industries where there is a great potential for harm. Of course, safety is not our only value. Efficiency and economy must also be considered. Presumably, however, a concept of *reasonable* risk will incorporate these values as well. To say that only the minimal standards set by governmental regulatory agencies qualify as reasonable once factors other than safety are taken into account is to suggest that these standards are as good as anyone should expect. But, in the present case, this is belied by the fact that two McDonnell Douglas competitors chose to *exceed* the existing regulations. So, whether or not one agrees with Curd and May's particular conclusions about the DC-10, their underlying standard of reasonable care has much to commend it.

3.3   Broadening the Scope of Responsibility

Two lines of resistance to broadening professional responsibility beyond the malpractice model warrant attention. First, we sometimes assume that in trying to determine who is responsible for harm or wrongdoing, we are engaged in a zero-sum pursuit. If the maintenance crew is at fault for not following proper servicing procedures, then McDonnell Douglas engineers bear no share of responsibility. Similarly, in the fictional case at the beginning of this chapter, if Carl Lawrence finds out that someone has negligently failed to close the valve, he can exempt himself from any responsibility for the accident. John Ladd labels this view negative, or task, responsibility—a view that regards responsibility as a kind of exclusivity ("It's my job, not his," or "It's his job, not mine").[6] Ladd argues that this is a much too narrow view of responsibility. The second line of resistance links responsibility essentially with *blame*. Ladd argues that this view is also too narrow. His critique of these lines of resistance and his alternative conception of responsibility deserve careful consideration.

Like Curd and May, Ladd finds the malpractice model of responsibility inadequate. He views this as too narrow and legalistic. Its exclusive search for blame, or fault, makes meaningful discussion of responsibility virtually impossible in situations like Union Carbide's disaster in Bhopal, India. This is because in such situations it is difficult, if not impossible, to identify specific, blameworthy individuals who can fairly be held accountable for the magnitude of the disaster. For Ladd, such a view of responsibility limits itself to asking "who is to pay for the damages and costs," with blame or punishment serving as the currency of moral "payment."[7] Ladd urges us to accept instead a conception of responsibility that is both broader and deeper. This conception appeals to desirable qualities of character, civic virtues that express direct concern for public welfare rather than simply the avoidance of blame.

What is needed, Ladd says, is a conception of positive responsibility. This is a view that, unlike negative, or task, responsibility, ascribes responsibility to an individual without having any special implications about the responsibilities of others. This is moral responsibility in the full sense: open-ended and a matter of varying degrees and stringency. Such a conception blocks escaping responsibility by trying to shift it to others.[8] Moral responsibility in this sense is best seen as a virtue—something positively good, something to be sought after. It becomes something that good people are ready and willing to acknowledge and embrace.[9]

Once we acknowledge this more positive conception, we can sever the essential tie between moral responsibility and blame, or fault. Responsibility may be necessary for blaming or punishing a person, but it is not sufficient. Blaming or punishing may be wrong—especially when excuses or mitigating factors are present.

The case with which we began this chapter illustrates these points. Eventually Carl Lawrence will have to try to determine what was responsible for the accident. In attempting this, what should Carl Lawrence be looking for? No doubt he should look for the cause of the accident. But, beyond this, he needs to ask if anyone should be held accountable for it. Clearly, not just any possible cause can be connected with the idea of accountability. If the cause is not traceable to a responsible agent, accountability does not apply. But, since the valve was opened, it is likely that a responsible agent was involved.

This does not mean that someone deliberately left the valve open. It could be a case of negligence. But whose negligence? Carl discovers, let us suppose, that Rick Duffy, a lead operator from the early shift, forgot to close the valve before leaving. Since that particular valve is in a remote and seldom-used section of Carl's unit, no one noticed the open valve until Kevin Rourke sent out his emergency notice. Does this settle the question of responsibility? It might seem so. As lead operator, Rick Duffy has the responsibility to open and close valves in his area at the appropriate times. He failed to remember to close the seldom-opened valve.

However, let us suppose that Carl reflects further. He recalls his first day on the job. After taking Carl around the facilities, Kevin Rourke asked Rick Duffy to show Carl how the distribution systems work. As Carl and Rick moved from the acid to the caustic distribution system, Carl noted a striking difference. The acid distribution piping had spring-loaded valves that close automatically when not in use. To pump acid into a remote receiving tank, a pump switch must be activated at the remote location. The operator has to hold the pump switch on while the tank is filling. Rick mentioned that the penalty for propping the switch on by other means is immediate dismissal. In contrast, no similar precautions apply to the caustic system. The caustic valves have to be manually opened and closed.

Carl remembers asking Rick why the caustic system was so different. Rick shrugged, "I don't really know. It's been this way at least as long as I've been here. I suppose it's because the acid distribution system is used so much more." Carl also asked Rick if the lead operators have written procedures for filling the caustic tanks. Rick answered that he had never seen any—nor did he recall any review of the practice during the four years he had been an operator. Carl then asked Rick if he was satisfied with this. Rick replied, "Well, I don't have any problems with it. Anyway, that's someone else's concern, not mine. I suppose they don't want to put out the money to change it. 'Don't fix the wheel if it's not broken' seems to be their attitude."

Carl remembers not being very impressed with this line of reasoning and wondering if he should ask his supervisor, Kevin Rourke, about it. However, not wishing to make a stir at the very beginning of his work for Emerson, Carl simply dropped the matter. He now wonders if he bears some of the responsibility for the caustic overflow. Perhaps he should have persisted. Further, he begins to wonder about Kevin's responsibility. Shouldn't people in Kevin's position be looking out for potential problem areas and encouraging others, including Carl and Rick, to do likewise? We can ask these questions as part of the query about who is to blame, or at fault, for the accident. But we need not. We might ask, instead, what virtues, or qualities of character, it is important for engineers, technicians, and others to have, especially those who work in environments in which accidents can occur.

Many industrial accidents, like natural disasters, may be thought of as situations beyond human control and, therefore, beyond responsibility. However, Ladd observes, these are actually situations in which human control has broken down. Rather than saying simply that these accidents are beyond human control, we should say that "there was no control where there ought to have been control."[10] Evidence that human control is relevant, Ladd claims, is that such accidents are unlikely to be repeated if we attend to them properly.[11] But, to a large extent, our ability to prevent them is developed only retrospectively. It seems too harsh, therefore, to blame everyone who contributes causally to such accidents.

Although we cannot expect to eliminate all industrial accidents, we can take preventive measures. In this regard, Ladd's basic message for engineers is: "Good engineering, and consequently good technological practice, requires constant testing."[12] However, if we restrict ourselves to the malpractice model of responsibility, this message will be taken too narrowly.

To see this, consider how the malpractice model looks retrospectively at responsibility. It focuses negatively on things that ought to have been done by someone, but were not. The aim is to determine whom, if anyone, to blame, or fault. Prospectively, the malpractice model focuses on what must be done in order to avoid being blamed or faulted in the future.

Ladd urges us to concentrate on responsibility prospectively, but in a different way than the malpractice model does. His more positive view of responsibility focuses on what ought to be done, without necessarily blaming or faulting those who fall short of this. Thus, prospectively, even though he was just beginning his job at Emerson Chemical, Carl Lawrence might have taken on the responsibility of discussing his concerns about the caustic system with Kevin Rourke. He should have done this not to avoid blame later, but to determine if the system needs to be improved.

Ladd's more positive conception of responsibility also permits a more positive retrospective view. Suppose, for example, that Carl Lawrence had immediately gone to Kevin Rourke with his concern about the caustic system, but Kevin had replied that no changes could be made at this time—and that they were not really needed anyway. After the caustic spill, Kevin might recall that earlier conversation with Carl: "Carl was right to bring it to my attention. I wish I'd taken his concern more seriously then." In such an instance, Kevin would be retrospectively regretting his inaction but praising Carl's responsible behavior.

What distinguishes Ladd's positive conception of responsibility from the malpractice model is that moral failure to do what one ought does not necessarily warrant blame. If we reject a necessary link between failure and blame, then "we can hold a large number of individuals responsible without holding any of them blamable."[13] Even if blame is difficult to determine in the Bhopal disaster, Ladd says:

> [T]he oughts still remain, however, and pertain to the conduct of all the various individuals whose acts or omissions made the accident at Bhopal possible: there are lots of things that they ought to have done, but did not do. [The problem at Bhopal was] a general lack of concern, especially on the part of the management and the government, for the safety of those around them. Safety was a low priority for almost everyone who was in any way connected with the disaster in Bhopal; other things came first, notably, jobs, positions, and careers. This lack of concern, almost indifference, for safety was manifested at all levels: the publication of and compliance with safety regulations relating to MIC from UC on down was pro forma rather than realistic and in day to day plant operations safety was sacrificed for the sake of cutting costs. Even at the lowest level, among the workers, concern for safety was less important than holding down a job.[14]

Rather than cast failure in terms of fault (blame), Ladd suggests that we focus on moral deficiency: "the lack of an appropriate attitude of concern or caring."[15] Thus, we should deplore the absence of a positive quality instead of blaming the presence of a positive evil. Ladd advocates shifting "from the presence of an evil to the absence of a good, and, in general, to an orientation towards humanity or lack thereof."[16]

Positive responsibility, for Ladd, is a virtue because "like other virtues, it is other-regarding, it is intrinsically motivational and it binds persons to each other."[17] Further, it is not just for saints and heroes—it is for everyone. Finally, Ladd makes a plea for civic virtue: "A virtuous citizen, and that should include everybody, should have a concern for the common good and for the long-range welfare of other people in the society, even where this concern demands individual sacrifices of one sort or another or simply gives less priority to one's own private interests and to one's advancement on the escalator to worldly success."[18]

For Ladd, it is clear that his plea for civic virtue is a matter of some urgency. He issues a warning:

> Only a resurgence of civic virtue or of what Bellah calls the "republican virtues" among the citizenry can save our society from self-destruction, brought on, say, through the irresponsible use of dangerous technology (nuclear armaments) and the irresponsibility by bureaucracies of fellow citizens for the sake of various narrow short-term goals.[19]

For some this may seem overstated, but we must at least acknowledge that a society lacking civic virtues is ill-equipped to address the very obvious social and environmental problems confronting us today. And the causal role engineers can play for good or ill in our handling of these problems is undeniable. How engineers should conceive their responsibilities is, of course, a function of the particular roles and opportunities available to them. But the growing professionalization of our society makes it very clear that professionals in general, and engineers in particular, will play a crucial role in how adequately we will deal with these problems. Realizing this, Ladd urges us to focus less on blame or fault and more on civic responsibility.

3.4   A Framework for Responsibility

So far we have discussed two different conceptions of responsibility: a malpractice conception that depends heavily on legal standards and John Ladd's more positive, open-ended conception of responsibility as a civic virtue. The malpractice conception focuses on minimal standards and blame for falling short of them. The positive conception has higher expectations, but falling short is regarded as an indication of moral deficiency rather than blame. However, what both have in common is a concern for reducing possible harms. The more minimalist conception stresses not causing harm, while the positive one includes the prevention of harm, even if that harm might be caused by people other than oneself.

It is not surprising that concern about harm plays such a central role in conceptions of engineering responsibility. Noting that technological knowledge greatly increases the power to affect the well-being of others, Kenneth A. Alpern suggests a fundamental moral principle for engineers, which he calls the principle of care: "Other things being equal, one should exercise due care to avoid contributing to significantly harming others."[20]

This principle, Alpern says, is a part of popular morality and is incorporated in virtually all ethical theories. Most engineering societies' codes of ethics seem to support this principle. For example, the National Society of Professional Engineers' Code of Ethics states in its first fundamental canon that engineers shall "hold paramount the safety, health and welfare of the public in the performance of their professional duties."[21]

Alpern next states a rule derivable from the principle of care, which he calls the corollary of proportionate care. "When one is in a position to contribute to greater harm or when one is in a position to play a more critical part in producing harm than is another person, one must exercise greater care to avoid doing so."[22] Alpern sees this corollary as having special relevance for engineers, since they often are in a privileged position in regard to understanding the potential for harm and having the ability to prevent it. This is because of their special expertise and the occupational role they are entrusted to play in its exercise.[23]

While most would agree with Alpern's principle of care and corollary of proportionate care, their implications for engineering practice are more problematic. Alpern himself, for example, concludes that there is "a basic obligation to avoid playing *any part* in the production of harm."[24] However, as Andrew Oldenquist points out: "This may require total withdrawal from organized society: no payment of taxes, for they buy instruments of death; no work for any corporation or government, for they all do some harm."[25]

In response to Alpern's claim that engineers would avoid harm if they "refused to submit the design when they had good reason to believe that it was dangerous,"[26] Samuel Florman comments:

> This ignores the fact that all designs contain some element of danger. In seeking to minimize danger, one usually increases cost, and therein lies a dilemma. . . . There is no real trick to making an automobile that is as strong as a tank and safe to ride in. The challenge is to make an automobile that ordinary people can afford and is as safe as the community thinks it should be. There are also considerations of style, economy of use, and effect on the environment.[27]

We should not expect to find a set of principles or rules that function like a recipe in yielding conclusions without the need for careful, and sometimes contestable, judgment. Nevertheless, principles and rules can be useful in bringing to mind the general sorts of moral considerations appropriate for responsible engineering. For example, Florman's criticism does not deny the great importance of not causing harm, and he does not offer frivolous reasons for resisting Alpern's applications. Rather, he cites other substantial, general values: usability, affordability, environmental impact, and consumer preference.

3.5   Good Works

There is another conception of responsibility that we have not discussed yet but which it is important to consider: what is sometimes called going "above and beyond the call of duty." We call this doing good works.

A simple example outside the engineering context illustrates what we mean by the concept of good works. Ralph wakes up at his usual time and prepares to go to work. When he looks out the window, he is shocked to see his long driveway drifted over with snow. He has only a snow shovel, not a plow. He realizes he will be very late to work—and very tired. As he bundles up to go out and shovel, Ralph is surprised to see his driveway being cleared by a neighbor with a snow plow. Although they are neighbors, they have never met before. No doubt Ralph appreciates what his neighbor is doing. What would he think if his neighbor had done nothing to help? Would he fault him? Would he think his neighbor had a moral deficiency? Either response is unlikely. His neighbor has gone "above and beyond the call of duty." His is not a saintly or heroic act, but it is a good one.

Such things happen in professional life as well. Here are two examples.

1. A statistician agrees to help analyze data to determine whether it is safe for residents in Love Canal to return to their homes. Although modestly compensated for his services, he realizes there are many much more lucrative consulting opportunities. Asked why he has accepted this task instead, he says: "Analyzing data just for the money doesn't mean anything to me. I want it to do some good."[28]

2. A design engineer devotes a great deal of time after regular working hours to see if the features of a safety rope for those who wash windows of high rises can be improved—even though the current design more than satisfies legal requirements. Asked why he is not satisfied with the current design, he comments, "You have to do the best you can—and that's usually inadequate."[29]

Here we have two examples of professionals who take on responsibilities that no one has a right to expect from them. If they did not do these things, no one would fault them. Most of us would not think that their not taking on these responsibilities would indicate a moral shortcoming or deficiency either. In short, although they might say of themselves, "This is what I *ought* to do," it is unlikely that we would feel it is appropriate for us to tell them that they ought to do what they are doing. Instead, we praise them for their good works.

Professional codes of ethics focus primarily on duties or obligations deemed so fundamental that failure to fulfill them warrants reproach or even formal sanctions.[30] We will refer to these as basic duties.[31] Although codes may commend ideals that go beyond basic duties, these commendations are stated quite abstractly, and they are often addressed to the profession as a whole, leaving it unclear how this applies to individual members of the profession.

Interpretations of codes typically focus on basic duties and their violations rather than on behavior that is ethically commendable. For example, the regularly issued *Opinions of the Board of Ethical Review* of the National Society for

Professional Engineers (NSPE) offers very helpful interpretations of NSPE's code. Its opinions, however, deal almost exclusively with whether certain courses of action under consideration are ethically required, prohibited, or permitted by the code. Left undiscussed are examples of engineers whose behavior is ethically commendable but not required by the code.

It is clear that John Ladd's appeal to civic responsibility as a professional aspiration goes beyond the basic moral requirements emphasized in typical professional codes of ethics, including those of engineering. Of course, fulfilling basic duties and avoiding wrongdoing should be a major concern of any comprehensive account of responsibility in professional life. However, Ladd urges us to broaden the notion of professional responsibility to include attitudes and behavior that go beyond this.

Rather than blaming those who lack such attitudes and behavior, Ladd suggests we may view them as being morally deficient. They ought to be disposed to do more than they do, but lacking this disposition indicates a kind of moral shortcoming. Although blame is absent, a negative judgment is still appropriate. Is there yet another level of morality—one that can be exemplified by professionals, but when absent does not imply either moral deficiency or fault, and thereby does not warrant a negative judgment at all? We suggest that there is, and our statistician and safety rope designer are examples.

Philosopher J. O. Urmson reminds us that there is a "vast array of actions, having moral significance, which frequently are performed by persons who are far from being moral saints or heroes but which are neither duties nor obligations, nor involve conformity to principle as I use that term."[32]

Let us consider another example in more detail. G. P. E. Meese describes the efforts of General Electric engineers to improve night driving in the late 1930s.[33] A group of engineers worked together to develop an automobile headlight that promised to dramatically reduce the number of fatalities caused by night driving. To accomplish this it was necessary to involve engineers in research, design, production, economic analysis, and governmental regulation. Although the need for headlight improvement was widely acknowledged, there was also widespread skepticism about its technical and economic feasibility.

That the resulting sealed beam headlight was no small accomplishment is made evident by Meese:

> The G.E. team was convinced that they *could* do something to lower drivers' risk.
> By 1937, they had already demonstrated the *technical* feasibility of the Sealed Beam.
> Their task, while refining G.E.'s production capabilities, was to get the car builders
> and designers to set aside traditional competitiveness, and to bring the regulators
> up to date concerning feasibility and performance of the new lamps.[34]

There is little reason to suppose that the G.E. engineers were simply doing what they were told—namely, to come up with a more adequate headlamp. Apparently the virtual consensus was that this could not be done. So the engineers had to overcome considerable resistance. That this was no ordinary task is evidenced by the remarks of another engineer of that era:

The reaching of the consensus embodied in the specifications of the Sealed Beam Headlamp is an achievement which commands the admiration of all who have any knowledge of the difficulties that were overcome. It is an achievement not only in illuminating engineering, but even more in safety engineering, in human engineering, in the art of cooperation.[35]

The difficulties this group of engineers faced put us on notice that enthusiasm for good works needs to be tempered with realism. Other demands and constraints may discourage undertaking such projects. Nevertheless, looking for opportunities to do good works, as well as taking advantage of these opportunities when they arise, is a desirable trait in an engineer.

How should we understand good works within the context of engineering responsibility? Whereas we hold each other responsible for certain things, it is also possible for us to assume certain responsibilities. The design engineer who has taken on the task of improving the quality of the safety rope is assuming additional responsibilities. These are self-imposed responsibilities. The statistician, otherwise fully employed, agrees to additional consulting responsibilities only when convinced this will "do some good"—a commendable but self-imposed standard. Finally, as the Sealed Beam Headlamp project illustrates, this need not be a solitary effort; engineers can undertake good works together.

It is easy to fail to notice that what we are calling good works commonly occur in professional life. Those who perform them may view themselves as simply doing what needs to be done. They may see requirements that we fail to notice, and they quietly do them. Or we may grow accustomed to what they do and simply take them for granted. Furthermore, once they accept a responsibility and the work is under way, it often is appropriate to hold them accountable for completing the work. What we may overlook is that taking on the responsibility in the first place was fully optional.

We might ask if it is really important to emphasize good works in professional life. Why not assume that if only professionals would meet their basic duties, they would fulfill the basic needs of those whom the professions acknowledge they should serve? A simple thought experiment shows that this is not a plausible assumption. Consider the implications of the absence of good works. Disasters are averted not only by professionals fulfilling their duties but also by their doing more than this requires. So are less severe, but nevertheless unwelcome, consequences. Also, the fact that not all professionals do meet their basic duties creates needs that will be unmet unless others occasionally do more than their basic duties call for.[36]

However, as we have noted, good works are not always welcome. In fact, sometimes they are discouraged, intentionally or not. We need to ask to what extent the organizations within which professionals work present obstacles to doing good works. For example, they may define professional tasks and responsibilities too narrowly, actively discouraging "do-gooders," or rewarding only those who do not "rock the boat." Good works may also be discouraged by the need to meet tight time schedules, by limited budgets, and by the press of other matters at hand. Some of these obstacles are simply realistic and justifiable limitations (particularly if good works can be accomplished only by neglecting basic duties). Others seem, in principle, alterable. When this is so, it is important to examine the extent to which changes might be desirable and feasible.

3.6   Do Engineers Need Virtues?

We have suggested that professional responsibility can include virtues that go beyond fulfilling the basic duties typically found in a professional code of ethics. Virtues are normally understood to include attitudes and dispositions, not just conduct. They reflect our moral character. William F. May urges that professional ethics pay more attention to matters of character and virtue.[37]

> Important to professional ethics is the moral disposition the professional brings to the structure in which he operates, and that shapes his or her approach to problems. . . . At the same time, his moral commitments, or lack of them, and the general ethos in which he and his colleagues function can frustrate the most well-intentioned structural reforms.[38]

May is talking about not just what professionals do, but also what they are ready (disposed) to do—and to see. Those who care about public safety and welfare and who are actively looking for ways to improve it, for example, are more likely to see what needs doing and how to go about it.

May suggests that attention to character and virtue is especially important because of the institutional settings within which most professionals work. He gives two reasons for saying this. First, large organizations have the ability to rather easily cover the mistakes of their employees. It is difficult to determine just where things went wrong and who bears responsibility. Second, large organizations are marked by highly specialized functions performed by professionals whose expertise is not shared by other professionals, let alone laypersons.

May says of the expert: "He had better be virtuous. Few may be in a position to discredit him. The knowledge explosion is also an ignorance explosion; if knowledge is power, then ignorance is powerlessness."[39] May offers a test of professional character and virtue: "One test of character and virtue is what a person does when no one else is watching. A society that rests on expertise needs more people who can pass that test."[40]

What counts as passing the test May suggests? There are virtues that are associated with basic duties: some degree of honesty, fair-mindedness, reliability, and a kind of integrity that goes with them. But we must add other elements if we are to go beyond basic duty. May's list also includes benevolence, perseverance, and public-spiritedness. These invite us to consider more than basic duties, as do compassion, kindness, generosity, and many other character traits and virtues.

One of the attractions of restricting the idea of the moral responsibility of professionals to basic duties is that this makes responsibility seem more precisely stateable and thereby more manageable. However, as Ladd points out, moral responsibility is more open-ended and admits of varying degrees and stringency. Unlike the malpractice model, Ladd's more positive notion of responsibility cannot be divided neatly into separate spheres warranting statements such as "It's my job, not his," or "It's his job, not mine." Further, although there are limits to what we can reasonably be expected to do, our work is never done—or, citing again the words of the safety rope design engineer, "You have to do the best you can—and that's usually inadequate."

3.7   Impediments to Responsibility

It is one thing to have a general understanding of engineering responsibility. It is quite another to apply this understanding in actual engineering practice. Unfortunately, many obstacles need to be confronted. We will discuss several of the more significant ones.

SELF-INTEREST

Engineering codes of ethics, like the codes of other professions, articulate standards of conduct for engineers as engineers. However, engineers are not simply engineers. They are, like everyone else, people with personal hopes and ambitions not restricted to professional ideals. Sometimes concern for our own interests tempts us to act contrary to the interests of others, perhaps even contrary to what others expect from us as professionals. Sometimes concern for self-interest blocks us from seeing or fully understanding our professional responsibilities. Taken to an extreme, concern for self-interest is a form of *egoism*—an exclusive concern to satisfy one's own interests, even at the possible expense of others. This is popularly characterized as "looking out for number one."

Whether a thoroughgoing egoist would act at the expense of others very much depends on the circumstances. All of us depend to some extent on others to get what we want; some degree of mutual support is necessary. But opportunities for personal gain at the expense of others do arise—or so it seems to most of us. Egoists are prepared to take advantage of this, unless they believe it is likely to work to their long-term disadvantage. But it is not just egoists who are tempted by such opportunities. All of us are, at least occasionally.

SELF-DECEPTION

One way of resisting these temptations is to confront ourselves honestly and ask if we would approve of others treating us in the same way we are contemplating treating them. This Golden Rule reasoning ("Do unto others as you would have them do unto you") can have a powerful psychological effect on us. However, for it to work, we must recognize what we are contemplating doing for what it is. *Rationalization* often gets in the way of this recognition. Some rationalizations show greater self-awareness than others, particularly those that exhibit self-defensiveness or excuse-making. ("I'm not really doing this just for myself." "Everyone takes shortcuts once in a while—it's the only way one can survive.") Other rationalizations seem to betray a willful lack of self-understanding. This is called *self-deception*, which Mike Martin characterizes as "the intentional avoiding of truths which are painful to recognize."[41] "One might suspect or have general knowledge about an unpleasant truth and then turn away before learning more about it. Or one might engage in *rationalization*: giving biased explanations of one's motives and actions in order to maintain a flattering view of oneself."[42]

Because of the nature of self-deception, it is particularly difficult to discover it in oneself. However, open communication with colleagues can help correct biases to which we are susceptible—unless, of course, they share the same biases (an illustration of "groupthink," to be discussed below).

WEAKNESS OF WILL

Sometimes we lack the courage to do what we think is right, or we give in to temptation, knowing that what we are doing is wrong. We may cover this over in self-deception, but sometimes we are fully aware of what we are doing. This is weakness of will. When this is a matter of lacking courage, fear is a major factor. When it is basically a matter of giving in to temptation, it is a form of self-indulgence. In either case, weakness of will is "infectious"; there often is comfort in numbers. If others with whom we associate display similar tendencies, we may be more likely to do likewise. So, to resist weakness of will, it may be important to find others who would also like to be able to display strength of will in doing what they believe is right.

IGNORANCE

An obvious barrier to responsible action is ignorance of vital information. If an engineer does not realize that, for example, a design poses a safety problem, he or she will not be in a position to do anything about it. Sometimes such lack of awareness is willful avoidance. But often it is due to a lack of persistence, a failure to look in the right places for necessary information, or the pressure of deadlines.

EGOCENTRIC THINKING

It is a common feature of human experience that we tend to interpret situations from very limited perspectives and that it takes some effort to take a more objective look. This is what psychologists call egocentricity. It is especially prevalent in us as young children, and it never completely leaves us. Is this just another aspect of self-interested thinking? Egocentric thinking is not always egoistic. It is actually a special form of ignorance.

It is not just self-interest that interferes with our ability to understand things from other perspectives. We may have good intentions for others but fail to realize that their perspectives are different from ours in important ways. For example, some people may not want to hear bad news about their health. They may also assume that others are like them in this respect. So, if they withhold bad news from others, this is done with the best of intentions—even if others would prefer hearing the bad news.

Egocentric thinking may be present in an engineering context as well. This can be seen when we have to examine a situation from several different perspectives, such as in the following fictional case study:

> You have been assigned the position of environmental engineer for one of several local plants whose water discharges flow into a lake in a flourishing tourist area. Although all the plants are marginally profitable, they compete for the same customers. Included in your responsibilities is the monitoring of water and air discharges at your plant and the periodic preparation of reports to be submitted to the Department of Natural Resources. You have just prepared a report that indicates that the level of pollution in the plant's water discharges slightly exceeds the legal limitations. Your boss, the plant manager, says you should regard the excess as a mere "technicality," and he asks you to "adjust" the data so that the plant appears to be in compliance. He says that the slight excess is not going to endanger human or fish life any more than if the plant were in compliance. On the other hand, he says, solving the problem would require a very heavy investment in new equipment. He explains, "We can't afford new equipment. It might even cost a few jobs. It will set us behind our competitors. Besides the bad publicity we'd get, it might scare off some of the tourist industry, making it worse for everybody." [43]

How do you think you should respond to your boss's request? Here we are asked to imagine ourselves in a specific role, an environmental engineer at a local plant. It is interesting to notice what happens when we consider this same situation from several other perspectives: the plant manager; environmental engineers from the competing companies; plant managers from the competing companies; the Department of Natural Resources; local merchants; parents of children who may swim in the lake; tourists; and so on. We may then see the problem take on strikingly different dimensions. We can ask students to go through several of these perspectives sequentially and then to make an "all things considered" assessment of what should be done. Or they can be divided into groups, with each group being given a different perspective to consider. After this the groups compare reflections and try to come up with an "all things considered" assessment. Considering the situation from these different perspectives is an important exercise in moral imagination.

Sometimes we need to critically examine our assumptions in order to gain a fuller understanding of a problem. For example, consider this seemingly uncomplicated case:

> Jack Strong is seated between Tom Evans and Judy Hanson at a dinner meeting of a local industrial engineering society. Jack and Judy have an extended discussion of a variety of concerns, some of which are related to their common engineering interests. At the conclusion of the dinner, Jack turns to Tom, smiles, and says, "I'm sorry not to have talked with you more tonight, but she's better looking than you."

Some men might comment, "I don't see anything wrong with a little flirting. It happens all the time, and it makes life more interesting. Besides, this was a dinner—a social event, not a business meeting." Many women, however, might react quite differently. They need not be opposed to flirtation in general in order to object to Jack's comment on this occasion. What, they might ask, is Judy's perspective?

If Judy is a typical female industrial engineer, she works mainly with male engineers.[44] Let us now imagine that, as a younger engineer, she is anxious to be recognized first and foremost as a good engineer. She is well aware of the stereotypical view that women are not as well suited for engineering as men. She did not often encounter open manifestations of this attitude while in college. More than 20 percent of her engineering classmates were women, the faculty were supportive, the male students did not make her feel she had chosen the wrong profession, and she graduated near the top of her class.

However, matters quickly changed on her first job. She found that she was the only woman engineer in her division. Now, even after a year on the job, she has to struggle to get others to take her ideas seriously. So she enjoyed "talking shop" with Jack at the dinner. But she was stunned by his remark to Tom, however innocently it may have been intended. Suddenly she saw the conversation in a very different light. Once again she sensed that she was not being taken seriously as an engineer.

What ethical questions does this scenario pose? We could focus on the appropriateness of Jack's remark, as well as its possible underlying attitude. However, equally important, we could ask what response to his remark might be appropriate. Judy is faced with a difficult situation. If she ignores the remark, she does nothing to improve her situation—or that of other women engineers—and she may suffer diminished self-esteem. Still, she may worry that nothing constructive will come from her making an issue of his remark.

However, Jack and Judy are not the only ones involved in the situation. How should Tom respond to Jack's remark? Does he have any special responsibility to try to discourage behavior like Jack's? Responding with the expected chuckle would simply reinforce Jack's behavior. Would a critical response be appropriate? Would it be more constructive to take Jack aside later to discuss the matter privately? Should Tom simply ignore the remark?

It might be objected that this little scenario is being taken too seriously. However, this fictional situation is based on an actual one experienced by a female engineer. In fact, this is the first example she offered when asked about ethical problems women typically face in engineering. She and other women interviewed observe that, especially early in their careers, they sense that their ideas are not taken as seriously as those of male colleagues—that they somehow have to "prove" themselves worthy of being listened to.[45] Those who have never had this sort of experience may not realize that others have to deal with problems like this.

MICROSCOPIC VISION

Engineers' typical working environment presents another obstacle to responsible engineering practice. Michael Davis calls this obstacle *microscopic vision*.[46] In his studies of wrongdoing, Davis concluded that the usual explanations of wrongdoing do not fit professionals very well. In reading extensively about professionals involved in wrongdoing, Davis found himself puzzled:

> Though the wrongdoers were usually well-educated and otherwise decent, much of what they did seemed obviously wrong. Surely they did not need a philosopher to tell them so. I also began to wonder at how little the wrongdoers themselves had to say about why they did what they did. . . . My wrongdoers did not seem to have done what they did simply because they were weak-willed, self-deceiving, evil-willed, ignorant, or morally immature—or even because they combined several of these failings. At most, those failings seemed to have played a subsidiary part in what my wrongdoers did.[47]

What, then, played a major part? Davis uses Robert Lund's circumstance in the Challenger disaster to illustrate what he has in mind.

In the face of Morton Thiokol's engineers' recommendation not to launch the Challenger, apparently Jerald Mason told his vice-president for engineering, Robert Lund, to "take off your engineering hat, and put on your management hat." Initially in agreement with his fellow Thiokol engineers, Lund changed his mind. Davis contends that none of the standard explanations of wrongdoing seem to account for what Lund did. He was not self-deceived, weak- or evil-willed, ignorant, or morally immature.[48] Davis's hypothesis is that when Lund took off his engineering hat and put on his management hat, he saw matters very differently. Davis uses the microscope as an analogy. When we look into a microscope, we see things that we could not see before—but only in the narrow field of resolution on which the microscope focuses. We gain accurate, detailed knowledge— at a microscopic level. At the same time, we cease to see things at the more ordinary level. This is the price of seeing things microscopically. Only when we lift our eyes from the microscope will we see what is obvious at the everyday level.

Every skill, says Davis, involves microscopic vision to some extent: "A shoemaker, for example, can tell more about a shoe in a few seconds than I could tell if I had a week to examine it. He can see that the shoe is well or poorly made, that the materials are good or bad, and so on. I can't see any of that. But the shoemaker's insight has its price. While he is paying attention to people's shoes, he may be missing what the people in them are saying or doing."[49] Applying this analogy to the professions, Davis's main point is that the microscopic worlds of engineers and managers are quite different.

The major contrast Davis draws concerns their respective attitudes toward risk. Engineers tend to be conservative in assessing acceptable risk:

> Often they work from tables approved by the appropriate professional association or other standard-setting agency. When they do not have such tables, they try not to go substantially beyond what experience has shown to be safe. Engineers do not, in general, balance risk against benefit. They reduce risk to permissible levels and only then proceed. Managers, on the other hand, generally do balance risk against benefit.[50]

Evidence that this contrast may fit the Challenger incident rather well can be found in some of the testimony before the Rogers Commission:

Mr. Boisjoly: One of my colleagues that was in the meeting summed it up best. This was a meeting where the determination was to launch, and it was up to us to prove beyond a shadow of a doubt that it was not safe to do so. This is in total reverse to what the usual is in a preflight conversation or a flight readiness review. It is usually exactly opposite that.

Mr. Lund: But that evening I guess I had never had those kinds of things come from the people at Marshall. We had to prove to them that we weren't ready, and so we got ourselves in the thought process that we were trying to find some way to prove to them it wouldn't work, and we were unable to do that. We couldn't prove absolutely that the motor wouldn't work.

Chairman Rogers: In other words, you honestly believed that you had a duty to prove that it would not work?

Mr. Lund: Well, that is kind of the mode we got ourselves into that evening. It seems like we have always been in the opposite mode. I should have detected that, but I did not, but the roles kind of switched.[51]

Of course, a complicating factor in this case is that Lund was both an engineer and a manager. The normal expectation is that he should wear both hats, thus having the apparent advantage of being able to see into two microscopes, lift his head, and place matters in a larger perspective than either alone permits. Yet, on this occasion, he was encouraged to look into only one microscope. Accepting the invitation, apparently Lund no longer saw what he normally, as an engineer, would see—and, thus, he lost sight of his basic engineering responsibility to microscopically focus on safety.

The important moral of Davis's account is that microscopic vision poses a constant danger. While such vision is necessary and valuable, its limitations need to be kept in mind. Professional training, with its emphasis on highly specialized expertise, makes professionals especially liable to be looking into microscopes when they should pause a moment and look up. Davis offers no easy solution to this problem of professionalization. However, he does suggest a way to minimize it.

> How might we change the environment? One way is simply to talk openly and often about what we want to have people notice. Lund would, for example, probably have refused to do as Mason suggested if the people back at Morton Thiokol's headquarters in Chicago had regularly reminded him that he was no ordinary manager: "We are counting on you to stand up for engineering considerations whatever anyone else does." Indeed, had *Mason* heard headquarters say that to Lund even a few times, he could hardly have said what he did say. He might well have deferred to Lund's judgment, even though NASA was pressuring him. "Sorry," he could have said, "my hands are tied."[52]

Whether or not it is realistic to suppose that companies might regularly remind their engineer/managers that they are to stand up for engineering considerations, engineer/managers can remind themselves of this. As well, they can remind themselves that they and others need to pause from time to time and lift their eyes from their microscopes.

ACCEPTANCE OF AUTHORITY

Engineering codes of ethics emphasize the importance of engineers' exercising independent, objective judgment in performing their functions. This is sometimes called professional *autonomy*. At the same time, the codes of ethics insist that engineers have a duty of fidelity to their employers and clients. Independent consulting engineers may have an easier time maintaining professional autonomy than the vast majority of engineers, who work in large, hierarchical organizations. Most engineers are not their own bosses, and they are expected to defer to authority in their organizations.

An important finding of the research of sociologist Stanley Milgram is that a surprisingly high percentage of people are inclined to defer uncritically to authority.[53] In his famous obedience experiments during the 1960s, Milgram asked volunteers to administer electric shocks to "learners" whenever they made a mistake in repeating word pairs (e.g., nice/day; rich/food) that volunteers presented to them earlier. He told volunteers that this was an experiment designed to determine the effects of punishment on learning. No shocks were actually administered, however. Milgram was really testing to see the extent to which volunteers would continue to follow the orders of the experimenter to administer what they believed were increasingly painful shocks. Surprisingly (even to Milgram) nearly two-thirds of the volunteers continued to follow orders all the way up to what they thought were 450-volt shocks—even when shouts and screams of agony were heard from the adjacent room of the "learner." The experiment was replicated many times to make sure that the original volunteers were a good representation of ordinary people, rather than especially cruel or insensitive people.

There is little reason to think that engineers are different from others in regard to obeying authority. In the Milgram experiments, the volunteers were told that "learners" would experience pain but no permanent harm or injury. Perhaps engineers would have had doubts about this as the apparent shock level moved toward the 450-volt level. This would mean only that the numbers need to be altered for engineers, not that they would be unwilling to administer what they thought were extremely painful shocks.

One of the interesting variables in the Milgram experiments was the respective locations of volunteers and "learners." The greatest compliance occurred when "learners" were not in the same room with the volunteers. Volunteers tended to accept the authority figure's reassurances that he would take all the responsibility for any unfortunate consequences. However, when volunteers and "learners" were in the same room and in full view of one another, volunteers found it much more difficult to divest themselves of responsibility.

Martin and Schinzinger observe that Milgram's experiments have special implications for engineers.[54] As we have already noted, engineers tend to work in large organizations in which the division of labor often makes it difficult to trace responsibility to specific individuals. Martin and Schinzinger comment, "The often massive bureaucracies within which most engineers work are designed to diffuse and delimit areas of personal accountability within hierarchies of authority."[55] Equally important, however, is the scale of projects involving engineers in large organizations. "Each person makes only a small contribution to something much vaster. Moreover, the final product is often physically removed from one's immediate workplace, creating the kind of "distancing" that Milgram identified as encouraging a lessened sense of personal accountability."[56]

Martin and Schinzinger suggest that engineers can reduce the effects of this distancing somewhat by reminding themselves of the experimental and risky nature of much of their work. Further, they need to bear in mind that, although distance might make it easier psychologically to be indifferent to the ultimate consequences of their work, it does not really relieve them of at least partial responsibility for those consequences.

One further interesting feature of Milgram's experiments is that volunteers were less likely to continue to administer what they took to be shocks when they were in the presence of other volunteers. Apparently they reinforced each other's discomfort at continuing, and this made it easier for them to disobey the experimenter. However, as we shall see in the next section, group dynamics does not always support critical response. Often quite the opposite occurs, and only concerted effort can overcome the kind of uncritical conformity so often characteristic of cohesive groups.

GROUPTHINK

A noteworthy feature of the organizational settings within which engineers work is that individuals tend to work and deliberate in groups. This means that an engineer will often participate in group decision making, rather than as an individual decision maker. Although this may contribute to better decisions ("two heads are better than one"), it also creates well-known, but commonly overlooked, tendencies to engage in what Irving Janis calls *groupthink*—a situation in which groups come to agreement at the expense of critical thinking.[57] Janis documents instances of groupthink in a variety of settings, including a number of historical fiascos (e.g., the bombing of Pearl Harbor, the Bay of Pigs invasion, the decision to cross the 38th parallel in the Korean War).

Concentrating on groups that are characterized by high cohesiveness, solidarity, and loyalty (all of which are prized in organizations), Janis identifies eight symptoms of groupthink:

1. An *illusion of invulnerability* of the group to failure
2. A strong "we-feeling" that views outsiders as adversaries or enemies and encourages *shared stereotypes* of others
3. *Rationalizations* that tend to shift responsibilities to others
4. An *illusion of morality* that assumes the inherent morality of the group and thereby discourages careful examination of the moral implications of what the group is contemplating
5. A tendency of individual members toward *self-censorship*, resulting from a desire not to "rock the boat"

6. An *illusion of unanimity*, construing silence of a group member as consent

7. An application of *direct pressure* on those who show signs of disagreement, often exercised by the group leader who intervenes in an effort to keep the group unified

8. *Mindguarding*, protecting the group from dissenting views by preventing their introduction (by, for example, outsiders who wish to present their views to the group)

A useful exercise would be to examine group dynamics the night before the launch of the Challenger. For example, Roger Boisjoly and Arnold Thompson, the two engineers most vocally opposed to the launch, were not invited to participate in the management meeting that convened after Robert Lund was encouraged to take off his engineering hat and put on his management hat. This seems to illustrate mindguarding. The final silence of the vast majority of the engineers involved seems, in retrospect, to have been taken by Lund to be agreement with his recommendation to launch.

Traditionally, engineers have prided themselves on being good team players, which compounds the potential difficulties with groupthink. How can the problem of groupthink be minimized for engineers? Much depends on the attitudes of group leaders, whether they are managers or engineers (or both). Janis suggests that leaders need to be aware of the tendency of groups toward groupthink and take constructive steps to resist it. Janis notes that, after the ill-advised Cuban Bay of Pigs invasion, President John F. Kennedy began to assign each member of his advisory group the role of critic. He also invited outsiders to some of the meetings, and he often absented himself from meetings in order not to unduly influence its deliberations. In the Challenger case, perhaps Robert Lund would have better fulfilled his managerial role as vice-president for engineering if he had invited his concerned engineers to directly communicate their concerns to the Marshall Space Flight Readiness Review team, or even to the top NASA readiness review team (which denied knowledge of the problem Boisjoly identified).

3.8   Chapter Summary

In this chapter we explored different conceptions of the responsibilities of engineers. These conceptions range from a minimalist, malpractice model that is primarily concerned with staying out of trouble to the idea of taking on responsibilities that go "beyond the call of duty"—what we called good works. In between these extremes are other conceptions, such as Curd and May's reasonable care model of being concerned to satisfy a standard of care that a prudent nonprofessional would advocate, and Ladd's more open-ended notion of positive responsibility, or civic virtue.

While each of these conceptions has something positive to contribute to our understanding of engineering responsibility, each also has some difficulties. The malpractice model rightly points to the importance of avoiding wrongful behavior. But strict adherence to its minimal standards can also contribute to avoidable harms and an overemphasis on attributing blame instead of seeking better understanding of what went wrong. The reasonable care model insists that minimal standards may not be enough, but it is not clear that what prudent nonprofessionals expect is always attainable. This is one of Florman and Oldenquist's concerns about Alpern's principle of care, as well as his corollary of proportionate harm. Where can the line reasonably be drawn? Ladd's notion of civic virtue and our notion of good works remind us that, in an important sense, one's work is never done, especially in professions like engineering, where the safety and welfare of others is so clearly at stake. Yet, there are limitations of time and money, and other responsibilities. One may even meet with active resistance from employers, supervisors, and colleagues.

We might wish for some sort of algorithm for determining what our responsibilities are in particular circumstances. But this is an idle wish. As we will see in the next chapter, even the written codes of ethics of professional engineering societies can only provide general guidance. The determination of responsibilities in particular circumstances depends on discernment and judgment on the part of engineers.

We have noted several possible impediments to the kind of discernment and judgment that responsible engineering practice requires. Self-interest, self-deception, weakness of will, ignorance, egocentric thinking, microscopic vision, uncritical acceptance of authority, and groupthink are commonplace and require special vigilance if engineers are to resist them.

Case Analyses

Case 3.1 To Dissent or Not to Dissent[58]

I

Alison Turner is a department manager at a large commercial nuclear generating plant. She is also a member of the Plant Nuclear Safety Review Committee (PNSRC). The committee's responsibilities include reviewing and approving design changes, procedural changes, and submittals to the Nuclear Regulatory Commission (NRC).

Today Alison finds herself in a difficult situation. PNSRC is meeting to decide what to do about a heat exchanger problem. Routine testing on the previous morning revealed degraded cooling water flow and high differential pressure in one of the containment spray heat exchangers of one of the two generating units. This unit has just returned to service after two months of repairs. Test results on the second heat exchanger were similar. Although the other generating unit has been in continuous service, testing reveals that its two heat exchangers are operating at less than full capacity. The most likely cause of the problem is sand blockage on the lake water side of the four heat exchangers.

After extensive analysis by engineers in the mechanical engineering and nuclear safety and licensing departments, they have concluded that the cooling water flow falls slightly below the minimum requirement set by the technical specifications under which the plant is licensed. Nevertheless, based on mechanical engineering's analysis, nuclear safety and licensing has prepared a Justification for Continued Operation (JCO) for submission to NRC. PNSRC is now meeting to decide whether to approve the JCO and forward it to NRC.

As Alison reviews the JCO, she is uncomfortable with one assumption made in the analysis. The analysis assumes that the heat exchangers still have 95 percent of their original heat transfer capability. The conclusion is that this would be satisfactory. However, in anticipating possible accidents, single failure criteria require the plant to assume the loss of one heat exchanger. Alison wonders if, under those conditions, the heat transfer problem would be manageable. The JCO does not discuss what might happen under that contingency.

Seven members of PNSRC are present, enough for a quorum. Alison is the least senior member present. From the outset of the meeting, committee chair Rich Robinson has made it clear that it is important to act quickly, since any shutdown will cost the company, and ultimately the rate payers, a lot of money in additional fuel costs. "Repairs," he says, "might take a couple of weeks. If we don't approve this, we may be facing a multi-million-dollar proposition. Fortunately, the JCO seems fine. What do you think?" Brad Louks and Joe Carpello immediately concur. Rich then says, "Well, if no one sees any problems here, let's go with it." There is a moment of silence. Should Alison express her reservations?

II

Alison Turner expresses her reservations. Brad Louks replies, "We're talking about containment heat exchangers. It's an accident mitigation system, and it's never had to be used here—or at any other commercial nuclear plant that we know of, for that matter. In fact, lots of plants don't even have containment spray systems." "Right," adds Joe Carpello, "we're ahead of the game on this one. I don't see any problem here. Nothing's totally risk free, but we've always been leaders in safety. Let's not get carried away with 'possibilities.'"

"I don't think Alison meant to have us get carried away with anything," Mark Reynolds interjects. "She's just wondering if the JCO should address the question of how things would look if we lost one of the heat exchangers. How much time would it take the nuclear safety and licensing department to make a calculation for us—another three hours? It's only 1:30 P.M., you know." "What's the point, Mark?" asks Joe. "Our track record is excellent, and the system is optional. It's not as though we're taking any extraordinary risks."

Nothing further is said, and Rich Robinson calls for the vote. Though not a committee requirement, PNSRC has always acted unanimously. It often rejects, sometimes approves, but always unanimously. As the call goes around the room, each member approves. The last member called on to vote is Alison. She still has serious reservations about approving the JCO without the nuclear safety and licensing department making further calculations. How should she vote?

III

Suppose Alison casts a negative vote and subsequent calculations show that her worries were unfounded. In the event of an accident, perhaps a single heat exchanger would be adequate to manage any likely heat transfer problems. Would it follow that it was wrong for her to cast a dissenting vote? [Recall that a single dissenting vote would not defeat approval. It would only set a precedent of proceeding without unanimity.]

Analysis

Alison Turner is concerned about the safety assumptions being made in her workplace.[59] This is an important question, but it takes on even more significance in Alison's workplace—a nuclear power plant. This case revolves around two important ethical issues: (1) How can a group make the best decision about safety? and (2) What is an ethical employee's responsibility in terms of expressing his or her opinion?

In terms of its safety decisions, it seems that the company who runs this nuclear power plant has asked the committee Alison is part of (the PNSRC—Plant Nuclear Safety Review Committee) to wear two different and potentially conflicting hats. In a famous example from the discussion that occurred before the Challenger explosion several years ago, a manager at Morton Thiokol asked an engineer who had opposed the launch to take off his "engineering hat" and put on his "management hat." When he responded to the question as a manager, he recommended launching the space shuttle under the conditions specified. This example illustrates that the decision recommended by an engineer may not be the same as the decision recommended by a manager. Asking people on one committee to play both roles may lead to disastrous results.

One reason for the potential danger in this situation is a phenomenon called "groupthink," discussed by Irving Janis in his book, *Groupthink* (Houghton Mifflin, 1982). In situations of groupthink, members of a group don't want to "rock the boat." They agree to a consensus to support the group even though individuals may disagree with the decision. Rich Robinson, the chair of the committee, has made it clear that it is important to act quickly to avoid a costly shutdown. He has set the tone for the meeting and set the stage for groupthink. It seems as if he has a decision made before the group even discusses

anything. When someone suggests that additional calculations could easily be made, one person reminds another not to rock the boat by saying, "Our track record is excellent, and the system is optional. It's not as though we're taking any extraordinary risks." The group never has a chance to critically examine the situation.

When the vote is being cast, Alison must decide her responsibility to express her doubts about the decision. According to Albert Hirschman in the book, *Exit, Voice and Loyalty* (Harvard University Press, 1970), employees have three options in situations such as this one: exit, voice, or loyalty. In other words, they may decide that the problem is significant enough that they are forced to quit their jobs and leave the corporation (exit). They may speak to their supervisors or anyone else who might be involved and try to convince them of their concerns (voice). Or they may remain loyal to the company and do nothing believing that the company knows best and the problem will be solved in due time. If Alison decided to use the voice option in this situation, she would cast a negative vote. In this way, she would be communicating her dissatisfaction with the committee's decision. Of course, she could abstain (in essence, the exit option) or vote for the decision (loyalty). Each decision is significant and each carries its own risks. If she casts a negative vote, she remains true to her doubts but has the potential not to be seen as a team player. Her future promotions could be affected. If she abstains, she walks a middle ground—she expresses some dissatisfaction, but may still be seen as a reluctant member of the team. If she casts a positive vote, she goes along with the group, remains part of the team, but her voice has been lost.

To avoid putting any individual in this difficult position, this group could have used a more systematic method of assessing the risk involved in the important decisions they are asked to make. For example, in their book, *Acceptable Risk* (Cambridge University Press, 1981), Fischhoff and his colleagues present seven objectives that they believe a method for assessing risk should meet: comprehensive, logically sound, practical, open to evaluation, politically acceptable, compatible with institutions, and conducive to learning. They note that not all methods meet these criteria, but any method can be examined in light of the criteria. The PNSRC might have avoided groupthink if they had made an attempt to examine their decision-making procedure more systematically. Of course, these criteria do not assure that any decision is sound, but they are one more way of checking to make sure that all areas have been explored before a group chooses a solution to an important problem.

Decision making about risk is a difficult thing to do. It is even more difficult when it is done by a committee that has to consider the implications of the decision for a number of different constituencies. Nevertheless, this area of decision making is extremely important. The committee must be structured so that each employee has a voice and can act as ethically as possible within the parameters of the decision to be made.

Case 3.2   The Catalyst[60]

I

A recent graduate of Engineering Tech, Bernie Reston has been employed in the Research and Development (R&D) Chemical Engineering Division of Larom, Inc. for the past several months. Bernie was recommended to Larom as the top Engineering Tech graduate in chemical engineering.

Alex Smith, the head of Bernie's unit, showed immediate interest in Bernie's research on processes using a particular catalyst (call it B). However, until last week, his primary research assignments at Larom were in other areas.

A meeting of engineers in Bernie's unit is called by Alex. He announces that the unit must make a recommendation within the next two days on what catalyst should be used by Larom in processing a major product. It is clear to everyone that Alex is anticipating a brief, decisive meeting. One of the senior engineers volunteers, "We've been working on projects like this for years, and catalyst A seems to be the obvious choice." Several others immediately concur. Alex looks around the room and, hearing no further comments, says, "Well, it looks like we're in accord on this. Do we have consensus?"

So far Bernie has said nothing. He is not sure what further testing will show, but the testing he has been doing for the past week provides preliminary evidence that catalyst B may actually be best for this process. This is also in line with what his research at Engineering Tech suggested with somewhat similar processes. If catalyst B should turn out to be preferable, a great deal of money will be saved; and, in the long run, a fair amount of time will be saved as well. He wonders if he should mention his findings at this time, or should he simply defer to the senior engineers, who seem as determined as Alex to bring matters to closure.

What would you advise Bernie to do? Identify and discuss any ethical issues this case raises.

II

Bernie somewhat hesitantly raises his hand. He briefly explains his test results and the advantages catalyst B might provide. Then he suggests that the unit might want to delay its recommendation for another two weeks so that he can conduct further tests.

Alex replies, "We don't have two weeks. We have two days." He then asks Bernie to write up the report, leaving out the preliminary data he has gathered about catalyst B. He says, "It would be nice to do some more testing, but we just don't have the time. Besides, I doubt if anything would show up in the next two weeks to change our minds. This is one of those times we have to be decisive—and we have to *look* decisive and quit beating around the bush. They're really getting impatient on this one. Anyway, we've had a lot of experience in this area."

Bernie replies that, even if the data on B is left out, the data on A is hardly conclusive. Alex replies, "Look you're a bright person. You can make the numbers look good without much difficulty—do the math backwards if you have to. Just get the report done in the next two days!"

Bernie likes working for Larom, and he feels lucky to have landed such a good job right out of Engineering Tech. He is also due for a significant pay raise soon if he plays his cards right.

What do you think Bernie should do? Explain your choice.

1. Write up the report as Alex says.

2. Refuse to write up the report, saying he will have no part in falsifying a report.

3. Other.

III

Bernie decides to write up the report. When he is finished, Alex asks him to sign it. Bernie now has second thoughts. He wonders if he should sign his name to a report that omits his preliminary research on catalyst B.

What options does Bernie have at this point? Which one would you advise him to take? Discuss.

IV

After reluctantly signing the report, Bernie continues to have second thoughts about what his unit has recommended. He now has an opportunity to do more research on catalyst B. After several weeks his research quite decisively indicates that, contrary to the expectations of Alex and the other more experienced engineers in the unit, catalyst B really would have been, far and away, the better choice. What should Bernie do now?

1. Keep the data to himself—don't make trouble.

2. Tell Alex and let him decide what, if anything, to do.

3. Other.

Analysis

We will now offer some commentary on the challenges Bernie Reston faced. Although convinced there may be reason to prefer catalyst B to A, Bernie may also be convinced that deferring to the judgment of the more experienced engineers is the best course of action—especially in this kind of situation. He may actually be persuaded that the others are probably right. His is a minority view, and he is considerably less experienced. The recommendation apparently cannot wait for further testing. Besides, Alex is Bernie's division head, and Bernie may believe that his job is to do as he is told. So, Bernie may conclude, it is best to support his colleagues' recommendation—both from the standpoint of Larom, Inc. and his own self-interest.

However, four cautions should be noted from the outset. First, although Bernie may have a general obligation to do what he is told by his superiors, blind or unthinking obedience is not obligatory. He has no obligation to do anything illegal or unethical, regardless of which "authority" requests it. [We will discuss obedience and the limits of authority in Chapter 9.] In this case, it is not at all clear that Alex's superiors at Larom would approve of his effort to falsify the report, or that they would fault Bernie for refusing to comply with Alex's request. After all, the report is for them. Why would they willingly agree to be duped—especially since approving the wrong catalyst could turn out to be very costly to Larom?

Second, Bernie should be alert to the possibility of *groupthink*, discussed in this chapter. Several of these symptoms seem to be present at the initial meeting. There is evidence that at least some of the senior members of the group share the illusion of invulnerability ("We've been working on projects like this for years. . . ."). Rationalizations for not having done more research on catalyst B follow on the heels of this illusion. Given the shared purpose of recommending the best catalyst for the job, the members may believe in the inherent morality of the group ("We know we're on the right side"). Silence in response to Alex's final look around the room for further comments may be the result of some self-censorship (especially if Bernie fails to speak up). This, in turn, feeds the illusion of unanimity. Finally, Alex's evident desire to orchestrate the group to a quick and decisive resolution indicates a readiness to apply direct pressure to any dissenters. Given that much may be at stake for Larom in this situation, Bernie is well advised to be alert to such group dynamics, rather than simply deferring to his more senior colleagues.

Third, Bernie seems to be the only one with evidence that catalyst B might be preferable, and his previous work with catalyst B has already impressed Alex. If he does not speak up, who will? It is unfortunate that Alex did not assign Bernie to work on catalyst B earlier.

Perhaps sometime earlier Bernie should have made a special point of discussing with his colleagues some of his previous work with catalyst B. But why didn't Alex take the lead? It seems that an opportunity for significant research when Bernie first joined the R&D division was lost. However, shifting responsibility to Alex for lacking foresight does not relieve Bernie of responsibility for speaking up now.

Fourth, Bernie is not only asked to suppress data about catalyst B but also to alter the other data. That is, he is asked to *lie*. Alex no doubt sees this as a lie intended to "protect the truth," since he believes that catalyst A really is best. However, as Sissela Bok convincingly argues, even lies of this sort are ethically questionable. She points out that we have a tendency to overestimate the good that comes from lying and to underestimate the harm that comes from lying. Individually and collectively lies do much to undermine trust. Also, by deceiving others, lies often lead people to make decisions they would not make if they had more reliable information, thus undermining their autonomy. Bok concludes that we should lie only after looking carefully to see if any alternatives preferable to lying are available.[61]

One alternative that might work is for Bernie to suggest that they include all the available data but still recommend catalyst A. [This is what, in Chapter 5, we call the "creative middle way" of resolving conflicts.] Since the data has not discouraged them from recommending catalyst A, why should they fear being forthright with others? This tactic could have unfortunate consequences for Bernie, too. But this is ethically preferable to submitting a falsified report—signed or unsigned. No option guarantees there will not be complications. Why not do what seems right and let the "chips fall" where they will?

Although it might seem to Bernie throughout this case that it would be *prudent* not to "rock the boat," it is not at all clear that this would be a correct assessment on his part. There are too many ways in which things can go wrong for him to be sure what a prudent course of action would be. However, prudence and ethics are not the same, and it seems that we can be more certain about what it would be ethical for Bernie to do.

Three basic lines of thought might help Bernie sort out what is at stake ethically when he is facing the initial question of whether to falsify data. One has already been discussed— that of thinking through the possible *consequences* of doing as Alex says, and of comparing this with other alternatives. In doing this Bernie needs to consider his basic responsibilities to Larom. (How what he does might affect Larom's customers and society generally is perhaps too indeterminate to be of much relevance here.) Although in the "heat of the moment" Bernie may find it difficult to think of little else than Alex and the others pressing for closure, his responsibilities are not exhausted by relationships to his divisional colleagues.

A second line of thought rests on the idea of *universalizability* [a notion we discuss in Chapter 6]: Whatever is right for Bernie in this situation is right for similar persons in similar circumstances. It may not be easy to determine just what should count as relevantly similar circumstances, but any serious thinking about this will conclude that Bernie's situation is hardly unique—and this thinking will not confine itself just to engineers who are deciding whether to falsify data. Bernie needs to think about the more general phenomenon of lying. Just how sweeping must his acceptance of lying be in order for him to conclude, in good faith, that falsifying data in this case is justifiable from an ethical point of view? To say that the sweep is very wide indeed is not to *predict* that doing what Alex requests will result in widespread lying. Rather, it is to point to the *principle* of action that Bernie must implicitly accept if he does falsify the data. Once Bernie looks at his situation in terms of this broader principle, he will likely find it much more difficult to find falsifying the data acceptable than if he asks only what the likely consequences are of doing as Alex requests.

Case 3.3 Sunnyvale[61]

I

Jim Grimaldi, projects manager in the Sunnyvale division of Universal Corporation, has just learned that in two weeks the headquarters in Los Angeles will be sending him a project engineer, Joan Dreer. Her job will be to supervise small groups of engineers involved in automotive brake design. The Los Angeles headquarters is anxious to move women into all company levels, and it has targeted Grimaldi's engineering division at Sunnyvale as a good place for Joan Dreer.

Joan Dreer will be the first woman engineer at Sunnyvale. On learning that their new supervisor will be a woman, several of the engineers inform Jim Grimaldi that they don't like the idea of a woman supervising their work.

What, if anything, should Jim Grimaldi do to prepare for Joan Dreer's arrival?

II

Joan Dreer has been with the Sunnyvale division for several months now. As project engineer she has been supervising the work of several engineering groups involved in automotive brake design. As a projects manager, Jim Grimaldi is Joan Dreer's supervisor. The contracts Joan Dreer's groups have been working on have tight deadlines and allow only extremely narrow margins for error. So, the engineering groups have had to work at maximum speed and under a great deal of pressure. Jim Grimaldi has become increasingly concerned about the work of the groups under Joan Dreer's supervision. He comments:

> A couple of months ago I was sent a new engineer from our plant in Los Angeles, Joan Dreer, and told to put her to work right away as a project engineer. The company was making a push to move women into all company levels but had apparently run into a lot of problems with their engineers down in Los Angeles. They had decided that our place would have the fewest problems adjusting to women and they were pretty insistent that we find a way to work things out. When I first took Joan around our plant so she could get to know the men and the kind of work we do, several of the engineers took me aside and let me know in no uncertain terms that they didn't want a woman to supervise their work. To make matters worse, Joan came on as a pushy and somewhat aggressive feminist. When one of the young engineers asked her if she was a "Miss" or a "Mrs.," she retorted that her private life was her own affair and that he should get used to calling her "Ms."

Jim Grimaldi has not found any of the groups under Joan Dreer's supervision outrightly refusing to work. But they do seem to have been dragging their feet in small ways so that sometimes they miss their deadlines. The other groups have also been showing some reluctance to cooperate with the groups under her supervision. So, Jim Grimaldi has become increasingly concerned about the impact Joan Dreer's presence seems to be having on his ability to meet deadlines, and he is concerned about how

this might affect his own career. He is also worried about the safety factor involved in the brake design. He concludes:

> I agree that it's important to move women into supervisory positions in the company, but I don't know whether we can really afford to do it just yet. Women aren't really suited for this kind of work. I don't want to fire any of my engineers. That would be unfair since they have worked hard in the past under a lot of pressure. What should I do?

What do you think Jim Grimaldi should do? Explain. What are the ethical issues involved, and how should they be approached?[63]

III

Parts I and II provide little information about Joan Dreer and how she happened to come to the Sunnyvale division. Consider the following possible background information.

Joan Dreer was excited about her transfer to Sunnyvale. But she was also apprehensive. Although she had received very high marks for her work at the Los Angeles headquarters of Universal, she had just gone through an extremely unpleasant experience. Her immediate supervisor in Los Angeles made it very clear that, in return for a recent promotion, he expected sexual favors. When she resisted, he became verbally abusive and tried his best to make life miserable for her at Universal. His derisive remarks about women engineers did not go unnoticed by others—several of whom found them quite amusing. Fortunately, her complaints to the corporate ombudsman were taken seriously. Disciplinary action was taken against Joan Dreer's supervisor. Joan Dreer also requested a transfer to a division that would be more receptive to women engineers. So, she hoped the Sunnyvale division would give her a fresh start.

Unfortunately, Joan Dreer's first day at Sunnyvale proved quite challenging. She took a small group of engineers by surprise when she entered the Sunnyvale lounge. A young engineer with his back to the door was commenting that he didn't like the idea of being told how to do his work by a woman, but that he would figure out how to handle the situation once he found out whether she was a "Miss" or a "Mrs." Another added, "Right, Johnson, what are you going to say to her, 'Should we call you Miss Honey or Mrs. Honey'?"

The laughter ended abruptly when Joan Dreer's entrance was noticed. Realizing that she was facing her first challenge, she tersely announced, "Mr. Johnson, my private life is my own affair. You'd better get used to calling me 'Ms.'"

How, if at all, does this background information change your understanding of the situation described in Part II? What do you now think are the major ethical concerns? How would you suggest they be approached?

Case 3.4 Working Overtime[64]

I

Ryan Redgrave was young, inexperienced in industry, and naive about industry methods of operating. He did, however, possess superb qualifications in statistics and in computer programming and applications. He was hired by XYZ to improve quality control in plastic parts.

Ryan began implementing elements of statistical process control, and steady improvement in the quality of plastic parts was observed. Ryan noted that one vendor, IMP, a small company, produced a high-quality raw material that gave a superior part except that frequently, when color was involved, their batch-to-batch color consistency was not good. He called this to the attention of IMP's sales representative, Mark, a personable young man about Ryan's age. Mark asked for Ryan's help in solving the inconsistency problem, and over dinner one evening Ryan outlined a series of experiments to get to the root cause of the color inconsistency.

Mark agreed that IMP would supply the necessary material samples, and Ryan worked late several nights to conduct the experiments he had devised. As a result of these experiments, Ryan was able to suggest some formulation changes to Mark to improve the color consistency of their raw material. To show his gratitude, Mark took Ryan and his wife to an expensive restaurant for dinner. "This will make up for some of the late hours you worked trying to solve our mutual quality problem," Mark exclaimed.

The formulation changes Ryan suggested did work and the color consistency of the IMP material improved markedly. Mark continued to check its performance on frequent sales calls at XYZ. The friendship between Mark and Ryan grew, with Mark frequently taking Ryan to lunch. On several of these occasions, Mark urged Ryan to recommend that XYZ buy more of its plastic from IMP.

Ryan did recommend to his procurement department that XYZ buy more from IMP because of the improved quality of the material. A small increase was put into effect, although procurement told Ryan that IMP's price was the highest of any of the plastics vendors with which XYZ dealt.

Identify and discuss any ethical issues this case raises. Has Ryan done anything wrong? Mark? Since Ryan worked extra hours, without pay, to improve IMP's color consistency, is this an instance of "good works" on his part?

II

Shortly after IMP was granted a larger order, Mark stopped by Ryan's office at XYZ to invite him to accompany several other IMP customers on a short ski trip to Colorado. Although he was only a beginning skier, Ryan accepted the invitation because the thrill of skiing the Colorado slopes was so appealing.

XYZ policy prohibited accepting favors from vendors, but this had never been communicated to Ryan and he saw nothing wrong with accepting the invitation. He did not know that two members of XYZ's procurement department had also been invited on the trip but declined because of the company's policy.

When Ryan mentioned the ski trip to a fellow employee in quality control, he was told he was violating a company policy. But Ryan decided he had earned the trip and would go anyway, and he told his fellow employee to say nothing. Ryan advised his supervisor he was going to take a couple of days vacation "to catch up on some repairs on the house."

Ryan enjoyed the skiing trip immensely— especially as its cost was beyond anything he could have managed on his own budget. Unfortunately, he was not as expert a skier as he should have been. On the last day he took a bad fall, strained his shoulder, and returned home with his arm in a sling. At work the following Monday he explained that he had fallen off a ladder while cleaning ice from the eaves of his house.

Secrets are difficult to keep, even in industrial plants. Word reached Ryan's supervisor about the ski trip, and he called Ryan in to discuss the policy violation. Ryan pleaded ignorance of the policy and the supervisor let him off with a verbal reprimand and the instruction that he contact IMP and repay the cost of the trip.

Ryan telephoned Mark, asked how much the trip cost, and told him why he needed to know. Mark laughed. "Forget it, Ryan, you earned that trip for what you did in helping us with our quality. If anyone asks us, we'll tell them you paid for your share. We may need your help again!" Ryan was greatly relieved because there was no room in his family budget to repay such a trip.

Identify and discuss the ethical issues in this case. Should Ryan have accepted Mark's final offer? Why would XYZ have a policy prohibiting free ski trips? Did Ryan's co-worker have any special responsibility to more aggressively discourage Ryan from taking the trip? Do you think Ryan's supervisor handled the situation well?

Case 3.5 "Why Won't They Read?"[65]

Sid Fisher was fuming. The manager of mechanical engineering research for XYZ had spent most of the morning in a research project review. He had listened patiently at first, then impatiently, to two young engineers review their research efforts on the development of a more efficient heat transfer surface. Realizing they were reporting efforts that had been unsuccessful, he finally interrupted and exclaimed, "Do you men realize that you have gone down the same blind path that Edwards and O'Malley did about five years ago? Their detailed research report is in our technical library. Did you read it before you began your work?"

The two engineers admitted they had not heard of Edwards and O'Malley's previous work, had not read the report covering it, and, in fact, had made no effort to check the current technical literature for related publications.

Sid thought about these wasted efforts and the money the unproductive research had cost his company. He remembered, painfully, at least two other recent efforts where inadequate literature research had cost XYZ the expense of wasted research and development activities. In one case a team of XYZ engineers worked hard for two years on a project only to discover that one of XYZ's competitors had a four-year-old patent covering almost precisely the same innovation they were developing. Until one of XYZ's patent attorneys called attention to the competitive patent after reading a monthly research report mentioning the engineers' project, none of the engineers on the development team had made any effort to review the patent literature.

In the second case, there had been a long, tedious research effort to modify the properties of a material for use in a new component part of one of XYZ's products. No progress at all was made until one of XYZ's scientists got a clue at a technical society meeting that it might be useful to check an article in a foreign technical journal. The article provided major help in accelerating the materials development significantly.

Sid thought to himself, "Why won't my engineers read?" Certainly XYZ provided the wherewithal—a modern technical library adequately supplied with current and past engineering and scientific journals, facilities for computerized literature searching, and a staff to assist engineers and scientists in using literature resources. Most of his engineers seemed to lack the incentive to read the literature, Sid thought. At best they seemed to confine their reading to a current trade journal or two.

Looking for clues to cure the "won't read" syndrome, Sid called an old friend, who was head of the mechanical engineering department at a nearby university. He asked him what sort of reading requirements were part of an engineer's course of study at present. The department head explained that engineering students, because of demanding course loads, did well to read the assigned textbooks and related technical handbooks and computer manuals. Significant outside reading began only in the M.S. or Ph.D. thesis research program. Not overly encouraged by this response, Sid began to think about what he could do to encourage greater use of available technical literature on the part of his engineers.

Discuss the responsibilities XYZ engineers have to keep up with readings relevant to their research. What responsibilities does Sid Fisher have in this regard? What might Sid Fisher do to deal effectively with this problem? Do university engineering programs have any special responsibility to help companies like XYZ with this problem?

Case 3.6 The "Underground" Project[66]

Joe Hall walked out of Tom Evers's office feeling "on top of the world." A young and relatively inexperienced development engineer with XYZ Appliance, Joe had just been given the green light to develop an idea he had for a modular water purification device for the home. Not only had director of new product development Tom Evers liked the idea, he asked Joe to form and head a project team to develop a prototype of the device.

Joe found the task to be more challenging than he had expected. To keep costs down, Joe had to select team members with less experience than he wanted. Because of the inexperience of the team, some of Joe's design ideas and materials choices had to be corrected, and he soon realized that the cost of the prototype (and the ultimate selling price of the appliance) would be higher than he originally estimated.

However, finally the day came when the project team ran a successful series of tests on an operating prototype. Joe set up a review and demonstration with Tom. Tom then agreed to arrange a review with XYZ's vice-president of marketing to ascertain marketing's interest in the water purification device. Unfortunately, the meeting with marketing did not go well. The marketing vice-president interrupted Joe's presentation of product cost, saying "I wish you guys in development would ask for marketing input *before* you begin to work on a new product. I can tell you our department is not interested in any type of a water appliance! I think you've wasted company money and created an albatross. From my viewpoint, you can shut off the project and put your prototype 'on the shelf.' I'll get back to you if we ever develop interest in this area but don't expect that to be soon!"

Tom instructed Joe to write a final report and consign the prototype to the development "morgue." All team members were assigned to other projects.

Upset that his first project team leader assignment failed, Joe decided he could not give up so easily. XYZ had a policy of permitting R&D employees to use 10 percent of their time to pursue new ideas without any further authorization. So, Joe continued to work on his project during this time.

Although Joe had every intention of confining his time on the project to 10 percent, he soon got so absorbed that he spent more and more time. He made some additional vendor contacts to get improved materials, "conned" a friend in electronics research to work on the control system, and had the machine shop do some additional work on the prototype (charging the shop time to another project of his).

Although progress on Joe's other assignments suffered, he was able to make substantial improvements in the water purification appliance. He debated with himself about when to confess to Tom that he had not really closed out the project. He wished that he could somehow get market research data that would convince Tom it had been the right move to continue on the project, and to get Tom to push for a marketing go-ahead.

Joe often discussed the project with his wife, and one day she gave him an idea about how to get some quick market data. She had seen a food products exhibitor in a local shopping mall get passers-by to answer questionnaires about the products displayed. Joe arranged for members of his wife's garden club to demonstrate the water purification appliance at the local mall and ask viewers to fill out a questionnaire determining their interest in the appliance and the price they would pay if it were for sale. Joe was careful not to show any XYZ identification on the prototype, particularly since he had no authorization to remove it from the XYZ laboratory.

Despite an amateurish approach, the club members collected a considerable amount of data. Reviewing the data, Joe was more convinced than ever that he had developed a marketable product and was anxious to convince Tom of this. He was sure he could make a very persuasive argument about the potential market, and that Tom would overlook the fact that Joe had overridden his orders to cease work on the appliance. Joe resolved to see Tom as soon as possible.

If you were Tom, how would you respond to Joe when he makes his presentation? Does the fact that Joe has a possible success on his hands justify what he did?

Case 3.7   The TV Antenna Tower[67]

About seven years ago, a TV station in Houston decided to strengthen its signal by erecting a new, taller (1,000-foot) transmission antenna in Missouri City, Texas. The station contracted with a TV antenna design firm to design the tower. The resulting design employed twenty 50-foot segments that would have to be lifted up into place sequentially by a jib crane that moved up with the tower. Each segment required a lifting lug to permit that segment to be hoisted off the flatbed delivery truck and then lifted into place by the crane. The actual construction of the tower was done by a separate rigging firm that specialized in such tasks.

When the rigging company received the twentieth and last tower segment, it faced a new problem. While the lifting lug was satisfactory for lifting the segment horizontally off the delivery truck, it would not enable the segment to be lifted vertically. The jib crane cable interfered with the antenna baskets at the top of the segment. The riggers asked permission from the design company to temporarily remove the antenna baskets and were refused. Officials at the design firm said that the last time they gave permission to make similar changes, they had to pay tens of thousands of dollars to repair the antenna baskets (which had been damaged on removal) and to remount and realign them correctly.

The riggers devised a solution that was seriously flawed. They bolted an extension arm to the tower section and calculated the size of the required bolts based on the model shown in Figure 3.1. Figure 3.2 shows what was really occurring and indicates what the riggers should have used as their model. Figures 3.3 and 3.4 complete the analysis, ending with the unforeseen magnification factor on the load of magnitude R.

Figure 3.4, which gives the solution, appears on the next page.

A sophomore-level engineering student who had taken a course in statics could

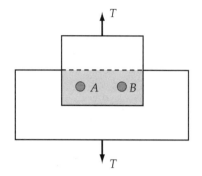

Figure 3.1
Model Riggers Thought Was Correct

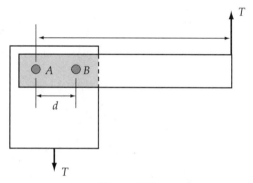

Figure 3.2
Model Riggers Should Have Used

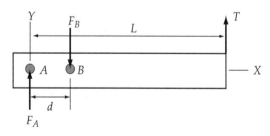

Figure 3.3
Free Body Diagram of Lifting Bar

have detected the flaw, but the riggers had no engineers on their staff. The riggers, knowing they lacked engineering expertise, asked the antenna design company engineers to review their proposed solution. The engineers again refused, having been ordered by company management not only not to look at the

---

$$\Sigma M_A = TL - F_b d = 0$$
$$\Sigma M_B = T(L - d) - F_A d = 0$$

Solving the above equations for F_A and F_B

$$F_A = \frac{T(L-d)}{d} \text{ and } F_B = \frac{TL}{d}$$

and the corresponding stress on each bolt is

$$\sigma_A = \frac{F_A}{A_{\text{bolt}}} = \frac{T(L-d)}{dA_{\text{bolt}}}$$

and

$$\sigma_B = \frac{F_B}{A_{\text{bolt}}} = \frac{TL}{dA_{\text{bolt}}}$$

where

F_A = force on bolt A
F_B = force on bolt B
A_{bolt} = cross-sectional area of bolt
d = distance between bolts

$$R = \frac{\text{shear stress calculation incl. moment arm}}{\text{shear stress calculation used by Riggers}}$$

$R \equiv$ error factor

$$R = \frac{TL/d\, A_{\text{bolt}}}{T/2\, A_{\text{bolt}}} = \frac{2L}{d}$$

Assuming one set of bolts was used, placed 1 ft apart, and the steel channel was 6 ft long:

$$R = \frac{2(6 \text{ ft})}{1 \text{ ft}} = 12$$

or, in other words, the stress (for these assumed numbers) in the new lug bolts is twelve times what Riggers thought it would be, based on its erroneous analysis.

Figure 3.4
Analysis of Riggers' Solution

drawings but also not to visit the construction site during the lifting of the last segment. Management of the design firm feared that they would be held liable if there were an accident. The designers also failed to suggest to the riggers that they should hire an engineering consultant to look over their lifting plans.

When the riggers attempted to lift the top section of the tower with the microwave baskets, the tower fell, killing seven men. The TV company was taping the lift of the last segment for future TV promotions, and the videotape shows the riggers falling to their death.

Consider how you would react to watching that tape if you were the design engineer who refused to look at the lifting plans or if you were the company executive who ordered the design engineer not to examine the plans.

To take an analogy, consider a physician who examines a patient and finds something suspicious in an area outside her specialty. When asking advice from a specialist, the physician is rebuffed, on the grounds that the specialist might incur a liability. Furthermore, the specialist does not suggest that the patient should see a specialist.

What conceptions of responsibility seemed most prevalent in this case? Can you suggest other conceptions that might have helped avoid this tragedy?

NOTES

1. This is a fictional case study, but it depicts the sort of situation that could arise for a chemical engineer.

2. For discussions of this issue see, for example, Peter A. French, *Collective and Corporate Responsibility* (New York: Columbia University Press, 1984); Kenneth E. Goodpaster and John B. Matthews, Jr., "Can a Corporation Have a Conscience?" *Harvard Business Review*, (60)(January/February 1982) 132–141; and Manuel Velasquez, "Why Corporations Are Not Morally Responsible for Anything They Do," *Business and Professional Ethics Journal*, 2, no. 3 (Spring 1983), 1–18.

3. Martin Curd and Larry May, *Professional Responsibility for Harmful Actions*, Module Series in Applied Ethics, Center for the Study of Ethics in the Professions, Illinois Institute of Technology (Dubuque, Iowa: Kendall/Hunt, 1984).

4. Ibid., p. 19.

5. Ibid., p. 18.

6. John Ladd, "Bhopal: An Essay on Moral Responsibility and Civic Virtue," *Journal of Social Philosophy*, Vol. XXII, no. 1 (Spring 1991), p. 81.

7. Ibid., p. 74.

8. Ibid., p. 82.

9. Ibid., p. 82.

10. Ibid., p. 78.

11. Actually, what Ladd says is, "These are unlikely to be repeated if we attend to them properly. However, this may be optimistic, as Martin and Schinzinger (*Ethics in Engineering*) point out in the case of the Titanic, and as the numerous fiascos discussed in Irving Janis's *Victims of Groupthink* suggest. Still, the point that we *can* (and *ought to*) learn and adapt is well taken.

12. Ladd, "Bhopal," p. 78.

13. Ibid.

14. Ibid.

15. Ibid.

16. Ibid.

17. Ibid.

18. Ibid., p. 90.

19. Ibid., p. 90. Ladd is referring to Robert Bellah et al., *Habits of the Heart: Individualism and Commitment in American Life* (New York: Harper and Row, 1985).

20. Kenneth A. Alpern, "Moral Responsibility for Engineers," in Deborah Johnson, ed., *Ethical Issues in Engineering* (Englewood Cliffs, N.J.: Prentice Hall, 1991), p. 188.

21. Most engineering societies have a similar provision. Engineering codes of ethics were discussed in detail in Chapter 2.

22. Alpern, "Moral Responsibility," p. 189.

23. But, as Andrew Oldenquist observes, it is not just engineers, nor even just professionals, who have special responsibilities to avoid causing harm. "Is a laborer less obliged to erect scaffolding safely and cover dangerous holes? A bus driver may find the schedule dangerously fast; a pilot may notice countless dangers his airline condones, mechanics may be asked to perform maintenance below minimum safety standards, workmen told to make concrete with what they know is too much sand, . . ." Andrew Oldenquist, "Commentary on Alpern's 'Moral Responsibility for Engineers,'" *Business & Professional Ethics,* 2, no. 2 (Winter 1983), p. 49.

24. Alpern, "Moral Responsibility," p. 41.

25. Oldenquist, "Commentary," p. 51.

26. Alpern, "Moral Responsibility," p. 44.

27. Florman, "Moral Blueprints," p. 54.

28. Personal communication with statistician Michael Stoline at Western Michigan University.

29. This is based on an interview with an engineer at Frost Engineering in Denver, Colorado. His analysis of the problem is that, when *used* by window washers, the safety rope does an excellent job of breaking falls. However, he worries that, despite legal requirements to use a safety mechanism, some workers will not use the mechanism because it does not permit them to lower themselves to the next level of windows as quickly as they like. His primary concern, he says, is that, like those who refuse to wear seatbelts, some will die or be seriously injured unnecessarily. Although the negligence (and liability) lies outside Frost Engineering, this engineer wants to do more. And, although Frost's customers do not complain about the quality of the safety rope, this does not satisfy him.

30. What follows in this section is adapted from Michael S. Pritchard, "Good Works."

31. Many basic duties of professionals are simply extensions of what J. O. Urmson more generally refers to as "rock-bottom duties which are duties for all and from every point of view, and to which anyone may draw attention." See his "Saints and Heroes," in A. I. Melden, ed., *Essays in Moral Philosophy* (Seattle: University of Washington Press, 1958), p. 205. However, other basic duties derive from the special roles of professionals. Even if those roles are themselves justified by principles of ordinary morality, the special basic duties apply only to those occupying professional roles. For example, professionals have special duties of confidentiality that are more stringent than those in ordinary, nonprofessional relations.

32. J. O. Urmson, "Hare on Intuitive Moral Thinking," in Douglas Seanor and N. Fotion, eds., *Hare and Critics* (Oxford, England: Clarendon Press, 1988), p. 168.

33. G. P. E. Meese, "The Sealed Beam Case," *Business & Professional Ethics, 1,* no. 3 (Spring 1982), pp. 1-20. This is one of several illustrations of good works that go beyond strict professional duty that Michael S. Pritchard discusses in "Good Works," *Professional Ethics, 1,* no. 1, (Fall 1992),

pp. 155–177. Much of the discussion of Ladd's views on responsibility below is based on similar discussion in "Good Works."

34. Ibid., p. 16.

35. H. H. Magsdick, "Some Engineering Aspects of Headlighting," *Illuminating Engineering* (June 1940), p. 533, cited in Meese, p. 17.

36. Of course, this may encourage laxity on the part of some. If Adams knows that someone else will pick up the slack when he neglects his responsibilities, this may encourage him all the more to neglect his duties. Eventually this may backfire; but it may not, thus perpetuating a basic unfairness to those who pick up the slack he creates. But there are other reasons than deliberate neglect for falling short of one's duties (e.g., illness). In any case, more than unfairness may be at stake. In some circumstances, if someone does not try to make up for Adams's shortcomings, others, too, may be seriously shortchanged or harmed.

37. William F. May, "Professional Virtue and Self-Regulation," in *Ethical Issues in Professional Life* (Oxford, England: Oxford University Press, 1988), pp. 408–411.

38. Ibid., p. 408.

39. Ibid.

40. Ibid.

41. Mike Martin and Roland Schinzinger, *Ethics in Engineering* (2nd ed.) (New York: McGraw-Hill, 1989), p. 200. For a detailed philosophical analysis of the complexities (and puzzling features) of self-deception, see Mike Martin's *Self-Deception and Morality* (Lawrence: University Press of Kansas, 1986).

42. Ibid.

43. This case is an adaptation of "Cover-up Temptation," one of several fictional vignettes appearing in Roger Ricklefs, "Executives Apply Stiffer Standards Than Public to Ethical Dilemmas," *Wall Street Journal* (November 3, 1983).

44. Although the number of women engineers is rapidly increasing, as recently as 1981 approximately 97 percent of the industrial engineers in the United States were men. See Manuel Velasquez, *Business Ethics* (2nd ed.) (Englewood Cliffs, N.J.: Prentice Hall, 1982), p. 4.

45. For a first-hand account of difficulties women often face in gaining full acceptance as engineers, see H. Patricia Hynes, "Women Working: A Field Report," *Technology Review* (November/December 1984), pp. 37–38 and p. 47.

For further discussion of women as engineers, see Samuel Florman, "Will Women Engineers Make a Difference," in the same issue, pp. 51–52.

46. Michael Davis, "Explaining Wrongdoing," *Journal of Social Philosophy*, Vol. XX, nos. 1 & 2 (Spring/Fall 1989), 74–90.

47. Ibid., p. 74.

48. Some might take issue with Davis on these matters in this case. Davis's hypothesis that something else accounts for Lund's response is valuable, nevertheless. Microscopic vision does occur, and Davis's application of this concept to Lund explains its distinctive features quite well.

49. Ibid., p. 80.

50. Ibid., p. 82.

51. Rogers Commission, Report to the President by the Presidential Commission on the Space Shuttle Challenger Accident, Washington, D.C., June 6, 1986, p. 93.

52. Ibid., p. 87.

53. Stanley Milgram, *Obedience to Authority* (New York: Harper & Row, 1974).

54. Martin and Schinzinger, *Ethics in Engineering*, pp. 76–77.

55. Ibid., p. 77.

56. Ibid.

57. Irving Janis, *Groupthink* (2nd ed.) (Boston: Houghton Mifflin, 1982).

58. Pritchard, *Teaching Engineering Ethics*, case and commentaries on pp. 92–113.

59. The following comments were written for this case by Professor Lea Stewart, Department of Communication, Rutgers University. Her comments were written for National Science Foundation Grant No. DIR-8820837, in Michael S. Pritchard, ed., *Teaching Engineering Ethics: A Case Study Approach* (Western Michigan University: Center for the Study of Ethics in Society, 1992).

60. The following set of case studies is inspired by two short fictional cases presented by Philip M. Cohn and Roy V. Hughson in *Chemical Engineer*, May 5, 1980. "The Falsified Data" and "The Falsified Data Strike Back" are just two of several fictional cases they present in this issue. They appear on pp. 100–107.

61. Sissela Bok, *Lying: Moral Choice in Public and Private Life* (London: Quort-Books, 1980).

62. Pritchard, *Teaching Engineering Ethics*, case and commentaries on pp. 391–401.

63. Parts I and II of this case study are from Manuel Velasquez, *Business Ethics* (1st ed.) (Englewood Cliffs, N.J.: Prentice Hall, 1981), p. 6.

64. This is an adaptation of W. Gale Cutler's fictional case, "Ryan Goes Skiing," *Research.Technology Management* (July/August, 1992), pp. 48–49.

65. This is based on W. Gale Cutler's fictional case, "When 'Johnny' Won't Read," *Research.Technology Management* (September/October 1988), p. 53.

66. This fictional case study is an adaptation of W. Gale Cutler's case study, "Joe Takes His Project 'Underground'," in *Research.Technology Management* (March/April), pp. 51–52.

67. This case study is presented in greater detail, complete with an instructor's guide and student handouts, in R. W. Flumerfelt, C. E. Harris, M. J. Rabins, and C. H. Samson, eds., *Introducing Ethics Case Studies into Required Undergraduate Engineering Courses*, final report to NSF on Grant No. DIR-9012252, November 1992, pp. 231–261. [Hereafter, Flumerfelt, Harris, Rabins, and Samson.]

Chapter 4

Introduction to Moral Thinking

In May of 1977 the Occupational Safety and Health Administration (OSHA) issued an emergency temporary standard (ETS) ordering that worker exposure to benzene be reduced from the regulated level of 10 parts per million (ppm) to l ppm. OSHA proposed to make this a permanent standard, because of a report to the National Institutes of Health in 1977 of excessive leukemia deaths due to benzene exposure. These deaths occurred in two rubber pliofilm plants in Ohio, both of which had benzene exposure levels in excess of 10 ppm No animal or human test data were available for lower exposure levels. Nevertheless, OSHA determined that there was no safe level of exposure to carcinogens and proposed that exposure to benzene be reduced to the lowest level that can be easily monitored. At the time the ETS was issued, little medical evidence existed of a relation between benzene and cancer at any level found in the industry. In fact, there was considerable evidence that there are levels at which exposure to benzene is harmless.

OSHA's authority seemed clear in the Occupational Safety and Health Act, which provides that "no employee will suffer material impairment of health or functional capacity even if such employee has regular exposure to the hazard dealt with by such standard for the period of his working life." The law went on to say that "other considerations shall be the latest available scientific data in the field, the feasibility of the standards, and experience gained under this and other health and safety laws."

On July 2, 1980 the U.S. Supreme Court ruled that the new OSHA standard was unjustifiably strict, because the law does not "give OSHA the unbridled discretion to adopt standards designed to create absolutely risk-free workplaces regardless of the costs." It said that, although the current limit is 10 ppm, the actual exposures are often considerably lower. It pointed out that a study by the petrochemical industry reported that, out of a total of 496 employees exposed to benzene, only 53 percent were exposed to levels between 1 and 5 ppm, and only seven were exposed to between 5 and 10 ppm Most of the scientific evidence, on the other hand, concerns exposure well above 10 ppm.

The Court held that a safe work environment is not necessarily a risk-free environment. "Unsafe" means the workplace has a substantial health risk. OSHA must adequately prove that there will be significant health benefits at a reduction to the 1 ppm level. OSHA, on the other hand, believed that in the face of scientific uncertainty, when lives are at risk, it should be able to promulgate strict standards given reasonable estimates of risk. OSHA officials were unhappy that the burden of proof that a certain level of chemical was dangerous was shifted to their shoulders, where formerly (and by the law, as they understood it), the burden of proof was with those who were willing to expose workers to possibly dangerous chemicals.

4.1   Introduction

The conflicting approaches of OSHA and the Supreme Court illustrate legal and probably also moral disagreement. OSHA officials were concerned about protecting workers, regardless of the cost. The Supreme Court justices apparently believed that OSHA officials had not sufficiently taken into account the small numbers of workers affected, the technological problems involved in implementing the new regulations, and the impact of regulations on the employers and the economy. OSHA officials seemed to be concerned almost exclusively with protecting the rights of individuals, whereas the justices were also concerned with promoting the overall good of society.

Despite this disagreement, OSHA officials and the justices probably agreed on many of their basic moral beliefs: that it is wrong to murder, that it is wrong to lie, that it is wrong to fail to keep obligations and responsibilities that one has accepted, that it is in general wrong to endanger the well-being and safety of others, and that one should not impose responsibilities on others that are greater than they can legitimately be expected to bear.

These observations point out the important fact that we usually experience moral disagreement and controversy within a context of agreement. Prior to our disagreement as to what ought to be done, we usually agree about many general moral precepts and factual beliefs. When we disagree, we are often simply not clear, and even here we often agree about the unclear areas and why they are important in the moral disagreement.

When we think about moral issues, we must keep the wide areas of agreement—including agreement as to what is unclear or simply unknown—in mind. The focus on moral problem solving in this book and in most discussions of morality tends to obscure the wide areas of moral agreement that most of us share. In this chapter we consider some of the concepts and distinctions that are useful in understanding both the areas in which we agree about morality and the areas in which we disagree. We begin with a discussion of "common morality," the basic moral beliefs most of us share. Then we focus on the importance of factual issues in moral debates. Next we consider "conceptual issues," or issues involving the meaning of concepts. Then we discuss "application issues," or the problems raised in applying concepts to particular situations. The chapter closes with a discussion of the distinction between two kinds of moral problems: general moral problems and specific moral problems.

4.2   Common Morality

We can call the stock of common moral beliefs *common morality*. The term is used by analogy with the term *common sense*. Just as most of us share a common body of beliefs about the world and about what we must do in order to survive—a body of beliefs that we call *common sense*—so we share a common stock of basic moral beliefs. While this common stock may differ to some extent from one person to another, there is a surprising degree of agreement about the content of common morality.

We also agree in many particular moral judgments. We not only agree that murder is wrong, but we often agree that particular actions are murders, and therefore wrong. We not only agree that for engineers to have undisclosed conflicts of interest is wrong, but that particular states of affairs are undisclosed conflicts of interest, and therefore wrong.

Despite this shared body of fundamental moral beliefs and judgments about particular cases, however, moral disagreement often occurs. Can we isolate the major factors that account for this? In the succeeding sections of this chapter we will do this, but first we focus on common morality.

We have said that there is a body of fundamental moral beliefs that most of us hold in common. Of course people do differ in their moral beliefs, due to such factors as family background and religious training, but most of these differences appear on the level of specific beliefs and judgments. The differences occur with respect to beliefs about specific practices (such as abortion, euthanasia, sexual morality, and capital punishment) or with respect to specific moral judgments (such as the judgment that a particular person should or should not have an abortion). The differences are not as prevalent on the level on which we are now focusing, our more fundamental moral beliefs.

To examine these fundamental moral beliefs more closely, we must formulate them—no easy matter. We shall look at two formulations. Even though these theorists did not necessarily have the concept of common morality in mind, we can take their formulations as summaries of many of its basic beliefs.

One theorist, W. D. Ross, constructed a list of basic duties or obligations, which he called "prima facie" or conditional duties.[1] In using these terms, Ross intended to convey the idea that, although these duties are generally obligatory, they can be overridden in special circumstances.

Ross disclaims "completeness or finality" for his list as an exhaustive account of common morality, but he believes that the list is reasonably complete. We can summarize his prima facie duties in the following list:

R1. Duties resting on our previous acts:
    (a) the duties of fidelity (not to tell lies and to keep promises)
    (b) the duties of reparation for wrong done
R2. Duties of gratitude (e.g., to parents and benefactors)
R3. Duties of justice (e.g., the promotion of a state of affairs in which happiness is proportional to merit)
R4. Duties of beneficence (to improve the condition of others)
R5. Duties of self-improvement (improving ourselves, either morally or intellectually)
R6. Duties not to injure others

Most engineers probably share these moral beliefs, and many engineering codes reflect them. Most codes enjoin engineers to be faithful agents of their employers, and this injunction can be seen to follow from the obligations to fidelity (R1) and gratitude (R2). Most codes oblige engineers to act in a way that protects the health, safety, and welfare of the public, and this obligation follows from the obligations of justice (R3) and beneficence (R4), and especially from the duty not to injure others (R6). Finally, most codes encourage engineers to improve their professional skills, an obligation reflected in R5.

Another theorist, Bernard Gert, has formulated a list of ten "moral rules," which have many similarities to Ross's list of prima facie duties. Although Gert did not offer these rules as a summary of common morality, they would serve that purpose:

G1. Don't kill.
G2. Don't cause pain.
G3. Don't disable.
G4. Don't deprive of freedom.
G5. Don't deprive of pleasure.
G6. Don't deceive.
G7. Keep your promise (or don't break your promise).
G8. Don't cheat.
G9. Obey the law (or don't disobey the law).
G10. Do your duty (or don't fail to do your duty).[2]

G1–G9 might be seen as specifications of Ross's duty not to injure others. G10 might be seen as including R1–R5. Gert, like Ross, believes these rules may on occasion conflict with one another. In this case, we must decide which rule takes priority, and this can only be done in the context of a particular situation.

Gert believes that the precepts of morality fall into two broad categories. The first consists of the ten moral rules. In addition to the ten moral rules, however,

Gert believes that common morality consists of ten "moral ideals," which differ from moral rules in at least two ways. First, while the rules are primarily negative and can be summarized as "Don't cause evil," the moral ideals are more positive in character and are oriented toward reducing the amount of evil in the world. Second, moral ideals are generally only encouraged by morality, whereas moral rules are required. We should not be punished for failing to follow moral ideals, but we often should be punished for failing to follow the moral rules.

The moral ideals can be formulated from the ten moral rules by introducing the word "prevent" and changing the wording of the rules slightly. Thus the moral ideal corresponding to "Don't kill" is "Prevent killing," and the moral ideal corresponding to "Don't cause pain" is "Prevent the causing of pain."

Note that, while the lists of Ross and Gert do not entirely agree, they have many features in common. G1–G5 and G8 appear to be special cases of R6. G6 and G7 are included in R1a. R2–R5 seem to be of a more positive nature, but they have close affinities with Gert's moral ideals. The duty of beneficence is the most obvious example of a prima facie duty that includes many of Gert's moral ideals, but many of the duties of gratitude and justice can be included here as well. Ross's inclusion of a duty to self-improvement may represent a more fundamental difference between himself and Gert, because Gert does not appear to recognize any "duty to ourselves" as a part of common morality.

Also remember that Ross and Gert recognize that the precepts of morality fall into two broad categories and that the most binding moral obligations are primarily negative in character and have to do with the avoidance of harm to others. Ross calls both the negative and positive obligations "duties," while Gert distinguishes between "rules" and "ideals." But Ross recognizes the fundamental distinction and gives greater weight to the negative duty of "non-maleficence."[3]

To understand our use of common morality, we should keep the following points in mind.

First, we should distinguish common morality from both personal morality and professional morality. While it is rare that common morality, personal morality, and professional morality will give three different answers to the same moral question, common morality may sometimes agree with personal morality and sometimes with professional morality. Taking a bribe is contrary to common morality and to professional morality, but it might not be contrary to the personal morality of some people. Likewise, an engineer's decision to refuse to design military hardware might be contrary to her personal morality, but it is not contrary to either professional engineering ethics or to common morality.

Second, many of the standard provisions of engineering codes are simply specific applications of common morality to the engineering profession. Prohibitions against dishonesty are an obvious example. The duty to hold paramount the health, safety, and welfare of the public is an instance of Ross's duty of beneficence and his duty not to injure others or Gert's rules against killing, causing pain, disabling, and depriving of freedom. Prohibitions against deception in representing professional qualifications or misrepresentation of data are instances of Ross's duty not to injure others or Gert's rule against deception. With respect to these provisions, there is no "special" engineering ethics.

Third, common morality recognizes the place of special duties and prerogatives attached to special roles. Ross's duties resting on our previous acts include our duties of loyalty to clients and employers. Gert accounts for "role morality" in terms of his rule requiring us to do our duty.[4] Many of the provisions of engineering codes embody the special role obligations of engineers. Even such provisions as the prohibition of dishonesty can be related to the role of engineers: scientific and technical information cannot be used for the good of clients and the public if engineers are dishonest. The obligations of engineers to hold paramount the health and safety of the public embody role morality, because these go beyond the obligations of nonengineers. Because of their special technical knowledge and their important role in creating the technology that can endanger the health and safety of the public, engineers have a special duty to protect the public from the harm that technological innovation can cause and to use their technical knowledge to benefit the public.

Fourth, the distinction between the negative and positive aspects of common morality, and the fact that priority is usually given to negative duties, enables us to understand some of the perplexing questions that engineers often encounter. But it also shows why this issue is troubling. Few engineers doubt that they should not design products that cause harm, but they differ on how much obligation they have to prevent harm caused by others. For example, does an engineer have an obligation to blow the whistle on wrongdoing committed by other engineers?

Fifth, the relationship of common morality to professional morality is complex. On the one hand, we have pointed out that many of the provisions of engineering codes simply transpose the provisions of common morality into the professional setting. Therefore, much of professional ethics is based on or derived from common morality. On the other hand, common morality is subject to criticism and change. While the prohibitions of dishonesty in common morality are unlikely to change, the beliefs about our obligations to the environment are in the process of modification. Future generations may take certain types of obligations to the environment as uncontroversial, even though today they are the subject of considerable debate. This change may in turn affect the content of the codes.

In this section we have emphasized our common morality. It is very important to remember this as we look at cases calling for ethical sensitivity or reflection. Common morality is an important resource in helping us assess the significance of factual information that is available to us. A primary task in ethically assessing any situation is to assemble information relevant to the resolution of the ethical problem(s) it presents. An ethics case study describes a set of circumstances that calls for ethical reflection. It is helpful to begin an analysis with two questions: (1) What are the relevant facts? (2) What are the relevant kinds of ethical considerations? These two questions are interconnected; they cannot be answered independently of one another. Let's see why.

What are the relevant facts? Note the key term here is "relevant." Relevant to what? To the ethical questions in need of attention. That is, we have to have our eye on what is ethically important in order to know which of the many facts available to us we should be considering. For example, it may be a fact that engineer Joe Smith was wearing a suit and tie on the day he was deciding whether or not to blow the whistle. But it is not obvious that this fact is relevant to the question of whether he should blow the whistle. As Ross and Gert's lists of moral duties and rules make clear, the fact that blowing the whistle might prevent serious injuries is relevant.

What are the relevant kinds of ethical considerations in any given case? Note, again, the key term "relevant." Relevant to what? To the facts of the case. For example, conflicts of interest are important to consider—but only when the facts of a case suggest that there might be a conflict of interest.

What are some of the resources we might use in framing the ethical considerations that might apply to a given case? These are the common, or shared, morality we discussed in this section; professional codes of ethics, discussed in Chapter 2; more general, comprehensive principles of ethics, to be discussed in Chapter 6; and our personal ethics. All of these may be helpful in determining what facts are relevant in any given case.

As we shall see, taking these resources into account can be very complicated and often quite controversial. However, it is not always this way, and it is important not to lose sight of this. The following fictional case illustrates this.

Thirty-four-year-old Steven Severson was in his last semester of the graduate program in mechanical engineering. Father of three small children, he was anxious to get his degree so that he could spend more time with his family. Going to school and holding down a full-time job not only kept him from his family, it shifted more parental responsibility to his wife, Sarah, than he felt was fair. But the end was in sight, and he could look forward both to a better job and to being a better father and husband.

Steven was following in the footsteps of his father, who received a graduate degree in mechanical engineering just months before tragically dying in an automobile accident. Sarah understood how important getting a graduate degree was to Steven, and she never complained about the long hours he spent studying. But she, too, was anxious for this chapter in their lives to end.

As part of his requirement to complete his graduate research and obtain his advanced degree, Steven was required to develop a research report. He compiled a vast amount of data pertaining to the subject of his report. Most of the data strongly supported Steven's conclusion as well as prior conclusions developed by others. However, a few aspects of the data were at variance and not fully consistent with the conclusions contained in his report. Convinced of the soundness of his report and concerned that inclusion of the ambiguous data would detract from and distort the essential thrust of the report, Steven decided to omit references to the ambiguous data in the report. Was it unethical for Steven to fail to include reference to the unsubstantiative data in his report?

We should first notice that there is a great deal of information in the above scenario that is not relevant to the ethical question. While they get our attention and are humanly interesting, the first two paragraphs have no real bearing on the ethical question. Even though they explain why Steven is doing the research, and why he is anxious to bring it to a successful close, none of this is relevant to the question of whether it is right to omit possibly important data from his report. No doubt there is also a great deal of irrelevant unmentioned information—like the size and color of the paper on which he prepared the report, whether or not Steven wears eyeglasses, how tall he is, what he ate for breakfast the day he completed the report, and so on.

In short, what we must do in resolving an ethical question is focus only on those facts that are relevant. Sometimes this may be an easy task, and sometimes the facts make the resolution seem obvious. But in these cases ethical criteria guide the sorting out of relevant from irrelevant facts. These criteria may come from our common morality, professional codes of ethics, or even our personal morality. Hence, we must remind ourselves of all three.

Readers may recognize a similarity between the above case and Case 2.9: Engineer's Duty to Report Data Relating to Research. That case, prepared by NSPE's Board of Ethical Review, consists basically of only the last paragraph of this case. That is, BER streamlined its presentation to include only relevant facts. In any actual case, however, much other information will be present and must be sifted through. We have simply embellished the original BER case with basically irrelevant information in the first two paragraphs of our case.

In the original BER case, the presentation of the scenario is followed by several relevant provisions in NSPE's Code of Ethics. (See the complete presentation of Case 2.9.) These provisions—calling for objectivity, truthfulness, and cooperative exchange of information—seem to settle the matter quite straightforwardly. Steven should not have omitted the data. However, as we shall now see, sorting out matters is often not so easy. Figure 4.1 illustrates the process of moral thinking described above.

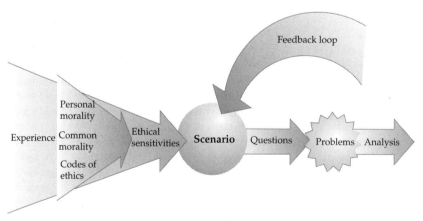

Figure 4.1
The First Phase of Moral Thinking

4.3   Factual Issues

We have seen that we cannot discuss moral issues intelligently apart from a knowledge of the relevant facts. If people disagree over the facts, they may well disagree over the moral judgments they make about a particular issue. To see the importance of facts in a moral controversy, we propose three theses regarding facts.

1. *Many times disagreements that appear to be over moral issues turn out to be disagreements over the relevant facts.* Imagine a conversation between two engineers, Tom and Jim, that might have taken place shortly before OSHA issued its directive in May 1977 that worker exposure to benzene emissions be reduced from 10 ppm to 1 ppm Their conversation might proceed like this:

Tom: I hear OSHA is about to issue stricter regulations regarding worker exposure to benzene. Oh, boy, here we go again! Complying with the new regulations is going to cost our company several million dollars. It's all well and good for the bureaucrats in Washington to make rules, as long as they don't have to pay the bills. I think OSHA is just irresponsible!

Jim: But Tom, human life is at stake! You know the dangers of benzene. Would you want to be out in the area where benzene exposure is an issue? Would you want your son or your daughter to be subjected to exposures as high as 10 ppm?

Tom: I wouldn't have any problem at all. In the first place, the exposure almost never gets that high. And there is just no scientific evidence that exposure to benzene below 10 ppm has any harmful effect. In fact, the scientific literature I have read and the data I have seen from our own studies indicates that exposure to benzene below 10 ppm is not harmful.

Tom shows Jim some of the evidence he has collected. The next day the conversation continues:

Jim: Well, Tom, maybe I was wrong. The data you showed me looks more convincing than anything I have seen. I thought the evidence was on my side, but now I believe it is on yours.

In this scenario, Jim and Tom agree when they see eye to eye on the facts. What looked like a moral disagreement was a lack of common agreement about the facts of the situation.

It is particularly important for engineering students to understand this: many apparent moral disagreements are reducible to disagreements over factual (in many cases technical) matters. Sometimes engineers and engineering students, after debate over professional ethics issues, come away with an attitude that might be stated like this: "Well, here was another dispute about ethics in which nobody could agree. I am glad that I am in engineering, where everything depends on the facts that everybody can agree on. Ethics is just too subjective."

Yet many times apparent moral disagreement is really disagreement over factual issues, not disagreement over moral issues.

Here is another example. Suppose two engineers, Judy and Jane, disagree over whether the government should enforce affirmative action policies in the workplace. They may think their disagreement is over the moral issue of the permissibility of affirmative action policies. Further discussion may reveal, however, that their real disagreement is over the factual question of how discrimination can be eliminated. On the one hand, Judy may think that, without affirmative action policies, women and minorities will continue to experience gross discrimination in the workplace. Jane, on the other hand, may believe that fair treatment in the workplace can be achieved without governmental intervention. Furthermore, Jane may admit that if governmental intervention is the only way to eliminate injustice in the hiring system, she would be in favor of it too. Thus the real difference between Judy and Jane is not over moral beliefs, but over a factual belief about what it takes to eliminate unjust hiring practices. If they could agree on the factual question as to how injustice to women and minorities could be eliminated, they could agree on their moral evaluation of the permissibility of government intervention.

2. *Factual issues are sometimes very difficult to resolve.* The dispute between Tom and Jim was very easy to resolve. Tom pointed out some facts that were common knowledge, but which Jim did not know. When Jim was shown the facts, he changed his position. Often, however, the factual issues are not easily resolved. Sometimes the information is not available, and sometimes it is difficult to imagine how it could be available. In the dispute over affirmative action, for example, it would be very difficult to resolve the factual issue over whether affirmative action is the only method for eliminating discrimination in the workplace. We would like to try each option for 100 years and compare the two, but such social experiments are impossible. Many technical and scientific issues are also in dispute and are not capable of resolution at a given time. When moral judgments depend on the resolution of these issues, the moral judgments are going to be controversial.

3. *Once the factual issues are clearly isolated, moral disagreement can re-emerge on another and often more clearly defined level.* Suppose Judy and Jane finally agree that their dispute over whether affirmative action policies are necessary to eliminate injustice in hiring policies cannot be resolved. Then they might have the following conversation:

Judy: So we both agree that if we knew affirmative action policies were the only way to eliminate injustice in hiring practices, we would say affirmative action was a good thing. You say you are convinced affirmative action is not the only way to eliminate injustice, and I believe it is. But I still think you are wrong in what you conclude from this. I believe we should promote affirmative action in the face of this factual uncertainty, because it is better to err on the side of promoting justice for women and minorities.

Jane: I think we still disagree, Judy. I believe we should give the benefit of the doubt to employers. If we don't know that affirmative action policies are really necessary to promote justice, we ought to let employers exercise their own judgment. This is more likely to promote economic efficiency.

Judy: But surely justice is more important than economic efficiency! If we don't know what the facts are, I believe we should give the benefit of the doubt to the employees. We ought to give more weight to considerations of justice.

Jane: Remember that if we enforce affirmative action we are only *possibly* preventing injustice, while we are very likely to diminish economic efficiency, because we might not be hiring the most appropriate person for the job. Besides, economic efficiency is not the only consideration. We also have to consider the freedom of the employer to do what he wants with his own company. Again, we are trading off almost certain losses in economic efficiency and certain losses in employer freedom against a possible increase in justice. I don't think this is a good trade-off.

Judy: But Jane, depriving people of equal opportunity in the workplace is very serious business. It strikes at the heart of people's self-esteem and ability to pursue their own goals in life. Surely even the chance of injuring people in this way is more important than the kinds of considerations you bring up. And with respect to your argument about employer freedom, I don't think affirmative action programs limit employer freedom in a very serious way.

Jane: Sorry, Judy, but I still disagree.

Here a value disagreement re-emerges, but now it is more precisely formulated. Now Judy and Jane understand that they are disagreeing over what should be done in the light of the factual uncertainty as to whether affirmative action is the only way to end discrimination. Jane thinks that in the light of this uncertainty the benefit of the doubt should go to employers and Judy thinks it should go to women and minorities. The considerations necessary to resolve this disagreement are different from the considerations necessary to resolve the original disagreement—which turned out to be over the facts. Now the disagreement is over what the best policy is in the face of factual uncertainty. This is more clearly a matter of moral disagreement.

Discerning Relevant Facts

We have seen that in many cases uncertainty and disagreement over moral issues can be traced to uncertainty and disagreement over facts. Not all facts are relevant to a moral issue. Call to mind the previous conversation between Tom and Jim about worker exposure to benzene. Whether the workers were male or female would not ordinarily be relevant to whether they deserved to be protected from exposure to benzene. It might be relevant under certain conditions, however. If research shows that males are more susceptible than females to the effects of benzene, then males might deserve special protection. This would be the result of their special vulnerability, however, not the result of their gender. If research shows that fetuses are even more likely to be harmed by exposure to benzene than adult males, then pregnant women would deserve more consideration than either men or nonpregnant women.

In both of these cases, the moral relevance of these facts will probably not be disputed by most people. The issue under consideration is protection from harm. If men are more likely to be harmed than women and fetuses still more likely to be harmed than men, then the degree of protection should correspond to the degree of vulnerability to harm.

The relevance of some facts to a moral issue can be more controversial. Suppose Engineer Edward must dismiss several of the technicians under his management. Should he dismiss the women and racial minorities because they were the last hired, or should he not dismiss them because of past inequities in the hiring of women and racial minorities? Here the relevance of race and gender is itself morally controversial. In disciplining an employee for theft, we would be much less inclined to take gender and race into account. If we did, it would probably be because of other factors that might be related to race or gender, such as degree of financial need.

Known and Unknown Facts

Many of the facts relevant to the resolution of moral disputes are known, but sometimes the facts are not known and therefore moral disagreements cannot be resolved. Thus it is important to distinguish not only between relevant and irrelevant facts, but between known relevant facts and unknown relevant facts. Their relationship is illustrated by Figure 4.2.

As this figure illustrates, we are concerned with the facts that are relevant to the resolution of a moral issue; some are known and some unknown. The known relevant facts are only some of the relevant facts about a moral issue. In this figure, more of the relevant facts are known than unknown. We must attempt to find answers to unanswered factual questions.

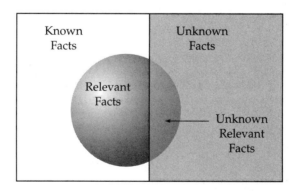

Figure 4.2
Analyzing the Facts

4.4   Conceptual Issues

Sometimes apparent moral disagreement turns out to be disagreement over conceptual issues, that is, over the meaning or definition of terms. In the benzene case, the most obvious conceptual issue has to do with the proper definition of "safe." Closely related to this is the definition of what constitutes a "substantial" health risk, or what constitutes a "material impairment" of health. Finally, the definition of "burden of proof" can be a point of controversy, especially if we are considering the issue from a moral and not merely a legal standpoint, where the term may be more clearly defined.

We can imagine a continuation of the conversation between Tom and Jim that illustrates the importance of some of these conceptual issues.

Jim: Tom, I've conceded that you are right about the facts. The evidence that exposures to benzene between 1 and 10 ppm is harmful is weak at best, but I think I was too hasty in concluding that this is the end of the matter. I'll go back to one of my original points: human life is involved. I just don't believe we should take a chance on harming people when we aren't certain about the facts. I think we ought to provide a safe environment for our workers, and I wouldn't call an environment "safe" when there is even a chance that the disputed benzene levels are harmful.

Tom: Here we go again on that old saw, "How safe is safe?" How can you say that something is not safe when you don't have any evidence to back up your claim?

Jim: I think something is unsafe when there is any kind of substantial health risk.

Tom: But how can you say there is any substantial health risk when there is no evidence for your claim and when, in fact, the evidence that is available seems to point in the other direction?

Jim: Well, I would say that there is a substantial health risk when there is any reason to suspect that there is a problem, at least when something like carcinogens are involved. The burden of proof should rest on anyone who wants to expose a worker to even a possible danger.

Tom: I'll agree with you that workers should not be exposed to substantial health risks, but I think this is a strange definition of "substantial." Let me put the question another way. Suppose the risk of dying from cancer due to benzene exposure in the plant over a period of thirty years is no greater than the risk over the same period of time of dying from an automobile accident while driving home from the plant. Would you consider the health risk from benzene exposure in this case to be "substantial"?

Jim: Yes I would. The conditions are different. I believe we have made highways about as safe as we can. We have not made health conditions for workers in plants as safe as we can. We can lower the level of benzene exposure in the plant, and with a relatively moderate expenditure. Furthermore, everyone understands the risks involved in auto travel. Many of the workers don't understand the risk from benzene exposure. They aren't acting as free agents with informed consent.

Tom: Wow! I don't think we are going to get anywhere on this one. Let's try another approach. Suppose at the lower levels of benzene exposure—I mean under 10 ppm—the risk of cancer is virtually nil, but some workers find that the exposure causes the skin on their faces, hands, and arms to be drier than usual. They can treat this with skin lotion. Would you consider this a health problem?

Jim: Yes, I would. I think it would be what some people would call a "material impairment" of health, and I would agree. Workers should not have to endure *any* change in their health or bodily well-being as a result of working at our plant. People are selling their time to the company, but not their bodies and their health. And dry skin is certainly unhealthy.

Tom: Well, this just seems too strict. I guess we really do disagree. We don't even seem to be able to agree over what we mean by the words we use.

Here genuine disagreement over moral issues has reappeared, but this time in the form of disagreement over the definitions of crucial terms. Many concepts, such as "safe," "substantial," "health," and "material impairment," are a blend of factual elements and value elements. Tom and Jim might agree on the effects of exposure to benzene at various levels and still disagree as to what is "safe" or "healthy" and what is not. In order to know whether benzene is safe, we have to have some notion of what the risks are at various exposure levels, but we also have to have a notion of what we consider "acceptable risk." The use of the term "acceptable" should be sufficient to alert us that there is a value element here that cannot be determined by the facts.

Here is another example. Suppose Bill is an engineer who represents his U.S. company in the foreign country of Morotavia. One day he is told by a Morotavian official that his company's warehouses may catch fire and the firemen may not arrive in time to extinguish the fire unless Bill's company contributes $100,000 to the official's reelection campaign. What should Bill do?

The Foreign Corrupt Practices Act of 1977 distinguishes between "bribes" and "extortion." It allows American companies to pay extortion in some cases, but not bribes, so it is important to know whether the payment would be a bribe or an extortion. It is not easy to give a complete definition of either bribery or extortion, i.e., the set of conditions both necessary and sufficient for something to qualify. It is easier to give a "characterization," a condition that, if met, is sufficient for something to count as either bribery or extortion. The following characterizations will be adequate for our purposes:

Bribery = Voluntary offering of goods, services, or money by the briber to secure an unjustified privilege to the briber.

Extortion = Nonvoluntary provision of goods, services, or money to the extortioner to secure treatment, to which one is already lawfully and morally entitled, from the extortioner.

According to these characterizations, Bill's company is being asked to pay extortion, not bribery.

Not only do the characterizations of these terms involve value terms, such as "unjustified privilege" and "morally entitled," but the question of moral permissibility raises ethical questions as well. In general, paying bribery, which is voluntary, seems more morally serious than paying extortion, which is nonvoluntary. Furthermore, extortion merely allows one to obtain what she is entitled to anyhow, whereas bribery enables one to obtain something she does not deserve—at least not as a result of bribery. While paying extortion may be unjustifiable in many situations (and extracting extortion is always unjustifiable), there are morally relevant differences between bribery and extortion. Regardless of how one resolves the question of what Bill should do, it is important to know which he is contemplating. And if one were to define these terms differently, their moral evaluation might be quite different.

The definitions or characterizations of some terms do not involve such obvious value issues. In thinking about the benzene case, we want to be sure that we agree about the meanings of such terms as "cancer" or "leukemia." Although scientists might well dispute the precise definitions of these diseases, no obvious value terms are present here. In debating what caused the leukemia, there could well be disagreements about what constitutes a "cause." Again, no obvious value terms are here. While some conceptual issues involve important value questions, some do not.

Usually the question of the meaning of a concept arises because we do not know how the concept applies to a particular situation. Sometimes such a question can be most appropriately resolved by a reexamination and further definition of the concept itself. Michael Davis provides an example of this tactic.[5] Most engineering codes require engineers to give priority to the health, safety, and welfare of the "public." How should we understand the scope of the term "public"? For example, how should this term have been interpreted by Roger Boisjoly when, on the night before the fateful launch of the Challenger, he was considering his obligations as an engineer? Are the astronauts part of the "public" and thus proper objects of the engineer's professional concern? Davis considers three ways in which we might interpret the term "public."

First, the "public" might include everyone. In this case, the astronauts are clearly a part of the public. Davis believes, however, that this is an unrealistic definition of "public," because few dangers are likely to threaten everyone, and the obligation would demand too little. The engineer's work might often threaten some of the public without threatening everyone.

A second possible definition takes this observation into account by defining "public" as "anyone" who might be threatened by the engineer's professional activities. This definition might imply that engineers should not do anything that threatens anyone who stands to be affected. If so, it is still too broad, for it would make engineering impossible. For example, it is difficult to imagine how we could have electric power stations or manufacturing plants that would not pose any threat to anyone.

A third and more plausible definition of "public" begins with the claim that what makes people part of the "public" is that they are liable to be affected by engineering services without being in a position to give free or informed consent to these effects. The "public," that is, is characterized by their relative innocence, helplessness, and passivity. On this interpretation, "public" would refer to those persons whose lack of information, technical knowledge, or time for deliberation renders them more or less vulnerable to the powers an engineer wields on behalf of his client or employer.[6]

As Davis points out, this interpretation implies that someone might be part of the public in one respect and not in another. For example, the astronauts would be a part of the public with respect to the danger of explosion due to the faulty O-rings, because they had no knowledge of the danger. They would not be a part of the public with respect to the ice formation on the booster rockets, for they were aware of this danger and evidently gave their informed consent to the risk involved. They could have chosen to abort the launch if they were unwilling to accept these risks.

Given this definition of "public," the moral principle that engineers should look after the health, welfare, and safety of the public does apply to the astronauts. Roger Boisjoly did have an obligation as an engineer to try to protect the astronauts from dangers to which they had not given their informed consent. We can of course question this definition of "public" and offer alternative definitions. However, if we accept it, Boisjoly's obligation seems to be settled. In this way, the resolution of a conceptual issue can help to resolve a moral issue.

4.5   Application Issues

We were able to trace part of Tom and Jim's disagreement to their different definitions of such terms as "safe" and "material impairment" of health. Sometimes, however, people appear to have the same definitions of terms, but disagree on their application in particular situations. There are several reasons why this might happen. First, because they may be operating from different factual premises, people who agree on meanings or definitions of key terms may apply them differently. Second, people may agree on the facts and the meanings or definitions of key terms but disagree about the relevance or importance of certain laws, policies, or ethical principles. All of these are, in some sense, application issues. However, in this section we emphasize a special kind, one that rests on a common feature of concepts. Attempts to specify the meanings of terms ahead of time can never anticipate all of the cases to which they do and do not apply. No matter how precisely one attempts to determine the meaning of a concept, it will always remain open-ended. That is, it will always remain insufficiently specified, so that some of its applications to particular circumstances will remain problematic. In such cases there is an *application issue*, which is closely related to a conceptual issue. Conceptual issues involve defining a concept; application issues involve applying the concept to a particular situation.

We can distinguish conceptual and application issues in a somewhat more formal way. If we let "*X*" refer to a concept, such as "keeping confidentiality" or "proprietary information," a conceptual issue has to do with what *X* is, that is, with what characteristics *X* has. An application issue has to do with whether a given situation *counts* as an instance of *X*. It is one thing to determine what we *mean* by "safe" and another thing to determine whether a given situation should *count* as safe, considering the definition. In many situations a clear definition of a term can make the application unproblematic. Many times the concept either clearly does or does not apply to a situation. Sometimes, however, this is not the case. As we have said, this is because definitions cannot possibly be so clear and complete that every possible situation clearly does or clearly does not count as an instance of the concept. It is this inherent limitation of all definitions and explanations of concepts that gives rise to application issues.

It is sometimes difficult to know whether two people disagree on the definitions of concepts or on their application to a particular situation. There are at least two reasons for this. First, as we have seen, all definitions are open-ended—they cannot cover all of the situations that one might find in his or her experience. That is, the definitions cannot be specified in enough detail so that in every possible situation it is clear whether the concept in question describes the situation. Second, we often may want to change or modify our definitions of crucial terms in the face of experience. Sometimes an experience may not appear to exemplify the concept as we have defined it, but we believe it should count as an instance of the concept. In this case the experience prompts us to modify the definition. We can summarize the process of analyzing a moral issue in Figure 4.3.

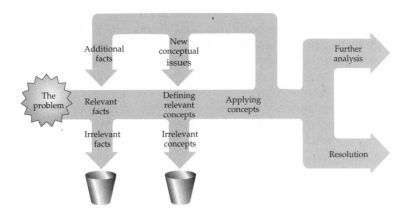

Figure 4.3
Analyzing a Moral Problem

A moral problem presents itself. We must determine the facts necessary to resolve the problem, then we must define the relevant concepts and apply them to the case. If there is still controversy, we must proceed to the types of moral analysis discussed in the next chapters. Sometimes the facts and concepts we need do not become apparent until the analysis is in process. The feedback arrows show that moral analysis helps to isolate the relevant facts and concepts through an iterative process.

4.6   General and Specific Moral Problems

One final distinction is helpful in moral thinking. Most moral disagreements occur on one of two levels of generality. The moral problems or issues we have dealt with so far have to do for the most part with what should be done in a specific situation. We shall call these *specific moral problems*. Bill's question as to whether he should pay the $100,000 to a Morotavian official's reelection campaign was a specific moral problem.

Some moral problems are more general in nature. Rather than having to do with what should be done in a particular situation, they raise more general questions about policy, about what should be done in situations of a certain general type. We shall refer to these as *general moral problems*. If Judy and Jane disagree over the moral acceptability of the affirmative action policy, they are not simply in disagreement over what should be done in a specific set of circumstances, but over what policies in general are morally appropriate.

Most of the moral problems that engineers face are specific, but sometimes more general issues arise, such as issues about the policies that should be adopted by the engineering community. When we consider how the professional engineering community should respond to such issues as the environment or the rights of professional employees, for example, we are dealing with general moral problems. As with specific moral problems, these disagreements often turn out to be over facts and over concepts. They might also involve disagreements over the applications of concepts to a general *type* of action rather than a specific action.

An example is the controversy over advertising and competitive pricing. Engineers in private practice constitute only a small percentage of the membership of the engineering profession. For them, however, advertising and competitive bidding are vital issues. Prior to the 1980s, most engineering codes contained provisions severely limiting advertising and price competition by engineers in private practice. Section 5 in the 1974 code of the Engineers' Council for Professional Development (ECPD), which has been superseded by the Accreditation Board for Engineering and Technology (ABET), reads:

> 5. Engineers shall build their professional reputation on the merit of their services and shall not compete unfairly with others.

As the following subsections reveal, "unfair" competition includes virtually all advertising and price competition.

> 5.c. Engineers should negotiate a method and rate of compensation commensurate with the agreed upon scope of services. A meeting of the minds of the parties to the contract is essential to mutual confidence. The public interest requires that the cost of engineering services be fair and reasonable, but not the controlling consideration in selection of individuals or firms to provide these services.

> 5.g. Engineers may advertise professional services only as a means of identification and limited to the following:

> (g.1) Professional cards and listings in recognized and dignified publications, provided they are consistent in size and are in a section of the publication regularly devoted to such professional cards and listings. The information displayed must be restricted to firm name, address, telephone number, appropriate symbol, names of principal participants and the fields of practice in which the firm is qualified. . . . . (g.4) Listings in the classified section of telephone directories, limited to name, address, telephone number and specialties in which the firm is qualified without resorting to special or bold type.

> 5.l. Engineers shall not enter competitions for designs for the purpose of obtaining commissions for specific projects, unless provision is made for reasonable compensation for all designs submitted.

These guidelines prohibited engineers from submitting bids without compensation and from advertising, except in highly restricted forms.

In the 1970s, however, the U.S. Supreme Court issued some important decisions that have fundamentally changed professional practice in the areas of advertising and price competition. In the 1977 decision, *Bates* v. *State Bar of Arizona*, the Supreme Court declared that it was a violation of the Sherman Antitrust Act for the Arizona state bar to forbid two lawyers, Bates and O'Steen, from advertising the services and prices at their legal clinic in the Phoenix newspaper.[7] The Court did place some restrictions on professional advertisements. (1) They should only be for routine services, (2) they should not be misleading or deceptive, and (3) they should be restrained as to claims for the quality of professional services.

In 1975 the Court ruled, in *Goldfarb* v. *Virginia State Bar*, that the state bar may not prohibit deviations from set fees for title insurance.[8] The Court suggested, however, that state legislatures could prohibit competitive pricing of professional services in a given profession if they (1) created a mechanism (such as a state board of registration) to regulate the profession, (2) promulgated a specific policy against competitive pricing in the professions, and (3) compelled professionals to comply with this policy. On April 25, 1978, the Court applied this doctrine directly to the engineering profession, ruling that the National Society of Professional Engineers' (NSPE) ban on competitive bidding was not permissible under the Sherman Antitrust Act.

These decisions resulted in changes in the codes of most engineering societies. They did not, however, put to rest the controversy over the desirability of advertising and competitive bidding by professionals, or over how the professional societies and state registration boards should regulate these two activities within the guidelines set out by the Court. In order to illustrate some of the controversies over advertising and competitive bidding, let us imagine a conversation between two consulting engineers, Caroline and Bill, which might have occurred in the late 1970s, at the time of the two Supreme Court decisions.

Caroline: I guess our world is about to change, Bill. It looks like we're going to be right in there with roofing contractors and pest exterminators as far as advertising and competitive bidding go. The Supreme Court has really knocked the wind out of our professional status with their decision that professional societies must not forbid advertising and competitive bidding for professional services.

Bill: Well, Caroline, maybe things aren't as bad as you think. After all, the Court's rulings against prohibitions of advertising and competitive bidding apply to all professions, not just engineering, so our professional status won't change relative to the other professions. Besides, some limitations on these activities are still allowed.

Caroline: I know, but things are going to change. I really think it's disgraceful. It's bad for our self-image as professionals, and if we think less of ourselves, we'll produce lower quality work. You know all the codes in engineering and every other profession have traditionally said that professionals may not advertise or engage in competitive bidding, except in special circumstances and within strict limitations.

Bill: I'm not so sure it's bad for either engineers or the public. As far as harming our self-image is concerned, I think it's a matter of what you get used to. When everybody gets used to professionals' advertising, it won't harm our self-image. And allowing advertising and competitive bidding may benefit the public. Advertising may give a client knowledge about other engineers, and competitive pricing might result in lower costs for professional services.

Caroline: I can't believe you've said that! Sure, the changes might result in lower prices for professional services, but it's going to lead to cost-cutting measures that will lower quality as well. As for the value of advertising, it will just lead potential clients to select an engineering firm on the basis of the firm's expertise in advertising and public relations, rather than its expertise in engineering. Besides, the cost of advertising must be added into the engineer's expense, so it could even increase the cost of engineering services.

Bill: I admit that this could be true, but I suspect it will not work out that way. Studies have been done that compare the price and quality of eyeglasses and prescription medicines in states where price competition is allowed with price and quality in states where it's not allowed. The results seem to show that price competition doesn't lower quality, although it does lower price.

I believe allowing advertising and competitive pricing might lower the price of professional services without decreasing the quality. You say that allowing advertising and competitive pricing will decrease the quality of professional services and might even increase the price. Anyhow, I think it's interesting that we both agree that engineers should practice their profession in accordance with policies that promote the public welfare. We just seem to disagree over the facts.

This conversation represents a disagreement over a general moral problem. The real disagreement between Caroline and Bill is not over the moral principle that "engineers should practice their profession in accordance with policies that promote the public welfare," but rather over the factual question of whether allowing advertising and competitive bidding in the professions (and engineering in particular) promotes the public welfare.

Will allowing advertising in engineering lower the quality of professional work or the professional status of engineers? Many engineers believe that it will "reduce" the professions to a "mere business" and perhaps even destroy professionalism itself. Milton Lunch, in his discussion of the 1977 decision on advertising, asks, "What is the next step down the 'slippery slope' as the drive against professional ethics continues and expands?" Later in the same article he wonders whether "the survival of the professions" is possible in the light of the decision.[9] But this rhetorical flourish falls short of empirical substantiation of his claims.

Some empirical studies suggest that advertising and competitive pricing may not be detrimental to quality. One of the studies referred to by Bill is Lee Benham's study of the effect of advertising on the price of eyeglasses.[10] Some states allow advertising eyeglasses and others prohibit it. Therefore a comparison of price structures in the two markets is instructive. In 1963, the most recent year for which data were available for the study, approximately three-quarters of the states had some restrictions on the advertising of eyeglasses. An example of a restrictive state is Florida:

> "Unprofessional conduct". . . is defined to mean any conduct of a character likely to deceive or defraud the public, including among other things free examination advertising, price advertising, billboard advertising, use of any advertising either directly or indirectly, whether printed, radio, display, or any nature which seeks to solicit practice on any installment payment or price plan. . . .[11]

The data were obtained from a subsample of 634 people covered in a 1963 survey of a national sample of those who underwent an eye examination and/or obtained eyeglasses in that year. Benham found "the difference in mean prices of eyeglasses between the two categories of states is $6.70, with the lower mean price found in states having no advertising restrictions. . . ."[12] Benham also states that he found no "systematic quality differences" between those firms that advertised and those that did not.[13] In July 1971, Benham surveyed nineteen retail outlets in Texas and New Mexico. The mean price sampled in New Mexico, a state with strict advertising laws, was $31.70; in Texas, a state without restrictions, the price was $25.90.[14]

Another empirical study of the effects of advertising on product price was done in 1976 by John Cady, this time on prescription drugs.[15] Regulation of advertising by pharmacies is enacted at the state level through legislation lobbied for by associations representing pharmacists and through state pharmacy boards. Since state pharmacy boards are composed primarily of licensed pharmacists, the profession of pharmacy is basically self-regulating. At the time of the study, laws and administrative regulations restricting retail pharmacists from advertising prescription drug prices were in force in thirty-three states. State restrictions on prescription drug advertising include controls on the use of outdoor signs, prohibitions on promotional schemes, on advertising prescription drug prices, and on advertising that implies a policy of discount drug pricing. For purposes of the study, states were classified as "regulated" if one or more of these restrictions was in effect in 1970.

The typical justification given by the pharmacy profession for price regulation is that deregulation will reduce pharmacy services, while not necessarily reducing prices. The method chosen for testing this claim was to compare services and prices in states prohibiting price advertising with those in states that do not. A national sample of more than 1,900 pharmacies was conducted in 1970 by R. A. Gosselin, a marketing research firm. An index of the prescription price level of each pharmacy was developed by taking the mean of the selling prices of ten widely used drugs in various pharmacological categories. Service was measured by whether the pharmacy did or did not offer consumers (1) delivery of prescription drugs, (2) prescription drug credit accounts, (3) prescription drug emergency service, (4) family prescription monitoring records, and (5) a waiting area for customers.

The study found that prescription drug prices were a statistically significant 5.20 percent higher in regulated states than unregulated states. The only significant difference in service was in category 4: pharmacists in regulated states were more likely to monitor drug use by families and individuals. It may be that these pharmacists, realizing such that record-keeping holds customers, use this method as one of the few competitive techniques available. Cady concludes that "the regulation of prescription drug price advertising, promulgated and defended by organizations representing retail pharmacists, appears to benefit pharmacists only."[16]

We can object in various ways to these studies as a basis for a claim that advertising in engineering should not be prohibited.[17] First, there is little if any confirmation (or, for that matter, disconfirmation) of Cady's results by other studies. Second, without knowing the income of pharmacists in states that do and do not permit advertising, we cannot be sure that the presence or absence of advertising is correlated with differences in income. Third, we do not know how directly either Benham's or Cady's studies apply to advertising in engineering. The studies do serve, however, to cast at least some measure of doubt on the claim that restriction of advertising and competitive pricing of engineering services benefits the public. More important for our purposes, they illustrate the kinds of empirical studies relevant to the dispute between Bill and Caroline.

The engineering profession has a responsibility to consider the issue of advertising and competitive pricing from the standpoint of the public interest, not from the standpoint of the economic self-interest of engineers. And empirical studies are important in determining what general policies are really in the public interest.

Conceptual issues also play a part in reasoning with general moral problems, just as with specific moral problems. In the argument between Caroline and Bill, one of the crucial terms is "welfare." In this case, we might define "welfare" as "the best professional services at the lowest possible price." Do we then consider service more important than price, or price more important than service? Even here there is a dispute about definitions. In other cases the conceptual issues may be equally or even more controversial. The reference in the ECPD code to "unfair" competition raises a conceptual issue. General moral problems can cover such topics as the importance of informed consent, the necessity for honesty in reporting research and test data, and many other conceptual issues.

There can also be application issues in arguments over general moral problems. While most of us believe that we should not deceive others, we may disagree as to whether "puffery" or exaggeration in advertising is a form of dishonesty. If it is, then common morality's prohibition of deception means that puffery is wrong. Others might argue that puffery, unless it is extreme, should not be counted as a form of deception. If this view is accepted and there are no other arguments against puffery, then a principle in an engineering code that prohibits puffery in advertising is unjustified.

Sometimes even when disagreements over facts, concepts, and their application have been sorted out, genuine moral disagreements remain. Here we must engage in moral problem solving, which is the subject of the next chapter.

4.7   Chapter Summary

Most of us agree about what is right and wrong in many particular situations, as well as over many moral rules or principles. Nevertheless, we are all familiar with moral disagreement, whether it occurs with respect to general rules or principles or with respect to what ought to be done in a particular situation.

It is possible to isolate several sources of ethical disagreement. We can disagree over the factual issues relevant to an ethical problem. If two people disagree over the relevant facts, they may disagree as to what ought to be done in a particular situation, even though they have the same moral beliefs. We can also disagree over conceptual issues, over the meanings of crucial terms in an ethical problem. We can further disagree over application issues, over whether and how certain crucial terms apply to a given situation. We might agree that deception is wrong but disagree over whether withholding information in a bargaining situation should count as deception.

Moral problems usually exist at various levels of generality; it is useful to divide them into two groups, however. Specific moral problems have to do with what should be done in a particular situation, such as whether John should correctly report the data on tests he had made. General moral problems apply to a class of issues, such as whether engineers should engage in advertising and competitive bidding.

Case Analyses

Case 4.1 The Co-Op Student[18]

Project leader Bruce Barton was being sorely pressed to complete the development of several engineering prototypes for a field test of a new appliance model for Innovation, Inc. One particular plastic component of the new model had given difficulty in laboratory tests, failing repeatedly before reaching the stress level necessary for successful operation. Bruce had directed a redesign of the component using a tough new engineering plastic recommended by the research laboratory's material science department. Stress tests had to be run on the redesigned component, but Bruce was running short of time and needed to get on with building the prototype.

Bruce sought out the manager of the material science department for help in running stress tests on samples of the new component. With this assistance he could go ahead with prototype building and conduct the tests concurrently. The prototypes, of course, would not be released to field test until the stress tests on the redesigned component proved its design to be satisfactory.

Tom Mason, manager of the material science department, was willing to assist because he knew how critical completion of the development was to Innovation's future appliance plans. However, this was also a busy time for Tom's department, so Tom suggested to Bruce that he could assign the test work to one of the engineering co-op students. Tom was also coordinator of engineering co-op students, and he liked to use them in demanding situations to give them practical experience.

Tom assigned the test work to Jack Jacobs, an engineering co-op student from the state university who was completing his second work session at Innovation. Jack was familiar with the test equipment and previously had done similar test work. Jack was a good student and his co-op work had been unusually well done. Tom commented to Jack that he would need to work diligently to complete the tests before he had to return to state university.

Jack completed the tests on schedule and turned in a report to Tom indicating the component had successfully passed the stress tests. Upon completion of the test report, Jack returned to the university for his next school session. Tom gave Bruce the good news. The prototypes were completed and the field test of these prototypes got under way on schedule.

A few weeks later, Bruce rushed into Tom's office to tell him that most of the prototypes were out of operation because of a catastrophic failure of the component that had been tested in Tom's lab. Bruce wanted to discuss the test immediately with Jack; but since Jack had already returned to the university, he and Tom settled for studying Jack's lab notebook.

After looking at Jack's notebook, Tom said, "Bruce, I hate to say it but these data look *too good*. I know the equipment and there should be more scatter in the measurements Jack took. I think some, if not all, these measurements are in error or they have been faked! At best, Jack probably took a few points and 'extrapolated' the rest!"

Analysis

Let us analyze this case in terms of the relevant facts, conceptual issues, and application issues. Before attempting to sort out these issues, however, we should think about the major moral issues involved in the case. This is because the factual, conceptual, and application issues that we consider are those that are important in resolving the moral problem. We also have to decide whose perspective we are going to take in answering the question. Several standpoints are possible, but it is most reasonable to take the perspective of Jack, the co-op student.

What is the moral issue that Jack faces? He has an obligation both to do the job well and to do it fast. Or, if he made the tests and found that the component failed, his problem may have been that he wanted both to please his superiors and to do the tests right, and he could not do both. But the first problem is probably the more plausible one.

The important factual issues are the following:

1. What happened in the testing? Did Jack fake the results or just make an error of some type?
2. Since the basic conflict was between doing the job right and doing it on time, did Jack in fact have enough time to do the job right?
3. If Jack could not do the job (either because he was incompetent or because he just did not have enough time), was it possible to get other people involved who could help him with his time problem or could show him how to do the job right?
4. Was it standard practice to let a co-op student do a job this important? If so, this is relevant to the question of who is *responsible* for the errors. This is not central to how Jack should resolve his problem, but it is central to another issue, that of responsibility. We will not consider this further here, but a key consideration in this case is Tom's responsibility as Jack's immediate supervisor.

Note that there are many other factual questions that can be raised, but the factual issues that are raised should be those that are important in resolving the moral issues in the case.

Now let us turn to the conceptual issues.

1. If one of the issues in understanding what Jack should do involves whether there was fakery or error, there is an obvious problem here. What do we mean by "fake"? Think of some ways to define "fake." For example, the basic idea of fakery is a deliberate misrepresentation of facts, that you lead people to have a belief that you know is wrong.

2. Another conceptual issue is, "What makes a 'satisfactory' design?" What are the criteria for satisfactorily passing the stress test? Here we do not know enough to state these criteria, and this does not seem like a conceptual issue that is likely to be controversial. Probably the criteria were clearly laid out and agreed on by all involved. Maybe we could say the design is "satisfactory" if it passes tests that are generally agreed on by the participants.

3. Since there is a possibility that Jack simply made an error, what do we mean by "error"? This again does not seem like a question that is likely to be controversial, and it is also a term that we would find hard to define without much more detailed knowledge of the case. Perhaps we could say that "error" is a failure to get or record accurate measurements.

The application issues are as follows.

1. What should *count* as faking the tests? You should provide some alternative resolutions to this issue, although you do not have to decide on the correct one in this exercise. Of course, since you do not know precisely what Jack did, you cannot say, "Here's what Jack did. Was it faking?" All you can do is suggest some things he *might* have done. For the purposes of this analysis, you do not even have to say which ones you would consider faking—just list some possibilities. Jack might have simply smoothed out a curve after taking a number of data points. He might have taken a single measure and filled in the rest. He might have taken two or three

measures and guessed at the rest. Which (if any) would we count as faking?

2. If we knew more of the facts of the case, we might have a major application problem trying to decide whether the component was "satisfactory" in terms of the tests. In other words, did the design pass the stress test in a way that could be called "satisfactory"? If the test numbers were just barely under minimal criteria, would the tests show the component is "satisfactory"?

3. What would count as "error" on Jack's part? Would something count as Jack's "error" if, unknown to Jack, the test equipment was faulty?

Case 4.2 Borrowed Tools[19]

Entil Corporation permits its employees to borrow company tools. Engineer Al House took full advantage of this privilege. He went one step further and ordered tools for his unit that would be useful for his home building projects even though they were of no significant use to his unit at Entil. Engineer Michael Green had suspected for some time that Al was ordering tools for personal rather than company use, but he had no unambiguous evidence until he overheard a revealing conversation between Al and Bob Deal, a contract salesman from whom Al frequently purchased tools.

Michael was reluctant to confront Al directly. They had never gotten along well, and Al was a senior engineer who wielded a great deal of power over Michael in their unit. Michael was also reluctant to discuss the matter with the chief engineer of their unit, in whom he had little confidence or trust.

Eventually Michael decided to talk to the contract procurement agent, whose immediate response was, "This really stinks." The contract procurement agent agreed not to reveal that Michael had talked with him. He then called the chief engineer, indicating only that a reliable source had informed him about Al House's inappropriate purchases. In turn, the chief engineer confronted Al. Finally, Al House directly confronted each of the engineers in his unit he thought might have "ratted" on him. When Al questioned Michael, Michael denied any knowledge of what took place.

Later Michael explained to his wife, "I was forced to lie. I told Al, 'I don't know anything about this.'"

Analyze the case from Michael's point of view in terms of the relevant facts, factual issues, conceptual issues, and application issues.

Case 4.3 Drinking in the Workplace[20]

Branch, Inc. has been losing ground to its competitors in recent years. Concerned that substance abuse may be responsible for much of Branch's decline, the company has just adopted a policy that imposes sanctions on those employees found to be working under the influence of alcohol or illegal drugs.

John Crane and Andy Pullman have worked together in one of the engineering divisions of Branch for several years. Frequently John has detected alcohol on Andy's breath when they were beginning work in the morning and after work breaks during the day. But until the new policy was announced it never occurred to John that he should say anything to Andy about it, let alone tell anyone else about it. Andy's work has always been first rate, and John is not the kind of person who feels comfortable discussing such matters with others.

Two days before the announcement of the new alcohol and drug policy, Andy tells John that he is being considered for the position of head of quality control. Although pleased at the prospect of Andy's promotion, John wonders if Andy's drinking will get in the way of meeting his responsibilities. John worries that, with additional job pressures, Andy's drinking problem will worsen.

Harvey Hillman, plant manager at Branch, knows that Andy and John have worked together many years. He has narrowed his choice for head of quality control to Andy and one other person. He invites John out for lunch to see if he can learn something more about Andy from John. Harvey says, "This is a really important decision. We need a top person for the quality control job. We've had some real problems the last few years with shoddy production, probably because of alcohol and drug abuse in the workplace. I had to move Jack Curtis out of head of quality control because *he* was drunk on the job. You can't expect a quality control person to keep others from abusing alcohol and drugs when he does it himself. We have to get this under control." Should John say anything about Andy's problem?

Analyze this case from John's point of view in terms of the relevant facts, factual issues, conceptual issues, and application issues.

Case 4.4 To Advise or Not Advise[21]

While carrying cardboard boxes filled with a powerful acidic solution, Edward Evans suffered serious burn injuries as a result of one of the bottles crashing to the floor. The bottle fell through the bottom of one of the boxes Edward was carrying for his employer.

Edward's attorney hired engineer Gregory Green to investigate the cause of the accident. Gregory quickly determined that, although the bottles had screw-on caps, the bottom of the box was damaged by leakage and that several of the other bottles in the box had loose caps. Gregory's analysis was reported by Edward's attorney during the court proceedings, but the attorney did not invite Gregory to come to court and testify as an expert witness. Edward and his attorney lost the case.

When Gregory learned of the disposition of the case, he wondered if he should have pressed Edward's attorney to invite him to testify in court as an expert witness. Gregory was quite convinced that Edward would have had no difficulty winning his case if Gregory had been given the opportunity to testify. At the same time, he realized that engineers are supposed to be "objective," making themselves available to provide truthful testimony, but serving simply as "advocates." (See, e.g., section II.3.a of the NSPE Code of Ethics: "Engineers shall be objective and truthful in professional reports, statements or testimony." See, also, section II.3.c: "Engineers shall issue no statements, criticisms or arguments on technical matters which are inspired or paid for by interested parties, unless they have prefaced their comments by explicitly identifying the interested parties on whose behalf they are speaking, and by revealing the existence of any interest the engineers may have in the matters.")

Would it have been appropriate for Gregory to advise Edward's attorney to have him testify as an expert witness? What relevant facts are presented? What factual, conceptual, or application issues does this case raise?

Case 4.5 The Corrected Estimate[22]

I

Several people were seriously injured by flying glass resulting from the explosion of a glass tank of water. Attorney Robert Raft represented two of the injured parties. He hired engineer Victor Swift to investigate the cause of the accident. Victor's preliminary determination was that the explosion most likely resulted from the presence of natural gas in the water. If Victor was right, this would support a finding against Cooler, Inc. However, the data did not warrant certainty. In court all Victor could testify was that the hypothesis that natural gas was the culprit was probably true. Robert Raft lost the case but decided he would appeal on behalf of his client.

Later Victor Swift recalculated and discovered he had been in error. The natural gas hypothesis, he concluded, was highly improbable. He also learned that another engineer, Sandra Burton, was hired by Robert Raft as he was preparing his appeal. Victor wondered if he should volunteer his new analysis to either Robert or Sandra.

What do you think Victor should do? Explain. What relevant facts are presented? Discuss any factual, conceptual, or application issues.

II

Victor Swift wrote to Robert Raft, explaining in detail his corrected estimate. Several days later Victor received a phone call from Robert. "I can't believe you'd send me a letter like this," Robert angrily shouted. "You took away my opportunity to appeal! You could at least have had the decency to call me about this first. That would have given me a chance to talk you out of it."

What should Victor say in reply? Does this angry call provide him with a good reason to change his mind about whether he acted appropriately in sending the letter to Robert?

Case 4.6 Spontaneous Explosion?[23]

Amy West suffered lacerations on her legs when a bottle of carbonated soda exploded. She claimed that it exploded on one of the lower grocery shelves as she reached up for another bottle of carbonated soda. Amy's attorney, Martin Leonard, hired engineer Dan Collins to testify.

During cross-examination, the opposing attorney asked Dan, "Wouldn't simultaneous explosion leave some residue on the shelf?" Dan knew that a *spontaneous* explosion would likely have left some residue on the shelf. He knew that the only residue was on the floor, suggesting that Amy West may have dropped the bottle. But he also knew that Amy's attorney did not want him to "volunteer" helpful information to the defendants. He pondered his options. Should he say "Yes," implicitly correcting the other attorney? Should he ask the other attorney if he meant to say "spontaneous"? Or should he respond in a way that would not provide the sort of answer the opposing attorney was undoubtedly seeking?

What relevant facts are presented? Discuss any factual, conceptual, or application questions this case raises.

Case 4.7 Forced-Sex Accusation

The New York Times (November 16, 1993, p. A12) reported that an engineer filed a lawsuit against her employer, claiming that her superiors "forced her to have sex with a Pentagon official so that the company could get millions of dollars in Government financing." She said her bosses told her she would lose her job unless she maintained a sexual relationship with a key Pentagon official. She contended that "in an act of desperation" she went to bed with the official and that talks between her company and the official began the very next day. Adding that she "refused to continue the relationship," the engineer said that one of her superiors "retaliated by abusing her and degrading and humiliating her."

What relevant facts are presented? What factual, conceptual, and application issues does this case raise? What bearing do they have on whether (and what kind of) wrongdoing occurred?

Other Cases

Reexamine any of the cases in the first three chapters to determine the relevant facts, as well as factual, conceptual, or application issues.

NOTES

1. W. D. Ross, *The Right and the Good* (Oxford, England: Oxford University Press, 1930), pp. 20–22.

2. See Bernard Gert, *Morality* (New York: Oxford University Press, 1988), Chapters 6 and 7.

3. ". . . even when we have come to recognize the duty of beneficence, it appears to me that the duty of non-maleficence is recognized as a distinct one, and as *prima facie* more binding. We should not in general consider it justifiable to kill one person in order to keep another alive, or to steal from one in order to give alms to another." Ross, *The Right and the Good*, p. 22.

4. Ross and Gert use the term "duty" in different ways. While Ross means by "duty" any moral consideration, Gert reserves the term for those special obligations associated with special roles, such as parent or professional.

5. Michael Davis, "Thinking Like an Engineer: The Place of a Code of Ethics in the Practice of a Profession," *Philosophy and Public Affairs, 20*, no. 2, (Spring 1991), 150–167.

6. Davis, "Thinking Like an Engineer, pp. 164–165.

7. *Bates* v. *State Bar of Arizona*, 433 U.S. 350, 53C, Ed. 2d. 810.

8. *Goldfarb* v. *Virginia State Bar*, 421 U.S. 773, 44L, Ed. 2d 572.

9. Milton F. Lunch, "Supreme Court Rules on Advertising for Professions," *Professional Engineer* (August 1977). Reprinted in Robert Baum and Albert Flores, *Ethical Problems in Engineering* (2nd ed.), Vol. 1 (Troy, N.Y.: Center for the Study of the Human Dimensions of Science and Technology, 1980), p. 123.

10. Lee Benham, "The Effect of Advertising on the Price of Eyeglasses," *Journal of Law and Economics, 15* (1972), 337–352.

11. *The Blue Book of Optometrists*, 87–88. Cited in Benham, "The Effect of Advertising," p. 340. Note the assumption that advertising is necessarily deceptive.

12. Benham, "The Effect of Advertising," p. 344. On pp. 344–345 Benham adds: "Despite the shortcomings of these estimates, they serve to indicate the direction and magnitude of the effect. The estimates of eyeglass prices alone [i.e., discounting the fee for eye examinations that are also included in these figures] suggest that advertising restrictions in this market increase the prices paid by 25 per cent to more than 100 per cent. Furthermore, these estimates are likely to underestimate the local savings to consumers occasioned by advertising, since the search process itself is less expensive when information is more readily and cheaply available."

13. Ibid., p. 348.

14. Ibid., p. 348 and note 14.

15. John F. Cady, *Restricted Advertising and Competition: The Case of Retail Drugs* (Washington, D.C.: American Enterprise Institute, 1976).

16. Ibid., p. 19.

17. We are indebted to Michael Davis for these cautionary observations.

18. From NSF Grant No. DIR-882-0837, presented with commentaries in Michael S. Pritchard, ed., *Teaching Engineering Ethics: A Case Study Approach*, pp. 37–47. This fictional case is an adaptation of W. Gale Cutler, "Did Jack 'Fake' It?," Research.Technology.Management (May/June 1988), p. 50.

19. Pritchard, *Teaching Engineering Ethics*, case and commentaries on pp. 25–36.

20. Ibid., case and commentaries on pp. 114–131.

21. Ibid.

22. Ibid.

23. Ibid.

Chapter 5

Methods for Moral Problem Solving

Charlie is assigned by his employer, Cartex, to work on an improvement in an ultrasonic range-finding device. While working on the improvement, he gets an idea for a modification of the equipment he is developing that might be applicable to military submarines. If this is successful, it could be worth a lot of money to his company. However, Charlie is a pacifist and does not want to contribute in any way to the development of military hardware. So he neither develops the idea himself nor mentions it to anybody else in the company. Charlie has signed an agreement that all inventions he produces on the job are the property of the company, but he does not believe the agreement applies to his situation. For one thing, his idea is not developed. For another, his superiors know of his anti-military sentiments. Yet he wonders if he is ethically correct in concealing his idea from his employer.

5.1 Introduction

Difficult ethical issues like the one Charlie faces call for techniques for resolving them. In the last chapter we considered some ways of sorting out the factual, conceptual, and application components of moral problems. Sometimes this sorting-out process resolves moral problems. For example, sometimes people know what to do when all of the facts are beyond dispute.

This is not always the case, however. Sometimes when all of the factual, conceptual, and application issues are settled, there is still uncertainty about what ought to be done or decided. In this case, there is a moral problem in the fullest sense of the term. That is, there is disagreement or uncertainty over the moral evaluation of the person or action. In this chapter we focus more directly on these kinds of moral problems and consider some techniques for resolving them.

Two common types are line-drawing problems and conflict problems. A *line-drawing problem* is one in which we view a moral problem as located on a spectrum, with the action at one end being clearly right and the action at the other end being clearly wrong. We are not sure, however, how to resolve the problem in question, because we are not sure whether the situation is more like the one where the action is clearly wrong or more like the one where the action is clearly right. A *conflict problem* is one in which we face a choice, as between two conflicting moral obligations or between two conflicting courses of action.

An appropriate metaphor for a line-drawing problem is a surveyor deciding where to set the boundary between two pieces of property. We know the hill to the right belongs to Jones and the hill to the left belongs to Brown, but who owns this particular tree? Where, precisely, should we draw the line?

Consider this example. The NSPE code says about disclosure of business and trade secrets: "Engineers shall not disclose confidential information concerning the business affairs or technical processes of any present or former client or employer without his consent (III.4)."

Suppose Engineer Mary signs an agreement with Company A that obligates her not to reveal the trade secrets of Company A. Mary later moves to Company B, where she finds a use for some ideas that she originally had at Company A. She never developed the ideas into an industrial process at Company A, and Company B is not in competition with Company A, but she still wonders whether using those ideas at Company B was a violation of the agreement she had with Company A. She has an uneasy feeling that she is in a grey area and wonders where to draw the line between the legitimate and illegitimate use of knowledge.

We can conceptualize many moral problems as either a line-drawing problem or a conflict problem, but usually one way of conceptualizing the problem seems more appropriate and natural than the other. Charlie's problem is probably most naturally viewed as a conflict between his obligation to his employer and to his own conscience, because he probably perceives his situation as one in which he would like to honor both of the conflicting obligations. The issue might also be seen as a line-drawing problem. On the one hand, Charlie knows that it would be wrong for him, as a pacifist, to actively take up arms. On the other hand, he knows that he should follow the directives of his employer in a situation in which there is no violation of his conscience. His question is whether the present situation is more like the first example or the second.

Mary's case is most naturally understood as a line-drawing problem, because Mary perceives the problem as an unclear case, opposed to others where she would know what to do. The case might, however, also be seen as a conflict problem, in which Mary believes she has obligations to both her old and her new employer.

Resolving line-drawing and conflict problems requires a kind of practical, problem-solving ability that is in some ways analogous to the skills developed by design engineers. Judgment is at a premium in this kind of activity, and there is no substitute for experience. There are no algorithms for resolving either line-drawing or conflict problems, but there are useful techniques in each case.

5.2   Resolving Line-Drawing Problems

In considering problem-solving methods, we begin with a method for resolving line-drawing problems.

The Method of Casuistry

In 1974 the United States Congress established the National Commission for the Protection of Human Subjects of Biomedical and Behavioral Research, which it asked to set up guidelines for human experimentation.[1] The members of the commission were from very different backgrounds, representing various disciplines and ideologies: lawyers, physicians, philosophers, theologians, and ordinary citizens. They quickly found themselves in an interesting situation. When they appealed to their most fundamental philosophical and theological principles in resolving issues having to do with human experimentation, they were in hopeless disagreement. When they focused on actual cases and principles such as justice and benevolence, they came to a remarkable degree of consensus.

They considered cases that everyone believed to be examples of morally wrong actions and other cases that everyone considered to be examples of morally correct actions. Finding that they could agree on such cases, they proceeded to examine cases on which they disagreed, pointing out the similarities and dissimilarities with the cases on which they agreed. The members of the commission found this to be a much more useful and profitable method for resolving moral problems than beginning with general principles.

At least one person on the committee recognized this approach as embodying the essentials of a very old method of moral analysis. It is called casuistry. For our purposes, we can define *casuistry* as a method for determining the proper moral evaluation of actions in a given case or cases by comparison with reference cases. The moral evaluation of the reference cases is not in question. Often the cases are arranged in a spectrum or series, with reference cases at the ends of the spectrum. The case at one end depicts an action that is unquestionably right, and the case at the other end depicts on action that is unquestionably wrong.

It is useful to develop some terminology for using the casuistic method. We shall call the cases on which there is agreement and which occupy the extreme ends of the spectrum the *paradigm* cases. The case that is uncontroversially morally permissible we shall call the *positive paradigm case* and the case that is uncontroversially morally impermissible the *negative paradigm case*. We shall call the controversial cases that are in dispute (and that are usually near the center of the spectrum) the *problematic* cases. We shall designate as the *test* case the one on which the analysis is to focus.

Figure 5.1 shows how the method of casuistry fits into the pattern of ethical analysis developed in Figure 4.1. If clarifying factual, conceptual, and application issues is not sufficient to resolve moral controversy, sometimes the remaining

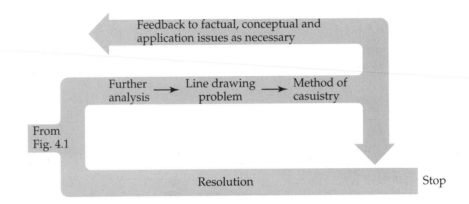

Figure 5.1
Line-Drawing Problems

problem is best understood as a line-drawing problem. The method of casuistry is then appropriate. In the casuistical analysis, we may need more facts and encounter further conceptual and application issues.

Figure 5.2 gives a more detailed graphic account of the method of casuistry for resolving line-drawing problems.

Case C+ is an action that most people would agree is morally permissible, and Case C– an action that most people would agree is morally impermissible. Cases C1 to C4 are more problematic cases, where the action is not as uncontroversially either right or wrong. Case C3 might be the test case, the case that is under discussion.

We should also make several general points about the method of casuistry in resolving line-drawing problems. First, the more ambiguous the case, the more we must know about its particular circumstances in order to determine whether it is morally permissible or impermissible. Whether failing to return money borrowed for a soda is theft may be decided only by reference to the particular lender

Positive Paradigm Case					Negative Paradigm Case
C+	C1	C2	C3	C4	C–

Figure 5.2
The Method of Casuistry for Resolving
Line-Drawing Problems

and his or her relationship to the borrower. Whether it is permissible to use some ideas you developed at Company A for a very different chemical process at Company B may be decided only by knowing the nature of the ideas and the policies of Company A and Company B. Similarly, whether to consider a payment of money as a bribe and therefore morally impermissible may depend upon the amount and timing of the payment, the influence it exerts on the person who accepts the payment, the appearance and taking of the action, and other factors.

Second, imposing a line of demarcation between some of the cases in a series involves an element of arbitrariness. It is erroneous to conclude from this, however, that there is no real moral difference between *any* of the cases in a series. The precise line between night and day may be arbitrary, but this does not mean there is no difference between night and day. Nevertheless, sometimes arbitrary conventions to separate permissible from impermissible actions are in order. Companies and in some cases professional societies should have policies that, for example, specify in some detail just what kinds of transfers of proprietary information from one job to the other are legitimate. Despite the rules, however, there will be many instances in which we cannot avoid an exercise of judgment. And of course judgment is called for in making the rules.

Third, in using the method of casuistry it is important to keep in mind that a single criterion will often be insufficient to separate acceptable from unacceptable cases. The method of casuistry is based on the isolation of analogies and disanalogies between various examples in a series. Unfortunately, we cannot depend on any single analogy or disanalogy to carry through all of the examples. This makes drawing the line more difficult.

Suppose you are an engineer working on a large construction job. One day you drive your car to the construction site to do some routine inspection, and when you return to your car you find a very nice selection of the latest CDs in the front seat. You know the gift has been put there by one of the foremen for the construction company that is building the project for your company. You suspect that if you ask why he did this, he will simply pass it off as "a gesture of good will." You also know that you can make things difficult for his company by refusing to make close judgment calls in his company's favor when you inspect the project. Should you accept the gift? Maybe you feel you should return it. But what about other situations where you are not so sure where to draw the line? Should you return the plastic pen he gave you that is worth about $2? What if the pen is worth $15?

An easy solution to the problem of accepting gifts would be for a company to establish a rule that employees should not accept any gift or gratuity worth more than a certain amount—for example, $25. Suppose, however, you are invited to attend an expense-paid meeting in Hawaii in which several vendors will demonstrate new models and present technical information about them. Even though the vendor's expenses for your attendance will far exceed the $25 limit, it might be proper for you to attend the meeting. Here a second criterion for acceptable gifts (the value of the gift to the company) appears to outweigh the criterion of the $25 limit.

Fourth, it is sometimes desirable to simplify the use of the method of casuistry. Figure 5.2 suggests that we must use a series of intermediate cases, as well as both a positive and a negative paradigm. Various methods of simplification, however, are possible. For example, the case to be decided can be compared with the positive and negative paradigms, without the use of a whole series of cases. The case can even be compared with only one paradigm, and this can be either the positive or the negative paradigm. Thus, we can use the method of casuistry with a minimum of two cases, although more are desirable with difficult issues.

Now let us look at some examples of the use of this method. We shall begin with a problem we have already considered.

Recall the problem of Engineer Mary described in the previous section. Was her use of ideas at Company B that she originally developed while at Company A wrong? Most people in our society believe that it is wrong to steal, or commit theft. Let us tentatively define stealing as taking the property of another without that person's consent. The prohibition of at least most instances of stealing can be justified by several of Gert's ten moral rules mentioned in the last chapter. Stealing is usually breaking the law, so its prohibition would follow from the rule against breaking the law. But even if theft is not against the law, it usually deprives a person of freedom, because loss of property means that a person cannot do what he or she might otherwise do. So let us agree that it is wrong to steal or commit theft.

There are some actions that virtually everyone agrees to as examples of theft. Breaking into a store at night and taking several thousand dollars' worth of merchandise is a clear violation of the moral rule against theft. So is shoplifting, or "borrowing" someone's car and failing to return it, or taking a bicycle that someone has forgotten to lock. By contrast, it seems peculiar to say that picking up a quarter on the street is theft, even though it fits our original definition of theft as taking the property of another without the person's consent. Here we can say that some examples fit our definition and are still not examples of theft. We can make our definition of theft more elaborate, but we can still find counterexamples to it. We might have the same kind of problem with calling our failure to return a sheet of paper that we borrowed from a friend "theft," although here there is an implicit understanding that we need not return the paper.

Some situations, however, are more problematic. We may not be entirely sure whether an engineer is guilty of theft because she uses some management techniques at Company B that she developed while at Company A. We may be even less sure about other examples. What should we say about an engineer who helped to develop a new chemical process at Company A and then moved to Company B, where she used some of the same ideas but applied them in a very different way to a different process? What should we say about an engineer who developed a computer program on company time for his company and then patented a considerably improved version under his own name? What about borrowing a book from a friend, forgetting about it, and then deciding not to return it because the friend has left town?

We can arrange such examples in a series, beginning with clear examples of stealing or theft, then moving into more problematic examples, and finally moving to examples that we would not consider instances of stealing or theft at all. Such a series might look like this:

C1. Breaking into a store and taking $3,000 in merchandise

C2. "Borrowing" someone's car and failing to return it

C3. Taking a bicycle that someone had forgotten to lock

C4. Developing a computer program on company time for your company and then patenting a considerably improved version of the program under your own name

C5. Using some management techniques you developed at Company A for your new employer, Company B

C6. Using some ideas you developed at Company A for a very different chemical process at Company B

C7. Borrowing a book from a friend, keeping it by mistake for a long time, and then failing to return it. (You discover the book after your friend has left town, and you decide to keep it.)

C8. Picking up a quarter that you saw someone drop on the street (assuming that you could probably catch up with the person and return the quarter if you made the effort)

C9. Picking up a quarter that someone (you don't know who) has dropped on the street

C10. Failing to return a sheet of paper (or a paper clip) you borrowed, with permission

There would probably be near universal agreement that cases C1–C3 are examples of theft. All of them can be negative paradigm cases. Or we could consider C1 the negative paradigm case and C2–C3 cases about which there would be little or no question. There would probably be near universal agreement that C9 and C10 are not theft. Either or both could be called a positive paradigm case. C4–C8 are problematic cases.

The problem in determining the moral status of C4–C8 is both an application issue and a line-drawing problem. Whether they should be counted as examples of theft is the same question as whether they should be considered morally permissible or impermissible. These problems are not easy to resolve without knowing more about the facts of the situation.

International Bribery

Consider again the example to which we refered in the last chapter.[2] In 1977 the U.S. Congress passed the Foreign Corrupt Practices Act (FCPA). The new law made it illegal for United States businesspersons and other United States citizens to "corruptly" pay, or otherwise authorize the payment, of money or anything of value to foreign government officials and foreign political parties. It was passed during the Carter administration, partially as a result of a discovery that nearly

400 American companies had paid approximately $300 million to foreign officials for business favors. For example, Lockheed had paid $22 million to foreign politicians over a five-year period to secure aircraft contracts. The Gulf Oil Corporation had made secret payments of $4 million to foreign politicians over the same period of time.

The FCPA was enacted, among other reasons, because of the widespread conviction that bribery is immoral. But it also raises the conceptual issue of the meaning of the concept of bribery and many application problems involving whether the prohibition of bribery applies in problematic situations. Consider the following series of cases:

C1. Paying money to a purchasing officer of a foreign government to obtain a contract

C2. Paying money to foreign government officials so that a product will at least be considered for possible purchase

C3. Paying money to expedite the processing of an application to do business in a foreign country

C4. Paying money to foreign government officials to ensure that your property will not be mysteriously destroyed by "vandals"

C5. Paying a normal registration fee to do business in a foreign country

C1 is a paradigm case of a bribe, if we use the characterization of "bribe" given in the last chapter. The role of a purchasing officer is to select the best product for her government. The bribe leads the official to violate this requirement.

C2 is more problematic. Unlike paradigm cases of bribery, this payment does not induce the foreign official to act contrary to her role. In fact, the foreign official should make her selection from all available products, so she should consider your product as well as the others. Also, the person who makes the payment does so to avoid an injustice that he and his company would otherwise suffer. In accordance with the characterization given earlier, perhaps this payment should be called an extortion fee rather than a bribe. Nevertheless, it has this feature in common with bribery: it gives the company that can afford to pay the fee an advantage over the company that cannot afford to pay it.

C3 usually involves small amounts of "grease money" and probably should not be considered a payment of bribery. In processing an application to do business in an efficient manner, the government official is only doing what she should do. Furthermore, the amount of money involved is so small that one's competitors can ordinarily afford to pay it.

C4 would usually be considered an example of an extortion or "protection" payment rather than a bribe because it involves paying a foreign official for what he should do anyhow. Furthermore, the payment is intended to avoid a harm rather than to obtain a benefit. If we apply the moral principle that it is wrong to pay or accept bribes and if we assume that extortion payments are not wrong in these circumstances, some might conclude that C4 is not a bribe. C5 is a paradigm case of a morally permissible action.

Accepting Gifts and Amenities

Tom was named the department manager of a large new chemical process unit that was to be designed and then constructed. Tom's responsibilities were to form the process unit staff; check the design for safety, ease of operation, and ease of maintenance; and then start up the plant after construction. In his previous experience Tom had found that a new type of valve and valve operator could often be used in place of more common gate valves and their operators. The new valves were consistently safer and less expensive and often gave a tighter shutoff than the gate valve. Tom convinced the project designer to add even more of these valves and operators to the design.

Suppose that, after a large number of the valves have been purchased, the salesman for the valves, Jim, visits Tom and gives him a $5 plastic pen with the name of Jim's company stamped on it. Very few people would consider Tom's acceptance of the gift ethically wrong. Call this case C1. Suppose, however, that Jim had visited Tom before he recommended Jim's valves and offered Tom $10,000 to recommend the valves. Suppose, further, that Jim's valves were, in Tom's estimation, actually less suitable than another product. In this case virtually everyone would agree that Tom's action was ethically inappropriate and actually was a case of accepting a bribe. Call this case C7.

In keeping with our terminology, we shall call the first case a positive paradigm case (C+) and the second a negative paradigm case (C–). Between these, however, there are a number of other possible cases whose ethical evaluation is more controversial. These are problematic cases. Consider the following examples.[3]

C2. After a large number of valves have been specified and purchased, Jim invites Tom to play golf with him at the local country club. Tom is an avid golfer and has wanted to play golf at the country club for some time. Should he accept Jim's invitation?

C3. After a large number of valves have been specified and purchased, Jim offers to sponsor Tom for membership in the local country club. Tom has wanted to be a member of the club for some time but has not found a sponsor. Should he accept Jim's invitation?

C4. After a large number of valves have been specified and purchased, Jim invites Tom to a seminar on valves to be held in South America. There will also be opportunities for fishing and recreation. Tom's company would have to pay for transportation, but Jim's company will cover all of the expenses in South America. Tom is sure his manager will authorize the trip if asked, but some managers are uneasy about such offers. Should he ask his manager for permission?

C5. After a large number of valves have been specified and purchased, Jim invites Tom to accompany him on a very nice fishing trip to South America. Jim's company will pay all expenses. Tom knows his manager will give permission to take the trip if asked, but some managers are uneasy about such offers. Should he ask his manager for permission?

C6. After the plant is constructed, Tom and Jim become very good friends and socialize on many occasions. They and their wives visit each other in their homes and in their lake houses. They also go fishing on each other's boats. Even after Tom leaves the original plant, he remains good friends with Jim. One day Jim invites Tom to fly in his plane to Mexico for a white-wing dove hunt. Tom never did anything to help Jim and his company other than recommend the valves, something that was done before Tom knew Jim. Nevertheless he wonders whether he should accept the invitation.

One way to answer the questions posed in C2—C6 is to compare the various cases with one another and with the two paradigm cases. The comparisons involve pointing out morally relevant similarities and dissimilarities. On the basis of these comparisons, we can come to some conclusions as to the proper evaluation of the problematic cases. Here are several of these morally relevant factors.

1. Perhaps the most obvious consideration is the monetary size of the gift. A $5 pen might not be considered significant enough to be a bribe, i.e., to influence Tom's decision. A $10,000 gift certainly is significant enough to do this.

2. The monetary size of the gift or amenity might be overridden by other considerations. For example, the trip to a seminar on valves in South America might involve a much larger monetary gift, but the knowledge that Tom would gain might be of considerable value to the company. This might even justify Tom's deciding to take the trip.

3. Another consideration is the degree to which Tom will feel obligated to Jim. Even though Jim's offer to sponsor Tom for membership in the local country club involves no money, accepting it might cause Tom to feel obligated to repay the favor, a feeling that would be reinforced every time the two meet at the club. Thus the potential for influence might be much greater here than with some of the gifts worth more money.

4. Another consideration is whether the offer comes before or after the crucial decision. In one of the paradigm cases the offer of $10,000 comes before the crucial decision and the product is not the most desirable. Here we can assume that Tom's decision was determined by the payment. The temporal relationship of the gift to the decision cannot in and of itself make the difference between morally permissible and impermissible actions, however. The reason for this is that we must consider two other related factors.

5. One of these factors is the appearance of the action. Businesspersons must be careful about how their actions will appear to other employees and managers and to the general public. Accepting a gift that appears to be a bribe may be detrimental to the business, even if the gift did not influence the decision. It can demoralize other suppliers and employees, perhaps leading them to assume that bribery is accepted practice. It can also harm the reputation of the firm.

6. Another closely related factor is that such an action can serve as an indirect bribe to other employees. If they see that a person who does business with Jim's company is likely to receive nice gifts, this is an inducement to them to do business with Jim's firm, even though the gift was not a bribe.

In some cases, we need additional factual knowledge before we can make an intelligent decision. For instance, what policies does Tom's firm have regarding gifts? How easily does Tom allow himself to feel obligated to others? Whether Tom accepts gifts from all vendors, even if he does not make purchases from them, may also be relevant. Using these and other similarities and differences between the various cases, most people will probably arrive at a high degree of consensus about what should be done in the individual cases.

Notice that we cannot resolve the issue as to what should be done simply by deciding which actions constitute accepting a bribe.

C1–C5 are not bribes, since they are given after the purchases of the valves. They might be considered improper for other reasons, however.

5.3   Resolving Conflict Problems

We have already pointed out that the rules of common morality can conflict with one another. There are situations when two or more moral rules or duties seem to apply and when they appear to imply different and incompatible moral judgments. This situation often arises in engineering ethics, as in other areas. Let us consider three techniques for resolving conflict problems: easy choices, creative middle ways, and hard choices.

1. Sometimes we have what we can call *easy choices*, where one conflicting obligation clearly has a higher priority than the other. Suppose you are driving along a freeway on your way to a dinner engagement. You have promised to meet a friend at 6 and are almost late. You see a person waving for help and realize there has been an accident. If you stop to assist, you will not be on time for your appointment. In a situation such as this, you would probably stop, even though you will violate your obligation to meet your friend at 6. The obligation to render assistance has a higher priority than the obligation to be on time for dinner.

Examples occur in engineering also. James is an engineer in private practice. He is approached by a potential client who asks him to design a project that clearly involves illegal activity. Engineer Susan is asked to design a product that will require the use of outmoded technology that, although less expensive and still legal, poses substantially greater threat to human life. James and Susan should simply reject such requests out of hand, even though they could dramatically increase the profits of their firms. The obligations to obey the law and to protect human life so clearly outweigh any obligation to maximize profits that James and Susan should have no difficulty in deciding what to do.

In such situations as the ones just described, it may sometimes be difficult to do what is right, but it is not difficult to *know* what is right. We might not even want to refer to this as a conflict situation at all, for the obligations involved have very different weights. In many real-life situations, however, the values are more evenly matched, and no hierarchy of values can give an easy answer. For example, the value of human life always overrides other considerations, but this is often not the choice we face. Usually, the trade-off is between a slightly increased *risk* to human life, as opposed to some other value. And we make trade-offs like this all the time. Automobile manufacturers could make their products much safer if they could sell them for $100,000, but then few people could afford automobiles. The following situations are more likely to produce problems for the morally conscientious professional.

2. Sometimes we must find a *creative middle way* between conflicting obligations, a resolution in which both of the conflicting demands are met. In many situations all of the moral obligations make strong claims on us, so that the ideal resolution of a conflict problem is to find some way to honor each of them.

This situation often occurs in the law as well. In 1974, the U.S. Supreme Court addressed a case in which Mr. Doyle, an untenured teacher, was not rehired by the Mt. Healthy, New York, school district after he disseminated information relating to the school district's dress code for teachers.[4] Mr. Doyle alleged that the school district dismissed him because he utilized his constitutional rights to protest the school district's policies. The district alleged that he had not been rehired because of his "notable lack of tact in handling professional matters," including publicizing the teachers' dress code and using "obscene gestures" to correct students.

The Court desired to honor two seemingly incompatible obligations. On the one hand, it wanted to protect the right of an employer to release a disgruntled or nonperforming employee. On the other hand, it wanted to protect the legitimate right of an employee to exercise his or her constitutional right to free speech. The Court found a creative middle way to accomplish this task. It ruled that the employee must first show that he did perform a constitutionally protected act. If this can be shown, the burden of proof shifts to the employer, who must then show that the disciplinary action was based solely on the employee's nonprotected activities. The Court apparently believed that in this way it had given due weight to both of the competing (and legitimate) legal considerations.

The philosophy of protest against racial discrimination developed by Martin Luther King, Jr., is also an example of a creative middle way.[5] Dr. King felt deeply the moral imperative to protest the racial injustice in this country. At the same time, he respected the rule of law and he did not want to take the stance of a revolutionary. His solution to this conflict issue was the theory of nonviolent resistance, according to which one violates laws that he or she believes to be immoral, but does not use violence and is willing to take the consequences of illegal activity. In many cases this may mean that a person must go to jail. While this philosophy may not have always been followed by protestors of racial injustice, it is an attempt to find a creative middle way between two conflicting moral demands, so that each of the demands is given due consideration.

Notice that in this example (and in many conflict issues) neither of the moral demands were honored in what we might call their original or "pure" form. Dr. King did disobey the law, so the obligation to obey the law was partially violated. At the same time, the obligation to oppose immoral laws was also not followed in an unrestrained fashion, for Dr. King refused to use violence and was willing to take the consequences of disobeying laws that he considered immoral. Instead, a middle position was found that incorporated some features of both of the conflicting moral demands.

To take another example, suppose an engineer, John, is representing his company in a foreign country where bribery is common.[6] If John does not pay a bribe, valuable business opportunities may be lost. If he makes payments, he may be doing something illegal under the Foreign Corrupt Practices Act, or he may at the very least be violating his own conscience. Instead of yielding to either of these unattractive alternatives, one writer has proposed a "donation strategy," according to which donations are given to a community rather than to individuals. A corporation might construct a hospital or dig new wells. In the 1970s, for example, Coca-Cola hired hundreds of Egyptians to plant orange trees on thousands of acres of desert, creating more goodwill than it would have generated by giving bribes to individuals. In 1983 the British gained goodwill for themselves in Tanzania by assembling thousands of dollars worth of tools and vehicle parts. They also trained the Tanzanians to service the vehicles, enabling the Tanzanians to continue patrolling their wild game preserves, which they had almost stopped doing due to the weakened economy. This gift was given in place of a cash donation, which might well have been interpreted as a bribe.

We can of course object to this solution. Not all creative middle ways are satisfactory, or at least equally satisfactory. We might argue that such gifts are still really bribes and are morally wrong. The evidence for this is that the effect of the gift is the same as the effect of an outright bribe: the person giving the gift gets the desired business contract. Furthermore, the motivation of the gift-giver is the same as the motivation of the briber—securing the business. There are also certain disanalogies, such as the gift-giving not being done in secret and its satisfying something more than the self-interest of an individual. We shall not attempt to resolve the application problems raised by this solution, which depend heavily on the details of particular circumstances, but simply to point out that it is an example of a creative-middle-way solution.

Here is another example. Suppose Barbara, a young engineer on her first job, finds that a chemical process at her plant is both dangerous and polluting. She knows from her college training that another process would be less dangerous and polluting and would even save the plant money in the long run. By suggesting this new process to her superior, she honors her obligation both to be a "faithful agent or trustee" of her employer and to look out for the safety of the public.

Consider the study of Florida's solution to the problem of competitive pricing. The Consultants' Competitive Negotiation Act of 1973 gives directions for negotiation for "professional services" for state agencies in Florida. According to the act, the negotiation procedure should consist of the following steps:

1. By reviewing qualifications, the state agency selects "no less than three firms deemed to be most highly qualified to perform the required services."

2. The agency will then "negotiate a contract with the most qualified firm for professional services at compensation which the agency determines is fair, competitive and reasonable."

3. "Should the agency be unable to negotiate a satisfactory contract with the firm considered to be the most qualified at a price the agency determines to be fair, competitive and reasonable, negotiations with that firm shall be formally terminated. The agency shall then undertake negotiations with the second most qualified firm. Failing accord with the second most qualified firm, the agency shall terminate negotiations. The agency shall then undertake negotiations with the third most qualified firm."

4. Should the agency be unable to negotiate a satisfactory contract with any of the selected firms, the agency shall select additional firms in order of their competence and qualification and continue negotiations in accordance with this subsection until an agreement is reached.[7]

Advocates of this procedure might well argue that it is a middle way between prohibiting all competitive bidding and allowing unrestricted competitive bidding. Or they might argue that it fulfills two obligations that engineers have to the public: to allow the operation of market forces, in order to reduce price, and to uphold high standards of quality. Engineering firms are originally selected on the basis of the reputation of the firm for quality and the appropriateness of the firm for the task. Only after a selection on the basis of quality do cost considerations play a role in the negotiation.

In thinking about creative-middle-way solutions to conflict problems, it is often helpful to consider a *range* of solutions, rather than a single one. We can then evaluate them in terms of their moral acceptability. For example, in the following case, Brad is in the second year of his first full-time job after graduating from Engineering Tech.[8] He enjoys design, but he is becoming increasingly concerned that his work is not being adequately checked by more experienced engineers. He has been assigned to assist in the design of a number of projects that involve issues of public safety, such as schools and overhead walkways between buildings. He has already spoken to his supervisor, whose engineering competence he respects, and he has been told that more experienced engineers check his work. Later he discovers that his work is often not adequately checked. Instead, his drawings are stamped and passed on to the contractor. Sometimes the smaller projects he designs are under construction within a few weeks after the designs are completed.

At this point Brad calls one of his former professors at Engineering Tech for advice. "I am really scared that I am going to make a mistake that will kill someone," Brad says. "I try to overdesign, but the projects I am being assigned to are becoming increasingly difficult. What should I do?" Brad's professor tells him that he cannot ethically continue on his present course, for he is engaging in engineering work that surpasses his qualifications and may endanger the public. What should Brad do?

Brad's case illustrates one of the most common conflict problems faced by engineers, one in which an engineer's obligations to employers seem to conflict with obligations to the public. These dual obligations are stated in engineering codes themselves. Canons 1 and 4 of the NSPE code illustrate this conflict:

Engineers, in the fulfillment of their professional duties, shall:

1. Hold paramount the safety, health and welfare of the public in the performance of their professional duties. . . .

4. Act in professional matters for each employer or client as faithful agents or trustees.

Although the obligation to the public is paramount, Brad should also honor his obligation to his employer if possible. A range of options is open to him.

1. Brad could go to his supervisor again and suggest in the most tactful way he can that he is uncomfortable about the fact that his designs are not being properly checked, pointing out that it is not in the firm's interests to produce designs that may be flawed.

2. He might talk to others in the organization with whom he has a good working relationship and ask them to help him persuade his supervisor that he (Brad) should be given more supervision.

3. He might tell his supervisor that he does not believe that he can continue to engage in design work that is beyond his abilities and experience and that he might have to consider changing jobs.

4. He could find another job and then, after his employment is secure, reveal the information to the state registration board for engineers or others who could stop the practice.

5. He could go to the press or his professional society and blow the whistle immediately.

6. He could simply find another job and keep the information about his employer's conduct to himself, allowing the practice to continue with another young engineer.

7. He could continue in his present course without protest.

In order to be ethically and professionally responsible, Brad should spend a considerable amount of time thinking about his options. He should attempt to find a course of action that honors both his obligation to protect the public and his obligation to his employer. It is also completely legitimate for Brad to try to protect and promote his own career, insofar as he can while still protecting the public.

With these guidelines in mind, we can see that the first option is probably the one he should try first. The second is also a good choice if the first one is ineffective. The third option is less desirable, because it places him in a position of opposition to his employer, but he may have to choose it if the first two are unsuccessful. The fourth option produces a break in the relationship with his employer, but it does protect the public and Brad's career. The fifth also causes a break with his employer and threatens his career. The sixth and seventh are clearly impermissible, because they do not protect the public.

There are, of course, still other options Brad can consider. The important point is that Brad should exercise his imagination to its fullest extent before he takes any action. He must learn to "brainstorm" to find a number of creative-middle-way solutions to his conflict problem. Then he should attempt to rate the solutions and begin with the most satisfactory one. Only after this has failed is one justified in proceeding to the less satisfactory solution.

3. Notice that in going down the list of possible resolutions, Brad may be forced to make some *hard choices*, some choices in which he is not able to honor some real and important obligations in the way that he would consider desirable. Options three to five in the above list require Brad to place himself in opposition to his employer, and they also require him to jeopardize his own career. The sixth and seventh options require Brad to overlook his obligation to protect the safety of the public and are thus not acceptable. Figure 5.3 illustrates this procedure.

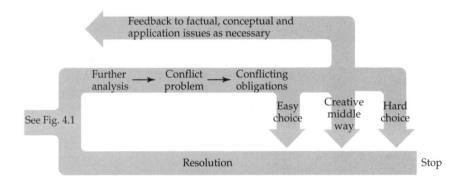

Figure 5.2
Resolving Conflict Problems

If the resolution of factual, conceptual, and application issues is insufficient to resolve a moral issue, sometimes the remaining problem is best understood as a conflict problem. In resolving this, we begin by enumerating the conflicting obligations. Then we must decide whether it is best to resolve by an easy choice, a creative-middle-way solution, or a hard choice. In this further analysis, we may need more facts and encounter further conceptual and application issues.

Gilbane Gold

Now here is a final example involving ethical problem solving, where resolving conflicting moral obligations is required. The case is the one presented in the popular videotape, *Gilbane Gold*.[9] The tape focuses on David Jackson, a young engineer in the environmental affairs department of ZCORP. The firm, which manufactures computer parts, discharges lead and arsenic into the sanitary sewer of the city of Gilbane. The city has a lucrative business in processing the sludge into fertilizer, which is used by farmers in the area.

To protect its valuable product, Gilbane Gold, from contamination by toxic discharges from the new high-tech industries, the city has imposed highly restrictive regulations on the amount of arsenic and lead that can be discharged into the sanitary sewer system. However, recent tests indicate that ZCORP may be violating the standards. David believes that ZCORP must invest more money in pollution-control equipment, but management believes the costs will be prohibitive. What should David do?

David faces a conflict situation that can be characterized by the convergence of four moral obligations. First, David has an obligation as a good employee to promote the interests of his company. He should not take actions which unnecessarily cost the company money or damage its reputation. Second, David has an obligation to protect and promote his own career. Third, David has an obligation to be honest with the city in reporting data on the discharge of the heavy metals, based on David's personal integrity, and also his professional integrity as an engineer. Fourth, David has an obligation as an engineer to protect the health of the public.

The problem David faces is this: How can he do justice to all of these obligations? If they are all legitimate moral obligations, he should try to honor all of them, and yet they appear to conflict in the situation. This produces the conflict problem.

Since the obligations are all legitimate, David's first option should be to attempt to find a creative-middle-way solution, despite the fact that the obligations appear to be incompatible in the situation. What are some of the creative middle ways?

1. One would be to find a cheap technical way to eliminate the heavy metals. If David could do this, he would provide a way out of a difficult situation for ZCORP. He would also enhance his professional career. He would keep trust with the city, because he would be able to honestly report that the city's regulations have been met. Finally, he would be upholding his professional obligation to protect the health of the public by finding a way to reduce the discharge of heavy metals.

2. Assuming a technical solution is impossible, David might suggest a management solution to Diane, the manager of the plant. She could approach the city about the problem, perhaps in consort with other managers of high-tech plants in the area. If, indeed, product lines are in danger of becoming unprofitable and perhaps removed, with the consequent loss of jobs, managers could present these facts to the city. Positive suggestions could be made for a compromise whereby the city would grant additional tax incentives or other advantages to the plants, in exchange for further purification of their effluent.

This approach, like the first one, would satisfy all four of David's obligations. It would provide a service to ZCORP, by suggesting a way to avoid an almost inevitable public relations disaster. It would, like the first alternative, enhance David's stature within the firm. It would manifest good faith with the city. Finally, it would again provide a means for David to fulfill his obligation to protect the public's health.

If David cannot find a way to honor all of his obligations, he must make some hard choices, deciding which obligation(s) have priority. His conclusion should almost certainly be that, as the engineering codes stipulate, his first obligation is to protect the health of the public. He might think of several ways in which he could do this.

3. David could alert corporate headquarters to the problems at the Gilbane plant, informing Diane of his action. He could argue that Diane is following a course of action that can only lead to a public relations disaster. The problems at the plant are already public knowledge and David has been summoned to appear before city officials, which means that the issue of toxic waste is not going to disappear. He could argue that he wants to be a loyal employee and that he has thought long and hard about circumventing his superiors. He could also say that alerting corporate headquarters is the most reasonable course of action, because the first two options are not available or have failed. He could point out that he is attempting to protect the company from bad publicity and possible lawsuits, and to protect his own professional integrity. He could also make some of the same suggestions to corporate management that were made to Diane in 2 above.

This option would precipitate a break with the management of the local plant, but it would show a larger loyalty to the company. This is another way of manifesting David's obligation to the public, since one of his aims in alerting corporate management is to encourage a more rational response to the problem of toxic waste. Finally, it would be an attempt to preserve good faith with the city and to preserve his own career.

4. According to the videotape, David has been summoned to appear before city authorities, so another option would be to tell Diane that, if asked by city officials about the discharge of heavy metals, he will be completely truthful. As a conscientious employee, he will attempt to present ZCORP in a favorable light, but he will not misrepresent the situation or withhold knowledge.

This alternative would be at least a step in the direction of protecting the public. It would also satisfy David's obligation to the city. While it would not manifest loyalty to the company in the sense of unqualified promotion of the company's interests, it would offer the possibility of an honest resolution of the issue. This poses risks for David's career, but management might view it as an honest attempt by David to be loyal to the company while preserving his own integrity.

5. David might announce to his supervisor that he can no longer in good conscience sign the documents that state that ZCORP is in compliance with city regulations on the discharge of toxic substances. He could emphasize that he wants to be a loyal employee, but that his professional career is at stake. In the light of the new tests, he cannot misrepresent the situation.

By taking this option, David has clearly placed the health of the public above loyalty to the firm or protecting his career, which might well be jeopardized by his action. If the previous options are not possible or are not successful, however, he may be forced to take it.

6. David could talk to the reporter about the problems ZCORP is having with the emission of heavy metals. This option would give a clear priority to protecting the health of the public and keeping good faith with the city and give a lower priority to being loyal to the company and promoting his own career.

7. David could resign from ZCORP and then talk to the reporter about the problems with the emission of heavy metals. This would of course constitute a break with ZCORP and would endanger his own career, since David would have the label of a whistleblower. It would again acknowledge the higher priority of keeping faith with the city and protecting public health.

There are many other possible options that David could examine, but these are sufficient to show a gradual progression from creative-middle-way solutions in which all four of the competing obligations can be honored, to courses of action in which some of the obligations are given priority over the others.

5.4   Standpoints of the Agent and the Judge

A person can take one of two different standpoints in resolving moral problems.[10] The first is that of a judge who observes a person attempting to resolve a moral problem and then evaluates the success of the resolution. This external evaluator or judge usually has the benefit of knowing the consequences of the choices made and the success of the person's choice.

Many well-known cases in engineering ethics are often approached in this fashion. Examinations of the Challenger case often raise certain questions. Should Roger Boisjoly have protested the launch decision even more strenuously? In light of the consequences, what do you think about Robert Lund's decision to agree to the decision to launch? How could Robert Lund have responded differently to Jerald Mason's directive to take off his engineering hat and put on his management hat? Should Roger Boisjoly have refused to continue to work on the field joints, once he concluded that their design was seriously flawed?

These are all important questions, and it is often instructive to ask and attempt to answer them. Engineers spend a great deal of time learning from past mistakes, and they can learn from past ethical as well as technical mistakes. But this approach is not the only way—and perhaps not the best way—to learn how to be a successful ethical problem solver.

A second standpoint one can take in resolving moral problems is that of the agent, the person actually facing a moral problem. We believe that this perspective is the best way to learn how to be a successful problem solver. This involves looking at the issue with the information that is available or could be available to the person facing the necessity of a decision; analyzing the moral, factual, and conceptual issues; and coming out with a conclusion as to what we would do if we were in that situation.

The most appropriate cases for doing this may not be the highly publicized ones whose outcomes we already know. In the Challenger case, for example, we all know that the decision to launch led to a terrible disaster. This fact so influences our thinking that it is difficult to look at the situation from the perspective of those who were making the decisions, people who did not know the consequences of their choices ahead of time. Rather, the most appropriate cases are often ones with which we are not familiar, whether fictional or actual. Here we can realistically test our skills at anticipating outcomes, analyzing conceptual issues, and resolving conflict and line-drawing problems.

Now let us turn to the topic of the next chapter: tests in moral problem solving. The methods we have proposed for resolving line-drawing and conflict problems assume that we have a strong resource in common morality. We have assumed, that is, that at least much of common morality is valid. For example, we have taken it for granted that there is no reason to doubt many of the paradigms of unquestionably right or unquestionably wrong actions to which we appeal in resolving line-drawing problems. Likewise, we have not questioned the validity of many of the competing obligations in conflict situations.

Nevertheless, our discussion of moral thinking so far leaves several questions unanswered. For example, when resolving conflict problems where all of the obligations cannot be met, which obligation takes priority? In resolving line-drawing problems, which similarities and differences between cases are morally relevant? The resources of common morality may be sufficient to answer many of the questions such decisions suggest, but we are inevitably inclined to ask whether there are any additional sources of moral insight.

Finally, there are still more basic questions that we have not addressed. Is there any way to find moral principles that are more fundamental or basic than the principles supplied by Ross and Gert? Could these more fundamental principles explain, organize, or justify common morality? Could they be used as a basis for criticizing or reforming common morality?

In the next chapter we shall address some of these questions.

5.5   Chapter Summary

A line-drawing problem is one in which we do not know how to distinguish between permissible and impermissible actions. The method of casuistry is often helpful in resolving such problems. By comparing problematic cases with those where it is clear what we should do, we can often decide what we should do in the problematic cases.

A conflict problem is a situation in which two or more conflicting obligations apply or in which we are faced with two or more courses of action and can only choose one. Sometimes one obligation seems to be so much more important than the other that we must choose to honor the more important one and neglect the other. At other times, however, we should try to come up with a solution to the conflict that enables us to honor all of the relevant obligations. Sometimes we must make hard choices between competing obligations or alternative actions. Often it is useful to think of a range of solutions to a conflict problem. We should first attempt to act in accordance with the solution that most satisfactorily honors the competing obligations. If the optimum solution is not possible or does not work, we should continue to the next most desirable solution, and so on until the issue has been resolved.

In evaluating the resolution of conflict issues, we can take either the standpoint of an external judge or of an agent actually immersed in the situation who does not know the outcome ahead of time. Usually the latter standpoint is a better way to learn the art of moral problem solving.

Case Analyses

Case 5.1 Tom's Problem

Now let us return to the case presented at the beginning of this chapter. Rather than developing both a positive and a negative paradigm case, we shall develop a negative paradigm case, one in which it is clear that Tom's action is wrong. Then we shall ask whether the case in question (the test case) is enough like the negative paradigm to warrant the same moral evaluation.

Suppose Tom is assigned by his employer, Cartex, to work on an improvement of an ultrasonic range-finding device. On company time and using company equipment, he conceives and develops a modification of the improvement that can be applied to military submarines. This improvement could be very valuable to Tom's company, and Tom has signed an agreement acknowledging that all inventions on company time are the property of the company. However, Tom conceals the potential military applications of his work from his superiors. Managers at Volram, the major competitor of Cartex, learn of the mili-

tary adaptation and offer Tom a large increase in salary if he will leave his company and join them, bringing his ideas with him. Tom accepts the offer and develops the military application. It turns out to be very profitable for Volram. Here Tom's action was clearly wrong.

There are several similarities between the test case and the negative paradigm case:

1. In both cases Tom deprives Cartex of an idea that could have been of great financial benefit.

2. In both cases Tom had an agreement with Cartex that his inventions on company time belonged to the company.

3. In both cases, Tom develops the idea on company time.

There are also differences between the test case and the negative paradigm case:

1. In the test case Tom does not know that his idea will be beneficial to Cartex.

2. In the test case Tom has strong moral objections to contributing to military weaponry.

3. In the test case Tom does not change employment or profit from the invention.

4. In the test case Tom does not develop the military application on company time. For that matter, he does not develop the idea at all.

5. In the test case there is (presumably) no clear violation of the agreement with Cartex.

The conflict in the test case is between Tom's obligation to his employer and his obligation to his own conscience. The fact that Tom has signed an agreement regarding his inventions is important, but there is an application issue as to whether his idea counts as an invention. We think that it does not. Therefore Tom has probably not violated the letter of his agreement with Cartex, although some might contend that he has violated its spirit. The fact that Tom does not profit from the idea for a military application himself and does not allow others to profit from it indicates he does indeed have a sincere commitment to pacifism.

The final resolution of this issue is difficult. The differences between the test case and the negative paradigm seem both more numerous and more important than the similarities, however, so we conclude that Tom is at least not morally obligated to reveal his ideas to his employer.

Case 5.2 A Vacation[11]

I

Dan Dorset had been looking forward to this trip for weeks. Once he was assigned to help Rancott install its equipment for Boulding, Inc., he arranged his vacation at a nearby ski resort. The installation would be completed on the twelfth, and his vacation would begin on the thirteenth—a full week of skiing with three of his old college buddies.

Unfortunately, not all of Rancott's equipment arrived on time. Eight of the ten identical units were installed by mid-morning on the twelfth. Even if the remaining two units had arrived that morning, it would have taken another full day to install them. However, Dan was informed that it might take as long as two more days for the units to arrive.

"Terrific," Dan sighed, "there goes my vacation—and all the money I put down for the condo."

"No problem," replied Boulding engineer, Jerry Taft. Jerry had worked side by side with Dan as each of the first eight units was installed. "I can handle this for you. We did the first eight together. It's silly for you to have to hang around and blow your vacation." Jerry knew why Rancott had sent Dan to supervise the installation of his firm's new equipment. Rancott's equipment had to be properly installed in order to avoid risking serious injuries to those who use the equipment. For years Rancott trusted its clients to follow the carefully stated directions for installation. But several recent accidents were directly traceable to failure to follow proper installation procedures. It was now Rancott's policy to send one of its engineers to supervise all installations.

Dan was confident that Jerry was as fully capable as he to supervise the installation of the remaining two units. What should Dan do?

II

Tempting as it is to leave early, Dan decides to stay until the job is completed. He loses all but the last two days of his vacation, but he feels he has done the right thing. Some time later Dan and his unit's chief of engineering, Ed Addison, are having a drink after work. Eventually the conversation turns to Dan's vacation.

Dan: What would you have done if you found out I left before all the units were installed?

Ed: Honestly? Probably nothing. It sounds like Jerry Taft had everything under control.

Dan: So if I had called, you would have told me it was okay to leave before the job was completed?

Ed: I didn't say that. I don't think it would be wise for me to *officially* approve something like that. Then it would be my neck, too, if anything went wrong.

Dan: Meaning it would have been on my neck if anything had gone wrong?

Ed: Sure. My only point is that I probably wouldn't have done anything about your leaving early—unless something went wrong. That's a chance you would have been taking. But it sounds like it wouldn't have been a very big risk.

Dan: Would you have taken it?

Ed: That depends on how badly I wanted to ski. Actually, I never have cared for skiing—it's too risky.

What do you think of Ed's position on this matter? If Dan had known Ed's position when he was at Boulding, would it have been all right for Dan to leave early? Identify relevant facts, as well as factual, conceptual, and application issues. Do you see any opportunities for casuistic reasoning, line-drawing, or creative-middle-way reasoning?

Analyses

The following two analyses were prepared by students in Michael Pritchard's undergraduate Ethics in Engineering class at Western Michigan University. These are examples of very good student analyses.

Analysis 1: Douglas A. Hunt

Dan Dorset, Rancott engineer and main character of the "A Vacation" case study, has the dilemma of staying on a past-schedule project or starting his planned vacation. Dan's predicament has been caused by the delayed arrival of some equipment, the installation of which will conflict with his vacation plans. To choose a course of action, Dan must sort through facts, issues, and obligations and decide whether he prefers to make a hard choice or come up with a creative-middle-way solution.

To define the ethical predicament more clearly, Dan must consider the relevant and irrelevant known facts, unknown facts, conceptual issues, and application issues in this case.

Foremost, some facts have to be recognized as irrelevant. The facts that the ski resort is nearby, that the vacation was to last a week, that Dan has made a deposit on a condominium, that Jerry Taft has helped Dan supervise the installation of the first eight units, and that Jerry knew why Dan was there (as required by Rancott policy) are all irrelevant. The locale, duration, and level of financial involvement should have no bearing on Dan's decision. Likewise, Jerry's understanding that Dan was there because of Rancott policy and his subsequent suggestion to ignore it does not affect Dan's duty to uphold the National Society of Professional Engineers Code of Ethics first fundamental canon to hold paramount the safety, health, and welfare of the public. This idea is supported by the fact that Dan is likely to be more experienced with the equipment and installation procedures than Jerry, regardless of Jerry's experience, and thus is in a better position to uphold this principle (an application of the corollary of proportionate care).

There are many relevant known facts in this case and a few relevant unknown facts. First, the known relevant facts are that the installation was to be complete on the twelfth, the vacation was to begin on the thirteenth, two units were late and would probably delay the start of the vacation, recent accidents were directly related to failure to follow installation procedures, and Rancott's policy dictated that Dan be present. However, Rancott's policy is somewhat irrelevant, because an ethical engineer, given an opportunity to supervise an installation that might result in injury if done improperly, would probably elect to perform this supervision in light of the first NSPE code canon. The unknown relevant facts include the exact arrival and installation times of the other equipment.

Finally, there are some significant conceptual and application issues. What do "there goes my vacation" and "blow your vacation" mean? Is the vacation really "gone" or "blown" if Dan is a couple of days late? Furthermore, would he not retain the vacation time if he never made it to his vacation because of the prolonged project? Also, how are we to understand Jerry's claim to be able to "handle this for Dan" or Dan's "confidence" in Jerry's being "as fully capable" as Dan to supervise the other two installations? On what are these claims based? The application issue related to these conceptual issues is: Does Jerry's experience really make him an adequate supervisor?

In creating and choosing a solution to his dilemma, Dan must both weigh the facts and issues and consider their specific applications in this case. The applications are best considered in terms of his obligations and the principles of sound, responsible engineering.

Foremost, Dan has some responsibilities as the engineer overseeing these installations. This assignment, as well as his job in general, is to supervise the complete installation. To stay and do this, he must sacrifice his vacation (in part or whole), which could be considered "good works," an application of the corollary of proportionate care, and an exemplary case of proper engineering decision making. To call Rancott and attempt to have another qualified engineer sent as a replacement would be a case of devising a creative middle way. If the installation did not require him to stay Saturday and Sunday, another creative-middle-way solution would be for Dan to ski during the weekend and return on Monday, assuming that he can account for the risks of injury over the weekend.

Whatever course of action that Dan chooses to pursue, the results must be viewed from the perspective of his obligations. His obligations are to Rancott (his employer), Boulding (the client relying on his expertise), the public (Boulding's employees), his career, his friends (who will be waiting for him to join them on vacation), and himself. By staying on the assignment at the cost of some or all of his vacation, Dan will satisfy all of the obligations except the last two. If he attempts to ski over the weekend and return to Boulding Monday morning, Dan may partially satisfy all of the obligations (assuming he does not get injured or killed). Similarly, having Rancott send another engineer would satisfy all of the obligations except possibly protecting his career (Rancott management might see Dan in a different light for placing a higher priority on his vacation). However, if Dan elects to go skiing and leave Jerry in charge, he will definitely not satisfy any of the obligations except possibly to himself and his friends, and he risks losing the opportunity to have such responsibility (or employment) should something go tragically wrong in his absence.

Analysis 2: Ken Calopisis [12]

The method of casuistry can be used in this situation. At one extreme is the negative paradigm case. In this case, Dan could leave for his vacation without leaving anyone who is competent enough to supervise the installation of the remaining two units. Dan could then take his skiing vacation, but he would be violating company policy. At the other end of the spectrum is the positive paradigm case. In this case, Dan could be relieved by another engineer from the Rancott corporation. Dan would still be able to go on his skiing trip while meeting Rancott's policy of having one of its engineers supervise the installation of its equipment.

Dan's situation falls between these two paradigm cases. In his case he can leave someone in charge who is competent to supervise the installation of the equipment, but the person does not work for Rancott as required by company policy. Using the method of casuistry, it can be determined whether Dan's case is more like the positive or negative paradigm cases.

However, I decided to examine the facts and came to the conclusion that Dan should stay until the equipment is completely installed. The fact is that it is company policy to have one of its engineers supervise the installation of its equipment. Dan did not make this policy, and he shouldn't unilaterally and arbitrarily decide whether or not he will follow this policy. The policy was made because several accidents occurred due to faulty installation of its equipment. Although it is not explicitly stated in the problem, it is conceivable that these accidents could or did jeopardize the safety of other people. I think it is Dan's moral duty and obligation as an engineer to ensure that public safety is not endangered.

There is also the matter of project and social scheduling. The project was scheduled to be completed on the twelfth, and Dan scheduled his vacation to start on the thirteenth. The date of completion was not guaranteed to be the twelfth. Although it is not wrong for Dan to schedule his vacation around planned company projects, it certainly is unrealistic for Dan to assume that no

problems would arise during the installation process. As an educated and supposedly competent engineer, Dan should realize that problems can and do arise in situations involving engineering. I feel that Dan, as a professional engineer, should be able to foresee this type of situation, and meet his professional obligations as an engineer before satisfying his personal objectives.

Case 5.3 The Deadline[13]

Ruskin Manufacturing has guaranteed Parker Products that it will deliver the complete order of small machines by the tenth of the month, a Friday. Parker has already extended its deadline once; this time, it insists, the date must be met. Tim Vinson, head of quality control, has been confident the deadline will be met. But on the eighth he learns that a new component of the machines is in short supply.

Tim realizes that he must decide whether to try to meet the deadline by using the old component (or by some other means) or to inform Parker Products that Ruskin will not be able to deliver the product on time. Before making a decision, Tim decides to consult with Chuck Davidson, the chief design engineer for this product. Chuck says, "I don't have a good answer for you. There's no time to come up with a completely satisfactory alternative. You could regrind, but given the time frame you might get a lot of impurities. Or you could just use the old components. But I'm not going to advise either of those. I don't want this hanging over my head. Maybe you should call Arnold."

Arnold Peterson is vice-president of product engineering. Years ago, like Tim Vinson, Arnold served as head of quality control. Tim is somewhat uneasy about calling Arnold for two reasons. First, Tim feels responsible for not seeing the problem earlier, and he is reluctant to admit failure to the vice-president of product engineering. Second, he wonders if Arnold really wants to be bothered by something like this. He might simply tell Tim that the problem is his to solve—somehow. So Tim decides to resolve the problem by himself. How should he resolve it?

Analyze the problem in terms of factual, conceptual, and conflict issues and then show how Tim should resolve his problem— and why.

Case 5.4 Gilbane Gold

In Chapter 3 we considered different conceptions of responsibility, ranging from avoiding breaking the law to doing good works. Examine the attitudes toward responsibility expressed by the various characters in the video, *Gilbane Gold*. To help you do this, we include relevant portions of the video's transcript. As you read through this, also identify any factual, conceptual, or application issues that might account for some of the differences among the characters. Finally, look for opportunities to employ casuistic reasoning, line-drawing techniques, or creative-middle-way thinking.

Characters: Phil Port, manager in charge of environmental affairs; David Jackson, engineer working under Phil Port; Tom Richards, environmental engineering consultant fired by ZCORP; Winslow Massin, retired professor of engineering; Diane Collins, vice-president of the local plant.

Phil Port: We here at ZCORP hold the environment as a top priority. Its the only way I would take the job. We do business strictly by adhering to the law. . . .

David Jackson: I'm getting higher levels from the discharge tests than ever before, lev-

els that are consistently, if only a little, above what the city allows. . . . Why hasn't the city gotten on our case?

Phil Port: This data is right on the line. We're probably not over the limit at all.

David Jackson: I need to run more tests, I guess.

Phil Port: We can't afford to spend a lot of time and a lot of money double checking everything. This isn't college, David. This is business.

David Jackson: These metals are serious business. This is arsenic and lead we're talking about.

Phil Port: I've been doing this for 15 years and it looks okay to me.

David Jackson: But I'm the one that's ultimately responsible to the city, and I need to know that the data I'm signing off on is accurate. Now I suspect that at peak production we are releasing a lot more arsenic and lead than they can handle downstream.

Phil Port: But you don't know that. The data doesn't tell us anything about what's going on downstream. Look, if we were causing a problem, we would have heard about it from the water people, right? It's their responsibility, you know. They tell us what they want coming out of our pipes and then it's their job. . . .

Tom Richards: You've got a serious problem here. This plant is dumping heavy metals into a water treatment system that simply can't handle them.

Phil Port: I don't think we are, Tom. I mean data from the test system the city requires shows we're within acceptable limits.

Tom Richards: The test is flawed and you know it. The test isn't sensitive enough to accurately reflect the levels. . . . [It is announced that ZCORP has signed a contract that will increase production five-fold.]

David Jackson: We may have a serious problem here, Phil. We're going to have to invest some serious dollars into water treatment.

Phil Port: It's real simple, David. Just do some calculations on how much more filtration we need with increased flow so that we don't pass the concentrations allowed by discharge.

David Jackson: But we'll still be putting out a lot of poison, Phil, and you know it. A lot more than they can handle downstream. Now, why can't we just go to the city and talk to them and alert them to the situation?

Phil Port: If you can solve this problem without spending a lot of extra money, people are going to view you in a completely different light. This may be your opportunity to shine. . . .

Diane Collins: Are we still in compliance with city regulations?

Phil Port: Technically yes. But with the increased production anticipated—

Diane Collins: Have we heard from the Gilbane water treatment people? No. Are we in the sludge business? No. You don't even know if the sludge will be unsafe. The problem as I see it is not with the city but with my environmental affairs department. Now I want solutions. And that does not mean spending money we can't afford.

David Jackson: You just don't get it, do you, Diane? We are dumping poison into the city sewer system. Now, whether the law allows it or not, that poison is going to collect in substantial amounts in the sludge, and that'll be passed on to the farmers.

Diane Collins: Look, Dave, I eat vegetables, too. I would not intentionally poison anyone any more than you would. But you don't have the data to substantiate your concerns. We are within city regs now, and will continue to be until the City Council changes the law.

David Jackson: I think we have a broader responsibility to the public.

Diane Collins: You are exactly right. We provide this city with thousands of jobs and a substantial tax base. We are in the computer business. They are in the sludge business. They can stop selling it if they think it's dangerous. . . .

David Jackson: Winslow, what are we talking about here? Forcing ZCORP to upgrade their water treatment system, that's not going to break their back.

Winslow Massin: Who are we to make the decision for them?

David Jackson: Is it the company's fault the law allows this much poison?

Tom Richards: The law is flawed.

Winslow Massin: It's not our responsibility. It's the city's.

Tom Richards: You've got to go with your conscience on this. I mean, people might get hurt and you're going to have to live with it.

Winslow Massin: If you go public, you'll most certainly lose your job. Tom, we go back a long way, but I don't agree with you. I don't think David should go public.

Case 5.5 Benzene in the Workplace

At the beginning of Chapter 4 we described a case involving the regulation of worker exposure to benzene. We gave an analysis of the factual and conceptual issues, but we did not attempt to resolve the moral issues. Continue the analysis offered there in order to resolve the moral issue, bearing in mind this chapter's methods of resolving disagreements.

Case 5.6 An Oil Spill?[14]

Peter has been working with the Bigness Oil Company's local affiliate for several years, and he has established a strong, trusting relationship with Jesse, manager of the local facility.

The facility, on Peter's recommendations, has followed all of the environmental regulations to the letter, and it has a solid reputation with the state regulatory agency. The local facility receives various petrochemical products via pipelines and tank trucks, and it blends them for resale to the private sector.

Jesse has been so pleased with Peter's work that he has recommended that Peter be retained as the corporate consulting engineer. This would be a significant advancement for Peter and his consulting firm, cementing Peter's steady and impressive rise in the firm. There is talk of a vice presidency in a few years.

One day, over coffee, Jesse starts telling Peter a story about a mysterious loss in one of the raw petrochemicals he receives by pipeline. Sometime during the 1950s, when operations were more lax, a loss of one of the process chemicals was discovered when the books were audited. There were apparently 10,000 gallons of the chemical missing. After running pressure tests on the pipelines, the plant manager found that one of the pipes had corroded and had been leaking the chemical into the ground. After stopping the leak, the company sank observation and sampling wells and found that the product was sitting in a vertical plume, slowly diffusing into a deep aquifer. Because there was no surface or groundwater pollution off the plant property, the plant manager decided to do nothing. Jesse thought that somewhere under the plant there still sits this plume, although the last tests from the sampling wells showed that the concentration of the chemical in the groundwater within 400 feet of the surface was essentially zero. The wells were capped, and the story never appeared in the press.

Peter is taken aback by this apparently innocent revelation. He recognizes that state law requires him to report all spills, but what about spills that occurred years ago, where

the effects of the spill seem to have dissipated? He frowns and says to Jesse, "We have to report this spill to the state, you know."

Jesse is incredulous. "But there *is* no spill. If the state made us look for it, we probably could not find it; and even if we did, it makes no sense whatever to pump it out or contain it in any way."

"But the law says that we have to report . . . ," argues Peter.

"Hey, look. I told you this in confidence. Your own engineering code of ethics requires client confidentiality. And what would be the good of going to the state? There is nothing to be done. The only thing that would happen is that the company would get into trouble and have to spend useless dollars to correct a situation that cannot be corrected and does not need remediation."

"But. . . ."

"Peter, let me be frank. If you go to the state with this, you will not be doing anyone any good—not the company, not the environment, and certainly not your own career. I cannot have a consulting engineer who does not value client loyalty."

What are the ethical issues in this case? Are there any factual, conceptual, or application issues? How do you think Peter should resolve this situation?

Other Cases

You might try applying the methods of problem solving discussed in this chapter and Chapter 4 to the following cases in earlier chapters:

1.2 USAWAY
1.3 Whose Property?
2.4 Gifts for Engineers
2.5 Engineer's Dispute with Client over Design

3.2: The Catalyst
3.4: Working Overtime
4.4: To Advise or Not Advise
4.7: Forced-Sex Accusation

NOTES

1. See Albert R. Jonsen and Stephen Toulmin, *The Abuse of Casuistry* (Berkeley: University of California Press, 1988), pp. 1–20.

2. See also C. E. Harris, *Applying Moral Theories*, (2nd ed.). (Belmont, Calif.: Wadsworth, 1992), pp. 67–69.

3. The previous case could be considered either an application issue or a line-drawing problem, but this case is most naturally classified as a line-drawing problem. Sometimes accepting a gift may not be a bribe, yet still wrong. Therefore resolving the application issue of whether accepting a gift is equivalent to accepting a bribe will not resolve the moral issue as to whether accepting the gift is morally wrong. For further discussion of this case see pp. 24–54 of "Introducing Ethics Case Studies into Required Undergraduate Engi-neering Courses," final report to the National Science Foundation on Grant No. DIR-9012252 by Raymond W. Flumerfelt, Charles E. Harris, Jr., Michael J. Rabins, and Charles H. Samson, Jr., November 1992.

4. *Mt. Healthy School Board* v. *Doyle*, 429 U.S. 274 (1974). See the discussion of the case in John L. Howard, "Current Developments in Whistle-blower Protection," *Labor Law Journal*, (February 1988), p. 74.

5. This example is taken from Henry A. Richardson, "Specifying Norms," *Philosophy and Public Affairs*, *19*, no. 4 (1990), pp. 279–310.

6. For this example, see Jeffrey A. Fadiman, "A Traveler's Guide to Gifts and Bribes," *Harvard Business Review* (July/August 1986), pp. 122–126, 130–136.

7. James H. Schaub and Karl Pavlovic, *Engineering Professionalism and Ethics*. (New York: Wiley-Interscience, 1983), pp. 122–126.

8. This case is suggested by the experiences of a former engineering student at Texas A&M University.

9. See Case 5.4.

10. We are indebted to Dr. Caroline Whitbeck for pointing out the importance of this distinction.

11. This fictional case study is from NSF Grant No. DIR-8820837, presented with additional commentaries in Michael S. Pritchard, ed., *Teaching Engineering Ethics: A Case Study Approach*, pp. 445–461.

12. This is a shorter version of Ken Calopisis's fuller analysis. In the longer version, he makes several points already made by Douglas Hunt. However, he also brings in the method of casuistry.

13. This case is from NSF Grant No. DIR-8820837, presented with additional commentaries in Michael S. Pritchard, ed., *Teaching Engineering Ethics: A Case Study Approach*, pp. 445–461.

14. This case was developed by P. Aarne Vesilind, Department of Civil and Environmental Engineering at Duke University. Used with permission.

Chapter 6

Tests in Moral Problem Solving

Mark Matthews and David Parkinson have just been reappointed members of the Madison County Solid Waste Management Planning Committee (SWPC). Matthews is president of Efficient Disposal Service and Parkinson is an engineer who specializes in solid waste disposal. State law requires that the seats Matthews and Parkinson occupy be held by a solid waste industry representative and an expert in solid waste, respectively. Parkinson has provided consulting services to Efficient Disposal in the past.

Prior to the reappointments, Efficient Disposal developed a proposal that Baker Township be the site for a county landfill. After studying the proposal, Parkinson has come out in favor of it and has been its strongest public advocate. The SWPC has tentatively agreed that Baker Township is the best site. Madison County has a population of approximately 300,000 with 95,000 living in Madison City. Rural Baker Township is the least populated township in the county, with approximately 500 residents.

Residents in Baker Township strongly oppose the proposed site for the landfill. They believe that they have been unfairly treated because they are poor and have a small representation in the power centers of the county. They also believe that their area, one of the most beautiful parts of the county, should be preserved in its present condition. Matthews and Parkinson, however, believe they have made the best decision, all things considered.

Residents in Baker Township are represented by the Concerned Citizens of Baker and the Baker Association for Rural Ecology. They believe their only chance to defeat the proposal to locate the disposal site in their area is to mount a recall campaign, making charges of conflict of interest against Matthews and Parkinson. Matthews and Parkinson are angered that their professional judgment has been called into question and are not inclined to resign, believing that their decision is really the best for the majority of people in the county. With any other location, the land would be more expensive and the disposal site would be closer to population centers. Furthermore, they argue, state law requires that their seats be occupied by people with backgrounds like theirs. Nevertheless, residents of Baker Township believe they have been treated badly.

The focus of Matthews's and Parkinson's decision whether or not to resign is on whether they have in fact made the best decision. If you were in their position, would you believe that you had made the best decision, all things considered?[1]

6.1   Introduction

The above case illustrates a common issue in moral controversies, the conflict between the obligation to respect the rights of individuals and the obligation to do what seems best for the majority. It appears that Matthews and Parkinson have made the right decision in terms of maximizing the welfare of the public. As the case report says, "With any other location, the land would be more expensive and the disposal site would be closer to population centers." Residents of Baker Township argue against this on two grounds. Their rights have been unduly infringed, because their numbers are small and they are poor. They also argue that even from the standpoint of majority benefit the wrong decision has been made. Baker Township is an area of natural beauty and rural charm, whose advantages to the entire area will be lost if the landfill is placed in their area.

The appeal to individual rights and majority welfare is also present in the benzene case presented at the beginning of Chapter 4. OSHA took the standpoint of the workers, arguing that their rights would be unduly infringed by being exposed to benzene, even if the concentrations are below those proven to be a health hazard. Protecting the rights of workers, OSHA officials assumed, requires that the burden of proof be placed on those who want to expose workers to any level of a carcinogen. Industry must prove that the exposure level is not harmful.

The Supreme Court justices, while not unmindful of the rights of workers, were also concerned about the economic welfare of industry and of the nation at large. If firms are forced to reduce toxic substance exposure to levels far below those proven to be harmful, the economy may be unduly harmed, possibly without any corresponding benefit to the workers themselves. In this case, at least, the Court believed that overall human welfare must override a possible (and in their view unlikely) risk to workers.

There are thus two approaches to moral thinking—those that take the preservation of the rights of individuals as the primary good and those that take maximizing human well-being as the primary good. These provide the basis for a number of tests for the rightness of actions that are useful in practical moral problem solving. They are also related to two important traditions in ethics: respect for persons, which we shall refer to as RP morality, and utilitarianism.

The utilitarian and RP traditions have been formulated into moral theories. A *moral theory*, for our purposes, is a set of concepts and principles that organizes and in some sense explains or provides a foundation for common morality, or some portion of it. A moral theory formulates the fundamental moral ideas that underlie much of common morality. Moral theories have several functions: an organizing function, a justifying function, a critical function, and a problem-solving function.

1. They *organize* our moral thinking by showing how many different moral beliefs can be traced to a common set of ideas. Thus, utilitarian moral theory attempts to organize morality by showing that all valid or legitimate moral beliefs are connected with maximizing human welfare. RP morality often attempts to show that all valid moral beliefs are connected with protecting the rights of individuals.

2. They *justify* many of the precepts of common morality. By proving that a moral belief contributes to maximizing human well-being, for example, a utilitarian shows that the belief is justified from the utilitarian standpoint.

3. They *criticize* and *reform* common morality. We have been careful to say that a moral theory explains or justifies only some of the ideas of common morality, not all. Consider utilitarianism as an example. More than likely, only some of the ideas of common morality can be shown to have a utilitarian foundation. Utilitarians maintain that this is not a defect of utilitarianism. Rather, those parts of common morality that cannot be shown to have a utilitarian foundation should be rejected. In this way utilitarianism can not only explain and justify many ideas in common morality but also criticize and reject others. Similar comments can be made about the relationship of RP morality to common morality.[2]

4. Finally, they assist in moral *problem solving* by supplying tests for the moral acceptability of actions. These tests suggested by utilitarianism and the ethics of respect for persons can be applied directly to moral problems. They can also be utilized in the analysis of both line-drawing and conflict problems. In using the method of casuistry, for example, the tests can evaluate the validity of the paradigm cases of right and wrong actions and isolate the morally relevant similarities and differences between cases. In resolving conflict problems, the tests can determine which resolutions are the most desirable from an ethical standpoint and which moral obligations should be given priority, in case hard choices must be made. It is this fourth function of moral theories to which we shall devote most of our attention in this chapter.

A moral theory can have one or several moral principles from which we derive our other moral beliefs. Although they would not have thought of their principles in this way, we could think of Ross's six prima facie duties and Gert's ten moral rules as representing two different but closely related moral theories. For our purposes, they provide a summary (or at least a partial summary) of the main precepts of common morality. In this chapter, however, we consider two theories—utilitarianism and the ethics of respect for persons—that have a single moral principle as their basis. We shall call this a moral standard. The moral standard supplies the criterion that determines whether an action is right or wrong, according to the theory.

It is easy to see why a moral theorist searches for a single, underlying moral standard. When we look at the formulations of common morality by Gert and Ross discussed in Chapter 4, we ask, "Is it possible to find a single principle that provides the basis of these lists of moral rules or duties?" Such a principle would give us profound insight into the fundamental nature of morality. However, many theorists believe that it is not possible to find a single principle and thereby to construct a master theory of morality. More plausible, perhaps, is the notion that utilitarianism and the RP morality, taken together, can account for most of the moral beliefs embodied in common morality. A given rule or duty of common morality can usually be justified by either a utilitarian or an RP moral standard, or in some cases by both.

If utilitarian and RP ideas are the basis of most of common morality, it is not surprising that many practical moral problems reflect a tension between a concern for maximizing human welfare and an interest in protecting the rights of individuals. The case presented at the beginning of this chapter and the benzene case are just two of many examples.

We begin this chapter with a discussion of utilitarianism, developing three tests for moral problem solving: the act utilitarian test, the cost/benefit test, and the rule utilitarian test. Then we consider the RP perspective, developing three tests for moral problem solving from this perspective: the Golden Rule test, the self-defeating test, and the rights test. After this, we consider some of the issues that arise when the various tests yield divergent conclusions.

Although these tests can be of considerable use in moral problem solving, we must always keep in mind the necessity of good judgment in determining which tests are most appropriate in a given situation and in assessing the limitations of the test. The tests must be used with discrimination and moral sensitivity; otherwise they lead to implausible results. There is no simple algorithm for solving moral problems.

6.2   Utilitarianism

Utilitarianism favors bringing about the greatest total amount of good that we can. A utilitarian moral standard expresses this basic idea. As we shall see, however, there is some disagreement among utilitarians about just how to formulate this moral standard. We examine some of the different ways in which utilitarians have explained what is morally required of us. Utilitarian values play an important part in the professional ethics of engineers.

Let us begin with a general statement of the utilitarian standard:

> Those individual actions or rules that produce the greatest total amount of utility to those affected are right.

The codes enjoin engineers to promote the safety, health, and welfare of the public, and this principle seems very close to the utilitarian standard. The term "welfare" could even be interpreted as synonymous with "utility."

There is a problem, however, in defining "utility" more precisely. The most common definition is "happiness," but happiness for one individual may not be happiness for another. John Stuart Mill, one of the most important representatives of nineteenth-century utilitarianism, argued that human beings have capacities that animals do not have and that the fulfillment of these unique human capacities is the basis of human happiness. He went on to say that we must give "pleasures of the intellect, of the feeling and imagination, and of the moral sentiments a much higher value as pleasures than those of mere sensation."[3] Others might not agree with Mill, however, finding the pleasures of the senses or the pleasures of earning money or the pleasures of fame or power more satisfying.

Utilitarians have responded to this problem by proposing *preference utilitarianism*: we should promote those general conditions that allow each individual to pursue happiness as he or she conceives it.

Utilitarian theorists generally agree that at least two conditions are necessary for most people to pursue happiness effectively: freedom and well-being. *Freedom* is the ability to make unforced choices in following our preferences. It refers primarily to noninterference by others in making fundamental decisions about life. *Well-being* is the set of conditions necessary to make effective use of freedom. It includes such factors as health, a certain degree of material well-being, food, shelter, and education. If a person is poor, sick, and uneducated, for example, mere noninterference from others will be of little value in achieving happiness.

Utilitarians maintain that the precepts of common morality, insofar as they are morally valid, can be derived from the utilitarian standard, in the sense that they maximize utility. If they do not, the utilitarian believes they should be eliminated from common morality. For example, the moral rules against killing, deception, and cheating and many of the prima facie duties are necessary in order to protect people from interference by others. Many of the moral ideals and positive moral duties are necessary to promote human well-being.

Even though we have presented utilitarianism as a proposed way of explaining the rules or prima facia duties of common morality, it can also evaluate various specific courses of action. For example, cost/benefit analysis, a type of utilitarianism, can be applied to particular actions: the course of action that produces the greatest benefit relative to cost is the one that should be chosen. "Benefit" is usually defined in some relatively specific way, such as producing jobs or something else of value to society, but the utilitarian insists that these benefits be justified in terms of the more general conceptions of utility as providing the conditions of freedom and well-being. There are several problems with the utilitarian perspective, but we shall consider only three here.

First, sometimes it is difficult to come up with a directive for action from the utilitarian standpoint. We have seen that in order to know what we should do from the utilitarian perspective, we must know which course of action will produce the most utility for those affected. Unfortunately, this knowledge is sometimes impossible to obtain. For example, we do not yet know whether permitting advertising and competitive pricing for professional services will lead to some of the problems suggested by those who oppose it. So we cannot say whether these are good practices from the utilitarian perspective. Sometimes all we can do is try a certain course of action and see what happens. This may be very risky in some circumstances.

Utilitarians reply that if we do not know the consequences of an action, we should not be sure of its moral status. The problem is not with utilitarianism but with the limitations of human knowledge. Nevertheless, this difficulty does mean that in some situations the utilitarian perspective cannot provide clear practical guidance.

A second problem with utilitarianism is closely related to the first. Utilitarians want to bring about the greatest total amount of good that they can. We shall refer to the population over which the good is maximized as the *audience*. The problem for utilitarians is determining the scope of this audience. There may appear to be a dilemma over this issue. Their audience should be all human beings, or at least all human beings who might be affected by the action to be evaluated. Perhaps the audience should even include all beings capable of experiencing pleasure or pain. But then it becomes virtually impossible to calculate which actions actually produce the most good for so large an audience. If we limit the audience, so that it includes only our country, or our company, or our community, then we face the criticism that others have been arbitrarily excluded.

A third difficulty with the utilitarian perspective is that it can sometimes justify perpetrating injustice on individuals. Suppose a plant discharges a pollutant into the local river, where it is ingested by fish. If humans eat the fish, they experience significant health problems. Eliminating the pollutant will be so expensive that the plant will become unprofitable and will be closed. Allowing the discharge to continue will save jobs and perhaps even permit the local community to remain economically viable. The pollutant will adversely affect only a small proportion of the population, the most economically deprived members of the community who fish in the river.

Under these conditions, allowing the plant to continue to discharge the pollutant might be justifiable from a utilitarian perspective, even though it would be unjust to the poorer members of the community. Many would say that the utilitarian solution should be rejected for this reason. Thus utilitarianism sometimes leads to implausible moral judgments, as measured by our understanding of common morality. This indicates that utilitarianism is not a completely adequate account of common morality.

6.3   **Three Utilitarian Tests**

Despite the limitations discussed, the utilitarian perspective is often very useful in moral problem solving. Now let us consider three tests suggested by the utilitarian moral standard.

The Act Utilitarian Test

The act utilitarian test focuses on the consequences (measured in utility) of particular actions. It raises a question: "Will this course of action produce more utility than any alternative course of action that I could take?" To answer this question, the following procedure is useful. First, you must enumerate the available options, or courses of action open to you. Second, you must determine the audience for the options, keeping in mind the problems in determining the audience. Third, you must decide which action will produce the greatest total amount of utility.

The act utilitarian test is often a useful mode of analysis of options in moral problem solving. Consider the case presented at the beginning of this chapter. Mark and David evidently believed that a responsible decision on their part required them to make some assessment of the impact of the two options on all of the citizens in the county. This meant they had to make an act utilitarian analysis of the options. As the case illustrates, this is not the only morally relevant perspective: the question of whether the rights of rural people had been unduly infringed was also an important consideration.[4]

The Cost/Benefit Test

Cost/benefit analysis is a version of act utilitarianism, in which the negative and positive utilities are translated into monetary terms. It provides an appealing way to resolve moral problems (especially conflict problems), because of its quantitative orientation. Cost/benefit analysis involves three steps. First, you must assess the options open to you. Second, you must assess the costs (measured in monetary terms) and the benefits (measured in monetary terms) of each of the options. As with act utilitarianism, the costs and benefits must be assessed for the entire audience of the action, for all of those affected by the action. Third, the agent must choose the course of action that produces the greatest benefit relative to cost. That is, the course of action chosen must not be one in which the cost of implementing the option could produce greater benefit if spent on another option.

We can illustrate this method with an example of pollution from a chemical plant.[5] Suppose a large chemical plant is near a residential area. The plant emits a number of noxious odors, some of them posing mild risks to health. How do we determine the optimal level of pollution the plant should be allowed to contribute to the environment?

First, we must assess the options. The plant is emitting pollution into the air, which is a part of the commons. (The commons are those areas, such as the air, rivers, and oceans, which are not owned by anyone in particular.) Economists say that the plant is externalizing the cost of the pollution by forcing others, such as the surrounding residents, to pay the cost of the pollution, in the sense of living with the odors, suffering the health effects, and perhaps expending funds to counteract these effects. We have the option of either allowing the plant to continue its present course of action or of forcing it to bear the total cost of its pollution, even if this means the plant must be closed.

Second, we must calculate the costs and benefits of the pollution. To measure the cost for the obnoxious smells, we consider several factors. We compare the costs of homes near the plant with costs of homes in locations that are equivalent, except that the pollutants are not present. This gives us one cost. Then we obtain some measure of the effect of pollution on health. We estimate the lost earnings from days missed at work, the cost in suffering, and any other costs attributed to poorer health. We also assign a monetary value to the negative aesthetic effects of the odors, if these were not adequately accounted for by the other costs. These and perhaps other costs, added together, give us the full cost of the odors.

There are also benefits of the pollution, because the plant confers benefits on the community, providing jobs and a substantial tax base. Some measure of the decrease in jobs or tax base due to the cost of eliminating the pollution must be made, a form of disutility.

Third, we must compare the costs and benefits of eliminating the pollution. The plant can be forced to eliminate the pollution itself, or to pay a "pollution tax" to the government, which will enable the government to eliminate the pollution, or to compensate the residents for the ill effects of the pollution. Then the pollution must be eliminated up to that point at which the costs of elimination outweigh the benefits, when an optimal state of cleanness will have been reached. An optimal state is not a "perfectly" clean environment, but an environment that is as clean as a cost/benefit analysis will allow. This state may be one in which the plant is forced to close, but it may not be. It all depends on the results of the cost/benefit analysis.

An individual engineer is usually not in a position to perform a cost/benefit analysis. She also may not be in a managerial position to make a decision regarding an environmental matter. But sometimes such an analysis has already been performed. In any case, there are serious problems with using cost/benefit analysis as a sole guide for protecting the public from pollution that endangers health.

First, the cost/benefit analysis assumes that economic measures of cost and benefit override all other considerations. Cost/benefit analysis encourages the elimination of a pollutant only when it can be done in an economically efficient manner. In some cases, however, the pollutant so eliminated may not be the most harmful one from an environmental standpoint. Suppose the chemical plant we have been considering is near a wilderness area that is damaged by one of the plant's emissions. It might not be economically efficient to eliminate the pollutant, from the cost/benefit analysis standpoint. Of course the damage to the wilderness area must be included in the cost of the pollution, but this cost might still not justify the elimination—or even the reduction—of the pollution from the cost/benefit analysis standpoint. Yet it is not necessarily irrational to hold that the pollutant should be eliminated, even if the elimination is not justified by the analysis. The economic value that anyone would place on saving the wilderness is not a true measure of its value.

Second, it is often very difficult to ascertain the costs and benefits of the many factors that enter into a cost/benefit analysis. If the threat to human health posed by a substance is not known, it is impossible to execute a competent cost/benefit analysis. This problem becomes especially acute if we consider long-term costs and benefits, most of which are impossible to predict or measure.

Third, cost/benefit analysis often does not take into account the distribution of costs and benefits. Often those who bear the costs of pollution do not share in the benefits. Using an earlier example, suppose a plant dumps a pollutant into a river where many of the poorer members of the community fish, using the fish to supplement their diet. Suppose further that, after all of the costs and benefits are calculated, continued pollution of the river is justified; that is, the costs of eliminating it outweigh all of the health costs to the poor. Still, if the costs are paid by the poor and the benefits are enjoyed by the rich, the costs and benefits are not equally shared. Even if the poor are compensated for the damage to their health, many would say that an injustice has still been done. After all, the wealthy members of the community do not have to suffer the same threat to their health.

Fourth, cost/benefit analysis might well have justified many practices in the past that most people would now consider morally wrong. In the nineteenth century, many people opposed child labor laws, arguing that they would lead to economic inefficiencies. They pointed out, for example, that tunnels and shafts in coal mines were too small to accommodate adults. Many arguments in favor of slavery were also based on considerations of economic efficiency. When our society did decide to eliminate child labor and slavery, it was not simply because they became economically inefficient, but rather that they came to be considered unjust. As we shall see in Chapter 10, most environmental legislation is based on values that transcend cost/benefit analysis.

Despite these problems, cost/benefit analysis is a useful method in ethical problem solving. We can hardly imagine constructing a large engineering project, such as the Aswan High Dam in Egypt, for example, without performing an elaborate cost/benefit analysis. While cost/benefit analysis has the typical weaknesses of any form of utilitarianism, it also has the typical strengths. Its ability to evaluate conflicting considerations in terms of a single measure, monetary value, makes it invaluable in certain circumstances. As with all other tools for ethical analysis, however, we must keep its limitations in mind.

The Rule Utilitarian Test

Sometimes it is not enough to ask whether a given action will produce greater utility than an alternative action. We must ask a question such as "Would utility be maximized if everyone did the same thing in the same circumstances?" From a more practical perspective, things we do will often be emulated by others. If engineers begin to reduce safety factors in design and their firm's profits are increased as a result, other engineers are likely to do the same thing. The question is: "What policy, if generally followed, would maximize utility?"

Given these considerations, rule utilitarianism is the only legitimate form of utilitarianism, and some theorists would agree with this claim. Others argue that it is not always appropriate to inquire about the utility of everyone's doing what we do. In the case presented at the beginning of this chapter, for example, it is not particularly helpful to ask about the utility of every engineer's deciding to place a landfill in a rural area rather than in an urban area. The circumstances of such cases vary too much to ask this sort of question. In situations where the rule utilitarian mode of analysis is useful, we should use the following procedure.

First, we must analyze the case in order to determine the alternative rules that are at issue. In the issues of advertising and competitive bidding in engineering, which were discussed in Chapter 4, two rules could be under consideration:

Rule 1: Engineers may engage in advertising and competitive bidding.
Rule 2: Engineers may not engage in advertising and competitive bidding.

Second, we must determine the proper audience for the rule. In this case, the audience includes both engineers and those who use engineering services.

Third, we must decide which rule produces the most utility for the relevant audience. As we saw in Chapter 4, the answer to this question involves a considerable amount of empirical knowledge about the consequences of each of the two rules. We would have to consider such issues as the self-image of engineers, the effect of advertising and competitive bidding on the price and quality of professional services, the value of advertising in conveying information to potential customers, the extent to which advertising places a premium on business ability rather than professional expertise, and the extent to which advertising of engineering services can mislead the layman. On the basis of these kinds of considerations, we must make a decision as to which rule, if generally followed, would lead to greater utility for the relevant audience.

Fourth, if we must make a decision in a particular situation, it should be on the basis of the rule that produces the most utility. If this is Rule 1, then the individual engineer should engage in advertising and competitive bidding. If it is Rule 2, the engineer should refrain from these practices.

Of course individual engineers would not establish rules such as Rule 1 and Rule 2; they would more likely be regulated by law or the professional codes. This method is the way to decide these regulations, however—from a rule utilitarian standpoint.

We can also use the rule utilitarian test to decide what should be done in particular circumstances. Suppose Engineer Mary is facing a decision as to whether to unilaterally substitute cheaper parts for those specified in a contract. In deciding what she should do from a rule utilitarian standpoint, she must first formulate the alternative rules:

Rule 1: Engineers may unilaterally substitute cheaper parts for those specified in the contract.

Rule 2: Engineers may not unilaterally substitute cheaper parts for those specified in the contract.

Mary must then determine the audience, which in this case is the producers and purchasers of such products and the general public. She must ask which of these two rules would produce more utility if generally followed. If she decides (as she surely will) on Rule 2, then she must follow this rule in her own action and not substitute the cheaper parts.

Notice that the rule utilitarian does not consider directly the utility of a particular action. Unlike the act utilitarian, the rule utilitarian judges the moral acceptability of particular actions by whether they conform to certain rules: those that produce the most utility. Notice also that the rules that may be subjected to a rule utilitarian analysis can be of very different types. The rules we examined in the arguments over advertising and competitive bidding in engineering are very general in nature and have to do with guidelines for a professional community. The rules we examined in Engineer Mary's case were much more specific, having to do with the permissibility of substituting inferior parts. Both are legitimate objects of a rule-utilitarian analysis.

6.4   The Ethics of Respect for Persons

The moral standard of the ethics of respect for persons is

> Those rules or actions are right which, if followed, would accord equal respect to each person as a moral agent.

For the purposes of this theory, we can say that moral agents are beings capable of formulating or pursuing goals and purposes of their own. They are autonomous. "Autonomy" comes from two Greek terms: *autos* meaning "self" and *nomos* meaning "rule" or "law." Thus a moral agent is autonomous in the sense of being self-governing. In the terminology of the RP theorist Immanuel Kant, moral agents are "ends in themselves," persons who are not to be treated as mere means to fulfilling the ends or goals of others. An autonomous action has three aspects. First, it is intentional, i.e., "willed in accordance with a plan."[6] Second, it is performed without external controlling influences. Third, it is made with understanding.

A moral agent must be distinguished from inanimate objects, such as knives or airplanes, which can only fulfill goals or purposes that are imposed externally. Inanimate objects certainly cannot evaluate actions from a moral standpoint. A paradigm example of a moral agent is a normal adult human being who, in contrast to inanimate objects, can formulate and pursue goals or purposes of his or her own. Since this moral theory has as its basic idea the requirement to respect the moral agency of persons, we have referred to it as the theory of respect for persons, or as "RP morality."

The RP explanation of common morality is that its precepts protect the moral agency of individual human beings. Maximizing the welfare of the majority must take second place to this goal. People cannot be killed, deceived, denied their freedom, or otherwise violated, even if doing so will lead to a greater total quantity of utility. While utilitarianism has a positive, forward-looking orientation, RP morality has a more defensive orientation. It has as its primary function the protection of individuals, so they can pursue their own aims within the parameters set by morality.

There are two principal difficulties with RP morality. First, it is sometimes hard to apply. In some cases, any alternative open to one individual involves interference with the moral agency of someone else. Suppose engineer Harry makes a promise to deliver a new product to a customer by a certain date. He finds that he can only keep this promise by delivering an inferior product. He must therefore infringe on the moral agency of the customer, no matter what he does. As a moral agent, the customer has purposes he or she is pursuing. These purposes will be hindered if Harry breaks a promise, but they will also be hindered if he delivers an inferior product that will not perform as expected. We shall consider shortly some of the ways in which RP theorists have responded to this problem. The implications of the theory in some situations remains.

A second problem with RP morality is that sometimes it seems justifiable to limit the moral agency of individuals for the sake of greater overall utility. Suppose engineer Jane owns a small engineering firm that is facing severe financial difficulties. She decides that the only way to save the firm is to institute a compulsory early retirement program. While this may infringe on the moral agency of those forced to retire, it may be the right thing to do under the circumstances. Utilitarians, however, can account for the rightness of this action more easily than proponents of RP morality.

6.5   Three Respect-for-Persons Tests

The Golden Rule Test

The RP moral standard requires us to treat everyone equally as a moral agent. This suggests a way of evaluating the resolution of moral issues, which we shall refer to as the universalizability criterion. The *universalizability criterion*, as we shall use the term, holds that, in order to be ethically valid, the resolution of a moral issue must be one that would be universally acceptable if others resolved similar issues in similar ways.

The universalizability criterion is grounded in an idea that is familiar to all of us. Most of us would acknowledge that if we act in a morally praiseworthy fashion, we are willing for others to do similar kinds of things in similar circumstances. This insight leads us to ask questions about fairness and equal treatment such as, "What if everyone did that?" and "Why should you make an exception for yourself?" Such questions highlight the fundamental issue in the universalizability test, but it can be formulated in more than one way.

The best-known version is the Golden Rule. A variant of the Golden Rule appears in the religious and ethical writings of most cultures, as the following list shows:

> Christian version: "Treat others as you would like them to treat you" (Luke 6:31, New English Bible).
>
> Hindu version: "Let not any man do unto another any act that he wisheth not done to himself by others, knowing it to be painful to himself" (*Mahabharata*, Shanti Parva, cclx.21).
>
> Confucian version: "Do not do to others what you would not want them to do to you" (*Analects*, Book xii, #2).
>
> Buddhist version: "Hurt not others with that which pains yourself" (*Udanavarga*, v. 18).
>
> Jewish version: "What is hateful to yourself do not do to your fellow man. That is the whole of the Torah" (*Babylonian Talmud*, Shabbath 31a).
>
> Muslim version: "No man is a true believer unless he desires for his brother that which he desires for himself" (*Hadith, Muslim, imam* 71-2).[7]

The Golden Rule requires us to evaluate the effects of our actions on others by asking whether we (the actors) would be willing to exchange places with those affected by our actions (the recipients). We might call the Golden Rule the principle of reversibility, because it asks whether a person would still consent to her action if the situations of the actor and recipient were reversed. Applied to line-drawing and conflict issues, it requires that the agent be willing to accept the consequences of his resolution of the issue even if he were to occupy the position of the recipient.

To apply the Golden Rule, I must take three steps. First, I must analyze the situation to determine the alternative actions available. Second, I must determine the consequences of the alternative actions. Third, I must place myself in the position of the one who would be affected by the consequences of each alternative and ask whether I would be willing to accept those consequences. An action is morally permissible if I would be willing to accept the consequences and morally impermissible if I would not.

We can informally consider some examples, without proceeding through the steps. Suppose I am an engineer trying to decide how to resolve the line-drawing issue of whether to accept a gift of a Thanksgiving turkey from a supplier. If I decide to reject the turkey because I believe it is a bribe, I must be willing to have the turkey returned to me if I were the supplier and the supplier were in my position.

Suppose again that I am a manager who orders a young engineer to remain silent about the discovery of an emission from the plant that might cause minor health problems for some people who live near the plant. In order for this resolution to be acceptable by the Golden Rule test, I must be willing to have my supervisor give a similar order to me if I were the young engineer. I must also be willing to place myself in the position of the people who live near the plant and would experience the health problem if the emission were not eliminated.

This last example highlights a problem in using the Golden Rule as a test for whether the resolution of a moral problem is acceptable. On the one hand, am I the kind of manager who believes that employees should obey their supervisors without question, especially if their supervisors are also professionals who have many years of experience? Then I would not object to remaining silent in accordance with my supervisor's orders if I were in the young engineer's position. Am I a member of the public whose health might be affected by the emission? Am I also very concerned with economic efficiency and skeptical of environmental regulations? Then I might even be willing to endure minor health problems in order to keep the plant from having to buy expensive new pollution-control equipment. Thus I could justify my action by the Golden Rule. On the other hand, if I do not have these beliefs, I cannot justify my action by the Golden Rule. The results of using the Golden Rule as a test of morally permissible action vary, then, depending on the values of the actor.

There is one possible way of avoiding some of these problems. The proponent of the Golden Rule might maintain that the Golden Rule requires not only that I place myself in the position of the recipient, but that I adopt the recipient's values and own individual circumstances as well. Thus I would not only have to put myself in the young engineer's place, but also to assume her values and her station in life. Since she was evidently troubled by my order to remain silent and probably is in a low position in the firm's hierarchy, I have to assume that I would find the order contrary to my own adopted wishes and values as well, and that I believe a professional has the right to question her supervisor's judgment. Thus I would not want to be ordered to remain silent, and my action as a manager in ordering the young engineer to remain silent would fail the test of the Golden Rule. I also have to assume the position of the people who would experience the minor health problems. Many of them—especially those whose health would be directly affected—would not be as concerned for economic considerations as I am and would object to the emissions.

Unfortunately, this tactic does not resolve all the problems. In other situations, placing myself in the position of the other people and assuming their values create a new set of problems. Suppose I am an engineer who supervises other engineers and I find that I must dismiss one of my supervisees because he is lazy and unproductive. The engineer whom I want to dismiss, however, believes that "the world owes me a living" and does not want to be punished for his irresponsibility. Now if I place myself in the position of the recipient of my own action, namely, the unproductive engineer, but retain my own values, I might use the Golden Rule to justify dismissing him. This is because I might believe that irresponsible employees should be dismissed and even be willing to be dismissed myself if I am lazy and unproductive. If I place myself in my supervisee's position and assume his values, however, I must admit that I would not want to be dismissed. Thus dismissing the young engineer fails this interpretation of the Golden Rule test, even though most of us probably believe that this is the right thing to do.

The Golden Rule can sometimes lead to counterintuitive conclusions, no matter which interpretation of it we give. This should not lead us to conclude that the Golden Rule is not a useful test in evaluating our resolution of line-drawing and conflict issues, but it should alert us to its limitations. These limitations stem from its reliance on the values and the circumstances of either the actor or the recipient in the specific situation to which the Golden Rule is applied. The next version of the universalizability test attempts to eliminate this problem.

The Self-Defeating Test

Another way of applying the fundamental idea of the universalizability criterion is to ask whether I would be able to perform the action in question if everyone else performed the same action in the same or similar circumstances. If everyone else did what I am doing, would this undermine my own ability to do the same thing?[8] If we must say yes to this question, we cannot allow others to do the same kind of thing we have done, and the universalizability criterion has not been met.

Three steps are involved in applying the self-defeating test. (1) I must analyze the situation and determine the options. (2) I must determine the consequences of the options. (3) I must determine whether the options, if universally adopted, are self-defeating. If they are, the action is impermissible. If they are not, the action is permissible.

Unlike the Golden Rule, the self-defeating test does not refer to the values or the particular circumstances of either the agent or the recipient. Rather, the question is more objective—whether everyone's performing the action would be self-defeating.

A universalized action can be self-defeating in either of two ways. First, the action itself cannot be performed if it is universalized. To use a famous example from the philosopher Immanuel Kant, if I borrow money on the promise to return it and do not keep the promise, my action would be self-defeating if universalized. If everyone borrowed money on the promise to return it and did not keep the promise, promises would not be taken seriously, and no one would loan money on the basis of a promise. Second, the purpose I have in performing the action can be undermined if everyone else does what I do, even if I can perform the action itself. If I cheat on an exam and everyone else cheats too, their cheating does not prevent me from cheating. My purpose, however, may be defeated. If my purpose is to make better grades than other students, it will be undermined if everyone else cheats, for I will no longer have an advantage over them.

In applying the self-defeating test, remember that when an action is universalized, others will not only do the same sort of thing that I do, but they will also know that others will do it as well. Suppose Engineer John decides to substitute an inferior and cheaper part in a product he is designing for one of his firm's large customers. He assumes that the customer will not check the product closely enough to detect the inferior part or will not have enough technical knowledge to know that the part is inferior. But if everyone practiced this sort of deception and expected others to practice it as well, customers would be far more inclined to have products very carefully checked by experts before they were purchased. This would make it much less likely that John's deception would be successful.

As with every other ethical test, the self-defeating test also has limitations. Some unethical actions might pass the self-defeating test. Engineer Bill is by nature an aggressive person who genuinely loves a highly competitive, even brutal, business climate. He enjoys an atmosphere in which everyone attempts to cheat the other person and to get away with as much deception as they can, and he conducts his business in this way. If everyone else follows his example, his ability to be ruthless in a ruthless business climate is not undermined. His action passes the self-defeating test, even though most of us would consider his practices immoral.

Engineer John, who has no concern for preserving the environment, could design projects that were highly destructive to the environment without his action's being self-defeating. The fact that other engineers knew what John was doing and even designed environmentally destructive projects themselves would not keep him from doing so or destroy the point he had in designing such projects, namely, to maximize his profit. The actions of both Bill and John would also pass the forms of the Golden Rule that do not require us to assume the values of others.

The Rights Test

The RP moral standard requires not only that we treat people equally but that we treat them as moral agents. Many theorists in the RP tradition have concluded that respecting the moral agency of others requires that we accord others the rights necessary to exercise it. A right may be defined as an entitlement to act or to have another individual act in a certain way. Rights serve as a protective barrier, shielding individuals from unjustified infringements of their moral agency by others.

Not surprisingly, these rights are essentially the rights to freedom and well-being. Freedom is immunity from interference by others in pursuing our own purposes. Well-being refers to the essential conditions necessary for the pursuit of our purposes. Note that these are the same two goods prized in utilitarianism. In RP morality, however, the goal is not the maximization of freedom and well-being overall. While one individual's rights may sometimes be overridden to protect another's that are considered to be more basic, those rights cannot be overridden merely to maximize overall freedom or well-being. Furthermore, generally, a more basic right cannot be sacrificed for a less basic right.

To implement this view, we must have a doctrine of a hierarchy of rights. Philosopher Alan Gewirth has provided a three-tiered hierarchy for distinguishing more basic from less basic rights.[9] The first tier includes the most basic rights, the essential preconditions of action: life, physical integrity, and mental health.

The second tier includes rights to maintaining the level of purpose-fulfillment an individual has already achieved. This category includes such rights as the right not to be deceived or cheated, the right not to have possessions stolen, the right not to be defamed, and the right not to suffer broken promises. The third tier includes those rights necessary to increase one's level of purpose-fulfillment, including the right to property, and the rights to self-respect and nondiscrimination.

Using this hierarchy, it would be wrong for a plant manager to attempt to save money by emitting a pollutant that is carcinogenic, because the right to life is a first-tier right and the right to maintain a level of purpose-fulfillment (including the right to property) is only a third-tier right. Sometimes, however, the hierarchy is more difficult to apply. How shall we balance a possible slight increase in the risk of death against a certain and substantial economic loss? Recall the benzene case presented in Chapter 4, where the Supreme Court had to balance a possible decrease in the risk of leukemia against the considerable expenses involved in mandating a reduction in exposure to benzene. The hierarchy of rights provides no automatic answer to such questions. The Court apparently believed that the introduction of utilitarian considerations was necessary to resolve the issue. Sometimes, the conflict of rights may be on the same level of the hierarchy, and here again the decisions as to which rights to violate are difficult.

People can forfeit their rights by violating the rights of others. When the state punishes a criminal, it denies him the exercise of rights he would otherwise have. But this denial is justified because he has violated the rights of others. Violating the rights of an employer may be justified when the employer has already violated the rights of the employees. In addition, some violations of the same right are more serious than others.

We can apply the rights test to the evaluation of general moral rules or laws (as, for example, in the benzene case), or to the evaluation of particular courses of action (as, for example, in a decision whether to reveal information about criminal activity to one's employer). In either case, we can apply the rights test in four stages.

1. Analyze the action to determine what options are available and what rights are at stake. When analyzing general rules, it is helpful to formulate a rule that describes the alternative actions. Usually this will be the same rule that would be used in a rule utilitarian analysis.

2. Determine the audience of the action. The audience consists of those whose rights would be affected.

3. Evaluate the seriousness of the rights infringements that would occur with a given action and compare the infringements with those of the alternative action.

4. Choose the principle or course of action that produces the least serious rights infringement.

Let us apply the rights test to a simplified version of the Gilbane Gold story recounted in Chapter 5. Suppose David Jackson is convinced that ZCORP can reduce the discharge of toxic chemicals without having to close the plant, and that the chemicals at the present rate of discharge are indeed harmful to the public. Here the contrast is between the public's right to health (a basic or first-tier right) and the firm's right to not have its present level of well-being interfered with (a second-tier right). In this case, ZCORP should reduce the discharge. While both ZCORP and the public are part of the audience, a second-tier right should be infringed before a first-tier right.

6.6   Tools for Moral Problem Solving

Moral problem solving is analogous to the work of a carpenter. The carpenter has a set of tools that are useful for various tasks. Each performs a valuable function, but each also has limitations. A hammer, for example, is effective for driving and pulling nails but not for turning screws or bolts. A carpenter must select the proper tool for a given task, keeping in mind the merits and limitations of each of the tools.

We now have four basic tools for moral problem solving. We can call these *methods of analysis, techniques,* or *modes of analysis.* They are the method of casuistry used in resolving line-drawing problems, the method of resolving conflict problems, the RP method or mode of analysis, and the utilitarian method or mode of analysis.

We can use these methods independently or combined in various ways. While the line-drawing and conflict-problem techniques, combined with common morality, are often sufficient to resolve moral issues, sometimes additional methods are useful. In the method of casuistry, for example, we compare cases with one another on the basis of similarities and differences that are morally relevant. We then decide whether the cases are more like those where the action is morally permissible or those where the action is morally impermissible. The tests suggested by utilitarian and RP theory often help in working with this method. If two cases are similar (or dissimilar) in that they both satisfy the act utilitarian test (or both fail to satisfy this test), this is important information. Similar things can be said of all the other tests developed from the two theories. Similarities and dissimilarities between cases based on a consideration of individual rights or the Golden Rule, for example, are always morally significant.

Suppose we are attempting to decide where to draw the line between legitimate and illegitimate cases of accepting gifts and amenities. Suppose further that we find that an important difference between two cases is their effect on the rights of individuals. Given what we have seen about the importance of rights in RP morality, we can be sure that this is a morally important difference. We should attach a similar importance to a difference between two cases based on the degree to which they promote overall human happiness or well-being.

Appeal to the two theories can also help us understand whether the paradigm cases in the method of casuistry are indeed paradigms of right or wrong actions. In some cases, all we need to know to explain why accepting $10,000 to specify an inferior product is wrong is that it is a bribe and that accepting bribes is wrong. Sometimes, however, we may be pressed for deeper reasons. Why is bribery wrong? The utilitarian could explain that bribery is wrong because it makes the capitalist system less efficient and therefore leads to disutility. The RP theorist could explain that bribery is wrong because it violates the rights of customers and supervisors to be given the correct information as to why a product was chosen.

The tests we have developed may also resolve conflict problems. We can appeal to the two theories to determine which obligations are most important, from a moral standpoint. We can also evaluate conflicting courses of action in terms of how effectively they protect or promote rights, and the extent to which they maximize utility.

Utilitarian and RP theories can assist in the resolution of line-drawing and conflict problems. In addition, using the step-by-step methods of analysis presented in this chapter, we can apply RP and utilitarian theory directly to moral problems. This approach is especially appropriate when one side of the moral issue in question takes a generally RP perspective and the other side takes a generally utilitarian perspective.

Consider the benzene case described in Chapter 4. The Supreme Court position embodied a limited or qualified form of utilitarianism by insisting that cost/benefit considerations (which are utilitarian in character) have a place in evaluating risk. By contrast, OSHA took the position that the rights of individual workers must always have priority, even in cases of considerable uncertainty. This position is, of course, more compatible with the ethics of respect for persons. We shall find, in fact, that many moral issues reveal a conflict between utilitarian and RP considerations.

Knowing that an argument represents a utilitarian or RP standpoint can also alert us to weaknesses characteristic of these standpoints. We can expect that any argument from the utilitarian standpoint may well give insufficient weight to considerations of justice and that any argument from the RP standpoint may give insufficient weight to considerations of the general welfare. Again the benzene case illustrates this claim. We can see the weaknesses in the perspectives of both the Supreme Court and OSHA. The Court's position can lead to an underestimation of the threat to the health of individual workers; OSHA's can lead to an underestimation of the importance of cost/benefit considerations.

A little practice enables us to become adept at recognizing characteristic utilitarian and RP approaches to issues. The same practice will enable us also to detect the characteristic weaknesses of these approaches. This is an important aid to critical thinking in morality.

Sometimes the RP and utilitarian modes of analysis lead to the same conclusion. We call this *convergence* of the two, which in such cases suggests the right course of action. Sometimes, however, the two modes of analysis lead to different conclusions. We call this *divergence*, and it leads to particularly difficult problems.

Several suggestions may aid in resolving divergence problems. First, when the violation of individual rights is minimal or questionable (as when there may be a small or uncertain threat to human health), utilitarian or cost/benefit considerations may in some cases justifiably prevail. Second, in cases of divergence, it may be useful to call upon the methods for resolving line-drawing and conflict problems, which may provide a clearer answer in some situation. Third, when the violation of individual rights is serious, RP considerations must usually prevail. Most ethicists agree that in a society that places such a high value on the protection of individual rights, no other option is appropriate.

6.7   Chapter Summary

Moral theories are attempts to explain common morality by showing that we can justify its precepts by reference to a moral standard that supplies a criterion for right and wrong. They are also useful in criticizing common morality and in providing tests for moral problem solving. The two most important moral theories are utilitarianism and the ethics of respect for persons (RP morality). The utilitarian moral standard says: Those individual actions or rules are right that produce the greatest utility to those affected. It suggests three tests for morally correct actions: the act utilitarian test, cost/benefit analysis, and the rule utilitarian test.

The moral standard of the ethics of respect for persons (RP morality) says: Those rules or actions are right that would accord equal respect to each person as a moral agent, if followed. This standard suggests three tests for morally correct action: the Golden Rule, the self-defeating test, and the rights test.

Utilitarian and RP theories can be combined in various ways with the methods for resolving line-drawing and conflict problems. The person who is skilled in ethical thinking must know which approach to moral problem solving is the most appropriate in a given situation.

Case Analyses

Case 6.1 Shameful Waste

We can probably best understand the case at the beginning of this chapter as a conflict problem. The two engineers can describe their conflict in several different ways. They can see it as a conflict between their obligation to the citizens of Baker Township and their obligations to the citizens of Madison City. But conflict problems should be stated in terms of competing moral obligations, not just obligations to various groups, which may not involve one in conflicting moral obligations at all.

Let us pursue this issue further. The engineers have an obligation to be fair to both groups. This means that they should not violate the right to equal treatment (a fundamental RP requirement) of either group. They also have an obligation to both groups to do what is in the best interests of the whole county, not just particular interest groups. Both the obligation to treat everyone fairly and the one to maximize the welfare of the entire county are obligations that the two engineers owe to each group.

It makes sense to treat the issue as a conflict problem, a conflict between two competing alternatives, each of which has reasons in its favor. More specifically, there is a conflict about the implications of the utilitarian approach in this situation. The problem is: assuming everyone is treated fairly and the claims of discrimination by Baker Township residents are false, do we maximize utility by placing the landfill near Madison City, or do we maximize utility by placing the landfill in Baker Township? To explore this issue further, we continue with the utilitarian analysis.

The relevant audience seems to be the residents of Madison County. Matthews and Parkinson argued that, with reference to this audience, the disposal site should be placed in Baker Township because (1) the alternative land is more expensive, (2) otherwise the disposal site would be closer to population centers (and therefore affect negatively a larger number), and (3) at the alternative site the contaminants would be more likely to seep into the underground water supply. These are all important considerations from a utilitarian standpoint.

The residents of Baker Township, however, offer reasons that they believe are also relevant from the perspective of the overall welfare of the county. They argue that (1) the beauty of their area is an advantage to the whole county, not just to them, and that (2) its preservation requires that the landfill be placed elsewhere. They believe these considerations outweigh the arguments given by Parkinson and Matthews.

How does one weigh the value to the county of the beauty of the area against the value to the county of the three considerations offered by Parkinson and Matthews?

One possible method is cost/benefit analysis. One might begin by establishing a monetary value for the preservation of the beauty in Baker Township. This might be done by estimating how much the tourist business in the area would decline if the landfill were located there, or by calculating the value of property in the area, as compared with property in less picturesque areas in the county.

These numbers would then have to be compared with the costs associated with the three considerations offered by Parkinson and Matthews. The difference in land costs in the two areas is presumably already available. The economic impact of locating the landfill near Madison City might be more difficult to determine. Presumably the cost of locating the landfill there would include such factors as the decline in property values near the landfill, the cost of curing any diseases caused by the landfill, and the loss (if any) of tourist business in Madison City.

We do not have enough factual information to make these calculations, and so we can only outline the considerations that would have to be a part of a cost/benefit analysis. However, we can anticipate some criticisms of this cost/benefit approach. First, critics might contend that the manner of computing the value of the rural landscape is flawed. Perhaps the increased value of property in the area or the value of the tourist trade are not adequate measures. Many people may drive through the area to enjoy its beauty without stopping to spend the night or even to eat at the restaurants. Furthermore, the method outlined so far only takes account of the values that people actually place on the beauty of the area. Perhaps the average person does not accord sufficient value to it.

A second problem with the cost/benefit approach as outlined so far is that it does not consider of the value of the beauty of Baker Township to future generations. As more and more of the countryside succumbs to urban development, the preservation of places like Baker Township in a relatively pristine condition may have far more value to future generations than to present residents of Madison County. One can attempt to estimate the costs and benefits for future generations of the two options for locating the landfill. Such estimates will, however, necessarily be highly speculative.

The advocate of the cost/benefit approach may argue that these additional considerations can be assigned monetary value as well. Often the vote citizens make at the ballot box (for example, in a referendum on where the landfill should be placed) is different from the "vote" they make in determining how to spend their money. One could, therefore, advocate a referendum on the issue, or look at past votes on similar issues. But even this is evidence only for the values people do have, not the values that perhaps they should have.

Perhaps we should turn to other forms of utilitarianism. Using rule utilitarianism, we could compare two rules such as "Engineers should always recommend that landfills be placed in rural areas," and "Engineers should always recommend that landfills be placed near urban areas."

It is unlikely, however, that either of these is justified as a general policy. More than likely, engineers should sometimes recommend that landfills be placed in rural areas and sometimes that they be placed near urban centers. One could think of other rules, such as, "Engineers should make recommendations for public policy in the most impartial and objective way possible." While it would not be difficult to justify this rule, it does not resolve the problems. The question

is what in fact the impartial recommendation should be. Thus, the rule utilitarian approach does not seem to help in this situation.

This leaves the act utilitarian perspective. Since this is similar to CBA, but without the numbers, some of the same issues arise. Perhaps we could more plausibly take account of the values that we think should prevail in the situation, rather than the values that the citizens actually have. For example, we could assign values to ecological preservation and to the importance of a rural landscape to future generations.

Without knowing more facts, resolution is probably impossible. The difficulty of weighing some of these issues, however, suggests that a creative middle way should be found, if possible. When there are strong value considerations on both sides of an issue that are not easily resolved, a creative-middle-way solution is especially appropriate. One such solution might be to locate the landfill in a part of Baker Township that is so remote that it would destroy little if any of the natural beauty of the area.

If a creative middle way cannot be found and if the value of preserving Baker Township for future generations cannot be established convincingly, or if the damage to the township is minimal, the original arguments made by Matthews and Parkinson may look more convincing. After all, even from the standpoint of future generations, the possible contamination of groundwater is a serious consideration, and this also favors locating the landfill in Baker Township.

Case 6.2 Inside Tool & Die[10]

At T&D Manufacturing, the procedure to obtain needed tooling is to have the tools designed in house by company tool engineers. When the design is approved, part prints and specifications are mailed to at least three approved outside vendors. The outside shop supplying the best price and delivery date is usually awarded a contract to produce the tool.

T&D also has an internal tool and die department. In the past this department has been used primarily to resharpen and repair the tools that are purchased outside. However, now the head of the department has requested management to allow them to offer a price to produce the tooling internally. This request is approved. Next the department head places a call to the purchasing department and asks for the prices obtained from the outside vendors before he submits his quote. "Look," he says, "we are all part of the same company. We should be working together." Is this an ethically acceptable procedure?

Analyze this case from the standpoint of factual, conceptual, and conflict issues. Then decide what should be done.

A Student Analysis

This chapter completes our introduction to methods of ethical analysis. Readers might wish to see an example of a student employing these methods in wrestling with a case study. We offer the following student's response as a model essay. Douglas Hunt was a student in Michael Pritchard's Ethics in Engineering class at Western Michigan University when he wrote this essay about the T&D case.

Introduction

The setting for this ethical dilemma is the desire of the head of a T&D Manufacturing's tool and die department, as a potential internal supplier, to obtain knowledge of the competitors' bids prior to submitting their own "best price" for a job that is to be awarded based on price and delivery. The pretense of the head of the internal supplier department is that he and the purchasing department "are all part of the same company. (They) should be working together" and that he should have access to the other bids before submitting his department's bid.

This scenario presents several factual, conceptual, and application issues, as well as a unique opportunity to apply the act, rule, and cost/benefit utilitarian tests and the universalizability, reversibility, self-defeating, and rights respect-for-persons tests. All of the preceding are discussed below.

Issues

Factual, conceptual, and application issues exist in this case study scenario. All of these issues arise from the assumptions and actions of the head of T&D's tool and die department.

The factual issue is a disagreement over the relevance of the statement "we're all part of the same company." While it is true that the tool and die department and purchasing department both are part of T&D manufacturing, the question that must be asked regarding this statement is whether or not this is relevant to the issue of the head of the tool and die department obtaining knowledge of competitors' offers before he bids on the job. While a business sense may lead one to think that it is relevant (because it allows him to underbid the lowest price), a moral perspective, as discussed later in the tests section of this essay, should lead one to believe that it is not (ethically) relevant. Thus, the following rhetorical question is offered for further consideration: Is it possible that our "judgment" regarding such issues in the business world has been clouded by the prioritization of money over ethics by logic such as what is offered by the head of the tool and die department and the subsequent decisions to make such information available?[!]

The conceptual issues hinge on the statement of "working together" and the concept of a supplier's "best price." First, there is disagreement over the idea (and assumption) of "working together." Again, a rhetorical question: would the two parties not be working together if the purchasing department did not allow the head of the tool and die department to learn of the other bids? Indeed, they are still working together by not making the competitors' offers known; they are working together *ethically,* with all bidding being conducted "above the table" (as discussed further in the following section). The second conceptual disagreement is over what is meant by the term "best price" (in this case, between suppliers bidding for a job). To the head of the T&D tool and die department, "best price" means being able to undercut the other suppliers bidding for this job. To the other suppliers, "best price" means offering their services at the most reasonable price they see fit making them available for, *without* knowledge of the competitions' offers from the contracting company.

The application issues stem from the agreement that an offer is defined as putting forth a (competitive) price to perform a job or service: when the (internal) offer is submitted and what it is based upon. There is disagreement over when the head of the tool and die department submits his offer. Should it be before or after he learns what the other offers were? Of course, the deeper question is, should he ever obtain this information? Without this knowledge, his bid is legitimate and would be based on the same information the other offers are based upon (neglecting the fact that he already probably has a better understanding of the product and the subsequent needs of the company in this job). Another application issue arises out of this

"sameness" concept: if the head of the tool and die department learns the competitions' prices after, let alone before, the job is awarded, would the other suppliers attempting to obtain the job receive this information? The illegality of insider trading comes to mind. Essentially, the application issue is the difference between a bid being based on knowledge of competitors' prices or knowledge of your processes and what it costs you to perform the job.

Tests

Many of the tests presented in the text can be applied to this case. They include the act, rule, and cost/benefit utilitarian tests and the universalizability, reversibility, self-defeating, and rights respect-for-persons tests.

The utilitarian tests pose some interesting questions, primarily based on financial considerations. The utilitarian tests would consider the utility to T&D, the bidding suppliers, the employees of all these companies, and government(s) and general public of the community(s) in which they each are located, depending on how the audience is defined. Ideally, the audience should include all of the (above) listed parties.

The act utilitarian test would consider the utility of providing the head of the tool and die department with the information for bidding on this job while the rule utilitarian test would consider the utility of providing the head of the tool and die department with the competitions' offers each time the tool and die department wished to bid on a job. In both cases, the T&D's profits and labor force would be increased (at least initially) by allowing the tool and die department to (likely) underbid the other suppliers. However, the disutility of the other companies having to downsize their labor force due to lack of work would probably outweigh the additional jobs created by keeping the T&D

work internal. Thus, utility is maximized by not sharing the information.

Similar to the act and rule utilitarian tests, the cost/benefit analysis would allow the company to obtain a price lower than the bid, but at the expense of taking the work from the other suppliers. It is possible that once the T&D tool department has successfully ousted the competition by winning successive bids due to underbidding the competition through insider knowledge, the "best price" may no longer exist for T&D; the head of the tool and die department would have established a monopoly on the market and the economic advantage to T&D as a company will have been lost due to the fact that outsiders would have stopped bidding, thus no longer providing competition. Therefore, again, the maximum utility is provided by not allowing the head of the tool and die department access to the bid information, as shown especially by the rule and cost/benefit tests.

The respect-for-persons tests serve to further support the utilitarian test results. First, the universalizability test would likely result in the common practice of no one bidding on other companies' jobs in which there was an internal job bidder (that had access to the competitions' bids and could do the job themselves); suppliers would likely consider bidding on jobs for companies with internal suppliers a waste of time and money. The self-defeating test using a universalized action would keep other companies from doing business with each other for fear of not having a fair chance, thus no longer allowing T&D to obtain the lowest price. The rights test would fail because it (1) interferes with the other companies' right to freedom, (2) interferes with the other companies' right to pursue well-being, and (3) violates Gewirth's second tier by deceiving the other companies in regard to the bidding procedure.

Recommendation

The recommended action to T&D's purchasing department is to not make available to the head of the tool and die department the bids of the other suppliers and to diplomatically suggest that he rethink his business tactics. A claim to company policy of not releasing the bids to anyone involved in the bidding process could be made. In a utilitarian sense, this action would allow the other companies to remain competitive and vital in the bidding process on a continual basis. From a respect-for-persons perspective, it would maintain their rights and standing as free moral agents.

Ultimately, the head of the tool and die department may significantly underbid the other suppliers purely out of desire to land the job and lack of knowledge regarding the competitions' bids, allowing T&D to improve its financial position. Of course, if this were to repeatedly take place, T&D may have to rethink its approval allowing internal departments to bid on jobs, due to a result similar to the outcome stated in the utilitarian and respect-for-persons test sections. It is also significant to point out that the purpose of a free market and capitalism is to allow for and take advantage of the opportunity for competition. If this is breached, then the advantages of a free market are lost.

Conclusion

In summary, this case highlights an excellent opportunity for one to act unethically in order to provide better "business opportunity" to one's company. This could be regarded as lack of foresight, as evidenced by the possible negative side effects of the utilitarian test results (lost jobs at suppliers). It is noteworthy, in closing, that the likely catalyst for this sort of lack of foresight is the (mis)identification of the audience for the course of action. If the audience is mistakenly defined as T&D (rather than all of the companies involved), the ultimate consequences may very well be lost utility and (dis)respect for persons to all involved.

Case 6.3 Highway Safety Improvements[11]

David Weber, age 23, is a civil engineer in charge of safety improvements for District 7 (an eight-county area within a midwestern state). Near the end of the fiscal year, the district engineer informs David that delivery of a new snow plow has been delayed, and as a consequence the district has $25,000 in uncommitted funds. He asks David to suggest a safety project (or projects) that can be put under contract within the current fiscal year.

From previous studies, David knows of two projects he believes should be completed as soon as funds are available. Site A is the intersection of Main and Oak Streets in the major city within the district; Site B is the intersection of Grape and Fir Roads in a rural area.

Pertinent data for the two intersections are as follows:

	Site A	Site B
Main road traffic (vehicles/day)	20,000	5,000
Minor road traffic (vehicles/day)	4,000	1,000
Fatalities per year (3-yr. average)	2	1
Injuries per year (3-yr. average)	6	2
PD* accidents per year (3-yr. average)	40	12
Proposed improvement	New signals with turn lanes	Install signal
Improvement cost	$50,000**	$25,000

*PD is abbreviation for property damage only
**Federal government will match state funds for this improvement since Main Street is part of the Federal Aid Primary System; hence, state will have to provide only $25,000.

A highway engineering textbook includes a table of average reductions in accidents resulting from the installation of the types of improvements David proposes. The tables are based on studies of intersections in urban and rural areas throughout the United States, over the past 20 years.

	Urban	Rural
% reduction in fatalities	50	60
% reduction in injuries	50	60
% reduction in PD accidents	25	–50*

*PD accidents are expected to increase because of the increase in rear-end accidents due to the stopping of high-speed traffic in rural areas.

Case 6.4: Fire Detectors   181

David recognizes that these reduction factors represent averages from intersections with a wide range of physical characteristics (number of approach lanes, angle of intersection, etc.); in all climates; with various mixes of trucks and passenger vehicles; various approach speeds; and so on.

Finally, here is some additional information that may be useful.

(1) In 1975, the National Safety Council and the National Highway Traffic Safety Administration both published dollar scales for comparing accident outcomes, as shown below:

	NSC	NHTSA
Fatality	$52,000	$235,000
Injury	3,000	11,200
PD	440	500

A neighboring state uses the following weighting scheme:

Fatality	9.5 PD
Injury	3.5 PD

(2) Note that the "exposure to hazard" is significantly higher for the drivers entering the rural intersection under present conditions. There are only one-quarter as many entering vehicles, but there are an equal number of fatalities and proportionately more injury and PD accidents.

(3) Individuals within the two groups pay roughly the same transportation taxes (licenses, gasoline taxes, etc.), hence, the collective taxes for the drivers entering the urban intersection are four times as much as for the group entering the rural intersection.

Where should David recommend that the money be spent? Analyze this case in terms of the relevant facts, conceptual issues, application issues, and conflict issues. Point out the utilitarian and respect-for-persons considerations.

Case 6.4 Fire Detectors

Residential fires cause many deaths each year. Several companies manufacture fire detectors in a highly competitive market. Jim's company is one of the firms that has a stake in this. Jim knows that there are two basic types of fire detectors. Type A is very good for certain types of fires, but for smoldering fires the detector will delay the alarm too long or fail to detect the fire at all, sometimes resulting in the loss of life. Most companies still manufacture Type A because it is cheap to build and generally performs well. Type A sells for $6 to $15. Both detectors perform well on most fires.

Type B detectors combine Type A detectors with a device for detecting smoldering fires, which constitute about 5 percent of all fires. Type B detectors sell for $15–$30, but they could be sold for almost the price of Type A detectors if they were manufactured in large quantities. In order to bring this about (short of government intervention prohibiting the sale of Type A detectors), many companies would have to decide that, in the interest of greater public safety, they will only sell Type B fire detectors.

There is little evidence that this is going to happen. As things stand, most companies either manufacture only Type A detectors, or at least depend on Type A detectors for the vast majority of their profit. Relatively few Type B detectors will sell under present market conditions. However, we do not know for sure what the actual effect of a company's example of selling only Type B detectors would be. It might stimulate other firms to follow the example, or it might cause the government to outlaw Type A detectors.

Jim's company could still stay in business if it manufactured only Type B detectors, because there is a market for them and fire detectors are only one of the products manufactured by Jim's company. Jim takes seriously the engineer's responsibility to hold paramount the safety and welfare of the public. He wonders what this obligation implies in this situation. As he sees it, there is no creative-middle-way solution. He must make what we have called a "hard choice," deciding on one or the other of the following options:

Option 1

He can make no attempt to change his firm's policy, which is to manufacture mostly Type A detectors and sell a few Type B detectors (20 percent of the firm's fire detector sales). Type A detectors, of course, are safety devices with a known deficiency, one of which can be corrected. However, they do work well 95 percent of the time. Also, far more people will buy Type A detectors than will buy Type B detectors, under present market conditions.

Option 2

He can urge his company to go out of the business of making Type A detectors and make only Type B detectors, arguing that this is the only ethical and responsible thing to do. In the long run, if other companies did the same thing, more lives would be saved and people would not be exposed to a danger of which they are generally not aware. (People generally do not know of the differences between Type A and Type B detectors.)

Questions

1. Analyze these two options from an act utilitarian (or cost/benefit) standpoint.

2. Analyze these two options from a rule utilitarian standpoint.

3. Analyze these two options from the standpoint of the Golden Rule, keeping in mind the questions and complications that can arise.

4. Do these modes of analysis converge on the same conclusion or diverge? If they converge, show how. If they diverge, explain what you think Jim should do and why.

Note: The factual assumption you make about the effect Jim's company's decision to stop manufacturing Type A detectors would have on the rest of the market (or other effects that it might have) is crucial in this case. State your assumption and stay with it throughout the analysis. One assumption, of course, is that you just don't have any idea what the effect would be. You could ask what conclusions you would get if you started with this. To complicate the situation, the assumption you make here may itself be in part governed by ethical considerations, even though it is about the facts. That is, when you don't know what the case will be in the future, what assumption is it most ethically justifiable to make? After all, a lot rides on this assumption.

Case 6.5 Trees[12]

Kevin Clearing is the engineering manager for the Verdant County Road Commission (VCRC), which has primary responsibility for maintaining the safety of county roads. Verdant County's population has increased by 30 percent in the past ten years. This has resulted in increased traffic flow on many secondary roads in the area. Forest Drive, still a two-lane road, has more than doubled its traffic flow during this period. It is now one of the main arteries leading into Verdant City, an industrial and commercial center of more than 60,000 people.

For each of the past seven years at least one person has suffered a fatal automobile accident by crashing into trees closely aligned along a three-mile stretch of Forest Drive. Many other accidents have also occurred, causing serious injuries, wrecked cars, and damaged trees. Some of the trees are quite close to the pavement. Two lawsuits have been filed against the road commission for not maintaining sufficient road safety along this three-mile stretch. Both were dismissed because the drivers were going well in excess of the 45 mph speed limit.

Other members of VCRC have been pressing Kevin Clearing to come up with a solution to the traffic problem on Forest Drive. They are concerned about safety, as well as lawsuits that may some day go against VCRC. Clearing now has a plan—widen the road. Unfortunately, this will require cutting down about thirty healthy, long-standing trees along the road.

Clearing's plan is accepted by VCRC and announced to the public. Immediately a citizen environmental group forms and registers a protest. Pat Northington, spokesperson for the group, complains, "These accidents are the fault of careless drivers. Cutting down trees to protect drivers from their own carelessness symbolizes the destruction of our natural environment for the sake of human 'progress.' It's time to turn things around. Sue the drivers if they don't drive sensibly. Let's preserve the natural beauty and ecological integrity around us while we can."

Many letters on both sides of the issue appear in the Verdant Press, the issue is heatedly discussed on local TV, and Pat Northington presents VCRC with a petition to save the trees signed by 150 local citizens.

What factual, conceptual, or application issues does this case raise? Discuss how Kevin Clearing should proceed at this point.

Case 6.6 Experimenting with Cadavers[13]

Germany's Heidelberg University used more than 200 corpses, including those of eight children, in automobile crash tests. The university claimed it received relatives' permission. The research ministry of Baden-Wuertemberg (the state in which the university is located) ordered the university to document these permissions. The revelation of these tests drew immediate protests in Germany. Rudolph Hammerschmidt, spokesman for the Roman Catholic German Bishops' Conference objected, "Even the dead possess human dignity. This research should be done with mannequins." ADAC, Germany's largest automobile club, issued a statement saying, "In an age when experiments on animals are being put into question, such tests must be carried out on dummies and not on children's cadavers."

German law permits the use of cadavers for research if relatives grant permission. In the crash tests, the bodies are strapped into cars that are smashed into other cars, walls, and barriers. The impact on humans is measured with cameras and electronic sensors. Heidelberg's Dr. Rainer Mattern, head of the forensic pathology department, indicated that children's cadavers had not been tested since 1989, but that testing of adult cadavers is continuing. He added that the tests have saved lives, including those of children.

Clarence Ditlow, head of the Center for Auto Safety (a public advocacy group in Washington, D.C.), reported that tests with cadavers were conducted by at least two research teams in the United States during the 1980s, including Detroit's Wayne State University. Ditlow said that the center advocates three criteria for such testing: (1) prior consent by the deceased person, (2) informed consent of the family, and (3) assurance that the data sought by the tests cannot be gained from using dummies.

Robert Wartner, a Wayne State spokesman, said the university's Bioengineering Center conducted tests as part of a study by the federal government's Centers for Disease Control. However, he added, "Cadavers are used only when alternatives could not produce useful safety research."

Time magazine (December 6, 1993, p. 70) reported that German parents were initially upset when asked if their children's bodies could be used in auto crash tests. However, nearly all, said *Time*, granted permission when they were told that data from the tests are "vital for constructing more than 120 types of instrumented dummies, ranging in size from infants to adults, that can simulate dozens of human reactions in a crash." *Time* also reported that, despite a 75 percent increase in the number of cars on the road over the last twenty years, the fatality rate decreased more than 50 percent. "Much of that improvement," *Time* said, "is due to the introduction of such devices as seat belts, air bags, safer windshields and stronger doors— all of which were developed with the aid of crash dummies."

Identify and discuss the ethical issues these experiments raise. What role(s) is played by engineers? In addition to considering factual, conceptual, and application issues, relate this case to leading ideas discussed in this chapter.

Case 6.7 The Ford Pinto[14]

In the late 1960s Ford designed a subcompact, the Pinto, weighing less than 2,000 pounds and selling for less than $2,000. Anxious to compete with foreign-made subcompacts, Ford brought the car into production in a little more than two years (compared with the usual three and one-half years). Given this shorter time frame, styling preceded much of the engineering, thus restricting engineering design more than usual. As a result, it was decided that the best place for the gas tank was between the rear axle and the bumper. The differential housing had exposed bolt heads that could puncture the gas tank if the tank were driven forward against them upon rear impact.

In court the crash tests were described in this way:

> These prototypes as well as two production Pintos were crash tested by Ford to determine, among other things, the integrity of the fuel system in rearend accidents. . . . Prototypes struck from the rear with a moving barrier at 21-miles-per-hour caused the fuel tank to be driven forward and to be punctured, causing fuel leakage. . . . A production Pinto crash tested at 21-miles-per-hour into a fixed barrier caused the fuel neck to be torn from the gas tank and the tank to be punctured by a bolt head on the differential housing. In at least one test, spilled fuel entered the driver's compartment. . . .[15]

Ford also tested rear impact when rubber bladders were installed in the tank, as well as when the tank was located above rather than behind the rear axle. Both passed the twenty-mile-per-hour rear impact tests.

Although the federal government was pressing to stiffen regulations on gas tank designs, the Pinto apparently met all applicable federal safety standards at the time. J. C. Echold, director of automotive safety for Ford, issued a study entitled "Fatalities Associated with Crash Induced Fuel Leakage and Fires."[16] This study claimed that the costs of improving the design ($11 per vehicle) outweighed its social benefits. A memorandum attached to the report described the costs and benefits in this way:

Benefits

Savings	180 burn deaths, 180 serious burn injuries, 2,100 burned vehicles
Unit cost	$200,000 per death, $67,000 per injury, $700 per vehicle
Total benefits	180 × $200,000 plus
	180 × $ 67,000 plus
	2100 × $ 700 = $49.15 million

Costs

Sales	11 million cars, 1.5 million light trucks
Unit cost	$11 per car, $11 per truck
Total costs	11,000,000 × $11 plus
	1,500,000 × $11 = $137 million

The estimate of the number of deaths, injuries, and damage to vehicles was based on statistical studies. The $200,000 for the loss of a human life was based on a National Highway Traffic Safety Administration study, which estimated social costs of a death in this way:[17]

Component	1971 Costs
Future productivity losses	
Direct	$132,000
Indirect	41,300
Medical costs	
Hospital	700
Other	425
Property damage	1,500
Insurance administration	4,700
Legal and court	3,000
Employer losses	1,000
Victim's pain and suffering	10,000
Funeral	900
Assets (lost consumption)	5,000
Miscellaneous accident cost	200
Total per Fatality:	$200,725

Discuss the appropriateness of using figures like the above in Ford's deciding whether or not to make a safety improvement in its engineering design. If you believe this is not appropriate, what would you suggest as an alternative?

Other Cases

The following cases already presented in this text might be examined in light of Chapters 4 and 5's leading ideas and this chapter's discussion of utilitarian and respect-for-persons-perspectives:

2.1: An Employment Opportunity
3.3: Sunnyvale

NOTES

1. Michael S. Pritchard, *Teaching Engineering Ethics: A Case Study Approach*, National Science Foundation, Grant No. DIR-8820837, p. 383.

2. The position we are taking in this book on the relationship of moral theories to common morality is a middle position between two extremes. One extreme is the belief that moral theories can only explain, but never serve as a basis for correcting or modifying, common morality. On this interpretation, if a moral theory leads to moral beliefs that contradict common morality, the theory must be rejected. One problem with this view is that it is not *always* possible to know what "the" view of common morality is on a given topic. Another problem is that common morality seems to change through time, and it may well change in the future. The cirtique of common morality offered by moral theories may well be an instrument for such change.

Another extreme is the view that moral theories might lead to a change in all of the views of common morality. On this view, all of the paradigms of right and wrong actions used in casuistry might be wrong and all of the moral requirements that generate conflict problems might be in error. This view is, at the very least, highly implausible. One would have to have a moral theory with an extremely powerful justification in order to warrant our allowing it to overthrow all of the beliefs of common morality. Probably no such justification for a moral theory exists.

Our own position is that the moral theories of utilitarianism and the ethics of respect for persons exist in dynamic relationship with common morality and perhaps also with each other. The theories can serve as a basis for evaluating and modifying common morality, but common morality can also serve as a basis for evaluating and modifying (or even rejecting) moral theories. On the one hand, a moral theory need not explain and justify all of common morality. On the other hand, a moral theory totally at variance with common morality would also be suspect. We shall also see that one theory can also serve as a basis of evaluating and modifying another theory.

3. John Stuart Mill, *Utilitarianism* (New York: Liberal Arts Press, 1957), p. 10. For a fuller exposition of utilitarianism, see C. E. Harris, *Applying Moral Theories* (2nd ed.) (Belmont, Calif.: Wadsworth, 1992), Chapter 7.

4. Utilitarians may object that they can account for rights. From the utilitarian perspective, people should be accorded rights when doing so maximizes utility in the long run. Whether giving rural people rights can be justified from a utilitarian perspective, even when doing so reduces the total amount of utility, is a complex question that we shall not consider further here. Even if utilitarians can give an account of rights, however, the account seems mistaken. Most of us probably want to say that people should have rights because they deserve them as human beings, not because giving people rights maximizes utility.

5. Baxter uses an example of "noise pollution" from an airport built near a residential area. See William F. Baxter, *People or Penguins: The Case of Optimal Pollution* (New York: Columbia University Press, 1974), pp. 49–58.

6. Ruth R. Faden and Tom L. Beauchamp, *A History and Theory of Informed Consent* (New York: Oxford University Press, 1986), p. 243.

7. These quotations, with the exception of the one from Luke, are taken from John Hick, *Disputed Questions in Theology and the Philosophy of Religion* (New Haven, Conn.: Yale Univerity Press, 1993), p. 93.

8. This version of the universalizability criterion is suggested by Immanuel Kant. For another exposition of it, see C. E. Harris, *Applying Moral Theories* (2nd ed.) (Belmont, Calif: Wadsworth, 1992, pp. 157–161).

9. See Alan Gewirth, *Reason and Morality* (Chicago: University of Chicago Press, 1978), especially pp. 199–271 and 338–354.

10. Pritchard, *Teaching Engineering Ethics*, case with commentaries, pp. 199–213.

11. This case study was developed by James Taylor of Notre Dame University.

12. Pritchard, *Teaching Engineering Ethics*, pp. 191–213.

13. This case is based on Terrence Petty, "Use of Corpses in Auto-Crash Tests Outrages Germans," *Kalamazoo Gazette* (November 24, 1993), p. A3.

14. Information for this case is based on a case study prepared by Manuel Velasquez, "The Ford Motor Car," in Manuel Velasquez, *Business Ethics: Concepts and Cases* (3rd ed.), (Englewood Cliffs, N.J.: Prentice Hall, 1992), pp. 110–113.

15. *Grimshaw* v. *Ford Motor Co.*, App., 174 Cal. Rptr. 348, p. 360.

16. This is reported in Ralph Drayton, "One Manufacturer's Approach to Automobile Safety Standards," *CTLA News*, VIII, no. 2 (February 1968), p. 11.

17. Mark Dowie, "Pinto Madness," *Mother Jones* (September/October 1977), p. 28.

Chapter 7

Honesty, Truthfulness, and Reliability

John is a co-op student who has a summer job with Oil Exploration, Inc., a company that does exploratory contract work for large oil firms.[1] The company drills, tests, and writes advisory reports to clients based on the test results. John, as an upper-level undergraduate student in petroleum engineering, is placed in charge of a field team of roustabouts and technicians who test-drill at various sites specified by the customer. John has the responsibility of transforming rough field data into succinct reports for the customer. Paul, an old high school friend of John's, is the foreman of John's team. In fact, Paul was instrumental in getting this well-paying summer job for John.

While reviewing the field data for the drilling report, John notices that a crucial step was omitted, one that would be impossible to correct without returning to the site and repeating the entire test, at great expense to the company. The omitted step involves the foreman's adding a certain test chemical to the lubricant being pumped into the test-drill site. The additive is a test for whether natural gas exists at the drill site. The test is important because it provides the data for deciding whether the drill site is worth developing for natural gas production. Unfortunately, Paul forgot to add the test chemical at the last drill site.

John knows that Paul is likely to lose his job if his mistake comes to light. Paul cannot afford to lose his job at a time when the oil business is slow and his wife is expecting a child. John learns from past company data files that the chemical additive indicates the presence of natural gas in approximately 1 percent of the tests.

Should John withhold the information that the test for natural gas was not performed from his superiors? Should the information be withheld from the customer?

7.1   Introduction

Employers, customers, and the general public rely on the information and professional judgments supplied by engineers in order to make important decisions. Many of these decisions involve very large amounts of money and issues of human health and safety. If the technical knowledge is inaccurate or incomplete, or if professional judgments are distorted by conflicts of interest or other factors, engineering services are useless. It is absolutely essential that engineering knowledge and judgment be reliable.

Reliability implies not only that professionals must be competent but that they can be trusted to convey their knowledge and judgment accurately to others. This is why the engineering codes place such emphasis on honesty and the avoidance of conflicts of interest. Yet the issue of honesty raises many difficult questions. Sometimes it is hard to be honest and forthright when we know we should be. In these cases, dishonesty is a matter of weakness of will. In other cases it may be difficult to know what honesty requires.

In this chapter we first review the statements of several codes of ethics on the subject of honesty. Next we look at the concepts of lying and withholding the truth, together with the moral foundations of truthfulness. Then we consider a series of special cases involving the obligation to tell the truth, beginning with the most blatant cases of misrepresentation and ending with cases involving conflicts of interest.

7.2   The Professional Codes on Honesty

The concern with truth-telling extends far beyond the boundaries of the engineering profession. Religious and secular literature contain many injunctions to tell the truth. One of the ten commandments forbids bearing false witness against one's neighbor. In Shakespeare's *Hamlet*, Polonius gives some advice regarding honesty to his son, Laertes, just before the son's first trip abroad from Denmark: "This above all: to thine own self be true, And it must follow, as the night the day, Thou canst not then be false to any man." John Bartlett's *Familiar Quotations* lists in the index two columns of entries on the word "true," another four on "truth," and a half column on "honesty." Miguel de Cervantes is the author of the famous aphorism, "Honesty's the best policy," which was used by George Washington in his 1796 Farewell Address. In 1381 John Wycliffe told the Duke of Lancaster, "I believe that in the end the truth will conquer."

In light of the long emphasis on honesty in our moral tradition, it is not surprising that engineering codes contain many references to honesty. The third canon of the IEEE Code of Ethics, which is reprinted in the appendix, encourages all members "to be honest and realistic in stating claims or estimates based on available data." Canon 7 requires engineers "to seek, accept, and offer honest criticism of technical work . . ."

The ASME Code of Ethics, which is also reprinted in the appendix, is equally straightforward. Fundamental Principle II states that engineers must practice the profession by "being honest and impartial." The seventh Fundamental Canon states: "Engineers shall issue public statements only in an objective and truthful manner."

The more detailed NSPE Code of Ethics, which appears in the appendix, admonishes engineers "to participate in none but honest enterprise." The preamble states that "the services provided by engineers require honesty, impartiality, fairness, and equity. . . ." The third Fundamental Canon (I.3) requires engineers to avoid deceptive acts in the solicitation of professional employment." In the Rules of Practice there are several references to honesty. In Item II.1.d, the code states, "Engineers shall not permit the use of their name or firm name nor associate in business ventures with any person or firm which they have reason to believe is engaging in fraudulent or dishonest business or professional practices." Items II.2.a through II.2.c and II.3.a through II.3.c in the Rules of Practice give more detailed direction for the practice of the profession. Item II.3 states that "Engineers shall issue public statements only in an objective and truthful manner." Items II.5 state that "Engineers shall avoid deceptive acts in the solicitation of professional employment." Items II.5.a and II.5.b give more detailed explanation as to how to implement this statement. In section III, "Professional Obligations," the code refers to the obligation for engineers to be honest and truthful and not to misrepresent facts in no less than six different locations (III.1.a, III.1.d, III.2.c, III.3.a, III.7, and III.8). In a statement that speaks directly to John's situation, part (a) of the third rule of practice states, "Engineers shall be objective and truthful in professional reports, statements or testimony. They shall include all relevant and pertinent information in such reports, statements or testimony."

Canon 3 of the ASCE code requires engineers to make "public statements only in an objective and truthful manner." A subsection enjoins engineers not to "participate in the dissemination of untrue, unfair or exaggerated statements regarding engineering."

In addition to the more explicit references to honesty, several of the codes require engineers to be responsible in other aspects of professional communication. The second canon of the IEEE code requires members to avoid conflicts of interest, and we have already pointed out that conflicts of interest can distort professional judgment. A subsection of canon 3 of the ASCE code requires members not to issue statements on engineering matters "which are inspired or paid for by interested parties, unless they indicate on whose behalf the statements are made." Here again is the emphasis on full disclosure. A subsection of canon 4 of the same code speaks to the matter of confidentiality, an area where withholding information is justified. It enjoins engineers to avoid conflicts of interest and forbids them from using "confidential information coming to them in the course of their assignments as a means of making personal profit if such action is adverse to the interests of their clients, employers or the public."

We have already cited the primary reason for the importance of honesty: without honesty, the value of engineering services is undermined. Unreliable engineering judgment is worse than none at all. We will now look more closely at the conceptual issues related to this topic.

7.3   A Taxonomy of Types of Misusing the Truth

An engineer can distort the truth in many different ways. The various ways that engineers can act irresponsibly in the communication of professional knowledge and judgment can be placed on a continuum, beginning with the paradigm cases of dishonesty, namely lying, and continuing to cases of failing to actively pursue the truth.

Lying

When we think of dishonesty, we usually think of lying. Ethicists have long struggled over the definition of lying. One of the reasons for the difficulty is that not every falsehood is a lie. If an engineer mistakenly conveys some test results on soil samples, she is not lying, even though she may not be telling the truth. In order to lie, a person must intentionally or at least knowingly convey false or misleading information. But even here complications arise. A person may give information that she believes to be false, even though it is actually true. In this case we may be perplexed as to whether we should describe her action as lying. Her intention is to lie, but what she says is actually true.

To make matters still more complicated, a person may give others false information by means other than making false statements. Gestures and nods, as well as indirect statements, can give a false impression in a conversation, even though the person has not told an outright lie.

In spite of these complications, most people believe that lies—or at least paradigm cases of lies—have three elements: First, a lie ordinarily involves something that is believed to be false or seriously misleading. Second, a lie is ordinarily stated in words. Third, a lie is made with the intention to deceive. So perhaps we can offer the following working definition: "A lie is a statement believed to be false or seriously misleading, made with the intention to deceive." Of course this definition leaves the term "seriously misleading" open for interpretation, but the open-ended nature of this working definition is deliberate. We call some misleading statements lies and others not.

Deliberate Deception

If an engineer discusses technical matters in a manner implying knowledge that he in fact does not have, to impress an employer or potential customer, he is certainly engaging in deliberate deception, even if he is not lying. In addition to misrepresenting one's own expertise, one can misrepresent the value of certain products or designs by praising their advantages inordinately. Such deception can sometimes have more disastrous consequences than outright lying.

Revealing Confidential or Proprietary Information

One can misuse the truth not only by lying or otherwise distorting or withholding it but also by disclosing it in inappropriate circumstances. Engineers in private practice can disclose confidential information without the consent of the client. Information may be confidential if it is either (1) given to the engineer by the client or (2) discovered by the engineer in the process of work done for the client.

Since most engineers are employees, a more common problem involving the improper disclosure of information is the violation of proprietary information. Using designs and other proprietary information of a former employer can be dishonest and may even result in litigation. Even using ideas one developed while working for a former employer can be questionable.

Withholding Information

Omitting or withholding information is another type of deceptive behavior. If Jane deliberately fails to bring up some of the negative aspects of a project she is promoting to her superior, she engages in serious deception, even though she is not lying. Failing to report that you own stock in a company whose product you are recommending is a form of dishonesty. Perhaps we can say in more general terms that one is practicing a form of dishonesty by omission (1) if he fails to convey information that the audience would reasonably expect would not be omitted and (2) if the intent of the omission is to deceive.

Failing to Adequately Promote the Dissemination of Information

The primary ethical obligation of engineers is to protect the health and safety of the public. This may require engineers not only to disclose information but to do what they can to see to it that this information is properly disseminated. Those affected must receive the information, especially if the information can avoid a disaster. Roger Boisjoly's attempts to inform his superiors of the dangers inherent in the O-ring design exemplify one engineer's recognition of this obligation.

Allowing One's Judgment to Be Corrupted

An important part of any professional service is professional judgment. Allowing this to be corrupted or unduly influenced by conflicts of interest or other extraneous considerations can lead to another type of dishonesty. Suppose Engineer Joe is designing a chemical plant and specifies several large pieces of equipment manufactured by a company whose salesman he has known for many years. The equipment is of good quality, but some newer and more innovative lines might actually be better. In specifying his friend's equipment, Joe is not giving his employer or client the benefit of his best and most unbiased professional judgment. In some cases this may be a form of dishonesty, but in any case Joe's judgment is unreliable.

Failure to Seek Out the Truth

Reliable judgment may include more than avoiding dishonesty in its various forms. The honest engineer is one who is committed to finding the truth, not simply avoiding dishonesty. Suppose Engineer Mary suspects that some of the data she has received from the test lab are inaccurate. In using the results as they are, she is not lying, nor is she concealing the truth. But she may be irresponsible in using the results without inquiring further into their accuracy. Honesty in this positive sense is part of what is involved in being a responsible engineer.

This taxonomy should not be interpreted as implying that lying is the most serious offense and failing to seek out the truth is the least serious. Sometimes the consequences of lying may not be as serious as the consequences of some of the other actions mentioned in the taxonomy. The taxonomy reflects primarily the degree to which one is actively distorting the truth, rather than the seriousness of the consequences of the actions.

7.4   Why Is Dishonesty Wrong?

The term "honest" has such a positive connotation and the term "dishonest" such a negative one that we forget that telling the full truth may sometimes be wrong and concealing the truth may sometimes be the right thing to do. A society in which people are totally honest with each other would be difficult to tolerate. The requirement of total honesty would mean that people would be brutally frank about their opinions of each other and unable to exercise the sort of tact and reticence that we associate with polite and civilized society. With regard to professionals, the requirement never to conceal or distort truth would mean that engineers, physicians, lawyers, and other professionals could not exercise confidentiality or protect proprietary information. Doctors could never lie or misrepresent the truth to their patients, even when there is strong evidence that this is what the patients prefer and that the truth could be devastating.

In spite of possible exceptions, however, dishonesty and the various other ways of mishandling the truth are generally wrong. The best way to see this is to consider dishonesty from the standpoints of utilitarianism and the ethics of respect-for-persons. Moral theories can provide valuable suggestions for thinking about moral issues. Here is a good illustration of their usefulness.

Let us review some of the major components of the respect-for-persons perspective. Actions are wrong if they violate the moral agency of individuals. Moral agents are beings capable of formulating and pursuing goals and purposes of their own—they are autonomous. "Autonomy" comes from two Greek terms: *autos* meaning "self" and *nomos* meaning "rule" or "law." Thus a moral agent is autonomous in the sense of being self-governing. In the terminology of the respect-for-persons theorist Immanuel Kant, moral agents are "ends in themselves," persons who are not to be treated as mere means to fulfilling the ends or goals of others. An autonomous action has three aspects.[2] First, it is intentional, "willed in accordance with a plan."[3] Second, it is performed without external controlling influences. Third, it is made with understanding.

This means that an autonomous action is one that is made with informed consent. Thus, in order to respect the moral agency of their patients, physicians must ensure that their patients make decisions about their medical treatment with informed consent. They must see to it that their patients are conscious and rational in making decisions that have some relationship to their life plans. They also have some responsibility to ensure that patients make decisions without undue coercive influences, such as stress, illness, and family pressures. Finally, physicians must see to it that patients are sufficiently informed about options for treatment and the consequences of the options.

Engineers have some degree of responsibility to see to it that employers, clients, and the general public make autonomous decisions, but their responsibilities are more limited than those of physicians. Their responsibilities probably extend only to the third of these three conditions of autonomy, ensuring that employers, clients, and the general public make decisions regarding technology with understanding, particularly understanding of their consequences. We have seen, for example, that the IEEE code requires members to "disclose promptly factors that might endanger the public or the environment" and that when the safety, health, and welfare of the public are endangered, ASCE members must "inform their clients or employers of the possible consequences."

In engineering this applies to such issues as product safety and the provision of professional advice and information. If customers do not know that a car has an unusual safety problem, they cannot make an informed decision as to whether to purchase it. If a customer is paying for professional engineering advice and is given misinformation, he again cannot make a free and informed decision.

The astronauts on the Challenger were informed on the morning of the flight about the ice build-up on the launching pad and were given the option of postponing the launch. They chose not to exercise that option. However, no one presented them with the information about the O-ring behavior at low temperatures. Therefore, they did not give their consent to launch despite the O-ring risk, since they were unaware of the risk. The Challenger incident is a tragic example of the violation of the engineer's obligation to protect informed consent. The fault, however, was not primarily with the engineers but with managers who supported the launch and did not inform the astronauts of the danger.

Many situations are more complex. In order to be informed, decision makers must not only have the relevant information but understand it. Furthermore, nobody has all of the relevant information or has complete understanding of it, so that being informed in both of these senses is a matter of degree. Therefore, the extent of the engineer's obligation regarding informed consent will sometimes be controversial, and whether or not the obligation has been fulfilled will also sometimes be controversial. We shall return to these considerations later.

Now let us turn to the utilitarian perspective on honesty. Utilitarianism requires that our actions promote human happiness and well-being. The profession of engineering contributes to this utilitarian goal by providing both technological innovations and information about technology that is important in decision making on individual, corporate, and public-policy levels.

Dishonesty in engineering research and testing can undermine these functions. If engineers report data falsely or omit crucial data, other researchers cannot depend on their results. This can undermine the relations of trust on which a scientific community is founded. Just as a designer who is untruthful about the strength of the materials she specifies for a building threatens the collapse of that building, so a researcher who falsifies the data reported in a professional journal threatens the collapse of the infrastructure of engineering.

Dishonesty can also undermine informed decision making. Managers in both business and government, as well as legislators, depend on the knowledge and judgments provided by engineers in making decisions. If these are unreliable, the ability of those who depend on engineers to make good decisions regarding technology is undermined. To the extent that this happens, engineers have failed in their obligation to promote the public welfare.

From both a respect-for-persons and a utilitarian perspective, then, dishonesty and other forms of irresponsibility with regard to technical information and judgment are usually wrong. These actions undermine the moral agency of individuals by preventing them from making decisions with free and informed consent. They also prevent engineers from promoting the public welfare. In the following sections we shall consider some areas in which this irresponsibility can occur.

7.5   Honesty on Campus

Three students were working on a senior capstone engineering design project.[4] The project was to design, build, and test an inexpensive meter that would be mounted on the dashboard of automobiles and would measure the distance the car could travel on a gallon of gasoline. Even though personal computers, microchip calculators, and "smart instruments" were not available at the time, the students came up with a very clever approach that had a good chance of success. They devised a scheme to instantaneously measure both voltage equivalents of gasoline flow to the engine and speedometer readings on the odometer, while keeping a cumulative record of the quotient of the two. That is, miles-per-hour divided by gallons-per-hour would give a figure for the miles the automobile would travel per gallon of gasoline. They even came up with a way to filter and smooth out instantaneous fluctuations in either signal to ensure time-averaged data. Finally, they devised a bench-top experiment to prove the feasibility of their concept. The only thing missing was a flow meter that would measure the flow of gasoline to the engine in gallons-per-hour and produce a proportional voltage signal.

Nowadays, customers can order this feature as an option on one of the more expensive automobiles, but at the time the design was remarkably innovative. The professor directing the project was so impressed that he found a source of funds to buy the flow meter. He also encouraged the three students to draft an article describing their design for a technical journal.

Several weeks later the professor was surprised to receive a letter from the editor of the journal, accepting for publication the "excellent article" that, according to the letter, he had "co-authored" with his three senior design students. The professor knew that the flow meter had not yet arrived, nor had he seen any draft version of the paper, so he asked the three students for an explanation. They explained that they had followed the professor's advice and prepared an article about their design. They had put the professor's name on the paper as senior author since, after all, it was his idea to write the paper and he was the faculty advisor. They did not want to bother the professor with the early draft. Further they really could not wait for the flow-measuring instrument to arrive, since they were all graduating in a few weeks and planned to begin new jobs.

Finally, since they were sure the data would give the predicted results, they simulated some time-varying voltages on a power-supply unit to replicate what they thought the flow-measuring voltages would be. They had every intention, they said, of checking the flow voltage and the overall system behavior after the flow meter arrived and, if necessary, making minor modifications in the paper.

As a matter of fact, the students incorrectly assumed that the flow and voltages would be related linearly. They also made some false assumptions about the response of the professor to their actions. The result was that the paper was withdrawn from the journal and the students sent letters of apology. Copies of the letters were also placed in their files, the students received an "F" in the senior design course, and their graduation was delayed six months. In spite of this, one of them requested that the professor write a letter of recommendation for a summer job he was seeking!

A student's experience in engineering school is a training period for his or her professional career. If dishonesty is as detrimental to engineering professionalism as we have suggested, part of this training should be in professional honesty. Yet surveys of students show that cheating on exams is not uncommon. Several years ago a respected liberal arts college in the Midwest surveyed its freshmen and found that 48 percent had cheated on exams or engaged in other forms of academic dishonesty.[5] There is no reason to believe that things are different in engineering schools.

If a student does not learn to avoid falsely presenting data or creating totally false data, she may be dishonest in her professional career. As we shall see in the next section, there are exact counterparts in the scientific and engineering communities to the types of dishonesty exhibited by students. Smoothing data points on the graph of a freshman physics laboratory report to get an "A" on the report, selecting the research data that support the desired conclusion, entirely inventing the data, and plagiarism of the words and ideas of others—all of these actions have obvious parallels in nonacademic settings.

Perhaps the ultimate irony in student dishonesty is to cheat on an exam in professional ethics. A recent comic strip shows a dejected student talking to his girlfriend about an ethics exam he took on some difficult questions about Kant, Hegel, and Mill. She asks how he did. "I got an 'A' on the ethics exam," he responds dejectedly. "Then why the sad face?" she asks smilingly. "I cheated," he answers.

7.6   Honesty in Engineering Research and Testing

David Baltimore was a Nobel laureate, a highly respected biologist, and institute director at Massachusetts Institute of Technology. In 1986, Margot O'Toole, a postdoctoral fellow at MIT, complained to Dr. Baltimore about some allegedly fraudulent data in a paper she, Dr. Thereza Imanishi-Kari, Dr. Baltimore, and several others had co-authored. Dr. O'Toole alleged that Dr. Imanishi-Kari had entered into her log book some false data that could not be replicated. Dr. Baltimore claimed total ignorance of the falsified data and at first refused to initiate an investigation. Finally he appointed a review committee, which exonerated Dr. Imanishi-Kari.

Still convinced that she was right, Dr. O'Toole alerted Representative John Dingell of Michigan, chairman of the U.S. House Committee on Science and Technology. The committee concluded that there was indeed scientific fraud and threatened criminal proceedings against Dr. Imanishi-Kari, but a federal judge dismissed the case.

During this period Dr. Baltimore accepted the presidency of Rockefeller University in New York City, but the suspicion surrounding his scientific work made it impossible for him to exercise his presidential responsibilities effectively. He tried to pacify his critics by withdrawing the disputed paper, but this tactic was unsuccessful. He finally resigned the presidency of the university. Whatever final evaluation we might give of Dr. Baltimore's handling of this situation, this case illustrates the seriousness with which the scientific community takes issues of honesty in research.

Dishonesty in science and engineering takes several forms: trimming, cooking, forging, and plagiarism.[6]

Trimming is "the smoothing of irregularities to make the data look extremely accurate and precise." This is a temptation to which not only engineering students but engineering researchers as well are susceptible. As one person guilty of this form of dishonesty put it, "I smoothed out the data. I took the curves and smoothed them out."[7]

Cooking is "retaining only those results that fit the theory and discarding others."[8] In one of the best-known cases of cooking, physicist Robert A. Millikan, who later received the Nobel prize, selected the data he reported in his famous paper on the electronic charge. The paper was based on a series of experiments on liquid droplets. It contained an explicit statement that his findings were not based on "a selected group of drops" but "all of the drops experimented upon during 60 consecutive days."[9] Evidently Millikan had enough data to make a sound case without selecting the data, but he chose to misrepresent the data anyhow.

Forging is "inventing some or all of the research data that are reported, and even reporting experiments to obtain those data that were never performed."[10] John Darsee was a Harvard Medical School graduate who went to work at Emory University. While at Emory, he published papers based on his research there that were subsequently withdrawn due to falsified data.[11] He gave the following justification for his dishonesty:

> I had too much to do, too little time to do it in, and was greatly fatigued mentally and almost childlike emotionally. I had not taken a vacation, sick day, or even a day off from work for six years. I had put myself on a track that I hoped would allow me to have a wonderful academic job and I knew I had to work very hard for it.[12]

Dr. Darsee's research was in medicine. The disastrous effects that inaccurate data could have had on medical practice are frightening. Equally disastrous effects could occur in engineering. Imagine the consequences of using a published theory on a new lightweight bridge design that was based on falsified data.

The difficulty in determining the full import of apparent forging and cooking of the data is illustrated by recent research on the so-called Goodrich A-7 brake case. The case, involving brake data falsification for the A-7 military aircraft at B. F. Goodrich, has long been a standard item in engineering ethics.[13] Two later accounts raise some serious questions as to what really was at stake.[14]

In 1968 the B. F. Goodrich Corporation won the competition for a subcontract to LTV, Inc. to design and build the brakes for the Navy A-7 aircraft. They won the contract because they entered the lowest bid and their design was the most innovative. They were anxious to win this contract because they had lost some aircraft business years before, due to a faulty component design, and wished to reestablish their reputation. The bid promised a lighter four-rotor brake. John Warren, an experienced design engineer, had designed the four-rotor brake for the proposal.

When the contract was awarded, Goodrich assigned Searle Lawson, a young recently graduated engineer, to take the laboratory data that would prove that the prototype four-rotor brake met all military standards, such as the required stopping time and maximum allowable temperature. Kermit Vandivier, a technical writer, was assigned to help write the reports based on the data Lawson was taking. Unfortunately, the data consistently showed that the four-rotor brakes did not meet military test standards, which had been established years earlier with the five-rotor brake performance in mind.

After a year of negative test results, none of which were reported to LTV, the brakes were flight tested. On one landing test (out of many uneventful tests) the brakes overheated. The pilot was never in danger, and he had plenty of extra runway to let the aircraft coast to a stop. Nevertheless, the overheating was further evidence of the inadequacy of the four-rotor brake. Lawson was present at the flight tests representing Goodrich.

Unknown to Lawson and Vandivier, Goodrich higher management had written off the four-rotor brake design as a failure and had started a parallel development program to design and test a five-rotor brake at Goodrich's expense. At a lower level, the Goodrich engineering management team decided to present the four-rotor brake test results in the best possible light. In order to keep the LTV contract, they directed that laboratory tests be modified. They specified that the brakes should be allowed to coast longer between applications than allowed by military specifications, be cooled by fans between and during test runs, and be remachined between test runs. When this cooking of the data still did not yield the desired test results, they decided that the data should be forged.

At this point Lawson and Vandivier informed the FBI, which in turn alerted the Government Auditing Office (GAO). The GAO's investigation resulted in a hearing in the U.S. Senate, chaired by Senator William Proxmire. The press coverage portrayed Vandivier and Lawson as heroes who voluntarily blew the whistle to protect the public safety. Vandivier was dismissed by Goodrich and took a job as a reporter for a local newspaper for which he had been writing part time. Lawson resigned and went to work for LTV, where he is currently employed.

Lawson and Vandivier knew nothing of the intentions of higher management. All they knew was what they observed. While the distortion of the data at Goodrich cannot be excused, the ignorance of Lawson and Vandivier regarding the ultimate intentions of higher management made it impossible for them to interpret the significance of this data falsification correctly. Thus the Goodrich case illustrates both the existence of data falsification and the difficulties that lower-level employees sometimes face in interpreting it correctly.

Plagiarism is the use of the intellectual property of others without proper permission or credit. It takes many different forms. Plagarism is really a type of theft. Drawing the line between legitimate and illegitimate use of the intellectual property of others is often difficult, and the method of casuistry is useful in helping us to discriminate between legitimate and illegitimate instances of the use of the words and ideas of others. Some cases are undeniable examples of plagiarism—as when the exact words or the data of another are used without proper permission or attribution. On the other side of the spectrum, the quotation of short statements by others with proper attribution is clearly permissible. Between these two extremes are many cases where drawing the line is more difficult.

A particularly vexing issue that might well be included under the category of plagiarism is the issue of multiple authorship of scientific papers.[15] Sometimes as many as forty or fifty researchers are listed as the authors of a scientific paper. One can think of several justifications for this practice. First, often a large number of scientists participate in some forms of contemporary research, and, furthermore, they all make genuine contributions. For example, there is the large number of people involved in research with a particle accelerator or the number of people required to perform some types of medical research. Second, the distinction between whether someone is the author of a paper or merely deserves to be cited may indeed be tenuous in some circumstances. The fairest or at least the most generous thing to do in such circumstances is to cite such people as authors.

There are, however, less honest motives for the practice, the most obvious one being the desire of most scientists for as many publications as possible. This is true both of academic and nonacademic scientists. In addition, many graduate and postdoctoral students need publications in order to secure jobs. Sometimes more senior scientists are tempted to list graduate students as authors, even though their contribution to the publication was minimal, in order to make their research record look as impressive as possible.

From a moral standpoint, there are at least two potential problems with multiple authorship. First, it is fraudulent to claim significant credit for scientific research when in fact a contribution is relatively insignificant. If claims to authorship are indeed fraudulent, those evaluating the scientist or engineer are not able to make informed decisions. Second, fraudulent claims to authorship give one an unfair advantage over others who do not make such claims. This results in an unfair advantage in the competition for jobs, promotions, and recognition in the scientific community. From the standpoint of the ethics of respect-for-persons, unsubstantiated claims to authorship should be avoided.

7.7   Honesty and Proprietary Information

Many companies require their employees to sign a patent assignment, whereby all patents and inventions of the employee become the property of the company, often in exchange for a token fee of $1. Sometimes employees find themselves caught between two employers with respect to such issues.

Consider the case of Tom, a senior engineering production manager of a tire manufacturing company, Roadrubber, Inc. Tom has been so successful in decreasing production costs for his company by developing innovative manufacturing techniques that he has captured the attention of the competition. One competing firm, Slippery Tire, Inc., offers Tom a senior management position at a greatly increased salary. Tom warns Slippery Tire that he has signed a standard agreement with Roadrubber not to use or divulge any of the ideas he developed or learned at Roadrubber for two years following any change of employment. Slippery Tire assures Tom that they understand and will not try to get him to reveal any secrets and that they want him as an employee because of his demonstrated managerial skills.

After a few months on the job at Slippery Tire, someone who was not a part of the earlier negotiations with Tom asks him to reveal some of the secret processes that he developed while at Roadrubber. When Tom refuses, he is told, "Come on, Tom, you know this is the reason you were hired at the inflated salary. If you don't tell us what we want to know, you're out of here."

This is a clear case of an attempt to steal information. If the managers who attracted Tom to Slippery Tire were engineers, they also in violated the NSPE code. Under "Professional Obligations," item III.1.d of the NSPE Code says, "Engineers shall not attempt to attract an engineer from another employer by false or misleading pretenses."

Some cases are not so clear. Sometimes an employee develops ideas at Company A and later finds that those same ideas can be useful—although perhaps in an entirely different application—to his new employer, Company B. Suppose Tom's new employer is not a competing tire company but one that manufactures rubber boats. A few months after being hired by Rubberboat, Tom comes up with a new process for Rubberboat. It is only later that he realizes that he probably thought of the idea because of his earlier work with Roadrubber. The processes are different in many ways, and Rubberboat is not a competitor of Roadrubber, but he still wonders whether it is right to offer his idea to Rubberboat.

Let's examine what the NSPE Code of Ethics has to say about such situations. Under "Rules of Practice," item II.1.c states, "Engineers shall not reveal facts, data or information obtained in a professional capacity without the prior consent of the client or employer except as authorized or required by law or this code." Item III.4 states,

> Engineers shall not disclose confidential information concerning the business affairs or technical processes of any present or former client or employer without his consent. (a) Engineers in the employ of others shall not without the consent of all interested parties enter promotional efforts or negotiations for work or make arrangements for other employment as a principal or to practice in connection with a specific project for which the engineer has gained particular and specialized knowledge. (b) Engineers shall not, without the consent of all interested parties, participate in or represent an adversary interest in connection with a specific project or proceedings in which the engineer has gained particular specialized knowledge on behalf of a former client or employer.

These code statements strongly suggest that even in this case Tom should tell the management at Rubberboat that they must enter into licensing negotiations with Roadrubber. In other words, he must be honest in fulfilling all of his obligations to Roadrubber.

Other cases can be even less clear, however. Suppose the ideas Tom developed while at Roadrubber were never used by Roadrubber. Tom realized they would be of no use and never even mentioned them to management at Roadrubber. Thus they might not be considered a part of any agreement between him and Roadrubber. Still, the ideas were developed using Roadrubber's computers and laboratory facilities. Or suppose Tom's ideas occurred to him at home while he was still an employee of Roadrubber, although the ideas probably would never have occurred to him if he had not been working on somewhat related problems at Roadrubber.

We can best deal with these problems in drawing the line between permissible and impermissible actions by means of the method of casuistry. As we have seen, the method involves pointing out similarities and dissimilarities between the cases whose moral status is clear and the cases whose moral status is less clear.

7.8   Honesty and Client-Professional Confidentiality

While most engineers are employees of large corporations, some, especially civil engineers, work for design firms that have clients. For these engineers, the obligation to protect the confidentiality of the client-professional relationship arises, much as it does for lawyers and physicians. Confidentiality would ordinarily cover both sensitive information given by the client and information gained by the professional in work paid for by the client.

An engineer can abuse client-professional confidentiality in two ways. First, an engineer may break confidentiality when it is not warranted. Second, an engineer may refuse to break confidentiality when the higher obligation to the public requires it.

Here is an example of the first type of abuse. Suppose Engineer A inspects a residence for a homeowner for a fee. He finds the residence in generally good condition, although in need of several minor repairs. Engineer A sends a copy of his one-page report to the homeowner, showing that a carbon copy was sent to the real estate firm handling the sale of the residence.

The NSPE Board of Ethical Review ruled that "Engineer A acted unethically in submitting a copy of the home inspection to the real estate firm representing the owners." It cites section II.1.c of the NSPE code, which states: "Engineers shall not reveal facts, data, or information obtained in a professional capacity without the prior consent of the client or employer except as authorized by law or this Code."[16]

This opinion seems correct. The clients paid for the information and therefore could lay claim to its exclusive possession. The residence was fundamentally sound, and there was no reason to believe that the welfare of the public was at stake. The case would have been more difficult if there had been a fundamental structural flaw. Even here, however, we can argue that there was no fundamental threat to life. Prospective buyers are always free to pay for an inspection themselves.

The following hypothetical case raises more serious difficulties. Suppose Engineer James inspects a building for a client before the client puts the building up for sale. James discovers fundamental structural defects that could pose a threat to public safety. James informs the client of these defects in the building and recommends its evacuation and repair before it is put up for sale. The client replies,

James, I am not going to evacuate the building, and I am certainly not going to spend a lot of money on the building before I put it up for sale. Furthermore, if you reveal the information to the authorities or to any potential buyer, I am going to take whatever legal action I can against you. Not only that, but I have a lot of friends. If I pass the word around, you will lose a lot of business. The information is mine. I paid for it, and you have no right to reveal it to anyone else without my permission.

James's obligation to his client is clearly at odds with his obligation to the public. While he may have an obligation to potential buyers, his more immediate and pressing one is to protect the safety of the present occupants of the building. Note that the section of the NSPE code quoted above requires engineers to keep the confidentiality of their clients and employers in all cases, except where exceptions are authorized "by law or this Code." This is probably a case where part of the code (specifically, the part emphasizing the higher obligation to the safety of the public) overrides the requirement of confidentiality.

Even here, however, James should probably try to find a creative middle way that allows him to honor his obligations to his client, to the occupants of the building, and to potential buyers. He might attempt to persuade the client that his intention to refuse to correct the structural defects is morally wrong and probably not even in his long-term self-interest. He might argue that the client may find himself in lawsuits, and that surely he would find it hard to live with himself if a catastrophe occurred.

Unfortunately, such an approach might not work. James's client might refuse to change his mind. Then James must rank his competing obligations. The codes are clear that the engineer's first obligation is to the safety of the public, so James must make the information about the structural defects of the building public.

The limits of client-professional confidentiality are controversial in most professions. Physicians must reveal cases of child abuse, even if it violates patient-physician confidentiality. The "Model Rules of Professional Conduct" of the American Bar Association says that lawyers "may" reveal confidential information when there is a threat of "imminent death or substantial bodily harm" (rule 1.6b).

One of the most famous legal cases involving professional confidentiality involves a psychologist whose client, Prosenjit Poddar, killed his girlfriend, Tatiana Tarasoff, after informing his psychologist of his intentions. Neither Tatiana nor her parents were warned of the danger, and, after Tatiana's death, the parents sued the University of California, where the psychologist was employed. A California court ruled in favor of the parents. Excerpts from the court's opinion are directly relevant to the situation sometimes faced by engineers:

When a therapist determines, or pursuant to the standards of his profession should determine, that his patient presents a serious danger of violence to another, he incurs an obligation to use reasonable care to protect the intended victim. . . . We conclude that the public policy favoring protection of the confidential character of patient-psychotherapist communications must yield to the extent to which disclosure is essential to avert danger to others. The protective privilege ends where the public peril begins.[17]

The California court agrees with engineering codes in placing the interests of the public above those of clients or employers. Still, all cases involving confidentiality will not be as clear-cut as the one James faced. In fact, his situation might serve as one extreme on a spectrum of cases. The other extreme might be a case in which an engineer breaks confidentiality to promote his own financial interests. Between these two extremes are many other cases where the decision might be difficult. Again, in such line-drawing cases, it is appropriate to use the method of casuistry.

7.9   Honesty and Expert Testimony

Engineers are sometimes hired as expert witnesses in cases involving accidents, defective products, structural defects, patent infringements, and other areas where competent technical knowledge is required. Calling upon an expert witness is one of the most important moves a lawyer can make in such cases, and engineers are usually well compensated for their testimony. However, being an expert witness is time consuming and often stressful, with considerable demands on the expert witness. Thomas A. Hunter is an engineering consultant from Westport, Connecticut, who often serves as an expert witness. Speaking at the winter annual meeting of the American Society of Mechanical Engineers in November 1992, he remarked, "Engineers must be credible in court. This credibility depends on the engineer's knowledge of engineering, the particular case, and especially the court process."[18] With regard to cases involving defective products, Hunter warned,

> To make a credible presentation to the jury, it is simply not enough to merely point out that there is a design defect. At a minimum, the expert must show three things. First, that the defect was recognizable by the designer; second, that there were means available to correct the defect when the product was designed; and third, that the costs of corrective features would not price the product out of the market or interfere with the product's effectiveness.[19]

When confronted with these demands, the expert witness faces certain ethical pitfalls. The most obvious is perjury on the witness stand. A more likely temptation is to withhold information that would be unfavorable to the client's case. In addition to being ethically questionable, such withholding can be an embarrassment to the engineer, for cross-examination often exposes it.

In order to avoid problems of this sort, an expert witness should follow several rules.[20] First, she should not take a case if she does not have adequate time for a thorough investigation. Rushed preparation can be disastrous for the reputation of the expert witness as well as for her client. This includes not only general technical knowledge but detailed knowledge of the particular case and the processes of the court before which the witness will testify. Second, she should not accept a case if she cannot do so with a good conscience. This means that she should be able to testify honestly and not feel the need of withholding information in order to make an adequate case for her client. Third, the engineer should consult extensively with the lawyer, so that the lawyer is as familiar as possible with the technical details of the case and can prepare the expert witness for cross-examination. Fourth, the witness should maintain an objective and unbiased demeanor on the witness stand. This includes sticking to the questions asked and keeping an even temper, especially under cross-examination. Fifth, the witness should always be open to new information, even during the course of the trial. During a trial of a recent accident case in Kansas, the defendant discovered in his basement an old document that conclusively showed that his company was culpable in the accident. He introduced this new evidence in court proceedings, even though it cost his company millions of dollars and resulted in the largest accident court judgment in the history of Kansas.[21]

7.10   Honesty and Failure to Inform the Public

Some types of irresponsibility in handling technical information do not involve withholding information but rather a failure to inform those whose decisions are impaired by the absence of the information. This is a serious impairment of moral agency. The responsibility of engineers to ensure that technical information is available to those who need it is especially strong where disasters can be avoided.

Dan Applegate was Convair's senior engineer directing a subcontract with McDonnell Douglas in 1972.[22] The contract was for the designing and building of a cargo hatch door for the DC-10.[23] The design for the latch of the cargo door was known to be faulty. When the first DC-10 was pressure-tested on the assembly line, the cargo hatch door blew out and the passenger cabin floor buckled, resulting in the destruction of several hydraulic and electrical power lines. Modifications in the design did not solve the problem. Later, a DC-10 flight over Windsor, Ontario, had to make an emergency landing in Detroit after the cargo hatch door flew open and the cabin floor again buckled. Fortunately, no one was injured.

In the light of these problems, Applegate wrote a memo to the vice-president of Convair, itemizing the dangers of the design. However, Convair managers decided not to pass this information on to McDonnell Douglas because of the possibility of financial penalties and litigation if accidents occurred. Applegate's memorandum was prophetic. Two years later, in 1974, a fully loaded DC-10 crashed just outside Orly Field in Paris, killing all 346 passengers. The crash happened for the reasons that Applegate had outlined in his memorandum. While there were genuine legal impediments to disclosing the dangers in the DC-10 design to the federal government or to the general public, this story emphasizes the fact that an engineer's failure to disclose information can have catastrophic consequences. In this case most of us would probably say that Dan Applegate's professional responsibility to protect the safety of the public required that he do something to make his professional concerns about the DC-10 known. Failing to do more to publicize concerns about the safety hazards in the aircraft resulted in massive expense and loss of life and denied passengers the ability to make an informed decision in accepting an unusual risk in flying in the aircraft.

Similar issues are raised in another well-known case involving the Ford Pinto gas tank case in the early 1970s. At the time the Pinto was introduced, Ford was making every effort to compete with the new compact Japanese imports by producing a car in less than two years that weighed less than 2,000 pounds and cost less than $2,000.[24] The project engineer, Lee Iacocca, and his management team believed that the American public wanted the product they were designing. They also believed that the American public would not be willing to pay the extra $11 to eliminate the risk of a rupturing gas tank. In the late 1960s and early 1970s that judgment was probably accurate, for at the time the American public was not much concerned about safety.

The engineers who were responsible for the rear-end crash tests of early prototype models of the Pinto knew that the Pinto met the current regulations for safety requirements in rear-end collisions; however, they also knew that the car failed the new higher standards that were to go into effect in just a few years. In fact, the car failed eleven of twelve rear-end collisions at the newly prescribed twenty-miles-per-hour tests. In the crashes the gas tanks ruptured and the vehicles caught fire. Thus many engineers at Ford knew that the drivers of the Pinto were subject to unusual risks of which they were unaware. They also knew that management was not sympathetic to their safety concerns. One of the engineers working on the Pinto test program found that the ignorance of potential drivers to the car's dangers was unacceptable and decided to resign and make the information public. The engineer thus gave car buyers the knowledge they needed to purchase the Pinto with informed consent.

Did Ford management have a callous disregard for safety? No, only a few years earlier this same management had voluntarily reported that some of their line employees, in a misguided show of company loyalty, had falsified EPA emissions data on new engines to bring Ford into compliance with EPA regulations on a new model. As a result of this honest disclosure, Ford was required to pay a very stiff fine and had to substitute an older model engine on the new car at even greater expense.

Still another such case involves the Chevrolet Corvair. Early prototype testing of the Corvair showed that it had a propensity to roll over in high-speed turns due to a flaw in the rear-end, roll-bar suspension design. The problem was compounded by the fact that the drivers of these cars were likely to be young people who tended to drive too fast. Tragically, the daughter of a GM executive was killed while driving an early model of the car.

Problems with the Corvair resulted in serious discussions at the highest levels of GM management about the proper course of action. The discussions were resolved when the head of the Chevrolet division of GM, "Bunkie" Knudsen, got a costly redesign and recall program approved. He threatened to resign and go public if his proposal was rejected. Knudsen subsequently became president of GM.

The obligation of engineers to protect the health and safety of the public requires more than refraining from telling lies, or simply refusing to withhold information. It sometimes requires that engineers aggressively do what they can to see to it that the consumers of technology are not forced to make uninformed decisions regarding the use of that technology. This is especially true when the use of technology involves unusual and unperceived risks. This obligation may require engineers to do what is necessary to either eliminate the unusual risks or at the very least inform those using the technology of the dangers. Otherwise their moral agency is seriously eroded. Placing yourself in the position of the seven Challenger astronauts, you probably would have wanted to hear all of the relevant engineering facts about the risky effects of low temperatures on the rocket booster O-ring seals before giving permission for liftoff. Similar considerations apply to those who flew the DC-10, or drove Pintos or Corvairs.

7.11   Conflicts of Interest

Consider the following fictional case. Anxious to upgrade its status as a first-rate research institution, Central Tech has just established a summer fellowship program for faculty research. Faculty may now submit proposals for research projects they wish to undertake.

As a young faculty member, engineer Roger Rhodes is excited about this new possibility. Although already a productive researcher, he has been frustrated at having too little time for research during his first few years of teaching. To make ends meet, he has had to take summer work in industry. A summer fellowship would not pay as much as industry, but it would provide enough for him to get by. More important, a fellowship would help him move ahead with his favorite research project. Besides, doing this research would help him get a promotion in the university.

As he is working on his proposal in his office, Roger's phone rings. It is David Dinsmore, vice-president for research at Central Tech. He says, "Roger, I'm calling to ask you to serve on the review panel for our new faculty fellowship program. It's important to have people on the panel who are highly respected and know good research when they see it."

What should Roger Rhodes say? He is flattered that David Dinsmore thinks so highly of him, but he wonders if it is all right to serve on the panel when he plans to submit a proposal himself. He mentions this to David Dinsmore, who replies, "Since this is a new program, we haven't worked out all the wrinkles yet. But it doesn't seem fair that our best people—the ones we want on the panel— should not have a chance at the fellowships. You can still apply. All we require is that you not be involved in evaluating your own proposal. Just leave the room when your proposal is being considered. The other panelists will rank your proposal in your absence, and you won't know where yours ranks until the entire process is complete."

Does this solve Roger Rhodes's problem? What *is* the problem? The answer that most readily comes to mind is that it is a conflict of interest. Roger has two conflicting interests—one in submitting his proposal for competitive evaluation, the other in serving as an evaluator. Either interest, taken by itself, is perfectly legitimate; taken together, however, they pose a serious problem. As evaluator, Roger has a responsibility to judge as impartially as he can, and so do the other panelists. But it is too much to expect him to be impartial in judging his own proposal. This is why David Dinsmore says Roger must absent himself from the room when his proposal comes up for consideration.

Still, two problems remain if Roger serves on the panel. First, his presence on the panel may bias the other panelists in his favor.[25] Second, even though he is not directly judging his own proposal, Roger may judge other proposals more harshly than he should, thus enhancing the chances of his own proposal's acceptance.[26] None of this possible distortion need be intentional or deliberate. Roger and the other panelists might be fully convinced that they are, after all, capable of objective judgment. But self-deception is possible, and it is notoriously difficult to discover in oneself. For that reason, it is difficult to eliminate.

So, it is not clear how Roger can serve on the panel and still avoid a conflict of interest. Roger should probably not accept the appointment.

NSPE's Board of Ethical Review (BER) periodically reviews cases that fall within the scope of NSPE's Code of Ethics. Of all the kinds of cases brought to the BER's attention, those concerning conflicts of interest are the most common. (Advertising issues are a distant second, and they relate more to how professional services may be promoted than how they are actually performed.) What exactly are conflicts of interest, and why do they generate so much concern in engineering practice?

Conflicts of interest are discussed in two places in NSPE's Code of Ethics. In neither place is "conflict of interest" defined. But an examination of those two occurrences will help us discover what a conflict of interest in engineering might involve and why this should be of ethical concern.

Fundamental canon 4 addresses the idea that engineers should act as "faithful agents or trustees" in performing their professional duties. The first entry under this heading is that engineers should disclose all "known" or "potential" conflicts of interest to their employers or clients. It is clear that one set of interests is that of an engineer's employer or client. This is mentioned in the context of engineers' performing their professional duties as agents or trustees. So far, then, three elements are present:

   1. Certain interests of an employer or client
   2. An engineer's professional duty to faithfully serve and protect those interests
   3. Competing interests that threaten to have an adverse impact on the engineer's fulfilling that duty

It is also clear that not just any possible interests of an employer or client count. An employer or client might have some interests that the engineer has no duty to serve or protect. For example, an employer or client might have an interest that can be served or protected only through illegal activity (e.g., fraud, theft, embezzlement, murder). An engineer has no professional duty to serve or protect such an interest. (However, he or she may have a duty to expose such an interest to external authorities.)

So, these interests must have some sort of legitimacy if an engineer has a duty to support or protect them. Further, they must relate to the engineer's professional role. Once it is understood that certain interests of an employer or client satisfy these conditions, we can understand why it is appropriate to say engineers should be seen as faithful agents, or trustees. The engineer is trusted to fulfill his or her duty to serve or protect those interests.

But what if an engineer finds that serving or protecting the interests of one employer or client may be compromised by serving or protecting the interests of someone else—either another employer or client, or even himself? Let us first consider the case of another employer or client. Suppose an engineer assumes a relationship of trust with a second employer or client. Were it not for the first relationship, there would be no problem. However, serving two clients who are in competition with each other in the same area of legitimate interest can easily create a conflict of interest. Or, simultaneously, being employed by two companies can create a conflict of interest, even if the companies are not direct competitors, for it may be difficult for an engineer to do quality work for two demanding employers.

Distinct from these possibilities is the following. Suppose an engineer is hired by a client to steal trade secrets from another client. This is not a conflict of interest because only one set of interests is legitimate. We have other ways of characterizing what has gone wrong. Of course, the engineer could be characterized as disloyal and as a thief, but this does not mean there is a conflict of interest.

Now for the second kind of case. In some instances we might talk about a conflict of interest when only the engineer and the employer or client is involved. Here we would refer to interests of the engineer that, in the absence of the other interests of the employer or client, it would be legitimate for the engineer to pursue. In this context, however, there is a conflict of interest. For example, in a hiring situation, normally one is pleased at seeing one's best friend hired. If asked to comment on a friend's qualifications, normally there is no problem with putting in a good word for the friend. But what if one is on the hiring committee, whose job it is to proceed objectively, without favoritism, in making its recommendations?

Nothing is inherently wrong with having a conflict of interest. What is at question is how it arises and what is done about it. Since it threatens fulfillment of one's professional duties, most codes of ethics urge professionals to guard against getting trapped in one. However, sometimes, through no fault of the professional, a conflict arises. Then the question is: What should be done about it?

This is what is said under fundamental canon 4: "a. Engineers shall disclose all known or potential conflicts of interest to their employers or clients by promptly informing them of any business association, interest, or other circumstances which could influence or appear to influence their judgement or the quality of their services."

Obviously employers and clients have a strong interest in engineers being free from conflicts of interest. One quite legitimate concern is that an engineer's other interests may unduly interfere with the kinds of judgment they expect their engineers to exercise in the performance of their professional duties to them. This in itself is a worry about the quality of service they will receive. In addition, employers and clients may be concerned about competing demands of time, energy, and loyalty affecting the quality of service provided.

However, as already noted, a conflict of interest may arise through no fault of the engineer. In any case, NSPE's code insists that engineers are to disclose known, or even potential, conflicts of interest to their employers or clients. Then employers or clients are given the opportunity to determine whether the continuance of the conflict of interest is acceptable to them. Deliberately withholding such information is dishonest, and it deprives employers or clients of the opportunity to decide for themselves how serious the situation is.

Fundamental canon 4 of the NSPE code emphasizes business associations, interests, or other circumstances that threaten to interfere with engineers' rendering the kinds of judgment and quality of service that their professional duties call for. But it requires only disclosure of these interests. Section III, professional obligations, goes further and specifies some prohibitions.

> 5. Engineers shall not be influenced in their professional duties by conflicting interests.
>
>   a. Engineers shall not accept financial or other considerations, including free engineering designs, from material or equipment suppliers for specifying their product.
>
>   b. Engineers shall not accept commissions or allowances, directly or indirectly, from contractors or other parties dealing with clients or employers of the Engineer in connection with work for which the Engineer is responsible.

We might object that this section assumes that acceptance of such material goods actually will interfere with engineers' meeting their professional duties. What proof is there that this will result? Actually, it is not necessary to provide proof in order to see why accepting substantial gifts and favors poses a problem. All we need to see is that their acceptance could and might appear to influence judgment and performance. Once the doubt is raised, how can the appearance of influence be shown to be merely that?

The problem of appearance has two important features. First, a sincere conviction that we have not been influenced by gifts or favors is not sufficient. We are especially prone to self-deception and rationalization about such matters, so we are not in an especially strong position to be self-assured about this in any particular case. Second, even if we could be certain in our own case, this does not mean that we can convincingly show others that we are right. So, the doubt remains—along with the damage to trust that doubt carries with it. This is why fundamental canon 4 stresses the importance of engineers' disclosing factors that "*could influence or appear to influence their judgment or the quality of their service.*"[27]

In characterizing conflicts of interest for lawyers, Michael Davis describes the conflict as "a collision between competent judgment and something that might make that judgment unable to function as the lawyer's role requires."[28] This seems to fit engineers particularly well, as in their professional roles, they are expected to exercise competent engineering judgment. This requires a kind of objectivity that is independent of incentives or disincentives that threaten to compromise engineering judgment.

These threats come in three basic forms. First, there are *actual* conflicts of interest that, unless removed, threaten to compromise independent engineering judgment. Second, there are *potential* conflicts of interest that can easily become actual conflicts. Finally, as we have seen, there is an *appearance* of a conflict of interest. Even if this is merely an appearance of, not an actual or potential, conflict of interest, it may generate sufficient distrust to cause problems.

What are the basic values at stake? First, Davis notes that problems concerning conflicts of interest are interpersonal. That is, what is at stake is a relationship between two or more individuals or groups, rather than simply conflicting interests within a particular individual. He emphasizes the duties involved in having professional roles or relationships. Corresponding to these duties are rights on the part of those to whom the duties are owed. Davis views failure to meet these duties as analogous to lying and promise-breaking. The problem that conflicts of interest pose is that trust in the independent judgment of the professional is threatened.

It is noteworthy that NSPE's code does not connect the problem of conflicts of interest to parties other than employers and clients. Neither do Davis or others who have recently written about conflicts of interest. However, it is important to realize that conflicts of interest may be of considerable moral interest to others as well. For example, when a special relationship between an engineer and a vendor unduly influences the engineer's recommendations about the purchase of materials or equipment, competing vendors might well complain of not getting fair consideration. Or they might complain of having to resort to unfair tactics themselves in order to get their feet in the door.

One consequence of such practices could be that materials and equipment are selected on the basis of gifts and special favors, not on the basis of their price and quality. This may harm the company, but it may also harm the public by offering the public inferior yet expensive—and possibly even unsafe—products. So, conflicts of interest are quite understandably of great concern in engineer/employer or client relationships, and they should be of some concern to the public as well.

Davis emphasizes the importance of reliable *judgment* on the part of engineers. Neil Luebke emphasizes the importance of *trust*.[29] Which view is right? Both. Luebke contrasts "Can I *trust* X to give me good advice?" with "Can I trust X to give me *good* advice?" However, he mistakenly thinks that Davis is more interested in the second question than the first. No one is interested in the services of an engineer who is incapable of giving good advice. Nor would they be interested in the services of an engineer who, however capable of giving good advice, cannot be trusted to render it. So, both trust and good advice are essential.

Luebke thinks Davis underplays the importance of trust. However, Davis's analysis of judgment actually reveals why trust is so important. Professional judgment, Davis insists, is about matters that require discretion, rather than simply routine application of an algorithm. Professional judgment requires the special expertise of engineers, and others must rely on responsible exercise of that expertise. The need for such reliance is based on two considerations:

1. Professional engineers have knowledge and skills not widely shared. This is why we say they have expertise. So most people have to defer to their judgment about engineering matters. (Even engineers may have difficulty understanding one another's work—especially when they have different specializations.)

2. Professional engineers have to be trusted to do their work competently. This is because usually there is not time, energy, or staff to check the detailed reliability of their judgment, even if someone is capable of doing so.

Engineers typically work in large organizations marked by highly specialized functions. Those working in one area do not necessarily know what specialists in other areas are doing, even if given the opportunity to observe their work. As already noted in Chapter 2, William F. May warns that experts (including engineers) had better be virtuous, since few are in a position directly to observe and understand what they do.

Luebke is right: trust is an essential value that is threatened by conflicts of interest. However, Davis is also right in focusing our attention on judgment. We expect engineers to exercise independent judgment about matters within their range of expertise in carrying out their responsibilities. Competence to make such judgments is, of course, a prerequisite. But, as Davis is no doubt aware, competence is not enough. Engineers must be as free as possible from influences that threaten to interfere with competent exercise of judgment.

We need not suppose that engineers, or any other professionals, have deliberately set out to compromise their judgment in situations raising questions about conflicts of interest. However, since employers and clients have a right to expect competent, independent judgment from their engineers, they also expect that engineers will inform them of any possible problems related to conflicts of interest. Not to do so is to disappoint a rightful expectation, and therefore to betray that trust.

We have mentioned that self-deception poses a special problem in conflict of interest situations. It can interfere with objectivity in ways that are hard to detect. We should mention two other kinds of problems. The first is simply the difficulty of recognizing a potential conflict of interest, especially before it is too late. This is sometimes quite difficult even for those who are otherwise attentive to the problem of conflicts of interest. (Readers might want to test this out by looking at Case 7.6 and Case 1.8.)

The second problem is the difficulty of knowing where to draw the line. There are clear-cut examples of conflicts of interest that should not be difficult to detect, at least not after a little reflection. Our fictional Roger Rhodes example is a case in point. There are other cases that clearly do not pose a conflict of interest, such as accepting a cup of coffee from a vendor. Unfortunately, most situations are not so clear-cut, and good judgment is required, as the following fictional case illustrates.

Scott Bennett is an engineer assigned to deal with vendors who supply needed parts to the Upscale Company. Larry Newman, sales representative from one of Upscale's regular vendors, plays in the same golf league as Scott. One evening they go off in the same foursome. Sometime during the round Scott mentions that he is really looking forward to vacationing in Florida next month. Larry says his uncle owns a condo in Florida that he rents out during the months he and his family are up north. Larry offers to see if the condo is available next month—assuring Scott that the rental cost is quite moderate.

Scott may interpret this simply as a friendly gesture on Larry's part and not consider possible implications for their business relationship—especially since he plans to be in Florida anyway. Suppose, next, that Larry calls Scott with good news: he can rent his uncle's condo for $100 a week. "My uncle," Larry says, "gets nervous when he rents to total strangers. He likes to have reliable people stay instead of making money on it—he just wants a little help meeting basic operating expenses and the taxes."

Scott accepts the offer and begins making plans for his vacation. Just before leaving, an Upscale vice-president sends out a new policy statement that says, among other things: "Accepting incentives from vendors is strictly prohibited."

What should Scott do? Is accepting Larry's offer in violation of the new policy statement? Is the condo offer an "incentive"? Scott has at least two reasons for not wanting to face this question squarely. First, he has already accepted the offer and may not wish to offend Larry by questioning his generosity. Second, he really *wants* to save money and stay in a nice condo. Actually, however, both reasons should give Scott pause for concern, for both are just the sorts of considerations that could affect his judgment in ways that do not serve his company well. If he does not want to offend Larry now, how will he feel about Larry later when he has made a difficult decision involving Larry's vending services—*after* he has used the condo? And if the anticipation of money and comfort interfere with his looking more carefully at the situation now, how will matters stand later?

It might be helpful for Scott to use some casuistic reasoning. If Larry offered to pay for Scott's plane fare, clearly this would be the sort of incentive prohibited by the policy. If Larry only suggested that Scott call his uncle for advice about local golf courses to play, there would be no problem. An inexpensive stay at the uncle's condo falls somewhere between these opposite paradigms.

Scott might be tempted to say to himself, "I'd already accepted the offer before the new policy was announced. So it doesn't apply—especially if I keep my mouth shut." But this is not likely to impress Upscale's vice-president, who no doubt feels he has substantial reasons for initiating the policy. So, if it hasn't already occurred to him, it seems that Scott should be asking himself what those reasons might be.

One question Scott needs to ask is at what point it is likely that one's professional judgment will be impaired by what happens. But this is not the only question. He also needs to ask at what point it is likely that others may believe they have reason to doubt the reliability of his professional judgment. He must avoid the appearance of a conflict of interest, too. Given the fact that the company has just announced the policy against incentives, the best thing to do in this case seems to be to consult with his superiors about the matter. What does the policy rule out, and should he turn down the offer?

7.12   Chapter Summary

Professional engineering codes stress the importance of honesty in engineering work. There are various ways to mishandle the truth. They include outright lying, deliberate deception, revealing confidential or proprietary information, withholding information, failing to adequately promote the dissemination of information, allowing one's judgment to be corrupted, and failing to actively seek out the truth when professional responsibilities are involved. The emphasis on honesty is justified from the standpoint of moral theory. From the standpoint of the ethics of respect-for-persons, dishonesty in engineering violates the moral agency of other people by limiting their ability to make free and informed decisions about issues that affect them or that they consider important. From the utilitarian standpoint, dishonesty in engineering distorts and obstructs the communication and advancement of technical knowledge, which in turn can contribute to human well-being.

Issues involving the proper handling of truth can occur in every area of engineering. Engineering students can engage in dishonesty in research projects and assignments and perhaps thereby acquire traits that will carry over into their professional life. Dishonesty in engineering research and testing can take various forms and can hinder the pursuit of knowledge. The misuse of proprietary information and of information gained in the engineer-client relationship can unjustifiably harm employers and clients (but other considerations, such as the welfare of the public, must sometimes also be considered). Expert witnesses have special obligations to present responsible, carefully prepared testimony. Engineers also have an obligation to actively pursue the truth in cases where the public welfare is at stake.

Conflicts of interest present especially difficult problems for engineers. They are morally troublesome because they can corrupt engineers' professional judgment and undermine trust in engineers. While there is nothing inherently wrong with having a conflict of interest, why the conflict arises and what is done about it are important considerations. Conflicts of interest can be actual, potential, or merely apparent. Self-deception poses a special problem in conflict-of-interest cases. Sometimes we do not even recognize a conflict of interest until it is too late. It is often difficult to draw the line between situations that do and do not pose a conflict of interest.

Case Analyses

Case 7.1 Oil Exploration, Inc.

Let us return to the case presented at the beginning of this chapter. John faces a conflict involving at least four moral obligations. First, he has an obligation to his employer to perform his duties in an honest and competent way and to be a loyal employee, insofar as this is possible within the bounds of morality. Second, he has an obligation to his company's customers to perform the services for which they have contracted and paid. Third, John has an obligation to his friend Paul. Friendship imposes mutual moral obligations, compounded by the fact that John probably owes his job to Paul. Paul could lose his job if his error is reported and Paul's wife is expecting a child, which make this obligation especially pressing. Fourth, John has an obligation to himself to preserve his own job and to promote his career, or at least a legitimate desire to do so. This obligation or desire might be overridden by other considerations, but it should be honored if possible.

Before making a decision, John should take some time to think of as many options as possible and to assess them in light of his conflicting moral obligations. He should attempt to find a way to satisfy as many of the competing obligations as possible, even if they are not satisfied in their fullest or most complete way.

The first opinion might be to simply overlook the error and indicate in his report that the test for gas was negative. If this option were successful, it would have the advantage of preserving Paul's reputation and probably his job. It would also allow John to continue in his job. It probably would not be congruent with his obligations to his employer. Presumably John's superiors want to perform services in an honest and competent way and to be informed when their employees make mistakes. This option would be even less successful in meeting the obligation to the customer. Even though the chances of overlooking a gas deposit are small, they do exist. Apart from this, the customer is not receiving the services for which it paid.

This first option fails to honor at least two of the relevant obligations. It also involves dishonesty. If John must explicitly indicate on the report that the missing test was performed, then he is guilty of lying. If he only omits mentioning the test that was not performed, then he is guilty of withholding information. Is this deception? Suppose we define deception as deliberately misleading someone with regard to some information to which the person had a right. By this definition, John is guilty of deception. While deception is sometimes justifiable, this exception to the rule against deception could probably not be universalized. If everyone falsified data in this way and it were generally know that this occurred, engineering reports could not be trusted.

In addition to these considerations, there is a good chance that John's deception would not be successful in the long run. If it were discovered, all of the relevant obligations would be violated. John would probably lose his job, as would Paul. The customer's rights have already been violated, and compensation might not be possible without the expense of a lawsuit. Finally, John's employer's reputation would have been harmed.

A second option is for John to report the error but take the blame himself. He might argue either (1) that he forgot to remind Paul to make the test or (2) that Paul told him that he had omitted the test and he forgot about this when he wrote the report. While the first option would probably not be successful, because the responsibility for making the test resides with Paul, the second might be successful. This option would honor John's obligation to Paul, to the company to some extent, and to the customer. It would not, of course, honor John's obligation to himself.

We might consider this option an act of supererogation—an act above and beyond the call of duty. Most of us would probably see something noble about it. It is not done out of self-interest, and it manifests a kind of loyalty to one's friend. It does, however, involve a lie. Can such a lie be justified? Would it be self-defeating if lies in such circumstances were generally practiced? The problem with universalizing such lies is that it does undermine trust between employer and employee. There would probably also be a suspicion that a lie was involved. If such behavior were universalized, this suspicion would be much greater. Therefore, it is doubtful if lying in such circumstances could be universalized without its being self-defeating. This option is therefore not justifiable.

A third option is to simply tell the truth, attempting in every way possible to ensure that the mistake will not happen again and to argue for Paul's retention by the company. John might even offer to help Paul remember to perform the test. This option seems to most adequately satisfy all of the moral demands on John. It manifests loyalty to the company and to the customer, and it preserves John's reputation and integrity. It does of course place Paul's job in jeopardy, but Paul made a mistake. Paul might argue that this option violates John's obligation to him, but John can argue that his obligation does not include a duty to lie for his friend.

Furthermore, John can strenuously attempt to defend Paul if his job is threatened. Paul might object that John's low position in the company as a summer student employee does not place him in a position to effectively defend him, but this might be wrong. John should probably go to a superior whom he trusts and reveal the situation. He should solicit the superior's advice and inform the superior of his concern for his friend and his own personal anguish over the situation. If John is fortunate in having an understanding superior, he may be able to save Paul's job.

Case 7.2 Disclosure of Previous Work by Consultant[30]

Facts

Engineer A agrees to provide consulting services to RMF, Inc., in connection with the development of a new product for manufacture. He develops a preliminary report, which is approved, then develops the design for the product. Engineer A and RMF, Inc., do not negotiate any terms in their agreement relating to the actual ownership of the design of the product. Neither takes any steps to seek patent protection. When the design reaches the production stage, RMF, Inc., terminates the services of Engineer A in accordance with their agreement. Thereafter, Engineer A agrees to provide consulting services to SYS, Inc., a competitor of RMF, Inc. As a part of those services, he divulges specific information unique to the product designed for RMF, Inc.

Question

Was it ethical for Engineer A to divulge specific information to SYS, Inc., unique to the product designed earlier by him for RMF, Inc.?

References

Code of Ethics—Section II.1.c.—"Engineers shall not reveal facts, data or information obtained in a professional capacity without the prior consent of the client or employer except as authorized or required by law or this Code."

Section III.4.—"Engineers shall not disclose confidential information concerning the business affairs or technical processes of any present or former client or employer without his consent."

Section III.10.c.—"Engineers, before undertaking work for others, in connection with which the Engineer may make improvements, plans, designs, inventions, or other records which may justify copyrights or patents, should enter into a positive agreement regarding ownership."

Analysis

[This analysis was prepared by Darrell Telgenhof, a student in Michael Pritchard's Ethics in Engineering class at Western Michigan University.]

Engineer A is currently working for SYS, and he has an obligation to provide them with the best service that he can. This may cause him to feel like he has conflicting duties in this situation. He may feel that he has an obligation to keep the designs from RMF confidential, but he also wants to provide SYS with a good product. If he feels that the unique designs are the best way to produce the new product, he will be more tempted to use them. He needs to keep in mind, though, that RMF and SYS are competitors and that RMF has a basic right to not have their design ideas copied by the competitors.

No laws have been broken here. Engineer A never signed any agreement and there are no patents on the design of the product developed at RMF. Strictly speaking, no one has legal ownership of the designs. Simply because his action is legal does not make it ethical. Maybe RMF should have taken the steps to get legal rights to the design. The fact that they didn't does not make their designs common property. It is somewhat irresponsible of Engineer A to say that it is RMF's fault for not being more careful, and then use the ideas to the advantage of the competitor.

Although the law does not forbid using this information for a competitor, the NSPE Code of Ethics does. Section III.4.b of the code states: "Engineers shall not, without the consent of all interested parties, participate in or represent an adversary interest in connection with a specific project or proceeding in which the Engineer has gained particular specialized knowledge on behalf of a former client or employer." Although we don't know for sure, it is most likely that Engineer A does not have consent from RMF to disclose the design information. RMF would not want their competitors using their technology. Under this assumption, Engineer A is in violation of the NSPE Code of Ethics. His conduct would likely be considered inappropriate for a professional engineer.

By applying the Golden Rule test, Engineer A could see that if he were in the position of his former employer he would not want the designs given to the competitors. His action may also be self-defeating if universalized. If all engineering consultants divulge this sort of information, it may only cause companies to be more careful to take care of legal rights first. It is probable, though, that companies would become much more suspicious of engineering consultants and would not want to hire them.

Competition between companies is what keeps companies striving to improve products and produce them economically. If a company has access to the designs of a competitor, it defeats the purpose of competition. From a utilitarian viewpoint it appears to be in the best interest of society to keep the competition fair.

This raises a conceptual issue about what "fair" competition is. Most companies have some aspects in which they surpass their competitors. Without this they would not be able to compete. Different people have different ideas about what "fair" is. To some people, if it's legal, it's "fair," but most people can agree that having access to a competitor's information gives a company an "unfair" advantage.

As a professional, Engineer A made a poor decision. He should have obtained consent from RMF for the use of their designs. The least that he should do now is inform RMF that he is reusing the design ideas.

Case 7.3 XYZ Hose Co.[31]

Farmers use anhydrous ammonia to fertilize their fields. The anhydrous ammonia reacts violently with water, so care must be exercised in disbursing it. Farmers' cooperatives rent anhydrous ammonia in pressurized tanks equipped with wheels, so the tanks can be pulled by tractors. The farmers also rent or purchase hoses that connect the tanks to perforated hollow blades that can be knifed through the soil to spread the ammonia. Leaks from the hose are potentially catastrophic.

For years the industry standard hose was one made of steel-meshed reinforced rubber, which was similar in construction to steel-reinforced automobile tires. Two separate trade associations had established these industry-wide standards.

About fifteen years ago a new, heavy-duty plastic became available that could replace the steel in the hoses. The plastic-reinforced hoses were less expensive, lighter, and easier to process than the steel-braided rubber. The new hose met the industry standards. One company, the XYZ Hose Company, began marketing the plastic-reinforced hose to farmers. Officials of XYZ knew, as a result of tests run by a consultant at a nearby state agricultural college, that the plastic did not react immediately to the anhydrous ammonia; however, over the years the plastic did degrade and lose some of its mechanical properties. Accordingly, they put warnings on all the hoses they manufactured, indicating that they should be replaced periodically.

After the product had been on the market a few years, several accidents occurred in which the XYZ hoses ruptured during use and blinded and severely injured the farmers using them. Litigation followed, and XYZ argued in its defense that the farmers had misused the hoses and not heeded the replacement warnings. This defense was unsuccessful, and XYZ made substantial out-of-court settlements.

XYZ has since dropped this product line and placed advertisements in farmers' trade journals and producers' cooperatives newsletters asking farmers to turn in their XYZ hoses for full refunds. The advertisements state that the hoses are "obsolete," not that they are unsafe.

Identify and discuss the ethical issues this case raises, paying special attention to relevant, key ideas presented in this chapter. What are the relevant facts? What factual, conceptual, and application issues are there? What methods for resolving these issues might be used?

Case 7.4 Forced Rankings[32]

I

Jim Peters leaned back in his office chair and sighed with relief. Supervisor of the metallurgical research section at XYZ, he had just finished writing the last of the annual performance appraisals on his twelve-person research team. Nearing the end of his first year as supervisor, this was Jim's first experience in appraising employees. Nevertheless, he felt he had done his appraisals well. He had held a thorough performance review discussion with each individual, going over progress toward specific annual objectives established early in the year. These discussions were open, frank, and, Jim believed, of value to him and to each employee.

XYZ's appraisal forms require giving each employee a ranking of high achiever, excellent, satisfactory, marginal, or deficient. Each ranking requires a supporting, written justification. Jim ranked eight of his twelve people at either high achiever or excellent. He ranked only one as marginal, and he ranked the other three as satisfactory.

Jim delivered his appraisals to his immediate supervisor, Jason "Mac" McDougal, manager of the materials research department at XYZ. Mac had to review Jim's appraisals, along with those of his other sections, approve them, and submit them to the human resource director for XYZ's total research operation. Jim assumed Mac would quickly and easily approve his appraisals.

Much to Jim's surprise, Mac stormed into Jim's office a few days later, threw the appraisals on his desk, and exclaimed: "Jim, these appraisals just won't do! You're over-rating your people! You know I have to force-rank everyone in materials research and turn that ranking in with all the appraisals. It looks to me like you've tried to assure that all your people will be placed high in the forced ranking. I want these appraisals rewritten and your ratings adjusted to something that more closely approximates a 'normal distribution'—you ought not to have more than a couple of high achievers and probably a couple of marginals or deficients. I want the revised appraisals back on my desk by the end of the working day tomorrow! Understand?"

Jim felt frustrated, disillusioned, and disappointed by this turn of events. It seemed to him the appraisal system was being manipulated to produce an expected result and was not truly reflecting the performance of people. He also felt pressed for time, since he had the next day fully committed to other projects. What options do you think Jim has? Which do you think he should select? Explain.

II

Jim Peters worked late into the night to meet Mac McDougal's deadline. As he approached the end of his task, he grew careless and changed two excellents to satisfactory without changing his comments on their performance.

Jim submitted his revised appraisals to Mac and went back to the daily routine of supervising the metallurgical section. Mac appeared satisfied with the revised appraisals and submitted them (along with his forced ranking) into the normal chain of approval in the laboratory.

Some weeks later the appraisals were returned to Jim, who then scheduled individual appointments with each of his people to inform them of their appraisal ratings and discuss plans for subsequent improvement.

Jim's individual meetings went reasonably well until he met with Pete Evans. (Pete's appraisal was one that had the changed rating without revised comments.) Pete listened to Jim as they reviewed the appraisal and finally burst out, "Jim, your comments seem to sound like I'm an excellent performer but you only rated me 'satisfactory'!"

Jim had been afraid of such an observation but hadn't carefully thought out a response. He simply blurted out, "I had to reduce most of the ratings I gave to conform to the distribution management expects!"

Pete stormed out of Jim's office muttering: "I thought my appraisal was supposed to motivate me to improve! It sure as hell didn't!"

Discuss Jim's handling of his reappraisal task. What might he have done differently that would have had better results? What would you suggest that he do now? What changes, if any, do you think XYZ should make in its appraisal system?

Case 7.5 Three Mile Island[33]

In March 1984, General Public Utilities' Metropolitan Edison pled guilty to criminal misconduct associated with its operation of the Three Mile Island nuclear plant in Harrisburg, Pennsylvania. GPU's Metropolitan Edison was ordered to pay $1 million to an emergency planning fund for the area around the Harrisburg plant, as well as a $45,000 fine, for falsifying tests relating to leaks from the reactor's cooling system.

David Dart Queen, the U.S. attorney handling the case against GPU, claimed to have evidence that "criminal conduct was all-pervasive" among control-room operators and supervisors who operated the reactor between September 1978 and March 1979. He found no evidence that company officers were guilty of misconduct.

Identify and discuss the ethical concerns this set of circumstances raises.

Case 7.6 *American Society of Mechanical Engineers* v. *Hydrolevel Corporation* [72 L Ed 2d 330][34]

"A conflict of interest is like dirt in a sensitive gauge," one that can not only soil one person's career but can also taint an entire profession.[35] Thus, as professionals, engineers must be ever alert to signs of conflict of interest. The case of the *American Society of Mechanical Engineers (ASME)* v. *Hydrolevel Corporation* shows how easily individuals, companies, and professional societies can find themselves embroiled in expensive legal battles that tarnish the reputation of the engineering profession as a whole.

In 1971, Eugene Mitchell, vice-president for sales at McDonnell and Miller, Inc., located in Chicago, was concerned about his company's continued dominance in the heating boiler low-water fuel cutoff valve market. Heating boilers must have a low-water fuel cutoff to ensure that boilers cannot be fired without sufficient water in them, for deficient water could cause an explosion.

Hydrolevel Corporation entered the low-water cutoff valve market with an electronic low-water fuel supply cutoff that included a time delay on some of its models. Hydrolevel's valve had won important approval for use from Brooklyn Gas

Company, one of the largest installers of heating boilers. Some Hydrolevel units added the time-delay devices so the normal turbulence of the water level at the electronic probe would not cause inappropriate and repeated fuel supply turn-on and turn-off. Mitchell felt that McDonnell and Miller's sales could be protected if he could secure an interpretation stating that the Hydrolevel time delay on the cutoff violated the ASME B-PV Code. He referred to this section of the ASME code: "Each automatically fired steam or vapor system boiler shall have an automatic low-water fuel cutoff, so located as to automatically cut off the fuel supply when the surface of the water falls to the lowest visible part of the water-gauge glass."[36] Thus, Mitchell asked for an ASME interpretation of the mechanism for operation of the Hydrolevel device as it pertained to the above section of the code. He did not, however, specifically mention the Hydrolevel device in his request.

Mitchell discussed his idea several times with John James, McDonnell and Miller's vice-president for research. In addition to his role at McDonnell and Miller, James was on the ASME subcommittee responsible for heating boilers and had played a leading role in writing the part of the boiler code that Mitchell was questioning.

James recommended that he and Mitchell approach the chairman of the ASME Heating Boiler Subcommittee, T. R. Hardin. Hardin was also vice-president of the Hartford Steam Boiler Inspection and Insurance Company. When Hardin arrived in Chicago in early April 1971 on other business, the three men went to dinner at the Drake Hotel. During dinner, Hardin agreed with Mitchell and James that their interpretation of the code was correct.

Shortly after the meeting with Hardin, James sent ASME a draft letter of inquiry and sent Hardin a copy. Hardin made some sug-

gestions, and James incorporated Hardin's suggestions in a final draft letter. James's finalized draft letter of inquiry was then addressed to W. Bradford Hoyt, secretary of the B-PV Boiler and Pressure Vessel Committee.

Hoyt received thousands of similar inquiries every year. Since Hoyt could not answer James's inquiry with a routine, prefabricated response, he directed the letter to the appropriate subcommittee chairman, T. R. Hardin. Hardin drafted a response without consulting the whole subcommittee, a task he had authorization for if the response was treated as an "unofficial communication."

Hardin's response, dated April 29, 1971, stated that a low-water fuel cutoff must operate immediately. Although this response did not say that Hydrolevel's time-delayed cutoff was dangerous, McDonnell and Miller's salesmen used Hardin's conclusion to argue against using the Hydrolevel product. This was done at Mitchell's direction.

In early 1972, Hydrolevel learned of the ASME letter through one of their former customers who had a copy of the letter. Hydrolevel then requested an official copy of the letter from ASME. On March 23, 1972, Hydrolevel requested an ASME review and ruling correction.

ASME's Heating and Boiler Subcommittee had a full meeting to discuss Hydrolevel's request, and confirmed part of the original Hardin interpretation. James, who had replaced Hardin as chairman of the subcommittee, refrained from participating in the discussion but subsequently helped draft a critical part of the subcommittee's response to Hydrolevel. The ASME response was dated June 9, 1972.

In 1975, Hydrolevel filed suit against McDonnell and Miller, Inc., ASME, and the Hartford Steam Boiler Inspection and Insurance Company, charging them with conspiracy to restrain trade under the Sherman Antitrust Act.

Hydrolevel reached an out-of-court settlement with McDonnell and Miller and Hartford for $750,000 and $75,000, respectively. ASME took the case to trial. ASME officials believed that, as a society, ASME had done nothing wrong and should not be liable for the misguided actions of individual volunteer members acting on their own behalf. After all, ASME gained nothing from such practices. ASME officials also believed that a pretrial settlement would set a dangerous precedent that would encourage other nuisance suits.

Despite ASME arguments, however, the jury decided against ASME, awarding Hydrolevel $3.3 million in damages. The trial judge deducted $800,000 in prior settlements, and tripled the remainder in accordance with the Clayton Act. This resulted in a decision of $7,500,000 for Hydrolevel.

On May 17, 1982, ASME's liability was upheld by the second circuit. The Supreme Court, in a controversial 6–3 vote, found ASME guilty of antitrust violations. The majority opinion, delivered by Justice Blackmun, read as follows:

> ASME wields great power in the nation's economy. Its codes and standards influence the policies of numerous states and cities, and as has been said about "so-called voluntary standards" generally, its interpretations of guidelines "may result in economic prosperity or economic failure, for a number of businesses of all sizes throughout the country," as well as entire segments of an industry. . . . ASME can be said to be "in reality an extragovernmental agency, which prescribes rules for the regulation and restraint of interstate commerce." When it cloaks its subcommittee officials with the authority of its reputation, ASME permits those agents to affect the destinies of businesses and thus gives them power to frustrate competition in the marketplace.[37]

The issue of damages was retried in a trial lasting for approximately one month. In June, the jury returned a verdict of $1.1 million, which was tripled to $3.3 million. Parties involved were claiming attorney's fees in excess of $4 million, and a final settlement of $4,750,000 was decreed.

Following the decision, ASME revised its procedures as follows:

> In the wake of the Hydrolevel ruling, the Society has changed the way it handles codes and standards interpretations, beefed up its enforcement and conflict-of-interest rules, and adopted new "sunset" review procedures for its working bodies.
>
> The most striking changes affect the Society's handling of codes and standards interpretations. All such interpretations must now be reviewed by at least five persons before release; before, the review of two people was necessary. Interpretations are available to the public, with replies to nonstandard inquiries published each month in the Codes and Standards section of ME or other ASME publications. Previously, such responses were kept between the inquirer and the involved committee or subcommittee. Lastly, ASME incorporates printed disclaimers on the letterhead used for code interpretations spelling out their limitations: that they are subject to change should additional information become available and that individuals have the right to appeal interpretations they consider unfair.
>
> Regarding conflict-of-interest, ASME now requires all staff and volunteer committee members to sign statements pledging their adherence to a comprehensive and well-defined set of guidelines regarding potential conflicts. Additionally, the Society now provides all staff and volunteers with copies of the engineering code of ethics along with a publication outlining the legal implications of standards activities.
>
> Finally, the Society now requires each of its councils, committees and subcommit-

tees to conduct a "sunset" review of their operations every two years. The criteria include whether their activities have served the public interest and whether they have acted cost-effectively, in accordance with Society procedures.[38]

Conflict of interest cases quickly become a mare's nest, as the following questions illustrate:

- How could McDonnell and Miller have avoided the appearance of a conflict of interest? This applies to both Eugene Mitchell and John James.
- What was T. R. Hardin's responsibility as chairman of the B-PV Code Heating Boiler Subcommittee? How could he have handled things differently to protect the interests of ASME?
- What can engineering societies do to protect their interests once a conflict of interest is revealed?
- Was the final judgment against ASME fair? Why or why not?
- Have ASME's revised conflict-of-interest procedures addressed the problem fully? Why or why not?

Case 7.7 The Last Resort?[39]

I

The New Wyoming State Board of Professional Engineers performs regulatory functions (e.g., licensing of engineers) for the state. Members of the board are appointed by the state governor. Most of the board members are also members of the New Wyoming Society of Professional Engineers (NWSPE), a voluntary umbrella organization of professional engineers in New Wyoming. Membership in NWSPE is controlled by its own board and is not subject to approval by the state board.

NWSPE holds annual meetings at a pleasant resort area in New Wyoming. This year the NWSPE meeting will begin the day after one of the state board meetings. Since they share many common concerns about the engineering profession, the executive committee of NWSPE has recently expressed a strong interest in improving communication between NWSPE and the state board. Ordinarily the state board meets in the state capitol building. Because the NWSPE annual meeting and the state board meeting will occur so close together—and most of the board members will be attending the NWSPE meeting anyway—the NWSPE executive committee extends an invitation to the state board to hold its meeting at the resort area. The board is invited to stay on for the NWSPE meeting, and an NWSPE session is planned for the board to conduct a roundtable discussion of state board activities and concerns. NWSPE offers to pay the travel and lodging expenses of state board members.

Should the state board accept the invitation? Discuss.

II

Suppose the state board accepts the invitation, agreeing that this would be a good opportunity to improve communication with NWSPE. Several days later Brian Simpson begins to have second thoughts. A new appointee to the board, and the only board member who does not belong to NWSPE, Brian wonders if the board has set itself up for a conflict-of-interest situation. Although he knows of no instances in which the board has directly ruled on any NWSPE activities, it occurs to him that NWSPE and its members come within the purview of the board's regulatory functions. Finally, Brian writes to Harold Brock, chair of the state board:

Dear Mr. Brock:

I have some serious reservations regarding our acceptance of the hospitality offered by NWSPE to hold our August meeting at the Lakeshore Resort. While I agree about the desirability for communication between the board and NWSPE, it is inappropriate for us as a regulatory body to accept anything of substantial value from the organization representing those whose profession we regulate. Acceptance of hospitality in the form of lodging and meals creates the appearance of a conflict of interest. Therefore, it is my intention to pay any expenses not otherwise covered by the state of New Wyoming.

Sincerely,

Brian Simpson, PE

Before sending the letter, Brian shows it to you. He discusses his concerns with you and asks your advice about the letter. What are the relevant facts with which you can work? Are there any factual, conceptual, or application issues to consider? What methods of moral reasoning might you use in resolving these issues? What is your advice to Brian?

III

Suppose Brian sends the letter as is. When Harold Brock receives the letter, he must decide what to do next. Should he

1. Share the letter with other board members, inviting each to decide for himself or herself whether to follow Brian's example
2. Call a special board meeting to discuss the matter
3. Decide, on behalf of the board, to withdraw acceptance of the hospitality
4. Other

Discuss your choice.

IV

Suppose Harold sends the letter to the other board members, inviting them to decide for themselves whether to follow Brian's example. One other member, Ellen Price, agrees with Brian and indicates that she, too, will pay her own expenses. None of the others, including Harold Brock, think the issue raised by Brian warrants refusal of the hospitality. Should Brian and Ellen do anything further, or should they simply quietly continue their rejection of the offer of hospitality? Discuss.

V

Suppose Brian and Ellen do not press the issue further but continue to insist that they will pay their own expenses. During the panel discussion at the NWSPE meeting, an engineer in the audience asks: "It seems like everyone is talking about ethics these days. What kinds of ethical questions does your board have to deal with?" Should either Brian or Ellen mention their concerns about a conflict of interest?

VI

Suppose Brian and Ellen do not press the issue further but continue to insist that they will pay their own expenses. While the annual NWSPE meeting is taking place, a resort area reporter learns (not through Brian or Ellen) that NWSPE is hosting the state board. Like Brian and Ellen, the reporter thinks this might create a conflict of interest. She attempts to interview members of the board about how they see the situation. She approaches Brian and Ellen. What should they say?

Other Cases

Many other cases that have already been presented in this text could be examined in light of the leading ideas in this chapter. The following are especially recommended:

1.4: The Thesis

1.5: Recommendation for a Friend

1.7: A Promotion

2.3: Signing and Sealing Plans Not Prepared by Engineer

2.6: Joint Authorship of Paper

2.7: Engineer Serving on Private Hospital Board and Performing Services

2.9: Engineer's Duty to Report Data Relating to Research

2.10: Engineer Misstating Professional Achievements on Resume

2.12: Signing of Drawings by Engineer in Industry

3.2: The Catalyst

3.4: Working Overtime

3.7: The TV Antenna Tower

4.4: To Advise or Not Advise

4.6: Spontaneous Explosion?

NOTES

1. We are indebted to Ray Flumerfelt, Jr., for this case. Names have been changed in order to protect those involved.

2. Ruth R. Faden and Tom L. Beauchamp, *A History and Theory of Informed Consent* (New York: Oxford University Press, 1986), p. 238.

3. Faden and Beauchamp, *A History and Theory of Informed Consent*, p. 243.

4. This case comes from the experience of one of the co-authors, M. J. Rabins.

5. Sigma Xi, *Honor in Science* (1986), p. 8.

6. See *Honor in Science*, pp. 11–18.

7. William Broad and Nicholas Wade, *Betrayers of the Truth* (New York: Simon & Schuster, 1982), p. 174. Cited in *Honor in Science*, p. 12.

8. *Honor in Science*, p. 11.

9. This statement is originally found in R. A. Millikan, "On the Elementary Electrical Charge and the Avogadro Constant," *Physical Review*, 2 (1913), 109–143. Quoted in *Honor in Science*, p. 12 and taken from Gerald Holton, "Subelectrons, Presuppositions, and the Millikan-Ehrenhaft Dispute," *Historical Studies in the Physical Sciences*, 9 (1978), 161–224. Recent correspondence from Sigma Xi suggests that Millikan may have been falsely accused of misrepresenting his data. Whether or not this is true, the case represents the *kind* of thing we mean by "cooking the data."

10. *Honor in Science*, p. 11.

11. Arnold Relman, "Lessons from the Darsee Affair," *The New England Journal of Medicine*, 308 (1983), 1415–1417.

12. "Conduct Unbecoming," *Sunday New York Times Magazine* (October 29, 1989), p. 41.

13. See Kermit Vandivier, "What? Me Be a Martyr," *Harper's Magazine* (July 1975), pp. 36–44.

14. John Fielder, "Tough Break for Goodrich," *Journal of Business and Professional Ethics*, 19, no. 3 (Spring 1986), 223–238; and Jocelyn Wills, "Goodrich Revisited," *Journal of Business and Professional Ethics*, forthcoming.

15. See *Honor in Science*, pp. 23–28.

16. *Opinions of the Board of Ethical Review*, Vol. VI (Alexandria, Va.: National Society of Professional Engineers, 1989), p. 15.

17. California Supreme Court, July 1, 1976. 131 *California Reporter*, pp. 14–33, West Publishing Co. Cited in Joan C. Callahan, *Ethical Issues in Professional Life* (New York: Oxford University Press, 1988), pp. 239–244.

18. "Engineers Face Risks As Expert Witnesses," *The Rochester Engineer* (December 1992), p. 27.

19. "Engineers Face Risks," p. 27.

20. For several of these suggestions, see "Engineers Face Risks," pp. 27 and 29.

21. See "Plaintiffs to Get $15.4 Million," *Miami County Republic* [Paola, Kansas] (April 27, 1992), p. 1.

22. Paul Eddy, *Destination Disaster: From the Tri-Motor to the DC-10* (New York: Quadrangle/The New York Times Book Co., 1976), pp. 175–188. Reprinted in Robert J. Baum, *Ethical Problems in Engineering*, Vol. 2 (Troy, N.Y.: Center for the Study of the Human Dimensions of Science and Technology, 1980), pp. 175–185.

23. Paul Eddy, *Destination Disaster: From the Tri-Motor to the DC-10*, pp. 175–188.

24. *Grimshaw* v. *Ford Motor Co.*, App., 174 Cal. Rptr. 348, p. 360.

25. Another possibility, of course, is that they will judge his proposal more severely in order to defuse the suspicion of bias. If Roger's proposal is thereby rejected, this might seem unfair to him. But if his proposal still survives, those whose proposals are rejected might still suspect bias.

26. If he judges them less harshly, he risks having his own proposal ranked lower or rejected. If it is still accepted, doubts will, again, not be removed.

27. Emphasis added.

28. Michael Davis, "Conflict of Interest," in Deborah Johnson, *Ethical Issues in Engineering* (Englewood Cliffs, N.J.: Prentice Hall, 1991), p. 319.

29. Neil R. Luebke, "Conflict of Interest as a Moral Category," *Business and Professional Ethics Journal*, 6, no. 1, pp. 66–81.

30. This is BER Case No. 87-2 in *Opinions of the Board of Ethical Review*, Vol. VI (Alexandria, Va.: National Society of Professional Engineers, 1989). The BER discussion of this case is on pp. 90–91.

31. This case is supplied by an engineering colleague who was an expert witness in the case. Since the litigation is ongoing, we have given the company the fictitious name of the "XYZ Hose Company." See Raymond W. Flumerfelt, Charles E. Harris, Jr., Michael J. Rabins, and Charles H. Samson, Jr. "Introducing Ethics Case Studies into Required Undergraduate Engineering Courses,"

Final Report to the NSF on Grant No. DIR-9012252, pp. 287–312.

32. This is an adaptation of W. Gale Cutler's fictional case, "What Should Jim Do?" *Research. Technology Management* (May/June, 1987), p. 44.

33. This case is based on a March 2, 1984 Wall Street Journal article, "GPU Unit Guilty Plea Is Accepted in Case on Three Mile Island."

34. This account is drawn from Flumerfelt, Harris, Rabins, and Samson, NSF Grant No. DIR-9012252.

35. Paula Wells, Hardy Jones, and Michael Davis, "Conflicts of Interest in Engineering," Module Series in Applied Ethics, Center for the Study of Ethics in the Professions, Illinois Institute of Technology (Dubuque, Iowa: Kendall/Hunt Publishing Company, 1986), p. 20.

36. American Society of Mechanical Engineers, Boiler and Pressure Vessel Code, section IV, paragraph HG-605a.

37. Charles W. Beardsley, "The Hydrolevel Case—A Retrospective," *Mechanical Engineering*, June 1984, p. 66.

38. Beardsley, The Hydrolevel Case—A Retrospective," p. 73.

39. This fictional case is drawn from NSF Grant No. DIR-8820837. It is presented, with commentaries, in Michael S. Pritchard, *Teaching Engineering Ethics: A Case Study Approach.*, pp. 368–382

Chapter 8

Risk, Safety, and Liability in Engineering

Don Hayward is employed as a chemical engineer at ABC Manufacturing.[1] Although he does not work with hot metals himself, he supervises workers who are exposed to hot metals eight hours a day, five days a week. Don becomes concerned when several workers develop respiratory problems and complain about "those bad smelling fumes from the hot metals." When Don asks his superior, Cal Brundage, about air quality in the workplace, the reply is that the workplace is in full compliance with OSHA guidelines. Don learns that OSHA guidelines do not apply to chemicals that have not been tested and that a relatively small percentage of chemicals in the workplace have actually been tested. This is also the case with the vast majority of chemicals workers are exposed to at ABC.

Don goes to ABC's science library, talks to the reference librarian about his concerns, and does a literature search to see if he can find anything that might be helpful in determining why the workers have developed respiratory problems. He finds the title of an article that looks promising and asks the reference librarian to send for a copy. The librarian tells Don that the formal request must have the signed approval of Cal Brundage, so Don fills out the request form and sends it to Cal's office for approval.

One month later the article has still not arrived. Don asks Cal about the request. Cal replies that he does not recall ever seeing it. He tells Don that it must have gotten "lost in the shuffle." Don fills out another form and this time personally hands it to Cal. Cal says he will send it to the reference librarian right away.

Another month passes and the article does not arrive. Don mentions his frustration to the reference librarian, who replies that he never received a request from Cal to order the paper.

What should Don do now?

8.1   Introduction

Don's concern for safety in the workplace is a common one for engineers. How should engineers deal with issues of risk and safety, especially when they involve possible liability for harm? In the case presented above, the risk arises from a manufacturing process. Other risks come from products, structures, and substances created by engineers.

Engineering necessarily involves risk. Even if engineers did not innovate but rather designed things in the same way year after year, the chance of producing harm would exist. New hazards could be found in products, processes, and chemicals once thought to be safe. But the element of risk is greatly increased because engineers are constantly involved in innovation. A bridge or building is constructed with new materials or with a new design. New machines are created and new compounds synthesized, always without full knowledge of their long-term effects on humans or the environment.

The presence of risk poses many value questions. Where should the burden of proof lie in controversies over the safety of a product, project, or substance? Should it lie with those who want to impose the risk, such as industry and government? Should they show that the risk is acceptable? Or should the public or its advocates show that a risk is unacceptable? Powerful moral arguments can be found for both positions. Proponents of the view that the burden of proof of showing that something is safe should be borne by those wanting to impose the risk argue that otherwise those who bear the risk may be subjected to dangers without their knowledge or consent. Proponents of the view that the burden of proof of showing that something is not safe should be borne by those on whom the risk is imposed argue that otherwise many benefits of technology will be kept from the public by excessive restrictions.

What constitutes "acceptable risk" is thus a normative question. Should we emphasize preserving public health and safety, or promoting technological innovation that can strengthen the economy and benefit everyone? But the "health/wealth" debate is not the only area of risk assessment and management that involves value issues. Even the definition of risk is controversial, as we shall see. The question of liability for risk also poses difficult issues for engineers and for those who make law and public policy. Engineers are often aware of risks they cannot make known without exposing themselves and their employers to legal liabilities. Should they and their employers be protected from these liabilities in order to more effectively protect the public?

These are just a few of the value issues that abound in the area of risk assessment and risk management. To be professionally responsible, engineers must first *be aware* of the ethical or value dimension of the risk debate. Second, they may also be called upon to resolve some of these issues. This chapter will be devoted to assisting engineers to more effectively meet both of these challenges.

We first examine statements in the codes having to do with safety. While the codes have little to say about risk, they do have something to say about the related concept of safety. Then we focus on the problem of identifying risk, pointing out that experts and laypeople often understand even the concept of risk differently. Next we consider the difficulties in evaluating the risks involved in technology, and the normative issues that these difficulties raise. Then we describe the task of determining acceptable risk and the conflict between individual rights and general welfare inherent in it. Next we proceed to the issue of communicating risk, then to the problems raised for engineers by liability for risk. Finally, we offer some summary thoughts on the responsibilities of engineers regarding risk.

8.2 The Codes and Engineering Practice Regarding Risk and Safety

Virtually all engineering codes give a prominent place to safety, stating that engineers must hold paramount the safety, health, and welfare of the public. The relationship of risk to safety is very close. If products, structures, processes, and substances are unsafe, they subject humans and the environment to undue risk. Therefore the statements in the codes having to do with safety are relevant to the topic of risk.

The NSPE's "Engineer's Creed" obligates engineers "to place service before profit, the honor and standing of the profession before personal advantage, and the public welfare above all other considerations." The first canon of the NSPE code requires engineers to "hold paramount the safety, health and welfare of the public in the performance of their professional duties."

The NSPE code, in sections II.1.b and III.2.b, requires engineers to design safely, defining this in terms of "accepted engineering standards." For example, item III.2.b instructs engineers not to "complete, sign or seal plans and/or specifications that are not of a design safe to the public health and welfare and in conformity with accepted engineering standards." Item II.1.a refers to informed consent, instructing engineers that if their professional judgment is overruled in "circumstances where the safety, health, property or welfare of the public are endangered" they are obligated to "notify their employer or client and such other authority as may be appropriate."

Many other engineering codes give similar instructions to engineers. For example, the IEEE Code of Ethics emphasizes members' responsibility for the public's health and safety in three ways. First, electrical engineers agree "to accept responsibility in making engineering decisions consistent with the safety, health, and welfare of the public, and to disclose promptly factors that might endanger the public or the environment." Second, they agree "to improve the understanding of technology, its appropriate application, and potential consequences." Third, they agree "to maintain and improve our technical competence and to undertake technological tasks for others only if qualified by training or experience, or after full disclosure of pertinent limitations." These last two items emphasize the importance of informed consent.

Although American engineering codes rarely use the term "risk," a new British code specifically addresses the issue. The London Institute of Mechanical Engineers' (IMechE) "Joint Code of Professional Practice on Risk Issues" became effective in March of 1993. This ten-point code discusses professional responsibility, the law, and professional conduct regarding risk.

Engineering practice is suffused with concern with safety. One of the most pervasive concepts is the notion of "factors of safety." If the largest load a walkway will have to carry at any one time is 1,000 pounds, for example, a prudent engineer might design the walkway geometry to carry 3,000 pounds. The walkway dimensions for normal usage would then be designed with a factor of safety of three.

Accepted engineering practice goes still further. In choosing materials to build the walkway, an engineer might begin with a material that has an advertised yield stress of a given number of pounds per square inch, and then treat this material as if it had only half of that capability in determining how much material to include in the walkway construction. This introduces an additional factor of safety of two. The final overall factor of safety at the walkway would be the product of the two separate factors, or six in this example.

Thus, a prudent engineer would design the walkway to be six times as strong as required for normal everyday use, in order to account for unpredictably high loads or unaccountably weak construction material. This approach is taught to all engineers early in their training, and factors of safety of six or higher are the norm rather than the exception.

8.3   The Identification of Risk

To assess a risk, an engineer must first identify it. To identify it, an engineer must first know what a risk is. Most people agree that the concept of risk involves the notion of adverse effect or harm. We might define a "harm" as an invasion or limitation of a person's freedom or well-being. Some of the most important types of well-being are physical well-being, psychological well-being, and economic well-being.

For the most part, engineering risks have to do with our physical and economic well-being. Engineering work can subject us to risks of health and accident or physical injury, which affects our physical well-being. Engineering work can also subject us to risks to our economic well-being. Faulty design of a building can cause it to collapse, resulting in economic loss to the owner. If a businessperson depends upon a chemical process for economic survival, faulty design of the process can be economically disastrous.

This account of risk is in accord with the thought of many risk experts. William W. Lowrance, for example, defines risk as "a compound measure of the probability and magnitude of adverse effect."[2] Risk is composed of two elements: the likelihood of an adverse effect or harm and the magnitude of that adverse effect or harm. By "compound," Lowrance means "the product." Risk is thus the product of the likelihood and the magnitude of the harm. A relatively slight harm that is highly likely might comprise a greater risk than a relatively large harm that is far less likely.

A recent National Public Radio story on the Environmental Protection Agency began with a quotation from EPA official Linda Fisher illustrating this objectivist conception of risk:

> A lot of our priorities are set by public opinion, and the public quite often is more worried about things that they perceive to cause greater risks than things that really cause risks. Our priorities often times are set through Congress . . . and those [decisions] may or may not reflect real risk, they may reflect people's opinions of risk or the Congressmen's opinions of risk.[3]

Every time Fisher refers to "risk" or "real risk," we can substitute Lowrance's definition, or perhaps even a simpler one, such as "probability of death or injury." Fisher believes that, while both members of the U.S. Congress and ordinary laypeople may be confused about risk, the experts know what it is. Risk is something that can be objectively measured, namely, the product of the likelihood and magnitude of harm.

Some experts believe, however, that the value element in risk is often more prominent than Fisher supposes. Fisher's comments were followed on the NPR program by comments by Granger Morgan of Carnegie Mellon University, who presented a different conception of risk:

> For many years there has been an argument among some technical experts that the public is all mixed up, that they just don't have their risk priorities right. But experimental results in psychology in recent years have suggested that that's not true. If you give the public a list of hazards and say, "Sort these in terms of how many people die each year from each of them," they can do it. If instead you give them the same list and they are asked, "Sort them in terms of how risky they are," you get a very different order. The point is that to most people risk does not equal expected numbers of deaths. It involves a lot of other things, things like equity and whether you can control the hazard, whether you understand it. And so partly the arguments about priorities derive from this difference between making judgments just on the basis of expected numbers of deaths versus considering all these other factors.[4]

Whether or not we believe that the public is always able to accurately assess the magnitude and likelihood of harm, Morgan's conception of risk is fundamentally different. He believes that "risk" in the public's mind involves not only expectation of a certain number of deaths or injuries, but also other issues, "like equity and whether you can control the hazard, whether you understand it."

Notice that these other factors involve values. "Equity" refers to justice or fairness. Is the risk fairly distributed? Do those who share the risk also get the benefits? References to whether one can control the hazard suggest that a risk that is voluntarily assumed, such as smoking, may be more acceptable than one that is not, such as having a nuclear plant built in one's neighborhood. Finally, a risk that is understood (one to which genuine informed consent is given) should be differently evaluated than one which is not understood.

We can think of other situations in which the identification of a risk may be controversial. Suppose Engineer Jane discovers that her plant is discharging a compound into the air that increases the chance of mild allergy attacks in 5 percent of the population within a radius of ten miles of the plant. While this effect might not have been considered a risk a hundred years ago, it probably would be today.

Nevertheless, the identification of the kinds of risk with which engineers are usually concerned involves the kinds of effects most people would be willing to classify as harms. For engineers, then, much risk identification is relatively noncontroversial.

8.4   Uncertainties and Value Judgments in Estimating Risk

Estimating risk has been described by one writer as looking "through a glass darkly."[5] If we could accurately predict the harm resulting from engineering work, there would be no risk; we would know precisely the harm to expect. Instead, we can only estimate the probability of harm. To make matters worse, we cannot even estimate the probability of harm with accuracy. In actual practice, therefore, estimating risk (or "risk assessment") is an *uncertain* prediction of the *probability* of harm. In this section we consider some of the methods of estimating risk, the uncertainties in these methods, and the value judgments these uncertainties necessitate.

Limitations in Detecting Failure Modes

With respect to new technologies, engineers and scientists must have some way of estimating the risks they impose on those affected. One of the methods for assessing risk involves the use of a fault tree, a diagram of the possible ways in which a malfunction or accident can occur. Fault trees are most often used to anticipate hazards for which there is little or no direct experience, such as nuclear meltdowns. They enable an engineer to analyze in a systematic fashion the various failure modes attendant to an engineering project. A failure mode is a way in which a structure, mechanism, or process can malfunction. For example, a structure can rip apart in tension, crumble to pieces in compression, crack and break in bending, lose its integrity due to corrosion (rusting), explode due to excessive internal pressure, or burn due to excessive temperature. Figure 8.1 illustrates how a fault-tree analysis can be used to discover why an automobile will not start.

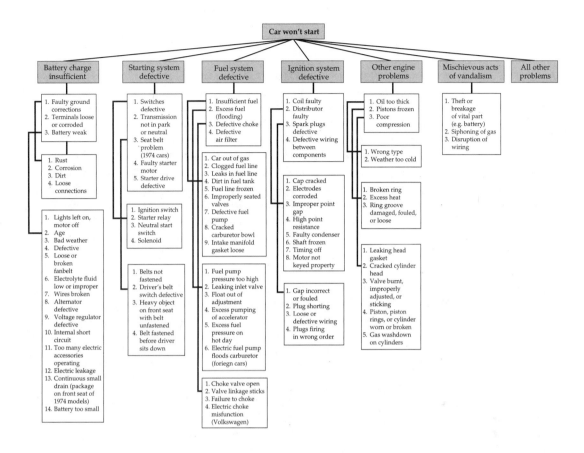

Source: This diagram is from B. Fischoff, P. Slovick, and S. Lichtenstein, "Fault Trees: Sensitivity and Estimated Failure Problem Representation," *Journal of Experimental Psychology: Human Perception and Performance*, 4 (1978): 342–355. Used with permission.

Figure 8.1
Fault-Tree Analysis of Failure of an Automobile to Start. The failure appears at the top of the fault tree, and the possible causes of the failure appear as "branches."

Another approach to a systematic examination of failure modes is the event-tree analysis. In a fault-tree analysis we begin with an undesirable event, such as a car not starting or the loss of electrical power to a nuclear power plant safety system. Then we reason backwards to determine what might have led to the event. By contrast, in an event-tree analysis, we begin with an initial event and determine the state of the system to which the event can lead. Figure 8.2 illustrates in schematic form an event-tree analysis.

This simplified event tree for an accident involving a loss of coolant in a typical nuclear power plant begins with a failure and enumerates the various events to which this failure could lead. This event tree shows the logical relationships between the possible ways that a pipe break can affect the safety systems in a nuclear plant. If both a pipe and on-site power fail simultaneously, the outcome will be a very large release of radioactive coolant. If these two systems are independent, the probability of this happening is the product of the two probabilities taken separately. For example, if there is one chance in 10^{-4} ($P_1 = 0.0001$) that the pipe will break and one chance in 10^{-5} ($P_2 = 0.00001$) that the on-site power will fail, then the chance of a loss of a very large release is one in 10^{-9} ($P = P_1 \times P_2$).

While it is necessary to go through such analyses to ensure that we have taken into account as many failure modes as possible, they have severe limitations. First, we cannot anticipate all of the mechanical, physical, electrical, and chemical problems that might lead to failure. Second, we cannot anticipate all of the points of human error that could lead to failure. Third, the probabilities assigned to the failure modes are largely conjectural and based on analyses that cannot be corroborated by experimental testing. We are not, for example, going to melt down

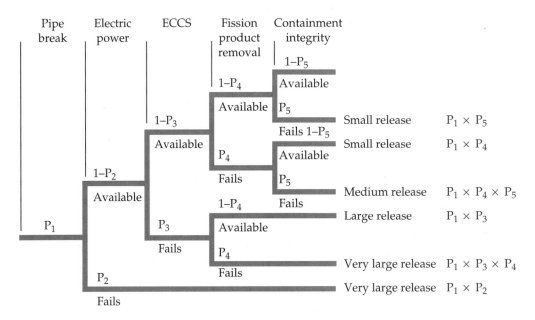

Reproduced, with permission, from the *Annual Review of Energy*, Volume 6, © 1981 by Annual Reviews, Inc. Courtesy N. C. Rasmussen.

Figure 8.2
Event-Tree Analysis of a Pipe Break in a Nuclear Plant

a nuclear reactor to determine the probability of such an occurrence leading to a chain reaction fission explosion. In many cases we do not know the probability of material behavior at extremely elevated temperatures. Fourth, we can never be sure we have all of the possible initiating events (even ones we know exist in different contexts) included on the event tree or placed in the right order.

An Unanticipated Tragedy

The following case illustrates the limitations of risk assessment. In the summer of 1962 the New York Telephone Company completed heating system additions to a new accounting building in Inwood, New York. The three-story, square-block building was a paradigm of safe design, using the latest technology.

In October of 1962, after the building was occupied and the workers were in place, final adjustments were being made on the building's new, expanded heating system located in the basement. This system consisted of three side-by-side, oil-fired boilers. The boilers were designed for low pressures of less than 60 psi and so were not covered by ASME boiler and pressure vessel codes. Each boiler was equipped with a spring-loaded safety relief valve designed to open and release steam into the atmosphere if the boiler pressure got too high. Each boiler was also equipped with a pressure-actuated cutoff valve designed to cut off oil flow to the boiler burners in the event of excessive pressure. The steam pressure from the boilers was delivered to the steam radiators, each of which had its own local relief valve. Finally, if all else failed, a one-foot diameter pressure gauge with a red danger zone painted on the face sat on the top of each boiler. If the pressure got too high, the gauge was supposed to alert a janitor who operated the boilers, so he could turn off the burners.

On October 2, 1962, the following events transpired.[6]

1. The building custodian decided to fire up boiler number 1 in the heating system for the first time that fall. The electricians had just wired the control system for the new companion boiler (boiler number 3) and successfully tested the electrical signal flows.

2. The custodian did not know that the electricians had left the fuel cutoff control system disconnected. The electricians had disconnected the system because they were planning to do additional work on boiler number 3 the following week. They intended to wire the fuel cutoffs for the three boilers in series (i.e., high pressure in any one would stop all three).

3. The custodian mechanically closed the header valve, because it was a warm Indian summer day and he did not want to send steam into the radiators on the floors above. Thus, the boiler was delivering steam pressure against a blocked valve.

4. As subsequent testing showed, the relief valve had rusted shut after some tests the previous spring in which the boilers had last been fired up. (Later, laws were enacted in New York state that require relief valves for low-pressure boiler

systems to be operated by hand once every twenty-four hours to ensure that they are not rusted shut. At the time, low-pressure boiler systems were not subject to this requirement.)

5. This was Thursday before payday, and the custodian made a short walk to his bank at the lunch hour to cash a check, shortly after turning on boiler number 1.

6. The cafeteria was on the other side of the wall against which the boiler end abutted. Employees were in line against that wall awaiting their turn at the cafeteria serving tables. There were more people in line than there would have been on Friday, because on payday many workers went out to cash their paychecks and have lunch at local restaurants.

7. Boiler number 1 exploded. The end of the boiler that was the most removed from the wall next to the cafeteria blew off, making the boiler into a rocket-like projectile. The boiler lifted off its stanchions and crashed into the cafeteria, after which it continued to rise at great velocity through all three stories of the building. Twenty-five people were killed and almost one hundred were injured.

We can make several observations about this scenario. First, there is no possible way that fault-tree or event-tree analyses could have predicted the chain of events in items 1–7. Second, breaking the sequence of events at any point would have prevented the explosion. For example, if the outside temperature had been cooler, the custodian would not have closed the header valve and the individual steam radiator valves in each upstairs room would have opened. If the relief valve had been hand-operated every day, its malfunction would have been discovered and probably corrected. If the time had not been noon and the day before payday, the custodian might have stayed in the basement and seen the high-pressure gauge-reading and turned off the burners. If it had not been lunch time, the unfortunate victims would not have been in the cafeteria line on the other side of the wall from the boiler.

We should make several concluding observations about assessing risk. First, it is not possible to anticipate all of the failures that can result in a catastrophe. Second, as this case illustrates, it is even more difficult to anticipate all of the human errors and the sequences of events that can result in a catastrophe. Third, we have already pointed out that the probabilities assigned to event-tree analyses are usually highly conjectural. For example, while we know that outside air temperature should have been a part of the event-tree analysis for the boiler explosion described above, the way the outside temperature entered into the chain of events leading to the catastrophe would probably never have been anticipated.

Despite these limitations, engineers must try to anticipate all possible failure modes. Unfortunately, in many instances a proper regard for past mistakes might have avoided catastrophes. Examples include the sinking of the Titanic, the collapse of Teton Dam, the nuclear reactor accident at Three Mile Island, and others.[7]

Estimating Risks from Toxic Substances

Now let us turn to another area of engineering in which the value judgments inherent in risk estimation are more evident. Industrial processes emit many compounds into the air and water that pose various degrees of risk to human health. Yet the estimation of these risks often contains hidden value dimensions and is often plagued by uncertainties. Here is an example.

Suppose Sue, a young engineer, is worried about a compound—call it Compound X—that her company is discharging into the air. Compound X is not regulated by the EPA, and she wonders whether its emission is a health hazard for the public. Her boss says he has looked at the epidemiological literature on Compound X, and it does not show any connection between Compound X and health problems.[8] Sue, however, is more sophisticated in her knowledge of the way such connections are established. How are the risks associated with such substances estimated?[9]

Assume that a scientist wants to investigate a causal link between a compound and cancer. In performing these studies (called "cohort studies"), the scientist especially wants to avoid claiming that there is a link between Compound X and cancer when there is none. In fact, a scientist is going to be more concerned to avoid claiming there is a link between Compound X and cancer when in fact there is none, than in claiming that there is not a link between Compound X and cancer when in fact there is. The reason for this is obvious: to make a claim about a causal relationship that is false is more damaging to one's reputation as a scientist than to fail to make a claim about a causal relationship that is true.

Unfortunately, as Sue is well aware, public-policy interests are not in agreement with scientific scruples at this point. From the standpoint of protecting the public from carcinogens, we are more interested in discovering a causal connection between Compound X and cancer if one in fact exists than in avoiding making a claim about a causal connection that does not exist. Only by adopting this policy can the public be adequately protected from carcinogens. Thus, whereas scientists have a bias against "false positives" (making a claim for a causal connection when there is not one), those whose highest priority is protecting the public have a bias against "false negatives" (claiming there is not a causal connection when there is one).

In addition to these considerations, Sue knows that there is another reason why scientists place primary emphasis on eliminating false positives. From a statistical standpoint, eliminating false negatives requires a larger sample than eliminating false positives, thus making the cohort studies more expensive and difficult to perform. Scientists therefore have a reason for avoiding false positives that is based on economics, as well as one based on an interest in preserving their scientific reputations.

Sue is also aware of a third reason why some scientists might favor eliminating false positives. Some scientific studies are privately funded, and many scientists have vested interests in conclusions that give compounds a clean bill of health. Many compounds have considerable value in the marketplace, and industrial firms are not anxious to have them declared a threat to the public health. Favoring the elimination of false positives tends to support the position of those who fund some studies.

Given these facts, Sue knows that scientific studies may not offer the public as much protection against carcinogens and other harmful substances as one might suppose. She is aware that there are value judgments involved in epidemiological estimates of risk. These favor the discovery of scientific truth, economic efficiency, and perhaps even the interests of those who sponsor the research rather than protecting the public. She wonders why this should be true, especially if public funding is supporting the scientific investigations. Perhaps, as one writer suggests, there should be two kinds of studies: those devoted to pure science and those that will form the basis of public-policy decisions.[10]

The estimation of risk from potentially toxic substances raises an issue that is implicit in all estimation of risk. In the face of the uncertainties inherent in the prediction of risk, how do we define "acceptable risk"?

8.5   Defining "Acceptable Risk"

In this section we explore the questions raised by the concept of "acceptable risk." This is an important concept in the discussion of engineers' responsibilities.

Promoting General Welfare Versus Promoting Individual Rights

Estimating the likelihood of harm from technology is far from an exact science, whether the harm be from the collapse of dams or buildings, explosions, mechanical failures, malfunctions of electrical systems, or the ingestion of toxic substances. Because of the element of uncertainty, the interpretation of the evidence involves a bias or predisposition in favor of one set of values rather than another. This is most clearly evident in the case of testing for toxicity. Shall we use the standards that favor the production of "good science" and the protection of producers from needless regulation or the standards most likely to protect the public from harmful substances? If we try to conceptualize the conflict problem in the most general terms, there is a choice between two sets of values.

On the one hand, in estimating risk, we can favor a less restrictive approach in which we try to avoid predicting threats to health and safety where there are none. From this standpoint, the burden of proof is on those who claim that a given risk is unacceptable. This approach favors "good science" in some areas, such as the evaluation of potentially toxic chemicals. It also favors the rights of producers of technology, because it emphasizes the importance of not burdening them with excessive regulations. Finally, it favors promoting economic growth, because reducing restrictions on economic activity often has this effect.

On the other hand, in estimating risk, we can favor a more restrictive approach in which we try to discover as many threats to health and safety as possible. From this standpoint, the burden of proof is on those who claim that a given risk is acceptable. This approach favors the protection of the public from threats to health and safety, even at the possible cost of economic efficiency. Put another way, it favors the rights of the users of technology over the rights of the producers of technology.

These two orientations or biases reflect in a general way two ethical positions with which we are familiar, utilitarianism and the ethics of respect-for-persons. Further discussion will make this connection clearer.

Utilitarianism holds that the answer to any moral question is in the course of action that maximizes human well-being. As we have seen, utilitarians often find cost/benefit analysis a useful tool in assessing risk. In applying this technique to risk, the technique is often called risk/benefit analysis, because the "cost" is measured in terms of the risk of deaths, injuries, or other harms associated with a given course of action. For simplicity, however, we shall continue to use the term "cost/benefit analysis."

Consider the case described at the beginning of this chapter from the cost/benefit standpoint. Is the risk to the workers from the fumes acceptable? Suppose Dan, in conducting a more thorough literature search, discovers that the risk imposed by exposure to the fumes is greater than he originally thought. In fact, the risk is one case of cancer each year for each 10,000 workers. To decide whether this is an acceptable risk from the cost/benefit perspective, he would have to compare the cost of preventing this rate of death with the cost of preventing or drastically reducing the risk.[11] To calculate the cost of preventing the deaths, we would have to include the costs of modifying the process that produces the fumes, the cost of providing protective masks, the cost of providing better ventilation systems, and the cost of any other safety measures necessary to prevent the deaths. Then we must calculate the cost of not preventing the deaths due to the fumes. Here we must include such factors as the cost of additional health care, the cost of possible lawsuits due to the deaths, the cost of bad publicity, and the loss of income to the families of the workers. If the total cost of preventing the loss of life is greater than the total cost of not preventing the deaths, then the present level of risk is acceptable. If the total cost of not preventing the loss of life is greater than the total cost of preventing the loss, then the present level of risk is unacceptable. And we must be careful not to overlook costs that are not immediately obvious and that could change the outcome of the analysis.

We might not be able to give monetary evaluations for all of the various costs and benefits of the two options, so a strict numerical analysis of acceptable risk might not be possible. The engineer might have to be content with a more intuitive assessment of the various options in terms of their contribution to the overall utility.

Suppose Dan is not able to find any conclusive evidence at all regarding the effects of the fumes. In the case of doubt, the utilitarian position might well favor placing the burden of proof on those who want to restrict worker exposure to the fumes. The argument might well be that regulations on industry not necessitated by scientific studies impose an undue burden on the productive sector of the economy. This in turn leads to economic inefficiency, fewer jobs, and a lower standard of living for the whole society. The harm that *might* result to a few workers if exposure is not restricted would probably be outweighed by the benefits to the larger society of less restriction.

Regardless of the precise form of utilitarian analysis employed, however, an exclusive reliance on this method of determining acceptable risk suffers from the characteristic limitations of utilitarianism. First, it might not be possible to anticipate all of the costs and benefits associated with each option, so that the cost/benefit method yields an inconclusive result. Second, we cannot always translate all of the risks and benefits into monetary terms. How do we assess the risks associated with a new technology, or with eliminating a wetland, or with eliminating the unique species in a part of a Brazilian rain forest? Again, this would render the cost/benefit approach inconclusive. Third, the method in its usual applications makes no allowance for the distributions of costs and benefits. Consider the case of noxious fumes again. If it produced more overall utility to expose the workers in the plant to serious risk of sickness and death, the exposure would be justified. As long as the good of the majority outweighs costs associated with the suffering and death of the workers, the risk is justified. Yet most of us would probably find this an unacceptable account of acceptable risk.

In spite of these limitations, cost/benefit analysis has a legitimate place in risk evaluation. When no serious threats to individual rights are involved, cost/benefit analysis may be decisive. In addition, cost/benefit analysis is systematic, offers a degree of objectivity, and provides a way of comparing risks, benefits, and costs by the use of a common measure, monetary cost.

Let us now consider the same situation from the standpoint of the ethics of respect-for-persons. According to this ethical perspective, it is wrong to deny the moral agency of individuals. We have seen that moral agents are beings capable of formulating and pursuing purposes of their own. We deny the moral agency of individuals when we deny their ability to do this. Moral agency is protected by rights, including the rights to life, health, and physical integrity; the right not to be deceived; and the right to free and informed consent to risks that might abridge these or other rights.

The ethics of respect-for-persons places great emphasis on individuals, regardless of the costs to the larger society. John Rawls expresses this thought in the statement that "each member of society is thought to have an inviolability founded upon justice . . . which even the welfare of everyone else cannot override."[12] As an example of the individualistic orientation of the ethics of respect-for-persons, consider the following statement by Mrs. Talbert, whose husband's health was severely damaged by byssinosis, caused by cotton dust:

> My husband worked in the cotton mill since 1937 to 1973. His breath was so short he couldn't walk from the parking lot to the gate the last two weeks he worked. . . .
>
> He was a big man, liked fishing, hunting, swimming, playing ball, and loved to camp. We liked to go to the mountains and watch the bears. He got so he could not breathe and walk any distance, so we had to stop going anywhere. So we sold our camper, boat and his truck as his doctor, hospital and medicine bills were so high. We don't go anywhere now.

The doctor said his lungs were as bad as they could get to still be alive. At first he used tank oxygen about two or three times a week, then it got so bad he used more and more. So now he has an oxygen concentrator, he has to stay on it 24 hours a day. When he goes to the doctor or hospital he has a little portable tank.

He is bedridden now. It's a shame the mill company doesn't want to pay compensation for brown lung. If they would just come and see him as he is now, and only 61 years old. . . .[13]

A utilitarian might be willing to trade off the very great harm to Mr. Talbert for smaller advantages to a very large number of people, resulting from failure to force cotton mills to protect their workers from the risk of byssinosis. After all, such protection is often very expensive, and these expenses must eventually be passed on to consumers in the form of higher prices for cotton products. Higher prices would also make American cotton products more expensive and thus less competitive in world markets, depriving American workers of jobs. Regulations protecting workers might even force many (perhaps all) American cotton mills to close. Such disutilities might well outweigh the disutilities to the Mr. Talberts of the world.

From the standpoint of the ethics of respect-for-persons, however, such considerations must not obscure the fact that Mr. Talbert's treatment violates at least two of the tests of RP morality. His rights have almost certainly been violated, because he has suffered severe damage to his health, almost certainly without his knowledge or consent. From the standpoint of the Golden Rule, probably few if any observers would want to be in the position of Mr. Talbert. Whether the test would violate the self-defeating test is perhaps more controversial, and we shall not consider it here.

In the light of the conflict between the utilitarian and respect-for-persons approaches to risk, it seems that an adequate account of acceptable risk must combine both utilitarian and respect-for-persons elements. From the respect-for-persons standpoint, we must emphasize the importance of informed consent and the rights of individuals. From the utilitarian standpoint, we must consider the consequences for the general welfare of the regulation of risk. Is it possible to find a creative middle way in the regulation of risk?

A Principle of Acceptable Risk

As a first step to formulating a resolution of the conflict over the regulation of risk, it will be helpful to review several laws relating to risk. The first observation is that the same divergence between utilitarian and RP perspectives also exists in the laws having to do with risk.[14] The chemical food additives amendments to the Food, Drug and Cosmetics Act, enacted in 1958, say that a chemical "deemed to be unsafe" may not be added to food unless it can be "safely used."[15] "Safe use" was defined by the Senate Committee on Labor and Public Welfare as meaning that "no harm will result" from its addition to food.[16] The well-known Delaney Amendment also prohibits the addition to food of any chemical known to cause cancer when ingested by animals.[17] In these laws, no attempt is made to balance risk and benefit, and anyone wishing to add a substance to food must bear the burden of proof of showing that it is not harmful. In most situations that involve benefits as well as risks, however, there is some attempt to strike a balance between the public welfare and the rights of individuals. Although the use of motor vehicles involves great risks, the legislatures have tried to minimize those risks while at the same time preserving the benefits of technology.

Similarly, the Toxic Substances Control Act of 1976 (TOSCA) authorizes the EPA to regulate any chemical upon a finding of "unreasonable risk of injury to health or the environment."[18] Since it is only "unreasonable risk" that triggers regulation, some degree of risk is clearly tolerated. The report of the House Commerce Committee defines "unreasonable risk" for TOSCA purposes as:

> . . . balancing the probabilities that harm will occur and the magnitude and severity of that harm against the effect of proposed regulatory action on the availability to society of the benefits of the substance or mixture, taking into account the availability of substitutes for the substance or mixture which do not require regulation, and other adverse effects which such proposed action may have on society.

The report goes on to say that "a formal benefit-cost analysis under which a monetary value is assigned to the risks . . . and to the cost of society" is not required.

The Atomic Energy Act of 1954 continually refers to the "health and safety of the public," but makes little attempt to define these terms.[19] The NRC rules, however, use the expression "without undue risk" and seem to suggest again a balancing of risks and benefits.[20] In the words of one legal commentator, in practice, especially in the earlier years, "the acceptability of risk was measured largely in terms of the extent to which industry was capable of reducing the risk without jeopardizing an economic and financial environment conducive to continuing development of the technology."[21] Again, we have an attempt to balance protection of individuals and promotion of the public welfare.

Sometimes the conflict between these two approaches is evident in a single debate. In the famous benzene case, for example, OSHA took an essentially respect-for-persons standpoint, arguing that the burden of proof should be on industry to prove that a given level of exposure to benzene was not carcinogenic. In its rebuke of OSHA, the Supreme Court argued that, in the light of the evidence that present standards did not lead to harm to workers, risk must be balanced against benefits in evaluating more stringent standards and that the burden of proof was on OSHA to show that the more stringent standards were justified.[22]

The law is far from clear on this issue. More than this, we cannot make an automatic inference from the law to what is morally correct. Still, the law, combined with the conclusions from moral theory considered above, may provide some useful suggestions for guidelines as to how to make the trade-offs between utility and respect for individual rights. Consider the following points.

First, an important consideration is how essential something is to human well-being. Several laws require protection of individuals, regardless of the cost. Chemical additives to food are not usually essential, and they must be free of the threat of harm. Yet, when a great benefit that cannot easily be replaced is threatened, trade-offs are allowed. Thus TOSCA requires us to take into account "the availability of substitutes" for a substance. As we have already pointed out, it is difficult to imagine regulations that would eliminate automobiles, even though they cause more than 50,000 deaths each year, as well as enormous numbers of injuries.

Second, a major requirement of the RP moral tradition is that people should not be subjected to unusual risks without their informed consent, Nevertheless, meaningful informed consent is often difficult to obtain for several reasons. (1) We cannot always know when consent is free. Have workers given their free consent when they continue to work at a plant with known safety hazards? Perhaps they have no alternative form of employment. (2) We cannot be sure that consent is informed. Laypeople often assess risk differently than experts. Should we count a risk as having been consented to, even if the understanding and assessment of the risk is quite different from the one an expert would make? (3) It is often just not possible to obtain any meaningful kind of informed consent from individuals who are subjected to risk as a result of engineering work. How would a plant manager obtain the consent of those who live near the plant for it to emit a substance into the atmosphere that causes mild respiratory problems in a small percentage of the population? Is the fact that the residents do not protest sufficient to say they have consented? What if they do not know about the substance, or do not know what it does, or do not understand its effects correctly, or are simply too distracted by other things?

The above considerations suggest a balancing of utilitarian and RP considerations. On the one hand, we must protect people from harm, especially with respect to substances that are ingested into their bodies or that pose a clear threat to life. On the other hand, this protection must be balanced against the need to preserve technologies that are irreplaceable and confer great benefits. Thus, RP morality requires that we should not subject people to dangers without their informed consent, and that harm should not be imposed unjustly. Conversely, we should be aware of the difficulties of obtaining free and informed consent in some circumstances.

In the light of these considerations, we can perhaps construct a *principle of acceptable risk* that may provide some guidance in determining when risk is within the bounds of moral permissibility.

> People should be protected from the harmful effects of technology, especially when the harms are not consented to or when they are unjustly distributed, except that this protection must sometimes be balanced against (a) the need to preserve great and irreplaceable benefits and (b) the limitations on our ability to obtain informed consent.

The principle does not offer an algorithm that we can apply mechanically to situations involving risk. Its use involves many conceptual and application problems, each of which must be considered on its own merits. We can enumerate some of the issues that arise in applying the principle.

First, we must define what we mean by "protecting" people from harm. This cannot mean that people are given certain assurance that a form of technology is free from risk. At best, "protection" can only be formulated in terms of probabilities of harm, and we have seen that even these are subject to considerable error.

Second, many disputes arise as to what constitutes a harm. Consider the case at the beginning of this chapter. Suppose the only effect of the fumes is the bad smell. Is having to breathe a foul odor all day long a harm? What about workers in a brewery or a sewage disposal plant? Here the foul odors cannot be eliminated, so the question of what harms should be eliminated cannot be divorced from the question of whether the harms can be eliminated without at the same time eliminating other goods.

Third, the determination of what constitutes a great and irreplaceable benefit must be made in the context of particular situations. We have given the example of automobiles as a benefit that most people would probably consider great and irreplaceable. A food additive that makes the colors of frozen vegetables more intense is clearly not a great and irreplaceable benefit, and if it is found to be a powerful carcinogen, it should be eliminated. Many other examples are more controversial. What about atomic power? What about cigarettes?

Fourth, we have already pointed out the conceptual and application problems that arise in determining informed consent and the limitations in obtaining informed consent in many situations. From the standpoint of RP morality, informed consent is a consideration of first importance. It is often difficult to interpret and apply, however.

Fifth, the criterion of unjust distribution of harm is also difficult to apply. Some harms associated with risk are probably unjustly distributed, for example, those associated with proximity to a toxic waste disposal area that is not well constructed or monitored. The risks associated with coal mining might also be considered to be unjustly distributed, but coal may also be considered a great and irreplaceable benefit. So the implementation of the requirement to reduce risk in the coal industry might be that the risks of coal mining should be reduced as much as possible without destroying the coal industry.

Sixth, an acceptable risk at a given time may not be an acceptable risk at another time. Engineers' responsibility to protect the health and safety of the public requires them to reduce risk, when this can be done as a result of the available technology.

8.6   Communicating Risk: Laypeople Versus Experts

The doctrine of informed consent derived from RP morality implies that engineers have a responsibility to promote the conditions in which individuals can give informed consent to risks they encounter as a result of technology. They must do what they can to ensure that the public understands the risks associated with technology and can consent to those risks, especially when they are unusual.

We have reviewed several statements in engineering codes that suggest the doctrine of informed consent. The NSPE code instructs engineers that if their professional judgment is overruled in "circumstances where the safety, health, property or welfare of the public are endangered" they are obligated to "notify their employer or client and such other authority as may be appropriate" (II.1.a). The first canon of the IEEE Code of Ethics requires IEEE members to "disclose promptly factors that might endanger the public or the environment." IEEE members must also "improve the understanding of technology, its appropriate application, and potential consequences."

One of the most serious problems is the disparity between the expert's and layperson's perception of risk. This disparity seems to have two different sources.

First, the public is sometimes mistaken in estimating the probability of death and injury from various activities or technologies. Risk expert Chauncey Starr notes that laypeople tend to overestimate the likelihood of low-probability risks and to underestimate the likelihood of high-probability risks associated with causes of death. The latter tendency can lead to overconfident biasing, or "anchoring." In *anchoring*, an original estimate of risk is made, an estimate which may be substantially erroneous. Even though the latter estimate is corrected, it is not sufficiently modified from the original. The original "anchors" all future estimates and precludes sufficient adjustment in the face of new evidence.[23]

A study by Slovic, Fischhoff, and Lichtenstein shows that while even experts can be mistaken in their estimations of various risks, they are not as seriously mistaken as laypeople. The study contrasts actual versus perceived deaths per year.[24] Experts and laypeople were asked their perception of the number of deaths per year for such activities as smoking, driving a car, riding a motorcycle, riding in a train, skiing, and so on. We can make a graph that plots perceived deaths against actual deaths. If the perception (by either laypeople or experts) of deaths were accurate, the graph would be a 45-degree line. That is, actual and perceived deaths would be the same. Instead, the experts were consistently about an order of magnitude (about ten times) low in their perceptions of the perceived risk, and the lay public still another order of magnitude (about 100 times) too conservative.

A second reason for the different attitudes toward risk by risk experts and laypeople is that laypeople think of risk in a different way from experts. Experts, as we have seen, usually define risk as the product of the magnitude and probability of harm. Laypeople do not evaluate risk in strict actuarial terms but consider other factors as well. According to Chauncey Starr, laypeople are generally willing to take voluntary risks that are 1,000 times (three orders of magnitude) as uncertain as involuntary risks.[25] For example, there is a perceived separation of three orders of magnitude between the "risk" involved in involuntary exposure to danger (as when a corporation places a toxic waste dump next door to one's house), and the "risk" involved in a voluntary activity (such as smoking). The amount of risk people are willing to accept in the workplace is generally proportional to the cube of the increase in the wages offered in compensation for the additional risk. For example, doubling wages would tend to convince a worker to take eight times the risk.

Another researcher, D. Litai, has analyzed risk into twenty-six factors, each having a dichotomous scale associated with it.[26] For example, a risk may have a natural or human origin. If the risk has a human origin, Litai concludes from an analysis of statistical data from insurance companies that the perceived risk is twenty times as great as a perceived risk having a natural origin. An involuntary risk is perceived as being 100 times greater than a voluntarily assumed one. An immediate risk is perceived as being thirty times greater than a delayed one. A catastrophic risk is perceived as being thirty times greater than an ordinary one. By contrast, a regular risk is perceived as being just as great as an occasional one and a necessary risk just as great as a luxury one.

While some of these differences may be attributable to factual errors of laypersons in estimating the probability or magnitude of harm, they may also be attributable to differences between experts and laypeople in the definition of risk itself. For example, laypeople often seem to think of an involuntarily assumed risk as inherently more "risky" than one that is voluntarily assumed.

These two types of differences may explain apparent discrepancies in public policy regarding risk. In his study of fifty-seven risk-abatement programs at five different government agencies in Washington (including the Environmental Protection Agency and the Occupational Safety and Health Administration), Starr shows that these programs vary greatly in the amount of money they spend to save a life. Some spend $170,000 a life, while others spend $3 million a life. If we assume that some of these widely different expenditures to prevent various kinds of risk reflect public pressure, this is further evidence that the public does not necessarily consider risks that can lead to the same probability and magnitude of harm to be equally risky.

These differences between the experts' and the public's approach to risk pose serious issues for engineers. What are the responsibilities of engineers regarding the communication of risk to the public? One option is to promote a policy of concealing the discussions from the public, under the assumption that the public's assessments of risk are often incorrect. In a country with democratic institutions such as the United States, however, this option is probably not politically (or even legally) possible.

This resolution of the problem is seriously deficient for other reasons as well. First, we have already seen that lay perceptions of risk often include value judgments. For example, a risk imposed involuntarily is more "risky" than one that is voluntarily assumed. This makes it all the more improper to make decisions about risk without the contribution of laypeople. Second, the experts are sometimes wrong. In evaluating the risks of a hazardous waste dump in Maxey Flats, Kentucky, experts calculated that plutonium would take 24,000 years to migrate one-half inch. Instead, ten years later plutonium and other radionuclides were discovered two miles off-site. The experts were in error by six orders of magnitude.[27]

Another option is to let authoritative bodies make decisions about risk. This still seems to isolate laypeople too much from decisions that affect their lives. Even if they are given membership in the authoritative bodies, their opinions tend to be overshadowed by those of the experts.

Still another option is to educate the public to see the problem the way the experts do. Experience has shown that this is possible only within limits. Laypeople persist in looking at risk differently from the experts, especially where value judgments are clearly involved.

Finally, there is the option of promoting a combination of lay and expert approaches, emphasizing (1) free and informed consent on the part of those subjected to risk, (2) fair distribution of risks and benefits, and (3) democratic processes in decision making. This option requires the engineering community to promote projects that inform the public of risk and to encourage engineers, who often possess the most reliable technical information, to participate in such projects.

8.7   Liability for Risk

Risks associated with technology can never be eliminated. Regardless of how careful we are, technology will sometimes produce harm. Accidents often lead to legal action, some of it involving millions of dollars. The threat of legal action has been a major issue in the professional life of physicians for some time and is increasingly becoming an issue for accountants, lawyers, engineers, and other professionals.

In this section we consider several issues raised for engineers by the threat of legal action. First is the controversy over the proper standards of evidence for conviction in liability cases. Second is the argument that engineers should be protected from liability in some areas, in order to be able to more effectively protect the public from risk. Third are the problems faced by governmental regulators in their attempt to prevent the kinds of situations that lead to legal action.

Liability in Tort Law

One of the issues engineers face in reducing risk is the problem of liability. Most of us are aware that the threat of malpractice litigation is an ever-present consideration for physicians. Engineering firms and even individual engineers are also increasingly concerned about liability and litigation in the event of product failure or design flaws.

Litigation seeking redress from harm most commonly appeals to the law of torts, which deals with injuries to one person caused by another, usually as a result of fault or negligence of the injuring party.[28] Many of the most famous legal cases involving claims of harm from technology have been brought under the law of torts. The litigation involving harm from asbestos is one example. In 1973 the estate of Clarence Borel, who began working as an industrial insulation worker in 1936, brought suit against Fiberboard Paper Products Corp.

During his career he was employed at numerous places usually in Texas, until disabled from the disease of asbestosis in 1969. Borel's employment necessarily exposed him to heavy concentrations of asbestos generated by insulation materials. In a pretrial deposition Borel testified that at the end of the day working with insulation materials containing asbestos his clothes were usually so dusty that he could "barely pick them up without shaking them." Borel stated, "You just move them a little bit and there is going to be dust, and I blowed this dust out of my nostrils by the handfuls by the end of the day. I even used Mentholatum in my nostrils to keep some of the dust from going down my throat, but it is impossible to get rid of all of it. Even your clothes just stay dusty continuously, unless you blow it off with an air hose." . . .

In 1964 doctors examined Borel in connection with an insurance policy and informed him that X-rays of his lungs were cloudy. The doctor told Borel that the cause could be his occupation as an installation worker and advised him to avoid asbestos dust as much as he possibly could. On January 19, 1969, Borel was hospitalized and a lung biopsy performed. Borel's condition was diagnosed as pulmonary asbestosis. Since the disease was considered irreversible Borel was sent home. . . . [His] condition gradually worsened during the remainder of 1969. On February 11, 1970 [he] underwent surgery for the removal of his right lung. The examining doctors determined that Borel had a form of lung cancer known as mesothelioma, which had been caused by asbestos. As a result of these diseases, Borel later died before the district case reached the trial stage.[29]

The federal district court in Texas decided in favor of the estate of Mr. Borel, and the fifth circuit court of appeals upheld the decision.

The standard of evidence in tort law is the preponderance of evidence, meaning that there is more and better evidence in favor of the plaintiff than the defendant. The plaintiff must show "(1) that the defendant violated a legal duty imposed by the tort law, (2) that the plaintiff suffered injuries compensable in the tort law, (3) that the defendant's violation of legal duty caused the plaintiff's injuries and (4) that the defendant's violation of legal duty was the proximate cause of the plaintiff's injuries."[30] This standard of proof that a given substance caused a harm is less stringent than that which would be demanded by a scientist, who might well call for 95 percent certainty. It is also less stringent than the standard of evidence in criminal proceedings, which calls for proof "beyond reasonable doubt."

As an illustration of this lower standard of evidence, consider the case of *Rubanick* v. *Witco Chemical Corporation and Monsanto Co.*[31] The plaintiff's sole expert witness, a retired cancer researcher at New York's Sloan-Kettering Cancer Center, testified that the deceased person's cancer was caused by exposure to polychlorinated biphenyls (PCBs). He based his opinion on:

(1) the low incidence of cancer in males under 30 (the deceased person was 29), (2) the deceased person's good dietary and nonsmoking habits and the absence of familial genetic predispositon to cancer, (3) 5 of 105 other Witco workers who developed some kind of cancer during the same period, (4) "'a large body of evidence' showing that PCB's cause cancer in laboratory animals," and (5) support in the scientific literature that PCB's cause cancer in human beings.[32]

The court did not require the expert to support his opinion by epidemiological studies, but merely that he have the appropriate "education, knowledge, training and experience in the specific field of science," and an appropriate factual basis for his opinion.[33] Other better-known cases, such as the case of Richard Ferebee, who alleged that he suffered lung damage as a result of spraying the herbicide paraquat, also accepted standards of evidence for causal claims that would not have been acceptable for research purposes.[34]

Some courts, however, have begun to impose higher standards of evidence for recovery of damages through tort, standards that are similar to those used in science.[35] In the Agent Orange case Judge Jack B. Weinstein argued that epidemiological studies were the "only useful studies having any bearing on causation," and that by this standard no plaintiff had been able to make a case. Bert Black, a legal commentator, has taken a similar view. He believes that the courts (i.e., judges) should actively scrutinize the arguments of expert witnesses, demanding that they be supported by peer-reviewed scientific studies or at least have solid scientific backing. In some cases, he believes, they should even overrule juries who have made judgments not based on scientific standards of evidence.[36]

Even though this view represents a departure from the normal rules of evidence in tort law, it might in some cases be fairer to the defendants, for some decisions in favor of plaintiffs may not be based on valid proof of responsibility for harm. The disadvantage is also equally obvious. By requiring higher standards of proof, the courts place burdens of evidence on plaintiffs that they often cannot meet. In many cases, scientific knowledge is simply not adequate to determine causal relationships, and this works to the disadvantage of the plaintiffs. There are also problems with encouraging judges to take such an activist role in legal proceedings.

The major ethical question, however, is whether we should be more concerned with protecting the rights of plaintiffs who may have been unjustly harmed or with promoting economic efficiency and protecting defendants against unjust charges of harm. We shall not attempt to settle this issue here but only point out its analogies with similar ethical conflicts already discussed in this chapter. Now let us turn to another issue involving liability.

Protecting Engineers from Liability

Engineers have a responsibility to protect public safety, but sometimes the threat of legal liability prevents them from assuming this responsibility. Engineers in private practice may face especially difficult considerations regarding liability and risk. In some cases, they may need increased protection from liability.

Consider, for example, the safety issues in excavating for foundations, pipelines, and sewers.[37] A deep, steep-sided trench is inherently unstable. Sooner or later the side walls will collapse. The length of time that trench walls will stand before collapsing depends on a number of factors, including the length and width of the cut, weather conditions, moisture in the soil, composition of the soil, and how the trench was excavated. People who work in deep trenches are subjected to considerable risk, and hundreds of laborers are injured or killed each year when the walls collapse.

To reduce the risk, construction engineers can specify the use of trench boxes in their designs. A trench box is a long box with an upside-down-u-shaped cross-section that is inserted inside the trench to protect the laborers. As long as workers remain inside the trench boxes, their risk of death or injury is greatly reduced. Unfortunately, the use of trench boxes considerably increases the expense and time involved in construction projects. The boxes must be purchased or rented, and then they must be moved as excavation proceeds, slowing construction work and adding further to the expense.

Engineers are placed in an awkward position with respect to the use of trench boxes, especially where the boxes are not required by building codes. If they do not specify the use of the boxes, they may be contributing to a situation that subjects workers to a very high risk of death and injury. If they do specify the use of the boxes, they may be incurring liability in case of an accident. With situations such as this in mind, the National Society of Professional Engineers has been actively lobbying the U.S. Congress to pass a law that specifically excludes engineers from liability for accidents where construction safety measures are specified by engineers but then either not used or used improperly. This would enable engineers to more effectively protect the safety of workers.

The problem with trench boxes illustrates a more general issue. If engineers were free to specify safety measures without being held liable for their neglect or improper use, they could more easily fulfill one aspect of their responsibility to protect the safety of the public.

Risk and Government Regulation

A great deal of governmental regulation is devoted to the control of risk. We shall close this section with a brief mention of the conflict problem faced by government regulators. It is important to see that regulators have problems similar to those we have discussed in other areas involving risk.

According to William Ruckelshaus, former administrator of the Environmental Protection Agency, regulators face a dilemma regarding risk management.[38] On the one hand, regulators could decide to regulate only when there is a provable connection between a substance and some undesirable effect, such as cancer. Given the element of uncertainty in many scientific estimations of risk and the difficulties in establishing the levels of exposure to toxic substances at which there is no danger, this option would expose the public to unacceptable risks. On the other hand, regulators could eliminate any possible risk, insofar as this is technologically possible. Choosing this option would result in the expenditure of large sums of money to eliminate minute amounts of any substance that might possibly pose risks to human beings. This would not be cost effective. Funds might better be spent elsewhere to eliminate much greater threats to public health.

The solution to this conflict problem probably involves a balancing of RP and utilitarian considerations similar to that suggested elsewhere in this chapter. Both considerations of cost and benefit and considerations of the rights of individuals must be employed. Engineers should be at the forefront in formulating rational regulations of risk.

8.8   Becoming a Responsible Engineer Regarding Risk

The development of new technology is intimately connected with risk. The obligation of engineers is to be ethically responsible in this regard. We believe this involves the following four elements.

First, engineers should be aware of the uncertainties and the value dimensions associated with all phases of the analysis and treatment of risk. Experts often differ widely in their estimation of risk. They are also often inclined to treat it as a matter of deaths or injuries produced by a certain type of activity. This oversimplified view tends to obscure the fact that even the identification and estimation of risk often involve a value dimension. The most obvious sense in which this is true is that risk involves the possibility of harm and what constitutes a harm can involve value judgments. We have also seen that value judgments are involved in setting the parameters in terms of which epidemiological studies of the effects of harmful substances are made. Unless engineers know that there are ethical considerations involved, they cannot be responsible in resolving them. Apart from this awareness, engineers cannot understand the difference between the experts' and the public's attitudes toward risk, for many of these differences hinge on different approaches to the value dimension.

Second, the ethically responsible engineer should be aware of the limits of cost/benefit analysis. Risk analyses that take account only of cost/benefit considerations omit important ethical considerations, such as the just distribution of risk, on which laypeople usually place great emphasis. It is ethically irresponsible to omit this. This does not mean, of course, that cost/benefit considerations should be eliminated, or that cost/benefit analysis is not an important tool for ethical analysis, but it should not be the only consideration.

Third, the ethically responsible engineer should, in general and where appropriate, promote free and informed consent and democratic decision making regarding risk. Of course engineers may have limited opportunity to do this, since such issues are usually the province of managers rather than ordinary engineers. Nevertheless, this is another area in which we believe the codes should be modified so that the engineering community has more responsibility for promoting these values. Even individual engineers, in their dealings with clients and customers and in their public statements about engineering products and projects, should promote free and informed consent, if this is possible.

Fourth, engineers owe it to the public to develop their abilities to think competently about such ethical issues as risk. Only if they do this will they be able to fulfill the three prior obligations adequately.

8.9   Chapter Summary

Engineering codes require engineers to hold paramount the safety, health, and welfare of the public. This implies that engineers must protect the public from unnecessary risk. Experts and laypeople differ, however, even in their conception of risk. Experts think of risk as the product of the probability and magnitude of harm, while laypeople are more apt to include such factors as the just distribution of risk in their conception of risk itself.

There is a large element of uncertainty in estimating risk. Engineers have an obligation to utilize all available methods, but they should be aware that all failure modes cannot be predicted, as the narrative of the boiler explosion in Yonkers, New York, illustrates. This element of uncertainty necessitates the introduction of normative considerations, primarily, promoting the general well-being of the public and protecting the rights of those subjected to risk. An attempt to combine these two perspectives is suggested both in the law and in moral theory.

The major problem in risk communication is created by the different perspectives on risk taken by experts and laypeople. In the light of these differences, engineers are morally and professionally obligated to promote the conditions in which the public understands the risks imposed by technology and is able to give free and informed consent to those risks if it chooses.

Risks impose liabilities on engineers and others involved in technological innovation, liabilities that often result in litigation. Some have proposed that the standards of proof in tort law, where most of the litigation occurs, be modified to be more congruent with the standards of proof in science. This would make it more difficult for plaintiffs to win damages. The arguments for and against this proposal involve both legal and moral considerations.

The threat of lawsuits also makes it more difficult for engineers to exercise their responsibility to protect the public from risk. As a partial remedy to this problem, the National Society of Professional Engineers has promoted the passage of legislation that enables engineers to specify risk-reducing factors in their design, without having to assume liability for the implementation of these specifications by contractors and owners.

Responsible engineers must be aware of the uncertainties and the value dimensions associated with risk, be aware of the limits of cost/benefit analysis, promote free and informed consent and democratic decision making regarding risk, and develop their capacities to think clearly about the ethical issues involved in risk.

Case Analyses

Case 8.1 Bad-Smelling Fumes

Let us continue with the case presented at the beginning of this chapter involving the foul-smelling fumes. Don faces two distinct moral decisions. He must first decide whether to pursue his attempt to get information about the possible impact of the fumes on his supervisees. If he gets additional information, he must then decide what to do with it.

The first issue is probably best understood as a conflict problem. As their supervisor, Don has an obligation to the workers. They should be protected from unnecessary risk to their health, especially when they have not given informed consent to the risk. The employer also has a right, within limits, to obedience from the employees. We can assume that Cal does not want the issue of the fumes raised, so Don has some obligation (which may be overridden by other considerations) not to raise it, simply out of obedience to his superior. The firm also should not have to bear unnecessary expenses for pollution control, and its employees should not contribute to this unnecessary burden.

Despite the existence of obligations on both sides, it seems clear that Don does have an obligation to get more information about the possible health effects of the fumes. If Don were to use the Golden Rule test, he could ask whether he, if he were in the position of the workers, would want to be exposed to a risk—or even a possible risk—without his knowledge or consent. The answer to this question would almost certainly be in the negative. He could also ask whether it would be self-defeating if everyone allowed workers to be exposed to actual or possible risks without the workers' knowledge or consent. The answer here is more difficult, but we can expect that the regulations on exposure to hazards in the workplace would be tightened further if such actions were widely practiced or widely known. Certainly workers would tend to be much more suspicious of their employers and would probably be more aggressive in demanding action, again contributing to the likelihood that such actions would be self-defeating if universalized. From the standpoint of rights, protection from physical harm or even death is a basic right. Even the threat of increased risk to health or increased risk of death is a serious infringement of basic rights.

Even the utilitarian standpoint suggests that the issue of the threat to the workers must be pursued. It is true that economic efficiency is an important consideration from a utilitarian standpoint. Thus we must realize that complete elimination of the fumes could be very expensive, in the extreme case even forcing the closing of the plant and eroding the economic base of the community. Nevertheless, the fumes almost certainly interfere to some extent with the efficiency and the morale of the workers. It also may be difficult to convince the workers that the fumes are entirely harmless, thus increasing worker mistrust of employers. Furthermore, even if scientific studies give the fumes a clean bill of health at the present time, problems with the fumes may be discovered in the future. Then the company may find itself saddled with a number of very expensive lawsuits, as well as some very bad publicity. These consequences could harm the economic viability of the firm, threaten the economic base of the community, and in general produce more negative utility than spending the money to eliminate the fumes.

Don might argue, however, that the problem is not his, that it is not his responsibility to press the issue, but this argument would not seem to be valid. This raises an interesting conceptual issue of how we should under-stand "responsibility" in an organization. Without attempting a complete definition of "responsibility," we can say that a person is, at the very least, responsible for the health and safety of those directly under his or her supervision. By this account, Don, as the supervisor of the workers, is responsible for their welfare. Even if he were not an engineer, therefore, Don would have responsibility to get additional information about the fumes.

His obligation is even stronger because he is an engineer. He has an obligation to hold paramount the health, safety, and welfare of the public. There is a conceptual issue as to what we mean by "public," and whether his supervisees should be included in this class. But if we assume that the "public" includes those (1) who are vulnerable to harm by technology without being aware of the dan-ger and (2) for whom one can be said to have a responsibility, then the employees are clearly part of the public. Therefore, Don also has an obligation as an engineer to pur-sue the matter.

Don still has the practical problem of how he can look for additional information with-out breaking the relationship with his super-visor completely. He does have a moral obligation to be obedient and cooperative with his superiors, insofar as his other moral obligations will permit. He might try several creative-middle-way solutions. He might first try once more to get approval from Cal to order the literature through the library, or he might attempt to get the literature through his local public or university library. He might talk to some of his friends who are managers on his level and ask them if they can order the literature for him. As a last resort, he might have to directly confront Cal and say that he will pursue the matter with Cal's superiors if Cal does not cooperate.

When Don gets the information he wants, he might find that there is overwhelming evidence that the fumes pose no health threat whatever. Even in this best possible scenario, however, Don still has a problem, for the fumes smell bad and are obviously an impediment to good morale and to effi-ciency in the workplace. Thus, even in this best possible scenario, Don will probably decide that he has an obligation to eliminate or reduce the fumes. More than likely, though, the literature search will not give the fumes such a clean bill of health. It might reveal that very little research has been done on the problem, or that the research is incon-clusive, or that the fumes pose some slight risk to health, or that the fumes raise the chance of serious illness or death by some amount. What should Don do in these cir-cumstances?

Without knowing either the results of the literature survey or the expenses and problems in eliminating the fumes, it is impossible to say precisely what we should do if we were in Don's situation. But it would be very difficult to justify tolerating the status quo. The argu-ments that we have already considered show this. Don should again, however, try to be as diplomatic as possible and honor his obliga-tions to his supervisor as well as to his super-visees. He should propose a specific plan to Cal for eliminating or greatly reducing the fumes, preferably with a cost estimate. He should attempt to make a convincing argu-ment that eliminating the fumes is good for the firm as well as for the workers: the workers are becoming concerned, worker productivity is decreasing (if this is the case), the company may be liable for lawsuits, and a proactive response to it is advisable. Only if Cal refuses to respond to the problem should Don con-sider circumventing his immediate superior.

It is possible that the cost of eliminating the fumes would be very large, in the extreme case endangering the financial via-bility of the company. Even here the degree of threat to the workers must be taken very seriously. At the very least, informed consent by the workers to the danger must be given.

Case 8.2 Containers[39]

Axtell, Inc. designs, manufactures, and installs large containers designed to store highly active chemicals. These containers require strong, reliable safety seals to prevent spills and leakage, precision temperature control units, and an automated valve system to control inflow and outflow.

For several years Axtell only manufactured the containers; its major customers installed them without supervision from Axtell. However, recent automated design innovations require intricate installation procedures. Mistakes can be very costly, ranging from damaged machinery and interrupted work flow to serious injuries to workers. So Axtell now sends engineers to each site to supervise installation.

As chief engineer of Axtell's installation division, Howard Hanson manages the installation supervisors. He is proud of his division's record during his five years on the job. There have been only two reported incidents of serious accidents involving Axtell containers. Both were determined to have resulted from negligence on the part of chemical companies rather than any flaws in the containers.

Axtell's good record is in no small way attributable to the work of Howard's division. Although the supervisory work is tedious, Howard insists that his engineers carefully supervise each phase of the installation. There are times when the workload is so heavy that it is difficult for the engineers to meet installation deadlines, and occasionally customers apply pressure on Axtell to be allowed to install containers without Axtell supervision. However, Howard realizes that quality, and perhaps even safety, may be compromised without proper supervision. Furthermore, he is concerned to minimize Axtell's legal liabilities. He has a motto on his office wall: "Better late than sorry!"

Normally only one Axtell engineer is sent to an installation site. Because the installations require several complex procedures, Howard has the work of new engineers double-checked by veteran engineers for the first few months on the job. The veteran supervisor's job is to coach and monitor the newcomer's work as they oversee the installation together. Each container is given a dated inspection number that can be traced to the engineer. Those that are double-checked are given two numbers, one traceable to the new engineer and the other to the veteran engineer. Axtell's requirement that new engineers have a one-month training period was Howard's idea. Although he realized that it was not required by law, Howard convinced Axtell management that such a requirement would enhance quality and safety.

Tom Banks was in the last week of his one-month trial period. He had been working with veteran engineer Charles Yost during the entire trial period. It was clear to Charles from the very first week that Tom had a real knack for thorough, efficient supervision. It seemed apparent to both of them by the end of the third week that Tom was more than ready to "go it alone." They reminded themselves that "rules are rules" and the training period is a full month. They would have to stick it out for the full trial period.

At the beginning of the final week Tom noticed that Charles seemed somewhat lethargic and inattentive. When he asked Charles if he was all right, Charles replied, "I'm just a little tired. I've been under a lot of pressure lately, and it's been cutting into my sleep." Tom suggested that Charles take a couple of days of sick leave to get rested. "We can ask Howard to assign someone else to me for these last couple of days." Charles replied that he had exhausted his sick and vacation leave time for the year and that he was too financially strapped to lose any pay. "Besides," he said, "Howard doesn't have anyone available to replace me this week, and this job can't wait. These guys are already champing at the bit." By Friday, however, Charles was too ill to concentrate on work.

Tom suggested that Charles go home for the day. Charles replied, "I thought about staying home today, but I just can't afford it—and we have to get the job done this week anyway. I'll get some rest this weekend and I'll be fine next week. We can get through today all right. Look, next week you're on your own anyway. I've been checking your work for three weeks. You're the best supervisor I've seen around here. Don't worry, you can handle it. Give 'em a good look and I'll just put my tag on."

What should Tom do? He could try to protect Charles and carry out the supervision by himself. He could stop the inspections and tell Charles that they need to talk to Howard. No doubt other options are available. Analyze this problem as a conflict or line-drawing problem, discuss relevant factual and conceptual issues, and justify your belief as to the proper course of action for Tom.

Case 8.3 A Tourist Problem[40]

Marvin Johnson is environmental engineer for Wolfog Manufacturing, one of several local plants whose water discharges flow into a lake in a flourishing tourist area. Included in Marvin's responsibilities are the monitoring of water and air discharges at his plant and the periodic preparation of reports to be submitted to the Department of Natural Resources.

Marvin has just prepared a report that indicates that the level of pollution in the plant's water discharges slightly exceeds the legal limitations. However, there is little reason to believe that this excessive amount poses any danger to people in the area; at worst, it will endanger a small number of fish. On the other hand, solving the problem will cost the plant more than $200,000.

Marvin's supervisor, plant manager Edgar Owens, says the excess should be regarded as a mere "technicality," and he asks Marvin to "adjust" the data so that the plant appears to be in compliance. He explains: "We can't afford the $200,000. It might even cost a few jobs. No doubt it would set us behind our competitors. Besides the bad publicity we'd get, it might scare off some of the tourist industry, making it worse for everybody."

How do you think Marvin should respond to Edgar's request? No doubt many people in the area besides Marvin Johnson and Edgar Owens have an important stake in Marvin's response. How many kinds of people who have a stake in this can you think of? For example, what about the employees at Wolfog?

Deborah Randle works for the Department of Natural Resources. One of her major responsibilities is to evaluate periodic water and air discharge reports from local industry to see if they are in compliance with antipollution requirements. Do you think Deborah would agree with the plant manager's idea that the excess should be regarded as a "mere technicality"?

How would local parents of children who swim in the lake view the situation? Would they agree that the excess is a "mere technicality"?

A basic ethical principle is "Whatever is right (or wrong) for one person is right (or wrong) for any relevantly similar persons in a relevantly similar situation." This is called the principle of universalizability. Suppose there are several plants in the area whose emissions, like Wolfog Manufacturing's, are slightly in excess of the legal limitations. According to the principle of universalizability, if it is right for Marvin Johnson to submit an inaccurate report, it is right for all the other environmental engineers to do likewise (and for the plant managers to ask them to do so). What if all the plants submitted reports like the one Edgar Owens wants Marvin Johnson to submit?

You should begin your answers to these questions by characterizing the questions as conflict or line-drawing problems and discuss the factual, conceptual, and application issues raised in the case.

Case 8.4 The XYZ Hose Company

Review the details of this case as presented in Case 7.3. Consider it from the perspective of responsibility for risk. What are the responsibilities of the project engineer at XYZ regarding the risk to the farmers? How would you have dealt with the data from the paper written by the agricultural engineering consultant about the long-term effects of anhydrous ammonia on the new plastic hose-reinforcing material? What would you have done about the advertisement that XYZ placed in the trade magazines recalling the "obsolete" hose?

Begin by characterizing the problems as line-drawing or conflict problems and by discussing the factual, conceptual, and application issues relevant to the case.

Case 8.5 Side-Saddle Gas Tanks

From mid-November 1992 through mid-February 1993, media coverage of the 1973–1987 Chevrolet and GMC pickup trucks was intense. In mid-November, two *New York Times* articles discussed a controversy about the fuel tank systems of 1973–1987 Chevrolet and GMC pickup trucks. These models place a gas tank on each side of the vehicle, both of which are outside the truck frame. The articles raised several important ethical questions about safety and responsibility. Although much that is contained in the articles is basically informational, their headlines make it clear that their primary intent is to help readers address these ethical questions: "Data Show G.M. Knew for Years of Risk in Pickup Trucks' Design"; "Despite Report that U.S. Standard Wasn't Cutting Fatal Car Fires, Little Was Done."[41]

Although the articles are by-lined (with Barry Meier listed as author), they are not offered as editorial opinions. Readers can expect primarily informative pieces—but perhaps with "slantings" in one direction or another. The question here is whether these articles provide readers with the sorts of relevant information they need to adequately address the ethical questions.

The first headline suggests to readers that GM may have been negligent. Why, readers may ask, did GM delay changing the location of the fuel tanks? Internal memos indicate that GM was trying to improve fuel tank safety as early as 1982. Yet, commenting on the change made in 1988, GM officials are credited with saying it was made for reasons of design rather than safety.

Although the articles indicate that the issues are very complex, several matters are not in dispute. It is clear to all that the GM vehicles are in compliance with existing safety regulations. It is also clear to all that the redesigned models (beginning in 1988) render the gas tanks less vulnerable to damage in collisions. Various internal documents mentioned in the articles reveal that GM considered plans to relocate the gas tanks as early as 1982, but it was noted that any significant change would require a "long lead time." The November 17 article cites a December 1983 internal GM document indicating its intention to change the fuel tank's position in 1987: "The fuel tank will be relocated inside the frame rails, ahead of the rear axle—a much less vulnerable location than today's tanks."[42]

According to the articles, one of GM's aims was to come up with a plan that would enable the vehicles to withstand collisions from the side without significant fuel leakage at speeds up to 50 mph—thus, far exceeding the 20-mph regulation in force since 1977. In 1984 a plastic shield for the tanks was introduced—successfully, according to GM director of engineering analysis, Robert A. Sinke, Jr.—but unsuccessfully, according to Clarence Ditlow, executive director of the Center for Auto Safety, who refers to this as a "Band-Aid fix." Despite introducing a redesign in 1988 that does seem to fulfill GM's aim to withstand 50-mph collisions, GM countered that the relocation of the gas tank was made for reasons of design rather than safety.

Aside from questions about whether GM bore any special responsibility for past harms or deaths associated with the 1973–1987 model fuel tanks, at issue were two related questions about the present: whether GM pickups during this period should be recalled and how safe or unsafe these vehicles are.

It was reported that the National Highway Traffic and Safety Administration (NHTSA) was contemplating ordering a recall of the vehicles. One problem with this is that the vehicles were in compliance with existing regulations. NHTSA would be questioning the adequacy of its own regulations. GM indicated it would resist any such recall as illegal. Further, a GM attorney, Chilton

Varner, was cited as saying in an interview that she believed the existing 20-mph standard is adequate to protect public safety. NHSTA, however, indicated that it might consider the question of whether the 20-mph standard is adequate. It might also consider whether the testing procedure itself should be changed. (The fuel tanks were tested by being struck with wide barriers at a 90-degree angle rather than with a narrower barrier at an oblique angle.)

The above summary gives some idea of the complexity of the controversy. Meanwhile, the millions of owners of the vehicles in question wondered how safe their pickups were. Did the two articles help them determine this? Various data were provided (by different sources). Thomas Carr, vice-president for the Motor Vehicles Manufacturers Association (a trade group in Detroit), claimed that 66 percent of all fatal car crashes involving fires are at speeds exceeding 50 mph. (What Carr did not mention is that, apparently, fully one-third are not.)

A 1990 study indicated that car fires have been reduced by 14 percent since the introduction of standards on fire safety, but that there is no observed reduction in the rate of fire-related deaths. (The report points out that the number of fires could decline without affecting the death rate if the fire deaths occur at speeds above the standard.)

Failure Analysis Associates (Houston consultant working with the auto industry) found that, from 1973–1989, GM pickups were involved in about 155 fatal side-impact collisions involving fires. Ford had 61 such accidents. The two companies had roughly the same number of pickups on the road.

However, federal investigators were still reviewing the fatal GM pickup accidents to see if the fires were actually caused by fuel tank leaks.

Sinke is quoted as saying that to determine the safety of a vehicle, one must consider the overall picture. "Any time you look at a small slice of the whole apple, one manufacturer's vehicles will not look as good as others. You have to look at the whole apple, and our overall safety record is as good or better than anyone's."

Brian O'Neill, director of the Insurance Institute for Highway Safety, is reported as insisting that it is possible for a vehicle to have a fire problem and a good overall safety record, since fire deaths are only 4 percent of the highway fatalities. "Fires can get very easily lost in overall pool data, but the fire statistics suggest that they have a problem. It has been well known for a long time that fuel tanks near the perimeter of the vehicle are not a good idea."

NHTSA estimated that about 5,200 pickups and other light trucks catch fire every year. Older vehicles are more likely to catch fire than newer ones because of corrosion and other factors that lead to fuel line and tank leakage.

Several days after the two *New York Times* articles were published, *Newsweek's* full-page account appeared. Entitled "Was GM Reckless?" the subtitle reads, "The troubled automaker is accused of ignoring an unsafe gas-tank design."[43] Complete with a color photo of a GM pickup truck in flames flanked by diagrams of the pre-1988 tank locations and the current model, the article recounts much of the information provided in the *New York Times* articles. But it makes one significant addition. It cites a September 7, 1970 internal memo from GM safety engineer George Carvil that warned of possible fuel leaks resulting from side collisions. "Moving these side tanks inboard," *Newsweek* cites the memo as saying, "might eliminate most of these potential dangers."

A later Barry Meier *New York Times* article carried the headline, "Courtroom Drama Pits G.M. Against a Former Engineer."[44]

Former GM safety engineer Ronald E. Elwell was reported to have testified in an Atlanta jury trial that GM altered documents, conducted secret tests, and ordered employees not to criticize its vehicles in writing. Meier reported:

> In his testimony, Mr. Elwell contended that company officials knew in the early 1980's that the side-saddle fuel tank design was "indefensible." Furthermore, he said, the company a decade ago was developing a steel plate to protect the tanks against punctures in collisions.
>
> But development of the steel plate was dropped because officials feared it would alert the public to the tanks' hazards, he testified. "It would produce the wrong image to the public," Mr. Elwell said.[45]

Working against the credibility of Elwell's testimony was the fact that, in 1971, GM put him in charge of fuel safety for pickups, and he worked on the side-saddle design and later defended it. However, Meier reported:

> Mr. Elwell has previously testified that he approved the tank's side location because the company, for marketing purposes, wanted to equip the pickups with large-capacity fuel tanks. But he said his views about the vehicle's safety changed in 1983, when he learned from his superior about company tests run from 1981 to 1983 that showed the tanks splitting open when a pickup was hit in the side by a car moving at 50 miles an hour.
>
> Mr. Elwell said he was outraged because G.M. had not made the tests available to him before he had testified in a San Francisco pickup case that year, leading him to feel he had perjured himself. "The tanks were split open like watermelons," he said.[46]

Although GM officials and attorneys in the Atlanta case were not allowed to comment publicly on the case, Meier indicated that

other lawyers not involved in the case predicted that GM would try to discredit Elwell's
testimony on the grounds that he is a disgruntled former employee. Elwell reportedly
complained that GM began easing him out of
serving as an expert witness shortly after the
1983 San Francisco case. The suggestion is
that Elwell might be seeking revenge for
being pushed into taking early retirement in
1986 after a thirty-year career at GM. (Elwell
was fifty-six in early 1993.)

Meier concluded his article:

> Though Mr. Elwell's motivations may
> never be fully clear, consumer advocates
> believe in him. "He could be out selling his
> testimony against General Motors, but he
> isn't doing that," said Clarence M. Ditlow,
> director of the Center for Auto Safety, a
> Washington consumer group.
>
> G.M. lawyers also indicated in pre-trial
> dispositions that they might assert that Mr.
> Elwell threatened the company, for not hir-
> ing him as a private consultant after he
> retired.[47]

On February 5, 1993, the result of the
Atlanta jury trial was announced.[48] The
court ruled that GM was to pay $101 million
to the parents of Shannon Moseley, a seven-
teen-year-old boy who burned to death in a
1989 crash in his GMC pickup. This was the
first punitive award among the many court
cases involving GM's side-saddle vehicles.
The court also awarded $4.2 million in com-
pensatory damages to Shannon Moseley's
parents. GM objected to the $105.2-million
verdict and indicated its intent to appeal.

Only three days later, on February 8, 1993,
GM launched a vigorous attack against NBC
for its November 1992 "Dateline NBC" por-
trayal of GM pickups.[49] "Dateline NBC" had
presented footage to demonstrate what
could happen to a GM pickup in a side-
impact crash. The film showed a 1977
Chevrolet pickup erupting into flames. The
NBC correspondent explicitly stated that the
demonstration was "unscientific" and that it
was not presented as a random experiment
to see what might happen. However, she
failed to mention that the private testing
company in Indiana attached tiny toy rockets
to the underside of the truck and ignited
them by remote control to make sure sparks
would be present when a Chevrolet Citation
struck the side of the pickup. Although NBC
initially defended its actions, it soon issued a
public apology. Public attention was suddenly shifted from safety issues to questions
of media responsibility.

Press coverage of the GM controversy also
made a decided shift. The May 10, 1993 issue
of *Newsweek* carried a full-page article entitled, "Just as Safe at Any Speed: The Feds
asked GM to recall its trucks, but has the
pickup-fire flap unfairly tainted the
automaker?"[50] In this article GM was
reported as challenging NHTSA's request for
a "voluntary" recall of GM pickups. GM
claimed that NHTSA's own data show that
GM trucks are safer to drive than most other
vehicles. NHTSA's data indicate that drivers
of GM pickups have 1 chance in 6,605 of
dying in an accident. Odds for Ford pickup
drivers are only slightly better (1 in 6,916).
For Dodge it is 1 in 8,606, while for Nissan's
light, compact model it is 1 in 4,521. For all
passenger cars it is 1 in 6,053.

However, *Newsweek* pointed out, these
data are about fatalities in general, not fatalities related to fires. William Boehly, the
NHTSA enforcement director who has asked
for the "voluntary" recall, conceded that the
GM pickups do well in overall safety—but
not in regard to fatalities resulting from fire.
Newsweek reported:

> The NHTSA's investigators, relying in part
> on information compiled in 120 lawsuits
> filed against GM by personal-injury
> lawyers, detected a tendency for GM

trucks to catch fire in fatal crashes more often than big Ford or Dodge trucks. Fires rarely happen—only 6 percent of all big-pickup fatalities involve fires. Unfortunately for GM, federal regulators have targeted fires that are caused by side-impact collisions for special concern. The chances of an individual owner dying from this subset of fires is infinitesimal: a driver could spend 31,673 lifetimes before meeting such a fate, assuming he kept the truck for 15 years. Still, the NHTSA calculates that this tiny risk is 50 percent greater than the chance of a fatal fire in a Ford pickup during a similar accident. Those numbers are too high for safety advocates like Clarence Ditlow, who called the GM trucks "rolling firebombs." And it is this small risk—in a truck basically as safe as Ford's—that has led the NHTSA to ask GM for a recall.[51]

According to *Newsweek*, Boehly claimed that NHTSA tests indicate that six lives a year might be saved if the pickups are fixed. GM's reply is that, to support this, NHTSA tests had to be highly selective for certain kinds of side-impact crashes—such as impacts against telephone poles at the point where cab and truck bed meet. GM's Ed Lechtzin was quoted as saying, "Our truck's safe. It's as if we get A-minus but still flunk the test."

Newsweek pointed out that the highway safety act requires that NHTSA focus its attention on flaws that pose "an unreasonable risk to safety." But it concludes:

In the GM case, the NHTSA seems to be asserting that any vehicle below average in even one tiny aspect of its design is unreasonably risky. Applied systematically, the NHTSA would be establishing a rule that recalls Garrison Keillor's community of Lake Wobegon—"where all the children are above average." But Keillor was joking. The problem for GM is that the NHTSA watchdogs are not.[52]

Identify the ethical issues surrounding the controversy over the GM side-saddle tanks. What are the relevant facts? What factual, conceptual, and application issues are there? Some more specific issues you might address are the following. Given that motor vehicles will always place us at some risk, how are we to understand 'safe'? If NHTSA is questioning its own standards, what kinds of criteria do (and should) they use? Can a product be unacceptably risky even though it satisfies current safety regulations? What does it mean to say that a design is changed that improves safety but is made for reasons of design rather than reasons of safety? Is this acceptable engineering practice? If a vehicle has an *overall* safety rating as good as its competitors, does it follow that it should not be required to improve any *particular* safety features?

Case 8.6 Faulty Heart Valves[53]

Shiley, Inc., a Pfizer subsidiary, was a pioneer in artificial heart valves. From 1965 to the late 1970s, Shiley manufactured and sold artificial heart valves that never had a fracturing problem. In the late 1970s it came up with a new model, the C-C, that allowed better blood flow than other models, thereby reducing the risk of blood clots. The new valve consisted of a metal ring through which blood flows, with two wire struts protruding from the ring that hold a small disk in place. The disk tilts up and down within the struts, opening and closing the valve according to the natural flow of blood. About 86,000 C-C valves have been implanted in patients.

Unfortunately, about 450 fractured C-C valves have been reported so far, with nearly 300 resulting deaths. Investigators have come up with disturbing findings. Since fractures can be fatal, Shiley inspectors were told to look very carefully (through microscopes) for any evidence of cracks. Each valve was hand-built, with one strut welded to the valve's metal ring at a much sharper angle than in earlier models. Then the wire strut was bent up and down, often several times, to insert the disk. Scratches had to be polished off to let blood flow through smoothly. If any cracks were discovered, the valve was to be rewelded or discarded. Each valve was accompanied by a card recording dates and the manufacturing operations performed. What investigators discovered was that many cards indicating rewelding were falsified. Many cards were signed off by Inspector No. 2832, an employee who had left Shiley six months before the valve was first manufactured.

Investigators learned that some cracks were simply polished over rather than rewelded. Further investigation revealed skepticism about the notion that rewelding was an acceptable practice. Nancy Wilcox, a Shiley employee, testified in a Houston court case that she had talked with Cabot Corp., supplier of the metal alloy Shiley used with its struts. She reported that a Cabot official said they do not normally recommend rewelding.

Shortly after this conversation, Shiley stopped rewelding, and it disposed of any valves observed to have cracks. Shiley also reduced the angle of the outlet strut, thereby making the initial weld of strut to ring easier.

A 1984 internal memo written by a member of Shiley's task force on valve fractures expressed concern about pressure on quality control inspectors to inspect valves at a rate that causes eyestrain, increasing the probability of not noticing some defects.

Pfizer apparently takes a different view. It is reported as holding that the major reason for fractures was an abnormal closure of the disk, causing it to hit the tip of one strut with too much force. Repeated striking can produce metal fatigue, ultimately resulting in a broken strut. In addressing this problem, Pfizer says that, in early 1984, it made design changes that avoided the abnormal disk closure—and that no valves with the new design have fractured.

The Federal Drug Aministration's position is that no specific cause of fractures has been proven.

Identify and discuss the ethical issues this case raises. What factual, conceptual, or application issues are there? Discuss the safety issues this case should raise for engineers.

Other Cases

Other cases already presented in this text might be considered from the standpoint of the leading ideas of this chapter.

Case 3.1: To Dissent or Not to Dissent
Case 3.7: The TV Antenna Tower
Case 4.5: The Corrected Estimate
Case 5.2: A Vacation
Case 5.3: The Deadline
Case 5.4: Gilbane Gold
Case 6.6: Experimenting with Cadavers

NOTES

1. See Michael S. Pritchard, ed., *Teaching Engineering Ethics: A Case Study Approach*, Center for the Study of Ethics in Society, Western Michigan University, NSF Report on Grant DIR-8820837, June 15, 1992, pp. 190–198.

2. William W. Lowrance, "The Nature of Risk," in Richard C. Schwing and Walter A. Albers, Jr., eds., *Societal Risk Assessment: How Safe Is Safe Enough?* (New York: Plenum Press, 1980), p. 6.

3. The National Public Radio story was aired on "Morning Edition," December 3, 1992. This account is taken from the *Newsletter* of the Center

for Biotechnology Policy and Ethics, Texas A&M University, 2, no. 1 (January 1, 1993), 1.

4. *Newsletter*, p. 1.

5. Carl F. Cranor, *Regulating Toxic Substances: A Philosophy of Science and the Law* (New York: Oxford University Press, 1993), p. 11.

6. See the *New York Times*, October 15, 1962 for an account of this tragic event. The engineering details are cited from an unpublished report by R. C. King, H. Margolin, and M. J. Rabins to the City of New York Building commission on the causes of the accident.

7. Martin and Schinzinger, *Ethics in Engineering*, p. 66.

8. Epidemiology is the study of the distribution of disease in human populations and the factors that causally influence this distribution.

9. See Carl F. Cranor, "Some Moral Issues in Risk Assessment," *Ethics*, 101 (October 1990), 123–143. See also Carl F. Cranor's *Regulating Toxic Substances* (New York: Oxford University Press, 1993), pp. 12–48.

10. Cranor, "Some Moral Issues," pp. 139–143.

11. For a more extended treatment of this issue, see the discussion in Chapter 6.

12. John Rawls, *A Theory of Justice* (Cambridge, Mass.: Harvard University Press, 1971), p. 3.

13. From the *Charlotte* (N.C.) *Observer*, February 10, 1980. Quoted in Carl F. Cranor, *Regulating Toxic Substances*, p. 152.

14. See Harold P. Green, "The Role of Law in Determining Acceptability of Risk," in *Societal Risk Assessment—How Safe Is Safe Enough?* (New York: Plenum Press, 1980), pp. 255–269.

15. Public Law No. 85-929, 72 Stat. 784 (1958).

16. Senate Report No. 85-2422, 85th Congress, 2d Session (1958).

17. 21 United States Code, sect. 348(c)(A) (1976).

18. Public Law No. 94-469, 90 Stat. 2003 (1976). The same criterion of "unreasonable risk" is found in the Flammable Fabrics Act. See Public Law No. 90-189, 81 Stat. 568 (1967).

19. Public Law No. 83-703, 68 Stat. 919 (1954), 42 United States Code 2011, et. seq. (1976).

20. 10 CFR 50.35(a)(4).

21. Green, "The Role of Law," p. 265.

22. *Industrial Union Department, AFL-CIO v. American Petroleum Institute et al.*, 448 U.S. 607 (1980).

23. Chauncey Starr, "Social Benefits Versus Technological Risk," *Science*, 165, (September 19, 1969), 1232–1238. Reprinted in Theodore S. Glickman and Michael Gough, *Readings in Risk* (Washington, D.C.: Resources for the Future, 1990), pp. 183–193.

24. Paul Slovic, Baruch Fischhoff, and Sarah Lichtenstein, "Rating the Risks," *Environment*, 21, no. 3 (April 1969), 14–20, 36–39. Reprinted in Glickman, pp. 61–74.

25. Starr, "Social Benefits," pp. 183–193.

26. D. Litai, "A Risk Comparison Methodology for the Assessment of Acceptable Risk," Ph.D. dissertation, Massachusetts Institute of Technology, Cambridge, Mass., 1980.

27. See K. S. Shrader-Frechette, *Risk and Rationality* (Berkeley: University of California Press, 1991), p. 52. See also M. Douglas and A. Wildavsky, *Risk and Culture* (Berkeley and Los Angeles: University of California Press, 1982), pp. 5–7, 167, 182.

28. Harold P. Green, "The Role of Law in Determining Acceptability of Risk." Reprinted in Glickman (1990), pp. 255–269.

29. *Borel* v. *Fiberboard Paper Products Corp. et al.*, 493 F.2d (1973) at 1076, 1083. Quoted in Cranor, *Regulating Toxic Substances*, (1993), p. 52.

30. Cranor, *Regulating Toxic Substances* (1993), p. 58.

31. 576A.2d4 (N.J. Super. Ct. A.D. 1990) at 15 (concurring opinion).

32. "New Jersey Supreme Court Applies Broader Test for Admitting Expert Testimony in Toxic Case." *Environmental Health Letter, 30* (August 27, 1991), 176.

33. Ibid.

34. *Ferebee* v. *Chevron Chemical Co.*, 736 F.2d 11529 (D.C. Cir. 1984).

35. Bert Black, "Evolving Legal Standards for the Admissibility of Scientific Evidence," *Science, 239* (1987), 1510–1512.

36. Bert Black, "A Unified Theory of Scientific Evidence," *Fordham Law Review, 55* (1988), 595–692.

37. See R. W. Flumerfelt, C. E. Harris, Jr., M. J. Rabins, and C. H. Samson, Jr., "Introducing Ethics Case Studies into Required Undergraduate Engineering Courses," final report to the NSF on Grant DIR-9012252, November 1992, pp. 262–285.

38. See William D. Ruckelshaus, "Risk, Science and Democracy," *Issues in Science and Technology, 1*, no. 3 (Spring 1985), 19–38. Reprinted in Glickman (1990), pp. 105–118.

39. Pritchard, *Teaching Engineering Ethics*, case and commentaries on pp. 61–76.

40. Ibid, pp. 411–418. This case is an adaptation of "Cover-up Temptation," one of several short scenarios in Roger Ricklefs, "Executives Apply Stiffer Standards Than Public to Ethical Dilemmas," *Wall Street Journal* (November 3, 1983).

41. Barry Meier, "Data Show G.M. Knew for Years of Risk in Pickup Trucks' Design," *New York Times*, November 17, 1992, pp. A1 and A10. Barry Meier, "Despite Report That U.S. Standard Wasn't Cutting Fatal Car Fires, Little Was Done," *New York Times* (November 21, 1992), p. A6.

42. Meier, "Data Show G.M. Knew," p. A10.

43. *Newsweek* (November 30, 1992), p. 61. The article is written by Thomas McCarroll.

44. Barry Meier, "Courtroom Drama Pits G.M. Against a Former Engineer," *New York Times* (January 19, 1993), pp. C1 and C14.

45. Meier, "Courtroom Drama," p. C14.

46. Meier, "Courtroom Drama."

47. Meier, "Courtroom Drama."

48. Michael J. McCarthy and Douglas Lavin, "GM Order by Jury to Pay $105.2 Million over Death," *Wall Street Journal*, February 5, 1993, p. A3.

49. Elizabeth Kolbert, "In TV 'Crash,' News and Law Collide," *New York Times* (February 10, 1993), p. A16.

50. Rich Thomas, with Frank Washington and Myron Stokes, "Just as Safe at Any Speed," *Newsweek* (May 10, 1993), p. 52.

51. Ibid.

52. Ibid.

53. The information for this case is drawn from William M. Carley, "Fatal Flaws: Artificial Heart Valves That Fail Are Linked to Falsified Records," *Wall Street Journal* (November 7, 1991), p. A6. For a discussion of ethical issues relating to this case, see John H. Fielder, "Ethical Issues in Biomedical Engineering: The Bjork-Shiley Heart Valve," *IEEE Engineering in Medicine and Biology*, March 1991, pp. 76–78.

Chapter 9

Engineers As Employees

In the mid-1970s the New York City Police Department had in operation an on-line computerized police car dispatching system called SPRINT. On receiving a telephoned request for police assistance, a dispatcher entered the address into a computer, and the computer responded within seconds by displaying the location of the nearest patrol car. By cutting the response time to emergency calls, the SPRINT system saved lives.

In 1977 the New York City prosecutors were considering another system, PROMIS. It would use the same host computer as SPRINT. The PROMIS system would provide names and addresses of witnesses, hearing dates, the probation status of defendants, and other information that would assist the prosecutors or arresting officers who wished to check on the current status of apprehended perpetrators. This project was managed by the Criminal Justice Coordinating Council or Circle Project, a committee of high-level city officials including the deputy mayor for criminal justice, the police commissioner, and, as chairman, Manhattan district attorney Robert Morgenthau.

The committee employed a computer specialist as project director, who in turn hired Virginia Edgerton, an experienced system analyst, as senior informa-tion scientist to work under his supervision. Soon after beginning the job, Edgerton expressed concern to the project director about the possible effect on the response time of SPRINT of loading the computer with an additional task, but he instructed her to drop the matter. Edgerton then sought advice from her professional society, the Institute of Electrical and Electronics Engineers (IEEE). After an electrical engineering professor at Columbia University agreed that her concerns merited further study, she sent a memorandum to the project director requesting a study of the overload problem. He rejected the memorandum out of hand, and Edgerton soon thereafter sent copies of the memorandum with a covering letter to the members of the Circle Committee. Immediately following this, Ms. Edgerton was discharged by the project director on the ground that she had, by communicating directly with the committee members, violated his orders. He also stated that the issues she had raised were in fact under continuing discussion with the police department computer staff; although he gave no documentation to support this claim.

The case was then investigated by the Working Group on Ethics and Employment Practices of the Committee on the Social Implications of Technology (CSIT) of the IEEE, and subsequently by the newly formed IEEE Member Conduct Committee. Both groups agreed that Virginia Edgerton's actions were fully justified. In 1979 she received the second IEEE-CSIT Award for Outstanding Service in the Public Interest. After her discharge, Ms. Edgerton formed a small company selling data processing services.[1]

9.1   Introduction

Virginia Edgerton's experience shows how a professional's concern for doing the right thing may place her in opposition to her employer. Because over 90 percent of all engineers are employees and because the perspectives of engineers and managers sometimes differ, this case has many parallels in the engineering profession. It is by no means unique to engineering, however. More and more physicians are being employed by health maintenance organizations and other corporate entities, and many lawyers work for corporations and large legal firms. Many certified public accountants work for accounting firms and corporations, and the accounting profession also includes management accountants, who are usually employees of large corporations. Most architects are employees of architectural firms. The issue of professional employee rights is destined to become more common in all professional ranks.

We begin with a brief look at what the engineering codes say about employer-employee relationships. Then we consider the changing legal status of employee rights. Next we examine several facets of the engineer-manager relationship, a central issue in the debate over professional employee rights for engineers. Then we develop some criteria for determining when managers should make decisions and when ordinary engineers should make them, applying the criteria to the decision to launch the Challenger. Since the appeal to loyalty to the organization is usually a part of the criticism of dissenting engineers, we examine the concept of organizational loyalty. Next we discuss the issue of professional employee dissent and how it can be done responsibly. Finally, we look at some ways that organizations can establish procedures for dealing with professional employee dissent in a positive and constructive way.

9.2   The Codes and Employer-Employee Relationships

The engineering codes provide some general guidelines for employer-employee relationships, but they also show many possibilities for conflict and line-drawing issues. We can use the code of the National Society for Professional Engineers (NSPE) as an example. On the one hand, the code provides a clear basis for loyalty to the employer. Canon 4 states: "Engineers shall act in professional matters for each employer or client as faithful agents or trustees." On the other hand, the same code gives directives that could easily lead to conflict problems. Canon 1 requires engineers to "hold paramount the safety, health and welfare of the public in the performance of their professional duties." These two canons can conflict, as they did in Virginia Edgerton's experience. While the health, safety, and welfare of the public are to be placed first, in many situations it may not be clear whether the obligations to the public are weighty enough to override the obligations to the employer. Canon 2 requires engineers to "perform services only in the areas of their competence," but a manager can ask an engineer to take a job in an area where she believes her qualifications are marginal at best. Canon 3 requires engineers to "issue public statements only in an objective and truthful manner." But Roger Boisjoly reported that his boss reminded him that in his testimony before Congress after the Challenger disaster he should not unnecessarily malign the company. Company officials had reprimanded him for revealing that Morton Thiokol had not honored his requests for more tests on possible O-ring failures.[2]

Another source of conflict and line-drawing issues is the guidelines regarding confidentiality. In the section on professional obligations, the NSPE code instructs engineers not to "disclose confidential information concerning the business affairs or technical processes of any present or former client or employer without his consent." Yet employers sometimes ask engineers to work on projects where information gained from a former employer can be used to good advantage. This has already been discussed in Chapter 7, with regard to honesty in engineering practice.

The codes also produce conceptual issues related to employer-employee relationships. The NSPE code requires engineers to protect the "public," but it does not say who counts as the public. We saw in Chapter 2 that in the Challenger disaster a good case can be made for including the astronauts in the category of the "public," at least with respect to the O-ring problem. The terms must be defined. Engineers are also required to act as "faithful agents or trustees" for their employers, but these terms are undefined in the codes. They are defined in the law, but the definitions may not always be adequate for ethical analysis. These terms are closely related to the concept of "loyalty" as it is commonly used, and we shall examine that term in more detail later.

Application issues also arise in applying the code. No matter how carefully we define such terms as "public" or "faithful agents or trustees," their application to real-world examples will often be problematic. Even if we define "public" as anyone who is ignorant of the dangers to which they are subjected by engineering work, the question arises as to how ignorant people must be before engineers have a professional obligation to protect them. Even if we have defined the terms "faithful agent and trustee" as carefully as we can, we may still have problems knowing whether a particular action conforms to the requirements of the code in this area.

This brief discussion is sufficient to show that the codes do not provide clear and easy answers to all of the deep issues that professional engineers face in relating to their employers. No code could possibly do this. In this chapter we attempt to interpret and extend the thinking embodied in the codes as it applies to employer-employee relationships. Since the legal context forms an important background for this discussion, it will be helpful to begin with a survey of the recent changes in the law and court decisions regarding employee rights.

9.3   The Changing Legal Status of Employee Rights

Until recently, American law has been governed by the common law doctrine of "employment at will." According to this, in the absence of a contract, an employer can discharge an employee at any time and for virtually any reason.[3] For example, this doctrine was the basis of a Pennsylvania court's decision in the 1967 case of *Geary* v. *United States Steel Corp.*[4] Mr. Geary was not educated as an engineer, but he had fourteen years of engineering experience with U.S. Steel. During the production phase of a new line of pipe, Mr. Geary became convinced that the pipe was unsafe under high pressure. He attempted to make his concerns known to management but was rebuffed. Finally a vice-president listened and ordered an investigation that vindicated Mr. Geary's concerns. A costly blunder was thus averted.

For his efforts Mr. Geary was fired on July 13, 1967, on grounds of insubordination. In a four-to-three decision, the Pennsylvania Supreme Court affirmed the traditional employment-at-will doctrine, reasoning as follows:

> There is nothing here from which we could infer that the company fired Geary for the specific purpose of causing him harm, or coercing him to break any law or otherwise to compromise himself. According to his own averments, Geary had already won his own battle within the company. The most natural inference from the chain of events . . . is that Geary had made a nuisance of himself, and the company discharged him to preserve administrative order in its own house.[5]

Thus, even in the relatively recent past, employees had little protection from their employers when acting out of the highest motives of concern for the public interest, or even the best long-range interests of their employer.

A move in a different direction was indicated in *Murray* v. *Microform Data*. In 1974 Marvin Murray noticed that a computer console marketed by his company was unsafe because it did not have a single switch for shutting off the electrical power. His protests resulted in his dismissal, and Mr. Murray was unemployed for almost a year. The judge allowed a jury trial, and Mr. Murray was awarded $20,000 for lost pay.

A still more important landmark was the 1980 case of *Pierce* v. *Ortho Pharmaceutical*. Dr. Grace Pierce, a physician, was involved in the development of

Loperamide, a drug for treating diarrhea in children and the elderly. Dr. Pierce believed the drug contained an excessive amount of saccharin, a drug suspected of being carcinogenic, and she objected to its use in tests on humans. Management overrode her objections, and she refused to continue work on the project. As a result, she was reprimanded and demoted. After resigning, she sued Ortho, alleging that her resignation was compelled by pressure from the company to violate her ethical principles.

A trial court judge dismissed her claim, invoking the doctrine of employment at will, but an appellate court found there were legal grounds for suit if her loss of employment was a violation of public policy. She appealed this ruling to the New Jersey Supreme Court.

Dr. Pierce lost her appeal because the majority of the justices believed there were defects in her case, among them the fact that she should have specified a section of the American Medical Association code of ethics in her defense. Nevertheless the decision broke new ground in the area of professional employee rights. In its majority opinion, the Supreme Court of New Jersey said:

> In certain instances, a professional code of ethics may contain an expression of public policy. However, not all such sources express a clear mandate of public policy. For example, a code of ethics designed to serve only the interests of the profession . . . probably would not be sufficient.

The Court went on to say that "employees who are professionals owe a special duty to abide not only by federal and state law, but also by the recognized codes of ethics of their professions. That duty may oblige them to decline to perform acts required by their employers."[6] The Court concluded by saying that wrongful discharge is a basis for a suit in contract law as well as tort law (the law governing injuries). Lawsuits in tort law might also allow for punitive damages, the Court said.

The wording of the decision provides grounds for an assertion of professional employee rights against an employer. At the same time, it sets limitations on the basis of this assertion of rights: it must be made in the name of the public interest rather than private benefit. The Pierce decision thus set the stage for modification of the common law.

Another important case, this time in 1981, was *Palmateer* v. *International Harvester*. Mr. Palmateer was not a professional, but his case in some ways affirmed the line of development suggested in *Pierce*. Mr. Palmateer discovered that some International Harvester employees were using company facilities to store stolen property. Instead of informing his superiors, he went to the police, who instructed him not to go to his employers but instead to continue to inform the police until an arrest could be made. He did as the police requested; as a result, company executives did not know of the illegal activity on their property until the arrests. When the matter was made public, Mr. Palmateer was fired for insubordination.

In the ensuing suit against International Harvester, the company argued that Mr. Palmateer's action violated the illegal search and seizure provisions of the

Constitution. The Illinois Supreme Court finally ruled against International Harvester, but it did not prescribe a remedy. In granting Mr. Palmateer a cause of action, the Court argued that if a corporation's actions violate public policy, the employee should be protected.

In a dissenting opinion, Justice Ryan made the following comment:

> By departing from the general rule that an at-will employment is terminable at the discretion of the employer, the courts are attempting to give recognition to the desire and expectation of an employee in continued employment. In doing so, however, the courts should not concentrate solely on promoting the employee's expectations. The courts must recognize that the allowance of a tort action for retaliatory discharge is a departure from, and an exception to, the general rule. The legitimate interest of the employer in guiding the policies and destiny of his operation cannot be ignored. The new tort for retaliatory discharge is in its infancy. In nurturing and shaping this remedy, the courts must balance the interests of the employers with the hope of fashioning a remedy that will accommodate the legitimate expectations of both. In the process of emerging from the harshness of the former rule, we must guard against swinging the pendulum to the opposite extreme.[7]

In a 1982 case, *Kalman* v. *Grand Union Co.*, Mr. Kalman, a pharmacist, insisted (correctly) that his professional regulations required keeping the pharmacy in the store where he was employed open when the rest of the store was open. Part of the rationale for this regulation was that unauthorized employees might otherwise get into the pharmacy and dispense drugs, thus endangering the public. The manager wanted to close the pharmacy on July 4, while keeping the rest of the store open, and he fired Mr. Kalman for insisting on adherence to state regulations. The New Jersey Superior Court agreed with Mr. Kalman, while pointing out that the professional's behavior in such situations must be mandated by professional ethics, not the individual's personal ethics:

> . . . employees who are professionals owe a special duty to abide not only by federal and state law, but also by the recognized codes of ethics of their professions. That duty may oblige them to decline to perform acts required by their employers. However, an employee should not have the right to prevent his or her employer from pursuing its business because the employee perceives that a particular business decision violates the employee's personal morals, as distinguished from the recognized code of ethics of the employee's profession.[8]

The 1983 case in Pennsylvania of *Novosel* v. *Nationwide Insurance Co.* concerns an employee who was asked to assist his company in a lobbying effort that was to the advantage of the firm. Novosel refused, and in fact spoke out for the opposite side. He was summarily dismissed. Drawing on Palmateer, the Pennsylvania court said that violating a "clearly mandated public policy" was "striking at the heart of citizens' social rights, duties and responsibilities."[9] Refusing to assist the corporation in a lobbying effort, and even speaking out against it, was protected activity.

Members of the court itself criticized the actions of the Pennsylvania court. In a dissenting opinion, one of the Novosel judges said, "My concern is that the panel has announced an extremely broad public policy exception."[10] He gave three reasons. First, it ignores the difference between the public and the private employee. While public employees may well have to consider the public within the scope of their jobs, private employees seem to not have the public as a constituency. Second, the ruling fails to consider, "other public policy interests such as the economic interest of the public in efficient corporate performance."[11] Third, it does not take into account the first amendment rights of the corporation and the corporation's legitimate expectation of loyalty from its employees.

These arguments are unconvincing, at least as applied to professional employees. First, professionals have obligations to the public, even if they are the employees of private corporations. Second, although economic efficiency is a legitimate concern, it should not override all other considerations. Third, loyalty to the company need not require that an employee to give up his rights as a citizen.

Despite a series of groundbreaking court decisions, the public policy exception to the doctrine of employment at will is still controversial. Some states do not recognize the exception. The states of Alabama, Florida, Georgia, Louisiana, Mississippi, Missouri, North Carolina, and South Carolina have recently specifically refused to recognize any exceptions to the employer's right to terminate an employee.[12] Even in those jurisdictions where the exception is recognized, there is still disagreement as to how far it should extend. These jurisdictions agree that discharging an employee violates public policy if it is because he exercises a right guaranteed by law or because he refuses to undertake an illegal action. For example, workers fired because they filed worker's compensation claims, refused to commit perjury, served on a jury, or refused to participate in an illegal price-fixing scheme have often found protection. Whether discharging an employee for whistleblowing or upholding professional standards violates public policy, however, is still in dispute.[13]

In addition to the judicial modification of the common law doctrine of employment at will, dissenting employees have also achieved statutory protection, primarily through whistleblower laws. In April 1981 Michigan became the first state to pass a "Whistle Blowers Protection Act." According to the *Wall Street Journal*, the provisions are as follows:

> Any employee in private industry fired or disciplined for reporting alleged violations of federal, state or local law to public authorities can now bring an action in state court for unjust reprisal. If the employer cannot show that treatment of the employee was based on proper personnel standards or valid business reasons, the court can award back pay, reinstatement to the job, costs of litigation and attorney's fees. The employer can also be fined up to $500. . . . Every employer in Michigan must post a notice of this new law in the workplace.[14]

The law's protection is weak. It protects an employee from discharge only for reporting illegal actions, not actions contrary to professional ethics or conscience. Furthermore, the penalties to employers are negligible. Nevertheless, the law is significant as an indication of another departure from the doctrine of employment at will. Since 1981 approximately half the states have legislated some form of whistleblower protection.

The attempt to limit management autonomy will no doubt continue. Many people believe this is justified and that employees, particularly professional employees, must be granted more rights in the workplace. But there are arguments in favor of protecting management autonomy as well. We now begin an examination of the moral issues raised by the disagreements professionals can have with their employers, first considering the types of disagreements.

9.4   Professional Employee Disobedience: A Taxonomy

When we think of disagreements between employees and their employers, the term that most often comes to mind is "whistleblowing." But whistleblowing usually refers to an employee's "going public" when she believes a company is guilty of serious wrongdoing. This may be the most dramatic instance of employee-employer disagreement, but it is not the most common one, especially for professionals. Jim Otten finds the expression "organizational disobedience" more appropriate as a generic term covering all types of employee actions that are contrary to the wishes of the employer. Given the similarities between this kind of action and civil disobedience, the term seems appropriate.[15] We shall not follow Otten's definition exactly, but we shall use his expression and define *organizational disobedience* as a protest against, or refusal to follow, an organization's policy *or* action.

It is helpful to keep these two points in mind. First, the policy a professional employee disobeys or protests may be either specific or general. It may be a specific directive of a superior or a general corporate policy, either a single act or a continuing series of actions. Second, the employer may not intend to do anything morally wrong. For example, when Mr. Geary objected to the production of a faulty type of steel pipe, he did not argue that U.S. Steel intended to manufacture a shoddy product. Rather, he was protesting a series of actions that would probably result in unfortunate consequences, however unintended.

If we decide to adopt the term "organizational disobedience," the next question is, "What are the types of organizational disobedience in which the professional employee might engage?" There are primarily three types.

1. One type of organizational disobedience, *disobedience by contrary action*, is illustrated by Mr. Palmateer's cooperation with the police in the apprehension of criminal activity on International Harvester property. His action was neither a protest of a policy by International Harvester nor a refusal to participate in an activity directed by his firm, but rather an involvement in activities that officials at International Harvester considered to be contrary to corporate interests. Mr. Novosel's political activities are in the same category.

Here is a hypothetical example from engineering. Suppose Engineer Sue is the technical advisor for the Clean Water Coalition. The coalition is an environmental organization in her community that attempts to keep the surrounding rivers and lakes as free as possible from contamination by the chemical industries in the community. Sue traces one of the newest contaminants to her own company, Good Citizen Chemical. On the basis of Sue's recommendation, the Clean Water Coalition recommends legal action against Good Citizen Chemical. Sue's boss tells her she must sever her ties with Clean Water Coalition or lose her job with Good Citizen Chemical.

2. A second type of organizational disobedience, *disobedience by nonparticipation*, is a refusal to carry out an assignment given by a superior, as in Mr. Kalman's refusal to carry out his manager's order to close the pharmacy on July 4. Dr. Pierce's anticipated refusal to carry out potentially hazardous experiments of a new drug on human beings illustrates this category. An example from engineering would be an engineer's refusal to develop a product that he considers fundamentally unsafe.

3. A professional employee may feel called upon to protest a general policy or specific action of a firm. This is *disobedience by protest*. Virginia Edgerton's decision to object to the anticipated plan to place the PROMIS system on the same computer with SPRINT was an example of this type of organizational disobedience, as was Mr. Geary's protest of the manufacture of the faulty line of steel pipe. The protest can be of two types. A professional can make his objections known through the hierarchy of his organization, whether it be private or governmental. This was the option taken by Mr. Geary and, initially, by Virginia Edgerton. The second type of disobedience by protest takes the protest outside the organization, as Virginia Edgerton eventually did. Professionals who protest often begin with the first type and proceed to the second.

Organizational disobedience by professionals can occur only if professionals are employed by organizations. This includes most engineers (perhaps as many as 90 percent). There is reason to believe, however, that most professionals of all kinds will increasingly conduct their work in an organizational setting. As noted earlier, most accountants already work as salaried employees, and, increasingly, lawyers and physicians work in large organizations. So-called mega-law firms often hire hundreds of lawyers, and health maintenance and other corporate health-care organizations employ large numbers of physicians.

9.5 The Manager-Engineer Relationship

The conflicts of professionals with organizations are conflicts with managers, because managers wield the power. So let us turn directly to the manager-professional relationship in the context of engineering.

Differences in Perspective Between Managers and Engineers

Many ethical and professional issues faced by engineers involve a conflict between themselves and managers. The most serious conflict is over decision-making prerogatives. What decisions are appropriately made by engineers, and what decisions are appropriately made by managers? Because of their positions in the organizational structure, managers usually have the authority to overrule the decisions of engineers. The question here is an ethical one: when should managers (or at least management considerations) prevail and when should engineers (or at least engineering considerations) prevail?

Management theorist Joseph Raelin, reflecting the position of many management students, says, "There is a natural conflict between management and professionals because of their differences in educational background, socialization, values, vocational interests, work habits and outlook."[16] We can be more precise about the areas of conflict between engineers and managers.

First, although engineers may not always maintain as much identity with their wider professional community as some other professionals (such as research scientists), they often experience a conflict in loyalties.[17] Like other professionals, they have obligations to both their profession and their employers. Most engineers want to be loyal employees who are concerned about the financial well-being of their firms and who carry out instructions from their superiors without protest. In the words of many engineering codes, they want to be "faithful agents" of their employers. At the same time, as engineers they are also obligated to hold paramount the health, safety, and welfare of the public. This requires engineers to insist on high standards of quality and (especially) safety. Raelin believes professionals, including engineers, place greater importance on ethical responsibility than managers.[18]

Second, since many managers are not engineers and do not have engineering expertise, communication is often difficult. Engineers sometimes complain that they have to use oversimplified language in explaining technical matters to managers and that their managers do not really understand engineering issues.

Third, many engineers who are not managers aspire to the management role in the future, where they perceive the financial rewards and prestige to be greater. Thus, many who do not yet occupy the dual roles of engineer and manager probably expect to at some time in their careers. This conflict then is internalized within the same person. Many engineers already are both engineers and managers. An example is Robert Lund, vice-president for enginering at Morton Thiokol at the time of the Challenger disaster.

With the complexity of the relationship between engineers and managers and the likelihood of conflict, it would be helpful if we could find a way to distinguish the situation in which engineering considerations should predominate from the situation in which management considerations should prevail. (Of course agreement and consensus between engineers and managers is always preferable to a more adversarial relationship.) We can begin by isolating some characteristics of the engineering and management perspectives.

Two Empirical Studies

Investigators do not always agree about the nature of the engineer-manager relationship. Some have found a yawning gap between the perspectives of managers and professionals, including engineers. According to Robert Jackall, this gap is especially prominent in ethical issues. In his study of managers in several large American corporations, Jackall discovered that large organizations place a premium on "functional rationality," which is a "pragmatic habit of mind that seeks specific goals."[19] Jackall believed that the managers and firms he studied had several characteristics that were not conducive to respecting the moral commitments of conscientious professionals.

First, the organizational ethos does not allow genuine moral commitments to play a part in the decisions of corporate managers, especially highly placed ones. A person may have whatever private moral beliefs she chooses, as long as these beliefs do not influence behavior in the workplace. A person must learn to separate individual conscience from corporate action. Managers, according to Jackall, prefer to think in terms of trade-offs between moral principles on the one hand and expediency on the other. What we might think of as genuine moral considerations play very little part in managerial decisions. Faulty products are bad because they will ultimately harm the company's public image, and environmental spoilage is bad for business or will ultimately affect managers themselves, who are also consumers.

This attitude is in contrast to that of White, an employee who was concerned with a problem of excessive sound in his plant. White defined the issue of possible harm to employees as a moral concern instead of approaching it pragmatically. In another anecdote, Jackall recounts the story of Brady, an accountant who found financial irregularities that were traced to the CEO. While Brady saw the issue as a moral one, managers did not see the issue this way at all. In discussing the case, they held that Brady should have kept his mouth shut and dropped the matter. After all, the violations were small relative to the size of the corporation.[20]

Second, loyalty to peers and superiors is the primary virtue for managers. The successful manager is the team player, the person who can accept a challenge and get the job done in a way that reflects favorably upon himself and others. Of course loyalty in the corporate setting is always limited by self-interest, and must be distinguished from true friendship. It does not extend to those who are out of corporate favor. As one manager put it, ". . . it's difficult to make friends because the normal requirement for friendship—that is, *loyalty*—doesn't fit in this context."[21] Third, lines of responsibility are deliberately blurred in order to protect oneself, one's peers, and one's superiors. This supersedes all other considerations. Details are pushed down and credit is pushed up. Actions are separated from consequences if possible, to avoid responsibility. In making difficult and controversial decisions, a successful manager always gets as many people involved as possible, so he can point his finger at others if things go wrong. He should also avoid putting things in writing.

According to this account of managerial decision making, the scruples of professionals have no place. In such an atmosphere a principled professional often has no alternative to organizational disobedience. Such was the case with Joe Wilson, an engineer who found a problem with a crane that he believed involved public health and safety. Wilson wrote a memo to his boss, who replied that he did not need such a memo from Wilson, and that the memo was not constructive. After Wilson was fired and went public, a *New York Times* investigation cited a corporate official's comment that Wilson was someone who "was not a team player."[22]

Jackall does not generalize from his study, but if engineers typically work in an organizational environment like the one he describes, their professional and ethical concerns have little chance of being accorded respect. There is, however, a more constructive aspect to Jackall's study. He does suggest some characteristics of managerial decision making that are useful in analyzing the manager-engineer relationship. First, the study implies that managers have a strong (probably overriding) concern for the well-being of the organization. Well-being is measured primarily in financial terms, but it also includes a good public image and relatively conflict-free operation. Second, managers often have few loyalties outside the organization. In particular, they do not have professional loyalties that transcend their perceived obligations to the organization. Third, the managerial decision-making process involves trade-offs among the relevant considerations. Ethical considerations are only one type among others. Furthermore, if we are to believe Jackall, managers tend not to take these seriously, unless they can be translated into factors affecting the well-being (for example, the public image) of the firm.

Another empirical study, funded by the Hitachi Foundation, which we shall refer to as the Hitachi Report, examined the engineer-manager relationship in ten companies and arrived at a less discouraging picture.

First, the distinction between engineers and managers is not always clear in large organizations. While employees in small companies can usually distinguish between engineers and managers, employees in large companies often cannot do so easily. Two, three, or even four levels of organization might stand between employees regarded as "just bench engineers" and those regarded as "just managers." Sometimes some "group leaders" (those who supervise the work of four to six bench engineers) in an organization identify themselves as managers while others in the same organization identify themselves as "just engineers."[23]

Second, the report did find a difference in perspective between engineers and managers. The engineers and managers interviewed were "virtually unanimous in the way they distinguished the engineer's perspective from the manager's." They agreed that engineers had to change their perspective in order to become good managers, in three ways: (1) engineers must pay less attention to engineering details; (2) engineers must develop a broader horizon, to take account of nonengineering considerations; and (3) engineers must focus on people rather than things.[24]

A third finding of the Hitachi Report is that most managers and engineers conceded that engineering considerations should have priority in matters of safety, and usually in matters of quality. Engineers were expected to "go to the mat," as one engineer put it, on fundamental matters of safety and quality. On safety, they expressed little if any deference to management.[25] Even on questions of quality, customer satisfaction, and cost, engineers were willing to give managers the last word only after giving management what one engineer called an "ear full" first.[26]

We shall not attempt to make any final judgment as to whether the Jackall study or the Hitachi Report provides the most adequate description of the engineer-manager relationship as it actually exists in large organizations. There seems to be some validity to both accounts. On the one hand, many engineers report experiences with managers who seem to fit Jackall's description. Some engineers perceive these managers as people who have little concern for morality and who do not respect the professional integrity of engineers. On the other hand, most engineers, like most professionals, report a high degree of job satisfaction. This implies that they find their relationship with managers satisfactory.

9.6   Paradigmatic Engineering and Management Decisions

It is important to turn from the various *descriptive* accounts of how managers and engineers *do* relate to one another in the context of decision making to a *prescriptive* or normative account of how they *should* relate. How should we establish the boundary between decisions that should be made by engineers and those that should be made by managers?

Functions of Engineers and Managers

An answer to this question must begin with a delineation of the proper function of engineers and managers in an organization and of the contrasting points of view associated with these differing functions.

The primary function of engineers is to use their technical knowledge and training to create products and processes that are of value to the organization. But engineers are also professionals, and they must uphold the standards their profession has decided should guide the use of their technical knowledge. Thus engineers have a divided loyalty: to the organization and to their profession. Their professional loyalties go beyond their immediate employer.[27] These obligations include meeting the standards usually associated with good design and accepted engineering practice. The criteria embedded in these standards include such considerations as efficiency and economy of design, the degree of invulnerability to improper manufacturing and operation, and the extent to which state-of-the-art technology is used.[28] We could summarize these by saying that engineers have a special concern for quality.

Engineers also ascribe preeminent importance to safety. Moreover, they are inclined to be cautious in this regard, preferring to err on the conservative side. In the Challenger case, for example, the engineers did not have firm data on the behavior of the O-rings at low temperatures, even though their extrapolations indicated that there might be severe problems. So they recommended against the launch.

The function and consequent perspective of managers is different. They direct the activities of the organization, including those of engineers. Managers are not professionals in the strict sense. Rather than being oriented toward standards that transcend their organization, they are more likely to be governed by the standards that prevail within the organization, and in some cases perhaps by their own personal moral beliefs. Both the Jackall study and the Hitachi Report imply that managers see themselves as custodians of the organization and are primarily concerned with its present and future well-being. This well-being is measured for the most part in economic terms, but it also includes such considerations as public image and employee morale.

This perspective involves a somewhat different type of thinking than one finds among engineers. Rather than thinking in the context of professional practices and standards, managers enumerate all of the relevant considerations ("get everything on the table," as they sometimes put it), and then balance the various considerations against one another in order to come to a conclusion. This means that managers might be more willing than engineers to reduce quality or safety in favor of such matters as cost or marketability. By contrast, engineers assign a serial ordering to the various considerations relevant to design, so that minimal standards of safety and quality must be met before any other considerations are relevant.[29] Although they may also be willing to balance safety and quality against other factors to some extent, engineers believe that they have a special obligation to uphold safety and quality standards in negotiations with managers. They usually insist that a product or process must never violate accepted engineering standards and that changes be made incrementally.

This suggests a distinction between what we shall call a "proper engineering decision" (PED) and a "proper management decision" (PMD). Without giving a full definition of either PED or PMD in the sense of necessary and sufficient conditions, we can formulate some of the features that should ordinarily characterize these two types of decision procedures. Since the following two statements are not definitions, we shall refer to them as "characterizations" of proper engineering and proper management decisions.

> PED: A decision that should be made by engineers or at least governed by professional engineering practice, because it involves either (1) technical matters that fall within engineering expertise or (2) the ethical standards embodied in engineering codes, especially those requiring engineers to protect the health and safety of the public.
>
> PMD: A decision that should be made by managers or at least governed by management considerations, because (1) it involves factors relating to the well-being of the organization, such as cost, scheduling, marketing, and employee morale or well-being, and (2) the decision does not force engineers (or other professionals) to make unacceptable compromises with their own technical practices or ethical standards.

Two preliminary remarks about these characterizations of engineering and management decisions are in order.

First, the characterizations of the PED and PMD show that the distinction between management and engineering decisions is made in terms of the standards and practices that should predominate in the decision-making process. Furthermore, the PMD makes it clear that management standards should never override engineering standards when the two are in substantial conflict, especially with regard to safety and perhaps even quality.

Second, the PMD specifies that a legitimate management decision not only must not force engineers to violate their professional practices and standards, but also must not force other professionals to do so either. Even though the primary contrast here is the difference between engineering and management decisions, the specification of a legitimate management decision must include this wider prohibition against the violation of other professional standards. (A complete characterization of a legitimate management decision should also include prohibitions against violating the rights of nonprofessional employees, but this would make the characterization even more complicated and is not relevant for our purposes.)

Paradigmatic and Nonparadigmatic Examples

Several terms in both characterizations are purposely left undefined. The definition of the PED does not define "technical matters," and it certainly does not define "health" and "safety." PMD does not fully specify the kinds of considerations that are typical management ones, citing only "factors relating to the well-being of the company, such as cost, scheduling, marketing, and employee morale or well-being." The definition of the PMD requires that management decisions not force engineers to make "unacceptable compromises with their own professional standards," but it does not define "unacceptable."

We do not believe it useful to give any general definition of these terms. Their applications will be relatively noncontroversial in some examples, and no definition can furnish an a priori clarification of all the controversial cases. We shall refer to the relatively noncontroversial examples of PEDs and PMDs as *paradigmatic* PEDs and PMDs.[30] The characterizations of the PED and PMD given above describe such paradigms, which we can think of as marking the ends in a spectrum of cases.

We can easily imagine a paradigmatic PED. Suppose Engineer Jane is participating in the design of a chemical plant. She must choose between Valve A and Valve B. Valve B is sold by a friend of Jane's manager, but it fails to meet minimum specifications for the job. It has, in fact, been responsible for several disasters involving loss of life, and Jane is surprised that it is still on the market. Valve A, by contrast, is a state-of-the-art product. Among other things, it has a quicker shutoff mechanism and is also much less prone to malfunctions in emergencies. Although it is 25 percent more expensive, the expense is one that Jane's firm can well afford. Valve A, therefore, is the clear and unequivocal choice in terms of both quality and safety.

Here Jane or other engineers should make the decision in accordance with engineering considerations. This is because (1) the decision involves issues related to accepted technical standards and (2) the decision relates in important ways to the safety of the public, and therefore to the ethical standards of engineers. The choice between Valve A and Valve B is a paradigmatic PED.

We can modify the example to make it a paradigmatic PMD. Suppose Valve A and Valve B are equal in quality and safety, but Valve B can be supplied much faster than Valve A, is 5 percent cheaper, and is manufactured by a firm that is a potential customer for some of the products of Jane's firm. Valve A, however, is made by a firm that is potentially an even bigger customer, although cultivating the relationship with this firm will require a long-term commitment and will be more expensive. If there are no other relevant considerations, the decision as to whether to purchase Valve A or Valve B should be made by managers, or at least made in accordance with management considerations. Comparing the decision with the two criteria in the PMD, we can say that (1) management considerations (such as speed of delivery, cost, and the decision as to which customers should be cultivated) are important and (2) no violation of engineering considerations would result from either decision.

Most cases will lie between the two extremes of paradigmatic PEDs and paradigmatic PMDs. Some cases lie so near the center of the imaginary spectrum of cases that they might be classified as either a PED or PMD. Consider another version of the same case in which Valve A has a slightly better record of long-term reliability (and is therefore somewhat safer), but Valve B is 10 percent cheaper and can be delivered more quickly. Here rational and responsible people might well differ as to whether the final decision on which valve to buy should be made by engineers or managers. Considerations of reliability and safety are engineering considerations, but those of cost and scheduling are management considerations. Would ordering Valve B be an "unacceptable" compromise of engineering standards of safety and quality? Are the cost and scheduling problems significant enough to overbalance the engineering considerations?

Many issues about pollution also illustrate these problematic situations. Suppose Process A is so much more costly than Process B that the use of Process A might threaten the survival of the company. Suppose, furthermore, that Process B is more polluting, but it is not clear whether the pollution poses any substantial threat to human health. Here again, rational people of good will might differ as to whether management or engineering considerations should prevail.

9.7   The Ford Pinto Case

Now let us apply these paradigms to a real-world situation. In discussing the Ford Pinto case (Case 6.7), Richard De George points out that when tests were made in 1970 and 1971, Ford engineers sent a memo to management stating that an $11 modification would make the gas tank safer. This was what De George calls an "engineering assessment." He maintains, however, that the decision not to make the modification was properly an "administrative decision." That is, it was a decision for managers, not engineers, even though he believes it was "with hindsight, a poor one in almost every way."[31] Two paragraphs later he repeats his assertion, saying that "the decision not to add the part . . . was not an engineering but an executive decision." In the next paragraph he maintains that engineers "do not have the obligation to insist that their perceptions or their standards be accepted. They are not paid to do that, they are not expected to do that, and they have no moral or ethical obligation to do that."[32]

De George's conception of the relationship between engineers and managers appears to be fundamentally at odds with the one developed in the previous section. Rather than some decisions being the province of engineers and others of managers, De George asserts that managers have the right (and not simply the power) to make any decision in any area. Engineers are paid to render advice to managers, and presumably to make decisions when managers do not choose to intervene, but they never have the right to insist that "their perceptions or their standards" should prevail. Although Jackall's moral cynicism should not in any way be attributed to De George, the writers agree on a strong version of the claim that engineers are subordinate to managers.

By contrast, the distinction between proper engineering and proper management decisions that we have developed suggests that engineers have certain prerogatives in decision making that managers should not violate. Just as physicians should resist the invasion of government or management into areas that are clear and undisputed examples of medical decisions, so engineers should resist the incursions of management into areas that are clear and undisputed examples of engineering decisions. De George's notion of the subordination of engineers to managers does not allow for this notion of professional prerogatives for engineers.[33]

How does De George defend his position? In reading through his essay, we find three relevant considerations. Even though De George may not have intended these to be used as arguments, we can treat them as if they were.

One is that the decision involved economic, legal, and public-image considerations. Commenting on the decision not to add the part, De George says that "it ended up costing Ford a great deal more not to put in the part than it would have cost to put it in."[34] Later, he criticizes Ford's cost/benefit analysis as a poor one, because "it did not consider litigation, recalls, and bad publicity which have already cost Ford over $50 million."[35]

Economic, legal, and public-image considerations are indeed management considerations. They are just the kind of thing mentioned in (1) of the PMD. The fact that these were relevant to the decision is a reason (although perhaps not a conclusive one) for believing that the decision was a PMD. But in order for a decision to be a PMD, it must not violate the technical or ethical standards of engineers. We have yet to determine whether the second part of the PMD criterion has been met.

A second reason suggested by De George's analysis of the Pinto case is that the engineers disagreed about the seriousness of the safety issue. On the one hand, as De George points out, one engineer recommended that the $11 modification be made. On the other hand, another engineer, Francis Olsen, the assistant chief engineer in charge of design at Ford, testified that he bought two Pintos for his eighteen-year-old daughter, indicating his confidence in the car. He bought a 1973 Pinto, kept it a year, and then traded it in for a 1974 Pinto, which he kept two years.

Disagreement among engineers could well be a reason for designating the decision a PMD. Since some engineers evidently thought the Pinto was safe without out the modification, perhaps the decision against making it was not a clear violation of engineering standards, so that condition (2) of the PMD was also fulfilled. Again, this is relevant but by no means conclusive. Too many questions about Mr. Olsen's decision to buy a Pinto for his daughter remain unanswered. Was he the only engineer who did not have doubts about the Pinto? Was his confidence well founded or naive? Would outside experts have shared his confidence in the Pinto? Without answers to these questions, we cannot assess the importance of Mr. Olsen's testimony.

The third reason given by De George as to why engineers "need not have the last word" is that the decision should not have been made by either engineers or managers, but by representatives of the public. He says that "while the degree of risk, e.g., in a car, is an engineering problem, the acceptability of risk is not." A balance must be reached between safety and cost and "the final decision on where to draw the balance is not only an engineering decision. It is also a managerial decision, and probably even more appropriately a social decision."[36] De George speculates that perhaps there should be a "panel of informed people, not necessarily engineers," who should "decide what acceptable minimum standards are."[37]

In the years before the Pinto tragedy, however, no such mechanism of the type De George envisions existed—indeed, it does not exist today. In its absence, why should the decision have been made by managers rather than engineers? Certainly managers did not take it upon themselves to warn consumers of possible dangers. Moreover, the assumption that laws and public policy can solve all such problems is suspect. Laws are usually enacted after catastrophes, not before, and laws can never set standards that apply to every situation. It is difficult to believe that structural changes such as the ones De George proposes, however useful, can entirely take the place of individual engineers who are concerned with public safety.[38]

One principal reason remains why the decision about the $11 part was a PED. Whether or not the failure to modify the Pinto violated technical engineering standards, what transpired did violate engineers' ethical obligations to hold paramount the safety of the public. Engineers should have been allowed to have the final word on the modification, or they should have had the right to insist that the public be informed of the possible dangers.

De George himself believes that information about the degree to which an automobile satisfies safety standards is "information a car buyer is entitled to have." He admits that in 1978, after the publicity about the Pinto, sales fell dramatically, "an indication that consumers preferred a safer car for comparable money. . . ."[39]

De George is probably right at least to this extent: the decision about modifying the Pinto was not a paradigmatic PED. First, important management decisions were at stake. Second, we might dispute whether technical engineering standards were violated. Third, the right to insist that consumers be afforded the right to free and informed consent to what may have been unusual dangers is not the same as the right to insist that a modification be made. So it is not the most typical or paradigmatic engineering decision. Nevertheless, in the following important sense, the decision was a PED: to keep good faith with the public, engineers had the right to insist that either the modification be made or that other steps be taken to protect the public.

9.8   The Challenger Case

The Challenger case is another controversial example of the conflicting prerogatives of engineers and managers. In a teleconference on the evening before the fateful launch, Robert Lund, vice-president for engineering at Morton Thiokol and both an engineer and a manager, recommended against launch, in concert with the other engineers. The recommendation was based on a judgment that the primary and secondary O-rings might not seal properly at the low temperatures at which the vehicle would be launched. NASA officials expressed dismay at the no-launch recommendation, and Thiokol executives requested an interruption in the teleconference in order to reassess their decision. During the thirty-minute interruption, Jerald Mason, senior vice-president for Morton Thiokol, turned to Lund and told him to take off his engineering hat and put on his management hat. Lund reversed his no-launch recommendation.

In his admonishment, Mason was saying that the decision whether or not to launch should be made from the management rather than from the engineering perspective. Testifying before the Rogers Commission, Mason gave two reasons for this belief.

The first reason was similar to one given by De George with respect to the Pinto decision, namely, that the engineers were not unanimous. ". . . Well, at this point it was clear to me we were not going to get a unanimous decision."[40] We might take this as a reason for holding that (2) of the PMD was not violated and that (1) and (2) of the PED were not fulfilled. If engineers disagreed, there was presumably not a clear violation of their technical or ethical standards.

There are reasons to doubt the factual accuracy of Mason's claim, however. In his account of the events surrounding the Challenger disaster, given at MIT in 1987, Roger Boisjoly reported Mason's question whether he was "the only one who wanted to fly."[41] Whatever validity Mason could give to his argument that some engineers supported the launch (and therefore that the opposition of the engineers to the launch was not unanimous) was apparently based on conversations with individual engineers after the teleconference. So Mason probably had little justification at the time of the teleconference itself for believing that the non-management engineers were not unanimous.

Nevertheless, Mason may be correct that there was some difference of opinion among those most qualified to render judgment, even if this information was not confirmed until after the event. If engineers disagreed over the technical issues, the engineering considerations were perhaps not as compelling as they would have been if the engineers had been unanimous. Thus the first part of the PED criterion may not have been fully satisfied. Those who did not find a technical problem probably would not find an ethical problem either. So the second criterion of the PED may also not have been fully satisfied.

Mason's second reason was that no numbers could be assigned to the time required for the O-rings to seal at various temperatures:

> *Dr. Keel*: Since Mr. Lund was your vice president of engineering and since he presented the charts and the recommendations not to launch outside of your experience base—that is, below a temperature of 53 degrees for the O-rings—in the previous 8:45 Eastern Standard Time teleconference, what did you have in mind when you asked him to take off his engineering hat and put on his management hat?
>
> *Mr. Mason*: I had in mind the fact that we had identified that we could not quantify the movement of that, the time for movement of the primary [O-ring]. We didn't have the data to do that, and therefore it was going to take a judgment, rather than a precise engineering calculation, in order to conclude what we needed to conclude.[42]

This might also be a reason for holding that the decision to launch did not violate (2) of the PMD, and that it did not clearly satisfy (1) of the PED.

The fact that no calculations could be made to determine the time it would take the O-rings to seal at various temperatures does not necessarily justify the conclusion that a management judgment should be made. Surely the fact that failure of the O-rings to seal could destroy the Challenger implies that the engineering considerations were of paramount importance, even if they could not be adequately quantified. The engineer's concern for safety is still relevant.

Again, however, Mason's comment may make a valid observation. Since engineers generally prefer to make judgments on the basis of quantitative calculations, they may well have been uncomfortable that there were no precise numbers for the degree of degradation of the O-rings at lower temperatures. As a result, the engineering judgment did not have the same degree of decisiveness that it would have had otherwise. All that Roger Boisjoly could argue was that the degree of degradation seemed to be correlated with temperature, and even the data he used to back up this claim were limited.

Mason's arguments, taken together, might be seen as an attempt to meet criterion (2) of the PMD. If the decision to recommend launch is not a clear violation of engineering practice, an engineer does not violate his technical practices by recommending launch. Thus Mason's argument could be seen as a claim that the decision was at the very least not a paradigm instance of a PED. A paradigm PED would be one where (among other things) the experts clearly agree and where there are quantitative measures that unambiguously point to one option rather than another.

Mason might also have argued that criterion (1) of the PMD was satisfied. A renewed contract with NASA was not assured, and failure to recommend launch might have been the decisive factor that persuaded NASA officials not to renew the contract with Morton Thiokol. Thus the well-being of the company might have been substantially harmed by a no-launch recommendation.

Despite these arguments, we believe that the launch decision was properly an engineering decision, even though it perhaps was not a paradigm case of such a decision.

First, criterion (1) of the PMD was not as compelling a consideration as Mason might have supposed. There was no evidence that a no-launch decision would threaten the survival of Morton Thiokol, or even that it would in any fundamental way jeopardize Thiokol's financial well-being.

Second, criterion (2) of the PMD was not satisfied, because the decision to launch violated engineers' propensity to modify or change course only in small increments. The temperature was more than 20 degrees below any previous launch, an enormous change that should have given an engineer good reason to object to the launch.

Third, criterion (1) of the PED was fulfilled. Even though the quantitative data were limited and certainly did not give conclusive evidence that there would be a disaster, they did seem to point in that direction, so that the desire for quantitative measures was not wholly frustrated. Engineers, furthermore, are alert to the fact that composites, such as the ones the O-rings are made of, are temperature-sensitive and that they could reasonably expect substantially lower temperatures to produce substantially greater blow-by problems.

Fourth, criterion (2) of the PED was met, because human life was at stake, and engineers are trained to be unusually cautious when there are serious issues of health and safety. This should be particularly important when those at risk do not give informed consent to special dangers—the case with the astronauts, who did not have any knowledge of the problem with the O-rings.

The importance of the safety issue was further highlighted because the practice of requiring the burden of proof to be borne by anyone advocating a launch decision rather than a no-launch decision was violated. In testimony before the Rogers Commission, Robert Lund recounts this all-important shift in the locus of the burden of proof:

> *Chairman Rogers*: How do you explain the fact that you seemed to change your mind when you changed your hat?
> *Mr. Lund*: I guess we have got to go back a little further in the conversations than that. We have dealt with Marshall for a long time and have always been in the position of defending our position to make sure that we were ready to fly, and I

guess I didn't realize until after that meeting and after several days that we had absolutely changed our position from what we had been before. But that evening I guess I had never had those kinds of things come from the people at Marshall that we had to prove to them that we weren't ready. . . . And so we got ourselves in the thought process that we were trying to find some way to prove to them it wouldn't work, and we were unable to do that. We couldn't prove absolutely that motor wouldn't work.

Chairman Rogers: In other words, you honestly believed that you had a duty to prove that it would not work?

Mr. Lund: Well, that is kind of the mode we got ourselves into that evening. It seems like we have always been in the opposite mode. I should have detected that, but I did not, but the roles kind of switched. . . .[43]

This last-minute reversal of a long-standing policy, requiring the burden of proof to rest with anyone recommending a no-launch rather than a launch decision, was a serious threat to the integrity of the engineering obligation to protect human life.

9.9   Loyalty: Uncritical and Critical

Unfortunately managers and engineers are not always careful to restrict themselves to their proper roles. While it is certainly possible for engineers to make decisions that should be made by managers, it is much more likely, given the authority structures in business and governmental organizations, that managers such as Jerald Mason will overstep their management role and make decisions that should be made by engineers. In justifying their demand for engineers' compliance, one of the most common claims of managers is that engineers should show "loyalty" to the organization, that they should be "team players." For example, Kermit Vandivier, an employee of the B. F. Goodrich plant in Troy, Ohio, was uncomfortable with what he considered to be unwarranted test practices on a brake that Goodrich was designing for the Air Force. He therefore submitted a letter of resignation, to take effect in a few weeks, but the chief engineer informed Vandivier that his resignation was to be accepted immediately because of Vandivier's "disloyalty" to the company.[44]

The appeal to loyalty to an organization is not always illegitimate. We have seen that the NSPE code requires engineers to be "faithful agents or trustees" of their employers, i.e., to be loyal. But because this appeal is frequently abused, it is important for responsible engineers to be able to think clearly about the concept of loyalty. Specifically, they must be able to distinguish between uncritical loyalty and critical loyalty.

Uncritical loyalty to an employer may be defined as placing the interests of the employer, as the employer defines those interests, above any other consideration. Uncritical loyalty is often espoused by business managers. In a 1973 CBS report on Phillips Petroleum, Inc., one of Phillips's top executives said that a loyal employee will buy only Phillips products and vote for those candidates who are most likely to support policies that are congenial to the interests of the company.[45] Only slightly more qualified claims are made by Herbert Simon in his classic text *Administrative Behavior*. While admitting that all employees have limits to the direction they will accept from their employers, Simon holds that within these very broad limits an employee should accustom himself to "relaxing his own critical faculties" and permitting "his behavior to be guided by the decision of his superior, without independently examining the merits of that decision."[46] A subordinate accepts his superior's authority when he "holds in abeyance his own critical faculties for choosing between alternatives and uses the formal criterion of the receipt of a command or signal as the basis for choices."[47] This means that professionals should accept their superior's suggestions and orders "without any critical review or consideration."[48] At most, they aim their reasoning at anticipating commands by asking themselves how the superior would wish them to behave in given circumstances.[49]

What arguments can be made for this kind of uncritical, unquestioning—or "blind"—loyalty? The "role morality argument" begins with an analysis of the relationship of family members or team members to one another. People sometimes say that we should be loyal to our family or to our team simply because it is our family or our team. It would be strange indeed for a mother to say that she has no more obligation to provide for her children than for her neighbor's children or for children in another part of the world. And it would be shocking for a child to say that he had no more sense of loyalty to his parents than to any other adults. Most of us would say that a mother has a special obligation of loyalty to her children simply because they are *her* children and that children have a loyalty to their parents simply because they are *their* parents. Similarly, a team member has an obligation to her team simply because it is *her* team. The mere fact that one is a team member is reason enough to support it enthusiastically.

Special obligations of loyalty are also usually thought to apply to the relationships of professionals and their clients and teachers and their students: the lawyer to her clients because they are *her* clients, a teacher to his students because they are *his* students, and a physician to her patients because they are *her* patients.

This approach to the concept of loyalty has great appeal, and it does point out that *loyalty is a special obligation based on a role that one occupies*, whether that of an employee, a parent, a child, a lawyer, a teacher, or a physician.

A somewhat more practical argument for uncritical loyalty is given by engineer Samuel Florman. His argument is not specifically given in defense of uncritical loyalty to one's employer, but his reasoning can be seen as a basis for this position. Engineering employees should strive primarily for a high level of technical excellence, rather than concern themselves with ethical issues that might result in conflicts with management.[50] Florman notes the increased emphasis on ethics in engineering, but he is concerned about the "deceptive platitude that a professional's primary obligation is to the public." If this view were widely accepted, the engineer would no longer be guided by his employer's wishes or instructions, or his own creative imagination, as constrained by laws, regulation, and technical parameters. He would be guided primarily by what his conscience tells him is best for the common good. If this appeal to conscience were to be followed literally, Florman believes, there would be several unfortunate consequences.

First, organizational chaos would ensue. Ties of loyalty and discipline would dissolve, and blowing the whistle on one's superiors would become the norm instead of the last resort. This would decrease efficiency and productivity, which is clearly a loss in terms of the public good. The offsetting gains would probably be minimal. A professional should remember that any product can be made safer at greater cost, but absolute freedom from risk is an illusion.

Second, any engineer who refuses to take an assignment from her employer in deference to his own scruples will only pass the assignment along to a colleague of less refined sensibility. So her objections will not protect the public anyway. The faulty product will go on the market regardless of the objection of the supposedly conscientious professional, having been designed by someone else. If an engineer refuses to work on a project or continues to make objections, she may be fired, as Virginia Edgerton was, but the questionable activities will more than likely continue.

Third, the engineer is not an expert in public policy. As a professional group, engineers have neither the ability nor the right to plan social change. They may contribute to debates on public policy as private citizens, but this is very different from subjecting their everyday professional work to the scrutiny of their own conscience. Should we risk oil spills and increase our reserves by offshore drilling? Should we accept the hazards of pesticides in order to feed hungry people? Should we stop building a dam and thereby protect an endangered fish? These are political questions. The public should not abdicate its responsibility to decide these issues of public policy by expecting engineers to make the choices in the name of engineering ethics. It is better for an engineer to be loyal to his or her employer and leave ethical considerations to public policy, according to Florman.

It is important to point out in Florman's defense that the issue, he believes, is not whether toxic substances should be controlled, or the environment protected, but rather who should have the responsibility for making the decisions about such matters. Florman believes the decisions should be made as a result of public debate and implemented by laws and governmental regulations, not by individual professionals acting as a result of their own ethical convictions. If new regulations and clumsy bureaucracies have made life difficult for corporate executives, the solution is not to eliminate the controls but rather to make the control process more efficient.

Opposed to the notion of uncritical loyalty to the employer is the notion of *critical loyalty,* which is giving due regard to the interests of the employer, insofar as this is possible within the constraints of the employee's personal and professional ethics. The concept of critical loyalty is a creative middle way that seeks to honor both of these requirements: engineers should be loyal employees, but only as long as this does not conflict with fundamental personal or professional obligations. Instead of defining the precise scope of such terms as "due regard," "personal ethics," or "professional ethics," we give some examples to illustrate the implications of this concept.

By the standard of critical loyalty, the Phillips executive went too far in claiming that the concept of loyalty justified expecting Phillips employees to buy only Phillips products, and he also went too far when he appealed to loyalty to justify expecting Phillips employees to vote in a way that furthered the interests of the corporation. These expectations infringe on the rights of employees to exercise the prerogatives of citizenship and to shape the direction of their personal lives by making purchases according to their own inclinations. Parents owe loyalty to their children, but this does not mean that a parent should try to shield his child from legitimate criminal prosecution. Such loyalty is a violation of the rights of others to protection from criminal activity. Lawyers should be loyal to their clients, but this loyalty cannot justify humiliating and deliberately confusing truthful witnesses, for this may violate the rights of citizens to dignified treatment in the courtroom. Engineers owe loyalty to their company, but this loyalty cannot justify violation of professional obligations to protect the health and safety of the public. Thus, if Virginia Edgerton was convinced that her employer's plans to expand the use of the computer were a threat to the public, the obligation to the public would take precedence over loyalty to her employer.

What arguments can be given to support the concept of critical loyalty? One is to show the weakness in the arguments for uncritical loyalty. For example, with respect to the role morality argument, one criticism involves the application of the universalization test. Any appeal to loyalty must be universalized. If I appeal to loyalty to justify playing as hard as possible so that my team will win, I must be willing for others to appeal to loyalty to justify their side also playing as hard as possible in order to win. Similarly, if a manager appeals to loyalty to justify asking his employees to work hard for their company, he must be willing for managers in other companies to make the same appeal.

Now in circumstances of normal competition, most rational people would be willing to universalize these kinds of appeals but not to universalize some appeals. What if all coaches appealed to loyalty to justify various sorts of "dirty tricks" against the competition? What if all coaches violated recruiting rules or told players to attempt to break the legs of opponents or slip debilitating drugs in their food? Most people would not want these kinds of actions to be universally practiced, and this requires limitations in the appeal to loyalty. Similarly, most rational people would not want to have all parents protect their children from the law, regardless of what crimes they have committed. Only critical loyalty justifies these limitations in the appeal to loyalty.

There are also serious problems with Florman's argument as a justification of uncritical loyalty. First, Florman's position can involve a serious abridgement of the autonomy and moral integrity of individuals. Suppose I do not have the right to protest obvious wrongs and that my only options are to continue working on a project that I consider immoral or to resign my job. This severely restricts my own freedom as a moral agent, especially when obtaining new employment involves considerable personal sacrifice.

Florman could respond by saying that in return for a guarantee of steady employment, a professional owes loyalty in the form of a surrender of a certain degree of autonomy. In the words of Herbert Simon quoted earlier, the employee "holds in abeyance his own critical faculties." This response is unconvincing, however. While an employee does owe loyalty to his employer, this should not include the complete abrogation of his powers of moral judgment. Florman's argument cannot support the claim that organizational disobedience is always impermissible.

A second argument against Florman is based upon the value to the company of independent employees—and especially independent professional employees. Companies do not usually want to engage in blatantly immoral or illegal actions. If nothing else, such activities often give the firm a bad public image and frequently embroil it in costly and time-consuming legal battles. Upper-level management may know nothing about the problems until they become public. The B. F. Goodrich aircraft brake case to which we have already referred illustrates this.

Third, ethically aware professionals who are willing and able to protest, and in some cases refuse to participate in, morally questionable activities are a great resource for the public. It is not possible for the law to control all abuses in business.[51] Laws are usually enacted only after serious abuses, many of which might have been avoided by ethically responsible employees. Furthermore, the law tends to be clumsy and inept at regulating activities that are potential sources of abuse. There is no substitute for the ethically responsible professional.

Finally, Florman exaggerates the bad effects of occasional organizational disobedience. He forgets that such actions are a relatively rare exception, not the rule. He forgets that a protest of an employer's action or a refusal to participate in a particular engineering project is not the same thing as guiding social policy in general. His suggestion that the employer routinely replaces his employer's directives with the deliverance of his own conscience is misleading.

Neither the role morality argument nor Florman's argument justify uncritical loyalty of engineers to management. Instead, engineers must always keep in mind their professional obligations, while remaining loyal employees, if this is possible. For engineers, critical loyalty implies that managers should never be allowed to make engineering decisions, nor should they be given jurisdiction over one's conscience. Nevertheless, organizational disobedience should always be a last resort. When it is unavoidable, it should be done in such a way as to minimize the negative consequences to both employer and employee. In the following sections we examine some ways in which responsible engineers can avoid the necessity of organizational disobedience and minimize its negative consequences when it is necessary. We also examine some ways in which managers can forestall the necessity of organizational disobedience by their employees.[52]

9.10   The Responsible Engineer and Organizational Disobedience

We have seen that there are at least three distinct areas in which responsible engineers might be involved in organizational disobedience: (1) engaging in activities contrary to the interests of the company, as perceived by management (disobedience by contrary action), (2) refusing to carry out an assignment because of moral or professional objections (disobedience by nonparticipation), and (3) protesting a policy or action of the company (disobedience by protest). What guidelines should the responsible engineer use in deciding when to engage in organizational disobedience in these areas, and how should she carry out this disobedience? Let us consider each of these three areas.

Disobedience by Contrary Action

Engineers may sometimes find that their actions outside the workplace are objectionable to managers, usually in one of two areas. First, managers may find that a particular action or perhaps the general lifestyle of an employee reflects unfavorably on the organization. For example, an engineer might be a member of a political group that is generally held in low esteem by the community. Another might have a sexual orientation that is offensive to some members of the community. Second, managers may find that some activities of employees are contrary to the interests of the organization in a more direct way. For example, an engineer may be a member of a local environmental group that is pressuring his or her company to install antipollution equipment that is not required by law, or lobbying to keep the company from purchasing some wetland area that it intends to drain and use for plant expansion. How should an engineer handle such delicate situations?

There are conceptual issues, application issues, and conflict issues in the questions raised here. The conflict is between the organization's right to protect itself from harm and the employee's right to personal freedom. The application issues have to do with the questions whether particular outside activities or the general lifestyle of employees count as genuine "harms" to the organization and whether curtailment by the organization represent substantial limitations of individual freedom. Conceptual issues are raised by the need to investigate the meanings of "harm" and "substantial curtailment of freedom."

While we cannot investigate these issues fully here, a few observations are essential. Disobedience by contrary action is not a paradigm case of harm to the organization (compare with theft or fraud), and its restriction by the organization is not a paradigm case of restriction of individual freedom (compare with pressure to do something the employee thinks is seriously immoral). Nevertheless, they are examples of these two concepts. There are some arguments to confirm this claim.

On the one hand, there is no doubt that an organization can be harmed by the actions of employees outside the workplace. A company that has a reputation for hiring people whose lifestyles are offensive to the local community may not be able to hire some very desirable people, and it may lose business as well. The harm that an organization may suffer is even more obvious when employees engage in political activities that are directly contrary to the interests of the organization. A manager can argue with some persuasiveness that the simplistic assertion that nothing the employee does after 5 o'clock affects the organization does not do justice to the realities of business and community life. On these grounds, a manager may assert that the organization's right to the loyalty of its employees requires the employee not to harm the organization in these ways.

On the other hand, an employee's freedom suffers substantial curtailment if organizational restrictions force her to curtail activities to which she has a deep personal commitment. Nor should employees simply resign if management finds their activities outside the workplace objectionable. The same activities might harm other organizations in the same way. Thus the consistent application of the argument that employees should never do anything that harms the organization results in the conclusion that employees should never engage in lifestyles or political activities that are controversial.

In surveying these arguments, we believe a good case can be made that organizations should not punish employees for disobedience by contrary action, which is a considerable infringement on individual freedom. Moreover, employees may not be able to avoid this type of harm to organizations simply by changing jobs. Many other communities might find an employee's sexual orientation offensive, and many organizations might be harmed by an engineer's political views or efforts on behalf of the environment. Thus allowing this type of harm to count as justification for organizational control permits organizations to exert considerable influence over an employee's life outside the workplace. In a society that values individual freedom as much as ours does, such a substantial abridgement of individual freedom is difficult to justify.

Despite these considerations, however, many managers act strenuously when they believe they or their organizations are threatened by actions of employees outside the workplace. Therefore two observations are appropriate.

First, some such actions harm the organization in a much more direct fashion than others. An engineer's campaign for tighter restrictions on his or her own company's environmental pollution will probably have a more direct effect on her company than an engineer's private sexual life. Employees should be more careful in areas where the harm to their organization is more direct.

Second, there can be a major difference in the degree to which curtailment of an employee's activities outside the workplace encroaches on her freedom. Curtailment of activities closely associated with one's personal identity and with very strong moral or religious beliefs is more serious than limitation of activities connected with more peripheral beliefs. Therefore employees should allow themselves more freedom in areas closely related to their basic personal commitments than in areas more peripherally related.

Disobedience by Nonparticipation

Engineers are most likely to engage in disobedience by nonparticipation in projects related to the military and in projects that may adversely affect the environment. Engineer James, a pacifist, may discover that an underwater detection system for which his company has received a contract has military applications and thereupon request to be relieved of an assignment to the project. Engineer Betty may request not to be asked to design a condominium to be built in a wetland area.

Disobedience by nonparticipation can be based on professional ethics or personal ethics. Engineers who refuse to design a product that they believe is unsafe can base their objections on their professional codes, which require engineers to give preeminence to considerations of public safety, health, and welfare. Engineers who refuse to design a product that has military applications because of their personal objections to the use of violence must base their refusal on personal morality, because the codes do not prohibit engineers from participating in military projects. The basis of objections to participating in projects that engineers believe are harmful to the environment is more controversial. As we shall see in the next chapter, only two professional engineering codes have anything directly to say about the environment, and their interpretation is unclear.

Several things should be kept in mind about disobedience by nonparticipation. First, it is possible (although perhaps unlikely) for an employee to abuse the appeal to conscience, using it as a means to avoid projects he finds boring or unchallenging, or to avoid association with other employees with whom he has personal difficulties. An employee should try to avoid behavior that promotes this interpretation of his action. Second, it is sometimes difficult for employers to honor a request for removal from a work assignment, for several reasons. There may be no alternative assignments or there may be no other engineer who is qualified to do the work or the change may be disruptive to the organization. These problems are especially severe in small organizations.

Nevertheless, we believe an organization should honor most requests based on problems of conscience when it is possible to do so. We have seen that common morality holds that a violation of one's conscience is a serious moral matter. Employers should not force employees to make a choice between losing their job and violating their conscience. Of course there are situations in which employers do not have any alternative work assignments, but many organizations have found ways to respect their employees' conscience without undue economic sacrifice.[53]

Disobedience by Protest

In some situations engineers find the actions of the employer to be so objectionable that they believe mere nonparticipation in the objectionable activity is insufficient. Rather, some form of public protest (or "whistleblowing") is required. The protest may be either within or outside the organization. Such situations are best viewed as complex conflict situations in which engineers must balance obligations to their employers, their families, their careers, and the public. According to the codes, the obligation to the health, safety, and welfare of the public must take priority over these others, but this does not always make the choice an easy one. There are several reasons for the difficulties that sometimes occur in resolving these conflict situations. Sometimes it is not clear whether in the particular situation the interest is crucial enough to warrant the required extreme personal sacrifice (such as loss of career). The harm to the public may be minor, or whether or not the harm will occur may be questionable. Again, it may not be clear whether the protest will be successful in protecting the public.

Richard De George has provided a set of criteria that must be satisfied before whistleblowing can be morally justified.[54] De George believes that whistleblowing is morally *permissible* (1) if the harm that "will be done by the product to the public is serious and considerable," (2) if the employees report their concern to their superiors, and (3) if, "getting no satisfaction from their immediate superiors, they exhaust the channels available" within the organization. De George believes that whistleblowing is morally *obligatory* (4) if the employee has "documented evidence that would convince a responsible, impartial observer that his view of the situation is correct and the company policy wrong" and (5) if the employee has "strong evidence that making the information public will in fact prevent the threatened serious harm."

De George presents his five considerations as criteria for permissible and obligatory whistleblowing for unsafe products. How he intends his criteria to apply to other contexts is not clear. Insofar as these criteria are taken as general tests for justified or required whistleblowing, however, they are subject to criticisms.[55] Let us consider each in turn.

Criterion (1) appears too strong. De George seems to assume that the employee must know that harm will result and that the harm must be great. Perhaps just believing on the basis of the best evidence available is sufficient. Sometimes an employee is not in a position to gather evidence that is totally convincing. (2) It should not always be necessary for employees to report their criticisms to their superiors. Often one's immediate superiors are the cause of the problem and cannot be trusted to give an unbiased evaluation of the situation. (3) Nor is it always necessary to exhaust the organizational chain of command. Sometimes there is not time to do this before a disaster occurs. And sometimes employees have no effective way to make their protest known to higher management except by going public. (4) It is not always possible to get documented evidence of a problem. Often organizations deprive employees of access to vital information necessary to make a conclusive argument for their position—for example, access to computers and other sources of information. (5) Finally, it may not always be necessary to have strong evidence that a protest will be successful in preventing the harm in order to have an obligation to make the protest. Just giving those exposed to a harm the chance to give free and informed consent is often a sufficient justification.

The criteria offered by De George seem to have many exceptions, and it is probably not possible to construct a set of exceptionless criteria for justified or required employee protest. Rather than offering checklists of necessary conditions that must be met, it may be more useful to propose a procedure to follow in protesting an employer's action. Given the assumption that confrontation with an employer should usually be approached incrementally and that open protest should be a last resort, here are some considerations for responsible dissent by engineers.[56]

First, responsible engineers should exert every effort to assure themselves that their protest is justified, if possible, with the best available documented evidence. They should attempt to consult others who might have relevant information and to check their own judgment against the judgment of others.

Second, if their organization has an ombudsman, an "ethics hotline," or some other in-house mechanism for raising ethical issues, responsible engineers should take advantage of these organizational resources. Failing this, professional societies or outside consultants might be able to offer some assistance, either in the form of advice, expert technical evaluation, financial support, or public support if protest external to the organization seems inevitable.

Third, responsible engineers should try to get other professional colleagues to stand with them, showing them the documentation they have collected and asking for their support in approaching higher management. Again, this approach should not be done in a confrontational manner but with the attitude of exhibiting professional responsibility and promoting the long-term interests of the organization.

Fourth, responsible engineers should make their objections known to their immediate supervisors if this is appropriate. Discussion should be as nonconfrontational as possible. Focus should be on the problem, not on personalities. The problem can be posed by saying "I have a problem" or "We have a problem," not "You have a problem."

Fifth, responsible engineers should make positive and concrete suggestions as to how to resolve the problem they see. Rather than simply pointing out what should not be done, they should show what should be done. When no criminal activity is involved and especially when the problem seems to have arisen inadvertently, responsible engineers can often propose solutions that allow individuals or the entire organization to find a face-saving way out of the situation. Providing an easy way out of the difficulty is often the key to preventing escalation of the problem.

Sixth, responsible engineers should attempt to find other sympathetic managers if their supervisor is unsympathetic. It is almost always better, however, to avoid the appearance of making an "end run" around one's own supervisor. This can sometimes be done by strongly suggesting to other managers that any conversations with one's own manager be confidential and informal.

Seventh, if all else fails, responsible engineers may have to make the objectionable activity known to the public. This usually involves the press or governmental agencies in some form. Often the protest is most effective if they have already resigned from the organization, to minimize the tendency of others to interpret actions as motivated by self-interest.

Few if any studies have been done that show the effects of whistleblowing on organizations. Studies of whistleblowers have shown, however, that even though most say that they are proud of what they did and would do it again, they admit that both they and their families have often suffered considerable hardships.[57] In the next section we consider some actions that organizations can take to avoid the need for whistleblowing.

9.11   Implementing Professional Employee Rights

One of the most popular definitions of a right is that it is a "valid claim *to* something and *against* someone which is recognized by the principles of an enlightened conscience."[58] An "enlightened conscience" can be one described by the concept of critical loyalty. Employees should then have the right to engage in justified and responsible forms of the three types of organizational disobedience without fear of dismissal or reprisals. Reprisals may include denial of raises and promotions, harassment, and assignment to unimportant, uninteresting, or demeaning tasks.

Managers should take positive steps to implement employee rights because employers and employees—even professional employees—are unevenly matched. An individual employee is no match for a powerful corporation or governmental bureaucracy, and in many cases even for a small business. It is usually more difficult, and certainly more emotionally traumatic, for an employee to find a new job than for an employer to find a new employee. Employers and employees do not face one another as equals. The attitude of powerful corporations and bureaucracies toward their employees is sometimes like that of the proverbial elephant who exclaimed "Each for himself, and God for us all," as he danced among the chickens.

The policies implementing employee rights should have several features. (1) They should focus on issues rather than personalities. This helps to avoid excessive emotionalism and personality clashes, a prominent feature of many instances of organizational disobedience. (2) Written records should be kept on complaints. This is important if court proceedings are eventually involved. It also serves to keep the record straight as to what was said and when it was said. (3) Generally, the complaints should be kept as confidential as possible for the protection of both the firm or governmental agency and the complainant. (4) There should be provisions for neutral participants from outside the firm or governmental agency when the dispute requires it. Sometimes employees within the organization are too emotionally involved in the dispute or have too many personal ties to make a dispassionate evaluation of the issues. (5) Explicit provision for protection from retaliation should be made, with mechanisms for complaint if an employee believes he has experienced this. Next to the fear of immediate dismissal, probably the greatest fear of an employee contemplating organizational disobedience is that he or she will suffer discrimination in promotion and job assignment, even long after the controversy is resolved. Protection from this fear is one of the most important employee rights, although one of the most difficult to provide. (6) Finally, the procedure for handling organizational disobedience should proceed as quickly as possible. Delaying resolution of such issues can be a method of punishing dissent. Sufficient delay often allows management to perform the actions against which the protest was made. Prolonging the suspense and cloud of suspicion that accompanies an investigative process also punishes a protesting employee, even if his actions were completely justifiable.

During the past fifteen years many proposals for improving corporate and governmental responsiveness to the demand for employee rights have been made; many have been instituted, with varying degrees of success. Corporate codes of conduct, corporate policy statements, "social audits," corporate (or shareholder) democracy, and the introduction of public and employee advocates on boards of directors are only some of these proposals. We focus on four that seem especially important for professional employees.[59]

First, one of the simplest and most effective policies, especially suited to small firms and small governmental agencies, is the "open door" policy. Managers make themselves available for hearing complaints on a regular basis and without prejudice to the complainants. This method is particularly appropriate where a single manager has the power to correct the problem. If the manager against whose action or policy the complaint is made has an open door policy, the issue can often be resolved in a way that produces least harm to the manager and the employee.

Second, in large organizations a formal procedure to handle complaints is essential. A procedure developed by the Nuclear Regulatory Commission (NRC) might be used by other organizations. The NRC has a procedure for handling what it calls differing professional opinions (DPOs). The process begins when an employee submits a concise written statement to her supervisor, summarizing both her own and the opposing views. If no accommodation is reached at this level, the DPO can be submitted to a competent, impartial peer review group for evaluation. If the originator is not satisfied with the disposition of the DPO by the review group, she may appeal the decision to any higher level within the NRC, including a commissioner or the commission as a whole. If the issue raised involves the public health or safety, the appeal can also be sent to the Advisory Committee on Reactor Safeguards (ACRSs) for their comments.

Safeguards have been instituted in an attempt to eliminate subversions and abuses of the process. A special review panel consisting of two managers, two nonmanagers, and one person from outside the NRC monitors the operation of the system and recommends improvements. Written records are made of the entire proceedings and furnished to the originator of the DPO as soon as they are generated. There are also time limits attached to the proceedings so that managers cannot bury the DPOs by long delays. A potential problem with the procedure is that "national security" may be invoked to keep the complaint procedure secret, and managers might use this loophole to protect themselves.[60]

Third, professional employee rights can receive protection through a corporate (or governmental) ombudsman. Registering employee complaints can often be done in a confidential and anonymous way. The ombudsman or advocate must operate independently of the corporate hierarchy and should have direct access to top management and (in corporations) to the board of directors. An ombudsman might not have sufficient expertise or power within a governmental or corporate bureaucracy to directly mediate a dispute between a professional and a manager, but he can facilitate a mediation. An employee should be able to have confidence that any complaint she submits will be treated fairly and honestly. Obviously the ombudsman could be utilized by nonprofessionals, but his or her services would be available to professionals as well.

Fourth, some organizations have established an office, often at the vice-presidential level, whose primary concern is ethics and social responsibility. Such offices have as one of their duties the proper disposition of employee complaints. Any employee must have access to this office, which operates confidentially and in complete freedom from middle and lower-level management. Some corporate ethics offices also provide an "ethics hotline," which is accessible to employees and others, such as vendors, who may want to inquire about corporate ethics policies or get advice on how to handle troublesome situations. For example, at Lockheed International, formerly General Dynamics, the ethics hotline receives approximately 5,000 anonymous calls each year. Many of the calls involve relatively minor problems—personal disagreements between employees or employees and managers. Resolving these problems has resulted in a substantial increase in employee retention. Some of the calls, however, have resulted in rectification of serious problems and even in criminal prosecutions.

A small business, such as a small engineering, legal, or architectural firm, could not make use of some of the more elaborate mechanisms proposed here. But perhaps modified versions of the NRC's DPO procedure are not beyond their means. In any event, the protection of professional employee rights is an issue of increasing importance in the workplace.

9.12   Chapter Summary

Engineering codes require engineers to be faithful agents of their employers, but they also require them to hold paramount the safety, health, and welfare of the public. These two obligations can, on occasion, conflict, producing difficult moral and professional problems for engineers. The common law doctrine of "employment at will" has traditionally given little protection to dissenting employees, but recent court decisions and whistleblower protection laws have changed the situation to some extent.

Employee dissent can take at least three forms. Employees can engage in activities outside the workplace that employers believe are contrary to the interests of their organization. Employees can refuse to carry out directives of their employers to which they have serious objections. Finally, employees can protest actions of their employers to which they object.

The engineer-manager relationship is at the center of most of the issues engineers face as employed professionals. A study by Robert Jackall finds the engineer-manager relationship fundamentally adversarial; a study funded by the Hitachi Foundation comes to substantially different conclusions. It is useful to characterize the decisions that should be made by managers and those that should be made by engineers. Application of this distinction to the Pinto and Challenger cases shows that in both cases the decisions were ones in which engineers rather than managers should have had the decisive voice.

In justifying their claim to obedience from employees, managers usually appeal to the concept of loyalty. An analysis of this concept shows that it is necessary to distinguish between "critical loyalty" and "uncritical loyalty" and that what employees owe managers is critical loyalty. Critical loyalty, however, cannot justify unquestioning obedience. It is useful to develop some guidelines for the application of critical loyalty to the three types of organizational disobedience.

When engineers believe they must take actions contrary to the wishes of their employers, they should do so in a measured and responsible way, whether the dissenting actions are in the form of disobedience by contrary action, disobedience by nonparticipation, or disobedience by protest. In the last category, which is often called "whistleblowing," it is difficult to construct strict criteria for the justification of employee protest of an employer's actions. The criteria suggested by Richard De George, for example, appear to have many exceptions. It is possible, however, to suggest some guidelines for responsible employee dissent.

Employers have used several methods to improve communication with employees and provide avenues within the organization through which employees can register their concerns. These methods include an open door policy, a mechanism for registering differing professional opinions, an ombudsman system, and an office devoted to ethical issues, which may contain an "ethics hotline."

Case Analyses

Case 9.1 To Dissent or Not to Dissent?—Again

[This is the same as Case 3.1, our sample case at the end of Chapter 3. We analyze this case again, this time employing concepts on moral thinking developed in Chapters 4–6 and concepts introduced in this chapter.]

Alison Turner is a department manager at a large commercial nuclear generating plant. She is also a member of the Plant Nuclear Safety Review Committee (PNSRC). The committee's responsibilities include reviewing and approving design changes, procedural changes, and submittals to the Nuclear Regulatory Commission (NRC).

Today Alison finds herself in a difficult situation. PNSRC is meeting to decide what to do about a heat exchanger problem. Routine testing on the previous morning revealed degraded cooling water flow and high differential pressure in one of the containment spray heat exchangers of one of the two generating units. This unit has just returned to service after two months of repairs. Test results on the second heat exchanger were similar. Although the other generating unit has been in continuous service, testing reveals that its two heat exchangers are operating at less than full capacity. The most likely cause of the problem is sand blockage on the lake water side of the four heat exchangers.

After extensive analysis by engineers in the mechanical engineering and nuclear safety and licensing departments, it has been concluded that the cooling water flow falls slightly below the minimum requirement set by the technical specifications under which the plant is licensed. Nevertheless, based on mechanical engineering's analysis, nuclear safety and licensing has prepared a justification for continued operation (JCO) for submission to [the] NRC. The PNSRC is now meeting to decide whether to approve the JCO and forward it to NRC.

As Alison reviews the JCO, she is uncomfortable with one assumption made in the analysis. The analysis assumes that the heat exchangers still have 95 percent of their original heat transfer capacity. It is concluded that this is satisfactory. However, in anticipating possible accidents, Single Failure Criteria require the plant to assume the loss of one heat exchanger. The JCO does not discuss what might happen in that contingency.

Seven members of PNSRC are present, enough for a quorum. Alison is the least senior member present. From the outset of the meeting, committee chair Rich Robinson

has made it clear that it is important to act quickly, since any shutdown will cost the company, and ultimately the rate payers, a lot of money in additional fuel costs. "Repairs," he says, "might take a couple of weeks. If we don't approve this, we may be facing a multi-million dollar proposition. Fortunately, the JCO seems fine. What do you think?" Brad Louks and Joe Carpello immediately concur. Rich then says, "Well, if no one sees any problems here, let's go with it." There is a moment of silence. . . .

Alison Turner expresses her reservations. Brad Louks replies, "We're talking about containment heat exchangers. It's an accident mitigation system, and it's never had to be used here—or at any other commercial nuclear plant that we know of, for that matter. In fact, lots of plants don't even have containment spray systems." "Right," adds Joe Carpello, "we're ahead of the game on this one. I don't see any problem here. Nothing's totally risk free, but we've always been leaders in safety. Let's not get carried away with 'possibilities.'"

"I don't think Alison meant to have us get carried away with anything," Mark Reynolds interjects. "She's just wondering if the JCO should address the question of how things would look if we lost one of the heat exchangers. How much time would it take the nuclear safety and licensing department to make a calculation for us—another three hours? It's only 1:30 P.M., you know." "What's the point, Mark," asks Joe. "Our track record is excellent, and the system is optional. It's not as though we're taking any extraordinary risks."

Nothing further is said, and Rich Robinson calls for a vote. Though not a committee requirement, PNSRC has always acted unanimously. It often rejects, sometimes approves, but always unanimously. As the call goes around the room, each member approves. The last member called on to vote is Alison. She has serious reservations about approving the JCO without the nuclear safety and licensing department making further calculations. How should she vote?

Analysis

This case, like the Virginia Edgerton case, focuses on disagreement in professional judgment. We have chosen to discuss this case rather than the Virginia Edgerton case because it is perhaps more ambiguous from the moral standpoint. There are two primary questions: (1) How should Alison vote? and (2) Did the atmosphere in the committee promote responsible professional judgment?

A number of factual issues are important to Alison's decision. (1) The most obvious such issue is whether a single heat exchanger would be able to handle the heat transfer load in an emergency. The refusal of the committee to ask the nuclear safety and licensing department to examine this issue means that Alison will not have an authoritative answer to the question before she votes. (2) Another question that she should ask herself is, "Has the PNSRC been conscientious in carrying out its oversight responsibilities?" On the one hand, the fact that the plant has a good safety record and that the committee "often rejects" documents suggests that it has been. On the other hand, the insistence on unanimity suggests that the expression of professional disagreement may have been inhibited. (3) Another question is whether the plant is either already or potentially in violation of the law or NRC regulations. We are told that "the cooling water flow falls slightly below the minimum requirement set by the technical specifications under which the plant is licensed." This appears to mean that the plant is already violating the law or NRC regulations. Further, the Single Failure Criteria *require* that one assume the loss of

one heat exchanger. If these criteria are set by law or the NRC, then the committee's willingness to ignore them means that it intends to further violate legal requirements. If these are in-house criteria, the committee is still derelict in its duty. (4) Another question is how the NRC will look on the plant's actions. Will they notice the committee's not fulfilling regulations? Evidently the NRC has looked favorably on the plant until now, but this attitude may be about to change. (5) How great is the risk of an accident due to the failure of proper heat exchange? Joe Carpello says that the committee should not get carried away with "possibilities," but the committee is supposed to look at failure modes, which are "mere possibilities." (6) Why are the heat exchangers not functioning properly? Is the problem really sand blockage? If so, why is this a problem on a unit that has just undergone two months of repairs? (7) Will the heat exchange problem continue to deteriorate? If so, how fast will this deterioration progress, and what are the consequences? (8) Will the shutdown for repairs on the heat exchanger be costly enough to endanger the financial well-being of the company?

There are several important conceptual issues in this case.

1. There is a division of opinion on the committee over what we might call "responsible professional judgment." Rich Robinson, Joe Carpello, and Brad Louks think Alison's worries are trivial and irresponsible. Mark Reynolds is not so sure. What is meant by the term "responsible professional judgment"? We can give several criteria for responsible professional judgment in engineering. (a) It must be made in the light of professional knowledge and skill. (b) It must be made in the light of all information relevant to the particular case. (c) It should be made in accordance with appropriate professional "technical" standards, which include such

considerations as the use of state-of-the-art technology and quality. (d) It should be made in accordance with the appropriate professional ethical criteria, which include in particular a responsibility for the health and safety of the public.

2. A closely related issue is raised by the manner in which Rich Robinson, chair of the committee, conducted the meeting. What is the proper "professional climate" for the formation and expression of responsible professional opinions? A useful analogy is the working of the United States Supreme Court.[61] The justices of the Court rarely all agree on an opinion, but the atmosphere in their discussions is presumably one in which disagreement is respected. The justice who writes the majority opinion must circulate his or her draft opinion to all members of the Court, who respond with suggestions for changes and arguments for differing opinions. As they argue the issues in the case, some justices may change their minds, and the challenge to each justice to defend his or her position is a valuable part of the formation of responsible legal judgments. Using the Supreme Court example, we can say that the principal criteria for a "professional climate" are (a) that differing professional opinions should be encouraged and respected, and (b) that differing opinions should be subjected to as much criticism and evaluation by professional peers as possible.

3. Most of the committee members appear to be making the decision from a management standpoint at least as much as from an engineering one. Robinson, for example, is concerned about the time and expense if a shutdown is required. So a third question is whether the decision to approve the JCO is properly a management or an engineering decision. This necessitates a prior decision: What do we mean by a proper management

and a proper engineering decision? Here we can refer to the criteria for a PED and a PMD.

Now we can turn to the application issues raised by these three conceptual issues.

The first issue concerns responsible professional judgment. Let us consider the criteria enumerated earlier. (1) Responsible professional judgment must be made on the basis of professional expertise. We have no reason to doubt the professional expertise of the committee members. (2) Responsible professional judgment about a particular case must be made in the light of all of the facts relevant to the case. Here we have problems. Most of the members of the committee were willing to approve the JCO without the information about how the plant would function if one of the heat exchangers were lost. So we must say that the actions of the committee (with the exception of Alison) did not meet this criterion. (3) Responsible professional judgment should be made in accordance with appropriate professional technical standards. In this case, some of the technical standards are provided by NRC regulations, which the committee was willing to violate in at least two respects. It was willing to overlook the fact that the plant was already not meeting the minimum cooling water flow standards. It was willing to overlook the requirement to furnish data on the ability of the plant to operate properly with only one heat exchanger. (4) Responsible professional judgment should be made in accordance with the appropriate professional ethical standards.

The most important ethical standard here is the responsibility of the engineer to be concerned with the health and safety of the public. There was a difference of opinion. On the one hand, Brad Louks pointed out that the heat exchangers were a part of an accident mitigation system and they had never been used on this or any other commercial plant. Joe Carpello also insisted that nothing can be completely safe. On the other hand, Mark Reynolds and Alison pointed out that one of the possible failure modes, a failure of one of the heat exchangers, had not been thoroughly investigated. If a refusal to investigate a known but somewhat unlikely failure mode is a failure to look out for the health and safety of the public, this criterion for responsible professional judgment has not been met.

The full answer to this question involves the investigation of another conceptual issue ("What do we mean by looking out for the health and safety of the public?") and relevance issue ("Does the failure to investigate a possible but unlikely failure mode violate this criterion?"). But we shall assume that the criterion is not fulfilled by the committee's failure to investigate the heat exchange issue. The committee did not exhibit responsible professional judgment with respect to the approval of the JCO.

The second application issue is whether a "professional climate" has been preserved in the committee. (1) One criterion for a "professional climate" is that differing professional opinions must be encouraged and respected. The atmosphere set in the committee did not fulfill this criterion. There was an atmosphere of intimidation and a pressure for unanimity that were not conducive to the expression of differing professional opinions. (2) The second criterion is that professional opinions should be subjected to as much criticism and evaluation as possible. This criterion also was not fulfilled. While criticism of Alison's opinion was encouraged (as it should have been), criticism of opposing views was strongly discouraged by the chairman of the committee, as well as several of its members. A professional climate was not preserved in the committee. (One wonders whether part of the explanation for this failure to preserve a professional climate relates to Alison's being was the first female engineer to serve on the PNSRC.)

The third application issue is whether the decision to approve the JCO is a PED or a PMD. Our previous discussion has shown that there are good grounds for classifying the decision on the JCO as properly an engineering decision. The decision involved both technical engineering considerations and an application of standards from the codes, especially those requiring engineers to protect the health and safety of the public. The arguments of Louks, Carpello, and Robinson, however, can be grounds for maintaining that the decision was also properly a management decision. They argued that approval of the JCO did not violate criterion (2) of the PMD, because the heat exchangers were not required, and the possibility of a catastrophe due to their malfunction was remote. They also argued that the decision involved substantial management considerations, thereby fulfilling criterion (1) of the PMD. That the approval of the JCO would involve a violation of regulations governing plant operation gives the edge to the argument that the decision was primarily an engineering one. Perhaps even more decisive is the observation that the *committee's* responsibility was apparently to make an engineering decision. Therefore, the committee should have made its decision on the basis of engineering considerations.

Finally, we must turn to the conflict issue. The conflict Alison faced was between her obligation to be a responsible employee and to make a responsible engineering decision. In this case, however, there does not appear to be a genuine conflict, because her true responsibility as an employee was to make a responsible engineering decision. Presumably she was placed on the committee because her professional judgment was valued. The committee was supposed to render a competent and responsible engineering judgment. Whether or not she was ultimately right, her responsibility was to render the best professional judgment of which she was capable. She attempted to do this. Our analysis of the conceptual and relevance issues leads us to conclude that (1) she should vote against approval of the JCO and (2) the atmosphere in the committee did not promote responsible professional judgment.

Case 9.2 Defective Sensors?

Charlie Long is an electrical engineer working for a major automobile company in the year 2001. He works in the automatic sensors department, and his job is to design and test electronic sensors for use in different parts of cars.

The latest version of the Lightning-Z100 was recently launched into the national market, equipped with an electronic sensor crucial to an innovative safety feature of the vehicle. This sensor was designed and tested by Charlie's department. The Lightning-Z100's major competitor equipped its comparable model (the Bolt-Z100) with a somewhat similar sensor two years before, and it apparently was effective in reducing the number of fatalities in head-on collisions.

Convinced that they could quickly come up with a design for an electronic sensor to match the Bolt-Z100's, Charlie's department committed to preparing one in time for the 2001 Lightning-Z100 model. Unfortunately, the design challenge proved to be more formidable than they expected, and they fell behind schedule. At the same time, they were under pressure to have something ready for the 2001 model. This, they were told by management and marketing strategists, could be the key to competing successfully with the Bolt-Z100.

So, time was short, and Charlie's department could delay its recommendation no longer. Although the prototype was not subjected to as rigorous testing as usual, Charlie's department recommended a go-ahead. Charlie was uncomfortable with this decision. He objected that more testing was needed on sensors that served an important safety function. But he was overruled, and he pressed the issue no further.

Several months after the Lightning-Z100 was on the road, a disturbing set of data emerged. A very high percentage of head-on collisions resulted in the death of passengers in the Lightning-Z100, much higher than similar collisions involving the Bolt-Z100.

As Charlie thought about this, he realized that the problem could lie in the new electronic sensor. The National Highway Traffic Safety Administration (NHTSA) decided to do a detailed study of the Lightning-Z100. Although it could not determine the precise nature of the problem, NHTSA found that, for some reason, the new electronic sensor was not functioning according to the design. All the new Lightning-Z100s would have to be recalled as soon as possible in order to avoid any more deaths from malfunctioning sensors.

Charlie reexamined the design. Suddenly he realized that there was a very specific design flaw. He was not sure why this realization had come to him—it would not be obvious, even to experienced electrical engineers. But there it was, staring him in the face. Further testing might have revealed this earlier, but there had not been time for that.

Meanwhile, many expensive lawsuits were being pressed against Charlie's company. Called in to testify in court, Charlie had a tough problem. Should he reveal everything (his belief that the testing was inadequate and his recent discovery) and cost the company a great deal of money? Or should he testify that he had been convinced that the testing was adequate? Should he keep it to himself that he now knew that there was something wrong with the design?

Analyses

The following two analyses were prepared by students in Michael Pritchard's undergraduate Ethics in Engineering class at Western Michigan University. These are examples of very good student analyses.

Analysis 1: Darrell Telgenhof

Charlie has a conflict problem. As an employee of the automobile company, he has an obligation to do what is best for the company. It would clearly be in the company's best interest if Charlie were to say that he thought the testing was adequate and that he did not know of any complications in the design. Charlie must remember, though, that the accident victims have a right to be compensated for injuries or the loss of loved ones.

There may be a conflict of interest playing a part in this situation, also. Charlie probably wants to do the right thing, but his vision may be clouded by the fact that his job and his company's reputation are on the line. Charlie is going to have to make a hard choice in this situation. If he tells the truth, his company may have to pay some substantial damages, and he is likely to lose his job. On the other hand, if he doesn't tell what he knows about the situation, the victims may not get their deserved compensation. Some of them may desperately need this for expenses incurred by their injuries.

Even though Charlie objected, his department gave the go-ahead and the company used the sensors in the production of the Lightning-Z100. This violates the right of the customers to know what risks they are taking on. Drivers know that there is a potential for them to get killed or injured while driving. They bought the car, expecting to lower that risk. Since the company knew that there was a possibility that the sensors were inade-quate, it was substantially increasing drivers' risks without their consent. The fact that the sensors were used as a selling point for the automobile shows that the customers expected the Lightning-Z100 to be safer than other cars. The company made the wrong choice, and now they should take responsibility for the damages.

By applying the Golden Rule test it is obvious that Charlie should tell the truth. He should give the victims the respect that he would want if he were in their position. Looking at the situation from a victim's viewpoint, he could see that he would not have wanted to be deceived about the safety of the car. He would be very upset if he didn't get compensation for the damages from an accident because an engineer concealed vital information.

If Charlie chose to support the company's defense, his action would be self-defeating, if universalized. Professional engineers get respect in part because people rely on them to tell the truth. If engineers often misrepresent the truth, they will soon not be trusted. Charlie's testimony would not mean anything to the court if he wasn't expected to be honest.

The utilitarian viewpoint is also satisfied if Charlie tells the truth. If the automotive company has to pay damages for their mistake, then they will be much more careful to make sure that the parts are satisfactorily tested before putting them in future models of cars. This may save many future accident victims from injuries or loss of life. In the long run, this may also be beneficial to the automotive company. If they make attempts to produce cars with higher safety standards, they will regain their credibility and develop a reputation for safe cars.

Charlie has a duty as an engineer to be honest about his claims. This raises the conceptual issue of what is meant by being "honest." Of course it is not practical, and seldom prudent, to be completely honest, but common morality dictates that it is not right to blatantly lie. Applying this term to the situation that Charlie is in, we can say that it would not be "honest" of him to argue in defense of the company. He would be telling a falsehood in order to benefit himself and his company, while hurting the victims.

If Charlie were not completely honest he would be in clear violation of the NSPE Code of Ethics. Section II.3.a states that "Engineers shall be objective and truthful in professional reports, statements or testimony. They shall include all relevant and pertinent information in such reports, statements or testimony." As a professional engineer, Charlie has a duty to act impartially. If he distorts the facts about the testing, he is not being truthful in his testimony. Also, if he does not reveal the problems that he has found in the design, he will be withholding relevant and pertinent information.

Even though it appears to be in Charlie's best interest to conceal the truth, it may turn out for the worst for him. If he says that he thought the testing was adequate, and during the trial it comes out that he tried to oppose the recommendation, he may get charged with perjury. This situation could also produce another unfavorable possibility. Charlie's dishonesty could cost him a loss of the respect of others, a quality that is important as a professional engineer.

This is a difficult position to be in. There are many things for Charlie to be concerned about. Telling the truth may not be the most beneficial thing for him, but as a professional he should attempt to act with the most ethical conduct.

Analysis 2: Michael Turnauer

Charlie Long is confronted with the decision of whether he should testify about the inadequate testing. The only relevant facts are that the sensor was not tested as rigorously as usual and that fatality rates for head-on collisions are considerably higher than those of a competitor.

There is no question that the sensor had not been tested "as rigorously" as usual. Does this constitute inadequate testing? Could it be that the additional testing that would have been done ordinarily is merely overkill, or is that testing necessary to make absolutely certain the sensor will work properly? How many successful trials are necessary and sufficient to approve the design? Should more than one prototype be tested?

To evaluate these questions it may also be helpful to know how acceptable testing is established. Did the company have its own standard procedures for testing? The text states that the testing is usually more rigorous, which may imply a company-imposed standard. More importantly, did the testing satisfy government mandated standards? If not, then this is a negative paradigm case of inadequate testing. If the testing standards were met it must then be determined whether those standards are valid, given the state of technology of the industry.

It is clear that the automatic sensors department had put itself in a pressure situation to deliver the sensor production in time for the new model. A major competitor had already introduced a similar system which was proving to be very successful. Management and marketing told the department that a comparable system would be the key in competing successfully. The sensors department committed itself to developing one and is now under duress to approve a final design. The issue brought to light here is how the decision was made to approve the sensor. Charlie's objections were overruled on what grounds? Was he overruled by management or by his peers? Furthermore, if the decision was made by the engineers, were they making an engineering decision or a management decision? This could be considered a PED only if the initial test data were so conclusive that no further testing was warranted.

This issue may be more easily resolved by backtracking to the inadequate testing discussion. If a positive paradigmatic conclusion was rendered, then approval of the sensor satisfied at least one of the two criteria for a PED: quantitative measures were unambiguous. There is still one more condition to be satisfied. The experts must clearly agree. It must then be determined whether Charlie, the lone dissenter, can be considered an "expert." A paradigmatic PED would be one where Charlie could not be considered an expert. Perhaps his experience is far less than his co-workers. If he is in fact a senior engineer in his department, then the decision was at the very least a nonparadigmatic case of a PED.

A conceptual issue which must be addressed in light of the resulting lawsuits is what constitutes safety. The principle of acceptable risk may be helpful in defining safety in the context of this problem. The amount of risk may be defined as the product of the probability and magnitude of harm. This would be a difficult judgment to make were it not for the competitor's product, the Bolt-Z100. The Bolt has prevented a much higher percentage of deaths in comparable head-on collisions. This would imply that the risk associated with the Lightning system is unacceptably high. This does not even account for the fact that the risk was unknown to those who assumed it: the consumer. This further magnifies the degree of risk. There is surely a relevant safety issue here.

A cost/benefit approach might also be examined. It is easy to see in hindsight that the cost of delaying approval of the sensor would likely have been far less than the cost of defending lawsuits, possible damage awards, and implicit publicity costs.

The safety issue may also be resolved with the respect for persons test. The self-defeating test goes back to whether the sensors were properly tested. If testing procedures were acceptable, then the self-defeating test does not apply. The golden rule test may apply, however. It is doubtful that any of the test engineers would accept the risk ultimately taken by passengers of the Lightning. The rights test may also give precedence to additional testing over expedition of bringing the system to production. The higher tier rights of the public must be given priority over the less basic right of the company to make or increase profit.

Charlie is also faced with conflicting professional (and possibly moral) obligations and his loyalty to his employer (and possibly its effect on his career). Section II.1.a [of the NSPE code] states that engineers must at all times recognize the primary obligation to protect the safety, health, and welfare of the public. This conflicts with section II.1.c with respect to testifying. The section prohibits disclosure of facts or information without prior consent [of the company].

Charlie may feel morally and professionally obliged to the public to fully reveal the information. On the other hand, he may not see fit to allow his company to be unjustly punished for its part in the resulting injuries or deaths. Excessive punishment of the company does not serve the general public. His testimony may ultimately be dictated by his legal obligations, according to whether those take priority over his professional obligations.

Case 9.3 The Price Is Right?[62]

XYZ orders 5,000 custom-made parts from ABC for one of its products.[63] When the order is originally made, ABC indicates it will charge $75/part. The contract states that ABC will use the "highest quality materials in manufacture."

After the agreement is completed, but before production of the part begins, ABC engineer Christine Carsten decides to do a little reading in the literature to find out whether there is any other material that can be used to manufacture the product. To her surprise and delight, she finds that a new and much less expensive metal alloy (M-2) can be used instead of M-1, which is customarily used to manufacture the part. The use of M-2 will cut ABC's costs by $18/part. Christine fills out a Value Engineering Change Proposal (VECP) for the proposed material substitution. The VECP comes to the attention of ABC's Vernon Waller, the manager who authorized the sales agreement with XYZ. In discussing the substitution of M-2 for M-1, Vernon asks, "How would anyone know the difference?" Christine replies, "Probably no one would unless they were looking for a difference and did a fair amount of testing." He also asks whether there will be any difference in the quality of the final product for XYZ. "As far as we can tell," Christine replies, "there is no difference: the product will be no better, but no worse. Of course, the new material does not have the track record in actual use that the old material does, so we cannot be completely sure about long-term reliability."

"Great, Christine." Vernon replies "You've just made a bundle for ABC." Puzzled, Christine asks, "But shouldn't you tell XYZ about the change?" "Why?" Vernon asks, "The basic idea is to satisfy the customer with good quality parts, and you've just said we will. So what's the problem?"

The problem, Christine thinks to herself, is that the customer might not be getting a material with the same long-term reliability, although she admits that she does not know this is the case. Further, even if XYZ would be satisfied with the different part, shouldn't it be given the opportunity to decide if it

finds the change acceptable—and to benefit from lowered cost?

Christine shares her further thoughts with Vernon. He replies, "I just don't agree, Christine. This is a management decision, not an engineering decision. You tend to your job and I'll tend to mine. XYZ will be a satisfied customer, and we'll be a satisfied supplier. We're not in the business of giving away money, you know. Besides, it cost us some time and money to find the new material."

The less expensive part is produced. As the shipment is prepared to be sent to XYZ, Christine is asked to sign a report verifying that the specifications for the part have been met. She is not sure whether Vernon's action involves any explicit violation of the contract. She wonders whether she would be violating her professional integrity by signing the document. What do you think?

In answering this question, it may be useful to use the method of casuistry, constructing a version of this case where Vernon's decision does not violate engineering integrity and clearly could be made by management and another case where the decision does violate engineering integrity and clearly should not be approved by engineers. Note as many similarities and differences between these two cases and the original case as you can. You may find the PMD and PED helpful when constructing the hypothetical cases.

Case 9.4 Failure[64]

R&M Machinery had for years provided EXES with sophisticated equipment and reliable repair service. EXES returned a failed piece of equipment. A meeting was held, which included Archie Hunter, a representative from EXES; Norm Nash, R&M's returned goods area representative, and Walt Winters, an R&M engineer intimately acquainted with the kind of equipment EXES had returned.

Norm Nash represented R&M's "official position": the piece of equipment is all right. However, during the the meeting it becomes apparent to Walt Winters that the problem has to be R&M's. He suspects that the equipment was not properly tested by R&M and that it failed because of an internal problem.

Walt keeps silent during the meeting. After the meeting he talks with Norm about his diagnosis. He suggests they tell EXES that the problem is R&M's fault, and that R&M will replace the defective equipment. Norm replies, "I don't think it's wise to acknowledge that it's our fault. There's no need to hang out our wash and lessen EXES's confidence in the quality of our work. A 'good will' gesture to replace the equipment should suffice."

R&M management decides to tell EXES that they will adjust to the customer's needs "because you have been such a good customer all these years." Although R&M replaces the equipment at its own expense, it does not tell EXES the real nature of the problem. Should R&M's solution be of any concern to Walt Winters at this point, or is it basically a "management problem"?[65]

What do you think Walt should do? Taking into account leading ideas in this chapter, analyze the situation from the standpoint of the relevant facts, conceptual issues, application issues, and conflict issues.

Case 9.5 A Wonderful Development[66]

Philip Harding is an engineer at a small family business called Wonder Products, Inc. (WPI). The majority of WPI's work involves designing and producing parts for larger products that are sold by other companies.

WPI is under contract to design and produce a complex component for General Farming Implements' (GFI) farm harvesting equipment.

Despite a nagging, though small, problem that does not find a "perfect" solution, WPI designs the part to GFI's satisfaction. The price is set at $100 for each component. GFI orders 1,000 components, with the understanding that since things have gone so well, they will be talking to WPI and Philip about other contracts.

WPI begins production and ships the first portion of the order to GFI on time. GFI, at this point, is very happy with the component and wants WPI to ship the final three-quarters of the order as soon as feasible. As Philip is working on the component, he thinks of an apparent solution to the "nagging problem" that bothered him through design. It would be a small change in the production process while incurring one dollar more per part. The improvement in the part would be significant, but it would not be considered revolutionary in its design.

Since he is in a rush to complete the order, Philip does not have much time to work on anything other than the order. He wonders if he should investigate this new idea immediately, or wait until he has the time to test it. He decides he should check out his new idea.

Philip confirms the fact that the new design solves the problem. But he has gotten slightly behind in the order. Philip brings the development to the attention of other members of WPI. He says that although they can fulfill the contract and be safe from legal reproach if they say nothing to GFI, they have an ethical obligation to offer the new design to GFI immediately, whether or not WPI ends up picking up some of the costs for making changes. He contends that the flaw in the initial design was an oversight on WPI's part. "We contracted with GFI with the understanding that we would provide them with the best design we could come up with," Philip says. "So we ought to tell them about the improvement."

The financial leader of the company, Connie, expresses her concern about the one-dollar addition to production cost. She says that they are working on a narrow profit margin now; and, although this represents only a 1 percent increase in cost, it adds up to $750 plus costs associated with recalling and altering the components already sent to GFI. She thinks that WPI would be better off introducing the development if and when GFI makes another order.

Tim, in charge of sales and public relations, suggests a compromise between the two. He suggests that they offer to share in the cost of the new product. Concerned with the image WPI projects, Tim worries about GFI later complaining about WPI not coming to them with the development during the first order. Although they could insist that the design change was not conceived of until after the first order was complete, there would always remain the doubt, indeed a correct doubt, that WPI held out on GFI by not offering them the best product. In the long term this could mean mistrust and, in the worst scenario, a reducing or even severing of business ties between the two. "Granted," Tim acknowledges, "the withholding of this information would mean an increase in our short-term income. But it could mean a disaster to our future with GFI—and a setback in our standing in the business community! Besides, we are behind as it is."

What should WPI do?

1. Tell GFI that WPI is behind because it has come up with an improvement on the old design and offer to share expenses for the improvement.

2. Tell GFI that WPI is behind because it has come up with an improvement on the old design and offer to make the improvement immediately if GFI is willing to take care of the additional expenses.

3. Not tell GFI about the improved design until after the order is completed.

4. Other.

Discuss the relevant facts; factual, conceptual, and application issues; and methods that might be used to resolve the question. Is the decision a PMD or PED? If it is a PMD, should Philip simply volunteer what he has discovered and leave it to others to decide what to do about it? Or should he participate more fully in the deliberative process?

The amount of money at stake in this case may seem quite small. Suppose a much larger amount were at stake (say, $600 per unit). Would this alter the way in which you think through the options in this case? Explain.

Other Cases

7.4: Forced Rankings

7.5: Three Mile Island

NOTES

1. This case is summarized from a series of reports in *IEEE Technology and Society Newsletter*, No. 22, June 1978, pp. 1–10. Used with permission.

2. These comments are available on video-tapes of speeches given by Boisjoly at the University of New Mexico in Albuquerque and at Massachusetts Institute of Technology. Similar accounts are available in the transcripts of the Rogers Commission hearings.

3. Common law is the tradition of case law or "judge-made law" that originated in England and is also fundamental in American law. Roughly speaking, it is based on a tradition in which a judicial decision establishes a precedent, which is then used by succeeding jurists as the basis for their decision on similar cases. Common law is to be distinguished from statutory law, or laws made by legislative bodies.

4. 456 Pa. 171, 319 A.2d 147 (1974).

5. 319 A.2d at 178 (footnotes omitted).

6. 84 N.J. 58, 417 A.2d 505, 512 (1980). Cited in Stephen F. Unger, *Controlling Technology*, p. 99.

7. 421 N.E.2d at 884.

8. 115 LRRM 4803 (NJ Super Ct 1982)

9. 721 F.2d 894 (1983)

10. *Novosel* v. *Nationwide Insurance Co.* 721 F.2nd. 894 (3d. Cir 1983), p. 903.

11. *Novosel*, 903.

12. Martin H. Malin, "Protecting the Whistleblower from Retaliatory Discharge," *Journal of Law Reform*, 16 (Winter 1983), 277–318.

13. Ibid.

14. *Wall Street Journal*, April 13, 1981.

15. Jim Otten, "Organizational Disobedience," in Robert Baum and Albert Flores, eds., *Ethical Problems in Engineering* (Troy, N.Y.: Center for the Study of the Human Dimensions of Science and Technology, 1980), Vol. 1, pp. 182–186.

16. Joseph A. Raelin, *The Clash of Cultures: Managers and Professionals* (Boston: Harvard Business School Press, 1985), p. xiv.

17. Raelin, *The Clash of Cultures*, p. 12.

18. Raelin, *The Clash of Cultures*, p. 270.

19. Robert Jackall, *Moral Mazes: The World of Corporate Managers* (New York: Oxford University Press, 1988), p. 5. Jackall focuses only occasionally

on the relationship between managers and professionals. But his occasional references to the relationship of managers to engineers and other professionals make it clear that he believes his general description of the manager/employee relationship also applies to the relationship of managers to professionals, including engineers.

20. Jackall, *Moral Mazes*, pp. 105–107.

21. Jackall, *Moral Mazes*, p. 69.

22. Jackall, *Moral Mazes*, p. 112.

23. See the unpublished manuscript, "Technical Communications Between Engineers and Managers: Preventing Engineering Disasters." This is a report prepared under a grant from the Hitachi Foundation. The panel conducting the study was chaired by Vivian Weil. The other members of the panel were Michael Davis, Thomas Calero, David Krueger, Robert Growney, Lawrence Lavengood, and Elliot Lehman. Draft version, October 24, 1990, pp. 18–19. Citations are used with permission.

24. Hitachi Report, pp. 22–24.

25. Hitachi Report, pp. 64–65.

26. Hitachi Report, p. 65.

27. Raelin also points out the importance of professional loyalties that transcend the organization, contrasting the "local" orientation of managers with the "cosmopolitan" orientation of most professionals. While describing engineers as more locally oriented than most professionals, he does not deny that engineers have loyalties to professional norms that transcend loyalties to their own organiztion. See Raelin, *The Clash of Cultures*, pp. 15–18 for a description of the local/cosmopolitan distinciton.

28. State-of-the-art technology may not always be appropriate. If an engineer is designing a plow for use in third-world countries, simplicity, ease of repair, and availability of repair parts may be more important than the use of the most advanced technology.

29. We are indebted to Michael Davis for this insight, as well as for several others in this section. Davis uses John Rawls's term "lexical ordering" to describe the assigning of priorities. Rawls, however, seems to equate serial ordering with lexical ordering. He defines a lexical order as "an order which requires us to satisfy the first principle in the ordering before we can move on to the second, the second before we consider the third, and so on. A principle does not come into play until those previous to it are either fully met or do not apply. A serial ordering avoids, then, having

to balance principles at all; those earlier in the ordering have an absolute weight, so to speak, with respect to later ones, and hold without exception." John Rawls, *A Theory of Justice* (Cambridge, Mass.: Harvard University Press, 1971), p. 43. See also Michael Davis, "Explaining Wrongdoing," *Journal of Social Philosophy*, 20 (Spring/Fall, 1988), pp. 74–90.

30. I am again appealing to the method of casuistry as a way of resolving the line-drawing problems involving engineering and management decisions. For purposes of this analysis, I am assuming that all decisions are either PEDs or PMDs, i.e., that they should be made by either managers or engineers, rather than by anyone else.

31. Richard T. De George, "Ethical Responsibilities of Engineers in Large Organizations: The Pinto Case," in *Business and Professional Ethics Journal*, 1, no. 1 (1981), pp. 1–14. Reprinted in Deborah G. Johnson, *Ethical Issues in Engineering* (Englewood Cliffs, N.J.: j312 Prentice Hall, 1991), pp. 175–186. Citation from Johnson, p. 178. All future citations of this article are taken from Johnson.

32. De George, "Ethical Responsibilities of Engineers," p. 179.

33. In defense of De George, he does believe that there are some situations in which engineers, like other employees, should blow the whistle on employers. In the essay under discussion he provides his well-known (and very restrictive) criteria for justifiable whistleblowing. But this position is still different from the one suggested by the distinction between PEDs and PMDs, where engineers have the right to insist *as professionals* that their professional judgment and integrity not be violated. We believe that engineers should defend this right vigorously, as the engineers in the Hitachi Report appeared to do. Also, if the professional integrity of engineers were universally respected, the necessity for whistleblowing would probably be greatly reduced, though not eliminated.

34. Johnson, *Ethical Issues in Engineering*, p. 178.

35. Johnson, *Ethical Issues in Engineering*, p. 181.

36. Johnson, *Ethical Issues in Engineering*, p. 180. We have run together what De George considers two separate arguments, one the claim that degree of risk is not the same as acceptability of risk and another the claim that engineering cost/benefit analysis does not consider such factors as how to balance safety and cost. But since balancing safety and cost is one of the primary things that must be done in determining acceptable risk, the arguments are closely related.

37. Johnson, *Ethical Issues in Engineering*, p. 181.

38. Almost twenty years ago Christopher Stone pointed out the limitations in the law's ability to take the place of socially responsible individuals and corporations. Many of his arguments, some of which We have summarized here, seem to apply to De George's claims about the efficacy of structural and public-policy remedies. See Christopher D. Stone's *Where the Law Ends: The Social Control of Business Behavior* (Prospect Heights, Ill.: Waveland Press, 1991), pp. 93-110. This is a reissue of a HarperCollins book, published in 1975.

39. Johnson, *Ethical Issues in Engineering*, p. 181.

40. *Report of the Presidential Commission on the Space Shuttle Challenger Accident*, February 26, 1986 to May 2, 1986, Vol. IV, p. 764.

41. Roger Boisjoly, "The Challenger Disaster: Moral Responsibility and the Working Engineer" in Johnson, p. 9.

42. Johnson, *Ethical Issues in Engineering*, pp. 772–773.

43. Johnson, *Ethical Issues in Engineering*, p. 811.

44. Kermit Vandivier, "Why Should My Conscience Bother Me?" in Robert Heilbroner, ed., *In the Name of Profit* (Garden City, N.Y.: Doubleday, 1972), p. 29. Cited in Marcia Baron, "The Moral Status of Loyalty," in Deborah G. Johnson, *Ethical Issues in Engineering*, p. 226.

45. "The Corporation," CBS Reports, December 6, 1973. Cited in Marcia Baron, "The Moral Status of Loyalty," p. 225.

46. Herbert A. Simon, *Administrative Behavior* (3rd ed.) (New York: Free Press, 1976), pp. 151 and 11. The citations are taken from Mike W. Martin, "Professional Autonomy and Employers' Authority," in Albert Flores, ed., *Ethical Problems in Engineering* (Troy, N.Y.: Center for the Study of the Human Dimensions of Science and Technology, 1980), pp. 177–181.

47. Simon, *Administrative Behavior*, pp. 126–127.

48. Simon, *Administrative Behavior*, p. 22.

49. Simon, *Administrative Behavior*, p. 129.

50. Samuel Florman, "Moral Blueprints," *Harper's* (October 1978), pp. 30-33.

51. See Christopher D. Stone, *Where the Law Ends: The Social Control of Business Behavior.*

52. For further discussion of this issue, see Marcia Baron, *The Moral Status of Loyalty* (Dubuque, Iowa: Kendall/Hunt, 1984).

53. In Chapter 10 we shall consider at greater length the issue of problems of conscience for engineers.

54. Richard T. De George, *Business Ethics* (New York: Macmillan, 1982), p. 161. This account is taken directly from Richard T. De George, "Ethical Responsibilities of Engineers in Large Organizations."

55. Several of these criticisms are suggested by Gene G. James, "In Defense of Whistleblowing," copyrighted in 1990 by Gene G. James. Reprinted in Deborah G. Johnson, ed., *Ethical Issues in Engineering.*

56. Many of these suggestions are taken from several helpful essays on whistleblowing. In addition to the essays by De George and James already mentioned, see the following: Michael Davis, "Avoiding the Tragedy of Whistleblowing" *Business and Professional Ethics Journal, 8*, no. 4, 3–19 and Ronald Duska, "Whistle-Blowing and Employee Loyalty," copyrighted in 1983 and reprinted in Deborah Johnson, *Ethical Issues in Engineering.*

57. See Myron Glazer, "Ten Whistleblowers and How They Fared," *Hastings Center Report, 13,* no. 6 (1983), 33–41.

58. See Joel Feinberg's discussion in "Duties, Rights and Claims," *American Philosophical Quarterly, 3* (1966), 337-344. Also, Joel Feinberg, "The Nature and Value of Rights," *Journal of Value Inquiry, 4* (1970), 243-255.

59. See Michael Davis, "Avoiding the Tragedy of Whistleblowing," *Business and Professional Ethics Journal, 8*, no. 4 (Spring 1990), pp. 3–19.

60. See Unger, *Controlling Technology*, pp. 125–126.

61. See the commentary on this case by Wade L. Robison in Pritchard, *Teaching Engineering Ethics*, pp. 105–108.

62. This fictional case is drawn from NSF Grant No. DIR-8820837, presented, with commentaries, in Michael S. Pritchard, ed., *Teaching Engineering Ethics: A Case Study Approach*, pp. 310–324.

63. This case is a slightly modified version of the one in Pritchard, *Teaching Engineering Ethics*, pp. 310–311.

64. Pritchard, *Teaching Engineering Ethics*, p. 48.

65. Pritchard, *Teaching Engineering Ethics*, p. 148.

66. Pritchard, *Teaching Engineering Ethics*, case and commentaries on pp. 476–484.

Chapter 10

Engineers and the Environment

The U.S. Army has used the Aberdeen Proving Ground to develop, test, store, and dispose of chemical weapons since World War II. Periodic inspections between 1983 and 1986 revealed serious problems with a part of the facility known as the Pilot Plant. These problems included

> . . . flammable and cancer-causing substances left in the open; chemicals that become lethal if mixed were kept in the same room; drums of toxic substances were leaking. There were chemicals everywhere—misplaced, unlabeled or poorly contained. When part of the roof collapsed, smashing several chemical drums stored below, no one cleaned up or moved the spilled substance and broken containers for weeks.[1]

When an external sulfuric acid tank leaked 200 gallons of acid into a nearby river, state and federal investigators were summoned to investigate. They discovered that the chemical retaining dikes were in a state of disrepair and that the system designed to contain and treat hazardous chemicals was corroded, resulting in chemicals leaking into the ground.[2]

On June 28, 1988, after two years of investigation, three chemical engineers, Carl Gepp, William Dee, and Robert Lentz, now known as the "Aberdeen Three," were criminally indicted for illegally handling, storing, and disposing of hazardous wastes in violation of the Resource Conservation and Recovery Act (RCRA). The three engineers did not actually handle the chemicals, but they were the managers with the ultimate responsibility for the violations. Investigators for the Department of Justice concluded that no one above them was sufficiently aware of the problems at the Pilot Plant to be assigned responsibility for the violations.

The three engineers were competent professionals who played important roles in the development of chemical weapons for the United States. William Dee, the developer of the binary chemical weapon, headed the chemical weapons development team. Robert Lentz was in charge of developing the processes that would be used to manufacture the weapons. Carl Gepp, manager of the Pilot Plant, reported to Dee and Lentz.

Six months after the indictment, the Department of Justice took the three defendants to court. Each was charged with four counts of illegally storing and disposing of waste. William Dee was found guilty of one count, and Lentz and Gepp were found guilty on three counts each of violating RCRA. Each faced up to fifteen years in prison and $750,000 in fines, but they received sentences of 1,000 hours of community service and three years probation instead. The judge justified the relatively light sentence on the grounds of the high standing of the defendants in the community and the fact that they had already incurred enormous court costs. Since the three engineers were criminally indicted, the U.S. Army could not assist them in their legal defense. This was the first criminal conviction of federal employees under RCRA.

10.1   Introduction

Dee, Lentz, and Gepp were responsible for serious environmental pollution. Their case marks one of the few times that engineers have been criminally indicted and convicted for actions done in their professional capacity. Their actions illustrate in a dramatic way the importance of environmental issues for the engineering profession.

If environmental issues are important for the engineering profession, engineering is even more important for environmental issues. On the one hand, projects designed by engineers produce toxic chemicals, which pollute the land, air, and rivers. Engineers also design projects that flood farmlands, drain wetlands, and destroy forests. On the other hand, engineers design projects and processes that reduce or eliminate these same threats to environmental integrity. Engineers have contributed to our environmental problems (as have most of the rest of us), but they are also an essential part of their solution.

What obligations should the engineering profession (as opposed to engineers as private citizens) assume regarding the environment? We begin to answer this question by looking at some of the controversy within the engineering profession over what engineering codes should say about the environment. Then we examine the changing attitudes of business managers toward the environment, because it is important in the relationship of engineers to the environment. Next we consider the criterion for deciding when the environment is sufficiently "clean" with respect to contaminants that threaten human health. Then we discuss the animal liberation and environmental movements, as they raise the larger question of engineering obligations to the environment, where human health is not an issue. Finally, we present a proposal. We believe this would allow engineers more freedom to exercise their obligation to protect human health, while not violating the consciences of engineers who do not believe they have professional obligations to the environment, where human health is not at stake.

10.2   Engineering Codes and the Environment

Few engineering codes make any direct reference to the environment. We begin by considering two exceptions.

Controversy over the Environment

The 1977 revision of the American Society of Civil Engineers (ASCE) code included for the first time the following statement:

> 1.f. Engineers should be committed to improving the environment to enhance the quality of life.

As engineer P. Aarne Vesilind has pointed out, the use of the word "should" means that this part of the code cannot be enforced.[3] All enforceable sections of the code use the word "shall" instead.

In 1983 a new eighth canon for the ASCE code was proposed, which read:

> 8. Engineers shall perform service in such a manner as to husband the world's resources and the natural and cultured environment for the benefit of present and future generations.

This canon is phrased in terms of a requirement ("engineers shall") rather than a recommendation ("engineers should"). Several guidelines for interpreting the canon were also proposed, such as the following one:

> 8.g. Engineers, while giving proper attention to the economic well being of mankind and the need to provide for responsible human activity, shall be concerned with the preservation of high quality, unique and rare natural systems and natural areas and shall oppose or correct proposed actions which they consider, or which are considered by a reasonable consensus of recognized knowledgeable opinion, to be detrimental to those systems or areas.

This guideline emphasizes that concern for the environment must be balanced against economic considerations. Unlike canon 8 and the 1977 statement, it also conveys at least the suggestion that "natural systems" are to be valued for their own sake, rather than for their contribution to human welfare.

This proposed canon, with its accompanying guidelines, was never made a part of the ASCE code. In its January 1984 meeting, the Professional Activities Committee of the ASCE voted unanimously not to recommend approval of the canon. According to the minutes of the meeting, committee members cited the

1980 policy statement of the ASCE as sufficiently covering environmental matters. That policy statement "recommends" that civil engineers recognize the effect that their efforts have on the environment and inform clients of the environmental consequences of the design selected. It also recommends that members "utilize mechanisms within the Society which lend support to individual efforts to implement environmental considerations," and "recognize the urgent need to take the lead in development, modification and support of efficient government programs, to insure adequate environmental protection, but avoid the inhibition of the economy which can result from overregulation."

From the standpoint of environmental protection, this policy statement is inadequate in two respects. First, it merely "recommends" that civil engineers abide by the guidelines, so that they have no binding force. Second, some of the recommendations are hopelessly vague. What does it mean to "utilize mechanisms within the Society which lend support to individual efforts to implement environmental considerations"? Whatever it means, the statement refers to voluntary, not mandatory, activity on behalf of the environment.

The 1990 revision of the ethical code of the Institute of Electrical and Electronics Engineers (IEEE) also makes reference to the environment. The first canon of the code commits IEEE members

> . . . to accept responsibility in making engineering decisions consistent with the safety, health, and welfare of the public, and to disclose promptly factors that might endanger the public or the environment.

IEEE members are required only to "disclose" possible dangers to the public and the environment. Should such dangers be disclosed only to one's immediate superior? What if one's superior is part of the problem? Should an engineer disclose threats to the environment to those outside his or her organization if there appears to be no internal remedy? Does an engineer have any right as a professional to refuse to participate in projects to which she has strong objections from an environmental standpoint? The code does not address these questions.

No other major engineering code mentions the environment. A recent proposal to introduce a canon pertaining to the environment into the ASME (American Society of Mechanical Engineers) code, which presently contains no reference to the environment was considered. In 1991 a resolution to include a statement on the environment was discussed in the ASME Board on Professional Practices and Ethics, but the resolution has not been acted upon by the entire organization.[4]

What Do the Codes Really Say About the Environment?

As things now stand, only two of the major engineering codes explicitly refer to the environment. What kind of commitment do these two codes make? Do the other codes make any commitment at all, even implicitly? In order to answer this question, we need two distinctions.

The first distinction is between two different types of concern for the environment. Engineers can be concerned for the environment when environmental pollution poses a direct and clear threat to human health. We can call this a *health-related concern*. Engineers can also be concerned for the environment even when human health is not directly affected. We can call this a *non-health-related concern*.

When engineers are concerned for environmental protection because polluting the air or water introduces carcinogens, this is an example of a health-related concern. Engineering projects often have an impact on the environment, however, even when human health is not directly affected. An engineer may be asked to design a dam that will destroy a wild river or flood thousands of acres of farmland. Or she may be asked to design a sawmill that will be located in the middle of an old-growth forest, or to design a condominium that will be built on wetlands. If an engineer objects to these projects for reasons having to do with the environment, the objection must be based on a non-health-related concern.[5]

A second distinction is between the intrinsic and instrumental value of nature. Some people believe that trees, rivers, animals, mountains, and other natural objects have *intrinsic value*, i.e., value in themselves, apart from human use or appreciation. We could say they believe that natural objects (or at least some natural objects) are morally considerable. Some people believe that natural objects have only instrumental value, i.e., value insofar as they are used or appreciated by human beings. Another way to make the same point is to say that natural objects are not morally considerable.

If we do not believe that forests or lakes or mountains—or animals—have value in themselves, we can still justify their having instrumental value, even if they are not directly related to human health. Destruction of forests can affect the supply of wood and the availability of recreational opportunities. Destruction of plant and animal species can damage the ecosystem and limit recreational opportunities. Flooding farmlands can reduce the supply of food for present and future generations. Draining wetlands can damage the ecosystem in ways that ultimately affect human beings.

Now we are in a position to examine the codes with respect to environmental commitments.

First, most engineering codes already implicitly commit engineers to health-related environmental concerns, whether or not they use the word "environment." Most codes commit engineers to hold paramount the safety, health, and welfare of the public. Insofar as protecting the environment is necessary to protect human health and safety, the commitment is already present.

Second, at most only two codes commit engineers to non-health-related environmental concerns. This interpretation seems to be confirmed by the wording of the two codes that explicitly mention the environment. When the ASCE and IEEE codes specifically refer to the environment, we can infer that the intention is to include non-health-related environmental protection. For example, the ASCE code mandates concern for the environment "to enhance the quality of human life." This may refer to non-health-related issues, as they relate to human welfare; for example, it could refer to the way recreational opportunities enhance the quality of human life.

The IEEE code seems even clearer. It requires IEEE members to disclose factors that could endanger "the public or the environment." If concern for "the public" refers to health-related issues, concern for the environment must refer to non-health-related issues.

One could perhaps argue that, just as there is a commitment to health-related environmental concerns in the obligation to promote human health, so there is a commitment to non-health-related environmental concerns in the obligation to promote human welfare. After all, ample recreational opportunities, a stable ecosystem, an adequate supply of renewable natural resources, wild rivers, and sufficient farmland are important aspects of human welfare. But this may be too wide an interpretation of the term "welfare" as it appears in the codes. For example, if ASCE members had intended all along to interpret "welfare" in this way, they would probably not have objected to adopting guideline 8g.

Third, the obligations imposed on engineers with respect to both health-related and non-health-related environmental issues do not impose strong obligations on engineers, and they are stated in very general terms. As we have pointed out, the ASCE code used the term "should," and the ASCE policy statement only "recommends." No directions are given as to how to promote health. How do we decide, for example, when the environment is sufficiently "clean" with respect to a certain pollutant? When is a possible threat to health at an acceptable level? The codes do not provide any direction. With regard to non-health-related concerns, the ASCE code only commits engineers to environmental "improvement," and the IEEE code says only that its members should "disclose promptly" factors that pose dangers to the public or the environment. Perhaps we should not expect the codes to give any more detailed instructions, but engineers will at least need to think about the general parameters of their professional obligations to the environment.

Fourth, there is not much evidence that the codes attribute intrinsic value to nature. The ASCE code relates environmental improvement to improvement in the quality of human life. The proposed eighth canon to that code does appear to attribute intrinsic value to "high quality, unique and rare natural systems," but it was rejected. The statement in the IEEE code, with its reference to engineering decisions that might endanger the public or the environment, appears to be the closest that the codes come to attributing intrinsic value to nature.

Why are engineering societies so reticent to make forceful statements regarding the environment? One answer is that environmental issues are still controversial among engineers, just as they are for many other people in our society. As an example, we consider the changing attitudes of business managers toward the environment.

10.3   Changing Attitudes Toward the Environment

Even though most engineering codes do not yet make specific references to the environment, public attitudes toward environmental issues have shown considerable change over the past few decades.

The Beginnings of the Environmental Movement

Prior to the 1960s, most people probably had little concern for the environment. Economic and technological progress took a clear priority over environmental considerations. It is not surprising, therefore, that both business managers and engineers assigned a relatively low priority (or even no priority) to preserving and protecting the environment. They were reflecting the attitude of most citizens when they assumed that pollution of the air, land, and water had to be traded for an increase in the standard of living.

When the environmental movement began in the 1960s, things began to change. Technology came under heavy criticism for its detrimental effects on the air, soil, and water. Rachel Carson's *Silent Spring*, published in 1962, was one of the important books written in the early years of the environmental movement.[6] Carson focused mainly on the effects of pesticides, DDT being one of her principal concerns. The following partial list of chapter titles gives some idea of the content and tone of her book: "Elixirs of Death," "Needless Havoc," "And No Birds Sing," "Rivers of Death," "Indiscriminately from the Skies," "The Human Price," "Nature Fights Back," and "The Rumblings of an Avalanche." Carson, trained as a marine biologist and employed for many years by the Fish and Wildlife Service, painted a dismal picture of what the future would be like if we failed to control the deleterious effects of chemical pollution.

During the 1960s and 1970s the influence of the environmental movement continued to grow. Some of the predictions made by critics of technology were extreme. For example, a group from the Massachusetts Institute of Technology predicted that somewhere near the year 2005 there would be a catastrophic decline in world food supply and industrial output.[7] It is unlikely that this prediction will prove to be accurate. Nevertheless, most people probably agree that the environmental movement has made a significant, even essential, contribution to our own and future generations.

Management Attitudes Toward Environmental Issues

The attitudes of business managers toward environmental issues may also be changing. For evidence of attitudes during what may prove to have been a transitional period, consider the following survey. From 1982 until 1985 Joseph M. Petulla, Director of the Graduate Program in Environmental Management at the University of San Francisco, surveyed a number of industries with respect to hazardous waste disposal. He found that he could classify the companies he investigated into three categories. The first type of company, consisting of 29 percent of the firms surveyed, engaged in what Petulla called "crisis-oriented environmental management." Industries in this group generally had no full-time personnel assigned to environmental concerns, devoted as few financial resources as possible to environmental matters, and fought environmental regulations. As one representative of this group put it, "Why the hell should we cooperate with government or anyone else who takes us away from our primary goal (of making money)?"[8] He went on to say that it is cheaper to pay the fines and lobby than to devote resources to environmental matters.

David Roderick, chairman of U.S. Steel, made a similar argument in a 1982 interview when he said, " . . . the primary role and duty of management really is to make money."[9] Economist Milton Friedman supported this view in a famous article in *The New York Times Magazine* when he said that it is the responsibility of business managers to "make as much money as possible while conforming to the basic rules of the society, both those embodied in law and those embodied in ethical custom."[10] He specifically mentions "avoiding pollution" as one of the items for which stockholder money should not be spent. Although Friedman would apparently not advocate breaking the law, he might be sympathetic with legal resistance to environmental regulations that decrease profit.

There are several arguments that business managers of this persuasion might use to defend their position. One argument is that businesses will fail—especially in international competition—if excessive environmental regulations are enforced. Another argument is that some degree of conflict between manufacturers and environmental advocates will make regulations more responsible. Another argument is that the greater efficiency businesses have without environmental regulations will outweigh any other negative consequences—such as environmental degradation.

A second group, consisting of 58 percent of the firms surveyed by Petulla, adopted what he called "cost-oriented environmental management." Firms in this group accepted government regulation as a cost of doing business, but they often did so without enthusiasm or commitment. There was usually a great deal of skepticism about the value of environmental regulation. Nevertheless, the firms usually had established company policies regulating environmental matters and separate units devoted to them.

We can think of many reasons for the attitudes of managers in this second group, and one reason might be that environmental regulations are inconsistent and do not represent a rational balancing of costs and benefits. Consider some of the apparent anomalies in the law and its enforcement. Environmental standards are sometimes set without any consideration of cost. Trace carcinogens are controlled, while much greater risks go relatively unattended. We tend to focus strongly on equipment and physical processes, while giving relatively short shrift to considerations of human error and venality. We set stringent emission standards, but then pay insufficient attention to unsafe operation of the same plants.

Critics see the apparent inconsistencies in the law as nothing more than a reflection of the irrational elements in the attitude of the general public toward environmental issues. Two months after the Exxon *Valdez* oil spill, a survey indicated that 80 percent of the respondents were willing to pursue greater environmental protection regardless of cost. To take another example, a study by David Okrent concludes that in this country the risk of dam failures is much higher than the risk from nuclear reactors, but it would be hard to convince the general public of this.[11]

A third group, consisting of 9 percent of Petulla's sample, adopted what he called "enlightened environmental management." In these companies, responsiveness to environmental concerns had the complete support of the CEO. The companies had well-staffed environmental divisions, used state-of-the-art equipment, and generally had good relationships with government regulators. One manager said that people in his company saw themselves as good neighbors in the community. "Anyhow," he concluded, "in the long run it's in our own interest, to keep us from lawsuits and generate some good will."[12]

The manager suggested two arguments to support his views. The first is that business should be a good citizen of the community. One argument for this position is that business has an implied contract with the larger society, according to which it must be a responsible citizen of the community in return for enjoying the advantages of a profitable business enterprise. A second argument suggested by the manager is the self-interested one that a positive attitude of cooperation with the law will be good for business in the long run, by generating goodwill and avoiding lawsuits.

Recent Developments

There is some evidence that management attitudes, at least in some industries, have changed since the mid-1980s. Petulla himself found that managers' concern for environmental issues seemed to be increasing, even during the three-year period of his survey. One example of more recent developments is an initiative by the Chemical Manufacturers Association (CMA), the trade association of the chemical industry in the United States.

For a number of years, the chemical industry had received a considerable amount of public criticism. It was further shaken by the disaster at a Union Carbide plant in Bhopal, India, in 1984. In the early hours of the morning on December 3, a poisonous cloud of methyl isocynate escaped from a pesticide plant. The toxic chemical eventually killed more than 3,000 and injured more than 200,000 local residents.[13] In 1988, the CMA established a program called "Responsible Care: A Public Commitment." The major objective of Responsible Care was to respond to public criticisms of the chemical industry in a serious and constructive manner. On April 11, 1990, more than 170 member firms of CMA published the following set of Guiding Principles of the "Responsible Care" initiative in *The New York Times* and the *Wall Street Journal*:

> To recognize and respond to community concerns about chemicals and our operations
>
> To develop and produce chemicals that can be manufactured, transported, used and disposed of safely
>
> To make health, safety and environmental considerations a priority in our planning for all existing and new products and processes
>
> To report promptly to officials, employees, customers and the public, information on chemical-related health and environmental hazards and to recommend protective measures

To counsel customers on the safe use, transportation and disposal of chemical products

To operate our plants and facilities in a manner that protects the environment and the health and safety of our employees and the public

To extend knowledge by conducting or supporting research on the health, safety and environmental effects of our products, processes and waste materials

To work with others to resolve problems created by past handling and disposal of hazardous substances

To participate with government and others in creating responsible laws, regulations and standards to safeguard the community, workplace and environment

To promote the principles and practices of Responsible Care by sharing experiences and offering assistance to others who produce, handle, use, transport or dispose of chemicals

In addition to the Guiding Principles, the Responsible Care initiative has developed a series of more specific codes covering various aspects of management practice in the chemical industry. The "Waste and Release Reduction Code of Management Practices," for example, is designed to achieve "a long-term, substantial downward trend in the amount of wastes generated and contaminants and pollutants released." It also commits members to "ongoing reduction of wastes and releases, giving preference first to source reduction, second to recycle/reuse, and third to treatment." There is also a pollution prevention code, a product stewardship code, a process safety code, a code governing the distribution of chemicals, and an employee health and safety code.

Since the major objective of the Responsible Care initiative is to respond to public concerns, the CMA established a Public Advisory Panel (PAP), consisting of 15 nonindustry representatives of the public. The PAP meets five times a year to monitor the progress of Responsible Care. Mark Sagoff, an environmental ethicist whom we shall refer to later in this chapter, was one of the early members of the PAP.

The CMA made commitment to Responsible Care a condition of membership, so the codes are binding on all CMA members. Thus the codes are an attempt at self-regulation by the chemical industry. Member companies report their progress annually to CMA in self-evaluation forms.

Critics can pose various questions about the Responsible Care initiative. One such question is, "How effective is the enforcement program?" The PAP itself has pointed out that enforcement is based on self-reporting, with little external verification. Imposition of penalties is also a problem. The only power a trade association has is to cancel a firm's membership, and this may not be a powerful enough sanction to enforce its mandates. The CMA has not revoked any firm's membership as a result of failure to comply with the Responsible Care guidelines, although some firms have withdrawn from the CMA, perhaps because of difficulty in complying with the guidelines. The CMA has apparently taken the position that it is better to help a firm to comply rather than disciplining it for noncompliance. The guidelines require member firms to assist one another in complying with the Responsible Care initiative.

Another question might be, "Does Responsible Care address the larger issue of whether a chemical should be manufactured at all?" Suppose, for example, there is strong evidence that a pesticide is so damaging to humans or the environment that it should be eliminated from the market altogether. Would the Responsible Care program be ready to encourage its members to discontinue production of the pesticide and devote resources to other areas, perhaps to the development of another chemical pesticide or even to the development of biological substitutes for the pesticide? The third of the Guiding Principles and the Product Stewardship Code address this issue to some extent, but it probably should be further developed.[14]

The Responsible Care initiative is a continuing and expanding activity and no doubt needs further improvement. Nevertheless, some people believe that it is the most important response of an industry sector to public concerns about environmental protection. It may well represent a significant change of attitude of upper-level management in one industry sector, the chemical industry, toward environmental issues. Individual firms have also initiated important environmental protection programs. Case 10.4 describes Minnesota Mining and Manufacturing's new initiatives.

The increasing concern for environmental protection suggests that other engineering codes may soon make reference to the environment. How should these references be interpreted? What standard should be used in promoting a cleaner environment, especially where human health is concerned?

10.4   The Environment and Human Health

Environmental pollution, both in and outside the workplace, is often a threat to human health. Since engineers are obligated to protect human health, they are obligated to promote a clean environment. How do we determine what is clean? Engineers often ask, "How clean is clean?" What is an appropriate working criterion or definition of "clean" that can guide responsible engineers in thinking about health-related environmental pollution? Should the environment be "perfectly" clean? What would it be like to have such an environment? If the environment cannot be "perfectly" clean (or if this conception does not even make any sense), how clean should it be? Some possibilities exist for resolving this conceptual issue.

The Comparative Criterion

One possible answer to the question "How clean is clean?" is to say that *the environment is clean enough if it imposes no greater threat to human life or health than other risks that people accept.* This criterion can be construed in a wider or narrower way.

In the wide interpretation, an environment is clean enough if it poses no greater threat to human life or health than threats that people find acceptable in other areas of their lives, whether or not these other areas have to do with environmental pollution. For example, some believe that workers have no right to expect that their working conditions pose a smaller threat to their life and health than the threat they incur by driving home from work in the evening. If we accept a certain risk to life or health in one area of our lives, we should accept the same risk of death in another area.

The narrower interpretation of the comparative criterion is that risks due to pollution in one area of our lives should be acceptable if they are no greater than the risks due to pollution in other areas of our lives. If we accept a given level of risk to life and health from the pollution in the rivers and lakes in which we fish, we should be willing to accept the same level in the plant where we work.

There are several problems with this way of deciding what should count as clean. First, the application of this criterion might force the public to accept the highest levels of pollution found anywhere. If environmental groups object to industrial or governmental pollution in a given area, the polluters need only point out that the dangers to human health are no greater than in other areas where the pollution levels seem to be accepted.

A second objection is that levels of pollution in a given area may be "accepted" by the public only because people have not been alerted to the dangers or have not been able to do anything about them. The reference points themselves may be suspect, and the acceptable levels of pollution may themselves be revised downward in the future. The comparative criterion provides no basis for determining what these new levels should be.

The Normalcy Criterion

Another answer to the quest for a criterion for acceptable levels of pollution is that *the environment is clean enough if the pollutants present in it are normally present in nature to the same degree.* There are several problems with this criterion as well.

First, the levels of "natural" pollution vary and may themselves often be undesirable. The level of exposure to background radiation is unusually high in Denver, Colorado, because of its altitude. If we consider this a type of pollution, it might be said to be "natural" or "normal," but we might be hesitant to infer that radiation from a nuclear plant that poses the same amount of danger to the health of surrounding residents is therefore acceptable.

Second, acceptable pollution cannot be exempted from the need for free and informed consent, and this is not adequately accounted for in the normalcy criterion. It is probably not correct to say that people in Denver consent to the exposure to the level of ultraviolet radiation present in their area. Rather, they cannot do much about it. If they could, they might choose to eliminate it.

Third, natural pollution may not always be balanced by corresponding benefits. The risk to health from living in the vicinity of a chemical plant may be greater than the risk to health from drinking unpasteurized milk, but this does not necessarily imply that the risk in drinking unpasteurized milk is more acceptable. The dangers from the chemical plant may be balanced by certain advantages (such as jobs and the products the plant produces), while the dangers from drinking unpasteurized milk may not be balanced by any advantages, even though they are "natural."

The Criterion of Optimal Pollution Reduction

Cost/benefit analysis (CBA) provides another plausible guideline. CBA is a type of utilitarianism, in that its aim is to maximize human well-being. One aspect of well-being is health, and pollution is a threat to health. Unfortunately, reducing threats to health involves a cost. We cannot improve the environment with respect to human health without devoting resources to it, and this cannot be done without diverting those same resources from other areas. As economist William F. Baxter comments, even though low levels of pollution contribute to human well-being, "so do food and shelter and education and music."[15]

As we saw in Chapter 6, CBA provides an appealing way of resolving conflict issues between the good of reducing pollution or other harms and other competing goods that make demands on social resources. In this criterion, "we must divert resources to environmental causes only up to that point at which the resources can produce more overall human well-being if used in other ways." That is, *the environment is clean enough if making it cleaner would require the use of resources that would produce more overall human well-being if used in other ways.* Thus the goal of CBA is not a totally "clean" environment, but rather an environment such that making it any cleaner would divert financial resources from other areas, where they could promote more human well-being.

We discussed the method of applying CBA in Chapter 6, as well as some criticisms of CBA, and we shall not repeat this discussion here. It is important to keep in mind that, in performing a CBA, we must be careful to attribute the costs and benefits properly. Sometimes the costs/benefits are borne by industry and sometimes by the public. Sometimes they are shared equally and sometimes they are not. Therefore a CBA is almost never a sufficient moral evaluation. We believe that while the CBA test may be useful, as a utilitarian test, it may still suffer from distribution problems. It may not be sensitive to unfair distributions of the burdens of pollution.[16]

The Criterion of Maximum Protection

Another answer to the quest for a criterion for a clean environment is that *the environment is clean only if any identifiable risk from pollution that poses a possible threat to human health has been eliminated, up to the capacity of available technology and legal enforcement to do so.*[17] For example, any substance that is a carcinogen ought to be wholly eliminated from the environment, even in concentrations that are thought to be harmless.

The argument in favor of this position is that sometimes concentrations thought to be harmless turn out not to be harmless after all. Placing the burden of proof on those who argue that a given pollutant is harmful uses citizens as guinea pigs, and it is morally unacceptable to do this. There are, however, at least two problems with this criterion.

First, even this criterion would not provide absolute protection, but at best only near-absolute protection, because in many cases we do not know whether a substance poses a threat to human health. Thousands of new compounds are introduced each year, and it is impossible to test them all. When they are tested, whether they should be labeled as toxic is sometimes also a matter of dispute. After all, table salt is toxic in sufficient concentrations.

Second, implementation of this criterion would be enormously expensive and detrimental to human well-being. It would force the elimination of many useful substances whose toxicity is doubtful or extremely limited. It would also require enormous expenditures. What if removing even a small additional amount of a substance would cost $5 billion? Would this be a wise investment of our resources? Questions of cost and benefit cannot be eliminated, and the strong criterion fails to take account of this.

The Criterion of Demonstrable Harm

According to yet another criterion, *the environment is clean if every pollutant that is demonstrably harmful to human health has been eliminated.* As compared with the previous criterion, this shifts the burden of proof to the other side. A pollutant is assumed to be harmless unless shown to be otherwise. Those who would eliminate a pollutant must carry the burden of demonstrating the harm it causes.

This criterion has the advantage of being far less expensive to implement and less likely to eliminate substances that may benefit human beings. It has a serious disadvantage, however. It is often difficult to prove a connection between a substance and a health problem, or even to decide what proving such a connection would mean. A strict version of this criterion might exclude evidence from animal studies, because the existence of a connection between a substance and a health problem in animals does not establish beyond doubt that the same connection exists in humans. Yet if animal studies are disallowed, it would be very difficult to identify many threats to human health. Even with weaker versions, many actual health risks would go undetected, thus endangering public health.

None of the criteria developed so far seem adequate. It is no wonder that legislators and the courts have found it difficult to establish an adequate criterion for a clean environment, even where human health is concerned. Yet they usually attempt to construct laws that are plausible from a rational and moral standpoint. So, even though moral criteria cannot be taken uncritically from the law, it may be instructive to survey some legislation and court decisions regarding the environment and public health. These may serve as a basis for constructing a guideline for answering the question "How clean is clean?"

10.5   What Does the Law Say?

Environmental degradation was not the subject of serious federal regulation until the late 1960s.[18] Until that time, an individual who wanted to combat pollution was usually forced to appeal to the common law. If no single individual was sufficiently harmed by pollution to be motivated to bring suit against a polluter, no action was taken. The states were equally ineffective in controlling pollution. This situation opened the way for federal intervention.

In 1969 Congress passed the National Environmental Policy Act, which declared "a national policy which will encourage productive and enjoyable harmony between man and his environment. . . ." The act attempts to "assure for all Americans safe, healthful, productive and aesthetically and culturally pleasing surroundings."[19] One of the best-known mandates of the act is the environmental impact statement, which the law required of federal agencies when their decisions affected the environment. Congress then created the Environmental Protection Agency (EPA) to enforce its mandates.

Although directly concerned with worker health, the Occupational Safety and Health Act (1970) has important implications for the more general control of toxic substances. It authorizes the Secretary of Labor to set standards for "toxic materials or harmful physical agents." The standard for a given substance must be one that

> most adequately assures, to the extent feasible, on the basis of the best available evidence, that no employee will suffer material impairment of health or functional capacity even if such employee has regular exposure to the hazard dealt with by such standards for the period of his working life.[20]

The act imposes a strict standard: the employee must be protected from "material impairment of health or functional capacity" for his entire working life. But it also enters the qualifications that the feasibility of the protection must be considered and that it need last only for the "working life" of the employee.

In 1970 Congress passed the Clean Air Act, amending it in 1977. The act places health considerations ahead of a balancing of costs and benefits when dealing with hazardous pollutants.[21] It set a goal of a 90 percent reduction for auto emissions. It permitted the EPA to consider economic and technological feasibility in deciding when the goals were to be met, but not in setting the goals themselves.

In 1972 Congress enacted the Clean Water Act and amended it in 1972, 1977, and 1986. The act, designed to "restore and maintain the chemical, physical, and biological integrity of the Nation's waters," makes it unlawful for any person, business, or governmental body to discharge any pollutant into navigable waters without a permit. The act mandated pollution control measures in two stages. By 1977 all plants were to have installed water pollution control devices that represented the best practicable pollution control technology. By 1989 all plants were to have installed equipment that met more stringent standards. Plants discharging conventional pollutants must apply the best conventional pollutant control technology. Plants discharging toxic or unconventional pollutants must apply the best available technology economically achievable. The act requires polluters to do the best they possibly can to stop polluting, without reference to cost.[22]

In 1976 Congress enacted the Resource Conservation and Recovery Act, designed to control the transportation, storage, treatment, and disposal of hazardous wastes. The act requires the producer of a hazardous waste to complete a "manifest," a form that describes the nature of the hazardous waste and its method of disposal. The transporter must sign the manifest and the operator of the disposal site must do so as well, returning the manifest to the producer of the waste. This procedure is supposed to provide a complete record of the disposal of the waste. The EPA is also required to regulate the disposal sites. Standards regulating hazardous waste must be based solely on the protection of public health and the environment.[23]

This short list by no means enumerates all of the environmental and health-related legislation passed by Congress in the past twenty-five years. It does illustrate, however, the range of positions taken on the proper criterion for a clean environment, from the refusal to allow cost to play any part in the determination to the clear acceptance of cost considerations. None of these acts mandates cost/benefit analysis, although some allow cost to be considered in their implementation.

Critics still maintain, however, that congressional legislation is often unrealistic in the extent to which it ignores cost considerations. The courts must face even more directly both the costs of pollution control to industry and governmental agencies and the technological limits to our ability to control pollution. Hence they might provide a more useful guide to a criterion for a clean environment.

In *International Harvester* v. *Ruckelshaus*, the District of Columbia circuit court ruled in 1973 that EPA regulations might have been congruent with the Clean Air Act, but were defective in that they failed to justify their rulings by a consideration of the feasibility and practicality of the technology required.[24] The District of Columbia court of appeals rendered a decision in 1973 with similar import. It interpreted a relevant section of the Clean Air Act as permitting the EPA to consider costs, but not to impose a cost/benefit test.[25] In the famous "benzene" decision of 1980, a plurality of justices on the U.S. Supreme Court found that "safe" does not entail "risk free." Justice Stevens argued that OSHA could not regulate a chemical simply because it posed some risk. OSHA would also have to show that the risk was "significant."[26]

In 1986 a tribunal for the circuit court in the District of Columbia reviewed a decision by the EPA setting a standard for vinyl chloride emissions at levels less strict than industry might achieve at great effort and expense. The court ruled that when the EPA cannot determine a "safe" threshold for a pollutant, it may take not only health but also technological and economic factors into account. It may establish emission standards that industry can achieve without paying costs "grossly disproportionate" to the level of safety achieved.[27]

In an earlier decision regarding asbestos, the District of Columbia circuit court of appeals noted that Congress recognized that "employees would not be protected if their employers were put out of business." It also called attention to the fact that "standards do not become infeasible simply because they may impose substantial costs on an industry, force the development of new technology, or even force some employers out of business."[28]

Carl Cranor summarizes the implications of the circuit court's decisions.

> The implicit principles embodied in the D.C. Circuit Court's decisions suggest the following. On the one hand, OSHA may set standards more stringent than existing ones in pursuit of better health for workers, unless they threaten the economic viability of an entire industry; that is too steep a price to pay for improved health. On the other hand, even the court interprets Congress as being willing to tolerate the loss of some jobs, and even some firms in an industry, if failure to impose health regulations would materially impair the health or functional capacity for workers in that industry.[29]

Any rational criterion for a clean environment must take into account both the need to protect the health of workers and the general public and the need to protect the financial viability of industries on which workers and the general public depend. Yet the balance suggested by Cranor's summary may not be the correct one, for it appears to allow serious violations of the health of individuals if this is necessary to protect a whole "industry." According to Cranor's summary, we may impose stricter health regulations, even if the result is the closing of some firms; but we may not impose regulations that force the closing of a whole "industry."

There are also conceptual and application issues having to do with how we determine what constitutes an "industry." As Cranor himself asks, "Are plastic container and metal container manufacturers part of the same industry or are they two different industries?"[30] Suppose that protecting human health requires that we impose regulation on plastic production that would put all plastic container manufacturers out of business. If plastic container manufacturers are considered an "industry" in themselves, we may not impose these severe regulations, because it would eliminate an "industry." If, however, plastic container manufacturers and metal container manufacturers are part of the same industry, the regulations may be imposed, because an entire industry will not be eliminated. This limitation on our ability to protect human health would presumably apply, regardless of the severity of the health risks to workers or the public.

Mark Sagoff has proposed a more stringent criterion for determining an acceptable level of cleanness, which he also believes has a basis in some of the same court decisions. We need an environmental policy that "might permit governmental agencies to take technological and economic factors into account, on a case-by-case basis, as long as they act in good faith to make progress toward reducing and, it is hoped, eventually eliminating damage to the environment and risks to human safety and health."[31] This criterion, however, seems excessively stringent. Like the criterion of strong protection discussed in the previous section, it appears to justify enormous expenditures of money for very small increases in environmental purity. We must continue to "make progress" in the reduction of pollution, even if the small increases are enormously expensive and produce no appreciable improvement in human health.

The attempt of the Congress and especially the courts to balance economic considerations against the need to protect human health has been only partially successful. It does suggest, however, the overall form of the balance: considerations of cost and technical feasibility against considerations of human health. Put even more succinctly, we must balance considerations of wealth against considerations of health. A more direct analysis of the issues in terms of this familiar moral contrast may be helpful in constructing a criterion for determining when the environment is "clean."

10.6   Balancing Health and Wealth: A Criterion for "Clean"

In coming to grips with the issues with which the courts are struggling, we must begin with the assumption that we are trying to balance the goals of increasing job opportunities and income on the one hand with protecting the health of individuals on the other. Let us begin with the utilitarian approach to this issue.[32]

From the utilitarian standpoint, we want to increase income, job opportunities, and even overall public health. An increase in income produces utility, whether it is the income of workers or owners. Similarly, an increase in the number and the desirability of jobs also increases utility. Finally, even a utilitarian can consider health. Good health is a precondition for achieving most other goods, and so is desirable even from a utilitarian standpoint, along with increased income and more jobs.

Utilitarians, however, permit trade-offs between any of these goods, if the trade-off will produce a net increase in overall utility. Since utilitarians consider the well-being of individuals only insofar as it affects overall utility, minor benefits to many might outweigh severe harms to a few. Thus we might be justified in reducing health protection for some, in exchange for a net increase in overall utility.

Some environmental laws and (especially) some recent court decisions have apparently been attempting to guard against this unfortunate tendency of utilitarianism to forget the individual in the effort to promote greater overall utility. This often involves an appeal to considerations more compatible with RP morality. The ethics of respect for persons speaks to the distribution of goods and harm, and to the special weight that some goods (such as health) have. From the RP standpoint, an individual's health should not be sacrificed, even in order to increase the general welfare of everyone.[33]

We believe that the engineer's obligation to hold paramount the health of the public should not be interpreted in purely utilitarian terms. However, we must not forget to consider the economic effects of regulations protecting human health. The proper criterion for evaluating what is "clean" must cover a spectrum of cases, with two extremes. We delineate this spectrum in the following criterion, which we call the *degree-of-harm criterion*:

The environment is clean if pollutants that pose a clear and pressing threat to human health have been eliminated or reduced below any reasonable threshold of harm, with little or no regard for cost. With substances that pose an uncertain (but possible) risk to health or whose threshold of danger to health cannot be determined, economic factors may be considered.

This policy should guide the engineer's interpretation of the requirement in most engineering codes to protect the health of the public. If there are statements requiring engineers to protect the environment, this criterion should be a guide in interpreting this obligation, insofar as human health is affected.

According to this criterion, the task of protecting the environment where human health is concerned oscillates between two extremes. On one extreme, where the risk of causing harm to people is grave, the imperative of protecting human health must be primary. In some cases, this imperative might require the elimination of virtually all pollution, even if this involves great expense or shutting down the source of the pollution. On the other extreme, where the risk to human health appears to be small or is indeterminate, cost/benefit considerations are more appropriate. While cost/benefit analysis cannot determine the extent to which serious threats to health are eliminated, it may—within limits that cannot be precisely specified—determine the extent to which suspected but undetermined threats must be eliminated.

We can illustrate how the criterion might serve as a guide in line-drawing problems with a case in which the criterion has been violated. Suppose Engineer Vivian is employed by Shady Chemical, a firm that follows the policies described by Petulla as "crisis-oriented environmental management." The firm has a long history of producing pesticides that not only damage the environment, but also pose a threat to the workers who manufacture them, the farmers who apply them, and the consumers who eat the food to which they are applied. When one of its products is banned by the government, the usual procedure of Shady Chemical is to slightly modify its chemical formula, so that it no longer falls under the ban. When the new product is also banned, a new chemical is usually ready.

Vivian has been asked to participate in the development of an alternative to one of Shady Chemical's most successful products. The firm has learned on good authority that the product will shortly be banned because it is a virulent carcinogen. Following its usual policy, Shady wants to find a substitute for the active ingredient in the pesticide which is as close to the old product as possible. Although one can never be sure that the modified product has similar toxic properties to the old one until extensive testing has been done, Vivian has good reason to believe that the proposed substitute may be even worse. Shady Chemical has violated the degree-of-harm criterion.

Consider another example. The plant that employs Engineer Bob has just discovered that its discharge into the atmosphere includes a new chemical that comes from a new product line. The chemical is structurally similar to a class of chemicals that has been declared safe by the governmental regulatory agency. There is no reason to suspect the chemical, although its effect on humans has not been extensively tested. The management at Bob's plant follows the policy described by Petulla as "enlightened environmental management," and the environmental affairs department in the plant is monitoring the new chemical. The department is prepared to take action to eliminate it from the discharge if any reason to suspect it is found, even if it is not banned by the government. In this case Bob's firm is probably showing sufficient regard for human health.

Many intermediate cases are more difficult to decide. Suppose Engineer Melinda is employed by a plant whose management follows the policies described by Petulla as "cost-oriented environmental management." A new chemical has been identified in the plant's discharge into the local river. The chemical is not a regulated substance, although it is structurally similar to substances that have been found to be carcinogenic in large concentrations. Elimination of the substance would be expensive, but its elimination would be economically feasible. In this situation the degree-of-harm criterion would probably require that the plant begin to prepare to eliminate the substance from its discharge. Melinda would have to have more information, however, before she could be sure about the implications of the degree-of-harm criterion. We cannot overemphasize the importance of a thorough analysis of the facts, especially in nonparadigmatic line-drawing cases.

What should the codes say with regard to health-related environmental issues? We have maintained that the codes already implicitly commit engineers to protecting the environment, insofar as human health is concerned. From this perspective, there is no need for any additional statement. Nevertheless, we believe that the importance of environmental cases, together with the fact that many engineers do not recognize the implicit commitments in the codes regarding health-related issues, requires that there be an explicit reference to the environment. *As a minimum*, engineering codes should contain a statement such as the following: "Engineers shall hold paramount the health, safety, and welfare of the public and the integrity of the environment, insofar as it affects human health."

10.7   The Anthropocentric Approach to Environmental Ethics

At most only two codes commit engineers to non-health-related environmental concerns. There is not much evidence that the codes attribute intrinsic value to natural objects. The contemporary environmental movement challenges both of these positions. During the past two decades there have been many objections to such activities as the use of animals in testing consumer products and in scientific laboratories; raising chickens and other animals in cages and similar confining conditions; killing whales, dolphins and other higher mammals; destroying the natural habitats of animal and plant species; draining wetlands; cutting virgin forests; and flooding farmlands and wild areas. These objections go far beyond a concern for human health. Sometimes they go beyond a concern for human well-being of any type. And while environmentalists sometimes base these objections on a view that natural objects have only instrumental value, they sometimes hold that natural objects have intrinsic value.

It is useful to divide the movement to protect the nonhuman world into two parts: the animal liberation movement and the environmental movement. Increasingly, these have gone their separate ways, and they sometimes can work at cross-purposes. For example, forest fires are often caused by natural means and sometimes may produce beneficial results for plant life, but they may be highly destructive to animal life. In such situations, animal liberationists may find themselves in an adversarial relationship with other environmental groups. The environmental movement is considerably more important for engineering ethics than the animal liberation movement. Nevertheless, it will be helpful to consider the common elements in the two movements, as well as some of the differences between them.

The common element in both the animal liberation and environmental movements is a rejection of the strong anthropocentric orientation that is prominent in Western ethics. An *anthropocentric* ethics holds that only human beings are "morally considerable," i.e., have intrinsic value. Nonhuman natural objects have value only as they contribute to human well-being. A *nonanthropocentric* environmental ethics holds that at least some natural objects other than human beings (animals, plants, and perhaps even inanimate things such as rivers and mountains) have intrinsic value.

Most Western moral philosophies focus primarily—or even exclusively—on human beings. They consider nonhuman animals, plants, and the nonliving world only insofar as they are necessary means for promoting the utility of humans or the respect due to human persons. William Baxter has stated this anthropocentric position in the following way: "Penguins are important because people enjoy seeing them walk about rocks. . . . I have no interest in preserving penguins for their own sake."[34] (Notice that the penguins are not asked about their view of the matter!) Human beings are the measure of the good.

The animal liberation movement challenges this account of the value of penguins and other forms of animal life. One of the most important challenges to such anthropocentrism as it applies to animals is based on some forms of utilitarianism, and it is easy to see how a concern for at least some nonhuman animals can be extracted from the utilitarian way of thinking. For utilitarians, happiness or well-being includes, among other things, the experience of pleasure and the avoidance of pain. Few people would deny that animals are able to experience pleasure and pain. Why, then, should only the pleasure and pain of humans be morally considerable? Can we give any reason, other than the anthropocentric position itself, for this limitation? If we cannot, then limiting ethical concern exclusively to the human species is arbitrary and unfounded.

Peter Singer, a utilitarian advocate of the rights of animals, has referred to the anthropocentrism of Western ethics as *speciesism*, a viewpoint that excludes nonhuman animals from the ranks of the morally considerable.[35] Like racism and sexism, speciesism is arbitrary and morally unjustifiable, Singer believes. Racism

excludes some human beings on the basis of skin color or other racial characteristics, and sexism excludes some human beings on the basis of their sex;
speciesism excludes some living beings on the basis of the species to which they
belong. Singer does not deny that human interests may often justifiably outweigh
the interests of nonhuman animals. Humans may, after all, have the capacity for
more intense suffering because of their greater self-consciousness and ability to
anticipate the future. But if the suffering of a human being and an animal is really
equal in intensity, the suffering of the human does not deserve any more consideration than the suffering of animals.

The animal liberation movement has some relevance to engineering ethics.
Engineering projects sometimes destroy the habitats and the lives of animals, and
products developed by engineers are sometimes tested on animals in inhumane
ways. In such situations engineers may be forced to make moral decisions about
the proper attitude toward nonhuman animals.

The environmental movement, however, is much more relevant to the engineering profession. In its broadest aspects, the environmental movement is concerned with the living and nonliving aspects of the natural world that form what
Aldo Leopold, an important figure in the contemporary environmental movement, calls the "biotic community." According to many proponents of environ-
mentalism, contemporary technologically advanced civilization is guilty of massive assaults on the biotic community. Western society in particular has tended to
conceive of nature as passive, as the fit object of human manipulation and control.

This view of nature as passive is amply reflected in our language about the natural world. We "develop" land. We "improve" raw land. We "exploit" and "con-
sume" natural resources. We "harvest" trees. We "harness" the rivers to produce
electrical power. We "manage" the wilderness. Nature, like the rest of the nonhuman world, must be subservient to human purposes.

Aldo Leopold wrote in *A Sand County Almanac*:

> We abuse land because we regard it as a commodity belonging to us. When we see
> land as a community to which we belong, we may begin to use it with love and
> respect. . . . Perhaps such a shift in values can be achieved by reappraising things
> unnatural, tame, and confined in terms of things natural, wild, and free.[36]

If we can interpret the animal liberation movement as derived from utilitarianism, perhaps we can understand the environmental movement as derived from
the ethics of respect for persons. For many proponents of the environmental
movement, we must replace the traditional distinctions between things and
moral agents with a wider view. In this view it is wrong to treat nature, or "the
land," as a mere commodity that can be used in any way humans see fit.
Leopold's view interprets nature as something to which we belong rather than
something which belongs to us. It is something "wild" and "free" rather than a
passive object on which we work our purposes. Nature is "a fountain of energy
flowing through a circuit of soils, plants, and animals."[37]

Viewing nature as an interdependent biotic community, Leopold believed that
nature elicits an ethical response. He called this the "land ethic" and stated its

moral standard in these words: "A thing is right when it tends to preserve the integrity, stability, and beauty of the biotic community. It is wrong when it tends otherwise."[38]

In the light of this wider moral vision, some environmentalists have found that the importance of human beings must be reassessed. A dramatic and extreme statement of this idea is given by philosopher Paul Taylor:

> Every last man, woman, and child could disappear from the face of the Earth without any significant detrimental consequence for the good of wild animals and plants. On the contrary, many of them would be greatly benefitted. . . . If then, the total, final absolute extermination of our species should take place and if we should not carry all the others with us into oblivion, not only would the Earth's community of life continue to exist, but in all probability its well being would be enhanced. Our presence, in short, is not needed. If we were to take the standpoint of the community and give voice to its true interest, the ending of our . . . epoch would most likely be greeted with a healthy "Good riddance."[39]

A widespread belief that beings other than humans have intrinsic value has emerged from recent environmental thought. But there is disagreement as to how far the class of morally considerable beings should be extended. We do not need to settle the question of precisely what parts of the natural world have intrinsic value. It is sufficient to point out that non-health-related environmental concerns can be justified by way of their connection with human welfare.

One way in which non-health-related concerns can be related to human welfare is what some environmentalists call the experience of "the wild." Political theorist John Rodman expresses the need for this experience.

> The need for wilderness grows more acute every moment because it is, among other things, the need to experience a realm of reality beyond the manipulations of commodity production and technology . . . the need for realities that function as symbols of otherness that can arouse a response from the suppressed potentialities of human nature.[40]

If human welfare includes the need to experience a part of the natural world that is wholly beyond human life, which is characterized by mystery and "otherness," then there is a basis for concern for nature that goes beyond a consideration of human health. From this standpoint we can say that human welfare is adversely affected by the elimination of wilderness areas and other environmental assets, even if such elimination does not directly affect human health.

If one does not accept this argument, a concern for the nonhuman world is related to human welfare in an even more direct and obvious way. Activities that reduce available farmland or drain underground water supplies can vitally affect the ability of human beings to support themselves. A healthy natural environment is important to human survival in the long run and is thus related to human welfare in the most fundamental sense of the term—human survival.

While the integrity of the environment is vitally important for human welfare, should the codes require engineers to promote environmental integrity, even when human health is not at stake? It is doubtful that the framers of the codes had non-health-related envronmental concerns in mind when they referred to human "welfare." The engineering community could, of course, decide to extend the term "welfare" to include non-health-related environmental issues, regardless of what the framers had in mind. Or it could impose such obligations on engineers, independently of an appeal to the reference to human welfare in many professional codes. What should engineering *professional* ethics require of engineers with regard to non-health-related environmental issues?

10.8   The Scope of Professional Engineering Obligations to the Environment

We can begin by considering some of the arguments of those who believe that professional engineering obligations to the environment should be extended beyond a concern for factors that endanger human health.

First, since engineers are often morally responsible agents, both in environmental degradation and in environmental improvement, they should have a professional obligation to protect the environment. People are morally responsible for something when they bring it about or cause it to exist or happen. If I turn out the lights while friends are walking up the stairs, knowing full well that they may fall, then I am responsible if they fall. If I did not know that anyone was on the stairs and had no reason to believe that they were, then I am not responsible.

According to this argument, engineers should share in the responsibility for environmental concerns, for they are often causal agents in projects and activities that affect the environment for good or ill. Engineers design dams that flood farmlands and wild rivers. They design chemical plants that pollute the air and water. They also design solar energy systems that make hydroelectric projects unnecessary and pollution-control systems that eliminate the discharge of pollutants into the air and water. Furthermore, they usually are (or should be) aware of the consequences of their actions.

Many people believe that if engineers are morally responsible agents in issues affecting the environment, they should also be required as professionals to promote environmental integrity, even where human health is not at stake. If this is the case, this requirement should be a part of the codes.

Second, the engineering profession might well have a salutary impact on our attitudes and actions with respect to the environment. Engineers are, after all, major participants in virtually all of the projects that affect the environment. If even a substantial number of concerned engineers refused to contribute their professional skills to some of the most environmentally destructive projects, the result might well be the cancellation of the projects or at least a modification of them so they will produce less environmental devastation.

There are also arguments that engineers should not be assigned professional obligations where human health is not at stake.

First, many of the judgments that would have to be made fall outside the area of professional engineering expertise. When engineers make such judgments, critics might accuse them of violating their professional responsibility by speaking outside their area of expertise. The second fundamental canon of the NSPE code, for example, requires engineers to "perform services only in the areas of their competence." Another section says: "Engineers may express publicly a professional opinion on technical subjects only when that opinion is founded upon adequate knowledge of the facts and competence in the subject matter" (II.3.b.).

Many objections to actions of government or private industry made on the basis that they harm the environment are not based on professional engineering competence. They come rather from one of the biological sciences. Perhaps engineers should make the objections on the grounds of personal moral beliefs, not on the basis of professional ethics.

Suppose Engineer Mary is asked to participate in the design of a plant that will be built near a wilderness. She objects because she believes that the wilderness is especially important for the ecology of the area. This judgment is not a professional engineering judgment but one more appropriately made by a biologist. While an engineer may object to participating in the project on the ground of her personal moral beliefs, it might not be proper to object on professional grounds.

The same problem exists in many other areas related to the environment. An engineer may object to designing an entertainment park that will be built on several thousand acres of open countryside. Or he may object to designing pumps that will be used in areas where the water table has been falling rapidly. In all of these cases the judgments involve values or knowledge outside most engineers' professional expertise. An engineer may well object to these projects, but the question is whether he should object as an engineer. To do so, the critic will argue, is to invite public disrespect for the engineering profession.

We can summarize this argument in more concrete terms. Suppose the NSPE code contained a provision such as this: "Engineers will not participate in projects that are unnecessarily destructive to the environment, even if they do not endanger human life or health." Given the nature of present engineering education, the judgments necessary to comply with such a provision would often not be typically professional engineering judgments, because engineering education does not cover these areas. Thus, incorporating such a provision in the NSPE code might well involve violating section II.3.b. of the same code. So most engineers would have to rely on the judgment of others who do have expertise on such environmental issues.

Second, an extension of professional responsibility for the environment into areas not clearly related to public health or safety might cause considerable problems for engineering societies. Engineers disagree among themselves over environmental issues, especially where human health is not directly involved. Forcing members of professional societies to take policy stands on such issues will introduce a new source of divisiveness into the societies.

Another aspect of this same objection is that such issues will be especially troublesome for engineering managers who are members of engineering societies. As Petulla's survey demonstrates, managers cannot always be expected to lend a sympathetic ear to policies that will inevitably result in greater expense for their organizations. The effect of introducing these issues into the societies may weaken management support for the societies themselves.

Furthermore, extending the provisions of the codes into controversial areas might well further weaken the influence of the codes on the engineering profession. Many engineers have never seen a copy of their professional code, and relatively few have any detailed knowledge of its provisions, even though most engineers seem committed to protecting public health and safety. Some engineers may already view some aspects of the codes as unrealistic. Engineers might cite strong environmental provisions as a reason for regarding the codes as radical and politically biased and thus as a reason for ignoring them.

Third, requiring engineers to protect the environment even where human health is not an issue would produce problems of conscience for some. While there are probably few engineers who disagree with the provisions of engineering codes regarding such issues as conflict of interest, performing duties only in areas in which they are competent, and the necessity of avoiding deception, many would probably disagree with strong provisions requiring engineers to protect the environment, where human health is not an issue. Requiring them to take a position contrary to their personal beliefs could force them into a situation with no desirable options. They would have to either act contrary to their personal beliefs, withdraw from their engineering society, or simply disobey their professional code. Engineering societies should avoid forcing their members to make such choices.

We believe there is considerable validity in arguments on both sides of this issue. For this reason, a way should be found to accommodate as many of the conflicting arguments as possible. In the next section we present proposals for this.

10.9   Two Modest Proposals

Professional engineering obligations regarding non-health-related issues can best be handled in terms of two proposals. First, while engineers should be required to hold paramount human health in the performance of their engineering work (including health issues that are environmentally related), they should not be required as professionals to inject non-health-related environmental concerns into their engineering work. Second, engineers should have the right to organizational disobedience with regard to environmental issues, as this is required by their personal moral beliefs. Let us pursue this second proposal in more detail. In section 9.4 we considered three types of "organizational disobedience," all relevant to our second proposal.

First, engineers should have the right to disobedience by contrary action with regard to environmental issues. That is, they should have the right to promote their personal beliefs, including their beliefs about the environment, outside the workplace. For example, an engineer should be able to join an environmental group devoted to saving wetlands, even when her employer wants to drain a wetland to build a new plant. An engineer should be able to speak out against the building of a dam that will destroy a wild river, even when his firm may profit from construction of the dam.

Second, engineers should have the right to disobedience by nonparticipation with regard to environmental issues. That is, they should have the right to refuse to carry out assignments they believe are wrong, including environmentally related ones. An engineer should be able to refuse to participate in the design of a plant that will adversely affect human health or be built on a wetland. Similarly, she should have the right to refuse to design a dam that will destroy a wild river.

Third, engineers should have the right to disobedience by protest with regard to environmental issues. That is, they should have the right to protest employer actions they believe to be wrong, including actions they believe are harmful to human health or the environment. Within the bounds of discretion and due regard for the employer, an engineer should be able to protest an employer's plan to design or build a dam that will destroy a wild river or a project which will involve draining a wetland.

In order to make these rights clear, the following provision regarding the rights of engineers could be incorporated into engineering codes:

> Where organizational constraints permit, engineers shall not be required to participate in projects that violate their professional obligations or personal beliefs. Engineers shall also have the right to voice responsible objections, both inside and outside the workplace, to engineering projects they believe are wrong, without fear of reprisal. Engineers shall have the right to support programs and causes of their own choosing, outside the workplace. Engineers shall not, however, lend the weight of their professional status to public statements that go beyond their area of professional competence.

The following arguments support this provision.

First, there are precedents for such provisions as this, which asserts a right of engineers rather than imposes an obligation on them. The unusual nature of this provision deserves emphasis. Most engineering codes are composed of a set of obligations that engineers impose on themselves. This provision asserts a right of engineers against their employers. There are, however, precedents for the assertion of rights of professionals.

The code of the American Medical Association protects physicians from having to perform medical procedures to which they have personal moral objections. Article VI of the Principles of Medical Ethics of the American Medical Association (July 1980) says: "A physician shall, in the provision of appropriate patient care, except in emergencies, be free to choose whom to serve, with whom to associate, and the environment in which to provide medical care." Suppose a physician objects to performing abortions or prescribing contraceptives to unmarried people.[41] This provision of the AMA code allows physicians to refrain from performing these procedures and still comply with their professional code. We believe engineers deserve similar protection.

There is even some precedent in engineering for similar assertions. In the next chapter we discuss a case examined by the Board of Ethical Review (BER) of the National Society of Professional Engineers. In case 82-5, the board defended the right of an engineer to protest what he believed were excessive costs and time delays in a defense contract. The board concluded that, while the engineer did not have an ethical obligation to continue to protest his employer's tactics, he had "a right to do so as a matter of personal conscience." The proposed addition to professional engineering codes would serve a similar function of protecting engineers who have personal objections to projects they believe are harmful to the environment.

In his "model code" of engineering ethics, Stephen Unger also proposes a provision that gives similar protection to engineers. Engineers shall "endeavor to direct their professional skills toward conscientiously chosen ends they deem, on balance, to be of positive value to humanity; declining to pursue those skills for purposes they consider, on balance, to conflict with their moral values."[42] He points out that individual attorneys and physicians are not required to accept every client that asks for their services. The claim that even a guilty person deserves a lawyer and that every person desiring medical services deserves a physician has its limitations when applied to engineering. Some engineering projects may not deserve to be built at all, such as the gas chambers in the Nazi extermination camps. Even if an engineering project is legitimate, it does not follow that an engineer who has moral objections to it should design it.[43]

Second, the proposal recognizes the limitations of organizations to honor the right of an engineer to refuse to participate in a project to which she has personal moral objections. Some organizations may have such limited resources that they cannot afford to reassign an engineer who objects to a project. This limitation is recognized in the opening phrase, "Where organizational constraints permit . . ." While an employer can abuse this qualification, it is necessary in order to accommodate the legitimate limitations that employers face.

Third, this provision has the additional advantage of providing a means for nonmanagement engineers to fulfill their *professional* obligations in a wide variety of issues. Engineers who are not managers often do not have a way to fulfill even their code-mandated obligations. For example, how are engineers who do not have decision-making powers to fulfill their obligations to protect the health of the public? Suppose Engineer Jane believes that her plant's discharge into the local river violates the degree-of-harm criterion, but management has decided to do nothing about it. In the absence of decision-making powers, how is she to carry out her responsibility to the public? The proposed code provision says that she may protest her plant's decision, or even refuse to work on projects that contribute to this unjustified pollution.

Fourth, the provision would protect the personal conscience of engineers who do have strong personal objections to actions that perpetrate non-health-related harms on the environment. Suppose Engineer Joe has been asked by his manager to be a part of a team that will design a plant that will use land that is part of a wildlife preserve. Joe believes the plant should not be built, but he is not in a position to make the decision. Our proposed provision would allow Joe to protest the building of the plant and even to request not to be assigned the task of helping in its design.

Fifth, the provision would allow engineers who do not share the concern for environmental issues where human health is not at stake to follow their own beliefs as well. Suppose Engineer Rhonda's firm also has a contract to design a plant that will use land that is part of a wildlife preserve. Our proposed provision would allow Rhonda to help design the plant.

The question of the nature and extent of the rights and obligations of engineers regarding environmental issues is still highly controversial. The discussion is in a very early stage. The proposals offered in this chapter are intended to contribute to this discussion, as it takes place both within the engineering community and in the larger public arena.

10.10   Chapter Summary

Two engineering codes explicitly refer to the engineer's obligation to protect the environment, but the statements are weak and ambiguous. Only two codes require engineers to be concerned with the environment when human health is not at stake. A requirement to protect the health and safety of the public, which is a part of virtually all engineering codes, implies that engineers already have an obligation to promote a clean environment when human health is involved. There is not much evidence that the codes attribute intrinsic value to nature.

According to a survey by Petulla in 1982–1985, most managers had only limited sympathy with environmental concerns. There is reason to believe that the attitudes of business managers have become increasingly sympathetic to environmental concerns.

To promote a clean environment, engineers must have a criterion for determining what is meant by "clean." A number of possible criteria are clearly inadequate. It is useful to look at laws and the courts for suggestions in approaching this difficult issue. The law suggests that an acceptable criterion must contain a balance between cost considerations and technical feasibility on the one hand and the need to protect human health on the other.

The environmental movement has focused public attention on non-health-related environmental concerns. Many environmentalists believe that the environment should be protected for its own sake, but we can also justify attention to the environment on the grounds that it is essential to protecting human welfare in such areas as recreation and renewable natural resources.

It may not be advisable at the present time to require engineers to have obligations to protect the environment where human health is not at stake. The codes should, however, protect the rights of engineers to engage in public environmental protection efforts, to protest employer actions they believe are environmentally destructive, and to refuse to engage in projects they believe are environmentally destructive.

Case Analyses

Case 10.1 Parkville[44]

Elizabeth Dorsey is an engineer at CDC, Inc., a large corporation in a crowded metropolitan area. Elizabeth prefers living in a smaller community, so she commutes thirty miles daily from her home in Parkville, a community of fewer than 5,000 people.

Noted for her environmental concerns, Elizabeth is on Parkville's Committee for Environmental Quality, a small but active citizen's group. Last year the committee successfully spearheaded opposition to rezoning a Parkville recreational and wildlife area for commercial purposes. While acknowledging that commercial development would aid the local economy, the committee convinced the city council that economic progress should not come at the expense of the environment.

However, now Elizabeth is facing a difficult problem. She has learned that CDC needs to expand its operations, which will require a new facility. But the immediate area has little to offer. In surveying surrounding areas CDC's planning committee has determined that the most desirable location for its new facility would be in nearby Parkville's recreational and wildlife area. The planning committee is now authorized by CDC to approach Parkville's city council.

CDC makes what it considers to be a very generous offer to the city council. Presenting itself as an environmentally conscious corporation, CDC says it will need only 25 percent of the wildlife and recreational area; it will carefully monitor and control emissions into the air and water, using "beyond-the-state-of-the-art" equipment and standards; it will annually contribute funds for the preservation and maintenance of the remaining 75 percent of the area. In addition, CDC points out how its presence will increase the tax base of Parkville, create new jobs, and enhance the local economy.

A member of CDC's planning committee learns that one of CDC's engineers, Elizabeth Dorsey, lives in Parkville. He suggests to committee chair, Jim Bartlett, that someone talk to her to see if she might be able to "soften up" Parkville city council members. Jim thinks this is a good idea and calls David Jensen, chief engineer of Elizabeth's unit. "David," Jim says, "I'd like you to talk to one of your engineers, Elizabeth Dorsey, about our efforts to secure some land near Parkville." Jim goes on to detail CDC's plans and what he would like Elizabeth to be asked to do.

Shortly after his conversation with Jim Bartlett, David Jensen calls Elizabeth Dorsey into his office and relays Jim's message. Unaware of Elizabeth's participation on Parkville's Committee for Environmental Quality, David asks, "Is there anyone on the city council you know well enough to talk to about this?"

David Jensen reports back to Jim Bartlett that he is not sure that Elizabeth Dorsey will be much help. "She says she doesn't know any council members well enough to talk to them," David says.

Much to his surprise, Jim replies, "Guess what I learned just half an hour ago? I had a phone conversation with an old friend who moved away from Parkville last fall. He says Elizabeth Dorsey is on an environmental concerns committee in Parkville. She knows city council members all right—she and her committee members took on the council last year and blocked its effort to open up commercially the area we want! We're going to have to keep an eye on her. Tell her she'd better 'cool it' on this one."

Over the next two weeks Elizabeth Dorsey keeps CDC's plans to herself. Then she receives a phone message indicating that the Committee for Environmental Quality is having an urgent meeting. At the outset of the meeting the committee chair announces that he has just learned of CDC's intentions. "We have to act quickly to mobilize against this," he concludes.

Did Elizabeth misrepresent to her supervisors her relationship to the city council? Did she engage in withholding information about CDC's plans from the Committee for Environmental Quality? Should she now join with her fellow committee members in mobilizing against CDC's intentions?

Analysis

There are a number of unclear factual issues that are important in the resolution of the case. What would be the effects on the wildlife and recreational area of selling 25 percent of it to CDC? Will Parkville be able to pay for the upkeep of the wildlife and recreational area without the contributions from CDC? Does CDC have other viable options for expansion? How much less desirable are they than the land in the wildlife and recreational area? What kind of environmental record does CDC have? How important is Elizabeth's participation in the fight to preserve the wildlife and recreational area? Is her participation essential, or does she want to participate primarily as a matter of conscience? Does she in fact know any

members of the Parkville city council well enough to be of benefit to CDC?

One of the major conceptual issues is "deception." Elizabeth may be guilty of something akin to deception or dishonesty by telling her employer that she does not know any city council members well enough to influence them and by not alerting the Committee for Environmental Quality to CDC's plans. Without attempting to give a complete definition, we can say that deception is (1) affirming what we know to be false or denying what we know to be true or (2) failing to reveal information in a situation in which most would expect one to be forthcoming.

Another conceptual issue is "conflict of interest." Recalling our discussion in Chapter 7, two principal points about conflicts of interest should be borne in mind. (1) Occupying a certain role justifies another person's relying on our judgment to be objective. (2) We are (or might be) subject to influences that would make our judgment less objective and disinterested than others who rely on our judgment might expect.

Now let us turn to the application problems. There are two instances where Elizabeth might be accused of deception. First, she can be accused of deception in not being more forthright with her employers about her relationship with the city council members. Since she has already been successful in exerting influence on the council members, she must know them well enough to exert such influence. While it may be true that she cannot influence them to reverse their position, the reason is not that she does not know them well enough. Rather, it might be that the council members no longer respect her integrity, since she has reversed her position. She also has failed to reveal information her employers might have expected her to reveal, her involvement in the local environmental movement. Her action almost certainly has involved deception with respect to her employer.

The second instance of deception is in not revealing CDC's plans to the Committee for Environmental Quality. This seems to be a clear case of not revealing information where she would have been expected to reveal it. Information about CDC's plans would have been helpful to the members of the committee, giving them more time to prepare their response, and committee members might expect her to reveal such information. At the same time, CDC might regard its plans as confidential information at this time, thus placing Elizabeth in a conflict situation.

Whether Elizabeth's continued activity on the Committee for Environmental Quality represents a conflict of interest is a complex question. On the one hand, people probably rely on her judgment on environmental matters to be objective and in the interests of the general public, and her employment by CDC calls this judgment into question. On the other hand, if Elizabeth continues to oppose CDC's attempt to buy a portion of the recreational and wildlife area, most of the members of the community may conclude that she has resisted the influence of her employer and her continued presence on the committee is not objectionable. Nevertheless, there is always the danger that her views will be tempered in some way because of the actions of CDC. So it is not unreasonable to hold that there is still at least a potential conflict of interest from the committee's perspective.

It is also possible that CDC regards Elizabeth's serving on the Committee for Environmental Quality as a conflict of interest, because she might join the committee in opposition to CDC. Still, since she is not on CDC's planning committee, it is not clear that Elizabeth has any special responsibility to recommend or otherwise advocate CDC's Parkville plan. In this respect, CDC should not fault her for her unwillingness to seek to influence Parkville's city council.

Nevertheless, CDC might believe that company loyalty requires, at least, that Elizabeth not join forces with the opposition. This would place her in a difficult position, since she is also an environmentally concerned citizen in the community into which CDC wishes to move. As we have noted many times, engineering codes of ethics typically insist that an engineer's paramount obligation is to protect public health and safety. There is no indication that this obligation is meant to be restricted to the context of employment. Engineers are encouraged to take on broader responsibilities for the good of society. This is precisely what she took her involvement with the Committee for Environmental Quality to be.

So, Elizabeth faces several conflict issues. She faces a conflict in deciding whether to engage in deception with regard to CDC. On the one hand, she has an obligation to herself to protect her job if possible. On the other hand, she has an obligation to tell the truth to her employer. She resolves the conflict by slightly misrepresenting the truth. She also faces a conflict in deciding whether to withhold information about CDC's plans from the Committee for Environmental Quality. This time the conflict is between her obligations to herself and her employer and her obligations to the committee to supply them with valuable information.

Elizabeth has already decided to engage in a certain amount of deception. Her more immediate problem is whether to join with the other members of the Committee for Environmental Quality in opposing CDC's plan to acquire a portion of the recreational and wildlife area. If Elizabeth's employer respects the rights of their employees to follow their own conscience, especially in activities outside the workplace, Elizabeth would not have a problem. It is clear, however, that Elizabeth's supervisors expect her to either support the CDC position or at the very least to remain neutral. Therefore she faces a conflict, this time between a certain loyalty to her employer and to herself (since her job may be in jeopardy) and an obligation to her own beliefs and to the committee. How can she resolve the conflict?

The first possible resolution is to try to persuade CDC managers to consider purchasing another location for expansion that is not so environmentally sensitive. She can argue that the attempt to purchase the land will result in a bruising public fight that will damage CDC's reputation, whether the company wins or loses. Because of Elizabeth's position in the company and the evident determination of CDC managers to secure the land near Parkville, this option may not offer much promise, but it would have the advantage of preserving Elizabeth's integrity as an environmentalist and preserving her job.

The second possible resolution is to resign from the committee on the grounds of conflict of interest and then to remain neutral with respect to the controversy. Her claim that she has a conflict of interest has some justification, and the action might be enough to satisfy her supervisors. The problem with this alternative is that it would require her standing idly without taking sides on an issue about which she cares very deeply, and that it would probably tarnish her reputation in the community by making her look like a person who does not stand up for her convictions.

A third option is to resign from the Committee on Environmental Quality, or at least remove herself from the deliberations on the CDC issue, but continue to publicly oppose the purchase of the wildlife area. This would no doubt anger her employers, but it might be the best way to preserve her integrity in the community, for it would remove any problem of conflict of interest

and preserve her reputation as a staunch environmentalist.

The fourth possibility is to resign from the Committee on Environmental Quality and take the side of her employer. This solution would please her supervisors the most, but it would severely damage both Elizabeth's reputation in the community and her own self-esteem; and it might result in environmental degradation in the Parkville area. This seems to be her least attractive option.

In order to make a responsible decision, Elizabeth must have some knowledge of her chances of getting another job. If they are good, she should risk losing her job by choosing the first or third option. Clearly the first option is the most desirable, for if it is successful it will not only resolve the environmental crisis but also probably preserve her job. The third option would endanger her job but preserve her integrity in the community and her own self-esteem.

If losing her job would cause severe problems for her and the first option is not possible, Elizabeth faces a very serious conflict issue, and there may be no creative middle way out of it. She should certainly examine very carefully the arguments for and against selling 25 percent of the wildlife and recreational area to CDC. But if she decides to support the CDC position, she will find it difficult to preserve her reputation in the community, or at least with the Committee on Environmental Quality. If she finds the arguments are against selling the land to CDC, she may have to choose the second option.

Case 10.2 Waste Disposal[45]

I

ABC's chemical waste is stored in a warehouse at an off-site location. While inspecting the warehouse, engineer Scott Lewis notices several leaking drums. He calls Tom Treehorn, head of ABC's Division of Chemical Waste. Tom responds, "I'll be right over with a crew to bring the leaking drums over here." Scott points out that the law forbids returning chemical waste to the "home" site. Tom replies, "I know, but I don't have any confidence in the off-site folks handling this. We know how to handle this best. It might not be the letter of the law, but our handling it captures its spirit."

Scott believes that Tom Treehorn is serious about preventing environmental problems—especially those that might be caused by ABC. Still, he knows that the Environmental Protection Agency will be upset if it finds out about Tom's way of dealing with the problem; and if anything goes wrong, ABC could get into serious legal difficulties. After all, he thinks, ABC is not a waste disposal facility.

What should Scott do at this point?

1. Tell Tom that he will inform Tom's superior if Tom goes ahead with his plan.
2. Tell Tom that he will not interfere with Tom's plan, but he will not help him with it either.
3. Advise Tom not to go ahead with his plan, but not interfere if Tom insists on going ahead anyway.
4. Say nothing, and help Tom with his plan.
5. Other.

II

Although he is not sure they are doing the right thing, Scott says nothing further to Tom and helps him load the leaking drums onto the truck for their return to ABC. The chemical waste is disposed of on the ABC site, with no apparent complications.

In further justification of his actions, Tom points out to Scott that ABC also saved a lot of money by taking care of the problem themselves rather than having to pay someone else to dispose of the chemicals.

Do you agree that they chose the proper course of action?

III

It might well turn out that, for all practical purposes, this is the end of the matter—that no further complications ever arise. However, there is a "worst case" possible scenario. Consider the following:

It is now several years later. Tom Treehorn has retired and moved to Florida. Scott Lewis left ABC shortly after he discovered the chemical leaks in the warehouse. He is now a senior engineer in a company in a nearby city. He is startled by a front page story in the press. ABC is being charged with contaminating the groundwater in the community surrounding ABC. The paper claims there is substantial evidence that ABC had for years violated the law by dumping waste materials on site. Tom Treehorn is mentioned as the main person who was in charge of overseeing the handling of chemical waste during the years of most flagrant violation. Those years included the short time Scott spent at ABC. A local group of citizens has started a class action suit against ABC.

Three weeks later Scott Lewis receives a letter requesting his appearance at a court hearing concerning the charges against ABC. What should Scott say in his testimony if asked if he was aware of any violations on the part of ABC?

Case 10.3 An Excess?[46]

I

Stephanie Simon knew Environmental Manager Adam Baines would not be pleased with her report on the chemical spill. The data clearly indicated that the spill was large enough that regulations required it to be reported to the state. Stephanie perceived Adam to be someone who thinks industry is overregulated, especially in the environmental area. At the same time, he prided himself as a major player in maintaining XYZ's public reputation as an environmental leader in the chemical industry. "We do a terrific job," he often said. "And we don't need a bunch of hard to read, difficult to interpret, easily misunderstood state regulations to do it. We got along just fine before the regulators ran wild, and we're doing fine now."

When Stephanie presented her report to Adam, he lost his temper. "This is ridiculous! We're not going to send anything like this to the state. A few gallons over the limit isn't worth the time it's going to take to fill out those damned forms. I can't believe you'd submit a report like this. Stephanie, go back to your desk and rework those numbers until it comes out right. I don't want to see anything like this again!"

What factual, conceptual, or application issues does this case raise? Discuss what you think Stephanie should do.

II

Stephanie Simon decided not to change the report. Instead, she submitted an angry resignation to Adam and took a job elsewhere. Bruce Bennett was pleased to have the job vacated by Stephanie Simon. It was an advancement in both responsibility and pay. He had heard that Stephanie left in anger, but he never was told exactly what angered her—just that Adam was not pleased with her reports. All went well for the first several months. Then there was another spill. Bruce's preliminary calculations indicated that the spill exceeded the specified limit requiring a report to the state. He also suspected how Adam would react to the "bad news."

Bruce had worked hard to get his present position, and he looked forward to moving up the ladder at XYZ. He certainly did not want to go job hunting at this time in his career. He thought, "These numbers are so close to falling below the limit that a little 'rounding off' here or there might save us all a lot of grief."

Discuss the factual, conceptual, or application issues this case raises. Discuss what you think Bruce should do.

III

Imagine how the above situations would be evaluated from the following perspectives:

1. A member of the state's environmental protection agency
2. The CEO of XYZ
3. Attorneys at XYZ who handle environmental affairs
4. Other industries faced with similar environmental problems
5. Members of the community whose health may be adversely affected if XYZ and other industries do not responsibly handle environmental problems

To what extent do you think Stephanie, Bruce, and Adam should take into consideration these perspectives in determining what their responsibilities are?

Case 10.4 3M's 3P Plus Plan[47]

Long reputed to be one of the nation's major air polluters, the Minnesota Mining and Manufacturing Company (3M) initiated a vigorous environmental program in the summer of 1990. The Hutchinson, Minnesota, facility installed $26 million worth of equipment to recycle and burn off solvents from its two plants—even though these plants were already meeting EPA standards for emissions. Carol Neis, a 3M engineer, indicated that, after emitting twenty-five million pounds of volatile organic solvents into Hutchinson's air in 1989, "we are achieving 95 to 98 percent reductions" in emissions in 1990.

3M says it has now built its environmental strategy into all layers of management and production. Here are examples.

- 3M wants to make 25 percent of each division's sales come from products introduced within the past five years. Its engineers are expected to regularly revamp production processes with pollution reduction as a primary concern.
- 3M is investing pollution-control equipment in its older plants. It expects by 1993 to cut its emissions by 70 to 75 percent from its 1987 levels. It wants to cut all emissions 90 percent (from the 1987 levels) by the year 2000. It also wants to reduce its hazardous waste by 50 percent from the 1987 levels.
- 3M is forfeiting, rather than selling, its federal pollution-reduction credits. Thus it is reducing overall pollution rather than letting other companies purchase from 3M the right to pollute.
- 3M offers to help customers reduce their waste problems by taking back some of its packaging.
- For years 3M has been cleaning up its operations before it is forced to do so by state or federal regulations.

Whatever other reasons 3M might have for addressing environmental concerns, it views its efforts as good business, at least in the long run. Robert P. Bringer, 3M's vice-president for environmental engineering and pollution control, comments: "Like everyone else we are trying to develop new products more quickly. But regulations have the opposite effect; they are time expanding. So if we get rid of the pollution, we get out from under the regulations."

Alfred Marcus, associate professor at the University of Minnesota's School of Management, concurs. "Why spend the money to clean up pollution at the end of the pipe when you can redesign a process to avoid generating it in the first place?"

3M claims that its more than 2,500 Pollution Prevention Pays programs have saved the company $500 million since the 3P program began in 1975. In 1989 3M introduced its 3P Plus program, calling for each of its divisions to develop plans to minimize waste and increase recycling. These efforts are monitored at the corporate level, and meeting environmental goals is among the criteria used in annual reviews of executive performance.

Discuss the possible implications of 3M's environmental program for its engineers. Assuming 3M is serious about significantly reducing pollution, what kinds of attitudes toward the environmental responsibility do you think 3M would like in its engineers? Does the 3M example provide environmentally concerned engineers at other companies a useful model for advocating a proactive approach to protecting the environment?

Case 10.5 The Exotic Game Ranch[48]

One of the reasons Nathan moved to the rural community in Montana was to get away from the pressurized city life. What he did not count on was the difficulty of relocating his engineering practice. He had a small but profitable firm in Cleveland, but he decided to sell out and move west. Now he was finding that, without his network of friends and clients, getting work was not easy. Several small firms could do the same type of general environmental engineering work that Nathan could do, and these firms all had been able to build up a local history and clientele.

It was therefore with some relief and excitement that Nathan received a call one morning from a prospective client who would not discuss his needs over the telephone but wanted Nathan to drive out to his ranch. It did not take Nathan long to decide to make the drive, even though it was over an hour away. The directions led him into the mountains and onto a dirt road that snaked its way through a canyon, suddenly opening up into a large secluded valley. At the only house in sight he was greeted by his prospective client, who turned out to be a wealthy local rancher named Wayne.

"I won't waste your time," Wayne started right in. "I have big plans for this place and I need your engineering to help me do it. Several of my colleagues and I are planning to build an exotic game ranch here, bringing in tigers from India, lions from Africa, even polar bears from Greenland, and set them loose within a fenced-in area. Hunters who have always wanted to bag such game will come and shoot them. We will arrange the whole hunt, make sure they bag what they contract for, and mount the heads as trophies. There are people out there who are willing to pay very well indeed to get their tiger."

"What I need from you, Nathan," continued Wayne, "is for you to be my engineer for the entire construction phase. We will be doing the fence, holding bins for the animals, the club house, the shooting shed, and all of the water and wastewater systems. I've allotted $10 million for the construction. Your construction management fee will be about $200,000. I want you because I hear you are a darned good engineer. I also understand you are new to this area and wouldn't go blabbing about this to everyone, causing adverse publicity and getting the Eastern press all in an uproar. What do you say?"

Nathan was taken aback. He had heard of such ranches, but he never thought he'd be asked to be the construction engineer for one. He finally asked, rather meekly, if the ranch was legal.

"Of course it's legal," replied Wayne. "We'll be buying the animals from trappers all over the world and shipping them in."

"What about endangered species?" asked Nathan.

"No problem. We'll only use animals that are not on the endangered species list," assured Wayne. He added, with a wink, "But if our suppliers happen to make a mistake, we certainly wouldn't offend them by rejecting the shipment, would we?"

"Look, it's essentially on the up and up. We simply bring in some animals and shoot them. What's the big deal? People have been doing that since the caveman days. And your involvement here is only during the construction phase. If you're not a sportsman, no problem. You just do the construction supervision for us, and get well paid for doing it. You don't have to be here once we start operating. So, do we have a deal?"

"I don't know. Give me a little time to think about it," replied Nathan.

"Sure. Take as much time as you need. But don't take all week. I'm a busy man."

Why do you think Nathan hesitated in doing what, on the face of it, is a golden opportunity for him? What values might be involved in his decision? If you were given such an opportunity, what do you think you should do?

Case 10.6 The Box Turtle[49]

Carole was late to work, and she was stepping on it, scooting down the rural highway, her mind on the problems she was having with the state wildlife people. They kept talking about "ecosystems" and "habitat" and "endangered species." All she wanted to do was build a dam for her client, a dam that was going to create a water supply reservoir and that would bring a new source of much needed water to the community. The citizens of the community were paying good money for this reservoir. Why the state people kept wrangling about wildlife was a mystery to Carole. Didn't they know what was important?

As she kept her eyes on the road and her mind on the job, she spotted a dark brown blob in the middle of the road. As she got closer, she saw that it was a small box turtle, trying to make it across the road. She swerved her car to avoid hitting it and saw in her rear view mirror that it seemed to have survived and was continuing on its way. She smiled and felt pleased that she had avoided the turtle. It seemed the right thing to do.

But then she began thinking about why it was that she had avoided the turtle. Of what use was it to her—or anyone else, for that matter? And she could have caused an accident trying to avoid hitting it. Not very bright, she thought. She had gone to school all those years, had ten years of engineering experience, earned her professional engineering license, and was a respected member of the engineering community. And here she was, endangering her own life, and perhaps others—simply to avoid killing an insignificant box turtle.

As she continued she tried to construct arguments that would explain why she did what she did and why she thought she had done the right thing. But to her consternation, she could not come up with a single convincing argument as to why she ought not to have run over the turtle.

Carole arrived at work still puzzled about her actions. But her attention shifted quickly when she saw another letter from state wildlife people, proposing yet another delay

in the reservoir project. They wanted to do some more studies on the destruction of habitat for the Venus flytrap, an endangered species. She read the letter and stormed out of the office, headed for the state agency ready to do battle in behalf of her clients.

"Who's more important, anyway," she argued, "some so-called 'endangered species,' or people?"

The fish and wildlife agent had heard all this before. "Yes, I understand. But the law says we have to make sure that the habitats of endangered species are not destroyed. I'm just following orders. I agree that the dam and water supply are necessary, but my hands are tied by this law. Venus flytraps are indigenous to this area, and it has to be checked out."

"Well, this whole thing is crazy," Carole replied. "Engineering is supposed to be a people-serving profession. People come first. You are endangering the health, safety, and welfare of the community by holding up the project because of some rare carnivorous plant! It's my job to get this dam built, and I'll fight to get it done on time—endangered species or no endangered species."

How would you explain Carole's reluctance to run over the turtle but her unwillingness to worry about the Venus flytrap? Is she relying on a distinction between her private life and her professional life? Is she really inconsistent, and, if so, how might this inconsistency be resolved? What ethical issues does this case raise?

Other Cases

In light of the ideas and concepts presented in this chapter, consider the following cases already presented in this text.

NOTES

1. Steven Weisskoph, "The Aberdeen Mess," *The Washington Post Magazine* (January 15, 1989).

2. *The Aberdeen Three*, a case prepared under National Science Foundation Grant No. DIR-9012252. Principal investigators were Michael J. Rabins, Charles E. Harris, Jr., Charles Samson, and Raymond W. Flumerfelt.

3. P. Aarne Vesilind, "Environmental Ethics and Civil Engineering," *The Environmental Professional*, 9 (1987), 336–342. This discussion of ASCE activities relies on Vesilind's account.

4. It is important to keep in mind that such committees comprise volunteers, representing engineers in universities, government, and industry. Policy positions must be compromises that satisfy different interests and viewpoints.

5. Of course all issues will not fit neatly into these two categories. And if we interpret "health" broadly enough, all environmental issues may affect human health, either physical or psychological. Nevertheless, we believe the distinction is useful.

6. Rachel Carson, *Silent Spring* (Boston: Houghton Mifflin Co., 1962).

7. D. L. Meadows, D. H. Meadows, J. Randers, and W. W. Behrens, III, *The Limits of Growth: A Report for the Club of Rome's Project on the Predicament of Mankind* (New York: Potomac Associates, New American Library, 1974).

8. Joseph M. Petulla, "Environmental Management in Industry," in Albert Flores, ed., *Ethics and Risk Management in Engineering* (Lanham, Md.: University Press of America, 1989), p. 146. For a fuller discussion of the ethical aspects of this issue, see C. E. Harris, Jr., "Manufacturers and the Environment: Three Alternative Views," in Mo Jamshidi, Mo Shahinpoor, and J. H. Mullins, eds., *Environmentally Conscious Manufacturing: Recent Advances* (Albuquerque, N.M.: ECM Press, 1991), pp. 195–203.

9. From a 1982 documentary film, "The Business of America." (News Reel, San Francisco).

See Petulla, "Environmental Management in Industry," p. 143.

10. Milton Friedman, "The Social Responsibility of Business Is to Increase Its Profits," *The New York Times Magazine* (September 13, 1970).

11. David Okrent and Chris Whipple, *An Approach to Societal Risk Acceptance Criteria and Risk Management*. Report UCLA-Eng-7746 (Los Angeles: UCLA School of Engineering and Applied Sciences, 1977). For some skeptics, one of the prime examples of public fickleness is the discrepancy between market behavior and voting behavior on environmental issues. For example, a recent survey by the *Wall Street Journal* and NBC found that on the one hand, 53 percent of the public say that fundamental changes in lifestyle, rather than scientific advances, will be the source of the needed changes in quality of the environment. On the other hand, a thirty-seven-year-old insurance claims manager voiced a typical comment when he said he probably would not pay 15–20 cents more for a gallon of gasoline if it were significantly less polluting. However, he went on to say, "But if they passed a law, I would not mind it." The insurance manager might well argue that this response is not an example of fickleness on his part, but rather reflects the realization that his action would have no effect unless it is shared by others.

12. Petulla, "Environmental Management in Industry," p. 151.

13. For an account of the Bhopal incident, see Paul Shrivastava, *Bhopal: Anatomy of a Crisis* (Cambridge, Mass.: Ballinger Publishing, 1987).

14. Most of this information was taken from material published by the Responsible Care Information Center, 2501 M Street, NW, Washington, D.C. 20037.

15. William F. Baxter, *People or Penguins: The Case for Optimal Pollution* (New York: Columbia University Press, 1974), p. 9.

16. We are indebted to Michael Davis for making this point to us.

17. For the suggestions of this and the following criterion, see William D. Ruckelshaus, "Risk, Science, and Democracy," *Issues in Science and Technology*, 1, no. 3 (Spring 1985), 19–38. Mr. Ruckelshaus is a former administrator of the Environmental Protection Agency.

18. This section utilizes several sources, both for legal citations and ideas. See Mark Sagoff, "Where Ickes Went Right or Reason and Rationality in Environmental Law," *Ecology Law Quarterly* (1987), pp. 265-323. See also Al H.

Ringleb, Roger E. Meiners, and Frances L. Edwards, *Managing in the Legal Environment* (St. Paul, Minn.: West, 1990), pp. 553-583. See also Carl F. Cranor, *Regulating Toxic Substances: A Philosophy of Science and the Law* (New York: Oxford University Press, 1993), especially pp. 160–163.

19. 42 U.S.C. sect. 4331 (1982) [note 20].

20. 29 U.S.C., sect. 655(b)(5)(1976).

21. 42 U.S.C., sect. 7412(b)(1)(B)(1982) [note 21].

22. 33 U.S.C., sects. 1251-1376 (1982) & Sup. III 1985 [note 21].

23. 42 U.S.C., sect. 6901-6986 (1982) & Sup. (1985) [note 21].

24. *International Harvester* v. *Ruckelshaus,* 478 F.2d 615 (D.C. Cir 1973).

25. *Portland Cement Association* v. *Ruckelshaus,* 486 F.2d 375, 387 (D.C. Cir 1973) [note 197].

26. *Industrial Union Dept. AFL-CIO* v. *American Petroleum Institute,* 448 U.S. 607, 642 (1980).

27. *Natural Resources Defense Council* v. *EPA,* 804 F.2d 710 (D.C. Cir 1986).

28. *Industrial Union Dept., AFL-CIO* v. *Hodgson,* 162 U.S. App. D.C. at 342, 499 F.2d at 467, 477–78 (D.C. Cir 1974).

29. Cranor, *Regulating Toxic Substances*, p. 161.

30. Ibid., pp. 161–162.

31. Sagoff, "Where Ickes Went Right," p. 314.

32. For suggestions for this utilitarian argument, see Cranor, *Regulating Toxic Substances*, pp. 163–168.

33. Recall Mrs. Steve Talbert's description, quoted in section 8.5, of the tragic effects on her husband of brown lung disease.

34. Baxter, *People or Penguins*, p. 5.

35. For a discussion of speciesism, see Peter Singer, *Practical Ethics* (Cambridge, England: Cambridge University Press, 1979), chapter 3.

36. Aldo Leopold, *A Sand County Almanac* (New York: Oxford University Press, 1949), pp. viii, ix. Quoted in Edward Johnson, "Treating the

Dirt: Environmental Ethics and Moral Theory," in Tom Regan, ed., *Earthbound: New Introductory Essays in Environmental Ethics* (New York: Random House, 1984), p. 352.

37. Leopold, *A Sand County Almanac*, p. 216. Quoted in Johnson, p. 352.

38. Leopold, *A Sand County Almanac*, pp. 224–225. Quoted in Johnson, p. 352.

39. Paul W. Taylor, "The Ethics of Respect for Nature," *Environmental Ethics*, 3, no. 3 (Fall 1981), 208–209. Quoted in William Aiken, "Ethical Issues in Agriculture," in Tom Regan, ed., *Earthbound*, p. 269.

40. John Rodman, "The Liberation of Nature?" *Inquiry*, 20 (1977), 126. Quoted in Johnson in Regan, *Earthbound*, pp. 355–356.

41. The right not to perform an abortion is explicitly asserted in AMA opinion 2.01. However, the code provision has wider implications.

42. Stephen H. Unger, *Controlling Technology: Ethics and the Responsible Engineer* (New York: Holt, Rinehart & Winston, 1982), pp. 37–38.

43. See Unger, *Controlling Technology*, pp. 37–38.

44. This case is part of NSF Grant No. DIR-8820837. See Michael S. Pritchard, ed., *Teaching Engineering Ethics: A Case Study Approach*, case with commentaries, pp. 284–309.

45. Ibid.

46. Ibid.

47. The following information is drawn from John Holusha, "Hutchinson No Longer Holds Its Nose: At 3M Cleaning Up Pollution Has Become the Corporate Ethic. It's Paying Off," *New York Times* (February 3, 1991), section 3, pp. 1 and 6.

48. This fictional case was developed by P. Aarne Vesilind, Department of Civil and Environmental Engineering, Duke University. Used with permission.

49. Ibid.

Chapter 11

Promoting and Enforcing Ethics

James graduated from Engineering Tech two years ago. Since then he has been employed by Brian and Associates, a small civil engineering firm.[1] He has been assigned to design schools, overhead walkways between buildings, and other projects. For some time he has been concerned that he may not have the experience required for such assignments, and he has conveyed this concern to his employer, Charles Brian. Charles replied that he always checks James's work and has found it satisfactory.

Later James learns that in fact Charles does not always check his work, but places his seal on it and sends the designs to his clients. He further learns that Charles places his seal on many designs that he has not checked and even allows other engineers to use his seal and forge his signature.

James becomes increasingly concerned about his employment situation and finally decides to look for another job. He tells his prospective employer why he is leaving Brian and Associates, and the employer hires him at once. James is encouraged by his new employer to report his former employer to the state registration board, which initiates action against Brian and Associates.

11.1   Introduction

This fictionalized version of an actual case illustrates the importance of ethical and professional standards in the experience of one young engineer. For a community to function properly, there must be rules, along with some method of promoting and enforcing them. The responsibility for promoting and enforcing ethics also applies to a professional community.

In the engineering community the responsibility for promoting high standards of ethical and professional conduct falls on several groups. Educational institutions clearly have an obligation to teach professionsal ethics. Engineering instructors should raise ethical considerations in the classroom, and engineering schools should offer courses in professional ethics. Unlike Brian and Associates, business organizations should also support engineering ethics and professionalism and refrain from placing their employees in situations where they must resign in order to maintain professional integrity.

We also believe that a special responsibility for promoting ethics lies with professional engineering societies. Professional societies are the proper forum for debating the controversial ethical issues that face the engineering profession. By promulgating ethical codes and recognizing and supporting members who uphold professional standards, they can do much to make ethical issues important for their members. We begin by considering some historical aspects of professional societies in the United States. Then we examine some of the ways that professional engineering societies already promote ethical conduct and some of the ways in which they might do so in the future.

The primary responsibility for enforcing ethical standards in the engineering community should rest with state boards of registration. State boards have the power to investigate violations of their own codes of ethics, to administer penalties and, in extreme cases, to revoke the Professional Engineer (PE) license. We therefore describe the activities of state boards of registration and of a national organization for state boards. Then we look at the experiences of one state board in enforcing ethics, the Texas State Board of Registration for Professional Engineers.

Engineers are not required to have a PE license to engage in all types of engineering work. This weakens the powers of state boards of engineering registration to enforce ethical standards in the engineering profession, because their chief power is the right to revoke the PE license. Therefore we also consider some of the arguments for and against mandatory registration of engineers, as well as arguments for and against the so-called industry exemption from registration.

11.2   Professional Engineering Societies: Promoting Ethics

Professional societies occupy a special place in the engineering community. Undoubtedly, the major function of most engineering societies is to promote the discovery and dissemination of technical knowledge. Most societies recognize, however, that they also have responsibilities regarding professional ethics. Precisely what these functions are is open to discussion.

Engineering societies may have some obligations to enforce ethics. Engineering societies do engage in investigations of ethical misconduct, much of it in an unobtrusive way. Such investigation may be especially appropriate when members are not registered professional engineers and therefore do not come under the authority of state registration boards. In these cases the only kind of discipline for ethical violations comes from their professional societies.

The professional societies, however, should probably not be expected to be extensively involved in disciplining wayward members. One reason is that the most severe penalty that a professional society can impose is the revocation of an engineer's membership, and membership in a professional society is rarely if ever a requirement for performing engineering work. Another reason is that disciplining wayward members might involve expenses that would impose heavy and perhaps intolerable financial burdens on professional societies. The expenses involved in investigating wayward members could be considerable, and there might also be legal fees.

A 1979 legal case, involving the American Institute of Architects (AIA), illustrates the problems that professional societies could encounter in attempting to enforce their own codes.[2] Keep in mind that the AIA is *not* the registration board that confers the architect's license, but a professional society for architects. The greatest punishment that the AIA can administer is the revocation of society membership, and society membership is not required in order to pursue a career in architecture.

Mr. Mardirosian was hired by the city of Washington, D.C., to review the work of another architect who had designed the alteration and reconditioning of Union Station and its new National Visitor Center. The earlier architect's contract contained a provision that allowed the city government to terminate his services at its discretion. The city decided to take advantage of this provision and to employ Mr. Mardirosian to complete the architectural services for the visitor center.

Mr. Mardirosian was charged with supplanting another architect in violation of AIA Standard 9:

> An architect shall not attempt to obtain, offer to undertake or accept a commission for which the architect knows another legally qualified individual or firm has been selected or employed, until the architect has evidence that the latter's agreement has been terminated and the architect gives the latter written notice that the architect is so doing.

The AIA's National Judicial Board agreed with the charge against Mardirosian and recommended expulsion of Mardirosian from the AIA. After an appeal by Mr. Mardirosian, the discipline was modified to a one-year suspension of his membership.

The architect sued the AIA in the United States District Court for the District of Columbia, alleging that the ethics standards constituted unreasonable restraint of trade in violation of the Sherman Antitrust Act. The district court granted Mardirosian's motion for summary judgment as to liability. The amount of fines, including triple damages, was to be determined in a jury trial. In June 1980 the AIA voted to make compliance with its ethical standards voluntary rather than mandatory. In late 1981 the case was settled when AIA paid Mardirosian $700,000 in damages. It had also incurred approximately $500,000 in legal expenses.

The Mardirosian case is only a single example, and there are questions as to whether the AIA applied its own standards correctly. In this particular case, many might be inclined to agree with Mr. Mardirosian. Nevertheless, the case illustrates the difficulties that professional engineering societies might face if they made a serious and concerted effort to discipline and expel members who violated their codes of ethics.

The experiences of the AIA in the Mardirosian case may also explain why many professional societies prefer to investigate ethics cases in an atmosphere of confidentiality and outside the reach of the press. In a confidential setting both the societies and those accused of wrongdoing can more easily reach accommodation, and they can do so without the burden of large legal fees. Even with the protection of confidentiality, there are severe limits to the abilities of professional societies to enforce ethics.

Professional societies can, however, promote ethics. The promotion of ethics involves activities that support, reward, and encourage ethical conduct, rather than punish members who act in an unethical manner. Registration boards are more likely to have the legal and financial resources for ethics enforcement, but they are probably less equipped to perform other functions than professional societies. For example, professional societies are the proper forum for debating what should be in a professional code of ethics. Should engineering codes have more to say about the environment? Should they have more to say about the professional rights of engineers in the workplace? Should they have stronger statements about conflicts of interest? Members of state registration boards would probably be more inclined to follow the lead of professional societies on such issues.

Promoting ethics might also involve activities such as honoring and rewarding members for outstanding conduct in the area of ethics. Some societies already have such awards. They could also help with the legal expenses of engineers who have been unjustly dismissed for blowing the whistle in the public interest. Helping employees who have been unjustly dismissed to find new jobs would also be a service to the profession. Educating the public to the risk involved in new technologies and helping the public to avoid unnecessary fears of technology would be an invaluable service, provided it was not perceived as merely self-serving. Finally, rendering decisions on the application of their codes in disputed cases—an activity already engaged in by the Board of Ethical Review of the National Society of Professional Engineers—can help engineers to understand the practical implications of their codes.

Thus, there may be a natural division of labor between state registration boards and professional societies. While registration boards are more likely to have the legal and financial means to enforce ethical standards—at least within the community of registered professional engineers—professional societies may be better equipped to promote ethics.

Professional societies can do much to set the tone of a profession, probably more than state registration boards. One of the recurrent themes in the history of American technical and engineering societies, however, is the tension between a business orientation and a professional (or at least technical and scientific) orientation. Such tension does not appear to us to be necessary, and it can be destructive to the common interests of both business and engineering professionalism. Nevertheless, it has often existed. A look at the history of engineering societies in the United States demonstrates this claim.

11.3 American Engineering Societies: Business Versus Professionalism

The tension between the business and professional orientations of engineering societies often expresses itself in debates over membership criteria. Broad and inclusive criteria allow businesspeople, many with relatively scant engineering training or experience, to be members. More restrictive standards, which emphasize academic training and engineering experience (such as being in "responsible charge" of engineering projects), favor a more professional orientation.

As an illustration, consider the American Institute of Mining Engineers (AIME), founded in 1871. The requirements of education and experience for membership in the AIME were generally much lower than the criteria of the American Society of Civil Engineers (ASCE), organized in its present form in 1867. The AIME was consequently much more business oriented. The first secretary of the AIME, the respected and strong-willed Rossiter W. Raymond, boasted that the AIME's membership included "common miners, laborers, mine foremen, and people who cannot spell."[3] He was also proud of the fact that many distinguished "captains of industry" were on its membership rolls. As editor of the AIME journal, Raymond refused to print discussions of such matters as the social responsibilities of engineers, conservation, and professional ethics, calling these concerns a type of "hysteria."[4]

In 1908 H. M. Chance led a revolt against Raymond and eventually formed a new organization, the Mining and Metallurgical Society of America (MMSA). The charter members of this short-lived organization agreed that the organization should:

1. Represent professional mining engineers on matters of ethics and public welfare

2. Develop strict membership requirements similar to those of the ASCE, thereby excluding business interests

3. Create a strong regional organization to prevent the society from being controlled by a single clique[5]

Engineering has no single society that clearly represents the entire profession, which may be partially explained by the business/professionalism division in engineering. Engineers with a strong professional orientation tend to favor a single society. Those with a strong industry orientation often want a smaller society that focuses on their specialized interest. The American Society of Mechanical Engineers (ASME) was formed in 1880. In 1913 the ASME brought about the formation of a Joint Committee on a Proposed Universal Code of Ethics in an attempt to construct a code of ethics that would be acceptable to all engineering societies. The code that was produced was not acceptable to all engineering societies, and the attempt was a failure. Several later attempts have been made by other groups, but none has been successful. The ASME finally adopted a code for itself in 1914.[6]

The American Institute of Electrical Engineers (AIEE) was formed in 1884. In 1963 it merged with the Institute of Radio Engineers (IRE), founded in 1912, to become the American Institute of Electrical and Electronics Engineers, an organization that is now, as the Institute of Electrical and Electronics Engineers (IEEE), the largest engineering society in the United States. The AIEE adopted a code of ethics in 1912. The code was oriented toward consultants, even though consulting firms are much less common in electrical than in civil engineering. The code treated issues such as conflict of interest to the exclusion of issues faced by engineers in a bureaucratic setting. Schuyler S. Wheeler, an early president of the AIEE who was instrumental in the creation of the code, assumed that loyalty to the client was primary "and the one to which all others must give way if there is any conflict."[7] The code adopted gave a preeminent place to loyalty to the client or employer. Wheeler thought that the engineer's duty to the public was "largely educational."[8] On the other hand, the AIEE code of 1914 also begins with instructions to the engineer to "be guided by the highest principles of honor" and to "satisfy himself to the best of his ability that the enterprises with which he becomes identified are of legitimate character." It may be that the duties to the employer were assumed to be unlikely to harm the public.[9]

Engineering historian Edwin Layton sees the ASME and AIEE as attempting to occupy a middle ground between ASCE's more professional orientation and AIME's orientation toward industry. The manner in which the two societies constructed a middle ground took different forms, however. The ASME adopted a rather open membership policy, much like the AIME, so that many businesspeople could become members. Even so, until 1904 the ASME was dominated by engineers who wanted to distinguish themselves from businesspeople on the grounds that engineers are the producers of new knowledge and businesspeople are simply the users of new knowledge. The AIEE, by contrast, instituted high standards for membership from the beginning. In spite of this orientation, the AIEE was for some of its history dominated by officers who had a strong industry orientation.[10]

Around the turn of the century, new trends led to the AIEE's becoming more professionally oriented and the ASME's becoming more business oriented. The explanation for this change, according to Layton, is that electrical engineering shifted to a scientific basis earlier than mechanical engineering, because of developments such as advances in physics, the arrival of alternating current, and more sophisticated communications devices. Unlike mechanical engineering, electrical engineering does not have a centuries-old craft tradition. This may also have made the transition to a scientific basis easier. At any rate, inventors and scientists became more prominent in the AIEE.

These changes increased the influence of inventors and scientists in the AIEE. The ASME, by contrast, was dominated in its earlier years by the interests of utilities. Later, in the 1930s, the utilities came to have a powerful influence in the AIEE, leading to a prohibition of papers dealing with costs and rates in the utility industry. Some critics argued that this practice seriously limited the efforts of government agencies to regulate public utilities.[11]

The American Institute of Chemical Engineers (AIChE) was founded in 1908. The early energy of the AIChE was taken up in defending the legitimacy of chemical engineering as a branch of engineering rather than as an offshoot of chemistry. Richard K. Meade, who called the organizational meeting that developed the concept of a chemical engineering society, made the case that "chemicals" did indeed occupy a legitimate place in the engineering profession. He pointed out, for example, that neither chemists nor mechanical engineers were the most qualified to build a chemical plant. The expertise necessary to perform this function should, he believed, be a part of a new branch of engineering.

Perhaps because of the need to educate engineers and the public on the necessity of its existence, the AIChE was from the beginning a leader in educational activities. It also became the first engineering society to try to accredit university engineering departments. The AIChE adopted a code of ethics only four years after its founding.

This brief survey of engineering societies shows several themes, some of which we can review.

First, the engineering profession in the United States does not have as much organizational unity as the other professions, being splintered into a large number of specialized societies. There is no single engineering society that forcefully represents the interests and ideals of the engineering profession to the profession itself and to the general public. In spite of several attempts, engineering societies have not been able to agree on a code for all engineers.

Second, concern for issues of professionalism and ethics has not been prominent in engineering societies. While the ASCE may be, from a historical standpoint, the foremost proponent of engineering ethics, historian Layton comments that it refused to adopt a code of ethics for the first fifty years of its existence. Even then, those who advocated a code of ethics did so "for its prestige value, rather than for any serious concern with self-policing."[12] Summarizing his survey of engineering societies and their commitment to professional ethics, Layton concludes by noting that

> Only a handful [of engineering societies] manifest any real concern for the professional motivation and ethics of their members. If such concern is a basic attribute of a profession, then it is also a requirement of a 'professional' society. It would seem that relatively few organizations in engineering can claim that distinction. . . . profession-wide, the emphasis given in engineering to professional motivation and conduct is spotty at best, and is essentially nonexistent in far too many areas."[13]

This is not to say that engineers have been less ethical in their professional work than physicians, lawyers, dentists, architects, veterinarians, or other professionals. The more likely consequence is that engineers do not have the same sense of their identity as professionals as the others. Further, recall that these views were written by Layton more than twenty years ago and may not necessarily be representative now.

Third, engineers have disagreed over whether their societies should have a professional or an industry orientation. Some societies, such as the AIME, have been primarily industry-oriented. In the extreme cases, organizations such as the National Electric Light Association, which flourished in the 1920s, are little more than trade associations. Usually the term "engineer" is not present in the titles of these organizations. Societies such as the AIChE have been more oriented toward the professional concerns and obligations of their members. Still others, such as the ASME and the IEEE, have oscillated between the two orientations.

As Layton himself points out, however, the conflict between the business orientation and the engineering orientation should not be exaggerated.[14] Neither could make important contributions to society without the other. Rather, he characterizes the problem in the following way:

> The problem has been to find suitable mechanisms of balance and accommodation. One of the basic problems of American engineers is that the balance has tended to shift too far in the direction of business, and accommodation has taken place largely on terms laid down by employers. The professional independence of engineers has been drastically curtailed. The losers are not just engineers. The public would benefit greatly from the unbiased evaluations of technical matters that an independent profession would provide. American business too might profit in the long run from the presence of a loyal opposition.[15]

While most engineers might find the term "loyal opposition" disturbing and inappropriate, it does seem true that engineers do not have the same sense of their "professional autonomy" as do other professionals. That is, engineers may not have as strong a sense as they should of their prerogative to make judgments about matters within their professional expertise and to have those judgments respected by managers and the public, especially where the safety, health, and welfare of the public are concerned.

Layton believes that one reason for the influence of business on professional societies is that many engineers aspire to become managers. Even in 1946 a survey of the six largest American engineering societies revealed that over one-third of their members were engaged in management. As far back as 1924, a survey of 5,000 engineers by the Society for the Promotion of Engineering Education revealed that eventually over 60 percent of engineers in the survey made the transition to management.[16] Layton characterizes the problem posed by the aspirations of engineers to management positions in the following way:

> The promise of a lucrative career in business does much to ensure the loyalty of the engineering staff. Conversely, it undermines engineers' identification with their profession. Social mobility carries with it an alternative set of values associated with the businessman's ideology of individualism. These values compete with, and to some degree conflict with, those of professionalism. Thus, professionals stress the importance of expert knowledge, but businessmen stress the role of personal characteristics, such as loyalty, drive, initiative, and hard work. Professions value lifetime dedication. But business makes engineering a phase in a successful career rather than a career in itself. Insofar as business treats engineering merely as a stepping stone to management, it represents a denial of much that professions stand for.[17]

Layton's thesis, although it agrees with the opinions of some other students of the engineering profession, may be too extreme. A more plausible explanation of the interest of engineers in business may be that their work is so closely connected with business enterprises that they cannot realistically ignore business considerations. Nevertheless, engineering societies could probably do more to promote engineering ethics than they have done in the past. One notable example of promoting ethics is the NSPE's Board of Ethical Review.

11.4 The NSPE Board of Ethical Review

The National Society of Professional Engineers established its Board of Ethical Review (BER) in 1958. The board considers questions submitted by state societies or members, rendering opinions on the ethical and professional propriety of the actions described in the cases. It bases its judgments on the NSPE code of ethics and its judgments do not attempt to criticize the code or suggest modifications of it. The board emphasizes that its judgments are to have educational value only. It does not engage in any independent attempt to investigate and confirm the facts presented to it, and it has no legal power to enforce its judgments. Nevertheless, the activities of the board stimulate discussion of ethical issues. The opinions of the board, which are clear and well reasoned, usually provide helpful guidance for engineers.

The following list is a partial tabulation of the categories of cases the board has considered from 1958 to 1988. The board considered 328 cases during this period, but many of them are one-of-a-kind cases. The categories listed in Table 11.1 (with the number of cases in the category listed to the right) are those that contain significant numbers of cases or the categories that we believe are particularly important from an ethical standpoint.

Table 11.1
Partial Tabulation of the Cases Considered by the NSPE's Board of Ethical Review, 1958–1988

Category	Number of Cases
Advertising	36
Competitive Bidding	11
Conflict of Interest	35
Contingent Contracts	8
Contingent Fees	5
Environmental Concerns	3
Free Engineering	6
Gifts	6
Patents	3
Political Activities and Contributions	9
Recruitment of Engineers	5
Solicitation of Business	4
Supplanting Another Engineer	8
Whistleblowing	2

As this table suggests, most of the cases have to do with problems arising in the private practice of engineering. Most of the firms involved are civil engineering firms, where most of the private practice of engineering takes place. The cases involving engineering in the corporate setting are less numerous.

The cases are designated by the year in which they are considered and the order during the year in which they are considered. Thus case 87-4 is the fourth case considered in 1987. Case 87-4 involves accepting a gift and a possible conflict of interest.

The care and thoughtfulness displayed in the decisions of the board illustrate many of the concepts and distinctions we discussed in the preceding chapters. The board's primary limitation is that most of its decisions have to do with ethical problems that arise in private engineering practice, even though this sector accounts for only a small percentage of engineers. To be sure, the board can deal with only the cases presented to it, and most of the cases have been submitted by private firms. Perhaps the Board should be more aggressive in soliciting cases involving engineers in large corporate or government organizations, and engineers other than civil engineers. Rendering decisions on cases involving engineers in the corporate setting would probably increase the board's influence in the engineering profession.

Despite this limitation, the NSPE's Board of Ethical Review is an impressive example of the way an engineering society can promote professional ethics. The Board's opinions stimulate interest in and discussion of ethical issues, provide guidance in resolving the issues, and demonstrate the importance that a professional society attaches to ethics. We have already presented several examples of BER cases, but we shall present several more examples at the end of this chapter.

11.5   American Engineering Societies: Present Configurations and Trends

The engineering profession in the United States is represented by a number of societies. Most of the larger ones are Participating Bodies in the Accreditation Board for Engineering & Technology, an organization founded in 1935, which, is responsible, among other functions, for accrediting engineering schools. In addition to the 21 participating bodies, there is one Associate Body, and there are 5 Affiliate Bodies. Table 11.2 lists the ABET participating bodies and their memberships. It is a convenient summary of many of the most important engineering societies in the United States.

As we have pointed out, there is no equivalent in engineering to the American Medical Association or the American Bar Association, i.e., a single professional society to which a considerable portion of the members of the profession belong and which the public recognizes as representing the profession. Members of the engineering profession belong to more than eighty professional organizations.

Table 11.2
Participating Bodies in the Accreditation Board for
Engineering and Technology

American Academy of Environmental Engineers (AAEE):
Founded 1913. Membership (July 1993) 2,500

American Congress on Surveying and Mapping (ASCM)
Founded 1941. Membership (November 1993) 7,483, including students

American Institute of Aeronautics and Astronautics, Inc. (AIAA)
Consolidated in 1963 from the American Rocket Society (founded 1931) and
the Institute of the Aerospace Science (founded 1932). Membership (October
1993) 37,924, including students

American Institute of Chemical Engineers (AIChE)
Founded 1908. Membership (September 1993) 58,850, including students

American Nuclear Society (ANS)
Founded 1954. Membership (September 1993) 16,000, including students

American Society of Agricultural Engineers (ASAE)
Founded 1907. Membership (September 1993) 9,267, including students

American Society of Civil Engineers (ASCE)
Founded 1852. Membership (September 1993) 113,638, including students

American Society for Engineering Education (ASEE)
Founded 1893. Membership (October 1993) 10,600, including students

**American Society of Heating, Refrigerating and Air-Conditioning Engineers,
Inc. (ASHRAE)**
Consolidated in 1959 from the American Society of Heating and Air-
Conditioning Engineers (founded in 1894 as the American Society of Heating
and Ventilating Engineers) and the American Society of Refrigerating Engineers
(founded in 1904). Membership (September 1993) 47,655, including students

The American Society of Mechanical Engineers (ASME)
Founded 1880. Membership (October 1993) 147,748, including students

Institute of Industrial Engineers, Inc. (IIE)
Founded 1848. Membership (September 1993) 29,000, including students

The Institute of Electrical and Electronics Engineers (IEEE)
Founded 1884. Consolidated in 1963 from American Institute of Electrical
Engineers and Institute of Radio Engineers. Membership (June 1993) 320,000,
including students

The Minerals, Metals and Materials Society (TMS)
Founded 1959. Membership (October 1993) approximately 11,000, including
students

National Council of Examiners for Engineering and Surveying (NCEES)
Founded 1920. Membership (September 1993) approximately 650 members of
68 member boards. Number of Registered Professional Engineers 641,383

National Institute of Ceramic Engineers (NICE)
Founded 1938. Membership (September 1993) 1,665, including students

National Society of Professional Engineers (NSPE)
Founded 1934. Membership (September 1993) approximately 69,000, including students

Society of Automotive Engineers (SAE)
Founded 1905. Membership (September 1993) 75,000, including students

Society of Manufacturing Engineers (SME)
Founded 1932. Membership (October 1993) 70,276, including students

Society for Mining, Metallurgy, and Exploration, Inc. (SME-AIME)
Founded 1959. Membership (January 1993) 18,835, including students

Society of Naval Architects and Marine Engineers (SNAME)
Founded 1893. Membership (October 1993) 9,700, including students

Society of Petroleum Engineers (SPE)
Founded 1959. Membership (September 1993) approximately 53,100, including students

There have, however, been several attempts to form what are usually referred to as "umbrella" organizations to which all engineers could belong. One of the early such attempts was the American Association of Engineers, founded in 1915. Another attempt was the Engineers Joint Council, founded in 1944.

The most recent such attempt is the American Association of Engineering Societies, whose membership ranks include sixteen member societies (including the major organizations in chemical, electrical, mechanical, and civil engineering), seven associate societies, and six regional societies.[18]

While not a true "umbrella" organization, the National Society of Professional Engineers, founded in 1934, is especially concerned with the professional development of engineers. The society is comprised mostly of civil engineers, especially civil engineers in private practice. However, it is open to professional engineers in all engineering disciplines. A code for the society was proposed in 1935, but none was adopted until 1946.[19]

It is also important to take note of the very different orientations and functions of the various engineering societies. Some societies, such as the ASME, IEEE, AIChE, and ASCE, are primarily concerned with the advancement of technical knowledge in their respective branches of engineering. Their orientation may be especially appealing to academic and research-oriented engineers. Other societies, such as the Society of Automotive Engineers, are more oriented toward the application of engineering knowledge to manufacturing. Still other societies, such as the NSPE, are primarily concerned with professional issues, such as licensing and legal liabilities of engineers. Since the NSPE engages in lobbying in Washington and elsewhere, it does not have the tax-exempt status of societies such as the ASME. In its attempt to promote professionalism in engineering, the NSPE established the Board of Ethical Review. We considered the activities of the board in Section 11.4.

11.6 Should Engineering Societies Be More Aggressive in Promoting Ethics?

There are other examples of ways that professional engineering societies can and do promote ethics. Of course many activities that might best be classified as enforcing rather than promoting ethics should be done in a private and unobtrusive way. For example, professional societies usually conduct investigations of wrongdoing by members out of the light of publicity. This approach protects innocent engineers who have been accused of wrongdoing because of malice or false information. Those who are guilty of wrongdoing are also probably more likely to cooperate and to reform when they do not have to defend themselves from public criticism. Nevertheless, ethics cannot be effectively promoted without public evidence of the fact that professional societies take ethics seriously. Here are some additional ways that this is done or might be done.

First, professional societies must continue to serve as forums for open debate of ethical issues. Most of the time this debate will be centered on proposed modifications in a society's code of ethics. In the previous chapter we described some of the controversy over environmental provisions in the codes of the IEEE, ASCE, and ASME. We believe that public discussion of such issues, both in the meetings and in the publications of professional societies, is beneficial. State boards of registration are not proper forums for such debates. They are composed of only a handful of professionals, and they may or may not represent the beliefs of registered engineers in a state. Furthermore, most engineers are not registered. Finally, sometimes different groups of engineers treat many issues differently. For example, chemical engineers may have more knowledge of the effects of water pollution than other types of engineers. Electrical and computer science engineers may know more about the improper use of information from computers than other engineers.

Second, engineering societies should emphasize recognition of ethical engineers and ethical employers. Societies can give this recognition in the form of awards. Such awards stimulate thought and discussion about ethical issues and demonstrate the importance that the society attaches to ethics and professionalism. At the present time, two of the best known of such awards for employees are the Award for Outstanding Service in the Public Interest of the IEEE's Committee on Social Implications of Technology and a similar award given by the American Association for the Advancement of Science (AAAS). The IEEE gave its award to three Bay Area Rapid Transit engineers in San Francisco and to Virginia Edgerton. The AAAS award was given to Roger Boisjoly. We believe that every major engineering society should have such an award and give it a place of prominence in its meetings and in its literature.

There is no reason to limit such awards to employees. Employers who exhibit outstanding records in the area of ethics and professionalism should also be rewarded. Many employers have long traditions of adhering to ethical principles in their relationships with clients or customers and employees; they deserve to be honored and recognized as much as ethical employees.

Third, engineering societies could assist ethical professionals whose ethical conduct has led to retaliation by employers. They could establish funds to pay legal expenses of engineers who are contesting discharge or other types of retaliation. These funds would not only assist engineers in a time of financial and emotional stress but also signal the support of their professional colleagues.

Societies could also assist engineers who have been discharged to find new employment. Often such engineers have trouble finding new jobs even though their dismissal was unjustified and was a result of conduct in the public interest. Stephen Unger has pointed out that an ethics committee could ascertain the facts of the case and then, if a member warranted support, help in finding new employment. A society might even make a list of employers who would be particularly sympathetic to ethical employees who have been dismissed without just cause.[20] This kind of support would require investigation by a committee and could be controversial, time consuming, and expensive, but it would be of enormous help to ethical professionals.

Fourth, professional societies could establish "ethics hotlines" or other services whereby engineers could seek advice on difficult issues they face. The hotlines could also be a source of information as to what assistance an engineer might expect from his or her professional society. Many large organizations already have such hotlines, and they have often been an effective way of resolving problems, usually before they reach crisis proportions.

There are other things that professional societies might do to support ethics, but many societies are probably reluctant to endorse even these proposals for promoting ethics. They may fear being embroiled in controversy, litigation, and expense that could limit their ability to achieve their primary mission: encouraging the discovery and dissemination of technical knowledge.

Stephen Unger believes these fears are exaggerated.[21] Engineering societies can protect themselves from legal action by making an honest effort to find the truth in the cases they investigate and by displaying a consistent record of commitment to the public welfare rather than the self-interest of engineers. It is useful to keep in mind, he believes, that truth is an absolute defense against libel or slander in the American legal system, and evidence of a sincere attempt to find the truth is a strong defense.

At least two active organizations have, according to Unger, been successful in escaping significant legal action because of their commitment to objectivity. For over half a century the American Association of University Professors (AAUP) has been investigating universities that violate the academic freedom of professors but it has never been successfully sued for damages. The Consumers Union (CU) has also been publishing its reports on consumer products for about 50 years and has had only one judgment against it. This judgment (for less than $16,000) was overturned on appeal. These organizations have a strong reputation for investigating issues objectively and for acting in the public interest rather than in their self-interest. If professional societies act in a similar fashion, they will be reasonably successful in protecting themselves from litigation.

Many societies may be reluctant to actively support their members for fear of the loss of industry support. Unger believes this fear is also unfounded. Industry needs access to the technical information disseminated by technical societies. It also benefits from the participation of its employees in standards committees and the ability to advertise in society publications. Furthermore, "an organization that acquired a reputation for being hostile to engineering societies on the grounds of the latter's support for ethical engineers would thereby incur resentment on the part of many in the profession."[22]

Unger may have underestimated the difficulties professional societies can encounter in promoting ethics. Large organizations could attempt a boycott of engineering societies, and such boycotts might be more successful than Unger believes. Historian Layton points out that many firms contribute directly to professional engineering societies and that many employers pay the dues of their employees.[23] These organizations might join with others in withdrawing support from the professional societies. This might include forbidding their employees to attend meetings or serve as officers, discontinuing any financial support of the societies, and perhaps withdrawing advertising from society publications. Under certain conditions, such actions might deal a severe blow to the continued viability of the societies themselves. Unger may also underestimate the divisiveness that a more activist promotion of ethics would cause.

On the other side of the argument, many employers have a high concern for ethics. They would no doubt welcome increased support and recognition that the societies could give. Furthermore, from the standpoint of the professional societies, the very nature of the professions as communities with moral ideals requires that professional societies do as much as they can to promote these ideals. It is not consistent to promulgate an ethical code and then fail to honor and support those who adhere to it. We believe that the evidence of the past decade indicates that engineers are increasingly recognizing this. Now let us turn to the institutions that are in a better position to enforce ethics.

11.7   State Registration Boards and the National Council of Examiners for Engineering and Surveying

State boards of engineering registration govern only those engineers who apply for and practice with a Professional Engineer license. State boards, however, still have several advantages over voluntary professional societies for enforcing professional conduct. First, state boards do not have to rely on voluntary contributions. They depend on such sources as state funding and mandatory fees collected for renewal of PE licenses. Second, state boards have legal powers that are not available to voluntary societies. While professional societies can only expel engineers from their membership, state boards can revoke PE licenses and initiate prosecutions for violation of state laws regulating the conduct of registered engineers. Third, state boards usually have an in-house apparatus for investigating complaints of unprofessional conduct, whereas professional societies may have more limited investigative capacities.

In 1907 Wyoming passed the first act in the United States that defined the standards that engineers must meet in order to be licensed.[24] Since that time, every state has enacted similar laws. The state engineering registration boards are charged with the administration of the law. The state boards are in turn members of the National Council of Examiners for Engineering and Surveying (NCEES). The NCEES is a national organization of state registration boards which, among other functions, suggests policies on engineering registration and keeps records of disciplinary actions by state boards.

As an example of its function of suggesting policies on engineering registration, the NCEES has developed a model law that sets forth the criteria for licensing engineers to practice and for regulating their practice after they are licensed. Most state laws regulating the practice of engineering follow the broad outlines of the model law. The model law sets several criteria for engineering licensure. The criteria require that a licensed engineer have a degree from a school with an engineering program accredited by the Accreditation Board for Engineering and Technology (ABET). In order to be licensed, an engineer must also pass two written examinations. The "fundamentals" examination covers basic science, mathematics, and engineering science. This examination is usually taken while the applicant is in the senior year of the B.S. program. The "professional practice" examination requires applicants to give engineering solutions to problems that might arise in practice.

The model law also requires that an applicant must have four years of "creditable" engineering work experience under the supervision of a registered professional engineer before the "professional practice" examination may be taken. Most boards define "creditable" experience as work involving increasing levels of difficulty and responsibility. An application for a PE license also includes a detailed description of the work experience as well as information sufficient to verify the other requirements. The model law also requires the applicant to be of good moral character. Most states have reciprocity agreements, allowing engineers to practice in one state with a license from another state.

State licensing boards provide directions for the engineer's work after licensing. For example, they have rules describing the manner in which an engineering drawing must be made and rules for the procedure by which a licensed professional engineer approves them. The drawings must be sealed with the PE's own numbered seal and signed by the engineer.

The boards have the responsibility for enforcing their own rules. Penalties for violating the state laws governing engineering practice or the rules promulgated by the boards have increasing degrees of severity, usually following this order:

1. Informal reprimand
2. Formal reprimand
3. Suspension of the license for a short period of time, with a longer probation
4. Longer suspension of the license

5. Revocation of the license
6. Fines

The following list provides examples from the records of the NCEES of disciplinary actions taken by various state boards:

- A land surveyor was ordered to resurvey and pay restitution for negligence in improperly locating boundary lines.

- A professional engineer's license was suspended for one year for failure to comply with a board order to have work reviewed by a peer reviewer prior to submitting the work for construction.

- A professional engineer was reprimanded and ordered to have an architect make a building-code check for negligence because he accepted an architectural assignment outside his area of engineering registration.

- A professional engineer's license was revoked for violating the terms and conditions of probation.

- A board ordered a nonregistrant to stop practicing engineering without a license.

- A professional engineer's license was probated for two years due to the improper design of a roof. The engineer was required to submit quarterly reports of work performed.

- A professional engineer was publicly reprimanded for signing and sealing work not prepared by the engineer or under the engineer's supervision.

- A professional engineer was ordered to complete a technical competence seminar and the engineer's license was probated as a result of sealing work done by another engineer not under the engineer's supervision and for violating other board rules.

- A professional engineer's license was revoked after the engineer was convicted of a felony. The engineer's license was restored after he served time on probation, made a personal appearance before the state board, submitted a recommendation by his supervising parole officer, and took a three-hour college-credit course on professionalism and ethics.

- A professional engineer's license was restricted because of errors in the engineer's calculations and the absence of a detailed drawing.

- A professional engineer was placed on four year's probation, required to give 400 hours of community service, and required to complete an ethics correspondence course after being convicted of two felonies and the violation of board rules. The convictions and rules violations had to do with embezzlement.

Most state boards are restricted in their enforcement powers by limitations in staff and funding. A registration board probably needs at least one full-time investigator, but many do not meet this requirement. In many states, registration boards must rely on district attorneys or the state attorney general's office. Unfortunately, state law enforcement agencies often have time and resources for pursuing only the most serious violations.

11.8   Experiences of a State Board

It may be helpful to supplement the preceding general information with an account of the experiences of a particular state board, the Texas State Board of Registration for Professional Engineers.[25] In January of 1968 the Texas board found itself in the position that many state boards were in earlier. An engineering registration law had been in effect since 1937, but there was still no organized effort to enforce its provisions. In 1965 the Texas legislature, largely through the efforts of the Texas Society of Professional Engineers (the Texas branch of the National Society of Professional Engineers), significantly improved and strengthened the provisions of the Texas Engineering Practice Act. The legislature also appropriated funds specifically designated for enforcement. Prior to this time, enforcement efforts had been restricted to occasional letters to alleged offenders, with no follow-up inquiries by investigators. These letters had little effect and were largely ignored.

The board hired its first investigator in January 1968. The investigator discovered ninety-three investigative inquiries that had not been pursued because of the absence of personnel to do the necessary on-site investigation. All of the inquiries had been initiated by outside complainants. The latest correspondence in each file was usually an unanswered letter from the board or the attorney general seeking compliance, sometimes containing threats of legal action. The investigator found that the legal action was never taken.

The investigator estimated that there were 4,000–5,000 violators of the Texas Engineering Practice Act. There were many reasons for the violations. (1) Most of the engineers who violated the act had little or no knowledge of its existence, much less its provisions and purposes. (2) Local, county, and state officials, even those who had specific responsibilities under the act, were ignorant of the act and its provisions. (3) Most engineers seemed to have little interest in the enforcement of professional standards unless they were directly threatened financially by unethical competitors. (4) The members of the board, who were usually creative and successful engineers and laypeople, either in business or academia, were not anxious to get involved in essentially negative law-enforcement activities. (5) The history of nonenforcement produced a climate of apathy among engineers in the state regarding the enforcement of the act.

In 1971 a second investigator was hired, and in 1984 a third. By the end of fiscal year 1992, 20,101 enforcement cases had been initiated. The enforcement section of the board took an active posture, initiating many investigations on its own rather than waiting for complaints to be made. Even with these additional investigators, the board must still rely on registrants, public officials, and interested citizens to bring violators to its attention.

The board members set the guidelines for the enforcement program. The philosophy of the board is to inform the public as much as possible, to obtain voluntary compliance where possible, to provide face-saving resolutions for unwitting violators, and to seek legal action only when other methods have failed. The board members generally subscribe to the belief that most engineers who violate the act out of ignorance of its provisions will voluntarily comply if they can do so without formally admitting guilt or being branded as violators of the law. In such situations the board always agrees to a reasonable time in which firms or individuals can comply, usually without undue disruptions or expenses. A small number of violators will either refuse to answer correspondence from the board or otherwise fail to comply with its directions. In these cases personal visits and further action may be necessary.

Since January 1968, more than 125 court cases have been filed. The violations have included such activities as the illegal use of engineering company names or engineering titles, illegal claims to be professional engineers, and illegal claims to have a professional engineering license.

Cases opened by the board are given one of the following nine classifications:

A Applicant matters

B Illegal practice of engineering

C Illegal use of seal or certificate

D Inquiries involving PE registrants (These involve suspicious activities that could result in disciplinary action.)

E Illegal use of engineering title or term

F Corporate name inquiries

G Neglect by public officials

H Miscellaneous matters

Z Structural and product failures

Table 11.3 gives the classification of cases before the board for June 1993.

From September 1991 through June 1993, nineteen registrants were disciplined. Table 11.4 lists the sanctions that were given.

It is difficult to gauge the effectiveness of state registration boards. The number of court cases in Texas (125), relative to the number of cases investigated (20,101), seems small, but it is difficult to know what standard to use in evaluating the work of the Texas board, especially with its strategy of using the courts only as a last resort. Perhaps the best measure would be to see whether increasing the resources of the board would result in a significant increase in the number of court cases.

Table 11.3
Cases Before the Texas State Board of Registration
for Professional Engineers, June 1993

Classification	Pending	Opened	Closed	Pending
	6-1-93		6-30-93	
A	2	1	0	3
B	106	21	51	76
C	3	0	1	2
D	17	3	4	16
E	6	7	4	9
F	11	13	1	23
G	2	2	3	1
H	12	12	4	20
Z	0	0	0	0
Totals	159	59	68	150

Table 11.4
Sanctions Given by the Texas State Board of Registration
for Professional Engineers, September 1991 through June 1993

Category	Number of Registrants
Informal reprimand	4
Formal reprimand	7
Suspension	1 (2 years with no probation)
Suspension with probation	1 (2 years, last year probated)
	1 (1 year, total period probated)
	1 (6 months, total period probated)
	2 (2 years, probated upon receipt by the board of evidence of completion of a correspondence course in engineering ethics)
	1 (6 months, last 5 months probated)
License revocation	1 (mandatory revocation due to a felony conviction and incarceration; revocation mandated by the Texas Register and Administrative Procedures Act)

11.9   Universal Engineering Licensure and the Industry Exemption

The power of state registration boards would be greatly increased if states required engineers to have a Professional Engineer license in order to perform any (or at least most) engineering work. State boards of engineering registration are severely limited in their ability to punish unethical conduct because engineers need not have a PE license in order to perform many types of engineering. Only a relatively small percentage of engineers, in fact, have a PE license, usually those who must approve projects that could directly endanger the safety, health, and welfare of the public. Although a high percentage of academic engineers are registered, most engineers who work for large corporations, for example, do not have a PE license. If an engineer's license is suspended, the engineer can still engage in many forms of engineering, and his or her ability to earn a livelihood is not destroyed.

If all engineers were required to have a license in order to engage in engineering work, however, the engineering codes of state registration boards would then be legally binding on all engineers. Combined with sufficient resources for investigation and prosecution, state boards would be in a position to enforce ethical standards for all engineers.

The same enforcement procedures could also strengthen the position of the ethical engineer. Suppose a client or employer is attempting to persuade an engineer to engage in unethical conduct. If a PE license were required in order to engage in engineering work, an engineer could then say to such a client or an employer, "I am sorry, but I cannot do what you ask. My state professional code does not permit such conduct, and I might lose my license if I comply with your request. This same code applies to all engineers in the state, so I don't think you are going to be able to get any other engineer to do what you ask either."

There are also some general arguments against requiring all engineers to be registered. First, it might be difficult in some cases to decide whether an activity requires the services of a registered engineer. Second, the prices of products and services might also increase because they would now require the services of licensed engineers. Third, the cost to states of policing the vastly increased numbers of professional engineers would be greatly increased.

The argument over engineering registration, however, usually focuses on the so-called industry exemption. The industry exemption is probably a major reason that many engineers do not seek registration as professional engineers. Most states now allow corporate employees to practice engineering without a license, whether or not their work affects public safety, health, and welfare, as long as some licensed engineer places his or her PE seal on the finished work. And even some finished work does not require a seal.

Various arguments have been put forth for retaining the industry exemption.[26] (1) The evidence that requiring the licensing of all engineers who in any way work on projects that affect the public would improve the safety of those products is not convincing to everyone. (2) The license fee might be a considerable financial burden for some engineers. (3) Removing the industry exemption might raise the price of engineering services because engineers would have a monopoly on some types of services, which could otherwise be performed more cheaply by nonengineers. This would increase the cost to the public. (4) To comply with such a law, it might be necessary to break up teams of engineers and nonengineers (including scientists). This might be the only effective way to separate engineering work and nonengineering work. Such teams have been important in technological advance, and their loss could hinder the progress of technology.

There are also arguments in favor of eliminating the exemption.[27] (1) The industry exemption seems inconsistent. Industrial products can affect public health and safety as much as structures. If the public needs the protection of the licensure requirement for those who design structures, it also needs it for those who design products. (2) The industry exemption requires that the "person in responsible charge" be licensed, but often this person is hard to isolate and the determination is made arbitrarily. When products are designed by teams, the team leader of one of the teams may be designated as the "person in responsible charge." But this person may be no more responsible than the leader of another team or someone who is not a team leader at all. (3) Eliminating the industry exemption would increase the ability of engineers to enforce professional standards because more engineers would have to become registered engineers and thus meet registration standards. It would in fact move engineering closer to the position of law and medicine, where all practitioners must be licensed.

Eliminating the industry exemption would not require all engineers to be registered. The requirement for registration might be stated so that engineers involved in projects which clearly have no relation to public health and safety could avoid registration. It might be stated in such a way that those engineering managers not engaged in design could avoid registration. Nevertheless, eliminating the requirement would have a significant impact on both industry and the engineering profession.

For a number of years the NSPE has held a policy in favor of eliminating the industry exemption, but many engineers and engineering societies have not affirmed this policy. Many engineers are not sympathetic with the arguments for elimination, to say nothing of a policy requiring all engineers to be registered.

The question of universal licensure and the industry exemption is still a controversial issue in the professional engineering community. As with other issues, the engineering community must keep in mind that it must set ethical standards for itself in dialogue with the larger society it serves. The guiding principle has been established: Engineers must hold paramount the safety, health, and welfare of the public. The interpretation and application of this guideline is a continuing process.

11.10   Chapter Summary

A professional community must establish standards for the conduct of its members, support those members who act in accordance with those standards, and discipline those members who do not.

Professional engineering societies, however, are ill-equipped to enforce ethics. One of their few powers is to rescind an engineer's membership in the society, and this cannot keep an engineer from practicing engineering. As the case of Mr. Mardirosian against the American Institute of Architects illustrates, disciplining members can lead to expensive lawsuits.

The history of engineering societies reveals a conflict between an orientation toward professionalism and toward business. While the societies have been excellent mediums for the pursuit of knowledge and the exchange of technical information, they may be more suited to promoting ethics than enforcing ethical standards.

The NSPE Board of Ethical Review is an example of one way that a society can promote ethics, but there are other ways that professional societies can do so. Professional societies already serve as forums for discussions of ethical issues, including debates about how the codes should be modified. In the future, they could become more involved in such activities as honoring ethical engineers and ethical employers, assisting ethical engineers who are in trouble with their employers, and establishing ethics hotlines. The limits of the abilities of professional societies in this area have not yet been determined.

The primary responsibility for enforcing ethics lies with state boards of registration, all of whom are members of the National Council for Examiners of Engineering and Surveying. State boards of engineering registration may impose a variety of sanctions on engineers who violate the state code. The boards are sometimes restricted in their enforcement powers by limitations in funding and personnel and by the fact that only registered engineers fall under their jurisdiction. Whether all engineers should be registered and whether the so-called industry exemption should be removed are controversial issues within the engineering profession. The resolution of this issue—like all other issues facing the engineering profession—should follow the guideline that the public's safety, health, and welfare must come first.

Case Analyses

Case 11.1   Sharing of Hotel Suite [28]

Facts

Engineer B is director of engineering with a large government agency that uses many engineering consultants. Engineer A is a principal in a large engineering firm that performs services for that agency. Both are members of an engineering society that is conducting a two-day seminar in a distant city. Both plan to attend the seminar and they agree to share costs of a two bedroom hotel suite in order to have better accommodations.

Question

Was it ethical for Engineer A and B to share the hotel suite?

References

Code of Ethics—Section II.4.a.—"Engineers shall disclose all known or potential conflicts of interest to their employers or clients by promptly informing them of any business association, interest, or other circumstances which could influence or appear to influence their judgment or the quality of their services."

Section II.5.b.—"Engineers shall not offer, give, solicit or receive, either directly or indirectly, any political contribution in an amount intended to influence the award of a contract by public authority, or which may be reasonably construed by the public of having the effect or intent to influence the award of a contract. They shall not offer any gift, or other valuable consideration in order to secure work. They shall not pay a commission, percentage or brokerage fee in order to secure work except to a bona fide employee or bona fide established commercial or marketing agencies retained by them."

Section III.3.—"Engineers shall avoid all conduct or practice which is likely to discredit the profession or deceive the public."

Discussion

The ethical issues presented in this case relate more directly to questionable appearances than affirmative ethical wrongdoing or professional improprieties. We have here two engineers who appear to be attempting to economize on the costs of attending a professional seminar, at the same time seeking better accommodations. That certainly seems to be a worthy and prudent decision on the part of both.

Nevertheless, there are other aspects of this case that need to be examined because they raise sensitive appearance issues. The first and most obvious is the fact that Engineer A and Engineer B maintain a business relationship with each other. In addition, Engineer B employs the services of other engineering firms for his agency. It would seem that Engineer B's agreeing to share a suite at a professional society meeting with Engineer A might suggest an entanglement of personal and professional relationships between the two in the eyes of other engineers who perform services for the agency. The time spent together would appear to give Engineer A a distinct advantage in future selections and negotiations.

Another dimension to this problem is the appearance that Engineer A is somehow "subsidizing" Engineer B's attendance at the meeting and thereby providing "valuable consideration" in violation of the Code. (Section II.5.b.) Again, we note there is nothing in the facts to suggest that Engineer A is attempting to "pick up the tab" for Engineer B. Rather, they indicate that both are seeking to jointly reduce seminar costs. However, as we have said on numerous occasions as in

BER Cases 60-9, 76-6, 79-8, and 81-4, engineers need to be extremely sensitive to the charge that their conduct suggests neither favoritism nor bias for or against any particular party. Rather, they must be guided by objectivity and honesty, conducting their affairs to promote that view both in practice and appearance.

While it would seem on its face that neither Engineer A nor Engineer B is motivated by improper intentions in this case, we believe that the sharing agreement created an improper appearance under Section III.3. and Engineer B appears to be showing favoritism to Engineer A. We think this action is not within the spirit or intent of the Code.

Conclusion

It was unethical for Engineers A and B to agree to share a suite under the circustances described.

Note: This opinion is based on data submitted to the Board of Ethical Review and does not necessarily represent all of the pertinent facts when applied to a specific case. This opinion is for educational purposes only and should not be construed as expressing any opinion on the ethics of specific individuals. This opinion may be reprinted without further permission, provided that this statement is included before or after the text of the case.

Analysis

In rendering a judgment on this case, the members of the board attempted to do more than give a narrow, legalistic interpretation of the NSPE code. They took into account not only the actual words but also what they believed to be the "spirit or intent of the Code," and their conclusion went beyond the literal requirements of the three parts of the code that they cited. No part of the code that

they cited dealt with the issue of appearances. Section II.4.a. requires engineers to "disclose" all *apparent* conflicts of interest, but it does not suggest that apparent conflicts of interest must be avoided. Section II.5.b. requires engineers to avoid gift giving, but the board agreed that there was no actual gift giving in this case.

The board based its decision directly on Section III.3., which prohibits conduct that is likely to discredit the engineering profession or deceive the public. This is a very broad provision that is subject to many interpretations. According to the board, an instance of apparent gift giving can either discredit the profession (presumably by giving the appearance of impropriety) or deceive the public (presumably because the public might think there was impropriety).

Using our terminology, we can probably best describe case 87-4 as a line-drawing problem, involving the conceptual and application issues of whether we should count apparent conflicts of interest as a type of conflict of interest and, if so, whether they should count as "discrediting" the engineering profession and/or "deceiving" the public. This case illustrates what we have already seen in our attempts to apply engineering codes (and ethical principles in general) to concrete situations, namely that such application requires analysis and thought as well as moral sensitivity and discernment.

The categories with the largest number of cases considered by the board are "advertising," "conflict of interest," and "competitive bidding." These are problems most likely to be encountered by engineers in consulting practice. Nevertheless, some cases have to do with problems engineers have with their employers when employers act in a way that engineers believe is inappropriate or unethical.

Case 11.2   Blowing the Whistle on a Defense Contractor [29]

In a 1982 BER case, an engineer who was employed by a large industrial company that engaged in substantial work on defense projects objected to the plans of one contractor whose submission represented excessive cost and time delays. The employer rejected the engineer's objections and finally placed the engineer on three month's probation, with the warning that the engineer would be terminated unless his job performance improved.

The question formulated by the board was as follows: "Does Engineer A have an ethical obligation, or an ethical right, to continue his efforts to secure change in the policy of his employer under these circumstances, or to report his concerns to proper authority?" The board based its answer on the code's requirement that engineers must protect the safety, health, and welfare of the public. Their conclusion was that "engineer A does not have an ethical obligation to continue his efforts to secure a change in the policy of his employer under these circumstances, or to report his concerns to proper authority, but has an ethical right to do so as a matter of personal conscience."

This case illustrates how broadly the board is willing to interpret the code. It relies on two ideas that are not clearly present in the code: (1) the distinction between an obligation to do something and a mere right to do it if one chooses, and (2) the affirmation that the personal conscience of engineers should be respected. The board admitted that in this case there was no clear threat of danger to public health or safety. Rather, the plans of the subcontractor were unsatisfactory and involved an unnecessary expenditure of public funds. The board continued:

> We could dismiss the case on the narrow ground that the Code does not apply to a claim not involving public health or safety, but we think that is too narrow a reading of the ethical duties of engineers engaged in activities having a substantial impact on defense expenditures or other substantial public expenditures that relate to "welfare" as set forth in Section III.2.b.

Here the board faced the issue of what counts as a detriment to public "welfare." Its position was that public "welfare" included the efficient use of tax funds. Because the case involved public funds, the board concluded that the engineer had at least a right, although not a professional obligation, to protect the public. Why the engineer had a right and not an obligation to protect the public is not clear. This case does make the claim, however, that the engineer has a right to follow the demands of his own conscience if his conscience requires him to protest the actions of his employer.

The board's resolution of this case allowed it to count as an engineering decision what some might take as a management decision. It contrasted its decision with another case (61-10) in which engineers "objected to the redesign of a commercial product, but which did not entail any question of public health or safety." Here, because no public funds were involved, the engineer did not have a right to protest as a professional. If the engineer protested, he had to do so as a citizen, not as an engineer. Moreover, the NSPE code does not provide any protection for the right of an engineer to protest, or to refuse to participate in, a project to which he objects on personal grounds.[30]

Case 11.3   Whistleblowing in City Government [31]

Another case that the board described as "whistleblowing" involved a city engineer who was also the Director of Public Works (Engineer A). Engineer A was the only licensed professional engineer in a position of responsibility in the government of a medium-sized city. The city had several large food processing plants that discharged large amounts of vegetable material into the sewage system during the canning season. Engineer A concluded that if large storms occurred during the canning season, the disposal plant would be overburdened. She brought this to the attention of Administrator C, who told her that "we will handle the problem when it comes" and instructed her to discuss the problem only with him. Engineer A disobeyed these instructions and brought the problem to the attention of city council members. As a result, Engineer A was removed from her position of responsibility and replaced by Technician B.

During the next canning season, when large amounts of vegetable material were introduced into the sewage system by the canning plants in the city, there were indeed some particularly heavy storms. It became obvious to those involved that if waste water from the treatment plant containing domestic waste was not released into the local river, the ponds at the treatment plant would overflow the levees and dump all their waste into the river. Under state law this condition had to be reported to the state water pollution control authority.

The question placed before the board was whether Engineer A fulfilled her responsibilities as an engineer merely by informing Administrator C of the problem and then informing certain members of the city council when Administrator C ignored the problem. The board recognized this as what we have called a conflict problem:

As we have long known, ethics frequently involves a delicate balance between competing and, oft times, conflicting obligations. However, it seems clear that where the conflict is between one important obligation or loyalty [i.e. to Administrator C] and the protection of the public, for the engineer the latter must be viewed as the higher obligation.

In discussing this case, the board referred to another case (65-12) in which it concluded that a group of engineers were ethically justified in refusing to participate in the processing or production of a product that involved machinery they believed to be unsafe. In another case (82-5), it concluded that an engineer who believed the plans of a subcontractor were inadequate from both a cost and design standpoint had a right to protest to his employer, but the protest was not required. The Board justified its opinion by arguing that "the Code only requires that the engineer withdraw from a project and report to proper authorities when the circumstances involve endangerment to the public safety, health and welfare."

In case 88-6, however, the board decided that merely reporting her concerns to Administrator C or to certain members of the city council did not fulfill Engineer A's obligation to report the problem to the "proper authorities." They argued that the "proper authorities" were state officials responsible for water pollution control. Thus, the board's resolution of the conflict problem had two parts. First, the conflict between the obligation to protect public health was interpreted as overriding the obligation of loyalty to one's employer. Second, the obligation to notify a "proper authority" was interpreted as an obligation to notify state health officials, making the action a bona fide case of whistleblowing.

Other Cases

NOTES

1. This case was suggested by an actual case brought to our attention by a student of Professor Lee Lowrey. We have slightly modified the facts and changed the names.

2. *Mardirosian v. The American Institute of Architects* (*AIA*), 474 F Supp. 628 (1979).

3. Edwin T. Layton, Jr., *The Revolt of the Engineers* (Cleveland: The Press of Case Western Reserve University, 1971), p. 94.

4. Ibid., p. 10.

5. Ibid., p. 11.

6. William H. Wisley, "The Influence of Engineering Societies on Professionalism and Ethics." Printed for the first time in Schaub and Pavlovic (1983), pp. 28–37.

7. Layton, p. 84.

8. Ibid., p. 85.

9. We are indebted to Michael Davis for this observation.

10. Layton, p. 35ff.

11. Ibid., p. 16.

12. Ibid., p. 110.

13. Ibid., p. 35.

14. Ibid., pp. 18–19.

15. Ibid., p. 19.

16. Ibid., p. 9.

17. Ibid., pp. 8–9.

18. See "AAES Strives Toward Being Unified Voice of Engineering," *Engineering Times*, Vol. 15, No. 11, November, 1993, p. 1 and "U.S. Engineer Unity Elusive," *Engineering Times*, Vol. 15, No. 11, November, 1993, p. 15.

19. Ibid., p. 32.

20. Stephen H. Unger, *Controlling Technology: Ethics and the Responsible Engineer* (New York: Holt, Rinehart and Winston, 1982), p. 73.

21. Stephen H. Unger, "Would Helping Ethical Professionals Get Professional Societies into Trouble?" in *IEEE Technology and Society Magazine* (September 1987), Vol. 6, No. 3, pp. 17–21. Reprinted in Johnson (1991), pp. 368–375.

22. Ibid., Johnson, p. 374.

23. Layton, p. 18.

24. We are indebted to Mr. E. D. Dorchester for most of the material in this section. Used with permission.

25. We are indebted to Mr. Ronald E. Hall, Supervising Investigator of the Texas State Board of Registration for Professional Engineers, for most of the material in this section. Used with permission.

26. For some of these reasons, see M. J. Kolhoff, "For the Industry Exemption . . . ," *Professional Engineer* (March 1976). Reprinted in Schaub and Pavlovick (1983), pp. 526–530.

27. Many of these arguments are taken from G. J. Kettler, "Against the Industry Exemption . . . ," *Professional Engineer* (March 1976). Reprinted in Schaub and Povlovick (1983), pp. 531–534

28. This is BER Case No. 87-4 in NSPE's *Opinions of the Board of Ethical Review*, Vol. VI (Alexandria, VA: National Society of Professional Engineers, 1989), pp. 94–95.

29. This is BER Case No. 85-2 in NSPE's *Opinions of the Board of Ethical Review*, Vol. VI (Alexandria, VA: National Society of Professional Engineers, 1989), pp. 59–61.

30. Note that the position of the board (and of the NSPE code) is similar to the position that we took on environmental issues in Chapter 10, where we held that an engineering code should protect the right of engineers to decline to participate in projects that violate their conscience, even if they do not violate engineering codes.

31. This is BER Case No. 88-6 in NSPE's *Opinions of the Board of Ethical Review*, Vol. VI (Alexandria, VA: National Society of Professional Engineers, 1989), pp. 114–116.

Bibliography

Books and Monographs

Alger, Philip L., Christensen, N. A., and Olmsted, S. P. *Ethical Problems in Engineering*. New York: Wiley, 1965.

Alpern, K. D. "Moral Responsibilities for Engineers," *Business and Professional Ethics Journal*, Vol. 2, No. 2, 1983, 39–48.

Anderson, R. M., Perrucci, R., Schendel, D. E., and Trachtman, L. E. *Divided Loyalties: Whistle-Blowing at BART*. West Lafayette, IN: Purdue Research Foundation, 1980.

Bailey, M. J. *Reducing Risks to Life: Measurement of the Benefits*. Washington, DC: American Enterprise Institute for Public Policy Research, 1980.

Baker, D. "Social Mechanisms for Controlling Engineers' Performance." In Albert Flores, ed., *Designing for Safety: Engineering Ethics in Organizational Contexts*. Troy, NY: Rensselaer Polytechnic Institute, 1982.

Baram, M. S. "Regulation of Environmental Carcinogens: Why Cost-Benefit Analysis May Be Harmful to Your Health," *Technology Review*, Vol. 78 (July–August) 1976.

Baron, M. *The Moral Status of Loyalty*. Dubuque, Iowa: Center for the Study of Ethics in the Professions, Kendall/Hunt, 1984.

Baum, R. J. *Ethics and Engineering*. Hastings-on-Hudson, NY: The Hastings Center, 1980.

Baum, R. J. and Flores, A., eds. *Ethical Problems in Engineering*. Vols. 1 and 2. Troy, NY: Center for the Study of the Human Dimensions of Science and Technology, Rensselaer Polytechnic Institute, 1978.

Baxter, W. F. *People or Penguins: The Case for Optimal Pollution*. New York: Columbia University Press, 1974.

Bayles, M. D. *Professional Ethics*. 2nd ed. Belmont, CA: Wadsworth, 1989.

Bazelon, D. L. "Risk and Responsibility," *Science*, Vol. 205 (July 20) 1979, 277–280.

Beauchamp, T. L. *Case Studies in Business, Society and Ethics*. 2nd ed. Englewood Cliffs, NJ: Prentice-Hall, 1989.

Bellah, R., et al. *Habits of the Heart: Individualism and Commitment in American Life*. New York: Harper and Row, 1985.

Benham, L. "The Effect of Advertising on the Price of Eyeglasses," *Journal of Law and Economics*, Vol. 15, 1972, 337–352.

Benjamin, M. *Splitting the Difference: Compromise in Ethics and Politics*. Lawrence: University Press of Kansas, 1990.

Black, Bert. "Evolving Legal Standards for the Admissibility of Scientific Evidence," *Science*, Vol. 239, 1987, 1510–1512.

Blackstone, W. T. "On Rights and Responsibilities Pertaining to Toxic Substances and Trade Secrecy," *The Southern Journal of Philosophy*, Vol. 16, 1978, 589–603.

Blinn, K. W. *Legal and Ethical Concepts in Engineering*. Englewood Cliffs, NJ: Prentice-Hall, 1989.

Board of Ethical Review, NSPE, *Opinions of the Board of Ethical Review*, Vols. I–VII. Arlington, VA: NSPE Publications, National Society of Professional Engineers. Various dates.

Bok, S. *Lying: Moral Choice in Public and Private Life*. New York: Vintage Books, 1979.

Broad, W., and Wade, N. *Betrayers of the Truth*. New York: Simon & Schuster, 1982.

Buchanan, R. A. *The Engineers: A History of the Engineering Profession in Britain, 1750–1914*. London: Jessica Kingsley Publishers, 1989.

Cady, J. F. *Restricted Advertising and Competition: The Case of Retail Drugs*. Washington, DC: American Enterprise Institute, 1976.

Callahan, D., and Bok, S. *Ethics Teaching in Higher Education*. New York: Plenum Press, 1980.

Callahan, J. C., ed. *Ethical Issues in Professional Life*. New York: Oxford University Press, 1988.

Cameron, R., and Millard, A. J. *Technology Assessment: A Historical Approach*. Dubuque, IA: Center for the Study of Ethics in the Professions, Kendall/Hunt, 1985.

Chalk, R., Frankel, M., and Chafer, S. B. *AAAS Professional Ethics Project: Professional Ethics Activities of the Scientific and Engineering Societies.* Washington, DC: American Association for the Advancement of Science, 1980.

Cohen, R. M., and Witcover, J. *A Heartbeat Away: The Investigation and Resignation of Vice President Spiro T. Agnew.* New York: Viking Press, 1974.

Cranor, Carl F. "The Problem of Joint Causes for Workplace Health Protections [1]," *IEEE Technology and Society Magazine* (September) 1986, 10–12.

Cranor, Carl F. *Regulating Toxic Substances: A Philosophy of Science and the Law.* New York: Oxford University Press, 1993.

Curd, M., and May, L. *Professional Responsibility for Harmful Actions.* Dubuque, IA: Center for the Study of Ethics in the Professions, Kendall/Hunt, 1984.

Davis, M. "Conflict of Interest," *Business and Professional Ethics Journal,* (Summer) 1982, 17–27.

Davis, M. "Avoiding the Tragedy of Whistleblowing," *Business and Professional Ethics Journal,* Vol. 8, No. 4, 1989, 3–19.

Davis, M. "Thinking Like an Engineer: The Place of a Code of Ethics in the Practice of a Profession," *Philosophy and Public Affairs,* Vol. 20, No. 2 (Spring) 1991, 150–167.

De George, R. T. "Ethical Responsibilities of Engineers in Large Organizations: The Pinto Case," *Business and Professional Ethics Journal,* Vol. 1, No. 1 (Fall) 1981.

Douglas, M., and Wildavsky, A. *Risk and Culture.* Berkeley and Los Angeles: University of California Press, 1982.

Eddy, P., Potter, E., and Page, B. *Destination Disaster: From the Tri-Motor to the DC-10.* New York: Quadrangle Press, 1976.

Elbaz, S. W. *Professional Ethics and Engineering: A Resource Guide.* Arlington, VA: National Institute for Engineering Ethics, 1990.

Ethics Resource Center and Behavior Resource Center. *Ethics Policies and Programs in American Business.* Washington, DC.: The Ethics Resource Center, 1990.

Faden, R. R., and Beauchamp, T. L. *A History and Theory of Informed Consent.* New York: Oxford University Press, 1986.

Fadiman, J. A. "A Traveler's Guide to Gifts and Bribes." *Harvard Business Review,* (July–August) 1986, 122–126 and 130–136.

Feinberg, Joel. "Duties, Rights and Claims," *American Philosophical Quarterly,* Vol. 3, No. 2, 1966, 137–144.

Feliv, Alfred G. "The Role of the Law in Protecting Scientific and Technical Dissent," *IEEE Technology and Society Magazine* (June) 1985, 3–9.

Fielder, J. "Tough Break for Goodrich," *Journal of Business and Professional Ethics,* Vol. 19, No. 3, 1986.

Fielder, J. "Organizational Loyalty," *Business and Professional Ethics Journal,* Vol. 11, No. 1, 1991, 71–90.

Fielder, J., and Birsch, Douglass, eds. *The DC 10.* New York: State of New York Press, 1992.

Firmage, D. A. *Modern Engineering Practice: Ethical, Professional, and Legal Aspects.* New York: Garland STPM, 1980.

Flores, A., ed. *Designing for Safety.* Troy, NY: Rensselaer Polytechnic Institute, 1982.

Flores, A. *Ethics and Risk Management in Engineering.* Boulder, CO: Westview Press, 1988.

Flores, A., ed. *Professional Ideals.* Belmont, CA: Wadsworth, 1988.

Flores, A., and Johnson, D. G. "Collective Responsibility and Professional Roles," *Ethics,* Vol. 93 (April) 1983, 537–545.

Florman, S. C. "Moral Blueprints," *Harper's Magazine,* Vol. 257, No. 1541 (October) 1978, 30–33.

Florman, S. C. *The Existential Pleasures of Engineering.* New York: St. Martin's Press, 1976.

Florman, S. C. *Blaming Technology: The Irrational Search for Scapegoats.* New York: St. Martin's Press, 1981.

Florman, S. C. *The Civilized Engineer.* New York: St. Martin's Press, 1987.

Flumerfelt, R. W., Harris, C. E., Jr., Rabins, M. J., and Samson, C. H., Jr. *Introducing Ethics Case Studies into Required Undergraduate Engineering Courses."* Report on NSF Grant DIR-9012252, November 1992.

Ford, D. F. *Three Mile Island: Thirty Minutes to Meltdown.* New York: Viking Press, 1982.

Frankel, M., ed. *Science, Engineering and Ethics: State of the Art and Future Directions.* Report of an American Association for the Advancement of Science Workshop and Symposium, February 1988, AAAS.

Fredrich, A. J. *Sons of Martha: Civil Engineering Readings in Modern Literature.* New York: American Society of Civil Engineers, 1989.

French, P. A. *Collective and Corporate Responsibility.* New York: Columbia University Press, 1984.

Friedman, M. "The Social Responsibility of Business Is to Increase Its Profits." *The New York Times Magazine* (September 13) 1970.

Garrett, T. M., et al. *Cases in Business Ethics.* New York: Appleton Century Crofts, 1968.

General Dynamics Corporation. *The General Dynamics Ethics Program Update.* St. Louis, MO: General Dynamics Corporation, 1988.

Gert, B. "Moral Theory, and Applied and Professional Ethics," *Professional Ethics*, Vol. 1, Nos. 1 and 2, (Spring/Summer), 1992, 1–25.

Gert, B. *Morality.* New York: Oxford University Press, 1988.

Gewirth, A. *Reason and Morality.* Chicago: University of Chicago Press, 1978.

Glazer, M. "Ten Whistleblowers and How They Fared," *Hastings Center Report*, Vol. 13, No. 6, 1983, 33–41.

Glazer, M. *The Whistleblowers: Exposing Corruption in Government and Industry.* New York: Basic Books, 1989.

Glickman, T. S., and Gough, R. *Readings in Risk.* Washington, DC: Resources for the Future, 1990.

Goldman, A. H. *The Moral Foundations of Professional Ethics.* Totowa, NJ: Rowman and Littlefield, 1979.

Gorlin, R. A., ed. *Codes of Professional Responsibility.* 2nd ed. Washington, DC: Bureau of National Affairs, 1990.

Gray, M., and Rosen, I. *The Warning: Accident at Three Mile Island.* New York: W. W. Norton, 1982.

Greenwood, E. "Attributes of a Profession," *Social Work* (July) 1957, 45–55.

Gunn, A. S., and Vesilind, P. A. *Environmental Ethics for Engineers.* Chelsea, MI: Lewis Publishers, 1986.

Harris, C. E. *Applying Moral Theories.* Belmont, CA: Wasdsworth, 1990.

Heilbroner, Robert, ed. *In the Name of Profit.* Garden City: Doubleday, 1972.

Hick, J. *Disputed Questions in Theology and the Philosophy of Religion.* New Haven, CT: Yale University Press, 1986.

Howard, J. L. "Current Developments in Whistleblower Protection," *Labor Law Journal*, Vol. 39, No. 2 (February) 1988, 67–80.

Hunter, Thomas. "Engineers Face Risks as Expert Witnesses," *The Rochester Engineer* (December) 1992.

Hynes, H. P. "Women Working: A Field Report," *Technology Review* (November–December) 1984.

Jackall, R. "The Bureaucratic Ethos and Dissent," *IEEE Technology and Society Magazine* (June) 1985, 21–30.

Jackall, R. *Moral Mazes: The World of Corporate Managers.* New York: Oxford University Press, 1988.

Jaksa, J. A., and Pritchard, M. S. *Communication Ethics: Methods of Analysis.* 2nd ed. Belmont, CA: Wadsworth, 1994.

James, G. G. "In Defense of Whistle Blowing." In W. Michael Hoffman and Jennifer Mills Moore, eds., *Business Ethics.* New York: McGraw-Hill, 1984.

Jamshidi, Mo, Shahinpoor, Mo, and Mullins, J. H., eds. *Environmentally Conscious Manufacturing: Recent Advances.* Albuquerque, NM: ECM Press, 1991.

Janis, I. *Groupthink.* 2nd ed. Boston: Houghton Mifflin, 1982.

Johnson, D. G. *Ethical Issues in Engineering.* Englewood Cliffs, NJ: Prentice-Hall, 1991.

Johnson, D. G. *Computer Ethics.* 2nd ed. Englewood Cliffs, NJ: Prentice-Hall, 1993.

Johnson, D. G., and Snapper, J. W., eds. *Ethical Issues in the Use of Computers.* Belmont, CA: Wadsworth, 1985.

Johnson, E. "Treating Dirt: Environmental Ethics and Moral Theory." In Tom Regan, *Earthbound: New Introductory Essays in Environmental Ethics.* New York: Random House, 1984.

Jonsen, A. L., and Toulmin, Stephen. *The Abuse of Casuistry.* Berkeley: University of California Press, 1988.

Kahn, S. "Economic Estimates of the Value of Life," *IEEE Technology and Society Magazine* (June) 1986, 24–31.

Kant, I. *Foundations of the Metaphysics of Morals, with Critical Essays.* Robert Paul Wolff, ed., Indianapolis, IN: Bobbs-Merrill, 1969.

Kemper, J. D. *Engineers and Their Profession.* 3rd ed. New York: Holt, Rinehart & Winston, 1982.

Kettler, G. J. "Against the Industry Exemption." In James H. Schaub and Karl Pavlovic, eds. *Engineering Professionalism and Ethics.* New York: Wiley-Interscience, 1983.

Kipnis, K. "Engineers Who Kill: Professional Ethics and the Paramountcy of Public Safety," *Business and Professional Ethics Journal*, Vol. 1, No. 1, 1981.

Kolhoff, M. J. "For the Industry Exemption . . ." In James H. Schaub and Karl Pavlovic, eds. *Engineering Professionalism and Ethics.* New York: Wiley-Interscience, 1983.

Kultgen, J. "Evaluating Codes of Professional Ethics." In Wade L. Robison, Michael S. Pritchard, and Joseph Ellin, eds. *Profits and Professions*. Clifton, NJ: Humana Press, 1983, 225–264.

Kultgen, J. *Ethics and Professionalism*. Philadelphia: The University of Pennsylvania Press, 1988.

Ladd, J. "Bhopal: An Essay on Moral Responsibility and Civic Virtue," *Journal of Social Philosophy*, Vol. XXII, No. 1 (Spring) 1991.

Ladd, J. "The Quest for a Code of Professional Ethics." In Rosemary Chalk, Mark S. Frankel, and Sollie B. Chafer, eds. *AAAS Professional Ethics Project: Professional Ethics Activities of the Scientific and Engineering Societies*. Washington, DC: American Association for the Advancement of Science, 1980.

Ladenson, R. F., Choromokos, J., d'Anjou, E., Pimsler, M., and Rosen, H. *A Selected Annotated Bibliography of Professional Ethics and Social Responsibility in Engineering*. Chicago: Center for the Study of Ethics in the Professions, Illinois Institute of Technology, 1980.

Ladenson, R. F. "The Social Responsibility of Engineers and Scientists: A Philosophical Approach." In D. L. Babcock and C. A. Smith, eds. *Values and the Public Works Professional*. Rolla: University of Missouri-Rolla, 1980.

Ladenson, R. F. "Freedom of Expression in the Corporate Workplace: A Philosophical Inquiry." In Wade L. Robison, Michael S. Pritchard, and Joseph Ellin, eds. *Profits and Professions*. Clifton, NJ: Humana Press, 1983, 275–286.

Larson, M. S. *The Rise of Professionalism*. Berkeley: University of California Press, 1977.

Layton, E. T., Jr. *The Revolt of the Engineers: Social Responsibility and the American Engineering Profession*. Baltimore, MD: Johns Hopkins University Press, 1971, 1986.

Leopold, A. *A Sand County Almanac*. New York: Oxford University Press, 1966.

Litai, D. "A Risk Comparison Methodology for the Assessment of Acceptable Risk." Ph.D. Dissertation, Massachusetts Institute of Technology, Cambridge, MA, 1980.

Lockhart, T. W. "Safety Engineering and the Value of Life," *Technology and Society (IEEE)*, Vol. 9 (March) 1981, 3–5.

Lowrance, W. W. *Of Acceptable Risk*. Los Altos, CA: William Kaufmann, 1976.

Luebke, Neil R. "Conflict of Interest as a Moral Category," *Business and Professional Ethics Journal*, Vol. 6, No. 1, 1987, 66–81.

Luegenbiehl, H. C. "Codes of Ethics and the Moral Education of Engineers," *Business and Professional Ethics Journal*, Vol. 2, No. 4, 1983, 41–61.

Lunch, M. F. "Supreme Court Rules on Advertising for Professions," *Professional Engineer*, Vol. 1, No. 8 (August) 1977, 41–42.

MacIntyre, A. *A Short History of Ethics*. New York: Macmillan, 1966.

MacIntyre, A. "Regulation: A Substitute for Morality," *Hastings Center Report* (February) 1980, 31–41.

Magsdick, H. H. "Some Engineering Aspects of Headlighting," *Illuminating Engineering* (June) 1940, 533.

Malin, M. H. "Protecting the Whistleblower from Retaliatory Discharge," *Journal of Law Reform*, Vol. 16 (Winter) 1983, 277–318.

Mantell, M. I. *Ethics and Professionalism in Engineering*. New York: Macmillan, 1964.

Margolis, J. "Conflict of Interest and Conflicting Interests." In T. Beauchamp, and N. Bowie, eds., *Ethical Theory and Business*, 1st ed. Englewood Cliffs, NJ: Prentice-Hall, 1979, 361–372.

Marshall, E. "Feynman Issues His Own Shuttle Report Attacking NASA Risk Estimates," *Science*, Vol. 232 (June 27) 1986, 1596.

Martin, D. *Three Mile Island: Prologue or Epilogue?* Cambridge, MA: Ballinger, 1980.

Martin, M. W. *Everyday Morals*. Belmont, CA: Wadsworth, 1989.

Martin, M. W. and Schinzinger, R. *Engineering Ethics*. 2nd ed. New York: McGraw-Hill, 1988.

Martin, M. W. "Rights and the Meta-Ethics of Professional Morality," and "Professional and Ordinary Morality: A Reply to Freedman," *Ethics*, Vol. 91, July 1981, 619–625 and 631–633.

Martin, M. W. "Professional Autonomy and Employers' Authority." In A. Flores, *Ethical Problems in Engineering*. Vol. 1. Troy, NY: Rensselaer Polytechnic Institute, 1982, 177–181.

Martin, M. W. *Self-Deception and Morality*. Lawrence: University Press of Kansas, 1986.

Mason, J. F. "The Technical Blow-by-Blow: An Account of the Three Mile Island Accident," *IEEE Spectrum*, Vol. 16, No. 11 (November) 1979, 33–42.

May, W. F. "Professional Virtue and Self-Regulation." In J. L. Callahan, ed., *Ethical Issues in Professional Life*. New York: Oxford, 1988, 408–411.

McIlwee, J. S., and Robinson, J. G. *Women in Engineering: Gender, Power and Workplace Culture*. Albany: State University of New York Press, 1992.

Meese, G. P. E. "The Sealed Beam Case," *Business and Professional Ethics Journal*, Vol. 1, No. 3 (Spring) 1982, 1–20.

Milgram, S. *Obedience to Authority*. New York: Harper and Row, 1974.

Mill, J. S. *Utilitarianism, with Critical Essays*. Samuel Gorovitz, ed. Indianapolis, IN: Bobbs-Merrill, 1971.

Mill, J. S. *Utilitarianism*. G. Sher, ed. Indianapolis, IN: Hackett, 1979.

Millikan, R. A. "On the Elementary Electrical Charge and the Avogadro Constant." *Physical Review*, Vol. 2, 1913, 109–143.

Morrison, C., and Hughes, P. *Professional Engineering Practice: Ethical Aspects*. 2nd ed. Toronto, Canada: McGraw-Hill Ryerson, 1988.

Murdough Center for Engineering Professionalism, *Independent Study and Research Program in Engineering Ethics and Professionalism*. Lubbock: College of Engineering, Texas Technological University, October, 1990.

Nader, R. "Responsibility and the Professional Society," *Professional Engineer*, Vol. 41 (May) 1971, 14–17.

Nader, R., Petkas, Peter J., and Blackwell, Kate. *Whistle Blowing*. New York: Grossman, 1972.

National Academy of Science, Committee on the Conduct of Science. *On Being a Scientist*. Washington, DC: National Academy Press, 1989.

Okrent, David, and Whipple, Chris. *An Approach to Societal Risk Assessment Criteria and Risk Management*. Report, UCLA-Eng-7746. Los Angeles: UCLA School of Engineering and Applied Sciences, 1977.

Oldenquist, A. "Commentary on Alpern's 'Moral Responsibility for Engineers,'" *Business and Professional Ethics Journal*, Vol. 2, No. 2 (Winter) 1983.

Otten, J. "Organizational Disobedience." In A. Flores, *Ethical Problems in Engineering*. Vol. 1. Troy, NY: Center for the Study of the Human Dimensions of Science and Technology, Rensselaer Polytechnic Institute, 1978, 182–186.

Peterson, J. C., and Farrell, D. *Whistleblowing: Ethical and Legal Issues in Expressing Dissent*. Dubuque, IA: Center for the Study of Ethics in the Professions, Kendall/Hunt, 1986.

Petroski, H. *To Engineer Is Human: The Role of Failure in Successful Design*. New York: St. Martin's, 1982.

Petroski, H. *Beyond Engineering: Essays and Other Attempts to Figure Without Equations*. New York: St. Martin's, 1985.

Pletta, D. H. *The Engineering Profession: Its Heritage and Its Emerging Public Purpose*. Washington, DC: University Press of America, 1984.

Pritchard, M. S., "Beyond Disaster Ethics," *The Centennial Review*, Vol. XXXIV, No. 2 (Spring) 1990, 295–318.

Pritchard, M. S. "Good Works," *Professional Ethics*, Vol. 1, Nos. 1 and 2 (Spring/Summer) 1992, 155–177.

Pritchard, M. S. ed. *Teaching Engineering Ethics: A Case Study Approach*, National Science Foundation, Grant No. DIR-8820837, June 1992.

Rachels, J. *The Elements of Moral Philosophy*. New York: Random House, 1986.

Raelin, J. A. *The Clash of Cultures: Managers and Professionals*. Boston: Harvard Business School Press, 1985.

Rawls, John. *A Theory of Justice*. Cambridge, MA: Harvard University Press, 1971.

Relman, A. "Lessons from the Darsee Affair," *The New England Journal of Medicine*, Vol. 308, 1983, 1415–1417.

Richardson, "Specifying Norms," *Philosophy and Public Affairs*, Vol. 19., No. 4, 1990, 279–310.

Ringleb, Al H., Meiners, Roger E., and Edwards, Frances L. *Managing in the Legal Environment*. St. Paul, MN: West, 1990.

Rogers Commission, "Report to the President by the Presidential Commission on the Space Shuttle Challenger Accident," Washington, DC, June 6, 1986.

Ross, W. D. *The Right and the Good*. Oxford England: Oxford University Press, 1988.

Ruckelshaus, William D. "Risk, Science and Democracy," *Issues in Science and Technology*, Vol. 1, No. 3 (Spring), 1985, 19–38.

Sagoff, Mark, "Where Ickes Went Right or Reason and Rationality in Environmental Law," *Ecology Law Quarterly*, Vol. 14, 1987, 265–323.

Schaub, J. H., and Pavlovic, K. *Engineering Professionalism and Ethics*. New York: Wiley-Interscience, 1983.

Schlossberger, Eugene. *The Ethical Engineer*. Philadelphia, PA: Temple University Press, 1993.

Schwing, R. C., and Albers, W. A., Jr., eds. *Societal Risk Assessment: How Safe Is Safe Enough?* New York: Plenum Press, 1980.

Shrader-Frechette, K. S. *Risk and Ration-ality*. Berkeley: University of California Press, 1991.

Simon, Herbert A. *Administrative Behavior*. 3rd ed. New York: Free Press, 1976.

Singer, M. G., ed. *Morals and Values*. New York: Charles Scribner's Sons, 1977.

Singer, Peter. *Practical Ethics*. Cambridge, England: Cambridge University Press, 1979.

Slovic, Paul, Fischhoff, Baruch, and Lichtenstein, Sarah. "Rating the Risks," *Environment*, Vol. 21, No. 3 (April) 1969, 14–39.

Solomon, R. C., and Hanson, K. R. *Above the Bottom Line: An Introduction to Business Ethics*. New York: Harcourt Brace Jovanovich, 1983.

Starr, Chauncey. "Social Benefits Versus Technological Risk," *Science*, Vol. 165 (September 19) 1969, 1232–1238.

Stone, Christopher. *Where the Law Ends*. Prospect Heights, IL: Waveland Press, 1991.

Taeusch, C. F. *Professional and Business Ethics*. New York: Henry Holt & Co., 1926.

Taylor, P. W. *Principles of Ethics, An Introduction*. Encino, CA: Dickenson, 1975.

Taylor, P. W. "The Ethics of Respect for Nature," *Environmental Ethics*, Vol. 3, No. 3 (Fall) 1981, 197–218.

Toffler, A. *Tough Choices: Managers Talk Ethics*. New York: Wiley, 1986.

Unger, S. H. *Controlling Technology: Ethics and the Responsible Engineer*. New York: Holt, Rinehart & Winston, 1982.

Unger, S. H. "Would Helping Ethical Professionals Get Professional Societies into Trouble?" *IEEE Technology and Society Magazine*, Vol. 6, No. 3, (September) 1987, 17–21.

Urmson, J. O. "Saints and Heroes." In A. I. Meldon, ed., *Essays in Moral Philosophy*. Seattle: University of Washington Press, 1958.

Urmson, J. O. "Hare on Intuitive Moral Thinking." In S. Douglass and N. Fotion, eds., *Hare and Critics*. Oxford: Clarendon Press, 1988.

Vandivier, R. "What? Me Be a Martyr?" *Harper's Magazine* (July) 1975, 36–44.

Vaughn, R. C. *Legal Aspects of Engineering*. Dubuque, IA: Kendall/Hunt, 1977.

Velasquez, M. "Why Corporations Are Not Morally Responsible for Anything They Do," *Business and Professional Ethics Journal*, Vol. 2, No. 3 (Spring) 1983, 1–18.

Velasquez, M. *Business Ethics*. 3rd ed. Englewood Cliffs, NJ: Prentice-Hall, 1992.

Vesilind, P. A. "Environmental Ethics and Civil Engineering," *The Environmental Professional*, Vol. 9, 1987, 336–342.

Vogel, D. A. "A Survey of Ethical and Legal Issues in Engineering Curricula in the United States," Stanford Law School, Winter 1991.

Wall Street Journal, "Executives Apply Stiffer Standards Than Public to Ethical Dilemmas," (November 3) 1983.

Weil, V., ed. *Beyond Whistleblowing: Defining Engineers' Responsibilities*. Proceedings of the 2nd National Conference on Ethics in Engineering, March 1982.

Weil, Vivian, ed. *Moral Issues in Engineering: Selected Readings*. Chicago: Illinois Institute of Technology, 1988.

Weisskoph, Michael. "The Aberdeen Mess," *The Washington Post Magazine*, (January 15) 1989.

Wells, P., Jones, H., and Davis, M. *Conflicts of Interest in Engineering*. Dubuque, IA: Center for the Study of Ethics in the Professions, Kendall/Hunt, 1986.

Westin, A. F. *Individual Rights in the Corporation: A Reader on Employee Rights*. New York: Random House, 1980.

Westin, A. F. *Whistle Blowing: Loyalty and Dissent in the Corporation*. New York: McGraw-Hill, 1981.

Whitbeck, Caroline. "The Trouble with Dilemmas: Rethinking Applied Ethics," *Professional Ethics*, Vol. 1, Nos. 1 and 2, (Spring/Summer) 1992, 119–142.

Williams, B., and Smart, J. J. C. *Utilitarianism: For and Against*. New York: Cambridge University Press, 1973.

Wills, Jocelyn. "Goodrich Revisited." *Journal of Business and Professional Ethics*, forthcoming.

Appendix

National Society of Professional Engineers®

Code of Ethics for Engineers*

Preamble

Engineering is an important and learned profession. The members of the profession recognize that their work has a direct and vital impact on the quality of life for all people. Accordingly, the services provided by engineers require honesty, impartiality, fairness and equity, and must be dedicated to the protection of the public health, safety and welfare. In the practice of their profession, engineers must perform under a standard of professional behavior which requires adherence to the highest principles of ethical conduct on behalf of the public, clients, employers and the profession.

I. Fundamental Canons

Engineers, in the fulfillment of their professional duties, shall:

1. Hold paramount the safety, health and welfare of the public in the performance of their professional duties.
2. Perform services only in areas of their competence.
3. Issue public statements only in an objective and truthful manner.
4. Act in professional matters for each employer or client as faithful agents or trustees.
5. Avoid deceptive acts in the solicitation of professional employment.

---

* Reprinted by Permission of the NSPE.

II. Rules of Practice

1. Engineers shall hold paramount the safety, health and welfare of the public in the performance of their professional duties.
   a. Engineers shall at all times recognize that their primary obligation is to protect the safety, health, property and welfare of the public. If their professional judgment is overruled under circumstances where the safety, health, property or welfare of the public are endangered, they shall notify their employer or client and such other authority as may be appropriate.
   b. Engineers shall approve only those engineering documents which are safe for public health, property and welfare in conformity with accepted standards.
   c. Engineers shall not reveal facts, data or information obtained in a professional capacity without the prior consent of the client or employer except as authorized or required by law or this Code.
   d. Engineers shall not permit the use of their name or firm name nor associate in business ventures with any person or firm which they have reason to believe is engaging in fraudulent or dishonest business or professional practices.
   e. Engineers having knowledge of any alleged violation of this Code shall cooperate with the proper authorities in furnishing such information or assistance as may be required.

2. Engineers shall perform services only in the areas of their competence.
   a. Engineers shall undertake assignments only when qualified by education or experience in the specific technical fields involved.

b. Engineers shall not affix their signatures to any plans or documents dealing with subject matter in which they lack competence, nor to any plan or document not prepared under their direction and control.

c. Engineers may accept assignments and assume responsibility for coordination of an entire project and sign and seal the engineering documents for the entire project, provided that each technical segment is signed and sealed only by the qualified engineers who prepared the segment.

3. Engineers shall issue public statements only in an objective and truthful manner.

a. Engineers shall be objective and truthful in professional reports, statements or testimony. They shall include all relevant and pertinent information in such reports, statements or testimony.

b. Engineers may express publicly a professional opinion on technical subjects only when that opinion is founded upon adequate knowledge of the facts and competence in the subject matter.

c. Engineers shall issue no statements, criticisms or arguments on technical matters which are inspired or paid for by interested parties, unless they have prefaced their comments by explicitly identifying the interested parties on whose behalf they are speaking, and by revealing the existence of any interest the engineers may have in the matters.

4. Engineers shall act in professional matters for each employer or client as faithful agents or trustees.

a. Engineers shall disclose all known or potential conflicts of interest to their employers or clients by promptly informing them of any business association, interest, or other circumstances which could influence or appear to influence their judgment or the quality of their services.

b. Engineers shall not accept compensation, financial or otherwise, from more than one party for services on the same project, or for services pertaining to the same project, unless the circumstances are fully disclosed to, and agreed to by, all interested parties.

c. Engineers shall not solicit or accept financial or other valuable consideration directly or indirectly, from contractors, their agents, or other parties in connection with work for employers or clients for which they are responsible.

d. Engineers in public service as members, advisors or employees of a governmental or quasi-governmental body or department shall not participate in decisions with respect to professional services solicited or provided by them or their organizations in private or public engineering practice.

e. Engineers shall not solicit or accept a professional contract from a governmental body on which a principal or officer of their organization serves as a member.

5. Engineers shall avoid deceptive acts in the solicitation of professional employment.

a. Engineers shall not falsify or permit misrepresentation of their, or their associates', academic or professional qualifications. They shall not misrepresent or exaggerate their degree of responsibility in or for the subject matter of prior assignments. Brochures or other presentations incident to the solicitation of employment shall not misrepresent pertinent facts concerning employers, employees, associates, joint ventures or past accomplishments with the intent and purpose of enhancing their qualifications and their work.

b. Engineers shall not offer, give, solicit or receive, either directly or indirectly, any political contribution in an amount intended to influence the award of a contract by public authority, or which may be reasonably construed by the public of having the effect or intent to influence the award of a contract. They shall not offer any gift, or other valuable consideration in order to secure work. They shall not pay a commission, percentage or brokerage fee in order to secure work except to a bona fide employee or bona fide established commercial or marketing agencies retained by them.

III. Professional Obligations

1. Engineers shall be guided in all their professional relations by the highest standards of integrity.
   a. Engineers shall admit and accept their own errors when proven wrong and refrain from distorting or altering thfacts in an attempt to justify their desions.
   b. Engineers shall advise their clients or employers when they believe a project will not be successful.
   c. Engineers shall not accept outside employment to the detriment of their regular work or interest. Before accepting any outside employment they will notify their employers.
   d. Engineers shall not attempt to attract an engineer from another employer by false or misleading pretenses.
   e. Engineers shall not actively participate in strikes, picket lines, or other collective coercive action.
   f. Engineers shall avoid any act tending to promote their own interest at the expense of the dignity and integrity of the profession.

2. Engineers shall at all times strive to serve the public interest.
   a. Engineers shall seek opportunities to be of constructive service in civic affairs and work for the advancement of the safety, health and well-being of their community.
   b. Engineers shall not complete, sign or seal plans and/or specifications that are not of a design safe to the public health and welfare and in conformity with accepted engineering standards. If the client or employer insists on such unprofessional conduct, they shall notify the proper authorities and withdraw from further service on the project.
   c. Engineers shall endeavor to extend public knowledge and appreciation of engineering and its achievements and to protect the engineering profession from misrepresentation and misunderstanding.

3. Engineers shall avoid all conduct or practice which is likely to discredit the profession or deceive the public.
   a. Engineers shall avoid the use of statements containing a material misrepresentation of fact or omitting a material fact necessary to keep statements from being misleading or intended or likely to create an unjustified expectation, or statements containing prediction of future success.
   b. Consistent with the foregoing, Engineers may advertise for recrutment of personnel.
   c. Consistent with the foregoing, Engineers may prepare articles for the lay or technical press, but such articles shall not imply credit to the author for work performed by others.

4. Engineers shall not disclose confidential information concerning the business affairs or technical processes of any present or former client or employer without his consent.
   a. Engineers in the employ of others shall not without the consent of all interested parties enter promotional efforts or negotiations for work or make arrangements for other employment as a principal or to practice in connection with a specific project for which the Engineer has gained particular and specialized knowledge.
   b. Engineers shall not, without the consent of all interested parties, participate in or represent an adversary interest in connection with a specific project or proceeding in which the Engineer has gained particular specialized knowledge on behalf of a former client or employer.

5. Engineers shall not be influenced in their professional duties by conflicting interests.
   a. Engineers shall not accept financial or other considerations, including free engineering designs, from material or equipment suppliers for specifying their product.
   b. Engineers shall not accept commissions or allowances, directly or indirectly, from contractors or other parties dealing with clients or employers of the Engineer in connection with work for which the Engineer is responsible.

6. Engineers shall uphold the principle of appropriate and adequate compensation for those engaged in engineering work.

   a. Engineers shall not accept remuneration from either an employee or employment agency for giving employment.

   b. Engineers, when employing other engineers, shall offer a salary according to professional qualifications.

7. Engineers shall not attempt to obtain employment or advancement or professional engagements by untruthfully criticizing other engineers, or by other improper or questionable methods.

   a. Engineers shall not request, propose, or accept a professional commission on a contingent basis under circumstances in which their professional judgment may be compromised.

   b. Engineers in salaried positions shall accept part-time engineering work only to the extent consistent with policies of the employer and in accordance with ethical considerations.

   c. Engineers shall not use equipment, supplies, laboratory, or office facilities of an employer to carry on outside private practice without consent.

8. Engineers shall not attempt to injure, maliciously or falsely, directly or indirectly, the professional reputation, prospects, practice or employment of other engineers, nor untruthfully criticize other engineers' work. Engineers who believe others are guilty of unethical or illegal practice shall present such information to the proper authority for action.

   a. Engineers in private practice shall not review the work of another engineer for the same client, except with the knowledge of such engineer, or unless the connection of such engineer with the work has been terminated.

   b. Engineers in governmental, industrial or educational employ are entitled to review and evaluate the work of other engineers when so required by their employment duties.

   c. Engineers in sales or industrial employ are entitled to make engineering comparisons of represented products with products of other suppliers.

9. Engineers shall accept personal responsibility for their professional activities; provided, however, that Engineers may seek indemnification for professional services arising out of their practice for other than gross negligence, where the Engineer's interests cannot otherwise be protected.

   a. Engineers shall conform with state registration laws in the practice of engineering.

   b. Engineers shall not use association with a nonengineer, a corporation, or partnership as a "cloak" for unethical acts, but must accept personal responsibility for all professional acts.

10. Engineers shall give credit for engineering work to those to whom credit is due, and will recognize the proprietary interests of others.

    a. Engineers shall, whenever possible, name the person or persons who may be individually responsible for designs, inventions, writings, or other accomplishments.

    b. Engineers using designs supplied by a client recognize that the designs remain the property of the client and may not be duplicated by the Engineer for others without express permission.

    c. Engineers, before undertaking work for others in connection with which the Engineer may make improvements, plans, designs, inventions, or other records which may justify copyrights or patents, should enter into a positive agreement regarding ownership.

    d. Engineers' designs, data, records, and notes referring exclusively to an employer's work are the employer's property.

11. Engineers shall cooperate in extending the effectiveness of the profession by interchanging information and experience with other engineers and students, and will endeavor to provide opportunity for the professional development and advancement of engineers under their supervision.

    a. Engineers shall encourage engineering employees' efforts to improve their education.

    b. Engineers shall encourage engineering employees to attend and present papers at professional and technical society meetings.

c. Engineers shall urge engineering employees to become registered at the earliest possible date.

d. Engineers shall assign a professional engineer duties of a nature to utilize full training and experience, insofar as possible, and delegate lesser functions to subprofessionals or to technicians.

e. Engineers shall provide a prospective engineering employee with complete information on working conditions and proposed status of employment, and after employment will keep employees informed of any changes.

"By order of the United States District Court for the District of Columbia, former Section 11(c) of the NSPE Code of Ethics prohibiting competitive bidding, and all policy statements, opinions, rulings or other guidelines interpreting its scope, have been rescinded as unlawfully interfering with the legal right of engineers, protected under the antitrust laws, to provide price information to prospective clients; accordingly, nothing contained in the NSPE Code of Ethics, policy statements, opinions, rulings or other guidelines prohibits the submission of price quotations or competitive bids for engineering services at any time or in any amount."

Statement by NSPE Executive Committee

In order to correct misunderstandings which have been indicated in some instances since the issuance of the Supreme Court decision and the entry of the Final Judgment, it is noted that in its decision of April 25, 1978, the Supreme Court of the United States declared: "The Sherman Act does not require competitive bidding."

It is further noted that as made clear in the Supreme Court decision:

1. Engineers and firms may individually refuse to bid for engineering services.
2. Clients are not required to seek bids for engineering services.
3. Federal, state, and local laws governing procedures to procure engineering services are not affected, and remain in full force and effect.
4. State societies and local chapters are free to actively and aggressively seek legislation for professional selection and negotiation procedures by public agencies.
5. State registration board rules of professional conduct, including rules prohibiting competitive bidding for engineering services, are not affected and remain in full force and effect. State registration boards with authority to adopt rules of professional conduct may adopt rules governing procedures to obtain engineering services.
6. As noted by the Supreme Court, "nothing in the judgment prevents NSPE and its members from attempting to influence governmental action. . . ."

Note: In regard to the question of application of the Code to corporations vis-a-vis real persons, business form or type should not negate nor influence conformance of individuals to the Code. The Code deals with professional services, which services must be performed by real persons. Real persons in turn establish and implement policies within business structures. The Code is clearly written to apply to the Engineer and it is incumbent on a member of NSPE to endeavor to live up to its provisions. This applies to all pertinent sections of the Code.

Publication date as revised: July 1993. Publication #1102.

American Institute of Chemical Engineers

In 1992, the Council of the American Institute of Chemical Engineers adopted this Code of Ethics to which it expects that the professional conduct of its members shall conform and to which every applicant attests by signing his or her membership application.

Professional Ethics

The American Institute of Chemical Engineers has prepared this statement to guide its members in their professional attitudes and actions and to convey to all interested persons the nature of professional standards of the chemical engineer. This brief statement outlines the ethical principles that should govern the actions of professional persons. Some detailed discussions of professional conduct may be found in the bibliography.

Every calling is great when greatly pursued.

—Oliver Wendell Holmes

A professional is one who, by reason of education, experience, intellectual capacity and moral integrity, is fully aware of personal responsibility to devote skill and knowledge to the service of society and the profession. Whereas any graduate engineer has acquired the technology fundamental to an engineering career, the truly professional engineer integrates social consciousness into professional judgment. Recognizing the accomplishments of the past, the needs of the present and the challenges of the future, the professional engineer accepts special obligations in relations with society.

No set of laws could prevent chaos in a society that lacked rough agreement on certain moral assumptions.

—John W. Gardner

The Institute recognizes that ethics and ethical conduct are intimately related to moral values and hence cannot be expressed exactly for all engineers. Often dilemmas arise in which two or more moral obligations, duties, rights or ideals come into conflict in a situation in which not all of them can be respected or fulfilled.

Questions relating to issues such as proprietary information, conflicts of interest, discrimination, and whistle blowing can best be answered by thoughtful consideration of fundamental principles rather than reliance on a detailed regulation. In the final analysis, the responsibility for determining the ethical path for any situation rests with the individual.

Code of Ethics*

Members of the American Institute of Chemical Engineers shall uphold and advance the integrity, honor and dignity of the engineering profession by: being honest and impartial and serving with fidelity their employers, their clients, and the public; striving to increase the competence and prestige of the engineering profession; and using their knowledge and skill for the enhancement of human welfare. To achieve these goals, members shall

---

* Reprinted by permission of the American Institute of Chemical Engineers

1. Hold paramount the safety, health and welfare of the public in performance of their professional duties.
2. Formally advise their employers or clients (and consider further disclosure, if warranted) if they perceive that a consequence of their duties will adversely affect the present or future health or safety of their colleagues or the public.
3. Accept responsibility for their actions and recognize the contributions of others; seek critical review of their work and offer objective criticism of the work of others.
4. Issue statements or present information only in an objective and truthful manner.
5. Act in professional matters for each employer or client as faithful agents or trustees, and avoid conflicts of interest.
6. Treat fairly all colleagues and co-workers, recognizing their unique contributions and capabilities.
7. Perform professional services only in areas of their competence.
8. Build their professional reputations on the merits of their services.
9. Continue their professional development throughout their careers, and provide opportunities for the professional development of those under their supervision.

Institute of Electronic and Electrical Engineers (IEEE)

Code of Ethics**

We, the members of the IEEE, in recognition of the importance of our technologies in affecting the quality of life throughout the world, and in accepting a personal obligation to our profession, its members and the communities we serve, do hereby commit ourselves to the highest ethical and professional conduct and agree:

1. to accept responsibility in making engineering decisions consistent with the safety,

---

** © 1990 IEEE. Reprinted with permission, from the Institute of Electrical and Electronics Engineers.

health, and welfare of the public, and to disclose promptly factors that might endanger the public or the environment;

2. to avoid real or perceived conflicts of interest whenever possible, and to disclose them to affected parties when they do exist;
3. to be honest and realistic in stating claims or estimates based on available data;
4. to reject bribery in all its forms;
5. to improve the understanding of technology, its appropriate application, and potential consequences;
6. to maintain and improve our technical competence and to undertake technological tasks for others only if qualified by training or experience, or after full disclosure of pertinent limitations;
7. to seek, accept, and offer honest criticism of technical work, to acknowledge and correct errors, and to credit properly the contributions of others;
8. to treat fairly all persons regardless of such factors as race, religion, gender, disability, age, or national origin;
9. to avoid injuring others, their property, reputation, or employment by false or malicious action;
10. to assist colleagues and co-workers in their professional development and to support them in following this code of ethics.

Effective January 1, 1991

American Society of Civil Engineers

*ASCE Code of Ethics**

Effective January 1, 1977. (By ASCE Board of Direction action April 12–14, 1975)

Fundamental Principles**

Engineers uphold and advance the integrity, honor and dignity of the engineering profession by:

1. using their knowledge and skill for the enhancement of human welfare;
2. being honest and impartial and serving with

fidelity the public, their employers and clients;
3. striving to increase the competence and prestige of the engineering profession; and
4. supporting the professional and technical societies of their disciplines.

Fundamental Canons

1. Engineers shall hold paramount the safety, health and welfare of the public in the performance of their professional duties.
2. Engineers shall perform services only in areas of their competence.
3. Engineers shall issue public statements only in an objective and truthful manner.
4. Engineers shall act in professional matters for each employer or client as faithful agents or trustees, and shall avoid conflicts of interest.
5. Engineers shall build their professional reputation on the merit of their services and shall not compete unfairly with others.
6. Engineers shall act in such a manner as to uphold and enhance the honor, integrity, and dignity of the engineering profession.
7. Engineers shall continue their professional development throughout their careers, and shall provide opportunities for the professional development of those engineers under their supervision.

ASCE Guidelines to Practice under the Fundamental Canons of Ethics

Canon 1.

Engineers shall hold paramount the safety, health and welfare of the public in the performance of their professional duties.

a. Engineers shall recognize that the lives, safety, health and welfare of the general public are dependent upon engineering judgments, decisions and practices incorporated into structures, machines, products, processes and devices.
b. Engineers shall approve or seal only those design documents, reviewed or prepared by

---

* As adopted September 25, 1976 and amended Ocober 25, 1980 and April 17, 1993. Reprinted with permission of the ASCE.

** The American Society of Civil Engineers adopted THE FUNDAMENTAL PRINCIPLES of the ABET Code of Ethics of Engineers as accepted by the Accreditation Board for Engineering and Technology, Inc. (ABET).

them, which are determined to be safe for public health and welfare in conformity with accepted engineering standards.

c. Engineers whose professional judgment is overruled under circumstances where the safety, health and welfare of the public are endangered, shall inform their clients or employers of the possible consequences.

d. Engineers who have knowledge or reason to believe that another person or firm may be in violation of any of the provisions of Canon 1 shall present such information to the proper authority in writing and shall cooperate with the proper authority in furnishing such further information or assistance as may be required.

e. Engineers should seek opportunities to be of constructive service in civic affairs and work for the advancement of the safety, health and well-being of their communities.

f. Engineers should be committed to improving the environment to enhance the quality of life.

Canon 2.

Engineers shall perform services only in areas of their competence.

a. Engineers shall undertake to perform engineering assignments only when qualified by education or experience in the technical field of engineering involved.

b. Engineers may accept an assignment requiring education or experience outside of their own fields of competence, provided their services are restricted to those phases of the project in which they are qualified. All other phases of such project shall be performed by qualified associates, consultants, or employees.

c. Engineers shall not affix their signatures or seals to any engineering plan or document dealing with subject matter in which they lack competence by virtue of education or experience or to any such plan or document not reviewed or prepared under their supervisory control.

Canon 3.

Engineers shall issue public statements only in an objective and truthful manner.

a. Engineers should endeavor to extend the public knowledge of engineering, and shall not participate in the dissemination of untrue, unfair or exaggerated statements regarding engineering.

b. Engineers shall be objective and truthful in professional reports, statements, or testi-

mony. They shall include all relevant and pertinent information in such reports, statements, or testimony.

c. Engineers, when serving as expert witnesses, shall express an engineering opinion only when it is founded upon adequate knowledge of the facts, upon a background of technical competence, and upon honest conviction.

d. Engineers shall issue no statements, criticisms, or arguments on engineering matters which are inspired or paid for by interested parties, unless they indicate on whose behalf the statements are made.

e. Engineers shall be dignified and modest in explaining their work and merit, and will avoid any act tending to promote their own interests at the expense of the integrity, honor and dignity of the profession.

Canon 4.

Engineers shall act in professional matters for each employer or client as faithful agents or trustees, and shall avoid conflicts of interest.

a. Engineers shall avoid all known or potential conflicts of interest with their employers or clients and shall promptly inform their employers or clients of any business association, interests, or circumstances which could influence their judgment or the quality of their services.

b. Engineers shall not accept compensation from more than one party for services on the same project, or for services pertaining to the same project, unless the circumstances are fully disclosed to and agreed to, by all interested parties.

c. Engineers shall not solicit or accept gratuities, directly or indirectly, from contractors, their agents, or other parties dealing with their clients or employers in connection with work for which they are responsible.

d. Engineers in public service as members, advisors, or employees of a governmental body or department shall not participate in considerations or actions with respect to services solicited or provided by them or their organization in private or public engineering practice.

e. Engineers shall advise their employers or clients when, as a result of their studies, they believe a project will not be successful.

f. Engineers shall not use confidential information coming to them in the course of their assignments as a means of making personal profit if such action is adverse to the interests of their clients, employers or the public.

   g. Engineers shall not accept professional employment outside of their regular work or interest without the knowledge of their employers.

Canon 5.

Engineers shall build their professional reputation on the merit of their services and shall not compete unfairly with others.

   a. Engineers shall not give, solicit or receive either directly or indirectly, any political contribution, gratuity, or unlawful consideration in order to secure work, exclusive of securing salaried positions through employment agencies.

   b. Engineers should negotiate contracts for professional services fairly and on the basis of demonstrated competence and qualifications for the type of professional service required.

   c. Engineers may request, propose or accept professional commissions on a contingent basis only under circumstances in which their professional judgments would not be compromised.

   d. Engineers shall not falsify or permit misrepresentation of their academic or professional qualifications or experience.

   e. Engineers shall give proper credit for engineering work to those to whom credit is due, and shall recognize the proprietary interests of others. Whenever possible, they shall name the person or persons who may be responsible for designs, inventions, writings or other accomplishments.

   f. Engineers may advertise professional services in a way that does not contain misleading language or is in any other manner derogatory to the dignity of the profession. Examples of permissible advertising are as follows:

      Professional cards in recognized, dignified publications, and listings in rosters or directories published by responsible organizations, provided that the cards or listings are consistent in size and content and are in a section of the publication regularly devoted to such professional cards.

      Brochures which factually describe experience, facilities, personnel and capacity to render service, providing they are not misleading with respect to

the engineer's participation in projects-described.

      Display advertising in recognized dignified business and professional publications, providing it is factual and is not misleading with respect to the engineer's extent of participation in projects described.

      A statement of the engineers' names or the name of the firm and statement of the type of service posted on projects for which they render services.

      Preparation or authorization of descriptive articles for the lay or technical press, which are factual and dignified. Such articles shall not imply anything more than direct participation in the project described.

      Permission by engineers for their names to be used in commercial advertisements, such as may be published by contractors, material suppliers, etc., only by means of a modest, dignified notation acknowledging the engineers' participation in the project described. Such permission shall not include public endorsement of proprietary products.

   g. Engineers shall not maliciously or falsely, directly or indirectly, injure the professional reputation, prospects, practice or employment of another engineer or indiscriminately criticize another's work.

   h. Engineers shall not use equipment, supplies, laboratory or office facilities of their employers to carry on outside private practice without the consent of their employers.

Canon 6.

Engineers shall act in such a manner as to uphold and enhance the honor, integrity, and dignity of the engineering profession.

   a. Engineers shall not knowingly act in a manner which will be derogatory to the honor, integrity, or dignity of the engineering profession or knowingly engage in business or professional practices of a fraudulent, dishonest or unethical nature.

Canon 7.

Engineers shall continue their professional development throughout their careers, and shall provide opportunities for the professional development of those engineers under their supervision.

   a. Engineers should keep current in their specialty fields by engaging in professional practice, participating in continuing education courses, reading in the technical literature, and attending professional meetings and seminars.

b. Engineers should encourage their engineering employees to become registered at the earliest possible date.

c. Engineers should encourage engineering employees to attend and present papers at professional and technical society meetings.

d. Engineers shall uphold the principle of mutually satisfying relationships between employers and employees with respect to terms of employment including professional grade descriptions, salary ranges, and fringe benefits.

The American Society of Mechanical Engineers

Code of Ethics of Engineers*

The Fundamental Principles
Engineers uphold and advance the integrity, honor, and dignity of the Engineering profession by:
    I.   using their knowledge and skill for the enhancement of human welfare;
    II.   being honest and impartial, and serving with fidelity the public, their employers and clients, and
    III.   striving to increase the competence and prestige of the engineering profession.

The Fundamental Canons
1. Engineers shall hold paramount the safety, health and welfare of the public in the performance of their professional duties.
2. Engineers shall perform services only in the areas of their competence.
3. Engineers shall continue their professional development throughout their careers and shall provide opportunities for the professional and ethical development of those engineers under their supervision.
4. Engineers shall act in professional matters for each employer or client as faithful agents

---

* Reprinted with permission of the AME Board on Professional Practice and Ethics.

or trustees, and shall avoid conflicts of interest or the appearance of conflicts of interest.
5. Engineers shall build their professional reputation on the merit of their services and shall not compete unfairly with others.
6. Engineers shall associate only with reputable persons or organizations.
7. Engineers shall issue public statements only in an objective and truthful manner.

Society Policy

Ethics
ASME requires ethical practice by each of its members and has adopted the following Code of Ethics of Engineers as referenced in the ASME Constitution, Article C2.1.1.

Code of Ethics of Engineers

The Fundamental Principles
Engineers uphold and advance the integrity, honor and dignity of the engineering profession by:
    I.   using their knowledge and skill for the enhancement of human welfare;
    II.   being honest and impartial, and serving with fidelity the public, their employers and clients; and
    III.   striving to increase the competence and prestige of the engineering profession.

The Fundamental Canons
1. Engineers shall hold paramount the safety, health and welfare of the public in the performance of their professional duties.
2. Engineers shall perform services only in the areas of their competence.
3. Engineers shall continue their professional development throughout their careers and shall provide opportunities for the professional and ethical development of those engineers under their supervision.
4. Engineers shall act in professional matters for each employer or client as faithful agents or trustees, and shall avoid conflicts of interest or the appearance of conflicts of interest.
5. Engineers shall build their professional reputation on the merit of their services and shall not compete unfairly with others.
6. Engineers shall associate only with reputable persons or organizations.
7. Engineers shall issue public statements only in an objective and truthful manner.

The ASME Criteria for Interpretation of the Canons

The ASME criteria for interpretation of the Canons are advisory in character and represent the objectives toward which members of the engineering profession should strive. They constitute a body of principles upon which an engineer can rely for guidance in specific situations. In addition, they provide interpretive guidance to the ASME Board on Professional Practice and Ethics in applying the Code of Ethics of Engineers.

1. Engineers shall hold paramount the safety, health and welfare of the public in the performance of their professional duties.
   a. Engineers shall recognize that the lives, safety, health and welfare of general public are dependent upon engineering judgments, decisions and practices incorporated into structures, machines, products, processes and devices.
   b. Engineers shall not approve or seal plans and/or specifications that are not of a design safe to the public health and welfare and in conformity with accepted engineering standards.
   c. Whenever the Engineers' professional judgment is over-ruled under circumstances where the safety, health, and welfare of the public are endangered, the Engineers shall inform their clients and/or employers of the possible consequences.
      (1) Engineers shall endeavor to provide data such as published standards, test codes, and quality control procedures that will enable the users to understand safe use during life expectancy associated with the designs, products, or systems for which they are responsible.
      (2) Engineers shall conduct reviews of the safety and reliability of the designs, products, or systems for which they are responsible before giving their approval to the plans for the design.
      (3) Whenever Engineers observe conditions, directly related to their employment, which they believe will endanger public safety or health, they shall inform the proper authority of the situation.
      d. If engineers have knowledge of or reason to believe that another person or firm may be in violation of any of the provisions of these Canons, they shall present such information to the proper authority in writing and shall cooperate with the proper authority in furnishing such further information or assistance as may be required.
2. Engineers shall perform services only in areas of their competence.
   a. Engineers shall undertake to perform engineering assignments only when qualified by education and/or experience in the specific technical field of engineering involved.
   b. Engineers may accept an assignment requiring education and/or experience outside of their own fields of competence, but their services shall be restricted to other phases of the project in which they are qualified. All other phases of such project shall be performed by qualified associates, consultants, or employees.
3. Engineers shall continue their professional development throughout their careers, and should provide opportunities for the professional and ethical development of those engineers under their supervision.
4. Engineers shall act in professional matters for each employer or client as faithful agents or trustees, and shall avoid conflicts of interest or the appearance of conflicts of interest.
   a. Engineers shall avoid all known conflicts of interest with their employers or clients and shall promptly inform their employers or clients of any business association, interests, or circumstances which could influence their judgment or the quality of their services.
   b. Engineers shall not undertake any assignments which would knowingly create a potential conflict of interest between themselves and their clients of their employers.
   c. Engineers shall not accept compensation, financial or otherwise, from more then one party for services on the same project, or for services pertaining to the same project, unless the circumstances are fully disclosed to, and agreed to, by all interested parties.

d. Engineers shall not solicit or accept financial or other valuable considerations, for specifying products or material or equipment suppliers, without disclosure to their clients or employers.

e. Engineers shall not solicit or accept gratuities, directly or indirectly, from con tractors, their agents, or other parties dealing with their clients or employers in connection with work for which they are responsible.

f. When in public service as members, advisors, or employees of a governmental body or department, Engineers shall not participate in considerations or actions with respect to services provided by them or their organization(s) in private or product engineering practice.

g. Engineers shall not solicit an engineering contract from a governmental body on which a principal, officer, or employee of their organization serves as a member.

h. When, as a result of their studies, Engineers believe a project(s) will not be successful, they shall so advise their employer or client.

i. Engineers shall treat information coming to them in the course of their assignments as confidential, and shall not use such information as a means of making personal profit if such action is adverse to the interests of their clients, their employers or the public.

   i.1   They will not disclose confidential information concerning the business affairs or technical processes of any present or former employer or client or bidder under evaluation, without his consent, unless required by law.

   i.2   They shall not reveal confidential information or finding of any commission or board of which they are members unless required by law.

   i.3   Designs supplied to Engineers by clients shall not be duplicated by the Engineers for others without the express permission of the client(s).

j. The Engineer shall act with fairness and justice to all parties when administering a construction (or other) contract.

k. Before undertaking work for others in which the Engineer may make improvements, plans, designs, inventions, or other records which may justify seeking copyrights or patents, the Engineer shall enter into a positive agreement regarding the rights of respective parties.

l. Engineers shall admit their own errors when proven wrong and refrain from distorting or altering the facts to justify their decisions.

m. Engineers shall not accept professional employment outside of their regular work or interest without the knowledge of their employers.

n. Engineers shall not attempt to attract an employee from another employer by false or misleading representations.

5. Engineers shall build their professional reputation on the merit of their services and shall not compete unfairly with others.

a. Engineers shall negotiate contracts for professional services on the basis of demonstrated competence and qualifications for the type of professional service required and at fair and reasonable prices.

b. Engineers shall not request, propose, or accept professional commissions on a contingent basis under circumstances under which their professional judgments may be comprised.

c. Engineers shall not falsify or permit misrepresentation of their, or their associates, academic or professional qualification. They shall not misrepresent or exaggerate their degrees of responsibility in or for the subject matter of prior assignments. Brochures or other presentations incident to the solicitation of employment shall not misrepresent pertinent facts concerning employers, employees, associates, joint venturers, or their past accomplishments.

d. Engineers shall prepare only articles for the lay or technical press which are factual, dignified and free from ostentation or laudatory implications. Such articles shall not imply other than their direct participation in the work described unless credit is given to others for their share of the work.

e. Engineers shall not maliciously or falsely, directly or indirectly, injure the professional reputation, prospects, practice or employment of another engineer, nor shall they indiscriminately criticize another's work.

  f. Engineers shall not use equipment, supplies, laboratory or office facilities of their employers to carry on outside private practice without consent.

6. Engineers shall associate only with reputable persons or organizations.

  a. Engineers shall not knowingly associate with or permit the use of their names or firm names in business ventures by any person or firm which they know, or have reason to believe, are engaging in business or professional practices of a fraudulent or dishonest nature.

  b. Engineers shall not use association with non-engineers, corporations, or partnerships to disguise unethical acts.

7. Engineers shall issue public statements only in an objective and truthful manner.

  a. Engineers shall endeavor to extend public knowledge, and to prevent misunderstandings of the achievements of engineering.

  b. Engineers shall be completely objective and truthful in all professional reports, statements or testimony. They shall include all relevant and pertinent information in such reports, statements, or testimony.

  c. Engineers, when serving as expert or technical witnesses before any court, commission, or other tribunal, shall express an engineering opinion only when it is founded upon adequate knowledge of the facts in issue, upon a background of technical competence in the subject matter, and upon honest conviction of the accuracy and propriety of their testimony.

  d. Engineers shall issue no statements, criticisms, or arguments on engineering matters which are inspired or paid for by an interested party, or parties, unless they preface their comments by identifying themselves, by disclosing the identities of the party or parties on whose behalf they are speaking, and by revealing the existence of any pecuniary interest they may have in matters under discussion.

  e. Engineers shall be dignified and modest in explaining their work and merit, and shall avoid any act tending to promote their own interest at the expense of the integrity, honor and dignity of the profession or another individual.

8. Any Engineer accepting membership in The American Society of Mechanical Engineers by this action agrees to abide by this Society Policy on Ethics and procedures for implementation.

Responsibility: Council on Member Affairs/ Board on Professional Practice and Ethics

Adopted: March 7, 1976
Revised: December 9, 1976
          December 7, 1979
          November 9, 1982
          June 15, 1984
          (editorial changes 7/84)
          June 16, 1988
          September 12, 1991

Accreditation Board for Engineering and Technology*

*Code of Ethics of Engineers***

The Fundamental Principles
Engineers uphold and advance the integrity, honor and dignity of the engineering profession by:

  I. using their knowledge and skill for the enhancement of human welfare;

  II. being honest and impartial, and serving with fidelity the public, their employers and clients;

  III. striving to increase the competence and prestige of the engineering profession; and

  IV. supporting the professional and technical societies of their disciplines.

The Fundamental Canons
1. Engineers shall hold paramount the safety, health and welfare of the public in the performance of their professional duties.

---

*Formerly Engineers' Council for Professional Development. (Approved by the ECPD Board of Directors, October 5, 1977)

**Reprinted by permission of the ABET.

2. Engineers shall perform services only in the areas of their competence.
3. Engineers shall issue public statements only in an objective and truthful manner.
4. Engineers shall act in professional matters for each employer or client as faithful agents or trustees, and shall avoid conflicts of interest.
5. Engineers shall build their professional reputation on the merit of their services and shall not compete unfairly with others.
6. Engineers shall act in such a manner as to uphold and enhance the honor, integrity and dignity of the profession.
7. Engineers shall continue their professional development throughout their careers and shall provide opportunities for the professional development of those engineers under their supervision.

Index

Cases are not indexed. See pp. xiii–xvi for a categorized guide to the cases.